THE BUILDINGS OF ENGLAND

FOUNDING EDITOR: NIKOLAUS PEVSNER

JOINT EDITORS: BRIDGET CHERRY AND JUDY NAIRN

CHESHIRE

NIKOLAUS PEVSNER
AND EDWARD HUBBARD

Cheshire

*The publication of this volume has been made
possible by a grant from*
THE LEVERHULME TRUST
to cover all the necessary research work

THE BUILDINGS OF ENGLAND

Cheshire

BY
NIKOLAUS PEVSNER
AND EDWARD HUBBARD

PENGUIN BOOKS

PENGUIN BOOKS
Published by the Penguin Group
27 Wrights Lane, London W8 5TZ, England

Viking Penguin Inc., 40 West 23rd Street, New York, New York 10010, USA
Penguin Books Australia Ltd, Ringwood, Victoria, Australia
Penguin Books Canada Ltd, 2801 John Street, Markham, Ontario, Canada L3R 1B4
Penguin Books (NZ) Ltd, 182–190 Wairau Road, Auckland 10, New Zealand

Penguin Books Ltd, Registered Offices: Harmondsworth, Middlesex, England

—

First published 1971
Reprinted 1978, 1986, 1990

—

ISBN 0 14 071042 6

—

—

Made and printed in Great Britain
by Butler & Tanner Ltd, Frome and London
Set in Monotype Plantin

CONTENTS

★

Map References

★

The numbers printed in italic type in the margin against the place names in the gazetteer of the book indicate the position of the place in question on the index map (pages 2–3), which is divided into sections by the 10-kilometre reference lines of the National Grid. The reference given here omits the two initial letters (formerly numbers) which in a full grid reference refer to the 100-kilometre squares into which the country is divided. The first two numbers indicate the *western* boundary, and the last two the *southern* boundary, of the 10-kilometre square in which the place in question is situated. For example Wallasey (reference 3090) will be found in the 10-kilometre square bounded by grid lines 30 and 40 on the *west* and 90 and 00 on the *south*; Crewe (reference 7050) in the square bounded by grid lines 70 and 80 on the *west* and 50 and 60 on the *south*.

The map contains all those places, whether towns, villages, or isolated buildings, which are the subject of separate entries in the text.

FOREWORD

The preparation for this volume was in the hands of Mr Edward Hubbard. As far as I could see it was faultless even down to handwriting. Mr Hubbard also wrote parts of the book. His name appears, abbreviated to EH, at the start of Birkenhead, the Eaton Hall Estate, and Port Sunlight, and in connexion with a number of Wirral places and some other bits and pieces. They are all entirely his except for Eccleston church, which is a joint effort. Moreover, Mr Hubbard read my whole text and improved it by corrections and suggestions. Finally, Mr Hubbard drove me through Cheshire, and his even temper and his psychological treatment of my moments of despondency were invaluable. He spoiled me thoroughly. So did his parents while I stayed with them. I am very grateful for their generous hospitality, and I also want to thank warmly Dr and Mrs Andor Gomme for their hospitality and my friends Reggie and Camilla Bagg for theirs while I battled with the introduction to the book. Miss Dorothy Dorn once again did the typing from my very irritating handwriting to perfection, and my secretary Mrs Judith Tabner the extensive correspondence.

Next Mr Hubbard and I have to thank rectors, vicars, priests, ministers for answering inquiries and checking proofs, owners and occupiers of houses for allowing access, very often where the public had no access, the Ministry of Housing and Local Government (here abridged MHLG) for putting at our disposal their lists of buildings of architectural and historic interest, and the librarians and staffs of public libraries, large and small, for dealing so helpfully with questions often of a tricky nature. Among them I may mention particularly Mr H. H. G. Arthur and Mr S. Marchant (Birkenhead), Mr P. D. Pocklington (Chester), Mr J. Sankey (Crewe), Mr B. Schofield (Hyde), Mr W. J. Skillern (Stockport), Mr B. C. Redwood (County Archivist), Mrs E. Berry (Chester City Archivist).

In addition Mr Hubbard wants to express his gratitude to Viscount Leverhulme and Mr J. Lomax-Simpson for help with the architectural activities of the first Viscount, Mr T. M. T. Hopkins and Mr J. C. Roberts for help on Port Sunlight in particular, Mr A. R. Mitchell for help concerning the Eaton Estate, Mr J. E. Allison for help concerning the history of Birkenhead, and the Rev. R. J. McGown for help in connexion with Caldy.

I, also in addition, am much indebted to the Very Rev. G. W. O.

Addleshaw, Dean of Chester, Sir Robert Somerville, Clerk to the Council of the Duchy of Lancaster, Canon M. H. Ridgway, Mr Raymond Richards, Mr Peter Howell, and Mr Donald Buttress, and for more specific reasons to Mr Mallinson and Mr Sydney Lee (Crewe Hall), Mr A. C. Sewter (William Morris), Dr H. L. Turner (Walls of Chester), Mr Denis Evinson (Catholic churches), Mr W. H. Hoult (Marple), Mr David McLaughlin (Knutsford), and Mr John Clare (Lyme Park).

The Introduction to Prehistoric Remains and all the gazetteer entries on them are by Derek Simpson. The Introduction to, and the gazetteer entries about, Roman Remains are by Professor Barry Cunliffe. The Introduction to Building Materials is written by Alec Clifton-Taylor. The National Monuments Record (NMR) have as always been helpful and generous. Cheshire is not one of their show counties. There are so far for the whole county only fifty-seven boxes. For Victorian churches my own material was greatly increased by Mr Peter Ferriday's Index of Restorations, which he most generously gave on permanent loan to The Buildings of England *(abbreviated* PF*), and by the Goodhart-Rendel Index at the Royal Institute of British Architects (abbreviated* GR*). Sir Thomas Kendrick's Index of Stained Glass I have, thanks to his kindness, also had access to (abbreviated* TK*).*

The principles on which the following gazetteer is founded are the same as in the forty-one volumes of The Buildings of England *which precede it. I have myself seen everything that I describe. Where this is not the case the information obtained by other means is placed in brackets. Information ought to be as complete as the space of the volume permits for churches prior to c.1830 and all town houses, manor houses, and country houses of more than purely local interest. Movable furnishings are not included in secular buildings, though they are in churches. Exceptions to the latter rule are bells, hatchments, chests, chairs, plain fonts, and altar tables. Royal arms, coffin lids with foliate crosses, and brasses of post-Reformation date are mentioned occasionally, church plate of after 1830 only rarely. Crosses are omitted where only a plain base or a stump of the shaft survives. As for churches and chapels of after 1830, I had to make a selection, and this is dictated by significance otherwise in the light of architectural history. The same applies to secular buildings of the c19 and c20. The churches of the latter centuries are frequently not orientated. In these cases* W, E, N, *and* S *in my gazetteer are to be understood ritually, i.e. with the altar end called* E.

Finally, as in all previous volumes, it is necessary to end the foreword to this with an appeal to all users to draw my attention to errors and omissions.

INTRODUCTION

CHESHIRE is not a county much visited by architectural travellers. Nor is it often the specific goal of tourists. It would probably be right to say that it is one of the least known of English counties. The reason may be that Cheshire has more than one face, and the tourist usually has an image beforehand of what he intends to find in a county. What would he think of when Cheshire is mentioned ? There is a wonderful corner of the Peak, with bare hills and villages in the folds and churches on wind-swept brows, but there is little of that. There is also 'Lancashire across the Border', textile towns like Stalybridge and Dukinfield, close to Ashton-under-Lyne, and Stockport is Lancashire in all but administrative identification. The prosperous businessmen of Manchester live at Alderley Edge or Wilmslow and do some shopping at Prestbury, the prosperous businessmen of Liverpool live in Wirral. These areas of outer Manchester and outer Liverpool have been called the Surrey of the North, villas in gardens with rhododendron drives. But Cheshire is also the flat land of the NW parts of the border with Wales, and it is foremost and centrally the attractive rolling country of the Cheshire Plain, with lakes or meres (the largest being Rostherne Mere and Combermere),* crossed in a N–S direction by sudden rocks from the hills of Frodsham and Helsby to Delamere Forest, on to Beeston and Peckforton, and s i of a gap to Bickerton Hill. All this central Cheshire is land unaffected by the commuters, and in the county – as in Shropshire and Herefordshire – the old families are still on the estates in which their ancestors had lived for centuries and sometimes in successor houses to ancestral castles and manors of before the Reformation. Such families are the Broughtons of Doddington, the Cholmondeleys of Cholmondeley, the Davenports of Capesthorne, the Egertons of Oulton, the Greys of Dunham Massey, the Greens of Poulton Lancelyn, the Grosvenors of Eaton, the Leches of Carden, the Leghs of Adlington, the Leycesters of Tabley, the Warburtons of Arley, the Wilbrahams of Rode.‡

But while this contrast of rural and urban-cum-suburban

* And subsidence has created more.

‡ Families either extinct or no longer resident in the county include e.g. the Brookes of Norton, the Cholmondeleys of Vale Royal, the Crewes of

Cheshire is what stays in one's mind, Cheshire has not a single really large town. Birkenhead and Stockport both have less than 150,000 inhabitants, Wallasey – visually not a town anyway – only just over 100,000, and Chester and Crewe under 60,000. Still, the existence of these and such smaller towns as Bebington, Sale, Cheadle, Altrincham, Ellesmere Port account for the fact that Cheshire, being in area exactly midway between the largest county (the West Riding) and the smallest (Rutland), ranks twelfth of forty-two in population.*

All this is the tourist's thoughts and views, but what has Cheshire to offer the architectural traveller? Overwhelmingly much of interesting Victorian building, sufficient and more than sufficient of the C16 to C18, a limited number of outstanding Perp churches, and very little earlier than the C14. The economic reasons for the sudden burst of ambitious church architecture in the C15 and the first half of the C16 have never been sufficiently investigated. They were not wool and cloth as in East Anglia, in the Cotswolds, in Somerset. It seems that they were just prosperous husbandry.‡

So the survey of building before the C15 can be brief.§ ANGLO-SAXON not a single church, though a number of sculptural fragments, the finest by far the Sandbach Crosses probably of the mid C9.‖ They are by the same hand and have always been a pair, like those of Gosforth, Penrith, and Beckermet St Bridget in Cumberland – we do not know why. They have vine-scrolls of Northumbrian origin, coarsened interlace, and some dragons, but foremost some religious scenes and a uniquely large number of doll-like heads and beasts in panels of various kinds. Sandbach has no parallel in Cheshire, but there is a whole group of Anglo-Danish, probably C11, crosses centred at Macclesfield (the

Crewe, the Davenports of Bramall, the Egertons of Tatton, the Leighs of Lyme, the Stanleys of Alderley and of Hooton.

* Counting the three Yorkshire ridings as three counties and using the 1961 census as the yardstick.

‡ Salt of course was a source of great wealth, but its exploitation was confined to the three 'wiches', Nantwich, Middlewich, and Northwich. Nantwich was the most important. It had eight salthouses in Domesday Book, about two hundred in 1600. But in the mid C19, after a long decline, the industry ceased at Nantwich. That protected the visual attraction of the town. There was no such protection at Northwich, where – or, to be precise, at Winnington near Northwich – I.C.I. grew out of it.

§ For the introductions to Prehistoric and Roman Cheshire and an account of building materials *see* pp. 45–51.

‖ Earlier still but alien is the Early Christian (?) font in Chester Cathedral.

Macclesfield Crosses are now in West Park) and extending into North Staffordshire. The most characteristic feature is that the shafts are square only above, but round below, with a hanging lunette or lobe at the transition. Such are the crosses of Cleulow (Wincle), and Lyme Park, and also those of Gosforth, and of Bakewell (Derbyshire) and Stapleford (Notts). Coffin slabs of the Anglo-Danish period are at West Kirby and Winsford (Over), the latter with an interesting inscription. Other Saxon fragments are preserved at Astbury, Bromborough, St John Chester, Frodsham, Neston, and Prestbury.

Of NORMAN architecture there is of course quantitively more, though also not much compared with other counties. Only two major monuments survive and they only partially: the shortened nave and the crossing at the W end of the choir at St John in Chester, the cathedral from 1075 to 1095, i.e. just before the present church was built, and the N transept, some fragments of the choir, and the NW tower of Chester Cathedral, which became a cathedral only in 1540 and had until then been a Benedictine abbey. Of all these the N transept of the cathedral comes first. This looks c.1100. The choir had circular piers with multi-scalloped capitals, as two fragments in the N choir aisle prove. The undercroft of the W range of the cathedral cloister also has short circular piers with circular many-scalloped capitals. This undercroft belongs to the same build as the NW tower, which however may be a little later. The undercroft has groin-vaults without ribs, the NW tower rib-vaults of an early profile. St Anselm's Chapel, the original abbot's chapel above the undercroft, is early C12 too. The Abbot's Passage below it is later, say c.1150. It has a rib-vault later than that of the NW tower. Finally the portal from cloister to N aisle is sumptuous Late Norman of about 1180–90.

St John has a shortened nave, again with round piers and round many-scalloped capitals, the four crossing piers, one bay of the chancel with a gallery, and parts of a NW tower, the connexion of which with the church is not clear. All this is C12, but we have no precise date. Late Norman is the surviving portal of Norton Priory, the only survival there except for another undercroft, again with circular piers and circular many-scalloped capitals. Cheshire is not a MONASTIC county. Benedictine Chester, founded in 1092, was of course the principal house. Of Vale Royal, one of the grandest Cistercian abbeys in the country, hardly anything is now visible. It was a late foundation – c.1275. C12 foundations were Combermere, 1133, also Cistercian;

Norton Priory, c.1133, Augustinian; Chester St Mary, c.1140, a Benedictine nunnery; Birkenhead, c.1150, Benedictine; and Stanlow, 1172, Augustinian. At Combermere there is a shadow of the refectory, at Chester St Mary nothing except a re-erected arch in Grosvenor Park, at Norton Priory no more than what has just been mentioned, at Birkenhead hardly anything of the church but some monastic remains, especially the rib-vaulted mid-C12 chapter house and the guest hall, at Stanlow just bits of walls. Stanlow moved to Whalley in Lancashire in 1294. À propos the Norman doorways of Chester Cathedral and Norton, more Norman doorways are preserved in parish churches – at Barthomley, Bruera, Church Lawton, Shocklach, and Shotwick, and arcades or parts of arcades at Bebington (still with square abaci and single-stepped arches), Frodsham (with the clerestory above), and Middlewich. At Prestbury alone, though cruelly dealt with by the C19, is a complete little church of nave and chancel. This has a w portal and above it the unusual motif of a row of seven statuettes. Figural Normal SCULPTURE can also be seen at Acton, near Nantwich, but it is not *in situ*, and on the font of Mellor, where it is wholly barbaric. There are other Norman FONTS as well, none however calling for special comment.

The THIRTEENTH CENTURY is, if anything, yet scarcer than the twelfth. The only major relics are the beautiful chapter house of c.1250–60 and the Lady Chapel of c.1260–80 of the cathedral, though both have suffered drastic restorations. Both have long lancets, stepped in the Lady Chapel, and the Lady Chapel has a vault with ridge ribs and tiercerons. Yet a little later than the Lady Chapel is the refectory, with its delightful arcaded staircase up to the reading pulpit. The earliest E.E. in the cathedral, however, is the e chapel of the n transept, rebuilt c.1200 with a plain rib-vault of diagonal ribs much more elegant than its late C12 predecessor of the Abbot's Passage. At St John the nave triforium must be of about the same date, whereas the clerestory is full C13. In the parish churches evidence is of the scantiest: the tower of Eastham with its gauche late C13 or early C14 spire, the lower parts of the tower and the arcade piers at Acton near Nantwich, the w responds of the arcade of Macclesfield parish church, and the late C13 arcades of Prestbury. So Prestbury had the same size in the C13 as it has now.

Evidence of the DECORATED style is more frequent, but again it is nearly all minor. The exception is Chester Cathedral, where the big building programme, started with the Lady Chapel, was now carried on westward. The new choir was begun about 1300 and consists of arcade piers with four major and four minor shafts separated by small hollows, a triforium, and a (rebuilt) vault with diagonal and ridge ribs. The abnormally long s transept followed about 1340, the nave s side about 1360. The N side was only dealt with about 1490, yet as a copy of the Late Dec work of the s side – sign of a remarkable and very English conservatism. The nave E bay on both sides incidentally differs from all others by having continuous mouldings, and that is a favourite Dec motif, often found in Dec doorways of parish churches. Where they survive, where perhaps arcades or at least responds and where aisle windows survive, we can deduce that, as in the case of Prestbury, the C14 churches preceding those of the Perp style were as large as their successors. Such is the case e.g. at Astbury, Malpas, Bunbury, and Wilmslow. Essentially Dec throughout is Nantwich, with its memorable octagonal crossing 18 tower. The piers here have four shafts and four thin flat diagonal projections. The tracery is interesting as marking the precise moment of change from Dec to Perp. Unfortunately no dates are known. Important as a dated piece is the Astbury tower. A will of 1366 refers to it. So Dec was then still the style used. The Dec chancel of Nantwich is rich in ornate details and it has, moreover, 18 & a stone lierne-vault, the only one in the county. Stockport has a 19 Dec chancel too, and Chester Cathedral sumptuous sedilia and piscina with nodding ogee arches. They were originally in St John's church. Northwich has a Dec stone reredos. Among ornamental motifs incidentally it is worth noting that ballflower does not occur once, in spite of its popularity in such western counties as Herefordshire.

If we have no date for the introduction of the PERPENDICULAR style at Nantwich we have none either in other places, and in any case most Perp work in Cheshire is late, C15 and more often than not late C15 and early C16. The earlier windows, where sufficiently large, have cusped lights and panel tracery, the later uncusped arched lights and often straight heads and no tracery at all. As for dates, they are as a rule of wills, and as a rule refer to steeples. Crossley and later Mr Richards have listed Late Perp dates as follows: Bunbury 1386 etc. and c.1527, and then at once: Prestbury c.1480, Weaverham pre-1485 etc., Mottram-in-Longdendale c.1486, Wrenbury c.1488, Malpas 1488 and 1508, Wilmslow c.1490–1522, Pott Shrigley 1491 ?, Gawsworth 1497–1536, Great Budworth 1498, 1527, Northwich (Witton) 1498, 1525, Shotwick c.1500, Middlewich c.1500, Burton 1500 (demolished), Savage Chapel Macclesfield between 1501 and 1507,

Bidston (Birkenhead) 1504–21, Handley 1512, Cheadle 1520–58, Lymm 1521 (demolished), Disley c. 1520–58, Grappenhall c.1525–39, Little Budworth c.1526, Wallasey c.1527, Barthomley c.1528, Rostherne 1533 (demolished), Mobberley c.1533, Winsford (Over) 1543. Of twenty, eleven are of 1520 and after.

_{21 & 25} The principal Perp churches of Cheshire are Astbury, Great Budworth, Malpas, Northwich, Barthomley, Gawsworth. At Chester Cathedral the N aisle of about 1490 has already been ₂₇ mentioned; the w doorway of the cathedral and its surround are of the early C16, the cloister was rebuilt c. 1525–30. At Macclesfield the Savage Chapel has a three-storeyed porch. So has Astbury, where very high two-transomed w windows are l. and r. of it and the tower is Dec and stands N of the N aisle. It has a recessed spire, a rare motif in Cheshire (cf. Davenham). Nor are broach spires much more frequent. Those at Eastham and Bebington are both C14, the former perhaps even earlier. Cheshire towers are never as spectacular as those of Somerset. The most ambitious ones have some simple frieze decoration just below the battlements and eight instead of four pinnacles. Bell-openings, if more conspicuous than usual, have three lights (about a dozen and a half) or two-light twins, occasionally gathered under a pointed-arched hoodmould (Barthomley) or an ogee-arched hoodmould (Middlewich, Sandbach, Wybunbury). St Peter at Chester, Macclesfield, and Malpas have rib-vaults inside the tower.

As for the bodies of parish churches, one can list quite a number of characteristic Cheshire features. One is ROOFS. Cheshire has fine Perp roofs. They are of low pitch with camber-beams, panels, ₂₄ and many bosses. Such are at Astbury, Barthomley, Cheadle, Chester St Mary, Disley, Great Budworth, Malpas, and Northwich (Witton). The ceiling of the N transept of Chester Cathedral is similar.* Clerestories are here and there made most impressive outside and inside by placing the windows close together, two to a bay. Audlem (twelve windows), Astbury, Barthomley, Brereton, and Sandbach are examples. Sandbach by the way has a high w porch open to N and s as well as the w. Northwich on the other hand has a polygonal E apse (like Lichfield Cathedral, Lichfield, though in Staffordshire, being the medieval cathedral of Cheshire), and Middlewich an aisle canted at both the w and E ends.

Late Perp churches tend to omit the chancel arch, i.e. let the

* The early type, the single-framed roof, is represented by Tarvin, though as late as the late C14.

arcades run to the very E end without any halt. Such is the case
e.g. at Astbury and at Weaverham. Finally the arcades. By far
the most usual elements are octagonal piers and double-chamfered
arches. They can be called the standard elements. In other
counties standard Perp is four shafts and four diagonal hollows.
This is what in Cheshire Brereton, Bunbury, and Northwich 26
(Witton) do. But more sophisticated forms occur. The type of
Chester Cathedral is continued at Malpas, the type of Nantwich
at Barthomley. Astbury has instead of single shafts thin triple 28
shafts in the main directions; so has the S arcade of Great Budworth. Capitals are only rarely decorated with foliage or fleurons
(Chester Cathedral transepts and nave, Middlewich, Mobberley).
As a rule they are moulded, and in the C16 the mouldings are
often shockingly primitive.

But the main Cheshire speciality has been left to the last –
TIMBER-FRAMED CHURCHES. Of course they exist in Shropshire and Herefordshire as well, but according to Professor Horn
those of Marton and Lower Peover may well be C13 and are 33
certainly C14 at the latest and are thus the earliest of their kind &
in Europe. In other cases parts are still timber-framed (War- 34
burton, Chadkirk at Romiley, Siddington, Holmes Chapel), or 35
we know from old illustrations or other sources that the prede-
cessors of later churches had been timber-framed. Inside, this
means timber piers with longitudinal as well as transverse braces,
the former imitating the arcade arches of stone churches. Marton
has a W tower which is surrounded on the W, N, and S by an aisle
in the Essex way.

TIMBER-FRAMED HOUSES of the Perp period must once have
been far more frequent than they are now, and as timber-
framing remained a standard structural technique well into the
C17, one has to extricate pre-Reformation elements from later
work. Bramall and Little Moreton Hall are two of the half-
dozen most famous of English timber-framed houses. But that is
due to what was done to them in the later C16 and early C17.
However, the hall at Little Moreton Hall is C15 and the hall
porch too, and at Bramall the S range with the chapel is C15 –
see e.g. the straight-headed windows with cusped ogee-arched
lights. The roof of the range has wind-braces forming quatrefoils,
and the same is true of the splendid roof of Tatton Old Hall.
Square-headed windows also appear at the Old Rectory at
Gawsworth, which has in addition one queen-post truss of the
hall roof and the three service doors from the former screens
passage. These three doors incidentally are preserved also in a

41 stone hall, that of Chorley Hall, Alderley Edge, which must be
C14. The screen of course was of timber here too, and the spere
posts have been preserved. The spere-truss, i.e. the two main
posts of the screen carried up to the top of the hall to support a
roof truss, is a Lancashire and Cheshire speciality. The Great
Hall of 1505 of Adlington Hall has it also, and moreover the
grandest canopy of honour above the dais, a panelled hammerbeam roof, and a fragment of the screen itself with very delicate
small-scale tracery. It is the type of tracery one is used to finding
30 in CHURCH SCREENS in Cheshire and especially in Wales.
31 Cheshire has a number of very fine ones, foremost Mobberley and
Astbury. The parclose screens at Bunbury and Cheadle are dated
respectively 1527 and 1529, and that at Bunbury is memorable for
having – painted, not carved – the earliest Renaissance motifs in
the county. Of CHURCH WOODWORK otherwise the best by far
20 are of course the stalls of Chester Cathedral with gorgeous canopies and misericords, and those of Nantwich, also with canopies
and misericords, and both of the late C14.* Nantwich has a Perp
29 stone pulpit, Mellor and Marbury Perp timber pulpits. In other
materials hardly anything deserves inclusion here: an iron-bound
15 chest at Malpas, a Chalice and Paten of c.1370 at Aston-by-
Sutton and a Chalice of 1496 at Chester Cathedral, and some
stained glass of the Dec (Tattenhall) and Late Perp (Astbury
and St Mary-on-the-Hill, Chester) period.

To return to SECULAR ARCHITECTURE after this digression:
CASTLES are few. The surviving tower of Chester Castle is of the
13 late C12 or early C13 and has a rib-vaulted chapel. The walls
2 of Chester are, as everyone knows, among the most complete in
1 England. Beeston Castle is in ruins. Only the inner gatehouse
stands more or less complete. This and the rest of the towers and
walls of inner and outer bailey are C13 work, as may be a little of
the scanty remains of Halton Castle within Runcorn New Town.
Other castles have disappeared entirely, e.g. the royal castles of
Frodsham, Macclesfield, and Shotwick and the barons' castles of
Aldford, Dodleston, Dunham Massey, Kinderton near Middlewich, Malpas, Nantwich, Newhall near Combermere, Northwich,
Oldcastle near Malpas, Pulford, Shipbrook near Davenham,
Shocklach, and Stockport.

Of manor houses Storeton Hall of c.1360 has only a scanty
fragment of original work, Thurstaston Hall has in the w wing a
C15 roof with cusped wind-braces, Tabley Old Hall retained
medieval work prior to its collapse, but Tatton Old Hall has an

* Other MISERICORDS at Malpas and Bebington.

even finer (and also larger) roof, Ince an impressive fragment of
c.1500 belonging to a summer residence of the Abbots of
Chester. It has large, straight-headed windows. Another summer
residence of the Abbots, Saighton Grange of c.1490, has a monumental gatehouse with a spectacular oriel window. The northern ₃₂
type of fortified house, the so-called tower house, is represented
by two buildings: Doddington of 1365 or 1403, complete to the top
and with tunnel-vaulted basement, and Brimstage of after 1398 ₂₂
with two bays of rib-vaulting on the ground floor. Alvanley Hall
has two round piers in the basement, and Utkinton Hall one tall
octagonal wooden pier now running through two storeys. It is
entirely mysterious. Vaulted basements or crypts, as they are
wrongly called, were a feature of town-houses, and Chester still
has about twenty of them. They are listed on p. 132, but only a
few are mentioned in the gazetteer. Some have tunnel-vaults, but
the best have rib-vaults with single-chamfered ribs. The earliest
have no ridge-ribs (11 Watergate Street); later they have (40 ₁₆
Eastgate Street). No. 12 Bridge Street still has six bays of rib-
vaulting. The earliest are undoubtedly of before 1300. In the c 13
also the ROWS must have been invented, and nobody has yet
convincingly explained how they came about, and what specific
purpose they served. They are covered elevated walks at first-
floor level, though not raised high above the streets due to the
ground floors (the level of the so-called crypts) being sunk. The
Rows remain as continuous walkways, in many cases incorporated
in subsequent rebuildings.

It has been said *en passant* that the earliest Renaissance motifs
of Cheshire are those of the parclose screen at Bunbury of 1527.
One's experience in other counties is that one must watch
FUNERARY MONUMENTS to see how the Renaissance established
itself. But Cheshire in this respect disappoints. It has a number
of good medieval monuments but then a gap of relevant material
which extends over more than fifty years. As for the Middle Ages
the earliest is probably the stone knight at Rostherne (c 13), but
the best quality was obtained in alabaster – late c 14 Knights at
Acton († 1399, in a fine stone recess), Bunbury († 1394), and ₂₃
Barthomley, early c 15 at Over Peover († 1410), mid-c 15 at Over
Peover († 1456), Cheadle, and Macclesfield, late c 15 at Macclesfield (c.1475, † 1492, † 1495), and early c 16 at Macclesfield too ₃₆
(c.1500, † 1527, † 1528) and at Malpas († 1522). On the tomb- &₃₇
chests are mourners or angels with shields. They are types
frequent in other counties as well, where alabaster monuments were made or exported to. BRASSES are all but absent – one

of *c.*1460 at St Peter Chester, one † 1460 at Wilmslow, one † 1513 at Wybunbury, one of *c.*1543 at Winsford (Over), and the famous
266 Pardon Brass † 1506 at Macclesfield promising 26,000 days of relief from Purgatory for five Pater Noster, five Ave, and one Creed. The last of the pre-Reformation effigies are the brass one at Winsford (Over) and a stone one † 1536 at Wilmslow, the first of the post-Reformation ones are two good incised slabs at Over Peover with dates of death 1573 and 1586 and Sir John Warburton at Great Budworth who died in 1575. And then there is again nothing until the early years of James I. It is a strange situation; for between 1605 and 1645 ten at least are worth including in this survey. That at Malpas (Cholmondeleys) of 1605 is the traditional tomb-chest with recumbent effigies, that at Gawsworth (a Fitton † 1619) also, but with kneeling children along the tomb-chest and a big wall-plate, that at Bowdon (Breretons † 1630) has his effigy behind and above hers and an arch on columns. Sir John Savage and his wife at Macclesfield (*c.*1630) has her effigy behind and above his, and in addition also columns, and an arch. This kind of arrangement recurs at Wybunbury († 1614) and originally existed also in Sir Edward Fitton's tomb at Gawsworth († 1643). Variations in posture are the Oldfield in St Mary in Chester, † 1616, who is propped up on his side, the Gamul in the same church, also † 1616, who introduces a son sitting pensively at the feet of his mother, the Sir Edward Fitton † 1643 at Gawsworth a little daughter standing at the heads of the parents.
52 Dame Alice Fitton at Gawsworth, † 1627, is shown seated, and her children kneel not small against the tomb-chest but large in front and behind her. William Smethwick † 1643 and his wife at Brereton are shown as three-quarter figures frontally placed. But the most impressive of the Jacobean monuments is Francis Fitton's also at Gawsworth, 1608, a table-tomb with the effigy above and his skeleton below – and that is a medieval type.

From the monuments we must go to the houses of those whom they record, and here there is plenty. ELIZABETHAN HOUSES first. It has already been said that in timber-framed architecture structurally at least the Renaissance made no difference. It is decoration which distinguishes the new from the old, and little of that decoration is Renaissance – occasional small foliage motifs as e.g. in the N range of Little Moreton Hall, or among other black on white motifs the baluster. But the standard decoration is geometrical. The timber-framed house before the mid C16 had had closely set vertical struts and herringbone patterns of diagonal braces. Now we find the concave-sided lozenges, quatrefoils, and variations on the theme of a white cross, by cutting the shape upright or diagonally. When all these motifs first appeared has never been fully investigated. Quatrefoils are to be found at Little Moreton Hall already about 1500 (and are already imitated by painting instead of carving by 1559).* For 1559 is the date at Little Moreton Hall of the two large polygonal bay windows 38 which nearly touch one another and of the gloriously wonky S & range with the long gallery piled on top. Bramall also once had 39 such a long gallery on top. Bramall has inside the dates 1592, 1599, and 1609. It is hard to choose the few best Elizabethan timber-framed houses. Handforth Hall is dated 1562 and has the plan with recessed centre and projecting wings and a good stair- 47 case which, however, is probably later. Churche's Mansion at 40 Nantwich is dated 1577, Soss Moss Hall, Nether Alderley 1583, Hampton Old Hall, Malpas 1591. The District Bank at Prestbury is small but exceptionally pretty, Haslington Hall is unusually large. A speciality of Cheshire is overhangs hidden by coving. In Chester, one of the most notable timber-framed buildings is the Leche House. Others, with greater or lesser degrees of C19 and C20 restoration, are Stanley Palace, 1591, Bishop Lloyd's House, The Falcon, probably 1626, and the Bear and Billet, 1664.

The taste for black and white is an unsophisticated taste.‡ Black and white patterns rarely aspire to convincing composition, and their spread all over deprives a building of those areas of repose which the plain walls of stone or brick houses provide, though it must be admitted that the popular diapering of brick by vitrified, i.e. blackish, brick shows that the Elizabethan and Jacobean age liked the enlivening by elementary geometrical motifs. Moreover, many of the major monuments of the age prove that the taste of the patrons as well as the architects was indeed unsophisticated.

Take the frontispiece of Lyme Park of c.1570 with its crazy 42 columniation, wavering between a bipartite and a tripartite rhythm, or take even the frontispiece of Brereton Hall of 1586 43 with its formerly much higher turrets, more consistent though the composition is. And take the chimneypieces at Lyme, at 44 Brereton, at Bramall, at Crewe Hall (so far as they are original

* And Mr Richards told me that at Gawsworth Old Hall timber-framing altogether was imitated by painting on brick c.1700.

‡ Professor Mario Praz (*On Neo-Classicism*) says: '. . . as though the walls were playing cards – clubs'.

or facsimile), at Dorfold, at Gawsworth (rectory), at Tabley, and also at Audlem and Bromborough – how bad is often the carving, how naïve the characterization of figures.

Lyme Park, though now largely late C 17 and early C 18, must already in Elizabethan days have had the same size as it has now and is thus the largest house of its date in the county. On a hill near by stands the Cage, a tower with angle turrets which must have been built as a 'standing', i.e. a look-out to watch hunting from. Another standing is Leasowe Castle, Wallasey, as it was built in 1593. It is octagonal. 1597 is the date recorded for Ardern Hall near Bredbury, a mystery house with stepped gables and windows which have mullions and transoms, but in the gables stepped arched lights. Another problem building, though for different reasons, is Willaston Hall in Wirral. This looks a normal moderate-sized Elizabethan house on the familiar E-plan, but the hall is in the middle and entered in its middle, and that is the sign of a hankering after symmetry rare before the late Elizabethan years, and rare even then. Yet Willaston is said to have been dated 1558. There is another house which has the same motif, Bidston Hall, Birkenhead, and here two dates have been put forward with acceptable reasons: pre-1594 and c.1620–1. The latter fits better, especially as the entry is in a big bow, and behind the hall and axial with it is a three-bay loggia on Tuscan columns. This motif repeats at Woodhey Hall, Ridley, where it may have belonged to a summer house. Of the house itself nothing is left.

That leaves the two best Jacobean houses of Cheshire; Dorfold Hall of 1616 and Crewe Hall begun in 1615. Both are of brick. Dorfold has a recessed centre and two short wings and the porch and the hall bay as counterpieces in the re-entrant angles – the scheme of e.g. Chastleton in Oxfordshire and Ludstone in Shropshire. The windows are large, and above the hall is a gorgeous
48 Great Chamber with the stucco tunnel-vault with the character-istic Jacobean interlaced broad studded bands forming themselves into geometrical patterns. The Drawing Room at Lyme Park has
45 another such ceiling, though flat. Crewe Hall, completed in 1636 and internally much rebuilt after a fire in 1866, has a frontispiece and a number of bay windows and shaped gables. The staircase
46 is one of the most ingeniously planned and ornately executed in the whole of Jacobean England, and it is not the invention of the Victorian architect, *E. M. Barry*, as one may well think.

How long did this style, or at least did these motifs, continue? In the countryside remarkably long. Halton Old Hall is still Jacobean in type and dates from 1693, a house at Lower Kinner-

ton still has Dutch gables in 1685, and a house of the same year
at Crowton mullioned windows of Jacobean proportions.

Conservatism is even more universal in SEVENTEENTH
CENTURY CHURCHES. The latest church work so far observed
was that of the 1550s. Then, with one exception, there is a gap
of fifty years. The exception is High Legh of c.1581, built with
timber piers as the chapel to High Legh Hall. The next after that
is Harthill probably of 1609, and that has mullioned windows
with arched lights and a hammerbeam roof with Jacobean details.
Both the type of window and the type of roof are of course Henry
VIII tradition, and they are continued e.g. at Lower Whitley and
in 1627 at Hargrave. The hammerbeam roof even appears as late
as 1662 at Handley, and the mullioned windows with arched
lights appear in the Legh Chapel of Macclesfield parish church
in 1620, and in the great chapel window in the back of Crewe Hall
c.1615–36. Nor are these the latest dates; for the chancel of
Great Barrow as late as 1671 has the same windows and a hammerbeam truss, the chapel of Tabley Hall has the same windows
again and a shaped E gable as late as 1675–8, and the same is true
even in 1689–91 for the E window of Tushingham, though there
the side windows have straight tops, and mullioned windows
with arched lights were even the choice for Ashton-upon-
Mersey in 1714.

A particularly telling instance of conservatism is the three
almost identical UNITARIAN CHAPELS (originally Presbyterian)
of Knutsford 1689, Macclesfield also 1689, and Dean Row, 56
Wilmslow, 1693. They still have two-light mullioned windows,
and incidentally a peculiar arrangement of access to the gallery:
two staircases lead outwards from near the centre, parallel with
the front wall, to upper doors above the lower in the first and last
bays. The type was no longer used at Hale in 1723 and Nantwich
in 1726.

In the architecture of the established church the change to the
classical style is heralded much earlier by one exceptional piece,
the N (Mainwaring) Chapel in Over Peover church. This has an
arcade of columns, not piers, and yet dates from c.1648–50.* It
is no chance that it is at Over Peover Hall that the stables have 50
the earliest classical columns in secular architecture too. The
cubicles are separated by Tuscan columns, and this was done in
1654. On the other hand it is true that the loggias of Woodhey

* Farndon church has round piers in 1658 with an unselfconscious intention
no doubt of getting near the columnar shape. Church Minshull in 1702–4 still
does the same.

(Ridley) and Bidston (Birkenhead) already have Tuscan columns, and that above the columns of the stables there is still strapwork.

Strapwork is the distinguishing feature of C17 CHURCH FURNISHINGS. It characterizes such screens as those at Middlewich of 1632 and Prestbury, the very complete furnishings of the 51 chapel of Cholmondeley Castle of 1652–5, and still – the same conservatism again – the tower gallery at Mobberley of 1683.* The most typical Elizabethan and Jacobean motif of woodwork is the blank arch on stubby pilasters. It occurs in plenty of pulpits in Cheshire and all over the country. It also occurs e.g. in the Stanley Pew at Nether Alderley. Other kinds of church furnishings need only be mentioned in passing. Baddiley still has its wooden tympanum with the Commandments, the Creed, and the Lord's Prayer inscribed under arches – a rare survival. It is dated 1663. Fonts are not of special interest, except perhaps the small group of the 1660s (Brereton 1660, Bunbury 1663, Sandbach 1667) with the elementary geometrical motifs or very summarily treated leaves or flowers as they are typical of the immediate post-Civil-War fonts everywhere in England. Often wooden covers go 49 with the fonts. A splendid example is at Astbury. Church plate is negatively remarkable. In nearly all counties the Elizabethan Settlement brought a rush of orders for cups and covers or chalices and patens. The operative dates are round about 1570. In Cheshire for some reason there was no demand, and most church plate is C17 and later. Chester Cathedral has ten pieces of 1662. The prettiest C17 stained glass, to conclude with, is the panel at Farndon with scenes and figures depicting Cheshire Royalists at the time of the Civil War.

That leaves FUNERARY MONUMENTS. Cheshire has one speciality there, the painted heraldic tablets mostly connected with the four generations of the Holme family, all called *Randle Holme*, heralds, historians, and antiquarians. They all seem to have painted such tablets. The tablets range from 1611 to 1708 54 in Audlem church, from 1614 to 1698 in Chester Cathedral, from 1627 to 1702 at Stoak, and others are at Backford, Bunbury, and Thornton-le-Moors. Rather more eventful is a painted tablet † 1624 at Over Peover which shows the skeleton of the deceased. Carved effigies of course continue. Alabaster disappears, and white marble comes in – see Philip Mainwaring † 1647 at Over Peover (in the chapel which was the first effort at a classical C17 53 style in Cheshire) and Sir Richard Wilbraham † 1643 and his

---

* Birtles church has much C17 woodwork, but it is all brought in.

wife † 1660 at Acton near Nantwich. A later c 17 fashion was
cartouches without effigies or portraits. They are current everywhere, but that of 1668 at Stoak is exceptionally swagger. Before 55
the end of the century totally new and much more varied and
resourceful types began to appear. Then Earl Rivers is represented in 1696 at Macclesfield semi-reclining and with a
demonstrating hand. Curtains are looped over columns which
carry a segmental pediment. The monument is signed by
William Stanton. Similar is the Bretland monument at Mottram- 58
in-Longdendale († 1703), and much more novel still the monument to Diana Warburton at St John Chester † 1693. This is by 60
Pearce and has as its centre a skeleton upright. Reredos or
aedicule backgrounds now became popular too.

The aedicule motif is closer to the c 18 than to the earlier c 17,
and the same can be said of certain LATE SEVENTEENTH
CENTURY HOUSES. The elements now are symmetry of the
façade, regularly distributed cross windows, and hipped roofs.
Thurstaston Hall of *c*.1680 has the two former, Golborne Old
Hall, Handley, of 1682 has all these, and Golborne has in
addition a large doorway with pilasters and pediment. Mellor
Hall probably of 1688 is the same, though the excessively steep
open scrolly pediment is a conservative element. Glegg's Hall,
Broxton, of 1703 belongs to this group as well, and except for
the change from casement to sash windows the type goes on into
the Georgian period essentially unchanged.

Once more, in the countryside, conservatism prevailed. Thus
transomed windows and the horizontally placed ovals which one
has a right to connect with about 1675 are elements of the Old
School at Burton, Wirral, of 1724, a very steep triangular pediment occurs in the centre of a house of 1733 at Malpas, and two-
light mullioned windows, though now vertical and no longer horizontal and though with raised surrounds, are used at the Home
Farmhouse at Thelwall in 1745.

The purest late c 17 Classical of the Wren kind must be sought
out inside the houses. The best examples are the reredos in the
chapel of Dunham Massey (hardly possible as early as 1655), the
panelling and doorcases from Wolseley Hall in Staffordshire at
the White House, Gawsworth, at Adlington Hall (w range), and
Lyme Park.* An easy help in dating is the twisted baluster 57
replacing the various forms of Jacobean and Carolean balusters.
Early cases are in the communion rail in the chapel of Tabley

* Or is this as late as *c*.1720? It can hardly be.

which dates from *c.*1678 and the staircase of Thurstaston which must date from *c.*1680, and a surprisingly early case of balusters of a two-strand twist is the staircase at Highfields, Audlem, dated 1674.*

The EARLY EIGHTEENTH CENTURY has left only one mansion on the grandest scale in Cheshire, *Leoni*'s Lyme Park 59 with its monumental s front, and that, though of the 1720s, is in style still close to the late C17 of Chatsworth. It is also close to a design by Boffrand of 1717, but neither has the detached upper portico of Lyme, and that is a Palladio motif. Internally especially in the woodwork Lyme Park continues direct from the Wren–Gibbons style – so much so that in some cases one remains in doubt about the real dates. But Lyme is exceptional. What else one sees of the early C18 in the county is average rather than above average – brick houses of five or seven bays, perhaps with giant pilasters or pilaster strips, perhaps with a doorway with open scrolly pediment, perhaps with segment-headed windows. None need be named here, except perhaps the oldest part of Rode Hall of *c.*1700 and Ramsdell Hall, Rode, of *c.*1720 because of its curious L-shape with the portal set diagonally across the angle. Here and only here Cheshire touches the English Baroque. Of town-houses two merit a mention: Jordangate House at Macclesfield of 1728 and Overton House at Congleton of about the same time.

For now the Cheshire houses come into their own, and the whole development of the county changed direction. The INDUSTRIAL REVOLUTION started earlier in Cheshire than in most counties. The earliest English silk mill was Lombe's at Derby of 1717. Charles Roe was a Derbyshire man, and he set up the first silk mill at Macclesfield in 1743. The building does not survive, but the church which he donated does (Christ Church 1775–6) and other mills of 1785 (Frost's) and so on into the C19. In 1801 Macclesfield had thirty silk mills and several cotton mills. The earliest at least partly surviving mill is John Clayton's at Congleton of *c.*1752 (the two lowest floors). About 1775–80 Sir George Warren converted part of the castle of Stockport into a mill. It was circular and embattled, and it is a pity that it has 66 disappeared. The next date is Samuel Greg's silk mill at Styal of 1784. All these mills are of course essentially utilitarian. They have four, five, or six floors, but attempts were made to make them more decorous by a mid-pediment and a clock cupola. Of working

* Two-strand newel posts are in Calveley Hall, Handley.

conditions the less said the better. Samuel Oldknow at Marple, e.g., whose original twenty-five bay, five-storey mill of 1790 – he had started an earlier one at Stockport in 1785 – is not preserved, used pauper children a great deal. The cruelty of it all was not felt; for Oldknow no doubt believed himself a philanthropist in so far as he built a new church for Marple.* Philanthropy of a more acceptable kind is the two unexpectedly large Sunday Schools of Stockport and Macclesfield, of 1805–6 and 1835 and 1813–14, four-storeyed, of brick and fourteen and ten bays long respectively. It makes a traditional major school building of the early c18 such as the Bluecoat School at Chester of 1717 appear quite small.

With the Bluecoat School we are back in the EARLY GEORGIAN decades, and a few more facts must be put on record about them. No major houses – that has already been said – and few church MONUMENTS. *Andries Carpentière*, resident in London but probably a Belgian, did the fine and large one at Bowdon to the Earl of Warrington in 1734 and another less successful one in the same church in 1735. There are no more items of CHURCH FURNISHING to be mentioned either. Two left their mark, as they became a widely accepted fashion: fonts with baluster stems and fluted bowls and brass chandeliers. The former begin with the beautiful black marble piece of 1697 in Chester Cathedral, and over a dozen followed.‡ English brass chandeliers are inspired by those of the c17 in Holland. The earliest dated one in Cheshire is at Holmes Chapel, and the date is 1708. This is followed by one at Prestbury of 1712. There are two types of these chandeliers only, one with the centre piece a ball, the other a more complex, more Baroque shape, and the two go on into the c19. The latest has the date 1822 (Macclesfield).

In CHURCHES the noteworthy fact is that they at last abandoned the Jacobean conventions and used large round-arched windows and, where opportunity arose, some classical motifs, a

* 1808–12. Only the tower now stands.

‡ Adlington Hall, Alsager, Ashton-upon-Mersey, Bruera, Cheadle, Church Minshull, Congleton, Heswall, St Thomas Hyde, Knutsford, Macclesfield, All Saints Marple, Pott Shrigley, Swettenham. But the font at Great Barrow of 1713 is still the pre-baluster c17 type. SUNDIALS by the way were popular too. They have baluster stems as a rule. The gazetteer does not include all of them. Examples are at Ashton-upon-Mersey, Backford, Burton, Farndon, Grappenhall, Great Budworth, Heswall, Knutsford, Malpas, Middlewich, Neston, Plemstall, Rostherne, Shotwick, Stretton, and Warburton (old church). The sundials at Harthill and West Kirby are columns.

pediment perhaps or a cupola. Most of the new churches are
small: Woodhey Chapel, Ridley, c.1700, Cholmondeley Castle
Chapel, Burton (Wirral) 1721, Capesthorne Chapel 1720–2
(much embellished inside in 1888–9), Somerford Chapel 1725,
Jenkin Chapel, Rainow, 1733, Carrington 1757–9. The first
major new churches were Congleton of 1740–2 with galleries and
Tuscan columns inside and a Gothic tower of 1786, and Knutsford of 1741–4, brick with giant Tuscan columns between nave
and aisles.

The SECOND HALF OF THE EIGHTEENTH CENTURY did not
change this pattern. Few large churches and more small ones.
The large ones are St Peter at Stockport of 1768, a plain, modest
brick building, Christ Church Macclesfield of 1775–6, already
mentioned as the gift of Charles Roe, and Alsager of 1789–90,
also a donation and ashlar-faced. Small churches need not be
enumerated. It is easy enough to say that the type was still regarded as acceptable at Threapwood in 1815.

For LATER GEORGIAN HOUSES the position is much more
complicated. Examples abound, and few are the clues to precise
dating. What one can say is that about 1750 there was a vogue
for Venetian windows with tripartite lunette windows over (Rode
Hall, the new house, 1752; Wimbolds Trafford Hall 1756;
Lawton Hall, Church Lawton; Ramsdell Hall, Rode). Venetian
windows are also the principal motif in a fine house of 1758 at
Macclesfield (now Rural District Council). Then there is a group
of larger brick houses of the mid-century which have a centre
and wings – the Palladian scheme. Such are Mottram Hall
Mottram St Andrew of c.1753 (where the centre has giant pilasters), Belmont Hall Great Budworth of 1755, and Tabley by
63 *John Carr* of 1761–7. Tabley has a grand portico towards the
62 garden. So has Adlington Hall in the range rebuilt in the 1750s, and
the difference between the design of a competent architect and
an amateur or country builder is instructive. Also to the 1750s
64 belongs the sham castle on Mow Cop, a folly built by the
Wilbrahams of Rode Hall, larger than most and with the assigned
date 1754 very early indeed. The fashion had only begun with
Sanderson Miller's tower on Edge Hill of c.1746–7. So medi-
evalism starts in Cheshire in 1754, but there were no immediate
successors.

The main stream of the later C18 and early C19 in the domestic
architecture of the county is the work of the Wyatts, *Samuel
Wyatt* (1737–1807) brother of the more famous James, and their
nephew *Lewis Wyatt* (1777–1853). Robert Adam on the other

hand is not represented at all. The Wyatt style is unmistakable, but the specific varieties of Samuel and of Lewis are hard to recognize. Smooth ashlar is what one expects, windows cut in without any mouldings, tripartite windows with blank segmental arches over, and a few medallions or oblong panels with garlands were the only decoration. James Wyatt at Heaton Hall outside Manchester had started it *c*.1772. Samuel followed at Doddington Hall in 1777–98, Samuel and after his death Lewis at Tatton Park *c*.1788–91 and 1807 etc., and probably Samuel again at Winnington Hall of the late c 18.

All three have exquisite INTERIORS, and it must here be added 70 as a postscript to the earlier Georgian decades that quite splendid Rococo interiors, especially stucco ceilings, stucco wall panels, and overmantels are found in Cheshire houses as well: in the great hall of Dunham Massey of *c*.1740, in the former Bishop's Palace at Chester (now YMCA) of *c*.1750, in the dining room at Tatton Park, in Rode Hall, Tabley House, Belmont Hall, Lawton Hall, and other less promising houses. Among the Wyatt interiors particularly fine are the circular Saloon of Doddington (and two ingeniously planned hexagonal rooms above it), the gallery at Winnington, and the staircase hall and the adjoining hall, both sky-lit, at Tatton Park. Shrigley Hall, Pott Shrigley, a little-known Regency house, repeated this arrangement, but unfortunately the staircase has recently been taken out. Regency also are the fine interiors of Poole Hall, Nantwich (1817).

Just as James Wyatt, in spite of the London Pantheon, Heaton Park, and so many other designs, did Fonthill in Gothic, so in Cheshire, side by side with the classical, GOTHIC MANSIONS, or rather castellated mansions, now began to appear: first Cholmondeley Castle designed in 1801 by its owner and enlarged 74 by *Sir Robert Smirke* in 1817–19.* The enlargement of Leasowe Castle, Wallasey by *Foster* of Liverpool followed in 1818, Combermere Abbey by the *Morrisons* of Ireland about 1820, Bolesworth Castle by *William Cole c*.1830, and Great Moreton 75 Hall in 1841–3 by *Blore* (for a Manchester manufacturer).‡   78

Meanwhile the Classical Revival had become the GREEK REVIVAL, and here for the first time we have a local architect whose work is as good as that of any in London: *Thomas Harrison*, born in 1744, and whose new buildings at Chester

* A special ornament of Cholmondeley Hall are the GATES and RAILINGS 61 of wrought iron by the *Davies* brothers of Wrexham who worked in the first half of the c18.

‡ The interiors are surprisingly fully preserved.

Castle are among the best of their date – 1785–1822 – in England. The main building with its hexastyle portico of unfluted Doric columns and its mighty projecting wings is reached by a wide-
67 spreading propylaea of Greek Doric columns – a powerful and
68 sombre composition. The Shire Hall inside, semicircular with a half-ring of columns and a coffered semi-dome, tells at once of the source of Harrison's inspiration: it is the Paris of Gondoin's École de Médicine of 1771–6, a building of great international impact. Harrison also did the new Northgate, in 1808–10 – new gates were gradually replacing the medieval gates of Chester, the Eastgate in 1768–9, the Bridgegate in 1782, and the Watergate in 1788 – and gave it sturdy unfluted Doric columns, and a number of private buildings, both in streets (1, Northgate Street, and in Watergate Street Watergate House) and in their own gardens (Dee Hills, Dee Hills Park, 1814). But Harrison's best house in Cheshire is Woodbank at (then outside) Stockport (1812). It was built for a cotton manufacturer. For Knutsford in 1815–18 Harrison designed another Sessions House, grand and taciturn also this.

With the growth of the towns other public buildings became necessary, and they had to be on a scale larger than usual before. Thus we find the utilitarian but by and large classical workhouses of Nantwich (1780), Northwich (1837), Arclid, i.e. Sandbach (1844), Stockport (1841), and Great Boughton (Chester, 1857–8),* the Deva Hospital at Upton outside Chester (1827–9), nineteen bays long, the Stockport Infirmary by *Richard Lane* (1832), twenty-nine bays long, with a Greek Doric portico, the town halls of Macclesfield (1823–4 by *Francis Goodwin*), with a Tuscan portico duplicated most effectively later (1869–71 by *J. Stevens*), and Stalybridge (1831–2), and the two Sunday Schools already mentioned.

In the towns major groups of houses now began to be treated as one long façade – the arrangement long familiar in London and most monumentally done at Bath and Edinburgh. Examples are Abbey Square at Chester of the 1750s and the long terrace of 1781 in Nicholas Street, Dysart Buildings at Nantwich, and,
73 most ambitious, Hamilton Square at Birkenhead, ashlar-faced, and begun in 1825. It reminds one immediately of Edinburgh.

The growth of the population of Cheshire due to the growth of industry had yet one more architectural consequence. There were, it was universally recognized, too few churches, and no

* Demolished.

churches, so the argument ran, meant no Christianity and hence no law and order. So Parliament voted £1,000,000 in 1818 and another £500,000 in 1824 for the building of churches where they were most urgently needed. These areas of need were of course London and in addition Yorkshire and Lancashire and also, though later, Cheshire. Cheshire built out of the first grant only one church, St Thomas at Stockport by *Basevi*, but twenty- 72 one out of the second grant, which allowed only something like ten per cent of the cost of each of them. COMMISSIONERS' CHURCHES, as one calls them, are recognizable, if a rough and ready generalization be permitted, by a minimum Gothic with long, lean windows along the sides, separated by thin buttresses, by no separate chancels or very short chancels, by no towers or thin W towers, and by many clumsy pinnacles.* The windows can be lancets or pairs of lancets (Dukinfield), or triplets of lancets (Hurdsfield), or lancets with Y-tracery (Bollington near Macclesfield). There may be aisles with tall octagonal or round piers, and there are (or were) nearly always galleries. Churches not built with Commissioners' money often look quite the same. Hurdsfield is one example, *Rickman*'s St Mary at Birkenhead of 1819–21 with its cast-iron tracery another,‡ and even Nonconformist chapels such as the Unitarian Church at Stockport (by *Tattersall*) of 1841–2 and the Congregational Church at Hatherlow near Bredbury of 1846 have the Commissioners' look.§ But the best of the churches of these years, the Stockport parish church by *Lewis Wyatt*, built in 1812–14, is much more substantial, and besides it is Perp.

Other early C19 churches chose yet other styles, and it can indeed be seen that Victorian historicism was on its way. NEO-GRECIAN for churches is rare in Cheshire. One can only name two: *George Basevi*'s St Thomas Stockport of 1822–5 with a high 72 W tower, but at its E end a giant portico, an ingenious but confusing scheme used at the same moment in St Matthew, Brixton, one of the London Waterloo churches (by Porden, 1822), and the excellent St John at Egremont, Wallasey, of 1832–3 with a Greek Doric portico. The architect was the otherwise unknown *H. Edwards*.‖

---

* A very early case of Gothic Revival is the top of the tower of Acton church near Nantwich, which dates from 1757, and is by *William Baker*.
‡ St Anne at Sale by *Hayley* of 1854 has thin iron piers.
§ Just as the Congregational Church at Macclesfield of 1822–3 looks like a Georgian brick church (and in fact became the church of St George).
‖ Classical also is St Werburgh at Birkenhead of 1835–7.

CHURCH FURNISHINGS of the late C18 and early C19 require only a few words. A large painting by *Hayman* of *c*.1778 is in Malpas church, a large painting by *Westall* of 1826 in Christ
65 Church, Chester. The best MONUMENTS are one † 1778 by *Nollekens* at Bruera, several by *Bacon*, especially that of Samuel Egerton at Rostherne of 1792 and that of Charles Roe, the founder of the Macclesfield silk industry, in the parish church. It has reliefs of the church, the mill, and the copper works with its smoking chimneys. There are two more Bacons at Runcorn (1792 and 1796), *Bacon Jun.* at Wrenbury and in other places, a fine *Flaxman* at Marple, Samuel Oldknow by *Chantrey* at Marple
83 too, and a specially ambitious *Westmacott Jun.* at Rostherne. The date of death is 1845. By *Knowles* of Manchester is a decidedly
82 idiosyncratic tablet at Hyde († 1344 and 1844).

By 1845 architecture was in full HISTORICISM. Already between 1816 and 1822 *Lewis Wyatt* had decorated the new
71 Dining Room at Lyme in the Wren style. Already in 1829 the same architect did Eaton Hall near Congleton in the Elizabethan style, and the same style was used in the same year for Willington Hall, in 1835 for Arrowe Hall at Woodchurch (Birkenhead), and in 1836–8 for Walton Hall at Higher Walton. Then, in 1837–9, *Blore* had built Capesthorne as a Jacobean prodigy mansion with two turrets. It was rebuilt after a fire by *Salvin* in 1861. But
1 & Salvin had already *c*.1844–50 built Peckforton Castle for Lord
79 Tollemache as the facsimile of a very grand C13 castle, correct and substantial enough to deceive anyone. This *reality*, as the Victorians called it, distinguishes Peckforton from such houses
78 as Great Moreton Hall, which only had been completed one year when Salvin began Peckforton.

It is the same with the VICTORIAN CHURCHES. Comparisons between the old and the new attitude present themselves everywhere. Take the Norman fashion, virulent all over England in the forties – who would be deceived by churches such as Hoylake (by *Sir James Picton*) of 1833, St Mary at Hyde of 1838–9 (by *Hayley & Brown*), or Buglawton of 1840 (by *Rampling*), or Rock Ferry (Birkenhead) of 1841–2 (by *Hurst & Moffatt*), or Byley of 1846 (probably by *J. Matthews*), or Swettenham also of 1846 (by *Derrick*), or Timperley of 1849 (by *J. Bayley*), or High Lane of 1852? Or take more ambitious Romanesque churches, i.e. churches in the *Rundbogenstil* as well, but Italian or Italy-French-Rhenish rather than English – whom would they deceive? One thinks of the bizarre and naïve Holy Trinity Birkenhead of 1837–40 by *Cunningham & Holme* and of the gorgeous and pre-

posterous Hooton church by *Colling* of 1858–62, with its
Byzantine touches added for good measure.

Or one may even take a major early church by *Pugin* such as
St Alban at Macclesfield of 1839–41, and one would still have to 76
admit that it belongs to Romantic rather than Victorian gothicism, although Victorian gothicism, i.e. the accurate recreation of
real Gothic churches, was invented by Pugin in 1840–1 and propagated by the Cambridge Camden Society and their journal *The
Ecclesiologist*, which began to appear in 1841, and by a few architect admirers of Pugin such as *George Gilbert Scott*. The ideal
Gothic was the so-called Second or Middle Pointed, i.e. the style
of Westminster Abbey and of churches of the late C13 and the
early C14,* and that makes it worth noting that *Sharpe* did a
normal Commissioners' church at Stalybridge in 1838–40 and
gave its lancet windows geometrical, i.e. Second Pointed, tracery.
Now Pugin's St Alban is still Perp, which Pugin later regarded
as the beginning of the end (as being for instance Erastian), and
the slender soaring piers have a quality of enthusiasm more of the
early than of the mid C19. Yet the tower, alas unfinished, is substantial and correct.‡ *Scott* is represented in Cheshire by quite a
number of buildings, churches except for the early workhouse of
Macclesfield done in 1843–5 in the Tudor style (i.e. in opposition
to the utilitarian Classical of earlier workhouses) when Scott was
still in partnership with Moffat. The only other secular buildings
are Sandbach School and the Literary Institute at Sandbach of
1849–50 and 1857 respectively, both of course Gothic. Among
churches there is nothing outstanding in scale, but nearly everything is serious and competent, and everything is Second Pointed.
But Scott was not the first in Cheshire to present the Second
Pointed. That was, so it seems, *Richard Tattersall*, who designed
the Unitarian Church at Dukinfield in 1840–1, a fact worth
following up. Admittedly Tattersall's church is unconvinced and
undistinguished, whereas Scott's never lack a certain distinction.
They can be mechanical in the details, they may play safe. But
Scott always followed good precedent, and he knew it by heart.
Originality was confined to the flora of his capitals. In chrono-
logical order they are Antrobus (1847–8), Kingsley (1849–50),
Halton (1851–2), St James, New Brighton (Wallasey, 1854–6),
Hulme Walfield (1855–6), Crewe Green (1857–8), Sandbach St

---

* The *Handbook of English Ecclesiology* in 1847 writes indeed: 'The pre-
vailing character of the Cheshire churches is decidedly poor; the style is most
commonly late . . . Third Pointed.'
‡ *Pugin*'s St Winifrede at Neston of 1840 and 1843 is minor.
2—C.

86 John (1861), Bromborough, a fine composition from the s (1862–4), Rode (1864), Chester St Thomas (1869–72), Stretton near Appleton (1870). Scott's practice was enormous, and the result was a high *niveau* rather than individual achievement. He was, like many Victorian church architects, also keenly interested in furnishings. His iron screens are familiar and famous. An outstanding example of the type of ironwork he designed or promoted is the grand cross for Chester Cathedral (which Scott
87 restored), now at Dunham-on-the-Hill. No other London architect had anything like so many Cheshire commissions as Scott, and what e.g. *Salvin* and even *Street* and *Slater & Carpenter* did, is not worth recording. *Butterfield*'s Christleton, in spite of some internal polychromy, has nothing of his aggressiveness. *Sedding*'s St Martin Marple of 1869–70 is so quiet that one may well overlook some subtle touches. *Brooks*'s St Michael at Crewe of 1883 etc. is a piece of strong architecture, and the capitals are already – very early indeed – in the Arts and Crafts taste.* But the best Victorian churches of the last quarter of the century are *Pearson*'s masterly Norley of 1878–9, with a broad central tower, and his equally masterly Thurstaston of 1885, which, unlike
96 Norley, is vaulted throughout,‡ and *Bodley*'s Eccleston of 1899, one of the parish churches of the Duke of Westminster's Eaton Hall estate, large, soaring, solemn, and very subdued. The Duke used a famous London architect for his church, and, as we shall see, a famous London architect for his huge mansion.

Taking all in all the ecclesiastical building of the Victorian Age in Cheshire, that was not so. Cheshire and Lancashire architects had the lion's share and proved that they deserved it. *J. S. Crowther* of Manchester came first, and his or rather *Bowman & Crowther*'s Unitarian Church at Hyde of 1846–8 is a building of national importance. It is recognized as the first Nonconformist chapel in England to be built entirely like a Church of England church, with a long chancel and the altar table in it. Crowther also designed the parish church of Alderley Edge, begun in 1851, only two years after the railway had made this desirable Manchester retreat available to those who wanted villas with ample grounds. Other Crowther churches are St Paul at Stockport (1849–51; *Bowman & Crowther*), St Matthew at Stockport (1855–8), and Poynton (1858–9). Second, and again from Manchester, appeared an architect of very different character: *J. Medland Taylor* (1833 or 1834–1909). Whereas Crowther belongs

* Brooks's Wybunbury is less interesting.
‡ His Crowton of 1871 is disappointing; so is his Winnington of 1896–7.

to Scott and indeed the mainstream of Victorian ecclesiastical architecture, in his respect for the best work of the past and in the ambition to make it come to life again, Medland Taylor was one of those who knew the rules and indulged in breaking them. Butterfield often did the same, but the nationally best known architects representing this relatively rare attitude are E. B. Lamb, S. S. Teulon, and Bassett Keeling. Medland Taylor's name must be added to theirs if one wants to draw up a list of those Goodhart-Rendel called rogue architects, using the term in the sense of rogue elephants and also the other sense. The first Medland Taylor church in Cheshire is Cheadle Hulme of 1862–3, and then follow Romiley in 1864–6, St John at Altrincham in 1865–6,* St Thomas at Hyde in 1867–8, Holy Trinity at Hyde in 1873–4, Marple in 1878–80, St James at Cheadle in 1880–1, and so to Great Saughall built in 1895–1901.

The best Cheshire architect was *John Douglas* (1829–1911),‡ and that he was recognized can be taken from the house he built himself in 1896 in Dee Banks at Chester, a large house in a dominant position. When he started he still believed in the massiveness and the gross effects of the High Victorian style. This is evident in Oakmere Hall, Sandiway, a Gothic mansion with a few French motifs built for a Liverpool merchant in 1867, and, among his churches, in Aldford of 1866 with its granite columns and stiff-leaf capitals and the big N rose window. Helsby of 1868–70 also ought to be called High Victorian. The style is still Second Pointed, which in the hands of Bodley, and a few others, changed to a free Perp about 1870. In Douglas's work Perp e.g. appears at this date at Dodleston and side by side with E.E. at Moulton in 1876–7. But the development is not just one from E.E. to Perp; it is also a growing refinement and feeling for location. Whitegate of 1874–5 for instance is perfectly placed, and Warburton of 1883–5 and St Andrew West Kirby of 1889 etc. are strongly and freely composed and detailed. Aldford and Dodleston are Eaton Estate churches, as is Pulford of 1881–4. The boldest of Douglas's church designs is St Paul, Broughton, Chester of 1876 and 1902, a wide, spacious timbered interior. Bickley of 1892 also has timber posts, and Douglas still went on in 1902–3 when he built the church at Sandiway, where he was Lord of the Manor. Much work by him is to be found in North Wales as well as Cheshire. Douglas had been a pupil of Paley of Lancaster, and he belonged

* With its unbelievable font.

‡ He began practising in Chester in the mid fifties. His firm became *Douglas & Fordham* in 1885 and *Douglas & Minshull* in 1898.

to the generation of Paley's brilliant partner *H. J. Austin* (1841–1915), who raised the work of *Paley & Austin* and later *Austin & Paley* to the level of the best in the country. At Stockton Heath in 1868 Paley was still alone. With Austin he did e.g. St Cross at Knutsford in 1880–1 and St Barnabas at Crewe in 1885, and Austin & Paley did St Mary Magdalene at Alsager in 1894–8

97 and the grandiose St George at Stockport in 1896–7, the latter, side by side with Bodley's Eccleston, the most majestic of the representations of Victorian historicism – but historicism still. In Austin's best churches one can always find unexpected elements felicitously blending with those of the past style inspiring him, especially unexpected asymmetry. And Austin is never niggly, all is broadly conceived and boldly developed. This is true also with some limitations of *C. E. Deacon* (c.1844–1927), who practised in Liverpool. He also stands in his best buildings (e.g. Prenton, Birkenhead, 1897 and 1909) at the final point of historicism, not ambitious to leave it behind, as some of his generation were.*

One of the most adventurous of that generation, decorator more than architect, was *Henry Wilson*, and the stucco decoration

99 of the apse, the altar table and communion rail, the font cover, and the door furniture of St Martin at Marple which he did in the 1890s show him at his best – English Arts and Crafts touching the Continental Art Nouveau in many places. Later in the same church Wilson slipped into a Renaissancism of less vigour. A

95 very early case of such Renaissancism is *Frederic Shields*'s reredos at St Mary without the Walls at Chester. The date is 1888. Of other CHURCH FURNISHINGS of the late C19 only stained glass can find a place here. The mid C19 had made much use of *William Wailes* of Newcastle. Then in the seventies came *Kempe*, and there are more of his windows in Cheshire than the gazetteer can hold. They represent the *juste milieu*, *Morris* represents the way forward to clarity of composition, deep, rich colour, and above all a sense of what stained glass is really about. The Cheshire examples are Frankby (1873), Alderley Edge (1873), New Ferry (1876–7), All Saints Oxton, Birkenhead (1881 and later), St Paul Boughton, Chester (1881, 1899, etc.), Neston (1888, 1894), St Cross, Knutsford (c.1894, 1899), Tabley chapel (c.1895). After the deaths of Morris and Burne-Jones the quality of

* *Edmund Kirby* deserves at least a footnote. His Catholic churches belong to this same place in the development, and his brick details, especially the many-moulded brick doorways and other arches, are a hallmark. Little Leigh of 1878–9, Appleton Thorn of 1887, and St Hildeburgh, Hoylake, of 1897–9 are the best. High Legh of 1893 is unexpectedly gimmicky. None of these is Catholic, however.

the glass by Morris & Co. deteriorated, and a sentimentality flowed in more corny than that of Burne-Jones himself. Pure Arts and Crafts glass was done beautifully by *Shrigley & Hunt* for Pownall Hall, Wilmslow, and there we leave church art for art 94 in houses.

But we are not ready yet for the houses of the late c 19; for we have in domestic architecture not yet gone beyond the 1840s, and for Cheshire the VICTORIAN AGE is of outstanding importance. This importance lies beyond individual buildings, in the field of urban growth and planning. The two must be distinguished, as in the whole of England of planning proper there is pitifully little. The only major case is Birkenhead. Birkenhead in the Middle Ages was a priory and a ferry. The future town in 1801 had only 110 inhabitants. By *c.*1845 there were 40,000. It was growth on an American scale. Steam ferries from Liverpool started about 1815 to 1820. *Rickman*'s St Mary, as we have seen, was begun in 1819, Hamilton Square in 1825. Other churches, as we have also 73 seen, followed: 1835, 1837, 1845. *J. Gillespie Graham*'s town plan, a plain grid, of 1 by $\frac{1}{4}$ m. was drawn up in 1824. In the 1840s it was continued to the w, so that in the end the longest street was 2 m. long. To the 1840s also belong Birkenhead Park, laid out by 81 *Paxton*, and the first park ever to be provided at public expense (1843 etc.), the first dock (1844 etc.), leafy suburbs (Clifton Park and Claughton, both *c.*1843 etc.),* and the earliest working-class flats in all England (four-storeyed, built by the Dock Company in 1845; demolished).

So Birkenhead can be called a planned town. Planning is too grand a word to apply to the small grids of cottages, the single cottages, and the 'block-houses' put up by the railway at Crewe from 1840 onwards. Bromborough Pool Village on the other hand has its place in the history of working class housing as a planned estate, though a small one, for the employees of one factory, Price's Patent Candle Co. The estate was started in 1853, i.e. only two or three years after Saltaire. It is only with Port Sunlight 93 that Cheshire moved into the forefront of international planning for factory employees.

So much for planning. Urban growth in Cheshire is essentially the growth of outer Manchester and outer Liverpool and, as it happened, in both cases a growth from which entirely and spectacularly the affluent profited. The railway had reached Wilmslow and Alderley Edge in 1849. So those who now built themselves

* The Rock Park estate (1836 etc.) is at Rock Ferry, not then part of Birkenhead itself.

villas and what may well be called mansions were truly commuters. So were those who had gone to Bowdon, but there development had already begun in the 1830s. Liverpool across the
river depended until 1886 on ferries. The areas affected were
large parts of Wirral. The houses could afford ample gardens and
are often hidden by them from the road. The character is much
like that of the Surrey areas occupied by wealthy Londoners.
Early Birkenhead suburbs have already been mentioned, and
further examples of houses, including those of the late C19 and
C20, will be found in the gazetteer under Birkenhead (especially
Bidston, Noctorum, and Prenton), Caldy, *et al.* One hesitates to
pick out individual buildings, and perhaps – with a few exceptions
– one need not. The foremost exception is Abney Hall at Cheadle,
built for a rich Manchester merchant by *Travis & Mangnall* and
77 decorated in the most sumptuous Gothic of the Pugin kind by
Crace, the most successful English decorator, partly to designs
and largely inspired by the designs of *Pugin*. The work was done
from 1852 onwards.

With the forties and fifties one is, needless to say, in the full
swing of HISTORICISM. We have already looked at Lewis Wyatt
imitating Wren about 1820 and Elizabethan in 1829, Blore
imitating the Jacobean in the thirties, at Salvin's facsimile of a
C13 castle in the forties, and at Douglas's Gothic with French
touches in the sixties. We must now add *Salvin*'s Marbury Hall
of *c.*1850 etc., unfortunately pulled down. This was predominantly in a French Louis XIII, a unique choice at so early a
moment. The French C16 and C17 fashion is generally one of the
late fifties and sixties. Then there is the Italianate in the villa (not
the *palazzo**) variety of Osborne. This in Cheshire is well represented by Halton Grange, Runcorn (now the Town Hall), of
1853–6 (by *Verelst* alias *Reed*) and curiously enough by the
80 Chester General Station of 1847–8, one of the largest in the
country at that time. It is the work of *Francis Thompson*.

And as a Cheshire speciality there is the BLACK-AND-WHITE
REVIVAL. It became a speciality, that is obvious enough, but it
was not created in Cheshire. The earliest cases at Chester are of
the fifties by *T. M. Penson*. But at Worsley across the border in
Lancashire the Court House is of 1849, and the very earliest case
known to me – a freak admittedly – is Henry VIII's Lodge at
Woburn Sands in Bedfordshire by *J. A. Repton*, built in 1811.‡

* Town buildings of the forties in the *palazzo* style are Nos. 24–28 Hamilton
Street at Birkenhead.
‡ Mr Peter Howell adds to these a design for a cottage by James Malton,

Penson's half-timber premises are moderate in size and not very knowledgeable in detail. But these things changed when *Douglas* and *T. M. Lockwood* discovered the medium. The result is that Chester became one of the most thorough-going Victorian and Edwardian towns in the country, though the layman does not realize it. Douglas's best is the stretch of St Werburgh Street 91 close to the cathedral which he developed as a speculation of his own in 1895 etc., afraid that piecemeal development would spoil it.* *E. A. Ould* of *Grayson & Ould*, a pupil of Douglas, was another enthusiastic exponent of half-timbering, though there is nothing by him in this style at Chester itself. The firm's best is Hill Bark at Frankby, of 1891, and it found a surprising continuation in Portal near Tarporley, large and extremely competent, and by *W. E. Tower*, Kempe's partner, built c.1900–5. *Lockwood* even at his best is not, it seems to me, up to Douglas. His designs are more playful, and on the scale say of his corner premises of Bridge Street and Eastgate Street (1888) playfulness is not 90 what is wanted. Black-and-white, i.e. c16 and c17 historicism, went on at Chester unchecked into the 1920s. Lloyds Bank at Altrincham of c.1870, a strikingly ambitious half-timber job for its date, is not by a Cheshire architect but by *Truefitt*.

Douglas worked in the country too, and did much for the Grosvenor Estate,‡ i.e. the Duke of Westminster's Eaton Hall Estate. His work there included the churches already mentioned, and also schools, farms, cottages, and lodges. He designed Eccleston Hill for the Duke's secretary and The Paddocks at 92 Eccleston, a spectacular brick house of c.1883 for the Duke's agent. Estate housing is in fact another aspect of planned architecture, not in the sense of Birkenhead and Crewe but as a considered building programme on quite a large scale. The Duke, it has already been said, commissioned Bodley to build his Eccleston church. For the remodelling of his mansion he commissioned *Waterhouse*, made famous in the North by his early Manchester Assize Courts and Town Hall, and by the time he began Eaton Hall, i.e. in 1870, he had also begun the Natural History Museum in London and major work at Oxford (Balliol College) and Cambridge (Caius College). It is a great pity that Eaton Hall, except

1798 (ill. H. R. Hitchcock: *Early Victorian Architecture*, vol. 2, II, 1), a design for a villa by E. B. Lamb, 1836 (ill. *ib.*, II, 13), and Park Lodge Cottages, Basildon Park, Berkshire, by J. B. Papworth, 1842 (ill. A. Rowan: *Garden Buildings*, R.I.B.A., 1968, pl. 40).

* But even at Chester Douglas seems somehow more seriously engaged when he designed in brick, as in Grosvenor Park Road c.1879.

‡ For which *Lockwood* did a number of buildings in Chester.

for the chapel, has been demolished. It was the largest of all Victorian mansions and cost the Duke over £600,000–which he could afford. It was wonderfully picturesque in skyline, but clear and rational in composition, with a symmetrical centre and a total separation of state rooms from private rooms. The style was Gothic, and the detail had that hardness, or call it crispness, which makes Waterhouse so easy to recognize. An earlier Waterhouse is the Knutsford Town Hall (1870–2), also of course Gothic. A yet earlier and specially good Gothic town hall in Cheshire is *Godwin*'s at Congleton of 1864–6. Godwin is the same who later achieved the Late Victorian refinement of Whistler's house in Chelsea and of spindly Japanesish furniture. The Chester Town Hall of 1864–9 is much larger and again Gothic. The architect is *W. H. Lynn* of Belfast. Gothic too is the Sandbach Town Hall by *T. Bower* (1889).

But other town halls by the eighties had turned away from the Gothic to that English Baroque Classicism which remained the official idiom until after the First World War. The examples are Birkenhead by *C. O. Ellison & Son*, 1883–7, Stockport by *Sir A.* 100 *Brumwell Thomas* of 1904–8, and Wallasey by *Briggs, Wolstenholme & Thornely* of 1914–20. Less conventional and more enterprising, though too small to achieve its full effect, is *Hare*'s Crewe Municipal Buildings of 1902–5.

These are all public buildings. Private buildings in the towns produced nothing worth recording in this survey – except Messrs 89 Arighi, Bianchi's premises at Macclesfield with their glass and iron façade, though 1882–3 is a late date for that kind of job.

As for building in the countryside, Crewe Hall, like Eaton Hall for the villages s of Chester, was a centre of estate building in its own neighbourhood. The Jacobean mansion had been altered by *Blore* in the 1830s and then largely burnt out in 45 1866. *E. M. Barry* was entrusted with the reconstruction, & 46 and he did an extremely sumptuous job. E. M. Barry was not a disciplinarian. The details tend to go wild – High Victorian in self-confidence and grossness. On the estate Lord Crewe at first employed *Eden Nesfield*, a remarkable choice. When he designed the monument to the first Lord Crewe in 1856 in Barthomley church, he was only twenty-one, and the monument with a Gothic canopy is indeed still High Victorian in the Scott 88 sense.* But estate cottages such as Stowford Cottages at Crewe

* Only one other Victorian monument needs recording: the Rev. John 84 Armitstead at Sandbach, a white three-quarter figure designed by *George Frederick Watts* and executed by *George Nelson* in 1876.

dated 1864–5 are unquestionably LATE VICTORIAN. One need only compare them with say *William White*'s sombre Gothic brick cottages of the fifties for the Rode Hall estate to see the difference. Stowford Cottages is a pretty building, it is cheerful and just a little Kate Greenaway, though earlier than her work and Norman Shaw's work in the same spirit. Nesfield and Shaw were in fact partners from 1862 to 1868. But Shaw's Glen Andred is of 1866, i.e. after Stowford. Nesfield's importance in introducing tile-hanging, pargetting, and suchlike Home Counties devices is great. *Shaw* himself designed one major house in Cheshire, but much later: Dawpool at Thurstaston of 1882–4. It has alas gone, but a chimneypiece of black and white marble survives (in the Kingsland Dance Hall at Birkenhead). Another architect who, inspired by Norman Shaw, early moved from High to Late Victorian was *J. D. Sedding*. His Marple Vicarage of 1873 already has the new delicacy and is on the way from Gothic to a quiet William and Mary.

The cottagey character of Shaw's and Nesfield's Home County houses made W. H. Lever (born in 1851), later Viscount Leverhulme (1922), decide in favour of this style when in 1888 he began to build houses for employees next to his factory and to lay out Port Sunlight. Port Sunlight is the first employees' estate, not of the mechanical, joyless kind of Bromborough Pool Village and Saltaire, but with plenty of trees in the street, plenty of gardens 93 and cheerful gabled cottages. Bournville, though started earlier, developed a little later. Mr Lever's architect was first *W. Owen*. Besides him and his son *Segar Owen* those most extensively employed in the early years were *J. J. Talbot*, *Grayson & Ould*, and *Douglas & Fordham*. Architects commissioned for individual housing jobs included *Ernest Newton*, *George & Yeates*, *Lutyens*, and *Sir Charles Reilly*. Ultimately *J. Lomax-Simpson* became company architect. The Art Gallery by *W. & S. Owen*, of as late as 1914–22, is the most monumental – but not a very remarkable – public building on the estate. Lord Leverhulme, near his own country house at Thornton Hough, built another more rural model village mainly in the 1890s and up to the First World War.*

The story of how historicism was finally overcome is by now familiar. It is an international story, and the last step, the total opposition to period inspiration, belongs to Frank Lloyd Wright

---

* There is one other parallel to, or effect of, Port Sunlight in Cheshire – the Styal Cottage Homes of 1898, a home for 600 children built by the Chorlton Board of Guardians not as one huge pile but as a group of twenty-eight separate buildings. The architect is called *Overmann*.

in America, to Gaudí in Catalonia, to Garnier and Perret in France, to Endell and Behrens in Germany, to Horta and Van de Velde in Belgium. But England paved the way – Voysey on the one hand, with his smooth surfaces, and his unmoulded horizontal bands of window, Tudor as their origin may be, and the Arts and Crafts on the other, in the hands of such men as Mackmurdo anticipating Art Nouveau. Mackmurdo with Selwyn Image and Herbert Horne founded the *Century Guild*. That was in 1882, and the Century Guild, only four years after its foundation, did much of the furniture and decoration of Pownall Hall at Wilmslow, a house designed or rather enlarged by an architect called *William Ball*. The furniture is remarkably free of imitation, 94 the interior planning is full of surprises, the stained glass by *Shrigley & Hunt* is superb, and the Kate Greenaway aspect of this English Domestic Revival is made embarrassingly patent by a surfeit of inscriptions. Considering its early date Pownall Hall is a building of national importance. *Voysey* provided interiors for two houses at Oxton (Birkenhead) in 1902 and altered and added to one house at Alderley Edge. This is mature Voysey of 1905 and 1914–18; for Voysey country houses had begun to make their mark already in the early nineties. Now in the same years – or, to be exact, later by two or three years – the younger *Baillie Scott* had appeared on the scene. One of his first major jobs is in Cheshire, at Knutsford. Bexton Croft, though not large, has all the Baillie Scott motifs, including a hall running up through both floors. There is also typical Baillie Scott decoration, always more fanciful than Voysey's. Much less known, and unjustifiably so, is *C. E. Mallows*, who began c.1906–7 to build a large house with an inner courtyard or garth for Bruno Mond of the future ICI. 98 It is Tirley Garth at Willington, and it remained his only large-scale commission. The Voysey inspiration is patent, but Mallows did not just imitate, and the garth and some of the points of internal planning are all his. Finally, again of the same years, i.e. c.1890 to c.1910, are a number of houses by *Edgar Wood*, the most important post-historicist architect of Lancashire in these years. One cottage of 1905 is at Bramhall and there is quite a series in and around one street at Hale.

Compare that street at Hale with the series of villas in Legh Road, Knutsford, which during the same years were built, essentially, one feels sure, to his own designs, by *Mr Richard Harding Watt* (1842–1913). In the centre of Knutsford also in 101 1907–8 he designed the Gaskell Memorial Tower and King's Coffee House, and the Ruskin Rooms in 1899–1902. Any Royal

Fine Art Commission now would veto such monstrous desecration of a small and pleasant country town. Yet the young today are not far out in dubbing Mr Watt the Gaudí of England. His motifs mix wildly, Classical, Italianate, Byzantine, and Unprecedented, he likes towers of jagged outline and domes, and his fenestration is as random as any brutalist's today.

The brutalists have not yet invaded Cheshire, but there is quite a bit of good RECENT ARCHITECTURE, even if less 'with it'. The earliest is in fact of between the wars, an odd-man-out – the large, very interesting chapel of Shrigley Hall, Pott Shrigley, by *Philip Tilden*, 1936–8, centrally planned and domed. For the last fifteen years listing by types is enough: the Methodist Church at Cheadle Hulme by *Denys Hinton* of 1967–8, the Geigy factory at Hurdsfield outside Macclesfield by the Swiss *M. H. Burckhardt*, and the extensive Bowater factory at Ellesmere Port by *Farmer & Dark* of 1955 etc., the offices and research centre of Shell at Stanlow by the *Building Design Partnership*, and (another building) by *Sir Frederick Gibberd*, the Northwest Gas Board Offices 102 at Altrincham, again by the *Building Design Partnership*, a school at Wilmslow by *W. S. Hattrell & Partners* and the excellent Library and Police Headquarters by the same at Crewe, private houses by *R. Clayton* at Frodsham and Sandiway and *Tom Mellor* at Hale, and the new housing at Lancashire Hill and the new ingenious central shopping precinct, both at Stockport, and both by *J. S. Rank*, the borough architect.

That leaves the most thrilling building of the Cheshire countryside to the last – and it is not architecture. Jodrell Bank is a Radio Astronomy Laboratory. The engineers designed it, we laymen may not understand it, but its visual impact makes the new sculpture of wire and welded bits of metal appear inadequate.

FURTHER READING

The earliest book devoted to Cheshire is Daniel King's *Vale Royal of England* (1656), and this was reprinted in George Ormerod's *History of the County Palatine and City of Chester* (1819, second edition 1882, edited by Thomas Helsby), the indispensable source of information for the county. For the churches of the county as indispensable is *Old Cheshire Churches*, by Raymond Richards (1947). Then there are the *Transactions of the Historic Society of Lancashire and Cheshire* (from 1848), the *Transactions of the Lancashire and Cheshire Antiquarian Society* (from 1883), and the *Journal of the Chester and North Wales*

Architectural, Archaeological and Historic Society (from 1849). In the absence of any volumes by either the Victoria County History or the Royal Commission on Historic Monuments, these series are particularly useful. Special mention should be made of F. H. Crossley's numerous papers on churches which, over a period of years, appeared in all three. The several writers on Wirral include W. W. Mortimer (*History of the Hundred of Wirral*, 1847) and Philip Sulley (*The Hundred of Wirral*, 1889), but of the old histories the most notable, after Ormerod, is *East Cheshire*, by J. P. Earwaker (1877–80). The relevant volume of D. and S. Lysons's *Magna Britannia* (1810), Henry Taylor's *Old Halls in Lancashire and Cheshire* (1884), and Edward Twycross's *Mansions of England and Wales* (1850) may also profitably be consulted, as may White's Directory of 1860, in addition to Kelly. *The Historical Atlas of Cheshire*, edited by Dorothy Sylvester and Geoffrey Nulty (1958), is published by the Cheshire Community Council, which is also producing a series of books dealing with different periods of the county's history. *Chester Cathedral* (1958) and *The Monks of Chester* (1962), both by R. V. H. Burne, contain architectural information on the cathedral, and for Chester itself there is Joseph Hemingway (1831) and G. L. Fenwick (1896), and amongst many local histories e.g. for Altrincham Alfred Ingham (1879), for Birkenhead Philip Sulley (1907), for Congleton Robert Head (1887), for Crewe W. H. Chaloner (1950), for Macclesfield C. Stella Davies (1961), for Nantwich James Hall (1883), for Runcorn Charles Nickson (1887), for Sandbach J. P. Earwaker (1890), for Stockport Henry Heginbotham (1882–92), and for Wallasey E. Cuthbert Woods and P. Culverwell Brown (1960). With regard to general literature, all that need be said is that, as in all counties, valuable sources are, for country houses the volumes of *Country Life*, for biographies of architects and sculptors the dictionaries respectively of H. Colvin and R. Gunnis, for church screens A. Vallance, for brasses Mill Stephenson, for corporation plate L. C. Jowett and W. St John Hope, for medieval wall paintings Tristram, and so on.

BUILDING MATERIALS
BY ALEC CLIFTON-TAYLOR

Over most of Cheshire three kinds of building materials, and three only, are in evidence: red or buff-coloured sandstone, brick, and 'black-and-white'. Few English counties present so little geological variety. Much of the underlying rock is in fact concealed by a thick covering of glacial drift (Boulder clays and sand).

In the western part of the county, including most of the Wirral peninsula, the soft pinkish Bunter sandstones were freely available for building, often, as in Chester itself, quite close to where they were needed. Directly above these, through central Cheshire, runs an outcrop of sandstones from the Keuper beds, more varied in colour: to the reds, pinks, buffs and greys, lichens often add attractive patches of green. These are the stones, all Triassic, of which the churches of Cheshire, including the cathedral, were constructed; but, beautiful as they often are at the quarry, they have, through the years, given a great deal of trouble. Although they can sometimes be sawn into very large blocks (well seen at Brereton church) and ashlared without difficulty, they blacken easily upon exposure and, owing to their friability and lack of structural cohesion, stand up very indifferently as a rule to the onslaughts of the weather. The NW tower of St John's, Chester, fell as recently as 1881, and was not rebuilt. The ruin is interesting as an example of the state into which this sandstone decays if left unrestored. Its surface today is shockingly fretted. No exterior carving, one feels, could survive in this stone for more than about a century. Of the cathedral itself, Scott recorded in his *Recollections*, 'the external stonework' – this was in 1868 – 'was so horribly and lamentably decayed as to reduce it to a mere wreck, like a mouldering sandstone cliff'. Nantwich is another fine church at which, because of the weakness of the stone, the carved and masoned details, where not replaced, have become blurred almost beyond recognition. So most of the county's churches have suffered greatly from restoration, with consequent loss of 'patina', or have lost all their pristine crispness of detail.

Approaching the Pennines – that is to say, along the eastern fringes of the county – the geological picture changes. Here the surface rocks are much older: whether sandstones or limestones, they belong to the Carboniferous series. Limestones play only a small part in the Cheshire scene, being mainly confined to the hilly area E of Macclesfield; but Millstone Grits and sandstones from the Coal Measures were quarried in the NE (e.g. for Lyme Park) and also in the SE, along the Staffordshire border, where there were once flourishing gritstone quarries at Mow Cop, S of Congleton. The late C15 church at Astbury is notable not only for its architectural splendour but also for its stonework: after nearly five hundred years the external details are still comparatively crisp, and the colours, a mixture of grey and pale buff outside with, in addition, some pink within, are very pleasing. At Pott Shrigley the condition of the Coal Measures sandstone which was used for the main fabric of the church contrasts very favourably with that of the grey, buff and red Triassic sandstone employed for the dressings.

Carboniferous sandstones, notably from the Coal Measures quarries above Kerridge, near Macclesfield, also furnished those heavy roofing slabs which, despite their sombre colouring, are often the most attractive feature of Cheshire buildings, both ecclesiastical and domestic. For, despite their great weight, these slabs were used to roof half-timbered buildings as well as stone. This can be well seen at Gawsworth Old Hall, where it has been calculated that the weight of the roof alone may exceed 300 tons, and also, to grand effect, at Little Moreton Hall, where the gritstone slates came from Mow Cop. The much thinner, lighter, less expensive Welsh slate reached Chester as early as the C14, but was not exploited commercially until the reign of George III. It is no doubt a better partner for the urbanity of Georgian brickwork, but a far less interesting material in itself.

Except for a few houses like Saighton Grange, inhabited by men of wealth and influence (in this case an Abbot), stone was never used extensively in Cheshire for domestic purposes. Even until the early part of the C17 the large majority of this county's houses, as well as a fair sprinkling of village churches, were half-timbered, for oaks grew here in profusion until the extravagant felling under Elizabeth I. And it is still true that few English counties can show so high a proportion of timber-framed houses as Cheshire, even after due allowance has been made for the abundance of Victorian and later renewals, as at Bramall Hall, Bramhall, Stanley Palace Chester, and a good many other less famous houses in the county town and elsewhere. (Nor should the not infrequent instances of brick walls with black and white painting intended to simulate half-timbering be overlooked, although close to these never deceive for an instant. At Pott Shrigley, facing the church, black painted 'timbers' and whitewash have been applied to a good gritstone housefront: imagine it!) Most genuine half-timbering in Cheshire dates from the C16 and C17; the central hall of Baguley Hall, formerly in Cheshire but now within Manchester, is exceptional in going back to the C14. Little Moreton Hall, which is Early Tudor and Elizabethan, is beyond doubt the show-piece of the style: one of the most picturesque timber-framed houses not only in Cheshire but in all England.

In common with other counties along the Welsh border, Cheshire still has a number of cruck-framed cottages; but the very large majority are, of course, of the post-and-panel type. Humbler people had to be content with square or nearly square panels in order to economize in wood; the well-to-do could afford more oak and sometimes, especially in the showy Tudor period, indulged to excess a taste for profusely ornamented panels. A local characteristic of Cheshire half-timbering – though also found across the Mersey, in Lancashire – is the curved cove under the overhang, sometimes itself profusely decorated, as at Little Moreton. The infilling was always originally wattle and daub; this gave way, about the C15, to laths and lime-plaster. On a good many houses these in turn were gradually replaced, in the C18 and C19, by brick 'nogging', probably because by then bricks were actually cheaper. A common and very disagreeable practice of the last hundred years has been to replace the original lime-plaster with an infilling compounded largely of cement. Cheshire has all too many instances of this: the timber-framed churches of Lower Peover and Marton are but two of them. Blackening the timbers with tar or pitch and lamp black, and whitening the plaster, was a traditional practice in Cheshire, perhaps for preservative reasons, but a great deal of the 'black-and-white' in which the county abounds dates only from the last hundred years or so.

As in all the counties of the West and North-West, brick as a building material for general use reached Cheshire comparatively late, and at first only as a substitute for stone for the chimneys of houses that were otherwise half-timbered. For this purpose it was indeed much superior to Cheshire sandstone. When in the Georgian period brick became the favourite material in Cheshire, even churches (e.g. Knutsford, Congleton) were usually built of it. The quality of Cheshire brickwork varies a good deal, alike in colour, texture and crispness of edge, and sizes also vary, even with bricks of similar date: some old bricks measure, on the face, 3 by 9 in., dimensions never found in the South. On the whole it must be said that Cheshire clays, although abundant, do not yield bricks of a visual quality comparable with many of those to be seen in southern and eastern England; to confirm this, one has only to walk through the architecturally attractive Georgian precincts to the N and W of Chester Cathedral (Abbey Square and Street). In the C19 an addiction to black or dark grey pointing was aesthetically very unfortunate. Nor do the red sandstones commonly employed for door and window architraves, quoins and other dressings contrast nearly so effectively with red brick-work as the grey and white limestones of the Jurassic regions.

PREHISTORIC REMAINS
BY DEREK SIMPSON

Cheshire has so far produced no evidence for settlement by man during the glacial periods. The earliest finds consist of flint cores, microliths, and flakes left by Mesolithic hunters and marking their temporary camping sites. The majority of this material comes from upland areas which would have supported only a light forest cover (e.g., Frodsham, Alderley Edge) and is related to a whole series of such industries in the Pennines. Contemporary coastal settlement is also indicated by discoveries on the Meols shore (Hoylake). The flint industry here shows links with coastal industries in Wales and northwards on the shores of the Irish sea. These hunters must have formed a small and scattered population and the evidence for settlement by early farming communities is equally scanty, although they have left behind the earliest surviving structure in the county; the Megalithic tomb known as the Bridestones at Congleton. The principal surviving feature is a long gallery divided up into compartments by transverse slabs and approached from a crescent-shaped façade. The chamber was originally covered by a long barrow beneath which were two further galleries, but scant traces of these survive. The monument is a southerly outlier of a large group of architecturally related tombs in South-West Scotland and North-East Ireland. Stray finds provide the only other indication of Neolithic settlement. Most important among these are the ground and polished axes of igneous rock, products of the axe factories of Graig Llwyd in North Wales and Great Langdale in Westmorland, examples of which have been found at Tarporley and Acton Brook. Flint occurs only as pebbles in the drift or on the beaches in the county, and the superior flint necessary for the manufacture of flaked and polished axes (e.g. Stockton Heath) must have been imported either in the form of raw material or as finished products. Apart from stone and flint work no material remains belong to this Early Neolithic phase (from c.3000 B.C.), and for the Later Neolithic the only finds are sherds from Eddisbury (*see* Delamere), Betchton, and from the Meols shore (Hoylake). The final Late Neolithic immigrants to settle in Britain, the Beaker folk, appear to have made little impact on the region. None of their characteristic drinking cups have been found, nor their crouched inhumation burials which these vessels normally accompany. The only possible indications (and those inconclusive) for the presence of this group are stray barb and tang flint arrowheads (e.g., Meols shore, Hoylake), a stone battle axe from Tarporley, and a finely polished jadeite axe from Lyme Park, which must be continental import.

From c.1650 B.C., new peoples with new traditions appeared in the county. These traditions represent an amalgam of those of the Single Grave Beaker groups and of the existing aboriginal Neolithic cultures. The evidence comes entirely from graves, and these invariably contain cremations in the native tradition, generally in collared urns which represent a development from Late Neolithic and Beaker wares. Some of these burials are in simple flat graves either single (e.g. Macclesfield) or multiple (Eddisbury, Delamere). Others again lie beneath earthen round barrows or cairns in the Single Grave tradition (e.g. Gallowsclough Hill, Oakmere, Norley; Butley, Bollington). The only metal object which has been found in any of the graves was a bronze dagger accompanying one of the collared urns from Wilmslow. For the Later Bronze age the position is reversed, with a total absence of sites, both sepulchral and domestic, and pottery, the evidence being provided by metalwork alone. The majority of objects, swords, spearheads, and axes, of this period occur as stray finds, particularly in river valleys, indicating the main trade routes across the area. The two most important bronze groups are the hoards from Broxton, consisting of an axe and a chisel, and from Congleton, with two spearheads, a socketed axe, and a length of bronze tube possibly forming part of the bellows used by the bronzesmith. Both hoards are small personal hoards in contrast to the great collections of scrap metal known from elsewhere in Britain. The objects in the Broxton hoard indicate trade across the Irish sea, while the socketed axe in the Congleton group is of Yorkshire type.

The transition from Bronze Age to Iron Age in Cheshire is

ill-defined, and its understanding is made more difficult by the contrasting forms of evidence for the two periods. For the Late Bronze Age one has only metalwork, for the Iron Age only field monuments, and the few excavated examples have produced little in the way of diagnostic finds. These monuments are seven hillforts, the most impressive prehistoric structures to have survived in the county. Only two have been excavated extensively, Eddisbury (Delamere) and Maiden Castle (Broxton). Both show two main structural phases: an earlier univallate fort, tentatively dated to the C2 B.C., and a multivallate phase in the late CI B.C. or early CI A.D. From Eddisbury came sherds decorated with finger-tip impressions on the shoulder which show links with the Iron Age A pottery of Southern Britain, as does the timber lacing in the rampart at the same site. The forts, and the remodelling of their defences which is a feature of a number of them, reflect the unsettled conditions of this period, but excavation has provided little evidence of the way of their builders, and of their contemporary domestic sites, represented elsewhere in Britain, one knows nothing.

ROMAN REMAINS

BY BARRY CUNLIFFE

Cheshire does not appear to have been densely occupied in the pre-Roman period, apart from the sandstone ridge running between Malpas and Helsby, where hillforts might hint at some local opposition to the Roman advance. The region was, however, of great importance to the Romans, for in the early years of the occupation it lay between the hostile territory of the Ordovices in North Wales and the potentially dangerous Brigantes in the Pennines. The first recorded military advance through the area into the territory of the Deceangli in Flintshire in A.D. 49 caused a revolt among the Brigantes, who feared, no doubt, the consequences of being divided from their Welsh allies. Ten years later a second major advance was made by the governor Suetonius Paulinus, who may well have set up a fort on the site of Chester as a rearward base for his attack on the Druids in Anglesey. After a rapid success he, too, was called away by a revolt, this time in eastern England. The revolt delayed Roman aggressive policy for another decade, but eventually in A.D. 71, under the governor Cerialis, a widely based engulfing attack on the Brigantes was successfully carried out, the Ninth Legion moving N from Lincoln while the Twentieth Legion advanced along the w side of the country, under the command of the legate Agricola, passing through Cheshire and Lancashire.

The final campaign began in A.D. 74, with the last stage of the conquest of Wales by Frontinus. By 76 or 77 he had turned his attention to the Ordovices, having begun the construction of a fortress at Chester. The work was completed by the next governor, Agricola, in 78–9, and from thence forward Chester served as the base for one of the legions stationed in the province (p. 133).

Civilian development seems to have been somewhat retarded. Settlements sprang up at Northwich, Middlewich, Wilderspool (*see* Higher Walton), possibly replacing military installations, and each seems to have developed a decidedly industrial aspect, particularly Middlewich, the centre of the salt-producing area. Nearer to Chester, possibly at Heronbridge and certainly at Holt (Flintshire), industrial development was controlled by the army. Elsewhere, apart from peasant settlements the picture is blank, no villa estates are known, and town development was non-existent.

CHESHIRE

★

ST MARY. The lower parts of the W tower with thin lancets and
flat buttresses and three arches inside are of the C13, a rare
time for Cheshire churches. One capital of one of the arches
has a little dogtooth. The top of the tower fell in 1757, and
the present top with its intersecting tracery and ogee gables is
typical Early Gothic Revival.★ The body of the church is mostly Perp, but the N aisle windows have the cusped intersecting
tracery of the early C14. The striking chancel parapet is a C17
replacement. Inside the church *Paley & Austin* have made
things difficult by their restoration of 1897–8. The arcades are
largely a re-cutting of theirs. The capitals especially are clearly
late C19. Yet the piers are C13, i.e. of the time of the tower.
Were they heightened later in the Middle Ages? They are
too high now for the original roof-line against the tower. The
present clerestory is a rebuilding of 1879. The chancel arch
with continuous mouldings looks Dec. The chancel windows
however are Perp. They are set in giant blank arches. – FONT.
Round, of Norman date, with broad arches and alternately
flowers and figures. – SCULPTURE. A number of Norman 7
stones in the S aisle E wall. Two stones with intersecting arches
and little figures under. – Two stones with one figure each. –
One piece with Christ in a mandorla and angels l. and r. – One
piece with three heads under arches. – One piece with an
eagle. – One good ornamental piece. – ROOD SCREEN. The
dado alone is left, with Jacobean decoration. – SCREEN. With
widely set columns; 1685. – COMMUNION RAIL. With flat
balusters. – CHANDELIER, of brass, C18. – STAINED GLASS.
In the E window by *Kempe*, 1886. Also S aisle, 1885 and 1888.
– PLATE. Chalice inscribed 1633; Flagon 1706–7; another
Chalice undated. – MONUMENTS. In the N aisle recess, 23
with panelled back wall and panelled tomb-chest, elaborate
panelling and shields at the top, alabaster effigy of Sir William

★ It is by *William Baker.*

Mainwaring † 1399. – Mrs Wilbraham † 1632. Good tablet. –
53 Sir Richard Wilbraham † 1643 and wife † 1660. White, grey,
and black marble. Two white recumbent effigies. It could be
by *Edward Marshall*. – Samuel Edgley † 1721. Good cartouche
(chancel N). – In the churchyard SUNDIAL, C17. The shaft
is a cross-shaft, but the top and the ball-finial are C17.

VICARAGE, W of the church. A plain Georgian five-bay brick
house.

ALMSHOUSES, N of the church. Just one pair, with the two
heavily rusticated doorways in the centre.

WINDMILL, ¼ m. SW. The body of a brick tower-mill.

(DORFOLD COTTAGE, ½ m. out on the Wrexham road. Gothick
stucco-work inside. Information from Mr G. Clegg.)

5070   ACTON
                        Near Northwich

WOVERLEY, Cliff Road. Three-bay brick house of the early
C18 with a handsome late C18 doorcase and a lower l. attachment.

9080   ADLINGTON HALL

The house is a delightful mixture, half (N and E) C15 and C16
black and white, half (S and W) mid C18 brick. There is no
formality either in the one or the other or the two joining, and
indeed the classical S façade with its portico is quite homely
and not even built for state rooms.

One approaches the oldest part from the N through some
brick building of no special interest which was added
*c.*1660 to this oldest part for convenience's sake. The oldest
part then faces S but is part of the N range. On the N side of the
court is a timber porch inscribed by Thomas Legh in 1581,
with large Elizabethan windows and two Elizabethan brick
bays with gables to its l. The N range to the r. of the porch,
and all the E range, is half-timbered, also Elizabethan. All the
timbering is plain, just with herringbone bracing and no
fiddly bits.

On entering by the porch, however, one finds oneself in
the hall of another Thomas Legh, built about 1500 (dated in
fact 1505, as we shall see). The screen has gone to a large
extent, but two small service doorways survive with carved
heads and the bases of the imposts carved with little beasts.
The screen was and is a spere truss, the two speres decorated
with rude panelling, and to the S of the S spere there is still a

little of the screen, with panels with most intricate tracery to w and e as in Cheshire (and Welsh) church screens. Between the speres there seems to have been a movable screen as at Rufford Old Hall in Lancashire. The hall roof is of the hammerbeam type with (later) angels against the hammers. At the high-table end is the finest canopy in the county, of five tiers of panels (with later shields) with instead of bosses letters at the intersections making up an inscription with the date 1505. The wall-plates below and the wider fringe above are carved. The hall windows are clearly not of *c.*1505 but of *c.*1581. They have three transoms and are of two, four, three lights. The square bays to n and s with their fine first-floor balcony rails must be late c 17, and indeed yet another Thomas Legh did much work at Adlington after the Civil War. Of that time also are the absurdly bad wall paintings of the Story of Troy, and the splendid organ with the equally splendid gallery railing, as finely done as if it were metal. All this can hardly be earlier than 1675 to 1680, which makes the wall painting very reactionary in style. The stone chimneypiece on the other hand with the face of the sun looks a generation later.

The main staircase is in the w range, and this, with the s range, was built about 1750. Half of it, including the Ballroom, was demolished in 1928, and there is now only a corridor to connect the stump of the w range with the s range. In the stump, on the upper floor, is the Drawing Room, whose beautiful panelling with fluted pilasters and whose chimney-piece must be late c 17 rather than mid c 18, i.e. of the time of the refurnishing of the hall. The fireplace is of white marble, the overmantel of wood, carved in the Grinling Gibbons style, though with some Rococo additions. The Dining Room below is in the same style but much simpler. One small room close to the hall has a wooden overmantel typical of the mid c 17.

The pride of the mid c 18 work, which was done by *Charles Legh* quite possibly to his own design, is the s front. This has thirteen bays with a four-column portico with pediment dated 1757. The columns are on absurdly high bases in no way aligned on the windows.* Behind the portico are two round-arched ground-floor windows and a round-arched entrance, and the mid-window above has a Palladian pediment.

* This motif occurred in a similar way at Henbury Hall, now no longer extant.

Until 1928 the façade also had projecting wings. To the courtyard the s and w ranges have a cloister, of pillars carrying three-centred arches. The Elizabethan windows of six and five lights in the N range were only exposed when the w range was demolished.

In the s range are no important features, just some pretty mid C18 stucco ceilings on the upper floor, one of them with gothicizing motifs. In the N range in 1936 a small CHAPEL was made, and in it furnishings of the former chapel found a place: some ornamental carving, the communion rail, and the baluster font.

The STABLES are dated 1749. They are on higher ground, SE of the house, and their front is of nine bays with a three-bay pediment on giant Doric pilasters.

In the wood to the s are a ROTUNDA and a SHELL COTTAGE.

ADSWOOD HALL *see* CHEADLE

8070

ALDERLEY EDGE

The railway arrived in 1842, and at once Alderley Edge began to develop as a residential district for affluent Mancunians. The edge itself offered wonderful sites, but in the plain also houses in a decidedly Early Victorian style can be seen. Besides, the date and scale of the church tell the story.

ST PHILIP. 1851–2 by *J. S. Crowther* of Manchester, large, ambitious, and unmistakably prosperous-looking. sw porch-steeple, roof patterned in slates of two colours. Dec tracery. – STAINED GLASS. By *Morris & Co.* one s aisle window, 1873. Two excellent figures and Morris's dainty leaf quarries supported by fat symmetrical interlocked stems.

METHODIST CHURCH, Chapel Road. 1863 by *Hayley & Sons*. It also has a sw steeple and Dec tracery.

To do justice to the domestic architecture of Alderley Edge much more ought to be known. Here only a few houses can be referred to, and the choice is emphatically arbitrary. THE RYLEYS on the A535 is still entirely classical, with its Greek Doric porch, but was built for Peter Taylor, a Manchester cotton merchant. In MACCLESFIELD ROAD is BROOMFIELD, 1847, but enlarged in 1873 by *Thomas Worthington* for himself. In WOODBROOK ROAD, the rough road leading up to the edge, is BOLLIN TOWER, dated 1846,[*]

* Information from Miss Elizabeth Johnston.

picturesque and castellated, with a tower. Also in Woodbrook Road REDCLYFFE GRANGE by *J. S. Crowther*. Finally, again in Woodbrook Road a house enlarged and altered by *Voysey* in 1905 and 1914–18. The house before Voysey was yellow brick. He used his roughcast in his addition. The totally unmoulded mullioned windows are unmistakable too, and inside the staircase with the narrowly placed white slats and three remarkably large and unenriched tiled fireplaces, one with two Voyseyish columns. All the door furnishings and such-like things are preserved too.

(In the top part of BEECHFIELD ROAD is THE QUINTA, early C20 by *Frank Mee*. More C20 houses further s, e.g. LONG-MYND in CONGLETON ROAD, *c.*1926 by *Halliday & Agate*.)

Unconnected with Alderley Edge is the survival of CHORLEY HALL (also on the A535). This is a medieval house in its moat. The oldest part is a stone hall of the C14, with entrance and exit doorways and the three stone doorways inside from the screens passage to the buttery, kitchen, and pantry. The screen also has left its mark, i.e. the two spere-posts now part of a timber-framed wall. The hall originally, as the posts show, went up to the roof. Of pre-Reformation windows only two are left, one of the hall, of two lights, the other of the buttery. The further history in the C16 and C17 is complicated and need not concern us here, except that the spectacular timber-framed wing is Elizabethan and has a number of the 41 familiar Cheshire black-and-white ornamental motifs. At the same time a ceiling was put into the hall to make it two floors. The mullioned and transomed windows are yet later, *c.*1640, the experts say.

MESOLITHIC SITES. From various sites in this parish have come a series of flint cores, flakes, and microliths indicating the presence of Mesolithic hunters.

ALDERSEY GREEN *see* HANDLEY

ALDFORD   [EH] *4050*

ST JOHN BAPTIST. Built at the expense not of the first Duke of Westminster but of the second Marquess. 1866 by *John Douglas*. Late C13 style. The most distinctive feature is the w tower, which has a conical-roofed sw stair-turret and recessed shingled spire. Tower parapet, corbelled out, composed of quatrefoils. Ashlar interior. Polished granite columns, stiff-leaf capitals, and large angel hood-mould stops. Two-light clerestory windows with central free-standing shafts internally. Opening off the choir, a N transept with a rose window. Chancel ceiling decorated. Quite early Douglas, but there are indications of his mature manner, e.g. in the design of the tower and spire and in the detailing of the FURNISHINGS. – REREDOS. Mosaics made by *Salviati*. – STAINED GLASS. Whom is the E window by?

E of the church the former RECTORY, 1897 by *Thomas M. Lockwood & Sons*. Large. Elizabethan style, with straight gables. Brick, blue brick diapering, and stone bands and dressings. Renaissance ornament around the doorway etc.

CASTLE. N of the church earthworks of a motte-and-bailey stronghold known to have been in existence in the C12.

GROSVENOR ARMS. Dated 1892. Poor. Materials typical of the Eaton estate, but used unconvincingly.

EATON ESTATE HOUSING. Much dates from the time of the first Duke, 1890s and earlier. Also cottages of the 1850s and 60s, typical of those built in the time of the second Marquess and possibly by *Edward Hodkinson*. Common brick, low-pitched roofs and heavily diamond-patterned windows. In the westernmost of the two roads which lead s from the church is an early C17 half-timbered cottage, brick-nogged, to which a thatched *cottage orné* has been added. The pair of cottages slightly further s with indented pargetting patterns is by *Douglas*.

Estate buildings outside the village include ALDFORD HALL FARM, ¾ m. s, a model farm of 1876–81 by *Douglas*. The farmhouse has Dutch gables. ¼ m. E of this, approached by a separate lane from the village, is FORD LANE FARM, 1890 by *Douglas & Fordham*. ¾ m. SE of the village is LEA HALL FARM, also by *Douglas*. The farmhouse, 1875, is of brick and half-timber.

ALLOSTOCK

HULME HALL. The house is reached by a medieval bridge across the moat. Two segmental arches and two triangular projections. (Inside the house heavily moulded beams. MHLG)

ALSAGER

CHRIST CHURCH. A Georgian church lavishly built in ashlar in 1789–90 at the expense of the Misses Alsager to the design of

Thomas Stringer. w tower with a slightly projecting pedimented centre and in this a doorway with Tuscan columns and pediment. Sides with six bays of arched windows and two more such doorways in the second bay N and S. Giant pilasters separate bay from bay. Giant pilasters also for the apse. The interior does not hold what the exterior promises. – FONT. C18 baluster with an octagonal bowl. – PLATE. Set of 1789.

ST GABRIEL (R.C.), Lawton Road. 1953 by *F. X. Velarde*. Of no interest except perhaps for the motif of mullions carved into human figures.

ST MARY MAGDALENE. 1894–8 by *Austin & Paley*. It is a great pity that the w tower was never built; for the church is substantial and serious. The Austin touch is at once felt in the chancel, with an aisle of two high arches N but no aisle S and instead three very tall, straight-headed Dec windows. The pier shape throughout is original – a kind of ellipse – and the arches die into them.

CHESHIRE COLLEGE OF EDUCATION. Remarkable for quantity but not quality – architectural quality.

ALTRINCHAM   7080

Altrincham, Sale, Timperley, Hale, and Bowdon are one and all Outer Manchester. The railway to Manchester was opened in 1849. Altrincham has a town centre without any attraction and is trying to do something about it. Architectural events in the secular field are absent outside the centre too.

ST GEORGE, Church Street. This is a most puzzling church. The literature says: rebuilt by *Paley & Austin*, 1896–7, but that cannot be. It is also known that a previous church was of 1799 and was extended w and E in 1858–60 and 1869, that the present top of the tower and spire are of 1874, and that the chancel was rebuilt in 1886. The lower part of the tower may well be 1799, and the interior of the nave with its arcades is acceptable as Paley & Austin. But the exterior is all brick and red brick or terracotta enrichments, and all a blunt, drab Norman. The arcades go on to the w l. and r. of the tower; so Paley & Austin must have meant to do away with it and replace it. But for the rest dates ought to be provided.

ST ALBAN, Lindsell Road. 1900 by *Austin & Paley*. Unfinished at the w end. Only two bays were done. The N transept carries a high bellcote, detailed originally and facing E. Good interior with exposed brick. – The PARSONAGE shows

Norman Shaw influence and is by *J. N. Cocker* as late as 1914 (consultant *Roger Oldham*).

ST JOHN EVANGELIST, St John's Road. 1865–6 by *J. Medland Taylor*. Of his usual quirks there is only the way the vestry entrance and the window of the organ chamber are set diagonally. Otherwise conventional: SW steeple, polygonal apse, geometrical tracery. But inside the stone PULPIT and the FONT must be by Medland Taylor, and the font is quite unbelievable with the stubby supports holding the bowl by means of ridiculously short flying buttresses.

ST MARGARET, Dunham Road, really at Dunham Massey. Another puzzling church. The literature says: 1853–5 by *Hayley* and only the w end recent, by *Tapper*, 1923–5.* If that refers to the church as it now is, it is a very remarkable building, for a number of motifs look decidedly late C19. The style first of all is Perp, not E.E. to Dec. Then there is the mighty crossing tower, until 1927 with a spire. Then there are the piers, in so free a Perp that the fronts to the nave have become fluted pilasters. Finally the crossing arches differ N and S from E and W, and chancel N wall differs from S – both Paley & Austin motifs. The chancel altogether is dramatically high and has a huge E window and gorgeous Gothic panelling of the canted ceiling raised up by a clerestory. It looks as if it can't be earlier than the last quarter of the century, yet 1853–5 seems after all to be its date.‡

ST VINCENT DE PAUL (R.C.), Bentinck Road. 1904–5 by *Kirby*. Fiery red brick, lancets, no tower, and a typical Kirby W doorway with an arch of wavy outline and many fine continuous mouldings.

METHODIST CHURCH, Hale Road. Very red brick, typical 1900-Gothic with Art Nouveau touches. By *Potts, Son & Hennings*, 1896–7. The cost was £2,459.

UNITARIAN CHAPEL, Dunham Road. 1872 by *Thomas Worthington*. Very blunt Gothic, abrupt in shape.

TOWN HALL, Market Street. 1901 by *C. H. Hindle*. Long, low, of brick, with four gables, Elizabethan and free Jacobean. – INSIGNIA. Chain of Office with a silver medal of 1759.

MARKET HALL, Market Street. 1849 and 1879.

NORTH WESTERN GAS BOARD, Golf Road, 1965–6 by the *Building Design Partnership* (*P. Titherley*). Excellent long six-storey block of precast concrete parts. In front a lower brick

---

* The W end is part of a larger scheme which remains incomplete.
‡ And this is confirmed by the Rev. J. Heywood.

building including the copper-sheathed lecture theatre.

Y.M.C.A. HOSTEL, Ashley Road. 1968–9 by *Elsworth, Sykes & Partners*. Brick piers and vertical window strips. Good, if not welcoming.

No perambulation, but the following single buildings. An attempt at saving the centre is the SHOPPING PRECINCT with a high block as part of it, in REGENT ROAD and George Street. It is by *A. H. Brotherton & Partners*, 1966–9, and incorporates a low dome with shops around and an odd fountain of various wheels. The other high block of Altrincham is opposite the station, in STAMFORD NEW ROAD. The best building in the town is the STAMFORD ESTATE OFFICE at the E end of DUNHAM ROAD, late C18, brick, of four bays with a two-bay pediment and in bays one and four a tripartite window under a blank segmental arch. The most spectacular Victorian building is LLOYDS BANK in the MARKET PLACE, by *George Truefitt*, large and high super-black-and-white, yet as early as *c*.1870. It was originally Brooks's Bank, i.e. built for Sir William Cunliffe Brooks. Finally, outside, by the golf course in STOCKPORT ROAD, is the OLD HALL HOTEL, late C18, brick, of five bays and two storeys, with links of two bays of large Venetian windows leading to end bays just with a niche and a pediment.

ALVANLEY   ₄₀₇₀

ST JOHN EVANGELIST. 1861, by an architect not yet identified. That is a pity, as the church has some character and the SCHOOL of the same year yet more. The best thing about the church is the w front with three pitched roofs and a diagonally set bell-turret. The style is that of *c*.1300. In the chancel a four-light open traceried stone screen, like a large window, separates the organ chamber – a Butterfield motif.

s of the church is CHURCH HOUSE FARMHOUSE, Late Georgian, with a nice front. Three bays, brick, with a three-bay pediment.

ALVANLEY HALL, ¼ m. SE of the church. In the cellar are two large medieval piers *in situ*. They are circular, on big polygonal concave-sided bases. They must have belonged to quite a monumental room.

ALVASTON HALL *see* NANTWICH

ANDERTON   ₆₀₇₀

BOAT LIFT, opposite the ICI Winnington Works. Built in

1875 by *E. Leader Williams* to lift boats from the Weaver to the Trent and Mersey Canal, a black, impressive installation. The difference is 50 ft.

ANTROBUS
6080

ST MARK. By *Scott*, 1847–8. A Commissioners' church. Nave and chancel in one, Dec style, with a bell-turret on the E end of the nave. Priest's doorway in a broad S buttress. The typical Scott SCREEN is partly of wood, partly of iron.

FRIENDS' MEETING HOUSE, $\frac{1}{2}$ m. SW. 1726. A plain brick house, but with an outer stair.

APPLETON THORN
6080

ST CROSS. 1887 by *Edmund Kirby*, better than one expects him to be. The church could easily be by Paley & Austin. It is not large but has a sufficiently dominant central tower. The style chosen is Dec. Aisleless nave. Low W baptistery with a big rose window over. Chancel with organ chamber on the N side. On the S side is the vestry. – Stone PULPIT with access from the organ chamber.

(OBELISK, on High Warren, W of the A-road, $1\frac{3}{4}$ m. W of the church. On four lions. Erected in 1874. MHLG)

ARCLID
7060

CONGLETON WORKHOUSE, now Hospital. The r. half is of 1844, a long brick front, very simple yet not without dignity. The l. half larger and of 1899.

ARDERN HALL *see* BREDBURY

ARDERNE HALL *see* TARPORLEY

ARLEY HALL
6080

The present house is the substantial fragment of an Early Victorian mansion, built in 1833–41 on the site of an earlier house whose hall was incorporated into the Early Victorian Dining Room which was included in the part which has recently been torn out. The architect of the house is one *Latham* of Nantwich, but tradition has it that the owner, *Rowland Egerton Warburton*, had much to do with the design. The house is of red brick with blue brick diapers. It is in the Jacobean style with mullioned and transomed windows and small shaped gables. The entrance (S) side has in its centre a stone-faced porch with coupled columns. On this, until recently, rose a tower. Its absence does no damage to the visual qualities of the front. The garden (E) front on the other hand makes no sense now as a composition. The missing part connected it with the CHAPEL, which is of red sandstone and was designed by *Salvin* in 1845. The S aisle was added by *Street* in 1856–7. Street followed Salvin in applying the Dec style. Good roof on angel corbels. – Three corona CHANDEL-IERS. – Iron SCREEN to hide the central heating. It may well be by *Street*. – STAINED GLASS. The E window by *Kempe*, 1895. – The chapel has a S porch with a polygonal turret in the corner. The front wall of the porch is of course recent. While the reduction of the house went on, the opportunity was missed to show that old and new can set one another off to advantage.

Of the preceding house the principal survival is the BARN with seven splendid cruck trusses. Over the last one is an Early Victorian clock turret. The building after that continues in brick and has a date 1604. Windows with mullions and with and without arches to the lights.

ARLEY GREEN. A pleasant group all on its own in the grounds of Arley Hall. The group includes the CHAPLAIN'S COTTAGE by *William White*, 1854, with its high steep roof,* and the timber-framed SCHOOL.

CROWLEY LODGE, 1 m. W of Arley Hall. 1743. Brick, of five bays with a one-bay pediment. Good stone gatepiers.

ARROWE, *see* WOODCHURCH, BIRKENHEAD, p. 107

ASHLEY 7080

ST ELIZABETH. *The Builder* in 1880 said: 'Erected from the designs of the Hon. *Wilbraham Egerton*, M.P.'.‡ A competent job, of red brick and red terracotta, with nice fancy details in the windows.

ASHLEY HALL, ½ m. NW. The hall itself is irregular and of no architectural interest, but the MHLG tells of a room with very good late C18 decoration 'with a Gothic flavour'. Large forecourt of farm buildings, one of them impressive, long, with slightly projecting wings and a pedimented doorcase. Is it late C17?

* A discovery of Dr Stefan Muthesius.
‡ So Mr Spain told me.

ASHTON

ST JOHN EVANGELIST. 1849 by *Shellard* of Manchester, the
chancel altered in 1900 by *Douglas & Minshull*. The N aisle
also looks later than 1850. The church has a W tower with a
good recessed spire, and two transepts, a typical plan of before
the turn to archeological accuracy. Perp tracery. The N chapel
with shafts and a plaster vault is of 1932 (by *Theodore Fyfe*). –
PULPIT. Real Art Nouveau. – FRONTAL of brass, rather more
Arts and Crafts, but both probably of *c.*1900.

SCHOOL, opposite the church. Gothic and no doubt of *c.*1849.

ASHTON HALL, ⅝ m. S. The three-bay part with the mullioned
and transomed windows and the doorway placed asymmetrically
must be Jacobean or Carolean. The top storey is a later
addition.

PEEL HALL, ½ m. NW. 1637. The entrance side is symmetrical,
with a portal with columns and two identical chimneybreasts.
In the lower wing perhaps, and at the back certainly, pieces
were re-used – at the back e.g. the fine carved surround
containing the date 1637. (Staircase with open well and shaped
flat balusters. MHLG)

ASHTON-UPON-MERSEY

ST MARTIN. The church end of Ashton is not engulfed yet in
the Outer Manchester suburbia. A rebuilding was completed
in 1714, and the mullioned windows with arched lights belong
to that date, though one would take them to be C17. The big
SE tower with its gabled fancy half-timber top is dated 1887.
The lychgate, like a pavilion with its pyramid roof, is of the
same time. The architect was *George Truefitt*, and the work
was paid for by Sir William Cunliffe Brooks, banker and
M.P. Earlier, in 1874, *Brakspear* built the octagonal baptistery.
The E and W windows with intersecting tracery could also be
Victorian, but the singular lozenge motif and the springing
of the intersecting arches makes one consider whether they
might not be 1714. The double-hammerbeam roof is interesting. Crossley thought it probably not earlier than 1714. Would
this then be Gothic survival or Gothic revival? The box pews
have been used very effectively to make PANELLING in the
chancel, much higher than one expects. – WEST GALLERY. –
FONT. An C18 baluster.

(The STOCKS are in a recess in the churchyard wall. MHLG)

ASHTON NEW HALL, S of the church. Georgian, of five bays

and two storeys. Brick. Doorway with broken pediment on columns.

(CONGREGATIONAL CHAPEL, Cross Street. A window by *Morris & Co.*, i.e. *Burne-Jones.* Ingham)

BROOKS INSTITUTE, Carrington Lane. 1888 by *Truefitt.* Brick and quite ornate half-timber.

ST MARTIN'S SCHOOL, Green Lane. Close to the former. Also a Brooks donation. 1874, Gothic and irregular. By *Brakspear.* The tower was added in 1877.

One high block of flats has arrived at Ashton too. Was it necessary?

ASTBURY

8060

ST MARY. Astbury is one of the most exciting Cheshire churches. The excitement is all Perp, as in nearly all such cases in the county, but the church is older. It is also a very puzzling church. It has a N tower with a recessed spire, and this stands outside the N aisle and is clearly Dec in its details. Money to its building was willed in 1366. The W window of the N aisle adjoining the tower has flowing tracery too, but the N windows of the aisle are yet somewhat earlier. The earliest are those of the N chapel, with plain Y-tracery. That indicates the late C13. The N windows further W have Y-tracery cusped, say of *c.*1300 or 1310. The whole of the S aisle windows are the same, the S porch, a two-storeyed porch, is Dec too, and the S doorway (continuous mouldings, keels) and – as may be anticipated – the W responds of the aisle arcades are also Dec, corresponding to former Dec piers which must have been quatrefoil with fillets and very small hollows in the diagonals. So the church of the C14 was the same size as that of today, i.e. the Perp church.

The Perp church is seven bays long without any structural division of nave from chancel. It has piers of fine mouldings, with tripartite shafts in all four directions, the arches dying into them. The place of the chancel screen is marked by mouldings which make the piers a little broader, and the S chapel has again a slight difference in the mouldings. From the piers vertical shafts rise and go up to the roof, framing the gorgeously high four-light clerestory windows. These staves are crossed by horizontal staves one at arch-apex level, the other at clerestory-sill level. But that is not all. The W end is a uniform composition, all Perp. There is here what looks at first an unfinished W tower, but cannot be; for the

3—C.

builders of that nave, had they thought of replacing the N tower, would not have embarked on something so thin. So one must accept this as a three-storeyed W porch, like the W porch to the Savage Chapel at Macclesfield. The ground floor of the porch was to be fan-vaulted. Four demi-figures of musicians were to carry it. The porch being so narrow in comparison with the nave allowed for two exceedingly long two-transomed four-light windows l. and r. The interior by their help and by that of the clerestory is thus very light and airy. We have no dates for this Perp rebuilding, nor would the details, e.g. the panel tracery used throughout, allow a dating.

24 The late C15 is usually assumed. The roofs are one of the most thrilling things at Astbury, low-pitched with camber-beams, as they usually are in Cheshire, and with plenty of bosses and also some dainty openwork pendants.

49 FURNISHINGS. FONT COVER. A splendid Jacobean or mid C17 piece and the pedimented gallows from which it is wound down or up. – CHANCEL SCREEN. An even more splendid piece, even though the ribbed coving is largely C19. The top of the dado is intricate openwork tracery. Single-light divisions, several top friezes. – PARCLOSE SCREEN. The intricate tracery is here at the top. Both screens are probably of c.1500. – PULPIT. Jacobean, with two tiers of the usual blank arches. – LECTERN. A wooden eagle, probably C17, but is the stand with the odd tracery upside down? – COMMUNION RAIL. Probably mid C17. Of an unusual design, hard to describe. – SOUTH DOOR. C15. The frame with fleurons. – C17 BOX PEWS. – SCULPTURE. Small part of an C11 Anglo-Danish circular cross shaft with the typical interlace like guts (N aisle W bay). – Also, in the S porch, architectural fragments. – WALL PAINTING. Of c.1500, in one bay of the N clerestory. A coat of arms and probably the Virgin blessing St George. – STAINED GLASS. In the N aisle W window glass of c.1500, formerly in the clerestory. Three figures, rather pale, and many fragments. – In the S aisle W window small figures in the tracery. – Yet smaller fragments in one S aisle S window. – The E and N aisle E windows are by *Warrington*, c.1858 and c.1861. – S aisle E by *Hughes & Ward*, c.1872. – S aisle the two westernmost S windows by *O'Connor*, 1871. – PLATE. Two Chalices, London, 1707; two Plates, London, 1712; two Patens, 1707 and London, 1709; two Flagons given in 1716. – MONUMENTS. In the S chapel an effigy of a late C14 Knight. – In the chancel on the N side Lady

Egerton, 1609. Recumbent effigy. – In the s chapel tomb-chest
lid with inscription and shields, the initials T. B. (for Thomas
Bellot), and the date 1654. No effigy. –Peter Shakerley, 1796.
By *King* of Bath. So their clientele went that far north. – In
the churchyard a totally defaced couple under a cusped canopy,
inscribed in the c16 as Ralph Brereton, a Knight with
uncrossed legs, and a priest. All c14.

GATEWAY. An effective approach to the church at the end of the
short vista from the main road, with happy houses l. and r.
The archway is hard to date. It is round-arched and has been
assigned to the c17 as well as the c15.

RECTORY. A generously proportioned five-bay brick house of
c.1760 or a little later.* Basement and two-and-a-half storeys.
Three-bay pediment. Doorway with the Venetian motif
below a broken pediment. (Hefty Rococo chimneypiece. A.
Gomme)

(SCHOOL, in the rectory grounds. By *Scott*, *c*. 1850–2.
A. Gomme)

BRONZE AGE GRAVE. In the churchyard during grave digging
was found a collared urn containing a female cremation. The
vessel is now in the Grosvenor Museum at Chester.

ASTON-BY-SUTTON   5070

ST PETER. The chancel is of 1697, the nave of 1736. The work
of 1697 was done by Sir Willoughby Aston, who in his diaries
several times mentioned *Vanbrugh*. The difference between
chancel and nave is telling. The nave is clearly Georgian, with
the arched windows with pilasters and the open bell-cupola
on a projection in the w front, but the chancel E wall is
equally clearly pre-Georgian, see the quoins of stones of even
length, the two niches and the circular window, and the
pedimental gable. The arched chancel windows have no
pilasters. Low, broad, segmental chancel arch. Ceiled roofs. –
FONT, PANELLING, PEWS, etc. are of 1857. The motifs are
partly Jacobean, partly Georgian. – WEST GALLERY. On
columns; probably *c*.1736. – PLATE. Gilt Chalice of *c*.1370,
engraved with the Crucifixion and a coat of arms. The chalice
is of a highly unusual form. – Paten with the hand of God,
probably of the same date. – MONUMENTS. Two painted
tablets to the Aston family, probably early c18, with many
coats of arms. – Sir Thomas Aston and John Aston. Erected

* Local tradition, however, places the building *c*.1710–20.

1697, when the chancel was built. Simple tablet. – Sir Willoughby Aston † 1702 and his wife † 1712. Tablet with two putti on top. – The motif was repeated in tablets of † 1737 and † 1752.

ASTON HALL, a later C17 mansion, was demolished in 1938. The grounds were landscaped by *Repton*, c.1793. (There remains a brick DOVECOTE of 1696. R. Richards)

6040   AUDLEM

An exceptionally attractive village with the church right in the centre on a turfed eminence. The three main streets meet here, and in the little square is a MEMORIAL LAMP of cast iron, dated 1877, and the SHAMBLES, C17,* open, with Tuscan columns carrying the roof. In the streets are no houses of note, but around the village centre there are.

ST JAMES. As nearly always in Cheshire, the impression is Perp, though in this case not Late Perp, and one has to look for earlier features. They are these. First the s doorway, which cannot be later than the late C13. One order of shafts; one capital has a head with a stiff-leaf wreath. Arch mouldings with fillets. Then Dec, i.e. first half of the C14, the priest's doorway, the lower part of the NW tower,‡ and the two-light N aisle windows and s aisle windows narrower and starting lower than the present windows. The size of the C14 windows can be traced in the outer wall. Inside the C14 is represented by the E springer of the W arch of the N arcade, indicating a nave narrower than it is now, and the W respond of the s arcade, indicating a nave very much lower than it is now. As it is now it is very high and has large s aisle windows with two-centred arches and panel tracery, a splendid clerestory of twelve closely set windows, and battlements on aisle and clerestory. The E end, N, S, and E walls is a lengthening of 1885–6, when the church was restored by *Lynam & Rickman*, but the chancel E window of five lights was probably re-erected. In its tracery it is exactly on the watershed between Dec and Perp, whereas a N chapel window is decidedly Late Perp. In the N aisle wall are three unexplained niches close together but of different shapes. Good roofs of the usual Cheshire type but with relatively few bosses. – FONT. Flat octagonal bowl. The panelling of the stem and base looks C17.

* Or 1733 ? (MHLG)
‡ There are squinches at the top for a spire.

– PULPIT. Jacobean, with the usual two tiers of blank
arches, but here unusually simple. – (CHEST. C13, with ironwork.) – CHANDELIER of brass, given in 1751. – STAINED
GLASS. N aisle E and one N aisle N by *Wailes*, 1857, according
to Sir Thomas Kendrick. – S aisle by *Kempe* from 1882
(Nativity scenes) onwards, N aisle one 1893. – PLATE.
Chalice given in 1635; Paten *c*.1635–40 (?); two Almsdishes
given in 1685; Baptismal Bowl given in 1744. – MONU-
MENTS. Four painted heraldic tablets of the *Randle Holme*
type – 1611, 1622, and 1708.

BAPTIST CHAPEL, ¼ m. E of the church. 1840, with giant
pilasters front and side. The METHODIST CHAPEL, SW of
the church, is much fussier – yellow and red brick, pinnacles,
and a finial at the top. It dates from 1862–3.

GRAMMAR SCHOOL, School Lane, confusingly hemmed in by
later buildings. Built in 1652–5. Brick. Two tiers of windows
with mullions and mullions and transoms. Four small gables.

MOSS HALL, ½ m. NW. Dated 1616. Timber-framed and
symmetrical, on the E-scheme. Four gables and a small extra
gable for the porch. The timbering is mostly closely set
vertical struts – so much so that the impression is 1516 rather
than 1616. But there are enough little carved details, chiefly
brackets, to ensure the right century. Mullioned and transomed windows. In the l. wing two good chimneypieces with
pilasters below and three painted shields (à la *Randle Holme*)
under arches in the overmantel.

HIGHFIELDS, 1¾ m. SE. A largish timber-framed house, dated *See*
1615. The front is symmetrical except for a Victorian addition ^{p.} at the l. end. Two staircases have twisted balusters, i.e. are ⁴⁴¹
later. One has twisting of two detached strands, and that is
dated 1674. But one chimneypiece is early C17. It has two
atlantes and cartouches in the overmantel. A second consists
apparently of pieces from different sources.

AUSTERSON *see* NANTWICH

BACKFORD   3070

ST OSWALD. Mostly of 1877–9 by *Ewan Christian*, but the
chancel is of the early C14, and the tower is Perp. The chancel
E window has uncusped intersecting tracery, the tower eight
pinnacles and good gargoyles (reproducing the Perp ones
accurately). (Much painted decorative work and paintings in
the nave by *Frampton*. EH) – STAINED GLASS. The E window

looks *Wailes*. – MONUMENTS. Several of the *Randle Holme* heraldic tablets, the earliest 1624. – Samuel Griffiths † 1796. By *E. Spencer* of Chester. A refined tablet with urn in front of obelisk. – Baskervyle Glegg † 1843. By *Sanders* of London. Tablet with urn. – In the churchyard a coarse C18 SUNDIAL.

BACKFORD HALL. 1863. Brick, over-diapered. Basically neo-Elizabethan, but with all manner of bulgy licences – exactly what one means when one speaks of debased in the case of Victorian buildings. Symmetrical centre with shaped gables and a lower wing.

(CHORLTON HALL, ⅝ m. E. Mid C18, much extended in a Baronial style in 1846. Centre and two projecting wings. Plasterwork in the Jacobean style in the dining room, in the Gothic style in the drawing room.*)

BADDILEY
6050

ST MICHAEL. Of a timber-framed church the small chancel remains visible. The nave was encased in brick in 1811. Pointed windows, nicely glazed, and pilasters between them. – Marvellously well-preserved furnishings, especially lucky the survival of the TYMPANUM, dated 1663. It is painted and has the Royal Arms, the Creed, the Lord's Prayer, the Commandments, etc. – Three-decker PULPIT. – BOX PEWS. – COMMUNION RAIL of flat balusters (dated 1701). – WEST GALLERY. – Also one early C16 BENCH END, with linenfold panelling and poppy-head. – PLATE. Paten C16 by *J. Lingley*; Cup, 1624–5. – MONUMENT. Sir Thomas Mainwaring † 1726. With two columns and a decorated segmental pediment.

BADDILEY HALL. Georgian, brick, of three bays and two and a half storeys. One-bay pediment. Rusticated door surround.

BANKHEAD *see* BROXTON

BARNSTON [EH]
2080

CHRIST CHURCH. 1870–1 by *G. E. Street*. Aisleless, with simple, Streetish exterior. Rock-faced. Red-tiled roof. The lancets are cusped and the E window has geometrical tracery. w front with central buttress terminating in an octagonal bell-turret. The nave windows, their mullions etc. flush with the wall surface, are studiously varied. On the s a single lancet

---

* Information sent me by Dr David Watkin.

and three windows of three stepped lights. On the N three
irregularly spaced windows each of two lights under a trefoil.
The former SCHOOL (built in more than one stage, but its early
part almost certainly by *Street*) and the VICARAGE (a less
happy design by *J. Francis Doyle*) with its COACH HOUSE
combine with the church to form a pleasing group. Its Victorian rural character remains intact, though the village is
poised between the sprawls of Heswall and outer Birkenhead.
BARNSTON TOWERS, ¾ m. s on the road to Gayton. A circular
brick tower, castellated, adjoining house and former stables.
(1852 and a remodelling of earlier buildings. Formerly two
towers, but one has been demolished. MHLG)

BARNTON   6070

CHRIST CHURCH. 1842, enlarged 1900. Ashlar, lancets and
a double bellcote. – (PULPIT. Puginesquely elaborate.
Brought from St Helen, Witton, at Northwich.)
Impressive view over the Winnington works of ICI across the
river Weaver.

BARTHOMLEY   7050

A pretty village, with a number of black and white houses and
cottages, C17 (WHITE LION, 1614), but mostly C19, and built
for the Crewe estate.

ST BERTOLINE. A rare dedication. The oldest relic is a rather
raw Norman doorway, re-set on the N side of the church. One
order of columns, primitive leaf capitals, zigzag in the arch.
The church otherwise is Perp, but not of one build. The very
lively four-light N windows with a transom above the ogee
heads of the lights and below the panel tracery precede
the s (Crewe) Chapel windows with uncusped lights and panels.
The latter is of *c*.1528. Both aisles are embattled, and so is the
clerestory. This has eight close-set windows, to the four bays
of the arcades inside. The piers are chamfered squares with 28
four attached shafts. The capitals and abaci are extremely
primitive. Just one and the sw respond have a little leaf
decoration. Good C15 nave and N aisle roofs. The chancel,
including the chancel arch and the arcade to the Crewe
Chapel, is of 1925–6 by *Austin & Paley*. The w tower is Perp
again, broad and powerful, with pairs of two-light bell-
openings under hoodmoulds and eight pinnacles. Some top
decoration. – REREDOS. Now under the tower. Later C17,

but seems composed of a variety of fragments. – PARCLOSE
SCREEN. Good, Perp, of two-light divisions, with panelled
muntins, and close dado decoration. – SCULPTURE. Five
medallions of Saints, Baroque, probably Flemish or French.
– PAINTINGS. Moses and Aaron, two large paintings from
the reredos; for such English oil-paintings, uncommonly
good. – STAINED GLASS. W window 1873 by *Clayton &
Bell*; E window 1925 by *Shrigley & Hunt*, sad after their
early work. – PLATE. Cup 1669–70; Cup 1676–7. – MONU-
MENTS. In the Crewe Chapel. Late C14 alabaster effigy of a
Knight (probably Sir Robert Foulshurst); good. The tomb-
chest does not belong. Mourners on it in pairs under crocketed
ogee gables. – Robert Foulshurst † 1529, rector. Long and
lean alabaster figure praying. Tomb-chest with shields in
cusped frames. – Anne Crewe † 1711. Standing monument
without effigy. Three urns, garlands and flowers. – John
Crewe † 1749, architectural tablet. – First Lord Crewe,
erected 1856. This is, surprisingly enough, said to be a
design of *Nesfield*, then twenty-one years old. It is pure High
Victorian Gothic. Cusped and crocketed canopies to W and E,
in the soffit coloured decoration, very Puginian. – Lady
Houghton † 1887. By *Sir J. E. Boehm*. A white marble figure,
asleep.

BARTON *see* GUILDEN SUTTON

3080   BEBINGTON

ST ANDREW, Lower Bebington. Two bays of the S arcade are
Norman, the N arcade a Victorian duplication. Round piers
with square, many-scalloped capitals, single-stepped arches.
Next in order of time the S aisle widening with windows of
c.1300, and then the W extension of the S arcade and the W
tower with a blunt broach-spire. They are early or mid C14.
The N and S chapels are Perp, with transomed four-light
windows. The chancel E window however is Late Dec, if
it can be trusted. The arcade arches to the chapel are four-
centred, and the spandrels have blank tracery. The chapels
were to be the beginning of a big rebuilding; for a continuation to the W was at least started. There must have
been a Norman crossing, probably with a tower, and now the
crossing was brought up to date,* and the shafts indicate the

---

* The Rev. W. M. D. Persson does not believe this interpretation.

intention again to go higher. The scheme started on the N side, where all arches are cusped except those of the transeptal bay. On the S side the arches below the transoms are uncusped and so is the transept window. The N and S windows of the chapels are panelled below the glazing inside. To the l. of the chancel E window is a handsome canopied niche. There was formerly another one on the r. N aisle added in 1846, re-using material from the nave N wall. – FONT. Circular, just with moulded framing of panels. Is that really medieval? – STALLS. Three seats with MISERICORDS, a pelican, a bearded face, a dolphin. Also four traceried stall ends with poppyheads. – The SCREENS and the REREDOS in the S chapel etc. are by *C. E. Deacon*. – STAINED GLASS. N transept by *Wailes*, 1855 (TK), S transept by *Henry Holiday*, for *Powell's*, 1881 and 1886. – PLATE. Stand Paten, 1704–5; Chalice, 1736, Chalice, 1769, both by *Richard Richardson*.

CHRIST CHURCH, King's Road, Higher Bebington. 1857–9 by *Walter Scott*. With a NW steeple added in 1885 and a long nave. The style is late C13. – STAINED GLASS. S side *Kempe* 1905 and one late *Morris & Co*. By the same all the N aisle.

(COUNTY SECONDARY SCHOOL FOR GIRLS, Higher Bebington Road. A good recent building by *Paterson, Macaulay & Owens* in collaboration with *E. Taberner*, County Architect. Quadrangular, with a classroom block linked to the lower assembly hall etc. by an administrative block, and with a covered way forming the fourth side. EH)

A weak attempt at a Civic Centre in VILLAGE ROAD, with the MAYER LIBRARY of 1870 (a converted farmhouse with a new clock tower), the former MUNICIPAL OFFICES behind, which were the house in which Joseph Mayer lived (enlarged by *E. A. Heffer* who also did the farmhouse conversion), the new Municipal Offices opposite, completed recently (by *Gilling, Dod & Partners*, 1955–6 and 1965–6). A Civic Hall is to follow. Also more civic buildings, by *Paterson, Macaulay & Owens*, just started at the time of writing.

BEESTON

BEESTON CASTLE lies 740 ft up on its isolated rock. It was built by Randle Blundeville, Earl of Chester, *c.*1220 and reverted to the crown in 1237. Little survives of the buildings. They lay along the walls of an outer and an inner bailey, the inner bailey being in the NW corner separated from the outer by a rock-bed ditch. The total area is *c*.900 by *c*.500 ft. The only moderately well preserved part is the inner gatehouse. This is C13 work, with two semicircularly projecting towers and a room 60 ft long on the upper floor. E of the gatehouse is another tower with semicircular front and NE of that yet another. There is no indication of a living hall. The outer bailey still has much curtain walling and remains of the outer gatehouse and seven towers with semicircular fronts. There are no such towers on the W and N, where the rock falls steeply.

BEESTON TOWERS, 1¼ m. E on the A road. Fancy half-timbering with a tower and turrets and over-decorated gables.

BELGRAVE *see* PULFORD

BELMONT HALL *see* GREAT BUDWORTH

BETCHTON *see* DEAN HILL

BEXTON CROFT *see* KNUTSFORD

BICKERTON

5050

HOLY TRINITY. 1839 by *Edmund Sharpe*. Nave and chancel with bellcote. Lancet windows; short chancel. Chancel added in 1875–6 and baptistery in 1911. – In the baptistery STAINED GLASS by *Kempe*, *c*.1904.

BICKLEY

5040

ST WENEFREDE. 1892 by *Douglas & Fordham* for the fourth Marquess of Cholmondeley. Very good, with its extremely broad, low W tower, crowned by a typical Douglas spire with very low broaches. The tower arch is uncommonly wide and deliberately corresponds with the chancel arch. The most attractive feature inside however is the timber passage aisle on the N side. The posts carry a long longitudinal beam, and above it is a hammerbeam roof.

BIDSTON *see* BIRKENHEAD, p. 95

BIRKENHEAD   [EH]

INTRODUCTION

'Men moralize among ruins, or, in the throng and tumult of
successful cities, recall past visions of urban desolation for
prophetic warning. London is a modern Babylon; Paris has
aped imperial Rome, and may share its catastrophe. But what do
the sages say to DAMASCUS? It had municipal rights in the days
when God conversed with Abraham. Since then, the kings of the
great monarchies have swept over it; and the Greek, and the
Roman, the Tartar, the Arab, and the Turk have passed through
its walls, yet it still exists and still flourishes; is full of life,
wealth, and enjoyment. Here is a city that has quaffed the magical
elixir and secured the philosopher's stone, that is always young
and always rich. As yet, the disciples of progress have not been
able exactly to match this instance of Damascus, but it is said
that they have great faith in the future of BIRKENHEAD'
(Benjamin Disraeli: *Tancred*, 1847).

At the commencement of the C19, Birkenhead, with a population of 110, consisted of the ruins of its Benedictine priory and a
small group of houses and cottages, sited on an isolated headland,
looking across the estuary of the river Mersey to the great and
prosperous port of Liverpool. Woodside Ferry, the most ancient
of the Mersey ferries, and one of the few which still remain, had
existed in the C13, and in 1330 Edward III granted to the
priory the right of ferry and charging tolls. Steamers, which
appeared on the river first in 1815, more reliably in 1817, and
on the Woodside route in 1819, meant that the hitherto hazard-
ous crossing could be made safely and regularly. Aware of the
opportunities presented by this link with Liverpool, the lord of
the manor (Francis Richard Price of Flintshire) initiated the
expansion of ferry facilities, the laying out of a few streets, and
the building of a hotel and a church (St Mary, 1819–21 by
Thomas Rickman) with the intention of establishing a bathing
resort and place of residence. In 1828 *The Liverpool Mercury*
reported that Birkenhead 'may, at no very distant period,
become of considerable importance, if not as a watering place, at
least as a favourite sojourn of the merchants of Liverpool'. Its
existence as a town in its own right had, however, by then
already begun, for in 1824 the Scotsman William Laird established a boiler factory, soon expanded into a shipbuilding
yard, on the shore of Wallasey Pool (a tidal creek extending some

2 m. inland), and in the same year he employed *James Gillespie Graham* of Edinburgh to prepare a scheme for the laying out of a new town. The resulting rectangular street plan, sited s of and parallel to Wallasey Pool, is one of the most ambitious instances of c19 town planning anywhere in Britain. At the E end, near the river, Hamilton Square was begun *c.*1825 to designs by *Gillespie Graham*, and it was intended that the entire town should consist of stone-faced buildings of high architectural quality. Streets were however laid out long before there was a chance of their being built up, and little progress had been made by 1833, when Parliament vested the government of the town in Improvement Commissioners. In the ten years following 1836, Hamilton Square was completed, and some building took place in its neighbourhood, particularly from *c.*1839, though not all of it to the originally intended high standard. The gridiron plan proper is 1 m. by $\frac{1}{4}$ m., but rectangular blocks exist beyond these limits and, although it was largely still unbuilt upon by 1839, between that date and 1844 the layout was continued westward, beyond the present Duke Street, perhaps as an extension to, rather than a completion of, Gillespie Graham's original plan. As a result, the longest street of the layout extends for almost 2 m. *Paxton*'s park was begun in 1843, and villa layouts by *Walter Scott* (Clifton Park) and *Charles Reed* (at Claughton) date from about the same time, though some other projected residential estates failed to materialize. The project for the public park was fostered by (Sir) William Jackson, the Jacksons and the Lairds being the families most prominent in the early affairs of the town and in promoting its development.

A plan for constructing docks in Wallasey Pool, initiated by William Laird in the 1820s, was defeated by Liverpool corporation, alarmed by the threat of rival docks. On the revival of the idea, the laying of the foundation stone in 1844 was accompanied by the utmost rejoicing and festivity, repeated in 1847, when the first stage of the docks and also the park were opened. On the former occasion, the future prospects of the town were at their most promising, and a typical acclamation of its current and expected growth was the reference of *Chambers' Edinburgh Journal* in 1845 to 'the sudden rise of a new city in England ... one of the greatest wonders of the age'. The notice which its reputation earned for it in *Tancred* has already been quoted, and poetical efforts inspired by it included e.g. a sonnet, published in *The Illustrated London News* in 1847, beginning,

Another glory on the Mersey's side:
    A town springs up as from a magic wand.
Behold these noble docks – the merchants' pride,
    And the fair park extending o'er the strand.
The gallant bark that often had defied
    The wild Atlantic, may no longer dread
The treacherous shore; in safety, now 'twill ride
    Within the waters of fair Birkenhead.

By 1847, however, difficulties had set in, and a depression, originating the previous year, resulted in the suspension of work on both town and docks. The population, estimated at *c.*40,000 in the mid 1840s, had by 1851 dropped to 24,000. With the eventual return of prosperity, architectural aspirations were abandoned, and the streets of the gridiron, the widest as well as the narrowest, were for the most part slowly built up in mean and crowded fashion, and at the w end many remained vacant until the c20. As for the docks, they encountered structural as well as financial troubles, and in 1855 the new town suffered the humiliation of seeing them taken over by Liverpool, unfinished and insolvent.

F. R. Price's post-1817 development took place between Chester Street and the river, but in 1856 the Laird shipbuilding business was moved to that region, and no trace remains of the early villas, the Birkenhead Ferry Hotel of 1820 or the later Monks' Ferry Hotel, and other than Price's church, now sadly encroached upon, the only obvious survival of Birkenhead's existence as a resort is the Woodside Hotel of 1833. Of classical buildings erected in the gridiron prior to the 1847 revulsion, there remain nearly all the commercial buildings but, except for Hamilton Square, hardly any of the housing. There is no reason to suppose that Gillespie Graham designed anything other than the town plan and the square, and the most active local architects were probably *William Cole*, a pupil of Harrison of Chester, *R. B. Rampling*, *Charles Reed*, who changed his name to *Verelst*, and *Walter Scott*, whose work can be followed into the Mid-Victorian era and who is known to have been more prolific than the references in the following pages would suggest. A Greek Revival Town Hall, built *c.*1833–5 following the setting up of the Commissioners, was by *Rampling*. Containing a market hall, it was in due course replaced by the present Market Hall, *c.*1843–5 by *Fox, Henderson & Co.*, and Town Hall, 1883–7 by *C. O. Ellison & Son*, and by the Sessions House and Police

Station, 1884–7 by *T. D. Barry & Son*. Of the early churches, Holy Trinity is of 1837–40 by *Cunningham & Holme*, St Anne c.1846–50 by *Cole*, St John 1845–7 by *Reed*, and Christ Church, Claughton, 1845–9 by *William Jearrad*. All are un-Camdenian in their ecclesiology and seem reactionary in their architecture when compared with the distinguished classical and Italianate town-centre secular buildings and with the suburban villas which form notable examples of Early Victorian eclecticism. St Werburgh (R.C.), 1835–7, is classical. None of the early (i.e. pre-1847) Nonconformist chapels remain intact. The well-known blocks of working-class flats of 1845 by *C. E. Lang* – the so-called Dock Cottages built initially to house the labourers working on the construction of the docks – stood at the westernmost end of the rectangular layout. They have been demolished, but the church intended to serve them (St James), begun by *Lang*, remains. The railway from Chester was opened in 1840, and its later extensions included a line to the docks, 1847, cutting awkwardly across the gridiron streets. The former station of 1840, a nice Italianate building, was demolished in 1968, as was, even more deplorably, *Robert Edward Johnston*'s Woodside Station of 1878, one of the few post-1847 buildings of any note in the town centre, and one of the few really good main line termini outside London.

Even while streets in the gridiron remained vacant in the 1830s, piecemeal building had begun outside its limits, and as far as subsequent town centre development is concerned, it is worth noting that Borough Road, the principal thoroughfare southwards, owes its irregular line to having been built c.1850–70, along the course of a stream. The steady growth of the town, and the swallowing up of former townships and villages, is closely related to the history of improved transport and communications with Liverpool, as is the development of suburban areas elsewhere in Wirral. Significant factors were the introduction of street tramways in Birkenhead (1860, the first in Europe), improvements in the ferry services (e.g. saloon steamers and floating landing stages, 1860s), the opening of the Mersey Railway Tunnel under the river (1886), the extension and connecting up of railways further into Wirral (e.g. the linking of Liverpool with Hoylake and West Kirby, 1888), electrification of railways (1903–38), and the opening of the Mersey (road) Tunnel (1934).

Birkenhead was incorporated in 1877, John Laird, son of William, being the first mayor. It became a county borough in 1888. The population in 1961 was 141,700.

INNER BIRKENHEAD

PRIORY

The Benedictine priory of St James in Priory Street was originally isolated on a headland overlooking the river. The site is
now hemmed in by shipyard graving docks. Although said to
have been founded *c*.1150 by Hamo de Masci, third Baron of
Dunham Massey, the date of foundation may have been a
little later in the C12. A ferry across the Mersey existed in the
C13, and the lodging of travellers, who doubtless would often
be delayed waiting for good weather in which to make the
dangerous crossing, placed so great a strain on the limited
resources of the priory that, following a petition from the
prior, Edward II granted leave in 1317–18, for accommodation
to be built for the housing of travellers and for them to be
charged for their food. It was in 1330 that Edward III granted
the right of ferry and of charging tolls.

The CLOISTERS were N of the church. Their walks are
destroyed, but much remains of the N and W ranges, and, on
the E, the Norman chapter house doubtless dates from the time
of the original foundation. The church was rebuilt, probably
in its entirety, early in the thirteenth century. Of the C13
CHURCH there survives part of the W wall of the N aisle
including the W respond of the nave arcade (its shaft a half
quatrefoil), the N transept W wall, and the easternmost end of
the N aisle N wall with a jamb of the doorway between aisle
and cloisters and a corbel of the arch between aisle and
transept. The C12 CHAPTER HOUSE is of two bays, with roll- 9
moulded diagonal vaulting ribs and unmoulded transverse
arch. Ribs spring from corbels in the four corners, and in the
centre of either side wall is a cluster of three columns with
scalloped capitals and with bases which indicate the height,
above the present floor level, of wall seating. There is an
indication of a later central screen having been inserted. W
door and flanking windows round-headed but unmoulded.
The S window of the E bay is original, but the E window and the
N window of the E bay are Perp; five lights. Two doorway
openings opposite each other in the W bay above a string
course may, it has been suggested, be a post-Reformation
re-setting of earlier work. Since the Suppression the chapter
house has served as a chapel. The room above, added in the
C14, now re-roofed, has two-light traceried E and W windows.
It was apparently entered from the N transept. Its purpose is

unknown, and the suggestion of its being a scriptorium is not convincing. Remains N of the chapter house were interpreted by Sir Harold Brakspear* as indicating a passage leading E to the INFIRMARY, and also stairs, reached through the C13 doorway which remains at the N end of the E cloister wall, and rising southwards behind the cloister wall to the DORMITORY, which would have extended E.

The N range, C14, contained the REFECTORY above a vaulted undercroft which survives intact and consists of a room of four bays by two bays and, at the W end, a separate two-bay division. Quadripartite vaulting. Diagonal and cross ribs with ogee-chamfered mouldings. Ribs spring from moulded corbels at the walls and, in the larger room, from octagonal central columns without caps. Above vault level, the walls are post-Suppression, except for a section towards the E end of the N wall. This contains a doorway which communicated with a building extending N, the lower stage of which appears to have been vaulted.

The W range is largely C13 (including most of the S and W walls, though later in date than the rebuilding of the church) and the result of a C14 remodelling. The S end had two storeys, the upper room forming the PRIOR'S LODGING. N of this the GUEST HALL rose the full height of the building. Doorway at the S end of the W wall and window above it, altered when a porch was added. Transomed window of two cusped lights and quatrefoil tracery in the S wall of the upper room and a puzzling doorway across the SE corner. Both storeys have a flat-headed fireplace, the upper one moulded. Two doorways between lower storey and cloister, the northernmost with roll-mouldings and virtually flat though cusped head. This gave into a lobby; fragments of two chamfered arches belonging to this remain. A wall passage from here enters the guest hall through a moulded arch. A doorway in the E wall of the upper floor led to the PRIOR'S CHAPEL. Traces remain of the curious arrangement whereby the chapel was carried on transverse arches and a diagonal rib-vault above the W cloister walk. Of the hall's two W windows, the southernmost retains its two lights, transom, and simple circle tracery, but its fellow has Tudor mullions and transoms. The screens passage at the N end was partly divided from the hall by a fireplace extending across from the W wall. Traces of it

* His contribution to R. Stewart-Brown's *Birkenhead Priory and the Mersey Ferry*, 1925, remains the best account of the buildings.

include a head corbel in the w wall. Like the w door into the passage, heavily moulded and with hood-mould and head stops, the fireplace is a C14 insertion. Doorway at the E end of the passage, connecting with the N range undercroft, reduced in height when the undercroft vaulting was built. The roof-line of a passage leading to the kitchen is visible above the doorway in the N end of the hall. – STAINED GLASS. The chapter house E window is of 1921 by *Comper*. – PLATE. Paten inscribed 'Birkenhead chappel 1736'; two Chalices.

CHURCHES

ST MARY, Priory Street. 1819–21 by *Thomas Rickman*. Built, adjoining the priory ruins, at the expense of F. R. Price as part of his plan for developing Birkenhead as a resort. Like the priory, it commanded a view of the river until the shipyards came. Red ashlar. Pinnacles and battlements. Rickman's church had a five-bay aisleless nave, polygonal altar recess, and w tower with slender octagonal spire.* Flat plaster ceiling with patterned ribs. It must have been a pleasant building before monstrous transepts were added in 1832–5. Mullions and tracery of Rickman's Dec windows of cast iron, which is also used for the delicate arcading carrying the w gallery and for tracery and cusping to panels of bench ends and doors. Alterations of 1882–3 by *Aldridge & Deacon* included the addition of a turreted SE vestry. – PLATE. *See* Priory, above. – MONUMENTS. William and George Hetherington † 1844 and 1846. By *C. Lewis*. – Dr William Stevenson. 1854 by *J. A. P. Macbride*. The doctor attends his classically draped patients.

ST ANNE, Beckwith Street. By *William Cole*, c.1846–50. Awkward and papery Gothic, despite its date. It possesses a certain charm, though *The Ecclesiologist* was not enamoured. Red ashlar. Dec and Perp. w tower and crocketed spire richly treated. Statues in canopied niches flank the transept door-ways. No aisles. Transepts as deep as the length of the nave W of them and divided from the nave by stone triple arcades. The roof trying to be a hammerbeam. The chancel was more than doubled in length in 1892–3 by *Charles Aldridge*.

ST JAMES, Laird Street. Begun in 1845 by *C. E. Lang* and intended to serve the now demolished blocks of workers' flats near by (the Dock Cottages) also by Lang. Church and flats stood isolated at the extremity of the longest street in the

* Or were the tower and spire added at the same time as the transepts?

rectangular layout, far beyond the point at which any other
building had taken place. The church occupies an island site,
closing the view along the street. It stood unfinished, *The
Ecclesiologist* reporting that 'fowls occupy the nave; and a
venerable goat appears to have a partiality for the chancel',
until completed in 1858 by *Walter Scott*. E.E. Aisles,
transepts, clerestory, long chancel. NW tower and spire.
Formerly flying buttresses and S transept gallery. Tall nave
arcade. – FURNISHINGS by *Deacon*. They include a singularly
overdone LECTERN, 1913.

ST JOHN EVANGELIST, Grange Road. 1845–7 by *Charles Reed*
(later *Charles Verelst*). Red ashlar. Aisles, transepts, shallow
sanctuary, thin W tower and spire. Lancets and a clerestory of
three-sided windows. Formerly W and transept galleries. Reactionary, but even if Reed was a poor ecclesiologist and archaeo-
logist, he was a good architect. It is a well-proportioned and
consistent work, and the interior is really impressive, with a
lofty and elegant eight-bay arcade continuing in front of and
beyond the transepts, which correspond to its sixth and
seventh bays. Arcade piers and capitals differ in design.

OUR LADY OF THE IMMACULATE CONCEPTION (R.C.),
Cavendish Street. 1860–2 by *E. W. Pugin*. Chancel added in
1876–7 by *Pugin & Pugin* to a simplified design. Rock-faced.
Polygonal apse, clerestory, W rose window. Intended NE tower
and spire not built. – REREDOS. 1895 by *Pugin & Pugin*. Two
stages of blank arcading line the apse. Paintings by *Hardman
& Co*.

ST LAURENCE (R.C.), Beckwith Street. 1889–90 by *Edmund
Kirby*, replacing a church rendered unsafe by railway tunnel-
ling. Polygonal apse. Tall clerestory with grouped lancets.

ST PETER, Cathcart Street. 1866–8 by *David Walker*. Completed
1882–3. Brick with a little stone dressing. Polygonal apse.
Coupled lancets alternate with circular windows in the clerestory. The W front has three doorways between the buttresses
and a pair of two-light windows and a circular window above.
Tower with pinnacles and pyramidal slated spire. The internal
brickwork has unfortunately been painted, though not recently. Nave arcade capitals boldly carved, no two alike.

HOLY TRINITY, Price Street. 1837–40 by *Cunningham &
Holme*. Ashlar. A lively, bizarre, and naive adaptation of the
Norman style. Well proportioned, and the interior surprisingly
dignified. The exterior, particularly the W tower, is indescrib-
able in the profusion and oddity of its detail. Grotesque masks,

which adorn the cornice all round the building, reach a climax
of hilarity with the corbels over the doorway, the beak-heads
of the doorway itself, and the chubby winged face higher in
the tower. Five-bay arcade and a bay for the altar separated
from nave and aisles by transverse arches. Roof beams sort
of Perp on colonnettes and angel corbels. w and side galleries.
Plaster masks on the gallery fronts and below the galleries.
The heads outside the church are grim and grotesque. Those
inside are demure and serene. Is this a heavy-handed attempt
at symbolism? Like other Birkenhead churches, Holy
Trinity is at present threatened with demolition. The loss of
this unique and entertaining curiosity, which *The Ecclesiologist* considered 'so execrable as not to be worth criticism',
could be ill afforded.

St Werburgh (R.C.), Grange Road. 1835–7. It has been
attributed to *M. E. Hadfield*. Red ashlar. A competent
classical design. Rectangular and aisleless. Shallow pedimented projections with giant pilasters at the E and W ends.
The principal (s) elevation has five windows, with entablatures and brackets, above a rusticated base. The presbytery
adjoins on the other side. Inside, the altar end has giant
pilasters, and at the opposite end is a semicircular gallery on
iron columns.

Oxton Road Congregational Church, Woodchurch
Road. 1857–8 by *William Cole*, who even at this date has not
progressed beyond a thin, incorrect sort of Dec. The intended
spire was never built and the tower has lost its tall pinnacles.

PUBLIC BUILDINGS

Town Hall, Hamilton Square. 1883–7 by *C. O. Ellison &
Son*. Two storeys of nine bays above a rusticated granite
basement. Corinthian pilasters and hexastyle pedimented
portico which has a flight of steps at either end. Quite
restrainedly classical, though the tall clock tower with domical
top is more inventive. The design is obviously derived from
that of Bolton Town Hall, which was, less directly, inspired
by Leeds. The plan form at Birkenhead, however, differs
from both these precedents, with the assembly hall occupying
a less dominant position. The building was damaged by fire
in 1901 and restored by *Henry Hartley*, who rebuilt the upper
part of the tower to a new design. Of the principal interiors,
the staircase and council chamber are the most lavishly

treated. – STAINED GLASS. Staircase window 1904 by *Gilbert P. Gamon*.

SESSIONS HOUSE and POLICE STATION, Chester Street. 1884–7 by *T. D. Barry & Son*. Free but not over-elaborate classical. Corinthian order to the recessed centre of the upper storey. Entrance with atlantes. The building backs on to the Town Hall and differs from it in having had proper consideration given to the long side elevations. These both read as tall end pavilions linked by a lower two-storey range.

MUNICIPAL OFFICES, Cleveland Street. 1967–9 by *Biggins Sargent Partnership*. The best of the several recent public buildings w of Hamilton Square and a welcome contrast to the adjacent block which since 1958 has disfigured the corner of the square, and with which it is connected by a single-storey wing. Ten storeys below a windowless top storey which houses plant room etc. In situ reinforced concrete faced with glass mosaic. Windows of warmly-tinted solar glass. Detailing less good than the overall conception.

QUEEN VICTORIA MONUMENT, Hamilton Square. 1905 by *Edmund Kirby*. A large version of an Eleanor Cross. Also in Hamilton Square WAR MEMORIAL, 1925 by *Lionel B. Budden* with sculpture by *H. Tyson Smith*, and JOHN LAIRD STATUE, 1877 by *A. Bruce Joy*.

EDWARD VII MEMORIAL CLOCK TOWER, Clifton Crescent (not its original site). 1912 by *Edmund Kirby & Sons*. Engaged Roman Doric columns above rusticated base. Clock stage with domical top. Portland stone.

CENTRAL LIBRARY, Borough Road. 1931–4 by *Gray, Evans & Crossley*. Neo-Georgian. The arrangement of the plan handled better than the principal elevation with its over-heavy entrance feature.

WILLIAMSON ART GALLERY AND MUSEUM. *See* Claughton, p. 98.

MARKET HALL, Market Place South.* Of *c*.1843–5. The engineers were *Fox, Henderson & Co.*, later of Crystal Palace fame. Three naves, the middle one narrower than the outer ones. 430 ft long, twenty-four bays. Cast-iron arcades, brick outer walls. Light roof trusses divide each bay into three. Low-pitched roofs, glazed along the ridges. Additional supports have been inserted into the outer naves, but the centre retains its long vista of delicate ironwork uninterrupted.

---

* Or at least what was Market Place South prior to recent roadworks.

The naves are expressed on the triple-pedimented end elevation. Side bays with two storeys of lunette windows in blank arches between brick piers. The interior originally had two fountains made by *John Seeley*. They were moved to Arrowe Park, where one remains (*see* p. 107).

GENERAL POST OFFICE, Argyle Street. 1905–6 by *Walter Pott*.

TECHNICAL COLLEGE, Borough Road. 1949–54 by *Willink & Dod* with later additions. H-plan with five-storey link between single-storey workshop block and six-storey front range. Much brickwork, but the upper storeys of the front elevation have, on either side of the central feature, bands of continuous fenestration, passing in front of the stanchions of the steel frame. Assembly hall block with segmental foyer window.

PARK HIGH SCHOOL FOR BOYS, Park Road North. 1965 by *Bradshaw, Rowse & Harker*, replacing and incorporating earlier buildings. Concrete, brick, much glazing. Some 1960s chunkiness, e.g. projecting concrete beams, but all is handled with restraint and sensitivity.

CONWAY SECONDARY SCHOOL, Conway Street. 1905–6. Art Nouveau Baroque in red pressed brick and terracotta.

ALBERT MEMORIAL INDUSTRIAL SCHOOLS (former), Corporation Road. 1865–6 by *David Walker*. Rather grim Gothic with polychromatic brickwork. Sculptural tympanum over the entrance and, at a higher level, a bust of the Prince Consort.

GENERAL HOSPITAL, Park Road North. There remains the central portion of the former Borough Hospital, 1862–3 by *Walter Scott*, built at the expense of John Laird. Italianate. Common brick with stone dressings.

CHILDREN'S HOSPITAL, Woodchurch Road. 1882–3 by *John Clarke*. Red pressed brick with sandstone entrance arch, mullions, etc. Half-timbered gables. Quite friendly and domestic-looking.

MATERNITY HOSPITAL, Grange Mount. *See* Perambulations, p. 94.

BIRKENHEAD PARK. *See* Perambulations, p. 91.

HAMILTON SQUARE STATION, Hamilton Street. The first stage of the Mersey Railway, which included the tunnel under the river, was opened in 1886. The engineers were *James Brunlees* and *Charles Douglas Fox*. The rails are here 103 ft 6 in. below the street. Station building by *G. E. Grayson*. Common brick and terracotta. Enormous tower built in connexion with the provision of power for the original hydraulic lifts.

MERSEY TUNNEL. Its official but little-used name is Queensway. 1925–34, with *Sir Basil Mott* and *J. A. Brodie* as engineers. 2.13 m. long, with a total length, including the two branches, of 2.87 m. *Herbert J. Rowse* was appointed architect in 1931 and was responsible for the following: MAIN ENTRANCE, King's Square. Lodges, tunnel entrance, retaining walls, etc., Portland stone, with French-1925-*moderne* details, with Egyptian touches. All now much altered, but unlike its Liverpool counterpart, the monumental sixty-foot-high column remains. It is of polished black granite, fluted, with illuminated head.* DOCK ENTRANCE, Rendel Street. Much smaller. VENTILATION STATIONS. Steel-framed brick-faced towers housing giant fans. Of basic cubic shapes, with some geometrical brick ornamentation. Those at SIDNEY STREET and TAYLOR STREET consist of emphatically square towers (two in the former case) rising from larger blocks, but that at WOODSIDE, at the river's edge, is a more homogeneous diminishing composition, 210 ft high. It is the most impressive and successful of all the several tunnel structures. For those on the Liverpool side *see The Buildings of England: South Lancashire*.

DOCKS

The scheme to construct docks in Wallasey Pool, promoted by William Laird in the 1820s, was thwarted when Liverpool Corporation, alarmed by the prospect of rival docks, bought up the required land on the margin of the Pool. Inexplicably, Liverpool parted with this land in 1843, and the following year unsuccessfully opposed in Parliament revived proposals for docks at Birkenhead. With *J. M. Rendel* as engineer, construction began in 1844 and the first stage was opened in 1847, both events being marked by rejoicings to which reference has already been made. Rendel's plan was to enclose the upper part of Wallasey Pool (to be called the Great Float) and to form a low-water basin at the river entrance. These had not materialized by 1847, when only the small Egerton and Morpeth Docks were completed. After being suspended as a result of the town's economic difficulties, work proceeded slowly, hampered by over-

---

* The styling of the interior of the tunnel itself is not as Rowse left it. Since the above was written the layout of the entrance has been yet further altered, and the column moved some distance from its former axial position.

ambitious plans, lack of money, and the incompetence of Rendel (who was replaced by *James Abernethy*) until, incomplete and in hopeless financial straits, Birkenhead docks were taken over by Liverpool Corporation in 1855 and transferred to the newly formed Mersey Docks and Harbour Board in 1857. Under *John Bernard Hartley*, son of Jesse Hartley, construction continued to revised plans, and much of Rendel's work, which was found to be unsafe, was rebuilt. Hartley succeeded his father as engineer to the Dock Board in 1860, but resigned the following year, his place being taken by *George Fosberry Lyster*.

EGERTON DOCK. Opened in 1847. Its shape is recognizable on *Rendel*'s plans of 1844. Coursed rubble sandstone contrasts with the cyclopean granite, reminiscent of Jesse Hartley's Liverpool dock structures, which can be seen in post-Rendel work, e.g. at MORPETH DOCK. Although first opened in 1847, this was later reconstructed and enlarged, and re-opened in 1868. The site of Rendel's intended low-water basin is occupied by ALFRED DOCK, opened in 1866, and WALLASEY DOCK, opened as a low-water basin in 1863 and re-opened as a dock in 1877. The GREAT FLOAT, partially opened in 1851 and completed in 1860, is divided into the WEST and EAST FLOATS by DUKE STREET BRIDGE (first opened in 1861). Graving docks at the W end by *Lyster*, opened in 1864 and 1877. Later work includes VITTORIA DOCK, first opened in 1909, and BIDSTON DOCK, opened in 1933.

HYDRAULIC TOWER, Tower Road. Designed by *Hartley* but not completed till 1863. It provided power for dock gates, bridges, etc. Engine house of brick with heavily rusticated stone dressings. The tower itself, slender, is mostly rock-faced. Both are castellated and machicolated. The engine house has lost a storey at the S end, and the tower formerly rose much higher, with an open lantern in two stages.

On the S side of the East Float, immediately SE of Vittoria Dock, the original WAREHOUSES, 1847 by *Rendel*. Three parallel ranges which originally extended further towards Corporation Road. The adjoining railway goods station, Italianate, has been demolished. Of other C19 warehouses, the group of former CORN WAREHOUSES, N of the East Float, remains partially intact. By *Lyster*, dated 1868. Six-storey, with hoist loop-holes and towers. Formerly two blocks facing the dock (one remains) and a single long block (no longer continuous) behind. Between them a canal, opening off the dock.

PERAMBULATIONS

The following is divided into (a) the rectangular layout and the streets at its E end, (b) Birkenhead Park, (c) S of the rectangular layout.

(a) The Rectangular Layout and the Streets at its East End

This perambulation must largely be concerned with tracing the most notable of the remaining classical buildings, faced with white sandstone from the near-by Storeton quarries, erected in the rectangular layout and the neighbourhood of Hamilton Square prior to 1847. The dour dignity of many of them, particularly of now-demolished terrace houses, was markedly Scottish in character, perhaps attributable to the personal influence of William Laird, and HAMILTON SQUARE itself is reminiscent of the Edinburgh work of its architect, *James Gillespie Graham*. The square is exceptionally grand and dignified. It is also very large, almost too large to read as a related whole, and the present layout of the central garden, of facile formality and bereft of large trees, does not help. The basic elevational form is of three storeys, with a further storey above a cornice, and with rusticated ground floor, pilastered doorways, and first-floor iron balconies. Giant order of columns to the end pavilions and of pilasters to the central features. The ends and centres further emphasized, e.g. by round-headed ground-floor windows, columned porches, and combinations of entablatured and architrave-framed windows. Orders unfluted Roman Doric. No two sides of the square are identical, and on the E side the two blocks which flank the Town Hall differ from each other, e.g. in the height and number of storeys, and from the remaining sides, e.g. in the more extensive use of round-headed windows and columned porches. The first houses to be built, in or after 1825, were those at the N end of the E side (including the present No. 63, which was Laird's own house) and those opposite at the E end of the N side. The junction between the first and second houses on the N side suggests an early modification of the scheme. By 1839, only the N side had been completed. The S and W sides were built in 1839–44 and the E side completed soon after, a gap being left for the future Town Hall.

Buildings in the neighbouring streets here referred to date from the years 1839–44 unless otherwise stated. In ARGYLE STREET, adjoining the return elevation of Hamilton Square,

is a three-storey block with a further shallow storey above a
cornice. Rusticated ground floor with segment-headed shop
openings. Brackets to first-floor windows. Adjoining the
return elevation of the square in PRICE STREET is a small
rusticated building with round-headed first-floor windows.
During the years 1894 to 1906 it housed *Harold S. Rathbone*'s
so-called Della Robbia pottery factory, and panels on the
frontage incorporate products of this Morris-inspired venture.
Nos. 17–21 is all that remains of a pair of blocks which flanked
the Greek Revival Brunswick Methodist Chapel of 1830. It is
probably of the same date. In this region of the gridiron were
a number of interesting terraces with fine ashlar façades.
Some were apparently fragments of quite ambitious composi-
tions which remained unrealized after building had been cut
short in 1846 or 47. The recent housing which extends over a
very large area westwards from Hamilton Square* has
involved the simplification of the original street layout as well
as the demolition of these terraces, and although none of the
smallest, two-storey, terraces remain, an indication of what
some of the three-storey housing was like is given by the block
with rusticated ground floor in MORTIMER STREET beside
the Town Hall. Its date is mid 1840s.

At the N end of HAMILTON STREET, Nos. 24–28, meeting the
return elevation of Hamilton Square, is a remarkably good
palazzo-type building, built between 1844 and 1847. Two (or
perhaps more accurately one and a half) storeys above the
ground floor. Five bays of windows with architrave frames,
those on the first floor with entablatures, enriched brackets,
and segmental pediments and with further enrichment around
the central window. Quadrant corners with re-entrant angles,
windows following the curve and balustrading between the
two upper storeys. Heavy cornice. Two-bay side elevation.
Detailing of considerable subtlety and refinement. Who was
the very able architect? On the NW corner of BRIDGE
STREET a modest two-storey building, but of ashlar, and
carefully handled. Diagonally opposite, on the SE corner, is
WATERLOO BUILDINGS. Three storeys, the ground floor
with traces of original shop fronts. Some giant pilasters and
windows with entablatures, etc. Quadrant corners. The
Hamilton Street frontage is incomplete. Also incomplete is the

* The overall plan and many of the buildings were designed by *T. A.
Brittain*, former borough architect. The plan has undergone revision by
Edgar Hindle, Director of Architecture, Housing and Works.

range comprising Nos. 1–7 Bridge Street. It is of ashlar, though painted, and round the corner in CHESTER STREET, No. 18 commands greater attention when it is known that the elaborate ornamentation is of stone, ill-advisedly painted, not stucco. At the foot of the street, the WOODSIDE HOTEL, 1833, a survival of Birkenhead's existence as a resort. The once-symmetrical principal elevation is spoilt by recent alterations and additions. The river was formerly nearer, the present Woodside Ferry Approach being reclaimed land. ¼ m. s along Chester Street is MARKET CROSS by *Walter Scott*, completed in 1847 as a shopping centre. The site was rectangular and was bisected by a diagonal street (Cross Street) to form two separate triangular blocks. One was demolished to make way for the Mersey Tunnel entrance, but the other largely survives. It is a robust Italianate design of a type more usually seen executed in stucco than stone. The Chester Street and Cross Street frontages, and the corner which forms a junction between them, are all different, and the elevations of the demolished block were different again. Adjoining the n end of the Chester Street frontage is the former ASSEMBLY ROOMS by *Edward Welch*.* It is on the corner of MARKET STREET, where Nos. 11–13 is a good, restrained, three-storey seven-bay building. Entablatures to the first-floor windows and a segmental pediment etc. to the central one. Cornice. Nos. 25–27 is worth a glance, and at the s end of HAMILTON STREET mention should be made of Nos. 30–34 and of Nos. 42–44 which was probably the house which *William Cole* designed for himself. Also the red sandstone MIDLAND BANK, Gothic, of c.1880. Well detailed. It is by *Seddon*.

To the s, a very extensive area was, in the late 1960s, given over to a system of approach roads for the Mersey Tunnel, with attendant spaghetti of flyovers and underpass.

Finally, for two outlying items, westwards along CONWAY STREET (into which the flyover system now extends) which, with its continuations, is the longest street of the town layout with a straight length of almost 2 m. Off into CAMDEN STREET where, on the corner of BECKWITH STREET, is the ANGEL INN. Nothing special, but worth a mention as a mid-1840s building in the gridiron. Then, in PARK ROAD EAST, the Italianate QUEEN'S HOTEL, stucco, of three storeys and

---

* Who also designed the MONKS' FERRY HOTEL, now demolished, and may have been more active in the town than is known.

nine by four bays. Ground floor with Ionic pilasters and porch. Apparently early 1860s, i.e. later than it looks.

(b) Birkenhead Park

Birkenhead Park cannot conveniently be described in the form of a perambulation, but the following suggested route takes in the buildings mentioned below and allows the principal features of the landscape to be seen. Begin at the main entrance at the junction of Park Roads North and East where the previous perambulation ended. Into the Lower Park. Lower Lake with bridges and boathouse. Then follow the inner carriage drive in a clockwise direction round the entire layout, making excursions at Gothic Lodge for No. 2 Park Road South, at Italian Lodge for Nos. 90–92 Park Road South and Cannon Hill in Park Road West, at Ashville Road for Nos. 8–61. Continuing round the Upper Park take in Castellated and Norman Lodges and the Upper Lake. Excursions at Central Lodge for Cavendish Road and No. 1 Ashville Road and (back in the Lower Park) through a footpath gate for Royden House in Park Road North.

The park was laid out in 1843–7 by *Sir Joseph Paxton*, who was employed at the instigation of Sir William Jackson. Birkenhead Park is Paxton's most successful landscape design and the first park ever to be provided at public expense. It had considerable influence upon subsequent public park development in this country and upon Olmsted and his plan for Central Park, New York. It was created from marshland with Paxtonian ingenuity by draining the marshes into lakes, the spoil from the excavation of which contributed to the making of artificial hillocks. The execution was supervised by Paxton's pupil *Edward Kemp*. The layout is encircled by a carriage drive, and between this and the surrounding roads is a belt of housing to which about 100 of the park's 226 acres were originally intended to be devoted. This combination of residential suburb with public open space ensured, with the profitable selling of building plots, the financial success of the scheme. The whole is bisected by an unenclosed public road, dividing the layout into the LOWER PARK and UPPER PARK. Each has a broad open area and a more densely planted part with winding paths around an irregular lake with an island. Gently picturesque landscaping in a post-Repton manner. Some subsequent additions are sadly out of character.

ENTRANCE LODGES. Doubtless designed under *Paxton's*

supervision, apparently by *Lewis Hornblower* and *John Robertson*. The latter was Paxton's architectural assistant at the time, and is best remembered for the model village of Edensor at Chatsworth. Stone, mostly ashlar. For the most part exceptionally attractive and well detailed, redolent of the same unclouded Mendelssohnian romanticism that characterizes the landscaping. Some are similar to, but more sophisticated than, buildings on the Chatsworth estate and to designs drawn by Robertson for J. C. Loudon's *Encyclopaedia of . . . Villa Architecture* and other of his publications: there is Loudonish precedent not only for the small, picturesque lodges, but also for the monumental MAIN ENTRANCE, on a U-plan, with a pair of lodges linked by a triple-arcaded screen. Giant order of unfluted Ionic columns to the screen and the front of the lodges. Anta pilasters to the lodges. The entablature and the superstructure of the screen break forward above the columns. Elaborate scroll-like ornament terminates the central feature. – CASTELLATED LODGE, Park Road West. Irregular, with battlements, square tourelles, etc., and octagonal staircase tower. – CENTRAL LODGE, Ashville Road. Pilastered single-storey wing abutting against a block with rusticated ground floor and pilastered upper storey. – GOTHIC LODGE, Park Road East. Neo-Elizabethan. – ITALIAN LODGE, Park Road South. Composition of single and two-storey blocks and belvedere tower. – NORMAN LODGES, Park Road North. A Greek Revival pair. Each bi-axially symmetrical with single-storey wings flanking a two-storey centre. Doric porches *in antis*. Upper windows in the form of horizontal panels. – GATEPIERS. Unified designs for park entrances and perimeter housing. Little of the original IRONWORK, also uniformly designed, survives.

BOATHOUSE, Lower Lake. The pilastered and arcaded upper storey was intended as a bandstand. The pantile roof and the original balustrading have gone. The Lower Lake has lost one of its bridges, but the CAST IRON BRIDGE and the SWISS BRIDGE remain. The latter, a covered timber structure with red-tiled roof, has recently been admirably restored.

81

HOUSING. *Paxton*'s plan for the perimeter housing consisted of an informal combination of villas and terraces, ingeniously arranged so as almost everywhere to avoid straight rigid rows – an interesting development of Nash's Regent's Park with its enclosing terraces and isolated villas. Purchasers of building sites were governed by regulations as to the development

and maintenance of their property; designs had to be approved
by the Improvement Commissioners, and the only permissible
materials were, in effect, Storeton stone and, with stylistic
limitations, brick. Carried out over a long period of time, and
with many of the plots never being built up, the housing is
not in accord with Paxton's suggested layout. The best of
the houses are amongst those built before the mid 1860s.
Almost the only part to approximate to Paxton's plan is a
group of villas in ASHVILLE ROAD, late 1840s and early 50s:
No. 8, Gothic, harmed by later extensions; No. 10, more
attractive Gothic; No. 16, restrained and dignified Italianate
(the dormers are recent); Nos. 59–61, two semi-detached
houses, though asymmetrical, Jacobethan; No. 57, dated
1854, good Jacobethan. All are probably by *Walter Scott*.[*]
No. 1 is late 1850s or early 60s. – CAVENDISH ROAD. No. 1
and Nos. 2–3. Late 1840s or early 50s. – PARK ROAD
NORTH. A large Italianate semi-detached pair, late 1840s or
early 50s, now a nurses' home known as ROYDEN HOUSE. –
PARK ROAD SOUTH. No. 2. Late 1850s or early 60s. An
unusually pure classical design for so late a date. Nos. 90–92.
Mid 1850s, though restrainedly classical. – PARK ROAD
WEST. CANNON HILL. Late 1850s or early 60s. Almost the
only terrace and the only one of any architectural or group
value. Its symmetrical Italianate façade seen across the Lower
Park forms an important feature in the landscape.

(c) s of the Rectangular Layout

At the E end of GRANGE ROAD a large shopping centre by *Sir
John Burnet, Tait & Partners* is under construction at the time
of writing.

CLIFTON PARK was laid out as a villa estate *c.*1843 by *Walter
Scott*, who also designed most of the early houses. It was
originally enclosed within sets of lodge gates. Houses referred
to below are ashlar unless otherwise stated. CLIFTON ROAD.
Largely built up soon after the initial layout. There has been
some demolition. The pilastered MASONIC TEMPLE was
originally a house. Nos. 17–19 are brick, a semi-detached pair
in one of which *Scott* himself lived, but there are a number of
houses, undoubtedly by him, of better quality, e.g. No. 11.
Also Nos. 38–40, a semi-detached Italianate pair, in the form
of end pavilions linked by a lower block. The pavilions have

[*] Though the names *Hodgkinson & Mott* have been mentioned in connexion with these houses.

rusticated ground storeys with segmental bay windows, are pilastered above, and have three-bay side elevations and parapeted and balustraded roofs. The link has a balcony on heavy brackets. Equally notable is No. 42, Gothic. An irregular, gabled composition with traceried windows and heavily moulded doorway. Due to the fall of the ground, the entrance is at upper-storey level, and the house is larger than it first appears. Fluted chimney with spiral enrichment. Despite a certain heaviness, Georgian picturesque eclecticism is closer than Victorian seriousness. No. 47 is Italianate, with bracketed eaves. Columned porch and, on the garden side, a loggia. Like other of the houses it has tripartite windows with ornamented cast-iron mullions. – In WHETSTONE LANE (outside the Clifton Park layout) Nos. 140–142 form a Greco-Italianate pair with more of the rich detailing which can be safely attributed to *Scott*. – Back into Clifton Park for HOLLYBANK ROAD. Nos. 1–3, with pilasters, and Nos. 5–9, with pedimented windows, are Italianate, stucco, but the former group of villas beyond them is much depleted. There is little else of note in the irregularly planned streets w of Clifton Road, due to the siting of the estate near to the gas-works. After the first few years its fumes discouraged the originally-intended villas, and building was subsequently completed to inferior standards. Of early work there is, though, a little in LOWWOOD ROAD, and in THE WOODLANDS Nos. 53–55 and Nos. 57–59 are both classical semi-detached pairs, and No. 42 is Gothic, freely grouped, with an open octagonal turret on one of its gables.

Now NW to CHARING CROSS for an asymmetrical range, partly curved on plan, consisting of the former MARTINS BANK with shops either side. 1901 by *Douglas & Minshull*. Gothic. Mostly ashlar, but some brickwork. The bank itself has a symmetrical frontage with two octagonal turrets, but with an additional, larger and circular, turret to the r. Octagonal banking hall. Diminutive dormers characteristic of Douglas. The GRANGE HOTEL and PARK HOTEL date from the 1840s, and in this region can also be found vestiges of other variously engulfed early development. Particularly, further w in GRANGE MOUNT a chaste pre-1840 villa incorporated in the MATERNITY HOSPITAL. Almost opposite, Nos. 19–21 have first-floor windows with brackets, entablatures, etc., and a balcony on brackets.

Finally, *c.* ¾ m. to the s, in BOROUGH ROAD, the KINGSLAND

DANCE HALL. Its black and white marble entrance is the dining room chimneypiece from *Norman Shaw*'s Dawpool (*see* Thurstaston, p. 363) of *c.*1882–4. Sir Reginald Blomfield, whose book on Shaw woefully misinterprets the significance of his work, commented upon the failure of this item to obey the classical rules.

OUTER BIRKENHEAD

ARROWE *see* WOODCHURCH

BIDSTON   *2090*

ST OSWALD, Hoylake Road. Tower early C16. Heraldic evidence of shields over the W door dates it between 1504 and 1521. Doorway with label and four-centred head. W window under ogee hoodmould. Three-light bell-openings, battlements. The remainder of the church was rebuilt in 1855–6 by *W. & J. Hay*. The rather un-Victorian low proportions maintain the scale of the tower. Aisles with gable roofs. Short chancel extension 1882 by *G. E. Grayson*. – REREDOS. A mosaic 'Last Supper' made by *Salviati*. – STAINED GLASS. In the S aisle, from E to W, are windows by *Morris & Co.* (1912), *R. Anning Bell*, and *H. Gustave Hiller*. – S aisle W window by *H. Hughes*. – N aisle E window by *Powell*. – In the N aisle a window by *Frank O. Salisbury*.

HOLY CROSS (R.C.), Hoylake Road. 1959 by *F. X. Velarde*. Interior not without merit, but what is one to make of the exterior and its overscaled toy fort tower?

FLAYBRICK HILL CEMETERY, between Boundary and Tollemache Roads. 1862–4. BIC on the gatepiers is for Birkenhead Improvement Commissioners. Layout by *Edward Kemp*. Buildings in lively mid-Victorian Gothic by *Lucy & Littler*. Formal layout with axis aligned on a road running diagonally from the rectangular town plan. Office with a fanciful bell-turret. Pair of linked chapels and between them a spire under which the axis passes. To the N an informal, more closely planted area with lodge, chapel, and arched gateway beyond.

GRANGE SECONDARY SCHOOL, Tollemache Road. 1933 by *Richard Furniss*, chief architectural assistant to the Borough Engineer and Surveyor.

FLAYBRICK HILL WATERWORKS, Boundary Road. Of *c.*1860–5. Circular tower with two storeys of windows and engaged columns.

Bidston retains a well-preserved village centre, with cottages grouped round the hill on which stands the church. Stone predominates, though there is some brick and thatch. In HOYLAKE ROAD, immediately E of the church, is THE LILACS, C17, its small main block with symmetrically disposed mullioned windows. Across the road, YEW TREE FARM, dated 1697, has a half-timbered gable-end. To the W is CHURCH FARM, C17, quite a large gable-ended block with an irregular pattern of mullioned windows at different levels. Labels. Almost opposite this is CLOVER ALMSHOUSES, 1901 by *Woolfall & Eccles* in a free Elizabethan style with semicircular gable.

On higher ground at the E end of the village is BIDSTON HALL. Bidston became Stanley property late in the C14, and the present house was built by an Earl of Derby – either (according to W. Fergusson Irvine) by the fourth Earl before 1594 or by the sixth Earl *c.*1620–1. The balance of historical probability suggests the latter date, as does the plan form, with the entrance giving centrally into a symmetrically planned hall, rather than at one end in the medieval manner. The crude and rustic nature of the building and its detailing belie the aristocratic association and would be consistent with a C16 date. Two storeys. The front originally had four gables. Four- and three-light mullioned windows flank a central semicircular bow, fully windowed on the first floor and forming a porch on the ground floor. Arched entrance with pilasters and enriched voussoirs. The rear elevation has four-light windows and a four-bay loggia of semicircular arches on columns. All mullions unmoulded, of curved section. Hall with heavy stone surrounds to the doors and, as elsewhere in the house, to the fireplace. The forecourt is approached through an arched gateway surmounted by three strange finials, the centre one at a higher level.

¾ m. SE, No. 98 TOLLEMACHE ROAD is a stone cottage with mullioned windows, perhaps C16. In BOUNDARY ROAD, opposite Flaybrick Hill Cemetery, TAM O'SHANTER COTTAGE, single-storey, whitewashed, thatched.

On BIDSTON HILL a late C18 WINDMILL, much restored. Also a LIGHTHOUSE rebuilt in 1872–3. The adjoining OBSERVATORY dates from 1866. Extending 1 m. S along a ridge is NOCTORUM, which, together with the W side of Bidston Hill, forms a spacious, leafy district of Late Victorian houses, many very large and very red. Although a little building had taken place previously, it was from *c.*1880 onwards that Liverpool shipowners and cotton merchants began to invade on a large scale. Also C20 houses, including some acceptable modern ones. In ELEANOR ROAD, CHARLEVILLE, 1959 by *J. Roy Parker*, and BIRKENLAND, 1957 by *Dewi Prys Thomas*. In VYNER ROAD SOUTH stood BIDSTON COURT, 1891 by *Grayson & Ould*. It was re-erected at Frankby as Hill Bark (*see* p. 219), but there remain here the entrance lodge (with pargetting, timberwork, and twisted chimneys), stables (ruinous), and a gardener's cottage, the latter facing UPTON ROAD. In this latter road the garden of THE PRIORY, 1902, was laid out by *Thomas H. Mawson*, but is now partly built upon, and the pine glades, the Chinese summerhouse, etc., are no more. In STOKESAY (the site of a demolished house) No. 4 is by *Ivan Johnston & Partners*, 1966. Ground area largely open. Main block timber-framed with veranda on diagonally projecting posts. In NOCTORUM LANE are HA'PENNYFIELD, 1959–60 by *J. Quentin Hughes*, and MERE HALL, *c.*1880, the largest of the several houses in Noctorum designed by *Edmund Kirby*. Now divided up, and although partly stripped, many features of the rich interior, incorporating Flemish Baroque woodwork, remain.*

CLAUGHTON

₃₀₈₀

CHRIST CHURCH, Christchurch Road. 1844–9 by *William Jearrad*. One of the decidedly un-Camdenian churches of early Birkenhead and an interesting example of the breed, with an odd mixture of Gothic elements. Red ashlar. Tall, narrow nave without aisles. Transepts. Thin w tower and spire. w doorway with ogee hood. Lancets. Steep-pitched hammerbeam roof. w and transept galleries. Apparently structurally unaltered, except for the addition of the chancel aisle and organ chamber.

ST MARK, Devonshire Road. 1890–1 by *C. W. Harvey* and *Pennington & Bridgen*. Tower 1913. Rock-faced. Clerestory. The tower stands clear of the s aisle, which ends in a polygonal baptistery. 'Well intentioned but uninspired', said Goodhart-Rendel. – STAINED GLASS. E window by *Christopher Whall*, 1906, i.e. earlier than it looks.

TRINITY (Presbyterian), Alton Road. 1865–6 by *W. & J. Hay*.

* Hitherto open land to the w is now being built up, badly, and the nearby MENLO estate is a hotch-potch which provides an example of how not to redevelop the site of a demolished house. The more regrettable as a good, unexecuted plan for the layout had been made by *G. W. Dishman & Associates*.

4—C.

WILLIAMSON ART GALLERY AND MUSEUM, Slatey Road.
1928 by *Leonard G. Hannaford* and *Herbert G. Thearle*. Fresh
and sensitive Neo-Georgian, well detailed. Brick with stone
dressings. Single-storey and virtually windowless. The entrance and a single window feature both have Corinthian
columns. Corinthian pilasters on the side elevation. Rectangular pillars in the entrance hall.

ST AIDAN'S THEOLOGICAL COLLEGE, Howbeck Road. 1854–
6 by *T. H. Wyatt* and *Henry Cole*. Tudor Gothic. Brick, stone
dressings, blue brick diapering. Only two sides of the intended
quadrangle were built. The principal (N) front is High rather
than Early Victorian and symmetrical in massing but not in
detail. Formerly a central flèche. An interesting departure from
the original design by *Wyatt & Brandon*, 1850, which was
symmetrical and less awkward, though also with French
pavilion roofs. Dining hall 1912 by *Hastwell Grayson*. Chapel
1881–2 by *David Walker*, re-arranged in the early 1950s by
G. G. Pace. The fittings were stripped from the sanctuary and
an altar was placed at the W end of the sanctuary with a cross
suspended above and an ambo built on either side. Of significance in the development of the liturgical movement in this
country.

STEVEDORES AND DOCKERS BENEVOLENT SOCIETY SOCIAL
CENTRE, Bessborough Road. Formerly a Unitarian Church.
1901–3 by *J. J. Talbot*.

s of Birkenhead Park and dating from about the same time (i.e.
from *c.*1843) a series of roads was laid out by *Charles Verelst*,
then still *Charles Reed*, for Sir William Jackson. The park
formed a buffer between the gridiron town plan and this more
spacious suburb. The layout, which extended s of Devonshire
Road and as far w as Manor Hill, was to have included a church,
though not on the site on which St Mark was ultimately built.
Reed may well have been responsible for some of the earliest
houses. These include KENYON TERRACE in DEVONSHIRE
ROAD, built between 1844 and 1848, a distinguished group of
three long terraces, each three-storey, ashlar, with rusticated
ground storeys, entablatures and brackets to some windows
(more brackets on the central block than on the others), some
Ionic porches, etc. Of the same period are some of the semi-
detached pairs and small villas in this road – including the
delightful ASTON LODGE, Gothic, with arched gateway – and
in GROSVENOR ROAD.* In SLATEY ROAD, THE GABLES,

* In DEVONSHIRE ROAD an extremely early PILLAR BOX in the form of

1865 by *Walter Scott* for himself, and also probably by him
LANDOUR, *c.*1850, in PALM GROVE. Further w was a district of larger houses, including work by both *Scott* and *Reed*,
the latter designing Jackson's own house, *c.*1843, which seems
to have been a Greco-Italianate villa of exceptional quality
and refinement. In MANOR HILL there remains OUTWOOD,
now ST ANSELM'S COLLEGE, apparently early 1860s, ashlar
and much rustication, Italianate, with handsome entrance gates
and interior with top-lit staircase hall. ST AIDAN'S TER-
RACE was built at the same time as St Aidan's College (i.e.
mid 1850s), with which it is in axis. Ashlar. A long composition
of quite large houses, each five bays. Impressive, despite the
congestion of classical elements and the canted bow windows.
In DEVONSHIRE PLACE, REDCOURT, now ST ANSELM'S
JUNIOR SCHOOL, looks like a fugitive from Noctorum.
1876–9 by *Edmund Kirby*, for George Rae, banker and Pre-
Raphaelite patron.

LANDICAN *see* WOODCHURCH

NOCTORUM *see* BIDSTON

OXTON   *2080*

ST SAVIOUR, Bidston Road. 1889–92 by *C. W. Harvey* and
Pennington & Bridgen, replacing a church of 1846 rendered
inadequate by the growth of Oxton as a Victorian suburb. Dec.
Cruciform, with a broad central tower, clerestory, and narrow
passage aisles. Exterior of rock-faced red sandstone. Good interior of brick with stone dressings. E window blocked in the
post-war restoration. – REREDOS. A triptych by *G. F. Bodley*,
1906. – STAINED GLASS. N transept and w windows 1903 by
Morris's firm, incorporating *Burne-Jones* designs, though after
both their deaths. The w window commemorates George Rae,
the Pre-Raphaelite patron. – Chancel s window by *Kempe*, as
was the destroyed E window. – Glass in the vestry from a near-
by house (*see* below) also by *Kempe*. – ALTAR and REREDOS in
the s transept and CHANCEL SCREEN designed by *Edward Rae*,
son of George. Like the CHOIR STALLS they have unusual in-
laid ornament. – WAR MEMORIAL. 1920 by *Sir Giles Gilbert
Scott*. – (NEEDLEWORK. Frontals designed by *C. G. Hare*.)
ALL SAINTS, Shrewsbury Road. 1879. – STAINED GLASS. By

a fluted Doric column, with vertical slot. A later, octagonal pillar box is in
Alton Road.

Morris & Co. Centre light of E window 1881, side lights 1900. Also S aisle window *c.*1914 and chancel N window *c.*1922.*

HOLY NAME OF JESUS (R.C.), Beresford Road. 1899 by *Edmund Kirby,* in the grounds of his own house, Overdale. Small aisleless church of intimate scale with a brick interior. Polygonal apse.

FIRST CHURCH OF CHRIST, SCIENTIST, Village Road. Built as Oxton Public Offices. 1874 by *Joseph Brattan.*

BIRKENHEAD SCHOOL, Shrewsbury Road. Main building 1871 by *Lucy* and/or *Walter Scott.* Tudor Gothic. Brick with stone dressings. Large two-storey hall, later subdivided horizontally. Boarding house and headmaster's house 1878. Chapel 1882–3 by *F. W. Hornblower* and *H. Townsend.*

In SHREWSBURY ROAD, No. 59 is of *c.*1884 by *George Smith* of Chester, who seems to have been influenced by Douglas. In 1902 *C. F. A. Voysey* designed furniture and decorations for two houses, which retain work in his characteristic style. They are No. 30 SHREWSBURY ROAD, which has four rooms with chimneypieces, one of them also with built-in furniture, and No. 37 BIDSTON ROAD, which has two rooms with windows, chimneypieces, built-in furniture, etc. HOLLY LODGE in VILLAGE ROAD is Gothic. In TALBOT ROAD, OXTON HALL COTTAGE, *c.*1660 (MHLG). Small two-storey stone house. Mullioned windows, one with a label. ARKHOLME and COLONSAY are both by *J. J. Talbot, c.*1901. In MILL HILL, POINT OF AYR is the house from which *Kempe* glass was taken to St Saviour (*see* above). Externally an uneventful Italianate villa, probably *c.*1850, but with a Gothic interior, at least part of which dates from 1857. No. 1 INGESTRE ROAD was built in 1956 by *J. Roy Parker* for himself.

Extending from ROSE MOUNT and FAIRCLOUGH LANE to WOODCHURCH ROAD is a district which includes many pleasant Early Victorian houses and earlier cottages.

Recently, much demolition and rebuilding have taken place in Oxton. Of new housing, that by *Kingham Knight Associates* (ROSEMOUNT PARK in ROSE MOUNT and EVERSLEY PARK in STORETON ROAD) is of good standard, but inferior piece-meal redevelopment of individual sites is fast eroding the character of the area.

PRENTON

3080

ST STEPHEN, Prenton Lane. Begun in 1897 by *C. E. Deacon* and completed in 1909 by *Deacon & Horsburgh.* Deacon's master-

* Details supplied by Mr A. C. Sewter.

piece, though a flawed masterpiece. Basically Gothic, but with fresh and underivative detailing. Grouped lancets. Lofty, but no clerestory. Sandstone exterior. The design makes better sense when it is known that a tower and spire were intended over the choir and that the nave was to have been one bay shorter. The 1897 stage involved the building of the nave. The chancel etc. came in 1909, but with a further bay inserted at the E end of the nave. The internal proportions also suffer as a result of the over-long nave. Interior of brick with some stone dressings. Rectangular piers with chamfered corners and bands of stone. A narrow arch and closely-coupled piers at the w end of the arcade. Good chancel, with the choir defined by two transverse arches, carried on tall free-standing piers, the capitals of which are linked to the side walls and carved in a frieze-like Arts and Crafts manner. A small SE chapel, with transverse arch and panelled and boarded ceiling, is also most successful. *See* p. 441 The *Deacon* FURNISHINGS, particularly the ALTAR, REREDOS, STALLS, LECTERN, and PULPIT, are lively and original and quite un-Gothic. – Chapel ROOD SCREEN. 1949 by *Bernard A. Miller*, painted by *Martin Bell*. Sensitive and harmonious.

ST ALBAN, Northwood Road. 1961 by *Gerald R. Beech*. Grey brick and much glazing in small panes. Slender bell-tower. Triangular apse, over which the ridge of the roof continues, a theme taken up by the free-standing vestry.

CONGREGATIONAL CHURCH, Storeton Road. By *T. W. Cubbon*. Hall 1889. Church 1909 but left incomplete. Ashlar interior with narrow passage aisles.

WAR MEMORIAL, Prenton Lane. An unfortunate design by *Briggs & Thornely*, dating from 1919. Reconstructed after bomb damage.

At Prenton are some of the best examples on Merseyside of early c20 domestic architecture, and the summit of Prenton Hill forms an attractive Edwardian suburb, created amongst existing pinewoods, with views westwards across Wirral to North Wales. Most of the best houses are by *Sir Arnold Thornely* of *Briggs, Wolstenholme & Thornely*. In PINE WALKS, GREYSTOKE, 1907 by *Ashby Tabb*, a Liverpool furnisher and decorator, for himself. By *Briggs, Wolstenholme & Thornely* are BIRCH HOWE, *c*.1910, a neat rectangle of painted brick, and PINE RIDGE, 1910. Also by *Briggs, Wolstenholme & Thornely* are PINE GROVE, *c*.1910, THE HOMESTEAD, *c*.1909 (by *Sir Arnold Thornely* for himself), and MANOR HOUSE,

1909, L-shaped, rendered, with some half-timber and a two-storey galleried hall – all in MOUNTWOOD ROAD, as is LONG MYND, 1908 by *John C. Grierson*. Again by *Briggs, Wolstenholme & Thornely* is THE WHITE HOUSE in BURRELL ROAD. THE QUARRY, *c.*1927, has a remarkable garden made in a former quarry. In PROSPECT ROAD, No. 8 of 1926 is again by *Ashby Tabb* for himself. Curious Home Counties vernacular. In TOWER ROAD, PICARDY, 1908 by *Briggs, Wolstenholme & Thornely*, brick and timber gabled frontage, with a sundial. In PRENTON LANE, ORIEL COURT, 1900 by *J. J. Talbot*, with a later addition to the right of the gable, and BRAESIDE, 1908 by *William Glen Dobie* for himself, with a garden on which *Mawson* advised. Next door, at WEST HILL in GOLF LINKS ROAD, a garden by *Gertrude Jekyll*, 1923 (i.e. a late work), though not surviving in its original form, and the house, by *Briggs & Thornely*, reconstructed after bomb damage.

¼ m. W, engulfed by post-war housing, PRENTON HALL FARM in PRENTON DELL ROAD and LOWER FARM in ROMAN ROAD are fragments of the former hamlet.

3080   ROCK FERRY

ST PETER, St Peter's Road. 1841–2 by *Hurst & Moffatt*. Red ashlar. Thin sort of Norman, but with a W tower and recessed spire. Illiterate, but not entirely unattractive. Interior reconstructed after bomb damage.

ST ANNE (R.C.), Highfield Road. 1875–7. Designed by *E. W. Pugin* but completed after his death by *Pugin & Pugin*. Later additions and enrichments. No nave arcade, but a single column stands in the entrance of either transept. Barrel roof with trusses on colonnettes and angel corbels. Aisles 1934. The intended spire was not built.

ST BARNABAS, Bedford Place. 1903 by *Grayson & Ould*. The roof is continuous over the aisles. Nave arcade of timber.

HIGHFIELD CONGREGATIONAL CHURCH, Rock Lane West. 1870–1 by *David Walker*.

PRESBYTERIAN CHURCH, New Chester Road. 1857–8 by *W. & J. Hay*.

CONVENT OF THE HOLY FAMILY (R.C.), Highfield Road. Central block 1862–4 by *E. W. Pugin*. Later extensions include the enormous chapel block (the chapel occupying only the upper part), 1931.

SWIMMING BATHS, Byrne Avenue. 1933 by *Richard Furniss*.

A ferry existed here in the C18 and perhaps earlier. At the beginning of the C19 its facilities were improved and, apparently at this time, a hotel was built and pleasure grounds were laid out. Steamers were introduced on the ferry and an esplanade constructed upstream from the hotel *c.*1830. In 1836 the Royal Rock Ferry Company was formed and further improved both coaching and ferry facilities and extended the hotel and its grounds. The ferry closed in 1939.

The ROYAL ROCK HOTEL is in BEDFORD ROAD. Stucco. At the E end a three-storey block, three by two bays, with lettering in relief. This is almost certainly the 1836 extension. The remainder is probably a later alteration of the original early C19 building. The company also built in 1836 BATH HOUSES on the ESPLANADE. Stucco, single-storey. Now partially demolished, but originally with a central pedimented block linked to end pavilions by Doric colonnades.

ROCK PARK. A private residential estate, enclosed within lodge gates, laid out in 1836–7 by *Jonathan Bennison*. This attractive sylvan suburb is picturesquely planned with a serpentine looped driveway, has a frontage to the esplanade and river, and was described by Nathaniel Hawthorne, who lived here when serving as American consul in Liverpool. 'There being a toll,' he wrote, 'it precludes all unnecessary passage of carriages; and there never were more noiseless streets than those that give access to these pretty residences. On either side there is thick shrubbery, with glimpses through it at the ornamented portals, or into trim gardens, with smooth shaven lawns . . .' Most of the houses were built before 1843 and all were completed by *c.*1850. They include semi-detached pairs and individual villas, some of ashlar and some stuccoed, in a variety of styles. At the time of writing, the estate (which includes some houses in ROCK LANE EAST) is remarkably complete, there having been no demolition and hardly any infill. Shortly, however, a dual-carriageway by-pass road is to be constructed, cutting the layout in two and involving the demolition of several houses and the entrance lodge. A practicable alternative route exists for the road, and the unnecessary and shortsighted destruction of Rock Park is an unforgivable act of vandalism.

Of further Early Victorian residential development S and W of Rock Park, nothing requiring special mention remains. EGERTON PARK, ¾ m. W, is another enclosed estate, though later in date than Rock Park, pleasantly planned, but with no buildings of interest. In BEBINGTON ROAD, ⅝ m. S of Egerton Park, the

ESSOLDO CINEMA, originally the REGAL. Classically conceived, with strong rectangular emphasis. 1937 by *S. Colwyn Foulkes*, an architect whose work has included some good cinemas in North Wales.

ST CATHERINE, Church Road. A brick church of 1831 altered and enlarged in 1875–6 by *J. Francis Doyle*. Doyle removed a w gallery from the box-like 1831 nave, replaced a flat ceiling with an open roof, and added chancel and transepts in rockfaced sandstone. Nave windows doubtless also by him. NE tower and spire added in 1879.

ST JOSEPH (R.C.), North Road. 1899–1900 by *Edmund Kirby*. Red pressed brick. Tall, with clerestory.

ST LUKE, Old Chester Road. 1881 by *G. E. Grayson*. – STAINED GLASS. E window 1919 by *Hardman & Co.*

ST PAUL, Old Chester Road. 1854–5 by *W. & J. Hay*. Dec, but reactionary and unarchaeological, with transepts but no aisles. Droopy NE spire. – ROOD SCREEN. 1910 by *Hastwell Grayson*. A handsome piece in the C15 style.

METHODIST CHURCH, Church Road. 1966 by *Paterson, Macaulay & Owens*. This replaces a huge octagonal church of 1861–2 by *Walter Scott*.

ST PAUL (Presbyterian), North Road. 1899–1900 by *R. G. Sykes*.

ST CATHERINE'S HOSPITAL, Church Road. The part which is the former workhouse has a central entrance block with tower and short rectangular spire. 1862–3 by *Thomas Leyland*. The wings on either side have since been raised in height. The other symmetrical block, with a prominent central feature, further N, was the Union Schools, 1868. – STAINED GLASS. In the chapel, the E window and three smaller windows by *Kempe*, 1896.

TRANMERE CROSS, Victoria Park. Base and chamfered shaft of a cross, probably C15, re-erected here in 1937.*

CLIFTON PARK. *See* Inner Birkenhead, p. 93.

ST MARY, Ford Road. 1868 by *John Cunningham*, at the expense of William Inman of Upton Manor (*see* below). Aisleless, with polygonal apse, SW tower, and diagonally placed organ chamber (formerly vestry). – FONT. A small movable wooden font.

---

* Having been rediscovered by Mr J. E. Allison.

The quatrefoil plan suggests the late C18 or early C19. –
PLATE. Chalice and Paten, 1618 by *I. C.*

ST JOSEPH (R.C.), Moreton Road. 1953–4 by *Adrian Gilbert
Scott.* The exterior is tasteful and consistent, if anachronistic.
Inside, the straight-sided arches appear as unconvincing con-
cessions to the C20.

BRANCH LIBRARY, Ford Road. 1936 by *Richard Furniss.*

OVERCHURCH PRIMARY SCHOOL, Moreton Road. 1938 by
Richard Furniss.

UPTON HALL CONVENT SCHOOL, F.C.J., Moreton Road.
Main buildings 1863. There remains, however an early C19
house, two-storey, stucco, with four-column stone porch.

The village is now thoroughly suburban. Of prosperous mid C19
villas, the only one to remain is UPTON MANOR (now part of
the CONVENT SCHOOL) in MORETON ROAD. This is two-
storey, Italianate, ashlar, and was built *c.*1857 for the shipowner
William Inman, almost certainly by *John Cunningham.* Taller
extension, with elaborately decorated interiors and a belvedere
tower, added some time before 1875. Staircase reconstructed,
apparently in 1911. The original block contains a galleried hall
with splendid domed roof-light and plasterwork. To the E, in
WESTWOOD ROAD, is ENTWOOD, 1959 by *Dewi Prys
Thomas,* a group of three proportionally related square blocks,
rendered, with low-pitched quarter-pyramid roofs.

WOODCHURCH

2080

HOLY CROSS, Church Lane. To a C12 nave was added a C14
S aisle. Its four-bay arcade has double-chamfered arches and
octagonal piers with broad capitals. Passage arch at the E end
of the arcade. The present aisle itself and the porch are C16,
possibly post-Reformation.* Porch doorway and outer arch with
four-centred heads under labels, the outer arch moulded, etc.,
with canopied niche above. In the aisle a PISCINA. C14 chancel
arch and chancel, though the latter incorporates an earlier
small N window.‡ Arch-braced roofs. W tower C14, though the
massive NW and SW diagonal buttresses were added in 1675
and the tower was later refaced. C12 work remained *in situ* in
the N wall of the nave until a N aisle, with hidden steel frame,
was added in 1964–5 by *Sir Hubert Worthington.* It would have
been difficult to go far wrong as far as the re-setting of masonry

---

* The Rev. R. S. Wilkinson draws attention to a datestone of 1584.
‡ Part of a WHEEL CROSS is built into the wall above it.

and the re-use and reproduction of C17 windows is concerned, but the delicate problem of adding to a medieval church was not satisfactorily solved. The doorway at the E end of the N aisle was previously set in the nave N wall, though with its plain chamfered reveal it can hardly be C12. – FURNISHINGS by *Crispin Worthington*. – FONT. C15. Octagonal. Bowl with angel corbels. Emblems of the Passion on the stem. – ROOD SCREEN. 1934 by *Bernard A. Miller*, dating from the time of his sympathetic restoration of the church. Carving designed and executed by *Alan Durst*. Quite boldly unconventional for its date, and most sensitive, with a quality of timelessness. – BENCH ENDS. Four, in the chancel. Perp. Traceried, with poppyheads. – STAINED GLASS. Fragments of Perp glass in the porch. – Medallions in the E window, French or Flemish. – Chancel s window 1875 by *Kempe*. – Of later *Kempe* glass, some is destroyed and some removed, though there are fragments in the s aisle w window. – PLATE. Chalice dated 1625. – PROCESSIONAL CROSS. 1937. Carved in ivory by *Alan Durst*. – MONUMENTS, in the chancel. Margaret Hughes † 1802. By *W. Spence*. – Three painted wooden panels commemorate Mary Ball † 1680, Mary Hockenhull † 1681, William Hockenhull † 1698.

The church enjoys a beautiful approach – almost a *beau idéal* small churchyard pathway, flagged, with yew trees on either side, and aligned on the Tudor porch.

RECTORY, Church Lane. Rebuilt in 1861–2 in a Streetish parsonage manner. The Gothic interior survived a replanning *c.*1930, but in 1961 the house was partly demolished, and although the principal rooms remain, stencilling, texts, etc., and exposed brickwork were obliterated under paint and plaster. The architect responsible for destroying this important example of Victorian decorative art was *Felix Holt*.

ST MICHAEL AND ALL ANGELS (R.C.), New Hey Road. 1965 by *Richard O'Mahony & Partners*. T-plan, with nave and transepts focused on the sanctuary, and with a small E chapel. Low concrete walls and shallow clerestory. High roof structure, steel-framed, clad externally with aluminium and internally with timber, rising to a pyramid over the sanctuary. Lighting louvres on the w side of the pyramid. – SCULPTURE. Mother and Child by *Norman Dilworth*.

LANDICAN CEMETERY, Arrowe Park Road. 1934. Chapels, crematorium, etc., by *Richard Furniss*.

ARROWE PARK, Arrowe Park Road. The grounds are now a

public park and the house a hospital. ARROWE HALL is neo-Elizabethan, ashlar, dating from 1835. Enlarged in 1844 and altered and extended three or four times subsequently. *John Cunningham* was responsible for at least one stage. Near-symmetrical entrance front, almost certainly 1835. – LODGE GATES. The engagingly fanciful lodge is of 1856. The gates (recently resited), which have an arrow motif, are probably earlier. – WORLD BOY SCOUT JAMBOREE MEMORIAL. 1929. Sculpture by *E. Carter Preston*. – (FOUNTAIN, in the corporation nursery garden. One of the two made by *John Seeley*, from Birkenhead Market Hall; *see* p. 85.)

Woodchurch remained rural until after the Second World War, with the village consisting of cottages and a green (now all vanished) grouped round church, rectory, and school. In 1944 *Sir Charles Reilly* prepared a plan for the WOODCHURCH HOUSING ESTATE, with a 'village green' type of layout to which, in the mood of post-war idealism, considerable social significance was attached.* It was rejected in favour of a scheme by *H. J. Rowse*, building of which began in 1946 and which, if completed, would have been a visual success, even if reactionary in its planning and architecture. Rowse was however succeeded in 1952 by *T. A. Brittain*, Borough Architect, who continued building to inferior standards of design. By *Rowse* the housing with steep roofs and varied materials, e.g. in ACKERS ROAD, and also shops in HOME FARM ROAD. The Neo-Georgian shop fronts are hard to defend, but are they not preferable to the shops in HOOLE ROAD? These face the church across a dreary waste that was to have been part of the central parkway of Rowse's layout.

Finally, to the S, the hamlet of LANDICAN, worth a mention on account of its completely rural character, which is retained in spite of proximity to the housing estate and to the route of a motorway.

BIRTLES   8070

ST CATHERINE. 1840. With an octagonal SW tower and neo-Henry-VIII windows. Nave and short chancel. With the S porch corresponds the N baptistery. The church is full of WOODWORK and stained glass, all brought in by Thomas Hibbert of Birtles Hall. The W screen e.g. has panels which were stall-backs in the Netherlands and two figured groups of a late date. The elaborate PULPIT is dated 1686. The eagle

* See *The Reilly Plan. A New Way of Life*, Lawrence Wolfe, 1945.

LECTERN is pre-Reformation and more probably Continental than English. There is also the FAMILY PEW, also with assembled bits and pieces. Most of the STAINED GLASS is Netherlandish too, of the C16 and C17, but the three main figures in the E window, the Virgin, an angel, and St John, are Netherlandish of the early C16 at the latest.

BIRTLES HALL. A fine ashlar house of the early C19.* Two storeys and a top balustrade. Porch with two columns *in antis*. Round the corner a front with two canted bay windows. Gutted by fire in 1938 and reconstructed.

BLACKDEN HALL *see* GOOSTREY

BLACON *see* CHESTER, p. 171

4050
BOLESWORTH CASTLE

75 Beautifully placed halfway up a hill and overlooking the plain to the w. The house was built *c.*1830 by *William Cole*. It is of ashlar, two-storeyed, and castellated and turreted. The façade seems symmetrical but is not. It has a raised centre with a wide canted bay and wide bays at the two ends as well, but the r. one is canted, the l. one a bow. *Clough Williams-Ellis* in 1920–3 changed the interior thoroughly. He removed the Gothic decoration (except that of the staircase) and erected a much more sumptuous classical ensemble. The principal rooms are the central hall with pilasters in two tiers and a balcony with a chaste railing and the new entrance hall with columns. Fine formal GARDEN with terraces. Gothic LODGE of 1868.

7080
BOLLINGTON
Near Bowdon

HOLY TRINITY. By *Salvin*, 1854. Nave and chancel, lancets and geometrical tracery. Lacking personality and distinction.

MILL on the River Bollin, ½ m. NE. A high, four-storeyed block of five bays, Georgian in outline, but Early Victorian in all the details. It was built *c.* 1856.

9070
BOLLINGTON
Near Macclesfield

ST JOHN BAPTIST. 1832–4 by *Hayley & Brown*, a Commissioners' church. Lancets with Y-tracery, no aisles but galleries, and a W tower; not a small church.

---

* Or *c.*1795 according to Earwaker.

VICARAGE, Shrigley Road, lying back on the SE side. By *Ernest Newton*, 1898, a medium-sized house with Tudor motifs, plain and sensible and sensitive also. Typical Newton doorhood.

ST OSWALD, Bollington Cross. By *F. P. Oakley*, 1908. Towerless alas, but a well-thought-out job. Florid Dec tracery, nice original doorway arch. Stone outside, brick inside. S aisle, the arcade arches dying into the piers.

NONCONFORMIST CHAPELS. The CONGREGATIONAL in Palmerston Street of 1867 still has round-arched windows, the other CONGREGATIONAL is of 1862 (by one *Williamson*) and already Gothic; so is the METHODIST in Wellington Road of 1886. Both the latter have towers.

Bollington has much character, with its stone houses and stone cottages, the river and the canal and the railway viaduct, two large mills with their tank towers, and on the nearest hill WHITE NANCY, a white phallic folly built *c*.1820 to commemorate Waterloo.

(INGERSLEY HALL, Mill Lane, ½ m. SE of the church. Georgian. Five by eight bays, two storeys, ashlar. Porch with unfluted columns.)

CAIRN, at Butley, 1½ m. W. Large cairn revetted with a stone kerb covering a series of cremation burials, one accompanied by a Food Vessel.

BOSLEY
9060

ST MARY. Small Perp W tower, the nave of 1777, the chancel, by *James Green* (GR), of 1834, both the latter of brick. The arched nave windows are very slightly pointed. Open timber roof. – PULPIT. Mid C17, unusual in its detached angle colonnettes. – MONUMENT. John Willans Newell † 1851. Signed by *Sanders*, Euston Road. A seated female figure by a sarcophagus with an urn seen at an angle. Also an amphora with flowers.

(COLLEYMILL BRIDGE, 1¾ m. W. Two segmental arches. Jervoise calls it the most striking bridge in East Cheshire.)

BOSTOCK HALL see MOULTON

BOUGHTON see CHESTER, p. 172, 173

BOWDON
7080

Bowdon, Altrincham, and Hale are one and all Outer Manchester. But socially Bowdon is the West End, with a considerable number of wealthy Mancunians' houses of the 1850s, 1860s, and after. Ormerod's second edition (1882) calls it 'studded with the many commodious and handsomely designed villas and terraces [terraces?] of a large and flourishing community, chiefly composed of those who every evening seek a healthy and pleasant retirement from the toils of business' – i.e. commuters. Commuting began when the railway reached Bowdon in 1849. But there was already a village there, and one finds brick terraces of presumably the 1830s along STAMFORD ROAD – including one charming Gothick pair (No. 75) – and also in CHURCH BROW.

ST MARY. The church is by *W. H. Brakspear* and of 1858–60. It is a very grand, prosperous building, with a big four-stage w tower, large four- and five-light aisle windows, square-headed and with a transom, a six-bay nave, and notably good details of stone-carving. The aisles are very wide, but have early C16 roofs from the predecessor church. Plenty of furnishings from that church. – REREDOS. In the N transept fragments of a delicately carved reredos.* – SCULPTURE. Also in the N transept fragments of Saxon interlace, some Norman fragments, some small C14 heads. – STAINED GLASS. Chancel s of c.1840. – W, E, N transept, s transept all c.1860 and all by the same hand. But whose hand? – s transept E by *Kempe*, 1898. – PLATE. Almsdish, 1712–13; two Patens with two Cups and two Flagons, gilt, 1775–6. – MONUMENTS. Priest, defaced. Canon Ridgway tells me that Rosemary Crump now considers this a C10 figure of Christ. – Early C14 Knight, his legs not crossed. – William Brereton † 1630 and wife. Recumbent effigies, his behind and above hers. Arch and two columns. – First Earl of Warrington, 1734. Signed by *Andrew Carpenter*, i.e. Carpentière. He received £389 for it. Large standing monument. Sarcophagus with seated figures of Truth and Learning. Back plate with very long inscription. – Langham and Henry Booth, 1735. Also by *Carpenter*. Also a standing monument. 'Reredos' with columns carrying a segmental pediment. On it two cherubs. Against this architecture a sarcophagus and an obelisk, and l. and r. of this two oval portrait medallions. – Thomas Assheton Smith † 1774. Signed by *Richard Westmacott* (i.e. Sir Richard Westmacott's father). – Ninth Earl of Stamford † 1910. Neo-Wren, with twisted columns. – WAR MEMORIAL. Outside, N of the church. Of c.1920 by *Arthur*

See
p.
441

---

* Or perhaps a stone SCREEN or a TOMB front. But Canon Ridgway feels uneasy about this piece, which seems to him 'foreign to Cheshire in the Middle Ages'.

Hennings. Shaft with a small figure of St George. The architectural detailing remarkably original.

St Paul's Methodist Church, Enville Road. By *Brakspear*, 1874–80. This Gothic monstrosity with a crossing dome is being demolished. One regrets its disappearance. It was the most ambitious ecclesiastical building of Bowdon.

Grammar School, Marlborough Road. 1911 by *H. Beswick*, the then County Architect. Red brick and orange terracotta. The recent addition – 1962–4 – by *W. S. Hattrell & Partners* is gratifyingly crisp and unmannered.

The merchants' houses of Bowdon would deserve a special study. They begin still in the style of before and around 1850 near the church. A specially good early example is High Lawn, up a walk from Langham Road or at the end of East Downs Road. The prominent belvedere is later, but the house itself with its bow is still Georgian in character. Langham Road is particularly rewarding. Here is e.g. Merlewood, 1869 by *Waterhouse* – yellow brick and very matter-of-fact – and opposite, more fanciful with steep bargeboarded gables, Field Bank.

In Green Walk, running NW from the church, is a group of large stone villas of the 1860s and 70s. The first is Erlesdene, by *Mills & Murgatroyd*, typically High Victorian, with Elizabethan and Gothic motifs. Immediately N, in Dunham Road, the Denzell Hospital, a luscious villa of 1874 in which debased Jacobean mixes with Gothic and Italianate. It is really very bad. Houses of large size continue N along Dunham Road to around St Margaret's church (*see* Altrincham), N and W of which is a further series of leafy winding roads.

Further out is Spring Bank, Ashley Road, Late Georgian, brick with two canted bay windows and between them the doorway and round-arched upper window.

Also further out at the SE end of Grange Road is The Green Bend, built for himself by *Frank B. Dunkerley* in 1923. It looks more like 1913, i.e. Hampstead Garden Suburb in style.

BRAMHALL

St Michael, St Michael's Avenue. 1910 by *J. Gibbons* (but the N aisle 1938). A decent stone building in the best tradition. Dec tracery. The arches die into the piers. But the church is made something special by *G. G. Pace*'s W tower of 1960–3. This is brick, high and square, with extremely large windows in all

three exposed sides. They each have four transoms, but these
are treated intermittently. The lights have pointed heads and
below, at ground level, are rows of lancet lights. Inside – typical
Pace – an undisguised metal ladder up to the top.

BRAMALL HALL is one of the four best timber-framed mansions of England. The others are Little Moreton and, in
Lancashire, Speke Hall and Rufford Old Hall. Unfortunately,
for Bramall much research remains to be done to establish
a chronology and Victorian alterations. There were many of
these, mostly after 1883* – one, the most spectacular, is on the
entrance, i.e. w, side, especially the two gables and the bay
window gablets.‡ This centre of the house is very thrilling to
look at, with decoration by concave-sided lozenges and cross-
shapes. Also the broad polygonal projection of the bay window
(cf. Little Moreton and Speke) gives a splendid sense of ampli-
tude. Dates inside record 1592, 1599, and (formerly) 1609.
However, the s wing is the oldest – of the c15. Here, to the N,
is an oriel on the upper floor and windows with moulded
mullions and cusped ogee heads. In the E part of the s range
is the chapel, with another such window, now blocked. This
range was the solar wing, and the moulded beams on the ground
floor are probably original. The s side is now brick-faced. The
great hall was where it is now; only it was open to the roof. A
ceiling was put in about 1590–1600, and a long gallery was
added as a top storey. The E side of the E range is even more
confusing. It is entirely irregular and is so already in the c18
and c19 illustrations. Up to the second half of the c18 there
was also a w range, making the house (like Speke) quadrangular.

Inside there is little stucco decoration left – a pendant in the
hall bay, and some friezes. In the CHAPEL is a PEW from the
Davenport Chapel at Stockport. It consists of a stall end, a
bench end and some mixed woodwork. Against the w wall
WALL PAINTINGS almost obliterated by black-letter inscriptions. In the E window three small STAINED GLASS figures of
the Crucifixion; early c16. The roof of the s wing is splendid,
with cambered beams, arched braces, and two and a half tiers
of wind-braces, an arrangement more likely for halls than for
solars. Above the hall is the Withdrawing Room with a ceiling
with pendants in quatrefoils and a large stucco chimneypiece

---

* Said to have been by *J. Douglas* and *Harry S. Fairhurst*.
‡ A Buckler drawing of the house in 1826 is at Capesthorne.

with elaborate and preposterous caryatids. Elaborate doorcase. Elizabethan ornamental wall paintings.

The landscaping of the grounds is late C19.

In HOLLY ROAD, at the corner of Woodford Road, is HOLLY COTTAGE by *Edgar Wood*, 1905. Common brick, demonstratively used, gables, a totally asymmetrical composition, and typical unmoulded and absolutely flush wooden window casements.

In CARR WOOD ROAD, at the corner of the same A road, is CASTLE HOUSE of 1926 by *John Swarbrick*, Elizabethan in motifs, but not in composition. Roughcast, but the porch set diagonally across the angle of the two wings with the brick exposed, and there is a broad tower. In the same street GATE-PIERS are chimneystacks from *Philip Hardwick*'s Stockport Grammar School.*

BREDBURY   9090

ST MARK. 1847–8 by *Shellard*. Quite big. W tower, the sides of the church with paired lancets. Short, low chancel. It is in fact a Commissioners' Church.

CONGREGATIONAL CHURCH, Hatherlow. 1846. Like a rather wilful Commissioners' church, i.e. with thin lancets, but the bell-turret polygonal, and supported by flying buttresses.

ARDERN HALL, 1½ m. NW, off the Ashton Road on the hill to the W (up Castle Hill). A mysterious house which has long been ruinous. It is said to have been dated 1597. It has one high tower, and to the entrance two steep stepped gables (one now destroyed) and under them a tripartite stepped window with trefoiled heads to the lights – an unexpected motif. The ruin ought to be investigated.

GOYT HALL, 1¼ m. SW, on a track from the end of Osborne Street. Timber-framed, Elizabethan, originally with two projecting gabled wings (one now brick), and in the re-entrant angles the gabled porch and a corresponding projecting bay. No decorative motifs.

BRERETON   7060

Hall and church lie close together and on their own – a gorgeous Elizabethan Hall and a very complete Perp church. The group is reached by a GATEHOUSE with embattled lodges which look *c*.1800.

* So Mr Buttress reports.

43 BRERETON HALL. Dated 1586. The front is not easily forgotten. It is of brick, symmetrical, and with in the middle a frontispiece with two towers once yet higher than they are now and crowned by ogee caps. To the l. and r. of the frontispiece are two bays with cross windows and then two gabled end pavilions with canted bay windows, two storeys high and ending in pediments. Moreover, and this is uncommon, there are big canted bay windows round the corners too. The house is said once to have had four ranges round a courtyard. Now there is only one and parts of the two adjoining ones. The frontispiece has a doorway of c.1830, a highly decorated sill zone of the first floor, with tapering pilasters, more decoration above the first-floor windows, and finally a bridge across from tower to tower. The entrance hall is of c.1830, cf. the stucco-work, and it is followed by a curving-up staircase also Late Georgian in type. The dining room has a chimneypiece with columns below, tapering pilasters above. In a first-floor room a chimneypiece with caryatids and arms. This is dated 1633. The STABLES look early C18: wooden cross windows and a big pediment.

ST OSWALD. Late Perp throughout. The W tower is embraced. Big aisle windows not in line with the six closely set clerestory windows. The arches of all the windows are nearly segmental. Embattled two-bay chancel. Arcades of four bays, the piers very coarse. Section of four shafts and four hollows; elementary capitals, double-chamfered arches. Panelled roofs of low pitch. – FONT. Dated 1660, and with its initials and simple geometrical motifs one of many almost identical fonts of 1660 or 1661 all over the country. – STAINED GLASS. Who did the glass of the W window? It looks c.1845–50 and is quite interesting. – The E window is signed by *Wailes*, 1853. – PLATE. Chalice, 1653–4; Chalice and Paten, 1660–1. – MONUMENTS. Sir William Brereton † 1618. Latin inscription between columns and with strap decoration. – William Smethwick † 1643 and wife. Frontal three-quarter figures. – Rev. E. Royds † 1836. Draped urn.

BEAR'S HEAD, Brereton Green. Timber-framed. Dated 1615. Nice strapwork tablet on the porch. In the gable-end a window on brackets.

₃₀₈₀   BRIMSTAGE   [EH]

BRIMSTAGE HALL. In 1398 Sir Hugh Hulse and his wife obtained a licence to build an oratory at Brimstage, and the remarkable medieval work which forms a rectangular block at the s end of the present farmhouse is consistent with this date. The ground-floor room is rib-vaulted in two bays, with dia-[22] gonal and ridge ribs of hollow single chamfer. The ribs spring from semi-octagon and quarter-octagon piers, except in the SE corner, where there is a corbel which has been variously interpreted as lion, owl, or cat. There are carved bosses, that in the E bay showing three fishes, but except for the evidence of this symbolism, there is nothing to suggest that the room was Hugh Hulse's chapel. Neither is there reason to assume that the structure forms a fragment of a much larger building. It does appear to have extended further, at least at the E end, where the present external wall has obviously been much altered, but the building has every appearance of having been a tower house, i.e. a compactly planned fortified dwelling of the pele-tower type. There is a further storey above the vaulted chamber, and originally a third storey existed in place of the present pitched roof, as is shown by the masonry of the rect-angular turret at the SE corner. Containing garderobes and a newel stair, this turret rises to its full three storeys, and is machicolated. No parapet remains, and the machicolations, the topmost parts of which seem incomplete, may once have been open. Some original doorways remain in connection with the staircase turret, and there is a blocked doorway in the w wall of the ground floor. Later mullioned windows on the ground floor.

BROADBOTTOM 9090

ST MARY MAGDALENE. 1888–90 by *W. H. Lowder*. Well placed on falling ground.

IMMACULATE CONCEPTION (R.C.), beyond the bridge. 1896 by *Oswald Hill*.

The BRIDGE is of 1683. One segmental arch of 70 ft length, ribbed underneath. High above the bridge immediately is the railway bridge.

N of St Mary Magdalene, one good early C19 house of five bays and two storeys, with a three-bay pediment and a Tuscan porch.

BROMBOROUGH 3080

A village which became a mid-Victorian Eden of large houses. Of the few which remain, two may be singled out for a glance: THE MARFORDS in Dibbinsdale Road NW of the station, with a Gothic centre and additions, and PLYMYARD, by *Bell &*

Roper, now inside the cemetery on the A41. Behind this incidentally, in PLYMYARD AVENUE, W of and parallel with the
A41, is LOW TARN, a house by *J. Roy Parker*, 1968.

86 ST BARNABAS. By *Sir George Gilbert Scott*, 1862–4, the large
church of the village-gone-prosperous. Nave and aisles,
chancel and semicircular apse, NE steeple with broach spire,
geometrical tracery. The church presents itself very well
from the S, with the external blank arcading of the vestry. The
interior is sound, but not memorable. Blank arcading in the
apse. – STAINED GLASS. Some by *Clayton & Bell*. – The E
window is by *Ballantine & Son*, influenced by French and
Belgian glass. – CROSS. Outside the church two Anglo-Saxon
fragments – a damaged cross head and part of a shaft with
interlace.

The VILLAGE CROSS, SE of the church, has a head of 1874.

N of the church is STANHOPE HOUSE. The porch, which may
be an addition, is dated 1693. Three-storeyed with dormers
and with a flat façade of three bays. Mullioned and transomed
windows. In the dormers are vertically placed ovals, usually a
sign of the late C17. (Inside there is splendid panelling, and a
screen and chimneypiece, all from Chillingham Castle. Late
C16 or early C17. Ionic columns and pilasters, strapwork, etc.
EH)

3080   BROMBOROUGH POOL VILLAGE

This, within a mile of Port Sunlight (SE), is also a manufacturer's
village of cottages for his employees. But it is much earlier, and
its date makes it memorable and deserving of being better
known. It was created by Price's Patent Candle Co. in 1853.
By that time their original works at Battersea had over 700
workers. The new works (now Price's Chemicals) are next-
door to the village, and there is still one picturesque building
with a clock tower. The village was the initiative of George and
James Wilson, sons of the founder. The plan is very elementary,
ust a few parallel streets, and the houses are first in short
terraces and later in pairs. There is also a CHAPEL, 1889–90
by *Leach* of London, the original SCHOOL, 1858, yellow brick
and in a vague and elementary way Italianate, and the SCHOOL
of 1898 replacing the original one which became the village
Hall. There were also two hospitals (1878 and 1901). The
houses fall into three groups: 1853–8, the 1870s, and 1896–
1901. In the end there were 142 houses (some have been demolished). The earliest are in YORK STREET and MANOR

PLACE, the latest in SOUTH VIEW. They are planned with parlour, kitchen, and scullery below, and three bedrooms above. All houses had internal water closets. There were also from the start allotments. The historical interest of Bromborough Pool Village lies in the fact that the Wilsons were among the very first British manufacturers to take on reasonable housing for their workers. They had been preceded only by Robert Owen's New Lanark of the first years of the C19 and then Col. Akroyd's Copley of 1847–9 and Sir Titus Salt's famous Saltaire begun c.1850–1.

COURT HOUSE, Pool Lane. Brick, C17, centre and projecting wings. Three-storeyed, with two shaped gables.*

BROOK BOTTOM
2 m. SE of Marple

9080

(Mr W. H. Hoult tells of interesting WEAVERS' COTTAGES, one of five storeys. Brook Bottom is reached from New Mills in Derbyshire.)

BROXTON

4050

BROXTON OLD HALL (or Higher Hall). An ornate gabled black and white house, partly original, partly by *John Douglas, c.*1873. The original part, assigned to 1595, corresponds to the two centre gables with their decoration of cusped concave-sided lozenges. (In the gardens cut into the rock is a GROTTO.)

GLEGG'S HALL.* A fine stone façade of 1703 in front of an older house whose Elizabethan or Jacobean mullioned and transomed windows appear round the corner. The façade has a recessed centre and two wings. Three gables, wooden cross windows with raised stone surrounds. It is a good example of how things went in Cheshire building about 1700. (Staircase with sturdy turned balusters starting out of goblet shapes typical of the date. NMR)

BANKHEAD, ½ m. E of the main Chester road (A41) and immediately N of the A534. 1864 by *Waterhouse*. A simple, functional Victorian house, with straight-headed sash windows. Brick, stone dressings, red-tiled roof, hipped gables.

MAIDEN CASTLE. An Iron Age promontory fort of 1½ acres defended on the S and E by two lines of ramparts still surviving to a height of 7 ft. An entrance occurs through both ramparts on the E side, the inner being inturned at this point. Excavation

* Both Court House and Glegg's Hall are now demolished.

has shown the site to have two structural phases. The earlier
consists of the inner rampart, 20 ft thick and probably originally 10 ft or more in height, revetted with stone on its inner
and outer face and timber-laced internally; and an outer bank
of sand revetted externally with stone. In the second phase
this outer bank was remodelled and increased in width.

BRUERA

4060

ST MARY. The church is Norman, cf. the s doorway inside with
a few ornamented stones and the chancel arch, whose triple s
respond is genuine. Capitals with coarse foliage and also faces.
Down one of the three shafts four single beak-heads are disposed. The windows, especially the E window, are Dec. The s
chapel is a Perp addition. The shingled bell-turret with spirelet
is of 1896, when the church was restored by *W. M. Boden* for
the Duke of Westminster. – FONT. Just one long, elongated
baluster without a separate bowl. Is it later C17? – STAINED
GLASS. The N window of 1897 is strikingly good – in the Arts
and Crafts mood. One ought to recognize the artist. – PLATE.
Cup, 1713. – MONUMENTS. Both standing on the ground. Sir
Ellis Cunliffe † 1769. A putto holds a portrait medallion in
front of an obelisk. – Sir Robert Cunliffe † 1778. By *Nollekens*.
The putto this time is seated. But there are also the obelisk and
the medallion.

65

(Some Eaton estate COTTAGES and, ¾ m. SE, NEWBOLD FARM,
c.1877 by *Douglas*. The farmhouse is simple but sophisticated,
of brick, with varyingly-shaped gables and a pyramid-roofed
turret.* EH)

BUERTON

6040

No church, but as a vertical feature the brick body of a tower mill,
untidy at the top at the time of writing.

BUGLAWTON

8060

ST JOHN EVANGELIST. 1840 by *R. B. Rampling*. Norman, with
a w tower of the oddest details. The square part ends in four
gables, but behind the tower goes on octagonally. A recessed
spire continues the octagon. The church is aisleless and has a
shallow altar recess.

(BUGLAWTON HALL. Dr Gomme considers that a modest C16
house was absorbed into an early C18 one, which was brought

* ½m. SSW of the village a CHEESE FACTORY, 1874 by *Douglas*. Altered
and extended, and now only just recognizable as the building which, of all
those of the Eaton estate, Muthesius chose to illustrate.

up to date in the late C18 with castellations, a fine fanlight,
and fashionable Roman cement. He refers also to the STABLES:
mid C18, with round windows on the upper floor, but the
walls presumably replacing an earlier timber frame, as the roof
is C15, with extremely hefty tiebeams with a fan-shaped
arrangement of trusses. No king- or queenposts.)

BULKELEY   5050

BULKELEY HALL. Georgian, seven bays, three storeys, brick.
No special features.

BUNBURY   5050

ST BONIFACE. Like most of the major parish churches of
Cheshire, this strikes one as a Perp church. In fact much remains of the Dec predecessor. There is first the chancel with
its uncommonly fanciful E window – not much such flowing
tracery exists in Cheshire – its simpler side windows, the ogee-
headed tomb recesses under one of them inside, and the door
inside to the (much altered) treasury and the ogee-headed
PISCINA and SEDILIA. Secondly Dec is the lower part of the
tower – cf. the W window and the continuous moulding of the
tower arch. But the W doorway and the upper parts of the
tower are Perp. We have in fact dates for Dec as well as Perp.
In the E window some (not surviving) glass had a date 1343.*
Rebuilding took place after Sir Hugh Calveley established a
college in the church in 1386, and the Late Perp remodelling
ended in the S chancel chapel, which was built c.1527 by Sir
Ralph Egerton (see below). The Perp exterior has much in the
way of battlements and pinnacles. The aisles are eight bays
long. The windows are of four lights, different on the N from
the S side. The S porch is Dec again – cf. the doorways – and
has a good roof. On the S side the high parapet of openwork panelling is not original; it dates from 1840. Inside, the
Dec arcades can still be recognized at the W responds. They
are semi-octagonal. So the piers were probably octagonal too.
The springing of the arcades lay much lower than it is now.
The present arcades are of course Perp. The piers are of the 26
familiar section of four shafts and four hollows and very slim,
and, as the aisles have no stained glass left, the impression
is airy and clear. The clerestory is of 1863–6 by *Pennington
& Bridgen*, the roof of 1950 by *Marshall Sisson*. In the S aisle,

* The tracery is apparently not *in situ*: i.e. it was re-used when the chancel
was enlarged at the time of Sir Hugh Calveley's remodelling.

when the SE chapel was built, the surround of the former E
window was kept. This also indicates a Dec date. Next to it the
chapel has a small w doorway. In the N aisle the arcade spandrels have little angels.

FONT. Dated 1663. Octagonal, with simplified motifs such
as fleur-de-lys, tulip, lozenge, heart. – REREDOS. In the N
chapel, of stone. What survives is big leaf brackets. – SCREEN.
The chancel screen is by *F. H. Crossley*, 1921.* – The screen
to the SE chapel is an important piece, dated 1527. It is high,
of single lights with ogee heads, but the dado is painted in
grisaille on red and green grounds with Early Renaissance
motifs, the earliest in Cheshire. – The door has linenfold panelling, but the upper part very curiously a trellis as if of osiers. –
DOOR. In the S porch, with trellis battens. – COMMUNION
RAIL. Of strong turned balusters. They were made *c.*1717. –
STAINED GLASS. Small pieces of original glass in several windows. – By *Kempe*, 1905, chancel s. – (Chancel N by *R. C. Evetts*,
1952. EH) – ARCHITECTURAL FRAGMENTS. They tell of the
earlier stone church on the site. Norman zigzag, and quite
large Norman scalloped capitals, probably from a major doorway. – CHANDELIER. Of brass. Baroque shape. 1756. – PLATE.
Small Paten, early C17, made at Chester by *Griffith Edwardes*.
– All other pieces are made in London: Cup, 1632; Paten and
Salver by *Humphrey Payne*, 1716; two Flagons, 1735; two
Offertory Plates by *Richard Bayley*, 1737. – MONUMENTS. C13
coffin lids with foliated crosses. – Defaced Knight, late C14 or
early C15. – Defaced effigies of a Lady and a (truncated) Knight,
both early C14. – Defaced effigy of Joan de Spurstow, *c.*1375–
80. – Civilian, C14 or C15. – Sir Hugh Calveley † 1394, founder
of the college. Alabaster effigy on a sarcophagus with small
image niches which originally contained weepers. The
GRILLE around with the many spikes is original. – Sir George
Beeston † 1601 (aged 102). Recumbent effigy under a plain
arch with columns l. and r. – Sir Ralph Egerton. With the reproduction of his kneeling brass, quite small. Dated 1527. –
George Spurstow † 1669. A painted tablet no doubt by *Randle
Holme*, like a hatchment. The painting shows the coat of arms.
– Mrs Johnson † 1741. A shockingly bad upright portrait,
badly preserved from having been buried in the churchyard. –
Thomas Aldersey † 1824. Tablet with draped urn.

* A design for a screen was made by *Douglas & Fordham*, and some
existing furnishings are apparently theirs.

Good c18 GATEPIERS.

(s of the church OLD SCHOOL HOUSE, built in 1527 as the
chantry priest's house. Half-timbered, with closely-set uprights.
Two storeys, and quite tall. Being restored and enlarged by
Cecil F. Wright. EH)

(SCHOOL, ½ m. w, towards Bunbury Heath. 1874 by *Douglas*.
EH)

BURFORD LANE FARM *see* OUGHTRINGTON

BURLEYDAM   6040

ST MICHAEL. Built in 1769 at the expense of the Cottons of
Combermere Abbey. Brick, with arched windows. A three-bay
w front with pediment, and wide nave and short transepts. In
1886 the E end was extended, though the surround of the E
window was probably re-used. Of 1886 probably also the open
timber roof, which does not go at all with the Georgian proportions. – STAINED GLASS. The E window by *Kempe*, 1908. –
MONUMENT. Viscount Combermere † 1855 (cf. Wrenbury).
Bust under Gothic arch. – Nice iron GATEPIERS for the
churchyard gates. They come from Llewenny.

BURTON   5060
Near Tarvin

BURTON HALL. Said to be of 1569. A very interesting house,
square and high, and each side with one big gable all along.
One of them has disappeared. The windows are mullioned and
transomed and set in no exact order. Staircase with twisted
balusters.

BURTON   3070
Wirral

ST NICHOLAS. 1721, except for the E end of the N chapel with
its E window of *c.*1300 (intersecting tracery). The 1721 work*
includes a w tower whose bell-openings have Y-tracery. But is
the tracery of the N and S sides 1721 or a Victorian attempt at
doing tracery but keeping in harmony with 1721 ? The pattern
is two round-arched lights and a circle over. The chancel was
rebuilt in 1870 – not in keeping. The interior is really two-
naved. A rather coarse arcade of five bays separates them.
Columns and single-chamfered arches. – ARCHITECTURAL
FRAGMENTS. Two big, round scalloped Norman capitals

---

* The mason was *John Morfitt*.

(porch). – COMMUNION RAIL. Every second baluster is
twisted; C18. – STAINED GLASS. The E window by *Kempe*,
1903. – PLATE. Set of 1809. – MONUMENTS. Coffin lid with a
foliated cross; C13. It is unusual in that the leaf trails run up
all the way l. and r. of the shaft. – Richard Congreve † 1820.
By *S. Gibson*. With a big weeping putto. – In the churchyard
a baluster-shaped C18 SUNDIAL.

BURTON MANOR. Enlarged and completely remodelled in 1904
by *Sir Charles Nicholson* (*Nicholson & Corlette*) for a son of
Gladstone. It is a classical design of no great force. Pedimented
entrance side with the two sides l. and r. of the pediment not
identical. The most attractive feature is a small inner courtyard. White rendering and some red brick accents. On one side
an alcove behind two massive columns. The rooms have classical details too, such as the big chimneypiece in the largest room
towards the garden. The staircase is Jacobeanizing and rather
fussy. – ORANGERY by *Beresford Pite*, a little later. – The
GARDEN is by *T. H. Mawson*.

The village street is pleasant and varied with some thatch and
half-timbering. The group of estate cottages by *H. S. Goodhart-
Rendel* comes as a surprise, with their big roofs, some of them
mansard. They are towards the E end, and beyond them, up a
lane, is the VICARAGE by *Nicholson*.

At the other end of the village, really outside it, is the OLD
SCHOOL HOUSE, a school founded by Bishop Wilson in 1724.
It is a conservative design, the gables, the two ovals below
them, and the windows with their broad transoms looking
twenty-five years older at least than they are.

(NW of the village two quite sizeable houses by *Briggs & Thornely*,
FIDDLESTONE WOOD in DUNSTAN LANE, 1929, Neo-
Georgian, and PHEASANT FIELD in MUDHOUSE LANE,
*c.*1930, still in an Arts and Crafts manner.)

BURWARDSLEY

ST JOHN. The church has an inscription about putting it in
perfect order in 1795,* but it all looks as if the building is of
the C17 – cf. especially the mullioned windows with arched
lights, and also the shaft with capital in the w window. The
bell-turret of course is Victorian, probably of 1884–9 (Kelly),
when a new chancel was built. – ORGAN. A pretty piece, probably Late Georgian.

* Not 1735.

A HOUSE against the hillside, 1 m. SW, has its gable-end connected by a Gothic arcade with a barn whose gable-end has an
over-large cross-shaped arrow-slit. Does this belong to the
estate housing at Harthill?

BYLEY   7060

ST JOHN EVANGELIST. 1846–7, a Commissioners' church – by
whom? It is said that the Rev. *Henry Massey*, vicar of Goostrey,
designed it, but the Incorporated Church Building Society
gives the architect as *J. Matthews*. Whoever was the designer,
the building does him no credit. It is in the Norman fashion of
the forties, but really very ugly. Minimum motifs, but a maxi-
mum of materials: red brick, yellow terracotta, and yellow
stone. The S tower with pyramid roof is, according to Mr Port,
later.

CALDY   [EH] 2080

CALDY MANOR. An irregular Elizabethan-style house of red
sandstone. C17 parts are said to be incorporated, but the evolution of its present form dates from after 1832, when the Caldy
estate was bought by Richard Watson Barton, a Manchester
merchant, who was in 1861 succeeded by his son Richard
Barton. The C19 work included e.g. alterations and additions
by *W. & J. Hay*, 1864, but the present appearance of the house
owes much to the early C20, when alterations were made for
Alexander Percy Eccles, a Liverpool cotton broker. The SE end,
which encloses two sides of a small garden, is partly C20 and
partly earlier. The low wing which extends to the village street
was converted to a chapel by *C. E. Kempe*, in 1882, at the expense of Richard Barton's widow, Elizabeth, a daughter of Sir
Benjamin Heywood of the Manchester church-building family.
The chapel was dismantled when the church in the village was
built (*see* below), but the tower, designed by *Kempe*, remains.
A clock has replaced the original louvred bell-openings, and
with its flèche and gabled timber upper stage the tower groups
beautifully with the house as seen from the road. The central
room of the principal (i.e. SW or garden) front contains plasterwork dated 1877, but the NW end of the house, beyond this,
was remodelled in 1907, and contains a two-storey hall in the
'Wrenaissance' style, with gallery and canted bay window.*

* This work may be tentatively attributed to *Briggs, Wolstenholme &
Thornely*.

Other interiors have been much altered in connexion with the use of the building as a hospital.

RESURRECTION AND ALL SAINTS. Built originally as a school, 1868 by *G. E. Street*, at the expense of Elizabeth Barton.* Converted, and a chancel and saddleback tower added in 1906–7 by *Douglas & Minshull*. A large Gothic chimneypiece by *Street* is re-used in the vestry. – FURNISHINGS. Several items of 1882 by *Kempe* were brought from the chapel in Caldy Manor (*see* above), e.g. STALLS and REREDOS, the latter being reduced in size to fit its new position. They look less satisfactory than they seem to have done in their original setting, and the later SCREEN does not help. – STAINED GLASS. Some by *Kempe*. – The SW window by *A. J. Davies* of the *Bromsgrove Guild*.

Caldy Manor and the church both make significant contributions to the townscape of the village centre, the attractive character of which is largely due to Richard Watson Barton, who, in the 1830s or early 40s, rebuilt or renovated all the cottages on his estate, with *R. B. Rampling* as his architect. Opposite Caldy Manor is MANOR FARM, with a datestone of 1683. SUNNY-FOLD is dated 1698. Symmetrical, with central porch projection. Mullioned windows. Opposite the church is BANKS FARM-HOUSE, also with mullioned windows. Dated 1702. The present CHURCH HALL, nicely placed at a bend in the road, was built by Elizabeth Barton in 1883 as a village reading room.

The development of Caldy as a spacious residential district dates from 1906. In CALDY ROAD one of the earliest houses is CALDECOTT, by *Hastwell Grayson*. THE CROFT, *c*.1911, is perhaps by *Sir E. Guy Dawber*.‡ Further E is OROVALES, *c*.1930 by *Gilbert Fraser*. Next to each other in CROFT DRIVE are two octagonal houses, the larger one, NEWLANDS, 1914, of unusual design, with a flat roof. They are set in a curving, tree-lined road typical of many a delectable suburb, but on Caldy Hill houses in KING'S DRIVE and THORSWAY command glorious views over the Dee estuary to the mountains of Wales and across Hilbre Island out to sea. By reason of its prosperous commuter country Cheshire is something of a Surrey of the north, but Surrey has nothing to compare with this.

* Street designed churches for two of Elizabeth Barton's brothers: at Denstone, Staffordshire, for Sir Percival Heywood, and at Swinton, Lancashire, for the Rev. H. R. Heywood.

‡ The house as existing differs from Dawber's published design for it. Does this mean a change of design rather than a change of architect?

CALVELEY HALL *see* HANDLEY

CAPENHURST   3070

HOLY TRINITY. 1856–9 by *James Harrison* and internally quite gratifying, but the noteworthy feature is the w tower of 1889–90, and this must surely be by *Douglas*. Corner stair-turret less high than the tower, very low timber bell-stage, spire with low broaches. – STAINED GLASS. All by *Kempe*; the recorded dates from 1876 to after 1900.

U.K. ATOMIC ENERGY AUTHORITY. A vast establishment with any number of cooling towers.

CAPENHURST HALL, E of the church. 1792. (The original block has a five-bay E front. Pedimented Doric doorcase. MHLG)

CAPESTHORNE   8070

Capesthorne looks fantastic from the west, a prodigy mansion of Elizabethan character with a pair of elevated turreted main accents reminiscent of the wings of Hatfield and a middle colonnade reminiscent of the same house. It is only when one gets near that one feels the tension relax and the discipline lessen. It is a grand concept executed lamely. The history of the building to a certain extent explains that. There was a seven-bay Early Georgian house here of which a good deal survives at the back (seven bays, two and a half storeys, quoins), and it had detached wings, and their walling survives more evidently. An agreement exists between the owner John Ward and *William Smith* for the building of these wings. It is dated 1719. The design was probably by *Francis Smith*.* In 1720–2 the chapel was built. In 1748 the house came by marriage to the Davenport family. In 1837–9 for Edward Davies Davenport *Blore* made a mansion of the house, though keeping to brick. He also converted the wings, which are now of seven by seven bays with shaped gables; the main mansion also has shaped gables. Blore's building was burnt in 1861, and *Salvin* was called in to rebuild. He kept to Blore's ideas, kept the two main accents, kept the colonnade, but made behind it two very high instead of three lower floors, and at the back, where Blore, as has already been said, kept much of the Georgian house, Salvin

* Dr Gomme's discovery. He considers that the elder *John Wood*'s contribution to the house may have been confined to submitting a design for the central portion between the wings. The centre block was built *c.*1732, though not necessarily to Wood's design.

did his own in two campaigns and ended with an asymmetrical but not a convincingly composed front. The two side views have curious tower-like erections competing with the façade turrets. They are Blore's not Salvin's invention. The house contains a number of Salvin rooms, the best perhaps the staircase with its unusual metal balustrade. The Saloon is a Salvin addition of 1879. The Entrance Hall is Blore's. It has a chimneypiece the caryatid and the atlas of which came from the former reading desk in the chapel and are Flemish. The heraldic glass is by *Willement*. In the Drawing Room are two delicate chimneypieces of *Coade* stone, brought from the family house in Belgrave Square. They have pagan and Christian symbols.

CHAPEL. Built in 1720–2. A simple building of three bays with a balustrade and cupola. The PANELLING and CARVING of the W gallery, i.e. the family pew, was originally on the E wall around the altar. Much was internally stepped up in key in 1888–9. Of that time the white terracotta reliefs by *Tinworth*, and also no doubt the ceiling. The REREDOS in the Italian Quattrocento style was designed by *Alan Booker* and executed in mosaic by *Salviati*'s. – The COMMUNION RAIL is of *c*.1722. – The PULPIT is Flemish, with carved panels of sacred stories. – PLATE. Silver-gilt Chalice and Paten of 1723.

Between the house and the chapel *Paxton* built a long CONSERVATORY, probably about 1837. It was pulled down *c*.1920.

On the same side of the house as chapel and conservatory is a large GATEHOUSE by *Blore*, also with shaped gables, and *Blore* did the three-storeyed LODGE on the main road too.

The GARDEN GATES in a most ornate Early Rococo are Milanese of *c*.1750.

CARDEN *see* CLUTTON

CARLETT PARK *see* EASTHAM

CARRINGTON

7090

ST GEORGE, ½ m. from the old hamlet. The new development is mostly industrial. Brick, 1757–9, four bays with arched windows and a cupola. The short chancel is of 1872 (PF). – BOX PEWS. – (Two FAMILY PEWS. – PULPIT, altered. R. Richards) – PLATE. Flagon, 1688–9; Stand Paten, 1688–9; Chalice, given in 1739.

CHADKIRK see ROMILEY

CHEADLE

8080

ST MARY. Perp. The arcades of standard elements. The church took a long time to build. The clerestory is obviously Latest Perp; so is the S chapel. In fact the chapel was completed by 1530, the nave by 1541, money was given for the tower in 1520–40, and the chancel was rebuilt in 1556–8 by Lady Catherine Buckley, former Abbess of Godstow. These were the years of Queen Mary. The S porch is specially good. – FONT. C18; a rather coarse baluster. – SCREENS. The chancel screen has only a few original parts, but the S chapel screen is more rewarding. It has the Brereton rebus. The dado has linen-fold panelling, the intricate tracery was put later on top of the dado. – The screen to the N chapel has an inscription referring to Sir John Savage and the date 1529. – STAINED GLASS. Fragments only in the Brereton Chapel. – PLATE. Cup, early C17, inscribed R.W.; large Paten, London, 1666–7; Stand Paten, London, 1718–19; Paten, 1722; Flagon given in 1734. – MONUMENTS. Two alabaster Knights now on the same tomb-chest; both third quarter of the C15 and both probably members of the Handford family. – Sir Thomas Brereton † 1673. Stone effigy, recumbent. Tomb-chest with shields in cartouches.

ALL HALLOWS, Councillor Lane. Begun in 1969 to the designs of *Paterson & Macaulay*.

ST JAMES, Gatley Green. By *Medland & Henry Taylor*, 1880–1. NW tower with overhanging saddleback roof and an outer staircase from the E. Polygonal apse and polygonal baptistery.

CONGREGATIONAL CHURCH, Massie Street. 1860–1 by *Poulton & Woodman*. Not of any significance. Lancet windows. No tower.

ST COLUMBA PRESBYTERIAN CHURCH, Wilmslow Road, Handforth. 1968–9 by *J. P. Whittle* (of *Halliday, Meesham & Partners*).

ABNEY HALL (now the Town Hall). Abney Hall in its external appearance is a large red brick house in the Tudor-Gothic style, with divers steep gables, asymmetrical and sombre – the sort of thing affluent Manchester businessmen built themselves in the villages of Cheshire which had been caught into the magnetic zone of Manchester. It is the interior which distinguishes the house. As it now is it represents three building periods. The NW corner is of 1847, a villa of which only the

neo-Norman portal remains easily distinguishable. In 1849 James Watts bought the house and enlarged it. He was a wholesale draper and later Mayor of Manchester, and Watts's warehouse in Portland Street overlooking Piccadilly is the largest of them all. The architects were *Travis & Mangnall*, and they were in all probability responsible for the enlargement of Abney Hall to the s and se. Finally in 1893 more additions were made by *G. F. Armitage*, in the se corner, and also between what was then two projecting wings on the s front. As one enters by the Norman portal, one finds oneself in a Gothic corridor, with the staircase on the l. This should at once be experienced; it has the full flavour of the house, thanks to *John Gregory Crace*, the most successful interior decorator of his day in England. He worked at Abney Hall between 1852 and 1857. The staircase has an open well, a very heavily carved (machine-carved?) balustrade, and a panelled ceiling on arched braces. At the top landing is a lantern on ribs and tierceron ribs on the pattern of the Ely octagon and the central lobby of Barry and Pugin's Houses of Parliament. Next one ought to visit the sw corner room, the former Drawing Room. Here one finds Puginesque Gothic at its most sumptuous and hence its most oppressive. *Pugin* indeed, in the last months of his life, provided Watts and Crace with drawings, but they were not followed in the letter, though in the spirit, or at any rate in the spirit as understood and interpreted by Crace. Only a very little of the decoration is actually Pugin's, e.g. the frieze. The room otherwise has a panelled ceiling with a pendant in each
77 panel, very ornate doorcases of papier-mâché, a Gothic chimneypiece of white marble, and a huge sideboard with top coving. The chandelier was made by *Hardman*. The room next door, in the middle of the w side, also has a big chimneypiece and rich doorcase. The chimneypiece is, as the Early Victorians liked it, made up of bits of woodwork from various sources. There is also a smaller sideboard here. Other features of the Pugin style to be found in the principal rooms include *Minton* tiles. Armitage's work is not to be despised either. The large former Music Room in the se corner has a huge inglenook and very good heraldic stained glass. In the garden is a slender tower with spire. This served as a ventilating shaft and may have been connected with greenhouses. It is of the 1850s period.

BARNES HOSPITAL, Kingsway. 1871–5 by *Blackwell & Booth*. Large, Gothic, and grim. Common brick, red brick, black brick, and stone. Largely symmetrical, but with an asymmet-

rically placed thin tower. The top is totally debased. Steep
dormers in the various ranges.

MANCHESTER ROYAL MENTAL HOSPITAL, St Ann's Road,
Heald Green. 1848–9 by *Richard Lane*. Large, Jacobean, symmetrical, with two projecting wings and shaped gables.

In WILMSLOW ROAD (Schools Hill) several large houses, foremost BRUNTWOOD, 1861, Elizabethan, with a tower, gables,
and finials; also BELMONT, Italianate, and MOSELEY HALL,
black and white.

EDINBURGH CLOSE, Councillor Lane, is good recent small-
scale housing, by *Arthur Pell* of *Taylor, Young & Partners*.

(ADSWOOD HALL, 1¾ m. ESE, near the Stockport boundary.
C17 – a datestone says 1659. Brick, with mullioned windows
and arched lights. MHLG, NMR)

CHEADLE HULME
8080

ALL SAINTS, Church Road. 1862–3 and 1873 by *Medland
Taylor*, uninteresting outside. Inside at least one oddity – the
W and E termination of the arcades.

ST ANDREW, Cheadle Road. By *Taylor & Young*, 1957–9.
Blocky Neo-Georgian, even with a cupola.

METHODIST CHURCH, Station Road. By *Denys Hinton &
Partners*, 1967–8. Excellent. To the street largely bare walls of
sand-coloured brick and just two vertical slit windows. The
hall part is more domestic, with segmental window-heads.
(Very quiet interior.)

CHEADLE HULME SCHOOL. 1865–9 by *Bates*, with two wings
of 1899 and 1903.

HULME HALL, Hulme Hall Road. C17 timber-framing, with one
gable with cross ornament, incorporated into a house of 1867.

CHECKLEY
7040

CHECKLEY HALL. Late C17,* of five bays and two and a half
storeys. The windows had and partly still have wooden crosses.
Doorway with a moulded surround with lugs. Rusticated gatepiers. (Good staircase with twisted balusters. Secondary staircase with flat balusters. MHLG)

CHELFORD
8070

ST JOHN EVANGELIST. 1774–6, but the W tower 1840. It has a
recessed spire. The windows of the church are pointed with

* White's Directory says 1694.

Y-tracery, more probably 1840 than 1774. The same applies to the low chancel. – PANELLING, BOX PEWS, and WEST GALLERY no doubt 1774. – (Good Arts and Crafts PULPIT. NMR) – STAINED GLASS. Some late *Morris & Co.* – PLATE. Tazza, 1587; Cup, London, 1652–3.

STATION. A good example of the recent rebuilding of stations in Cheshire by the *Midland Region's Architect's Department* (*W. R. Headley* and others).

LODGE to Astle Hall. Picturesque in the *cottage orné* manner.

4060   CHESTER

INTRODUCTION

In the popular view Chester is the English medieval city *par excellence*. It has preserved its walls all around, and within them are half-timbered houses galore, and they are built with covered galleries on a level half-way up what would be the level of ground-floor ceilings in towns less quaint. These so-called Rows are indeed the most remarkable medieval feature of Chester; for they certainly existed already in the C13. But do they make Chester a medieval city? It is difficult to reach visual conclusions; for Chester is a busy town of about 60,000 inhabitants. It is not like Durham or Salisbury, let alone Wells or Ely, and not even like

Lincoln, where the cathedral is on the hill away from the main streets. At Chester the main shopping and the main traffic are right by the cathedral, hardly separated from it. One can come to conclusions on the character of the town only early in the morning or on a Sunday. If one then tries to make up accounts, Chester is not a medieval, it is a Victorian city. What deceives is the black and white. 95 per cent is Victorian and after. It is able to deceive because the motifs are accurately imitated. That the structure is often sham, i.e. not timber-framing, but nailed-on boards, one does not see. What betrays the real date is that Victorian black and white is bigger and better than C16 and C17 black and white – bigger i.e. in scale, and better i.e. in the variety of motifs, and their picturesque, free arrangement. *T. M. Penson* first and then *T. M. Lockwood* and *John Douglas* were the chief practitioners, and one may well find their work hard to take. A magpie façade, even if Elizabethan or Jacobean, is busier than one of stone or brick. The areas of rest between decorative passages are lacking. The result is gay – yes; it delights the eye in a country setting. But in the streets it jingles away too insistently. Still, the historic interest at least is undeniable – of the old as well as the revived half-timber. The revival belongs to the 1850s and can best be seen in Eastgate Street. Between the 1850s and the 1870s scale and resourcefulness grew, and the real prodigies are of the 1880s and after.

Chester is the Roman Deva, and was one of the principal towns of England, headquarters of the 20th Legion.* Little is preserved so that it makes a visual impact, but the principal axes of the street pattern inside the walls are pure Roman, and the Romano-medieval plan remained largely unaltered until about 1830, when Grosvenor Street was cut through diagonally and Grosvenor Bridge built as a relief road and relief bridge.

When Chester was deserted by the Romans it fell back to the Welsh. There followed centuries of struggle: Mercian supremacy, Danish occupation, return to English occupation, and finally Norman occupation. It is only then that visual evidence begins, at St John, which had cathedral rank for a short time between 1075 and 1095, and at the present cathedral, which was a Benedictine abbey until the Dissolution and became a cathedral only in 1541. Chester was given to William's nephew Hugh Lupus, who built up the powerful earldom of Chester which in 1237

---

* For more on Roman Chester, *see* below, p. 133.

became royal (Cheshire was County Palatine). One mighty tower of the castle survives, and the walls of Chester dating from the C 12 to C 14. They are more completely preserved than anywhere else in England. Chester was a prosperous port; how prosperous is shown for instance by the fact that the Blackfriars settled before 1236, the Greyfriars in 1238–40, and the Whitefriars in 1279.* The C 13 is the time too of the invention of the Rows. No convincing reason has yet been brought forward to explain them. They are colonnading or loggias or galleries at a level above the lowest which in its turn is sunk by a few steps. To call these sunk parts crypts is not strictly accurate.‡ Crypts and Rows are in a half-storey position looked at from the streets. This incidentally makes for visual pleasures. The Rows have all the qualities of our elevated pedestrian ways, pets of today's planners, and the medieval walls, restored to make an uninterrupted circuit possible, allow walking above streets, small houses, and gardens along direct ways. As for the explanation of the Rows, it might perhaps just be said that galleries at ground level are of course a medieval tradition in many parts of Europe – one may remember the French *bastides* such as Montpazier, or Innsbruck or Padua – and that the domestic arrangement of the upper as the chief living floor is quite common in England in say the Norman houses of Lincoln.

Medieval Chester – this is now easily forgotten – was an important port and remained so until in the C 15 and C 16 the Dee silted up. Yet architecture seems to prove that Chester managed to make up for the loss in shipping. It settled down to a comfortable county-town existence. Still it was a small town – population in 1801 was only 14,000. Hence it could keep its street pattern so successfully. Grosvenor Street did little visual damage, the new inner ring road does more. The new central shopping development immediately next to the town hall and reaching right back to Trinity Street and the ring road on the other hand is well planned and well managed, which is more than one can say in most towns of the size of Chester.

* Between *c.*1270 and *c.*1290 there were also Friars of the Sack. This little-known order had only nine houses in the whole of England, all founded between 1250 and 1275.

‡ About twenty of them have been identified. Several are vaulted and date from the C 13, or in some cases, early C 14. Some are mentioned in the Perambulation, and references to others are to be found in P. H. Lawson and J. T. Smith's papers on the Rows in the *Chester and North Wales Arch., Arch. & Hist. Soc.*, XLV, 1958.

ROMAN CHESTER

The earliest Roman occupation on the site of Chester (DEVA) consists of several cremation burials which may belong to a camp or auxiliary base so far undefined. The building of the fortress, as we now know it, was probably begun towards the end of the governorship of Frontinus in 76 or 77 as part of the increasing military activities against the Ordovices in North Wales. His successor, Agricola, completed the campaigns and, probably in the winter of 78–9, put the finishing touches to the fortress – a point suggested by a lead water-pipe stamped with Agricola's name and dating to 79. In these early years the fortress, manned by the Second Legion Adiutrix, formed a valuable buffer between the newly conquered tribes of North Wales and the very difficult Brigantes in the Pennines. Based on a navigable river as well as on a major line of road communication, it would have been vital in controlling the supplies pouring northwards to support Agricola's advance. When, in the late 80s, the Scottish conquests were relinquished, the Twentieth Legion returned southwards to take up permanent occupation of Chester.

For about a decade the soldiers continued to live and work in wooden buildings surrounded by an earth and timber defensive circuit, but soon after A.D. 100 the defences were strengthened with a masonry wall and most of the internal buildings reconstructed in stone or stone and timber. The construction of Hadrian's Wall and its subsequent garrisoning by contingents of the Twentieth Legion left the fortress only partly occupied by troops throughout much of the C2, but some rebuilding early in the C3 and the extensive reconstruction of the N wall about A.D. 300 show continued military interest, possibly as the threat of pirate activity in the Irish Sea increased.

The C4 saw the breakdown of the old military order. Legionary sizes were now decreased and the force was turned more and more into a peasant militia, which probably occupied the fortress more as a town. This state of affairs continued to the end of the C4; thereafter the picture is obscure.

There is not a great deal to be seen of the Roman fortress, but the encircling wall is reasonably displayed in some places. The best preserved section is the N wall E of the North Gate, where Roman facing 16 ft high can be seen surmounted by a cornice at wall-walk level. The battered face (unlike the Trajanic period wall) and the inclusion of old tombstones show that much of this stretch is a re-build, probably of early C4 date. Another length of foundation, outside the line of the present city wall, can be seen in Kaleyards. The internal angle turret at the SE corner is also displayed, near the Newgate, the Roman work surviving to several courses above the foundation offset plinth. The only evidence of the gates is a piece of wall which probably belongs to one of the guard chambers of the Eastgate, now preserved in the cellar of the Leeds Permanent Building Society, No. 48 EASTGATE STREET.

Several pieces of the *principia* (the headquarters), which lay towards the centre of the fortress fronting on to Watergate Street, have been seen from time to time. Of these the most impressive is a row of column bases belonging to the N colonnade of the aisled cross-hall. Some of these are still visible in the cellars of No. 23 NORTHGATE STREET ROW. Fragments of a tessellated pavement and the remains of part of a large colonnaded building can be seen in Nos. 18 and 22 ST MICHAEL'S ROW, while parts of the same building appear beneath Nos. 23–38 EASTGATE STREET.

Elsewhere in the walled area details of a number of buildings have been found in excavation. In the block bounded by Watergate Street, Old Hall Place, Commonhall Street, and Weaver Street, a battery of three massive buttressed granaries was discovered and excavated in 1954–6. N of the end of Goss Street lies a building of elliptical plan, not unlike a Roman theatre, and the entire N part of the area appears to have been filled with barrack accommodation of standard plan.

Outside the fortress wall, on the edge of the Roodeye below the city walls opposite Blackfriars, two Roman features can be seen: a small section of the quay wall close to the SW angle, and the amphitheatre immediately adjacent to the SE corner. The amphitheatre is now undergoing excavation with a view to exposing the entire N half of the structure to the public. It is now known that the masonry structure, which may have been built soon after A.D. 80, was preceded by a timber version, presumably in use only a few years after the founding of the fortress.

On the S side of the river, at Handbridge, are the remains of a quarry which began to be used *c*.100, when the fortress was largely rebuilt in stone. The exposed quarry-face can still be seen in Edgar's Field, where a small recess contains a very weathered sculptured figure beneath a gabled pediment. The figure, evidently Minerva, was probably the presiding deity worshipped by the quarrymen.★

★ Since this was written by Professor Cunliffe more excavations have taken place, and Mr G. M. R. Davies then of the Grosvenor Museum reports as

INNER CHESTER

Inner Chester is here circumscribed as follows: N to the top of Upper Northgate Street, i.e. the new fountain, NE to the Station and City Road, E to the end of Foregate Street, S and W to the river.

THE CATHEDRAL

Seeing Chester Cathedral in its setting in the centre of a busy town and its other setting close to a small secluded precinct, a

---

follows. Considerable commercial redevelopment, mainly within the walls of Chester, has allowed archaeological excavation to fill in several important gaps in the plan of the legionary fortress over the last decade and continues to do so. The lack of contemporary Roman documentation lays great stress on the need to excavate for historical evidence wherever possible.

The Roman W defences, though swept away in the Middle Ages together with those along the S side, have now been accurately located as a result of the construction of the inner ring road, which runs parallel to them on the outside, the W gate lying mainly under the Guildhall. The tower at the NW angle was found to have survived in the city wall, but the needs of modern transport required it to give place to St Martin's Gate, where its outline is marked out in stone setts on the pavement of City Walls Road.

Between the Kaleyards and Eastgate a trench dug at r. angles to a visible section of the Roman E wall revealed the position of the parade ground stretching out beyond the ditch towards Frodsham Street.

In the SE corner of the fortress extensive clearance between the E wall and Bridge Street for the shopping precinct made excavation possible from which the existence of barracks and the considerable complex of the legionary bath-house (thermae) became known. The discovery of the latter means that the suite of rooms with hypocausts and mosaics already known in St Michael's Row and Bridge Street has been recognized as part of the baths system. (A well preserved section of hypocaust still exists in the cellar of Lawleys Ltd, No. 39 Bridge Street.) Furthermore, the large colonnaded hall in St Michael's Row along the north side of the bath-house can be identified as the exercise hall (palaestra). Columns from this building have been resited outside the walls in the Roman Gardens, S of Newgate. Two more complete columns stand in the gardens of Eaton Hall, together with the altar dedicated by the Twentieth Legion to the Nymphs and Springs, which was found in 1821 near Boughton Cross at the source of the legion's water supply (see p. 211).

The largest scene of archaeological activity to date in Chester has been the Central Redevelopment Area between Princess Street and Hamilton Place, stretching from Linenhall Street through to Northgate Street. Where the underground car parks now are, were excavated from W to E the remains of workshops (fabricae), the elliptical building already mentioned above, with a bath-house along its S side, and the SW corner of a building which occupied the normal position of the commandant's house (praetorium). To the S of this the W half of the row of offices along the northern limit of the head-quarters building (principia) came to light, including the central shrine of the standards (sacellum). Part of that room, the focal point of the fortress, which has the rock-cut strong-room (aerarium) below it, is being preserved in the new building on the Old Market site for inspection from Hamilton Place.

mental effort is needed to visualize it as what it was until 1540 – a Benedictine abbey. It was only Henry VIII who raised it to cathedral rank, and the last Abbot became the first Dean. The abbey was founded in 1092 by Hugh Lupus, Earl of Chester, though an establishment of secular canons had existed before, probably from the c9. The buildings are of red sandstone, the church with its 355 ft not long as major abbeys, or indeed cathedrals, go.

EXTERIOR

10 From some angles the church is impressive indeed, but for the architectural scholar it is an extremely confusing building, owing to the fact that very little documentary evidence has come down to us, and even more owing to the fact that a whole series of c19 restorations has made the exterior what it is now and that in the majority of cases it has not yet been possible to determine whether the restorers – *Hussey* in 1844 etc., *Scott* in 1868 etc., *Blomfield* after 1882 – reproduced what had been there before or followed their own fancies.*

This examination of the exterior is arranged topographically, starting at the E end. The E end is the Lady Chapel, a beautiful vessel of *c.*1260–80 with side windows of three stepped lancets and an E window of five stepped lancets. The stonework is all *Hussey* and *Scott* (especially the gable and the high-pitched roof are Scott's own), but for a lancet-style building genuine-ness of surface is not so necessary. Moving s there follows the choir with its s aisle and at once a daring conceit of *Scott*'s for which, however, he said he had evidence: the s aisle ends in a polygonal apse and is covered by an absurdly high polygonal roof, reaching right up into the clerestory. Scott in his report said that he found evidence for this and reminded his audience of Norrey in Normandy. One cannot check now, and one is left with a suspicion of wishful thinking. The choir clerestory is Scott's, but two of the original windows, it is said, had re-mained, and again one has one's doubts. The windows are Dec, of three lights. The E window is by *Hussey*; the pinnacles are *Scott*'s. The aisle windows on the other hand have geo-metrical tracery of late c13 character, but those on the N side are by *Hussey*, those on the s by *Scott*. Hussey seems to have

* I am extremely grateful to the Dean of Chester for having helped me over the intricacies of the restorations, of which he knows far more than anyone else.

decided in favour of them on the strength of surviving minor internal features with geometrical details. The s transept has Dec aisle and Perp clerestory windows. How original are their designs? The great s window anyway is of 1887, by *Blomfield*. The s end of the transept was repaired by *Harrison*, who restored the cathedral in 1818–20, and the squat corner turrets etc. are his. The flying buttresses here and in the nave are *Scott*'s entirely. Outside on the s wall of the transept, at a nice height which makes them easily seen, is a row of figural corbels, and among them Gladstone and Disraeli can be recognized. The crossing tower is Perp, but the top with the big embattled pinnacles is by *Scott*. There should be eight pinnacles. The nave again has Dec aisle and Perp clerestory windows. The aisle windows are by *Hussey*. So to the s porch, the stump of a sw tower, and the w front. All this is work of the early c16, thoroughly restored and perhaps embellished by *Scott*. The s porch is of two storeys. The inner doorway is intact; so are the vaulting shafts in the corners. But the fan-vault is by *G. G. Scott Jun.* The over-decorated upper floor, except perhaps for the two two-light windows, is by *Sir G. G.*

The façade however seems mixed. On the lower level work is palpably original, the recessing of the doorway, some of the 27 niche-work of the recess (but probably not the larger outer niches), and the delightful frieze of little angels and yet littler people in the frieze above the doorway culminating in the Assumption of the Virgin. The eight-light window is also basically original, but battlements, pediment, and turret are by *Scott*. The w front is unfortunate in that the NW tower – a Norman tower as we shall see – is totally hidden by Barclays Bank, formerly the King's School, replacing the Bishop's Palace, originally the Abbot's Lodgings. So nearly one third of the façade is missing.

The N views are more complex. The church cannot be isolated from the MONASTIC PARTS. First the choir as on the s side, then at once to the E range of the cloister, hiding the fact that the N transept is again Norman. What one sees is the exterior of the chapter house, an exquisite exterior of long slender lancets of about 1250–60, on the N side two, three, and three and a blank, and the E side a curious system of lancets set in a system of giant blank lancet arches. This is largely due to *Blomfield*. The lower building after the chapter house is the warming room, all externally not original. The great refectory E window of reticulated tracery is by *Sir Giles G. Scott*, 1913, replacing something quite different. The N side windows are mostly Dec, but towards the W end Perp. To see more one must stand at the cloister garth: then the N side of the nave can be seen, like the S side. On the E side it is at once clear that the dormitory is gone entirely which ran along the upper floor of the E range.* On the N side appears the S wall of the refectory. This side has at the E end the five close Dec windows lighting the staircase to the reading pulpit (*see* below p. 147). They are of single lights, cinquecusped with an ogee top. More on the cloister will be said later. The high Norman walling of the W range belongs to St Anselm's Chapel (*see* p. 145).

INTERIOR

Norman work appears in three places: the N transept, the NW tower, and the cloister. For the latter *see* p. 145. The other two will be described now out of topographical order. The church was no doubt begun in 1092, and again no doubt at the E end. That at least was the overwhelmingly general custom. The E end is supposed to have had an apsed choir. The choir aisles ended in apses too, and their outline is marked in the floor. How long building took is not certain, but the details of the NORTH TRANSEPT do not look later than *c.*1100 or so. In the E wall is the opening to a chapel formerly also apsed. The opening, which is surprisingly decayed, has sturdy Early Norman details. Triple responds, two-scallop(?) capitals, two-step arch. The chapel itself – to anticipate – was replaced *c.*1200 by a straight-ended one of two bays. Vaulting-shafts with rings, capitals stiff-leaf as well as Late Norman; rib-vault. The E wall however has the three stepped lancets of the Lady Chapel, i.e. – if original – it is a later C13 alteration, and the PISCINA also is later C13 with its pointed-trefoiled head and its stiff-leaf capitals. Another such PISCINA is in the E wall of the transept between the openings into the chapel and the choir aisle, and this is cut into a wall-pier of the choir type (*see* below). The fragments S of this pier may have belonged to a screen. From the chapel an arch opens to the S into the N choir aisle. It is a later (*c.*1300) alteration, as it cuts into the architecture of the chapel. The arch has two head stops. Above the Norman arch into the chapel is a low triforium of six openings. Short columns with plain Early Norman single-scallop capitals and unmoulded

5

* Though Sir Harold Brakspear considered that it ran E from the NE corner.

arches. Above that is the Perp parapet with quatrefoils of open-work and the clerestory corresponding to that in the s transept (*see* below). In the w wall are some small blocked Norman windows at triforium level. The clerestory windows are Perp again, but of a different pattern. In the N wall is a small E.E. doorway. The big N window is by *Scott*. Excellent timber ceiling of *c.*1520 with many bosses.

If one enters the N choir aisle for a moment, one sees at once in the first bay on the r. the circular base of a round pier and that of a second which is a mighty round scalloped capital upside down. So the choir had round piers, like St John's church and e.g. Hereford Cathedral.

Now the NORTH TOWER. This also is Norman, but about forty or fifty years later than the transept, though the arches are still merely stepped. But among the shafts of the arches to s and E are keeled ones, and the capitals have many small scallops. A window in the N wall was placed high up because of the cloister. In the adjoining w bay of the N aisle is another such window, blocked.

For the rest of the interior topography is again preferable to chronology. Chronologically the latest item so far has been the E chapel of the N transept, i.e. a job of *c.*1200. Nothing is preserved in the church itself between this and the LADY CHAPEL, i.e. *c.*1260–80. The chapel is of three bays with a rib-vault with longitudinal ridge ribs and also short transverse ones caught up by two tiercerons. Three big bosses of the Trinity, the Virgin and Child, and the Murder of St Thomas Becket, and also smaller bosses. The vaulting-shafts are tripartite, the front ones with fillets. Thick leaf capitals. Are SEDILIA and PISCINA to be trusted? The piscina is of two lights, the sedilia has only a pendant instead of a mid-shaft.

The N choir aisle ends in the CHAPEL OF ST WERBURGH, a Late Perp addition. Vault of two bays with tierceron stars.

The CHOIR can confidently be dated to *c.*1300. It is five bays long. Strong piers of four major and four minor shafts connected by small hollows. The shafts have fillets, finer on the N, broader on the s side. The bases and the capitals are still in the E.E. tradition. Moulded arches, on the N side with dominant rolls, on the s side with dominant hollows. The E arch is not wholly original. Vaulting-shafts start in the spandrels of the arcade. They stand on corbel figures, larger on the s than on the N side. A triforium follows of four small openings per bay, consisting of shafts carrying depressed trefoiled arches. In the NE bay the details of the arches are a little simpler, and altogether it is likely that the N preceded the S side. The clerestory is Dec, and it is said (*see* above) that two of the windows are original. The vault of the choir has diagonal and both longitudinal and transverse ridge ribs. This vault is of timber and by *Scott*. The painted decoration is by *Clayton & Bell*. The SEDILIA are lusciously Dec and very largely by *Scott*. The original parts can easily be recognized, and they include three-dimensional ogee arches. The back towards the aisle consists of long thin panels separated by vertical leaf strips, also only very scantily original. The sedilia came from St John's church, but at an early date. The CHOIR AISLES have tripartite vaulting-shafts with a fillet as in the Lady Chapel. The vaults are again *Scott*'s. In the S aisle are two large genuine recesses, cusped, and still without ogees, and at the start of Scott's apse is a Perp image niche. In the S aisle apse are SEDILIA and PISCINA with simple geometrical tracery, and in the E bay of the N aisle is another PISCINA with such tracery – justifying *Hussey*'s geometrical windows.

The CROSSING piers continue from the choir into the early C14. Typical mouldings. The lantern stage has two large blank arches to each side, a wall passage, and a longitudinal and a transverse arch rising from the middle of each lantern wall. They differ in their section. The decoration of the ceiling is by *G. G. Pace*.

The SOUTH TRANSEPT takes us up to *c*.1340. It has the unusual length of five bays – exactly like the choir. Also, it has a W as well as an E aisle. The vault in the S bay of the latter is the only genuinely medieval rib-vault in the cathedral. It is of diagonal ribs and both longitudinal and transverse ridge ribs and has bosses. Also in the S wall are SEDILIA and a PISCINA. In the N bay of the same aisle is however a genuine vaulting springer, and it is remarkable that *Blomfield*, when he did the rest of the aisle vaults, did not continue what he had found. He thought he knew better. He also incidentally did not continue Scott's choir aisle ribs. The vault is of timber, whereas the W aisle vault is of stone. The S transept 'nave' has piers like those of the choir. The vaulting-shafts however start from the ground here, an attachment to the former pier shape, beset with fillets. Also the capitals are different. They have individual ornamental motifs, and those of the S wall leaf-bands. Are these latter to be trusted? Perp clerestory with wall passage.

Parapets of openwork quatrefoils. The W aisle vaulting-shafts are like the E aisle ones.

The most remarkable thing about the NAVE is that between the S side, which continues direct from the S transept, starting, say, about 1360, and the N side, which at first sight is identical with the S side, there should be well over a hundred years. The work was done by Abbot Ripley (1485–93). The capital of the W respond has his monogram. This self-conscious conservatism or, as it were, historicism is something typically English. The same case exists at Westminster Abbey and at Beverley Minster. Only the bases of the piers are Perp on the N, while they are Dec on the S, and the S capitals have individual fleurons etc., but whole leaf-bands on the N. The E bays adjoining the crossing differ from all the others on both sides. They have continuous mouldings of three sunk convex curves and should probably be explained as a necessary buttressing for the crossing while it was being built. The clerestory is Perp, and the parapet after that first E bay changes to bareness. The lierne-vault is of timber and by *Scott*. The W wall has high blank arcading below which cannot be later than *c.*1300 if it is original. Above it is the huge eight-light Perp W window. The S aisle has window surrounds which are original and Dec, justifying the Dec C19 aisle windows which *Hussey* introduced apparently without evidence. The aisle vaults are Scott's again. Access to the SW tower is by a panelled arch.

FURNISHINGS

From E to W, and always taking N before S.

LADY CHAPEL. STAINED GLASS by *Wailes*, 1859. Medallions à la C13. – ST WERBURGH'S SHRINE. Stone, Dec, of two bays by one, much restored by *Blomfield*, after fragments had been found to supplement the lower part which, since the Dissolution, had served as the Bishop's throne. On the upper stage several statuettes of kings and saints. – MONUMENT. Archdeacon Wrangham, a brass cross; 1846 by *Hardman*.

NORTH CHOIR CHAPEL. STAINED GLASS. E window by *O'Connor*, 1857, one large pictorial representation. – MONUMENTS. Bishop Graham, 1867. Designed by *Kelly & Edwards*. Recumbent effigy and Gothic architectural surround. – William Bispham † 1685. Brass plate and stone surround with short columns and an open scrolly segmental pediment.

20 CHOIR. REREDOS and FLOOR MOSAIC by *J. R. Clayton*, 1876. –
STALLS. One of the finest sets in the country. In the county
only Nantwich can compare, in the rest of the North of England only Manchester. The Manchester stalls are of the early
C16, both Chester and Nantwich are late C14. The type, however, is the same, with the high, spiky, closely set canopies with
crocketed arches and spirelets. The stalls themselves have
powerfully carved ends with poppyheads, some original, some
Victorian. Among the former the Dean's and the Vice-Dean's
stalls are noteworthy. The Dean's stall shows the Tree of
Jesse, as does an end on the N side as well. The carvings on the
arm rests are worth inspecting too, but the greatest glut is the
MISERICORDS. Here only a few can be singled out.* From the
Dean's stall (S side NW end) S and then E: Coronation of the
Virgin; Sir Gawain and the portcullis falling on his horse; a
Monster killing a Knight; Unicorn, Virgin, and Knight;
Wrestlers; a Man leading a Lion; Sow and Litter; Virgin and
Child; Quarrelling Couple; Reynard the Fox; Samson and the
Lion. – From the Vice-Dean's stall (N side SW end) first N and
then E: Pelican; Knight on horseback; Angels with the In-
struments of the Passion; Life of St Werburgh; Woman beat-
ing her Husband; Fox shamming dead; the Ascent of Alexander; Angel with Harp; Tristram and Iseult; Tiger Hunt;
Stag Hunt. This selection does not mean that other misericords are not aesthetically just as, or even more, rewarding,
e.g. the two Herons on the N side. – STONE SCREEN WALLS.
Visible from the N and S choir aisles. They are part of the
former PULPITUM and were re-set by *Scott*. They are high
and have blank single-light panels with crocketed ogee arches.
– BISHOP'S THRONE. 1876 by *Farmer & Brindley* to *Scott's*
design. – STAINED GLASS. E by *Heaton, Butler & Bayne*,
1884. – CANDLESTICKS. By *Censore*, a Bolognese gun-founder
who lived in Rome and died in 1622. – LECTERN. With a
wooden eagle, on a stem with wooden figurines. First half of
the C17.

NORTH CHOIR AISLE. The STONE SCREEN like that of a
chantry is by *Hussey*. – IRON GATE from Guadalajara; 1558. –
STAINED GLASS. The four first on the N side from the E by
Wailes; the first three 1859, the fourth 1853. – Then a good
Heaton, Butler & Bayne, 1863, and the westernmost *Clayton
& Bell*, 1863. – MONUMENTS. Tablet to Bishop Jacobson,
1887. By *Boehm*; the design by *Blomfield*. – George Travis

* The cathedral has a booklet with a complete list and a plan.

† 1797 by *Joseph Turner*, architect. With portrait in an oval.*

SOUTH CHOIR AISLE. The apse has STAINED GLASS by *Clayton & Bell*, 1872, and below good MOSAICS designed by *Clayton* and made by *Salviati*, 1879. – Fresco PAINTING also by *Clayton & Bell*, 1874. – The other STAINED GLASS is as follows: the first from the E, 1850 by *Hardman*, designed by *Pugin*. – Then two by *Wailes*; 1852. – IRON GATE. Also 1558, like the other. – MONUMENTS. Black tomb-chest with quatre-foil decoration and small painted figures between. C13 or early C14. The reference to the Emperor Henry IV is erroneous. – Bust of Thomas Brassey. The Italian Quattrocento design by *Blomfield*, 1882, the bust, made before 1877, by *Wag-müller*. – Bishop Peploe † 1752. Very fine architecture and decoration. – *Randle Holme* did three painted monuments: two heraldic (J. Leche † 1639, Katharine Wynne † 1698) and one with flat strap- or fretwork (Robert Bennet † 1614). 54

CROSSING. *Scott* moved the choir stalls to their present position (they had previously been moved further W by Hussey) and in place of the former stone pulpitum (*see above*) he provided the present SCREEN, 1876. Its GATES were made by *Skidmore*. – ROOD. 1913. Designed by *Sir Giles Gilbert Scott* and made by *F. Stuflesser*. The cross which formerly was here is now at Dunham-on-the-Hill (*see* p. 205). – The ORGAN SCREEN and ORGAN CASE on the N side of the crossing are also of 1876 by *Scott*.

NORTH TRANSEPT. STAINED GLASS. The two clerestory E windows by *Wailes*, 1853. – MONUMENTS. One to the C17 Bishop Pearson. 1863. Designed by *Blomfield*, with carving by *Earp*. – On the N wall Samuel Peploe, c.1784, by *Nollekens* (putto before an obelisk), and L. W. Halstead † 1829 by *Thomas Kelly* (with a pyramid and some heavy Grecian decoration). – On the W wall: Edward Massey † 1836. In a Gothic surround, but the representation curiously Baroque. He lies on a couch, an angel above him in a cloud. – Col. T. G. Egerton † 1835. By *Bedford*. He reclines, mourners stand by him. – Henry Trowbridge Moor † 1837. Large Gothic tablet with a gable at the top.

* By the entrance to the Lady Chapel a brass to the Rev. Mascie Domville Taylor † 1845. By *Hardman* and obviously influenced by *Pugin* if not actually designed by him. At the W end of the N wall are brasses, one above the other, to Dean J. S. Howson and to James Frater, clerk of works, both of whom played so considerable a part, with Scott, in the restoration of the cathedral (EH).

SOUTH TRANSEPT. Stone SCREEN to the S choir aisle. Only partly old. – REREDOS in the second chapel from the N by *Kempe*, 1906. – STAINED GLASS. The great S window by *Heaton, Butler & Bayne*, 1887. – In the E aisle the first from the N by *Heaton, Butler & Bayne*, 1876. Then three by *Kempe*, 1890, 1892, 1902, and at the S end by *Clayton & Bell*, 1890. – On the W side the first from the N by *Powell*, 1892 and the second by *Kempe*, 1904. – MONUMENTS. George Ogden † 1781 by *Hayward*. Kneeling female figure by an urn. – Anne Matthews † 1793. By *Banks*. Female figure leaning on a rock, an anchor in front of it. – John Philips Buchanan † at Waterloo 1815. Dramatic trophy with a big Grecian helmet. – First Duke of Westminster, 1902. Designed by *C. J. Blomfield*. Recumbent effigy by *Pomeroy*.

NAVE. FONT at the W end. A big baluster carrying a big bowl. Black marble; 1697. – LECTERN. 1876 by *Skidmore*. Very large, in the English Gothic tradition. – PULPIT. Stone; designed by *Hussey*. – WEST DOOR. Traceried; much restored. – STAINED GLASS. The E window by *W. T. Carter Shapland*, 1961. With large single figures. Strong colours. A work that will please many but can also please the few. – MONUMENTS. Gothic standing monument to Roger Barnston of 1838. By *John Blayney*. – Bishop Stratford, 1708. Large tablet with above the inscription three putto-heads and at the top a bust. – Bishop Hall † 1668. Noble black and white marble tablet with open scrolly pediment. No figures. – Edmund Entwisle, 1712. With two putto-heads and garland. – John and Thomas Wainwright † 1686 and 1720, signed by Bishop *George Berkeley* and *William Kent*, but lovably rustic in the execution. Two cherubs hold the inscription plate over which hangs a fat garland. It really looks 1670 rather than 1720. – Robert Bickerstaff † 1841. By *Blayney*. Weeping willow over an urn. – Mrs Dod, 1723. Oval medallion with frontal bust. – Dean Smith † 1787. By *Banks*. Mourning female figure by an urn. – Sir William Mainwaring, 1671. Large tablet with twisted columns and a segmental pediment; two putti squeezed in.

NORTH AISLE. On the wall MOSAICS. Stories in large figures. 1883–6. Designed by *Clayton*, executed by *Burke & Co*. – The MOSAIC FLOOR in the tower bay was designed by Dean *Howson* and made by *Burke & Co.*, 1885. – FONT. Early

3 Christian, square, with on one side two peacocks and the alpha and omega and the chi-rho sign. On the second two affronted winged lions, on the third two affronted winged eagles, and on

the fourth excellent interlace.* – STAINED GLASS. A series by *Heaton, Butler & Bayne*, 1890.

SOUTH AISLE. STAINED GLASS. One window by *Wailes*, 1862. – Under the SW tower the complete C17 furnishings of the CONSISTORY COURT, fitted up *c*.1636. The entrance is through a SCREEN. There is a wooden enclosure with a bench round, raised on the side in whose centre is the canopied Chancellor's throne.

PLATE. Chalice of 1496 with a grasshopper as its hallmark. – Ciborium, 1661, probably German. – Two Patens, two Patens, two Flagons, silver-gilt, two Maces, all 1662 and all London.– Almsdish, 1673, London. – Two Candlesticks, 1683, London. – Spoon, 1691, London. – Two small Almsdishes, 1737, by *Richard Richardson II*, Chester. – Also a Pastoral Staff designed by *Bodley & Garner*, 1890, made by *Krall*.

THE MONASTIC PARTS

A Norman cloister and Norman domestic quarters must of course have existed, and there is quite some evidence of them. The earliest is the UNDERCROFT of the W range, groin-vaulted in two naves with short round piers with round scalloped capitals – early C12. The ABBOT'S PASSAGE to its S, i.e. in the SW corner, came later, say *c*.1150. It is not bonded in. It has two bays of rib-vaulting, the ribs of a later profile than those of the tower (half-roll and two small half-hollows). Above the passage is the C12 CHAPEL OF ST ANSELM, of three bays, with a C19 Gothic plaster vault. This also is not bonded in, and it obscures the N window in the NW tower. The wall supports for the original transverse arches of the chapel have volute and scallop capitals. The chancel bay which extends over the cloister walk was remodelled in the early C17. Fine stucco ceiling of low pitch studded with motifs. – Good strap-topped DOORS. – C17 SCREEN and COMMUNION RAIL.

St Anselm's Chapel originally adjoined the Abbot's Lodging, which was above the W range of the cloister and later extended westward into the area now of Barclays Bank – a late medieval development often to be found. The W face of the E wall of the original lodging can still be seen from outside.

The whole S wall of the cloister, i.e. the N wall of the nave

* The genuineness of the font is in doubt.

is Norman too. It has two sets of three blank arches with patterned shafts. E of them is the major doorway from church to cloister, and this is the only example of Latest Norman in the cathedral. Three orders of columns, waterleaf capitals, as they are characteristic of say *c*.1175–90, moulded arch, the outer order with a kind of intermittent corn-cob motif. The contrast between this Latest Norman and the Earliest E.E. of the N transept E chapel is telling.

In the W walk N of the undercroft is another passage with a Norman doorway. Inside is the springing of a Norman rib-vault, and in the E range, near the S end, is a blocked perfectly simple Norman doorway. Much rebuilding of the ranges round the cloister took place in the C13. The best start is with the CHAPTER HOUSE. Its front is entirely by *Hussey*, but the VESTIBULE is genuine and memorable as one of the earliest cases of piers running into vaults without any intervening capitals. The piers have bundles of eight attached shafts, and the ribs do not strictly continue them, but break up each shaft into a triple rib. There are no bosses. The chapter house is the aesthetic climax of the cathedral, a wonderfully noble room, vaulted with rib-vaults, including ridge-ribs. The vaulting-shafts are triple, the middle one polygonal. They stand on stiff-leaf corbels and have stiff-leaf capitals. The windows are slim lancets as we have already seen. There are inside boldly detached shafts with rings repeating the forms of the windows. The proportions are admirable. The wall to the vestibule is in the usual way divided into a portal and two two-light windows over (quatrefoil in the spandrels). – (CUPBOARD, with C13 ironwork. NMR) – STAINED GLASS. The E window by *Heaton, Butler & Bayne*, 1872.

N of the chapter house is the SLYPE, formerly to the monastic infirmary. This is E.E. too. Its doorway has detached shafts. The vault is of four bays and has diagonal as well as ridge ribs.

The WARMING ROOM with two large former fireplaces is N of the slype. It is of four by two bays and it has single-chamfered ribs. The piers are octagonal. Taking up a little of the oblong space of this room is the DAY STAIR to the former dormitory, opened handsomely to the E walk by a big quatrefoil in a circle. E.E. also is the doorway into the warming room, in the NE corner. It has a cinquecusped head.

More E.E. work in the N walk. In the N range of course is

the refectory. Its doorway has two orders and a cusped arch. E of this is the LAVATORIUM, of three arches. The cloister vault interferes with it and other features with a ruthlessness now hard to understand.

The CLOISTER WALKS were in fact rebuilt about 1525–30. Proof of the date is the initials of an abbot of 1527–9 and the arms of Cardinal Wolsey. The S walk was rebuilt again by *Scott* on the pattern of the W walk, i.e. with detached piers forming niches. Of such detached piers there are only four in the W walk, forming a CARRELL, i.e. a reading space set aside. The vaults have diagonal and ridge-ribs, all hollow-chamfered, and bosses. They stand on wall corbels which look earlier than Perp in the E walk and which stand on big figures in the N and W ranges. The cloister windows are all Perp and of the same design except in the NE corner. In the same corner are the earliest-looking corbels; yet the window pattern as such is not earlier than the other.

In conclusion the REFECTORY. This is basically Norman – cf. the inside of the main doorway – but its present appearance is late C13 to early C14. The windows, as has already been said, are largely Dec, and the E window, of 1913, is by *Sir Giles Gilbert Scott*, who restored the refectory and other of the monastic parts. The roof is by *F. H. Crossley*, 1939. What can only be seen from the cloister garth is a set of five small, closely set windows in the S wall near the E end. They are cinquecusped, and their very raw ogee tops cannot be trusted. Their function is to light the steps which run up in the wall to the READING PULPIT. The stair is in the thickness of the 14 wall, and the arches to the room itself are pointed-trefoiled. The pulpit projects triangularly on a big corbel with three bands of stiff-leaf. The whole ensemble – in spite of the ogee detail just mentioned – is decidedly pre-ogee, say *c.*1290. So incidentally are the wall-shafts between the Dec windows.

THE PRECINCT

That is, Abbey Square and Abbey Street and no more. They both have Georgian terraces of brick houses and both retain cobbled paving. There is a green in the centre of the square; in it stands a column from the former Exchange of 1695–8.* The S side of the square marks the site of the Abbot's Lodging which, at the Dissolution, became the Bishop's Palace. For the building erected for the King's School on part of the site

* The date is taken from Hemingway.

see Barclays Bank, Northgate Street (p. 161). Adjoining this is the ABBEY GATEWAY. It has continuous chamfers, the outer ones enclosing the carriage as well as the pedestrian entrance. Three-bay vault with both diagonal and ridge ribs all of one chamfer. The date *c.*1377 (licence to crenellate the abbey walls) seems too late. The upper storey altered, early C19. Further N is the LITTLE ABBEY GATEWAY, a small segmental arch. On the W side of ABBEY SQUARE Nos. 1–2 date from the 1820s. Nos. 3–6 are of *c.*1754–61, and on the N side Nos. 7–11 are also of this date, though they form a more ambitious group. On the N side are three fine large doorways, with fluted pilasters, and one with a triangular, the other two with segmental pediments. No. 7 and No. 9 have staircase halls with heavy panelling and with skylighting. The staircase of No. 7 is Chippendale Chinese, that of No. 9 has three slim twisted balusters on each step. (Good staircase also in No. 11. Spacious top-lit stair well, but the stairs rise only to the first floor, and there is a gallery at second-floor level. EH) In the NE corner of the square is the BISHOP'S HOUSE (formerly the Deanery), late C18. On the E side No. 12 is Georgian, but Nos. 13 and 14 are the two remaining of four cottages built for lay clerks of the cathedral in 1626. In ABBEY STREET Nos. 5–9 are of 1764 and Nos. 4–10 of 1826–8.

THE TOWN

CHURCHES

ST JOHN BAPTIST. St John is a Saxon foundation of the C7 or C10. It was refounded as a collegiate establishment in 1057 by Leofric, Earl of Mercia. It became a cathedral in 1075, when Bishop Peter of Lichfield decided to move his see, but this was translated to Coventry by his successor in 1095. Even so, St John remained a cathedral by name, with Lichfield and Coventry, until the new diocese of Chester was formed at the time of the Dissolution. The external impression of the church is of Victorian E.E. This Victorian work is by *R. C. Hussey*, who restored the interior and the S side in 1859–66 and[*] was responsible for the restoration of the N side and the building of the NE bell-tower in 1886–7. The E window is by *T. M. Penson*. To the E of this seeming Victorian church, however, are medieval ruins, though they are not at first very telling, and there is the stump of a mighty NW tower, the E

[*] According to Dean Addleshaw.

arch of which is simply stepped. The C16 upper part of the tower fell in 1881, destroying the E.E. N porch, which was rebuilt by *Douglas* in 1882. As one enters the church, however, one is transported into the early C12. There is a Norman nave, 6 shorter now than it was, a splendid Norman crossing, and just the first bay of the Norman chancel. The rest, outside, is the Norman arch to the Lady Chapel and the remains of the C14 choir chapels. The choir as well as the nave have sturdy round piers with round many-scalloped capitals and double-stepped arches. The choir bay has its Norman gallery too, with very short round piers. The crossing has three shafts in the W and E piers, two in the N and S piers, and again arches simply stepped. The transepts have both been cut off. The decorative detail, what little there is, seems later E of the crossing than W. Also the entry arch into the S choir aisle (with fat rolls) seems later than its N counterpiece (just stepped). Although the Norman rebuilding may have begun before the seat of the diocese was moved away from Chester, the work remained incomplete when the see was removed, and indeed in the nave the triforium stage was built a good deal later, hardly before 1190. It has pointed arches, four per bay, the shafts with rings, and the clerestory is full C13 – cf. the leaf capitals. There are four clerestory arches per bay too, but only two windows, which makes for an awkward rhythm. Vaulting shafts rise from the triforium floor level, but there is no vault. The W end of the S chancel aisle shows blank arcading, and this continues outside the present E wall.

E of what was the S transept is what is called the CHAPTER HOUSE. It would be in a very odd position if it was that. Also it is on a lower level. It is of two by two bays with an octagonal pier and single-chamfered arches, and looks c.1300. There is an original doorway into the chancel aisle.

FONT. Small, square, with simple vegetable motifs, probably 1660s. – (REREDOS. 1876–7. Designed by *Douglas*, with a Last Supper painted by *Heaton, Butler & Bayne*. EH) – REREDOS, SE chapel. Formerly wider and for the Commandments, Creed, etc. Two sections are left. They each have a scrolly open pediment. It is a charming, rustic piece of 1692. (In the arch an aluminium figure of the Virgin by *Michael Murray*, 1969.) – GATE of wood and iron to the S chapel; C17. – WALL PAINTING. St John Baptist. In the N aisle E respond, barely visible. – STAINED GLASS. W window designed by *Edward Frampton*, 1887–90. – E window by

Clayton & Bell, 1863. – (N aisle first from E is a memorial to
Thomas M. Lockwood, the architect, 1901. By *Shrigley &
Hunt*. – ORGAN CASE. By *Lockwood*, 1895. The organ itself is
earlier, and was brought to Chester after first being erected in
Westminster Abbey for use at Queen Victoria's Coronation.
EH) – Two brass CHANDELIERS given in 1722. – PLATE. Two
Chalices, one 1633, London, inscribed 1674, the other a copy,
1674; Paten, 1664; Paten, inscribed 1683; Paten, 1717 by
Richard Richardson I of Chester; Chalice and Cover, 1725 by
the same; two Flagons, 1729 by *William Darker*; two Almsdishes, 1735 by *Richard Bayley*. – (Silver-gilt cross by *Michael
Murray*, 1969.) – MONUMENTS. Three medieval stone
effigies, an early C14 Knight with crossed legs, a Priest of
about the same time, and Agnes de Ridlegh † 1347. The lower
part of the slab was left intact with leaf carving and the
inscription, the upper part shows her upper part in relief. –
60 Diana Warburton † 1693. By *Edward Pearce*. Reredos
architecture and an upright skeleton holding the inscription.
– Cecil Warburton † 1729. Marble. In the centre a bust in
relief in an oval medallion. – (At the W end of the S aisle
several painted monuments by the *Randle Holme* family, with
dates of death ranging from 1628 to 1682. EH)

See Perambulation for the stone house S of the church
(p. 166) and for the former RECTORY, now Grosvenor Club
(p. 165). (The present VICARAGE, in Vicar's Lane, is a house
apparently designed by *Lockwood* for the Grosvenor estate.
Dated 1892. EH)

CHRIST CHURCH, Gloucester Street. Rebuilt in separate stages
from 1876 to 1900 by *Douglas*. A SW steeple was planned but
not built. Chancel and SE chapel of ashlar, inside and out. The
rest of red pressed brick with stone dressings. 'Sort of light
conventional E.E. with thin arcades ... [and] squattish
lancets', wrote Goodhart-Rendel. (By no means completely
conventional, however. See, e.g., the differing roofs in N and S
aisles, the corbelling out of wall-shafts, and the piers without
capitals. – By *Sir Charles Nicholson* the chancel FITTINGS,
c.1900–10, in a curious chunky neo-Perp. – ROOD BEAM, 1920,
by the same, and probably also the chapel GATES. – Chapel
REREDOS by *Kempe*, 1897. – STAINED GLASS. By *Kempe* are
windows in the chapel, 1897, and S aisle, 1901. – Also the W
window, 1902. – By *A. K. Nicholson* the baptistery, 1906. –
Also one N aisle window. – By *Bryams* the N aisle W, 1906. EH)
– PAINTING. Christ prepared for the Entombment. By

Westall, 1826. From Eccleston church. Quite an important painting. – PLATE. Credence Paten, 1725, London; two Chalices, 1821 by *William Bateman*; two Patens, 1838.

ST FRANCIS (R.C.), Grosvenor Street. 1874–5 by *J. O'Byrne* – a surprising building, wide and aisleless, without a tower. The treatment of the upper windows inside is very original.

LITTLE ST JOHN. *See* Perambulation, pp. 161–2.

ST MARY-ON-THE-HILL, St Mary's Hill. A Norman foundation. Externally the masonry looks Victorian, except for the lower part of the w tower,* and the church does indeed owe much to restorations of 1861–2 by *James Harrison* and of 1890–1 by *J. P. Seddon*. The upper part of the tower (the pinnacles of which were formerly taller than they are now) is *Harrison*'s. The interior is Perp except for the Dec tower arch and the Dec chancel arch, which dies into the responds. Three-bay arcades with octagonal piers. In the nave a good camber-beam roof,‡ in bays of eight by five panels, and with many bosses. In the s aisle the window reveals are original. They stand on animal corbels. The SE chapel was first built *c.*1443, which is probably somewhat earlier than the Perp remodelling of the rest of the church, but it was rebuilt in 1693. The responds of the arch to the chancel must be of this date. – RAILS. C17 rails re-used in the choir stalls. – PULPIT. Little of the woodwork is old. – WALL PAINTING. E wall of the s aisle. Crucifixion with three figures and a royal figure above. Not much can now be recognized. It is late medieval, like the architecture. – STAINED GLASS. The Late Perp glass in the tracery of the s chapel E window includes heraldic work, a series of Passion shields, and the Brereton rebus. The lights below are by *H. Hughes*, 1865. – E window (1857) and s chapel centre s (1850) by *Wailes*. – In the N chapel E window remains of the Crimean War memorial by *George Hedgeland*, *c.*1856. – N chapel N by *Ward & Hughes*, *c.*1861. – N porch by *Shrigley & Hunt*, 1892. – PLATE. From St Bridget (demolished). Silver-gilt Flagon, 1696, London, and two Patens of the same time; Chalice, 1718, Chester, by *Richard Richardson*; Chalice, 1783. – The plate which belonged to this church is now at St Mary-without-the-Walls (*see* p. 174). – MONUMENTS. Thomas Gamul † 1616 and wife. Erected by her. Recumbent effigies, and a son, who survived his father, sitting pensively by the feet

---

* This has an early C16 doorway, much weathered.
‡ Said to have been brought from Basingwerk Abbey, Flintshire, after the Dissolution, but this is most unlikely.

of his mother. Kneeling against the tomb-chest are figures of
children who died young. – Philip Oldfield † 1616. Alabaster.
He is lying on his side, his cheek propped up by his elbow.
Against the tomb-chest an incised skeleton. The children kneel
in front of it. Original railings. – William Currie † 1834. Big
Gothic tablet. By *James Harrison*. – (In the N aisle C17 monuments to the Randle Holme family.)

The present street frontage of the former RECTORY is by
Thomas Jones, 1835.* Brick and stone. Nicely stretched out.
Tudor.

ST MICHAEL, Bridge Street. Largely of 1849–50 by *James
Harrison*. Older work is, however, incorporated, particularly
the N arcade and the chancel roof. The arcade has octagonal
piers with fleurons in the capitals. The chancel roof is of
1496, and is narrower than the present chancel – an arrangement which may date from the enlargement of the church in
1678. Bridge Street Row passes beneath the tower. – STAINED
GLASS. N aisle E end by *Clayton & Bell*. – PLATE. Chalice
of the 1560s by *William Mutton* of Chester; silver-gilt Chalice,
1635, London; two Flagons, 1701, London; Chalice and
Paten 1723, by *Richard Richardson* of Chester; Flagon
1728; C17 Paten, altered 1725 by *Richard Richardson* of
Chester. – (MONUMENT. Roger Comberbach † 1771. By
Benjamin Bromfield. EH)

ST NICHOLAS. *See* St Werburgh Street, p. 162.

ST OLAVE, Lower Bridge Street. A mere chapel with a bellcote.
(Partly medieval, but restored in 1859 by *James Harrison*. EH)
– PLATE. C17 Cup.

ST PETER, The Cross. Dec, quite small, with a Perp outer N
aisle. The w tower, which once carried a spire, is embraced
and has Dec arches. Later vault with a large bell-hole. Two-
bay nave arcades. The church has been altered and restored
several times in the C17, C18, and C19. It still keeps two
galleries.‡ – PAINTING. On the N tower pier very dim
religious scenes. – PLATE. Paten, 1708; Chalice and Flagon,
1713, by *Richard Richardson*, Chester; Paten, 1736; Chalice,
1785. – (MONUMENT. George Johnson † 1818. By *S. & F.
Franceys*. EH) – BRASS of a Civilian, *c.*1460, a 37 in. figure.

HOLY TRINITY, Watergate Street. Now the Guildhall. 1865–9.
Designed by *James Harrison* and completed after his death by

* So Mr R. C. Williams kindly told me.
‡ The s side was refaced by *Harrison* following the demolition in 1803 of
the timber-framed pentice which adjoined the church.

Kelly & Edwards. A prominent building with a s w steeple and early C14 motifs. Nave and aisles; clerestory; no separate chancel. – STAINED GLASS. The E window by *Kempe*, 1885. – MONUMENTS. A palimpsest brass the reverse of which is part of the effigy of a Knight, early C16. – Also John Whitmore † 1374. In armour. Now hidden by flooring. – CIVIC PLATE. All silver, with Chester hallmark, and all now in the Guildhall Museum. Two Dessert Spoons, 1703; two Dessert Spoons, 1716; Tumbler Cup, 1721; Gravy Spoon, 1723; Tumbler Cup, 1726; Marrow Spoon, 1734; Pap Bowl, *c.*1739; Pap Bowl, 1743; Bread Basket, 1765; Sugar Basin, 1773; two large Spoons, 1784; Tumbler Cup, 1786; Cream or Sugar Pail, 1801. – For CHURCH PLATE etc. *see* Holy Trinity, Blacon, p. 171.

ST WERBURGH (R.C.), Grosvenor Park Road. By *Edmund Kirby*, 1873–5, the w end completed in 1913–14. White stone, apse, lancets, no tower. A large church, high and unembellished.

OLD ST WERBURGH (R.C.), Queen Street. Now a school. Built in 1799. Arched windows and an altered front with pediment across and two garlanded panels. Mr Howell states that originally there was a Doric porch, and that fine plasterwork remains inside.

BAPTIST CHURCH, Grosvenor Park Road. By *Douglas*, 1879–80, at the end of a row of houses also by him (*see* p. 164). Red brick, with a turret at either side. Details of *c.*1300.

CONGREGATIONAL CHURCH (former), Queen Street. 1772; enlarged in 1838. Five bays, ashlar, Grecian, with pediments over the angle bays and Doric columns *in antis*.

METHODIST CENTRAL HALL, City Road. 1872–3 by *W. Botterill* of Hull. Only nine years later than the classical Presbyterian chapel (*see* below) and now trying hard to be a church, i.e. with a steeple.

(METHODIST CHURCH, St John Street. Although refronted in 1906, the body of the church is of 1811 and is, according to Mr Howell, by *Harrison*. There are side galleries and a four-bay Ionic arcade, though the detailing must be 1906 rather than 1811. EH)

ENGLISH PRESBYTERIAN CHURCH OF WALES, City Road. 1864 by *Michael Gummow* of Wrexham. Classical; stuccoed. Five bays with two Ionic columns *in antis* and a three-bay pediment.

(WELSH PRESBYTERIAN CHURCH, St John Street. 1866 by

W. & G. Audsley of Liverpool. A lively High Victorian front
with an enormous rose window. EH)

PUBLIC BUILDINGS

CITY WALLS.* The present circuit of the walls, nearly two
miles in circumference, represents the area of the medieval
walled town. Roman foundations were incorporated in the
E and N walls, the W and S walls being buried below streets:
Holy Trinity Church marks the Roman West Gate, St
Michael the South Gate. Early C12 work is represented by an
extension of the Roman defences to the S and W to include the
castle. For Roman work *see* pp. 133–4. Much of the later
medieval work, in the local brown sandstone, was carried
out in the C13, and the defences again became of importance
during the Civil War. The damage inflicted then by the
Parliamentary troops was repaired in the time of Queen Anne,
with little respect for the preservation of medieval details. In
the C18 the walls seem to have been maintained for their value
as a pleasant promenade, and the medieval gates were replaced
by new gates in the form of bridges to preserve the wall walk. The
walls stand now to a height of 15 to 25 ft, and average 5 to 6 ft
in width. The wall-walk was probably originally defended to
the outside by crenellations, since replaced by triangular
coping, so that much of the wall above the walk is not original.
Its interior face appears to have been unprotected, except
perhaps by timber rails mounted on stone corbels. These
corbels can be seen in two places – by the Kaleyard Gate and
by St Martin's Gate. A base plinth, sometimes a single course,
occasionally a double-stepped plinth, can be seen on both
sides of the wall.

The walls are best surveyed from the wall walk. Starting at
the EASTGATE (*see* p. 163) and walking N, the visitor is on
medieval wall overlying Roman foundations. The steps to
Frodsham Street have partially obscured the semicircular
remains of a small bastion. At the E end of Abbey Street is the
KALEYARD GATE, for the cutting through of which Edward I
granted permission in 1275. The semicircular PHOENIX
TOWER marks the NE angle of both the Roman and the medieval defences, and was both rebuilt and refaced in the C18. In
common with most of the other towers it has been deprived of
its defensive characteristics by extensive restoration, at least

* This account of the walls was written by Dr Hilary L. Turner.

above the level of the wall-walk. The tower is about 70 ft high, rising on a stepped battered base. Perhaps the only original part of the tower to survive is the lower chamber, octagonal in plan, with a diameter of about 30 ft. Above the round-arched doorway is a plaque, cut in 1613, to commemorate the use of the tower by one of the City Guilds (the Painters, Glaziers, Embroiderers, and Stationers). Later steps lead to the upper storey, whose division from the lower is marked by a string course. The original fenestration probably corresponded to that of the lower room, five arrow-slits providing the widest possible cover. Access to the upper storey and to the roof is likely to have been by an internal stair.

Beyond the NORTHGATE (see p. 161) lie four towers. The first is the rectangular MORGAN'S MOUNT, now devoid of any medieval features. It is close to the NW angle of the Roman defences, discovered during the construction of the inner ring road, which here passes through the wall by way of ST MARTIN'S GATE (see p. 161). The other three towers lie on the medieval fortifications. The GOBLIN TOWER or PEMBERTON'S PARLOUR, originally a circular tower straddling the wall, was rebuilt as a semicircular tower in the time of Queen Anne, and was again reconstructed in 1894. It bears an inscription commemorating the Murengers, the officials responsible for the administration of the tax for the maintenance of the walls. The rectangular BONEWALDESTHORNE'S TOWER stands at the NW angle of the medieval walls; its rounded S side contains a fireplace and a stair, lit by a single loop, to the upper floor, not accessible to visitors. It is entered by a pointed archway, and the tower is little more than a defended entrance to the spur wall leading to the WATER TOWER, built between 1322 and probably 1326, to defend the former harbour. For this work a detailed contract specifying dimensions and cost (£100) was drawn up between the city and one *John Helpstone*; it also included the construction of the spur wall, which was crenellated on both sides; some of the cross-loops remain. The wall itself is 97 ft long, 11 ft 2 in. wide, and about 24 ft high. A sunken chamber, not open to visitors, was incorporated in its build. The Water Tower now stands about 75 ft high with a solid battered base to a height of 17 ft. A wide pointed archway with chamfered jambs leads into the lower chamber; to the r., a small latrine was enclosed in the junction of the tower and the wall. Stairs lead through the thickness of the wall (about 12 ft) into a vaulted octagonal room, whose moulded ribs spring from the angles of the walls. Each of the deep embrasures, now blocked off, functioned as arrow-loops, which are now visible only from the outside. A circular stair leads to the upper room, also octagonal, but with only four embrasures. A fireplace with a modern grate stands in the W wall, traces of whose original chimney remain at roof level. Corbels at the angles support the roof, with an extra one on the entrance projection. A raised fighting platform overlooks the tower entrance. This level is not accessible to the public. The projecting stones in the string course served both to carry away water and to provide a base for timber hoarding for the more effective protection of the base of the tower. Two cross-loops remain in the crenellated parapet.*

The W and S walls, on the line of City Walls Road, Nun's Road, and Castle Drive, are now little higher than the road level. (For the Watergate, see p. 170.) Opposite Nun's Field the base of a few crenellations remains, but an inscription N of Grosvenor Road marks a noticeable stretch of repairs done in 1674. The SHIPGATE, close to the Castle, was demolished in 1830, and its arch is now in Grosvenor Park (see p. 160). The length of wall SE of the castle, between it and the river, was re-aligned at this time. On the E side of the BRIDGEGATE (see p. 167) part of the medieval gate obtrudes. The external RECORDER'S STEPS were built only in 1700, and the WISHING STEPS of 1785 link the different levels of the S and E walls. Beyond the NEWGATE and the WOLF GATE (see p. 165), the position of the SE angle of the Roman defences, the truncated medieval base of THIMBLEBY'S TOWER remains; its groined roof and loopholes, reported to be in good condition, were destroyed by the Parliamentary offensive. The visitor has thus completed his perambulation.

CASTLE. Chester Castle was founded by William the Conqueror on, it has been said, the site of the Saxon fortification. It became the seat of the Earls of Chester and the centre of government of the County Palatine. Building work is known to have taken place in the mid C12, and also in the C13, following the annexation of the Earldom to the Crown in 1237, and under Edward I, who made Chester his base for the conquest of North Wales. But what remains of medieval

* See D. F. Renn, *Jnl. Chester & N. Wales Arch. Arch. & Hist. Soc.* vol. 44.

work is not at once visible, except from the river side. What occupies the site now is *Thomas Harrison*'s group of county buildings. Harrison won a competition for this rebuilding of the castle, and building work went on from 1788 to 1822.* What he has achieved here is one of the most powerful monuments of the Greek Revival in the whole of England. Propylaea of the Greek Doric order with a heavy attic and, 67 on either side, pedimented lodges. On the inner side the lodges are porticoed, and project beyond the central block. The main ranges form three sides of a large court. The three are of one and a half storeys and are connected by links of Greek Doric columns. The centre was built to contain the Shire Hall, the NE side barracks and exchequer court, the SW side the armoury. The gaol was behind the central block and has unfortunately been demolished. The central block is of nineteen bays. The middle part projects slightly, and has six giant unfluted Doric columns carrying a pediment lower than the heavy attic. The middle is ashlared, the side pieces rusticated. The two projecting ranges are of nine bays and have an order of unfluted giant Ionic demi-columns. The SHIRE HALL is 68 of great beauty. It is semicircular with a ring of ten Ionic columns, and there are ten more against the flat wall. Coffered semi-dome with a skylight à la Pantheon. The shape and treatment are derived from Gondoin's sensational École de Médicine (or Chirurgie) in Paris of 1771-6. Beyond lies AGRICOLA'S TOWER, or Caesar's Tower, the principal medieval survival. This was one of the towers of the inner bailey. The site of the outer bailey is approximately represented by Harrison's courtyard, the Shire Hall occupies the site of the Great Hall, and the barracks wing that of the outer gatehouse. The inner bailey was to the S, beyond Harrison's armoury wing, and Agricola's Tower was sited between the inner gatehouse and the inner and outer bailey walls. The tower was refaced by *Harrison* in 1818, but inside are two

* Dr J. Mordaunt Crook has discovered that the dates of the competition and of the commencement of building were earlier than had previously been thought. At the time of writing, the results of Dr Crook's research have not been published, and he has most kindly communicated the following set of dates: Harrison commissioned 1785 after winning the competition; plans for courts and gaol developed 1786-8; gaol, exchequer court, and grand jury room begun 1788; Shire Hall begun 1791, the portico under construction 1797, and the interior finished 1801; barracks and armoury wings planned in 1800 and built in 1804; propylaea begun 1810 (after contemplation by Harrison for nearly thirty years and with many variant schemes having been considered), and completed 1822.

rib-vaulted rooms. The lower room was redone after a fire of
1302, and has a very crude early C14 sexpartite vault. Above
13   it, the chapel of ST MARY DE CASTRO is late C12 or early C13,
with two bays of quadripartite vaulting. The ribs are slender,
and rise from thin detached circular shafts with waterleaf
capitals. – PAINTINGS. Fragments of ornamental C14 wall
paintings.

QUEEN VICTORIA STATUE, in the castle courtyard. 1903
by *Pomeroy*.

COUNTY POLICE HEADQUARTERS. 1964–7 by the County
Architect, *Edgar Taberner*. Extremely objectionably sited – an
eight-storey block immediately by the propylaea of the castle
and turning towards it a windowless wall with an aggressive
all-over concrete relief (by *W. G. Mitchell*).

COMBERMERE MONUMENT. In front of the castle propylaea.
Equestrian statue of Field-Marshal Viscount Combermere by
Marochetti, 1865.

COUNTY HALL, Castle Drive, occupying the site of Harrison's
gaol. By the former County Architect, *E. Mainwaring Parkes*,
1938–57. Not an ornament to the riverside view.

TOWN HALL, Northgate Street. 1864–9 by *W. H. Lynn* of
Belfast. Gothic, symmetrical. Ten bays. Above the central
two bays rises a tower which terminates with gables and a
short, diagonally placed spire. The style is late C13, the execution rather mechanical. The best feature is the staircase,
rising in an apse. At the half level it is joined by a straight
flight from a two-storeyed gallery which extends beyond the
apse. Council Chamber 1896–7 by *Lockwood* after a fire.
Several tympana with reliefs.* – INSIGNIA. Sword of State,
hilt C15, decoration and sheath 1668. – Great Mace, 1668. –
Oar by *Richard Richardson* of Chester, 1719–20. – Porter's
Staff, 1721. – PLATE. Two-Handled Cup, 1654; Tankards,
1668–9, 1669–70; Flagons, 1678–9, 1679–80; Ewer, 1679–80;
Flagons, 1684–5, 1685–6; three Salvers, 1701–2; Snuff Box,
1704–5; Flagon, 1725–6; Salver, 1729–30; two Punch Bowls,
1786, 1787; Tea Urn, obtained 1802.

GUILDHALL. See Holy Trinity, p. 152.

FIRE STATION, Northgate Street. The black and white part
with three semicircular oriels and three gables is of 1911.

(SWIMMING BATHS, Union Street. 1900–1 by *Douglas &*

---

* According to Mr Howell, those in the porch were designed by *S. F.
Lynn* and executed by *Williams* of Manchester.

Minshull. The front is of half-timbering above a brick and stone ground storey. Twisted chimneys. EH)

GROSVENOR MUSEUM, Grosvenor Street. 1885–6 by *Thomas M. Lockwood.*

BLUECOAT SCHOOL. *See* Perambulation, p. 161.

(QUEEN'S SCHOOL, City Walls Road. 1882–3 by *E. A. Ould.* Brick. Quite an enterprising Douglas-like building. EH)

(ST JOHN'S SCHOOL, Vicar's Lane. Built at the expense of the Duke of Westminster in 1882–3. Nothing special, even though the Duke employed *E. R. Robson* for this fairly sizable school job. EH)

(GATEWAY THEATRE. By *Michael Lyell Associates.* In the new shopping precinct by the Town Hall. 500 seats. The auditorium is cantilevered, and the entrance is below it.)

GENERAL STATION, Station Road. 1847–8 by *Francis Thompson.* [80] *C. H. Wild* was responsible for the original iron roofs, and *Robert Stephenson* was involved in his capacity as engineer of the Chester and Holyhead Railway. One of the most splendid early railway stations, extremely long, and, at least in its central part – very long in itself – excellently held together. This centre has as its l. and r. ends two frontispieces, both with two turrets. The style is Italianate, the material brick with ample stone dressings. A long extension on the l. side with arcading and a similar long wing on the r. side.*

DEE BRIDGE. Late C14, widened in 1826. (Seven irregular arches, some pointed, some segmental. The seventh arch from the city, i.e. that at the S end, is later. Originally there was a tower, the broad base of which remains, between the sixth and seventh arches, and this was probably approached by a drawbridge. The 1826 widening involved the corbelling out of the footwalk on the E side and the building of new arches in front of the E side of the first and third arches and the W side of the seventh, but the C14 moulded arch openings remain visible. Five of the six original arches have broad ribs. The power station W of the N end occupies the site of the celebrated Dee Mills which, like a predecessor of the present bridge, is known to have existed in Norman times. EH)

GROSVENOR BRIDGE. By *Harrison.* The proposal for a bridge to form a new link between the city centre and the road to

* (Altered behind the frontage, and the composition of the front itself suffers as a result of alterations and additions between the centre and the wings. Ornamental stonework by *John Thomas,* who, also for the Chester and Holyhead Railway, did the lions flanking the entrances of the Britannia Bridge. EH)

Wales originated in 1818. The present design dates from 1824, construction began in 1827 (under the supervision of *Jesse Hartley*, incidentally), and the bridge was finished in 1833 after Harrison's death. A beautiful single segmental arch with a span of 200 ft. The abutments have niches and carry pediments, and beyond them, at either end, a single semicircular arch links the bridge proper with the embankments on which the approach roads are carried.

QUEEN'S PARK BRIDGE, The Groves. A suspension bridge rebuilt in 1923.

(GROSVENOR PARK. Laid out at the expense of the second Marquess of Westminster. 1867 by *Edward Kemp*. The LODGE at the end of Grosvenor Park Road and a little Gothic structure near the river known as BILLY HOBBY'S WELL are by *John Douglas*. – STATUE of the second Marquess of Westminster. 1869 by *Thomas Thornycroft*. – RUINS. Three re-erected arches. They are the Shipgate from the City Walls, an arch from St Michael, Lower Bridge Street, and one from the Benedictine nunnery of St Mary, which stood near the castle. This arch is apparently C13. Two moulded orders and remains of shaft capitals. EH)

PERAMBULATION

The natural start is THE CROSS, the place where the two main Roman streets crossed.* First go N. The street is NORTHGATE STREET. On the E side little, though there are Rows.‡ On the W side No. 1, the CITY CLUB, originally COMMERCIAL NEWS ROOM. It is a beautiful ashlar-faced building by *Thomas Harrison*, 1808. Three rusticated segmental arches, and above them unfluted Ionic giant columns carrying a pediment. Chastely decorative panels above the main windows. Next is SHOEMAKERS' ROW, with a ground-level covered walkway, rebuilt from *c.*1897 onwards, replacing a true Row. Partly by *Douglas*. It is a very ambitious black and white group parts of which have Gothic decoration, oriels, etc. On the top corner is a statue of Edward VII. The street here widens out in front of the Town Hall, next to which the new shopping precinct by *Michael Lyell Associates* is under construction at the time of writing.§ For the &ATEWAY

---

* The remains of the High Cross are now re-set by the Newgate – see p. 165.

‡ Crypts under No. 8 and under No. 16 (Quaintways).

§ (It is unfortunate that the very effective Mid-Victorian Baroque frontage of the former market hall was not retained and incorporated. EH)

THEATRE, part of the same scheme, *see* p. 159. Opposite, BARCLAYS BANK is the former KING'S SCHOOL, occupying the site of the Bishop's Palace, a sizable Gothic stone building by *Sir A. W. Blomfield*, *c.*1875–7. The school hall is at once recognizable. For the ABBEY GATEWAY *see* p. 148. (Where the street again narrows is a typical *Harry Weedon* ODEON CINEMA. EH) Much plain Georgian, and the PIED BULL, with an C18 front, built out over the pavement, and with three segmental arches. (Late C16 or early C17 work inside, including a staircase. EH) Just before the Northgate, and set back from the street on the E side, is ABBEY GREEN, a Georgian brick terrace of two and a half storeys and thirteen bays overlooking a playing field.

The NORTHGATE is by *Harrison*, 1808–10, prominently signed and dated. Segmental arch, and l. and r. pairs of unfluted Doric demi-columns flanking pedestrian openings. Solid parapet.

Instead of passing through the Northgate, turn w into Water Tower Street and off its w end to KING'S BUILDINGS, a Georgian brick group dated 1776. Two Venetian doorways. King's Buildings lies by the new INNER RING ROAD, and here, opposite the new development, is one lonely survival, a Georgian four-bay house with a Gibbs doorway. (The inner ring road cuts through the city walls under ST MARTIN'S GATE, quite an elegant affair by the City Engineer, *A. H. F. Jiggens*, in association with the *Building Design Partnership*. In this region the walls, ring road, railway, and canal make a strangely complex pattern.* Slightly further w in TOWER ROAD is a remarkable survival – set against the city wall a model of the Grosvenor Bridge made for *Thomas Harrison*. EH)

Now back to the Northgate for UPPER NORTHGATE STREET, right at the start of which is the former BLUECOAT SCHOOL, built in 1717. Brick with stone dressings. Centre and two projecting wings. In the centre a pediment. Cupola. It has all the usual ingredients, but somehow the composition seems lame. Maybe the basket arches of the windows do it. (STATUE of a Bluecoat boy in a niche over the entrance, 1854 by *Edward Richardson*. At the rear ALMSHOUSES by *Morris & Hobson*, 1854. They are in connexion with the medieval foundation of the Hospital of St John, as is the CHAPEL, i.e. LITTLE

---

* Near by is the junction of the Chester Canal of *c.*1772–9 with *Telford*'s Ellesmere Canal of *c.*1793–5.

ST JOHN, which occupies the l. wing of the building. This also served the near-by gaol, and when the canal cutting was made, the now disused BRIDGE OF SIGHS was built in 1793 to maintain access. EH) (PLATE. Chalice, 1641; Paten by *Richard Richardson I*, 1716; Paten, *c.*1730; Chalice by *John Robins*, 1781.) On the same side of the street Nos. 11–13, mid C18, have a frontage projecting over the pavement and carried on columns, and at the N end the inner ring road breaks in. The roundabout with the well-intentioned fountains destroys the street continuity, and indeed the town scale.

Next EASTGATE STREET. (Prior to 1850, Georgian brick predominated, but in the second half of the C19 an almost complete transformation took place. An increase of scale and height was introduced, as well as stylistic variety, and, with its Rows, it is as a Victorian street of unique character that Eastgate Street must be viewed. EH) First the N side. Near the start, Nos. 9–13 (OWEN OWEN).* 1900. A late work of *Lockwood*, chief provider of late C19 black and white. No. 25 is by *T. A. Richardson*, 1861, of an early type of black and white to be looked at in greater detail on the other side of the street. The WESTMINSTER BANK is by *George Williams*, 1859–60. Stone, five bays, with a Corinthian giant order carrying a three-bay pediment. Then MARTINS BANK, stone ground floor, black and white above, plenty of Gothic details. It is by *Douglas* and part of his most ambitious scheme, the designing and building as his own developer of the whole E side of ST WERBURGH STREET, 1895–9. He first designed it in stone, but the Duke of Westminster wanted it in timber. The scheme was of course a speculation, but Douglas was moved by his respect for such an important site, close to the cathedral, and would not let it be built over piecemeal. The composition is Douglas at his best (though also at his showiest). He breaks it up into four units, all large, all going well with each other, but all having their own individualities.‡ The separate ST OSWALD'S CHAMBERS is also by *Douglas*. In the W part of St Werburgh Street is the former CHAPEL OF ST NICHOLAS, now a supermarket. All that remains of medieval work is along the S side. (This probably dates from an enlarging of the chapel in 1488. The Gothic front is of

* Where numbers are given they are those at street level, which differ from those at Row level.

‡ There is a plaque commemorating the architect on the St Werburgh Street side of Martins Bank.

1854–5 by *James Harrison*, who adapted the building as a concert hall. Beyond is St Werburgh Row, 1935 by *Maxwell Ayrton*. EH) Back into Eastgate Street. No. 37 is by *C. A. Ewing*, very high, and the Midland Bank, a high brick and stone building with turrets, is of 1883–4 by *Douglas & Fordham*, enlarged in 1908.

So to the Eastgate, 1768–9, with a rusticated elliptical arch. On it jolly ironwork carrying a Diamond Jubilee Clock, 1897–9. *Douglas* again, and surprisingly playful. (From the top of the Eastgate can be enjoyed a particularly good view of the street, with the vista closed by a glimpse of the Welsh hills. EH) On into Foregate Street (*see* below).

On the s side of Eastgate Street returning to The Cross there are the following. First the Grosvenor Hotel, 1863–6, large and dull. Begun by *T. M. Penson* and completed after his death by *R. K. Penson & Ritchie*. The client was the second Marquess of Westminster, i.e. the Grosvenor estate, which was responsible for much of the C19 rebuilding of Chester. Then an entrance to a new shopping precinct (*see* Bridge Street below), followed by No. 52 (Row number), the recent facsimile of a very handsome early C18 brick house with a big shaped gable.* No. 36 and No. 34, lowish and relatively modest, are both of 1856 by *T. M. Penson* and are the earliest remaining examples of the half-timber revival. No. 38, the original part of Browns of Chester, of *c*.1828, Greek Revival, has two unexpectedly solemn Doric columns. Then Browns Crypt Buildings, a big, asymmetrical E.E. stone job with a tower, by *Penson*, 1858, i.e. quite an early instance of High Victorian Gothic. Underneath is one of the best of the medieval crypts of Chester. Entrance with small 16 windows l. and r.; rib-vault with ridge ribs; four bays. The date is probably after 1300. No. 26 which follows has a half-timbered frontage dating from a *Penson* restoration of 1859 for the Marquess of Westminster. (Earlier work remaining includes an C18 staircase. MHLG) No. 22 is genuine – 1640 – and it is followed by some Georgian work, providing an indication of what the pre-Penson Eastgate Street was like.

---

* The Chester half-timber revival began *c*.1850 with the restoration, virtually a rebuilding, by *T. M. Penson* of a shop which occupied part of the site of the three-gabled half-timbered block which follows here. The revival was, in its early years, applauded and encouraged by the newly-formed local historical and archaeological society. Illustrations of Penson's work of the 1850s, with some significant comment, can also be found in *The Builder* (EH).

90 Towards the end of the street No. 2, of 1888 by *T. M. Lockwood* for the Duke of Westminster, is large, with a gable and much rich ornament. Far more knowledgeable than the earlier C19 half-timber. For the adjoining corner building *see* Bridge Street.

FOREGATE STREET ought to be walked before the return journey up Eastgate Street. It was one of the first streets to be built up outside the walls, though little of early date survives.

See p. 441

On the N side the DISTRICT BANK is ornate black and white and as late as 1921. No. 71 is mid Georgian and has Gibbs arches and columns. No. 77 is C17 timber-framing, small, with herringbone bracing and a coving under the eaves. (Towards the end of the street are two buildings with diapered brick, etc., reminiscent of the Eaton estate. They flank the entrance to PARKER'S BUILDINGS, 1889, built as tenements for retired Eaton employees. At THE BARS, the site of an outer defence work of the city, is WILLIAMS DEACONS BANK, by *Thomas M. Lockwood & Sons*, c.1893. In connexion with the inner ring road, much demolition is in progress here at the time of writing. EH) On the S side of Foregate Street, No. 142 is by *Douglas*, 1884, brick with a large gable, in Flemish Renaissance style. Now turn into GROSVENOR PARK ROAD for a brilliant group of brick houses by *Douglas*, c.1879. The composition is excellent, varied yet enough of a unity. How much more convincing Douglas is where the temptation to fussiness inherent in the magpie technique is avoided. The Baptist Church (*see* p. 153) is part of the group. Back into Foregate Street and now into BATH STREET for another *Douglas* group, this time of c.1902–3 (i.e. *Douglas & Minshull*). It starts with the LOMBARD BANK at the corner and is on a smaller scale – one storey and dormers. Most of it, with three of his round turrets, is symmetrical, but not all. Again back into Foregate Street and after a while into LOVE STREET for FOREST HOUSE, c. 1784, which must have been the grandest Georgian house in Chester. Originally it had a courtyard opening on to Foregate Street. The very high three-bay block which remains has a pedimented gable. High rusticated ground floor with arched windows. The main upper windows have balustrading.* Back into FOREGATE STREET yet again. (Further W is the ROYAL OAK, one of the numer-

---

* Mr Howell reports good plasterwork and an octagon room on the ground floor. Also a vestibule with, at either end, a screen of two Ionic columns carrying an arch. There is said to be a further octagon on the upper floor.

ous instances of the half-timber revival being continued into
the C20. It was rebuilt by *F. Davies*, 1920. A few yards further
on a ground-floor passage leads to the UNION HALL, built in
1809 for tradesmen attending the Chester fairs. A galleried
court, of which the E and part of the S sides remain. Three-
storey. Iron columns. EH) The BLOSSOMS HOTEL is of 1896
by *Thomas M. Lockwood & Sons* and 1911 probably by one of
the sons, i.e. either *P. H.* or *W. T. Lockwood*. Between this
and the Eastgate is LLOYDS BANK,* Greek Revival, of three
bays, ashlar-faced, with a central feature with engaged Tuscan
columns below and tripartite window and pediment above, and
then OLD BANK BUILDINGS, 1895 by *T. M. Lockwood &
Sons*. (Lockwood at his best. The frontage is all half-timber,
projecting over the pavement on piers. Asymmetrical with,
on the l., two jettied gables and, set further back, a turret.
Ornament is sparingly and effectively used, e.g. the brackets.
Some of the windows have the arched centre lights of which
Lockwood was so fond. EH)

Now S into ST JOHN'S STREET for No. 6, a very good mid C18
house of five bays and two storeys with raised ground floor.
Outer steps to a doorway with fluted Corinthian pilasters and
pediment. Also fluted Corinthian ground-floor angle pilasters.
At the end of the street and to the r. is the NEWGATE. (A
wide arch with two towers by *Sir Walter Tapper* and *Michael
Tapper*. Built in connexion with plans for the ring road and
completed in 1938. Immediately N of it is the WOLF GATE.
The present opening dates from the early C17, and is thus
the oldest remaining gateway in the city walls. EH) Outside the
Newgate, near the so-called Roman Garden, are the re-
erected remains of the HIGH CROSS which stood at The
Cross but which was demolished in the Civil War. Lantern
head with spire and ball-finial, part of which is original.
Through the Newgate to PARK STREET for the six left over of
the NINE HOUSES. They are genuine – mid C17 – and low,
each with a gable. The windows redone. Their neighbour (by
W. H. Kelly) is of 1881 and hence bigger and better. Out
again through the Newgate‡ to VICAR'S LANE for the
GROSVENOR CLUB, the former rectory of St John's. Mid
C18. Five bays, two and a half storeys. Doorway with Gibbs
surround and pediment. From here the YMCA building
above THE GROVES can be reached by way of the lane at the

* Mr Howell states that it is probably by *Lewis Wyatt*.
‡ (The ALMSHOUSES in LUMLEY PLACE are probably *Douglas*. EH)

w end of St John's church. Large. Two and a half storeys. It was built *c.*1750 by Bishop Peploe, and of this period is the portion with quoins, rusticated window heads, etc. The canted bay and the portion w of it came a little later, though the bay may mask part of the original building. Behind it is a room with the most exuberant C18 stucco decoration in Chester. It is typical 1750s. s of St John's is THE HERMITAGE, said to have been an anchorite's cell, but the present house is evidently built of materials from the church. (The Groves itself is a tree-lined riverside road, with a pleasant group of buildings beyond the suspension bridge. EH)

90 Next BRIDGE STREET. No. 1 adjoins the big gable in Eastgate Street already referred to, and like it is by *T. M. Lockwood,* 1888, for the Duke of Westminster. It forms an ornate corner half-timber, with a turret. (On the opposite corner, Nos. 2–4, 1892, is also by *Lockwood* for the Duke. High; a combination of half-timber with brick. Also blue brick diapering à la Eaton estate and stone bands and dressings. Lockwood's typical Renaissance ornament and round-headed centre window lights. Bridge Street is shorter and broader than Eastgate Street, with a higher proportion of pre-Victorian buildings remaining. It is not in direct line with Northgate Street, which makes for good townscape at The Cross, and the relationship of St Peter's to the street is particularly happy. As the Rows came to be adapted to serve the commercial needs of a flourishing county town, the most fashionable shops tended to concentrate on the s side of Eastgate Street and the E side of Bridge Street, both now entirely given over to shopping. The w side of Bridge Street, however, interestingly retains something of a domestic character, with generally low headroom. EH) As regards the E side, there is a sequence of specially conspicuous Rows. No. 15 has a crypt with two double-chamfered segmental arches. Midway down is ST MICHAEL'S BUILDINGS. Very large. Imitation black and white. As first rebuilt by *W. T. Lockwood* in 1910 for the Grosvenor estate, it was faced with white faience, but was given its present appearance by order of the second Duke of Westminster. Faience still remains at street level and in the spacious ST MICHAEL'S ARCADE, which extends back from the Row. Considering its date, it is remarkable to find an elevated shopping street, and it can have needed no effort to link it up with the new shopping precinct (the GROSVENOR-LAING development) which was built in 1963–5 to designs by

Sir Percy Thomas & Son. (No. 43 is a genuine half-timber survival. C17. Narrow frontage with a gable. EH)

The following are the notable buildings on the W side of Bridge Street, though first one should continue down Lower Bridge Street and also explore some side streets (*see* below). The THREE OLD ARCHES is so called after a row of three single-chamfered arches. (There are C13 cellars. Nos. 44–6 is the best of the several Georgian fronts in the street. Two storeys above the Row, with rusticated stone window heads. No. 40 is by *James Harrison*, 1858, minor, and on the opposite corner of Commonhall Street No. 38 is by *Douglas & Fordham*, 1897. Black and white with much Douglassy timber ornament. EH) Nos. 22–6 is mid C17. Timber framing, plastered over. It has on two upper storeys a system of engaged twisted columns. Also twisted balusters at Row level. No. 20, THE PLANE TREE, is by *Lockwood*, c.1873, and much less showy than he was to be later. Half-timbered, symmetrical, with some flower patterns in the plasterwork. No. 12, COWPER HOUSE, is mid C17, and has one uncommon motif in the gable. Windows not original. It has a fine crypt of six bays of plain rib-vaulting on plain corbels. Single-chamfered ribs. Three windows at the far end. Also a doorway with a trefoiled head. So back to The Cross.

LOWER BRIDGE STREET continues S down to the Dee Bridge. On the E side Nos. 29–31 probably of 1603, timber-framed, with ogee herringbone bracing. (It contains a now-enclosed Row, and fragments of this former Row are visible in buildings to the N. EH) The TALBOT HOTEL, originally Park House, is of 1715, with a Tuscan porch and an enriched surround to the window above the porch. No. 51 is yet a little older. Good stone doorcase with open scrolly pediment. The end on this side is a Georgian group called BRIDGE PLACE. The BRIDGEGATE is of 1782 by *Joseph Turner*. Segmental arch and two arched pedestrian passages. Balustrades and some rustication. Opposite Bridge Place, going back, there is first the BEAR AND BILLET, as late as 1664, with one gable. Three storeys below the gable. Continuous window bands on two floors. Enriched brackets, beams, etc. At least some of the fenestration dates from a C19 restoration. At the corner of Shipgate Street Nos. 86–88 is also timber-framed, with two gables and two projecting windows. (And in SHIPGATE STREET is the mid C18 SHIPGATE HOUSE. EH) Nos. 80–84 is brick, splayed at the upper corner of Shipgate Street.

Higher in Lower Bridge Street GAMUL HOUSE looks derelict at the time of writing. The façade rises off an elevated terrace and looks like that of a chapel. There are two (apparently formerly at least three) elliptical windows (the large segment-headed windows may be later insertions) and a central doorway with pediment. It is probably of *c.*1700. (Inside, a fireplace with the Gamul arms probably painted by *Randle Holme*. Also, according to the NMR, brackets and pendants of a Jacobean roof and a Jacobean chimneypiece with fancy pilasters.) In CASTLE STREET No. 23 has a nice door surround, No. 25 a quoined centre bay with pediment. Back in Lower Bridge Street, at the corner of Castle Street, is the OLD KING'S HEAD, C17, the top storey timber-framed, with some herringbone bracing and coving below two of the three gables. Further up are some Georgian brick houses in dilapidated condition, and BRIDGE HOUSE, early C18, of six bays with two tiers of pilasters. Bracketed cornice. Later shops obscure the lower stage. Good staircase with a Venetian window to the side elevation. The end is THE FALCON. Good C17 timber-framing (said to be 1626) above an earlier base which incorporates a C13 crypt. Two gables on coving. There is a continuous band of windows on the first floor with quatrefoils below. (Formerly a Row passed through the building. EH)*

GROSVENOR STREET was the first major alteration to the Romano-medieval street system. It was broken through diagonally from the foot of Bridge Street. In it is the TRUSTEE SAVINGS BANK, 1851-3 by *James Harrison*, Tudor Gothic, with a corner turret.‡ PEPPER STREET now carries the inner ring road, and the Grosvenor-Laing shopping precinct (*see* above) presents a long frontage to it. In WHITEFRIARS No. 1 is dated 1658. It is timber-framed and small, but with two gables. One of them is pargetted. The upper windows are on

* The Victorian enthusiasm for half-timber in Chester was not confined to the building of new specimens: the genuine ones underwent restoration, with Georgian sash windows being removed, etc., and the present appearance of The Falcon owes much to a restoration apparently by *Grayson & Ould*, *c.*1886, rather than, as has been stated, by *Douglas*, *c.*1893 (EH).

‡ The street was formed *c.*1825-30 and was planned by *Thomas Harrison* in connexion with his Grosvenor Bridge (*see* p. 159), i.e. as a new route between the city centre and the road to Wales. Apart from the castle itself, the only other building of Harrison's time to survive in the immediate neighbourhood is his own house – ST MARTIN'S LODGE in CASTLE ESPLANADE to the N. The Police Headquarters (*see* p. 158) is an unwelcome successor to a castellated barracks by *Penson* (EH).

carved corbels. Further on much undisturbed Georgian brick development.

The fourth main direction is w, i.e. down WATERGATE STREET (now the quietest and least commercialized of the main streets, with the Rows retaining something of a semi-domestic character: EH). First the s side. The *Lockwood* building at The Cross has already been mentioned. No. 9, GOD'S PROVIDENCE HOUSE, was of 1652 but was reconstructed in 1862.* No. 11 is of 1744. The Row has Tuscan columns. (C18 staircase. MHLG) Beneath‡ is a late C13 crypt. Two-naved, four bays, with octagonal columns and single-chamfered ribs without ridge ribs. The street has in fact more crypts than any other. The LECHE HOUSE is mid or late C16.§ Half-timbered frontage with a gable, and unusual in Chester in that its Georgian sash windows remain. Great hall set back at r. angles to the street. Jacobean work included the obscuring with a plaster ceiling of the open roof of the hall (though beams of the roof tell of it). A strikingly big plaster pendant. Plaster also the overmantel, Jacobean, with columns and an achievement of arms. There are scanty remains of plaster friezes, too. C17 extension at the back of the house, and also a nice open gallery on a fluted column. No. 23 has another rib-vaulted crypt with single-chamfered ribs on corbels. (Yet another crypt at No. 37.) Now for BISHOP LLOYD'S HOUSE, early C17, timber-framed, and perhaps the best in Chester. Two gables. Decorated posts and brackets at Row level. Also carved panels of religious subjects, and, in the r. gable, closely-set panels and caryatids. The windows all belong to *Lockwood*'s restoration of *c*.1899. (Chinese Chippendale staircase. Two good rooms above the Row.) (One room with modest stucco ceiling and an overmantel with a cupid on a lion and turreted pilasters. (In the other room a stucco ceiling with all-over geometrical patterns and a mid

* It is by *James Harrison*, larger and more elaborate than its predecessor, but incorporating some timberwork from it. Like many of the Victorian timber buildings it was dated (1862), but this has recently been obscured. Mr David Lloyd reports that, at a time when the Chester and North Wales Architectural, Archaeological, and Historical Society was regretting the loss of ancient buildings in Chester and encouraging the half-timber revival, the threatened destruction of the C17 house caused a storm of protest. The owner remained adamant in his intention to demolish, but agreed to the building of a timber replacement (EH).

‡ I.e. QUELLYN ROBERTS.

§ Mr Lloyd states that there are remains of a central hearth beneath the present floor of the hall.

C17 chimneypiece. NMR)* A little further on the OLD
CUSTOM HOUSE INN, dated 1637, small, with an asymmetrical oriel and a crypt. Below, the inner ring road intrudes. On
the w side of NICHOLAS STREET, the section which runs s
from here, a long, even terrace of brick houses survives. It
dates from 1781. Beyond, in Watergate Street, is the STANLEY
PALACE, dating from 1591. The three l. gables of the elevation
at r. angles to the street are of this date. The decoration is
mostly concave-sided lozenges. Some ornamented brackets
etc. Heavily restored in 1935, and the r. gable and street
frontage are of this time. WATERGATE HOUSE is by *Harrison*,
c.1820. Brick. It has the entrance at the angle and behind it a
fine square hall with canted corners, two-storey and top-lit.
Segmental projection on the garden front.

The WATERGATE was built in 1788. (The Dee formerly flowed
near to the Watergate. The quays etc. of the port of Chester
were in this region, and New Crane Street and Paradise Row
were laid out in connexion with a partial revival of maritime
trade in the 1730s. Nothing requiring an excursion outside
the walls remains, however. Instead turn r. into CITY WALLS
ROAD and r. again into STANLEY PLACE, a short street of
Georgian houses dating from c.1778. At the w end of the s
side, facing City Walls Road, is a sedan chair porch with a
door on two sides. EH)

Back on the N side of Watergate Street. First a sequence of
Georgian houses. Beyond Holy Trinity, No. 68 is Early
Georgian with segment-headed windows with ornamental
keystones. (Nos. 40–42 and No. 38 retain remains of medieval
cellars. Apparently a house with hall and chamber lay back
at the rear, behind three shops, and with a cellar extending
under the whole building.‡) Nos. 28–34, the BOOTH MAN-
SION, is early C18. Brick with stone quoins etc. Eight bays.
Two storeys above Row level. Tuscan columns at the Row.
Bracketed cornice. Medieval arches span the Row. (Nos. 28–30
has a cellar with a longitudinal arcade of four, originally five,
bays. Also a medieval cellar further back in Nos. 32–34.)
Further up the street some C18 brick frontages. (No. 4, DEVA
HOTEL, has an Elizabethan staircase and a Jacobean chimney-
piece. MHLG)

* According to Mr Howell, panelling and one chimneypiece were brought
from elsewhere.

‡ See P. A. Faulkner, 'Mediaeval Undercrofts and Town Houses',
Archaeological Journal, vol. 123, 1966.

That completes the main Perambulation. One extra item must however be added: the QUEEN HOTEL in STATION ROAD, opposite the General Station. This is four-storeyed and Italianate, with a big porch, the whole composition stodgy as these Italianate hotels tend to be. First built in 1860–1 by *T. M. Penson*; it was, however, burnt in 1861 and rebuilt by *Penson* and *Cornelius Sherlock* in 1862, without its original high roofs.

OUTER CHESTER

WEST, NORTH WEST, AND NORTH

(ST THERESA (R.C.), Blacon Avenue, Blacon. 1959 by *Reynolds & Scott*. Although a visit is not necessarily recommended, the building may be cited as an average example of the many churches put up in Cheshire and elsewhere by these architects. There is even another one in a different part of Chester. EH)

ST THOMAS OF CANTERBURY, Parkgate Road. 1869–72 by *Sir George Gilbert Scott*. Nave completed later by *J. O. Scott*. Unfortunately the intended SE tower was never built. Ashlar interior. Nave and chancel. Aisles but no clerestory. Pairs of shafted lancets. Quatrefoil piers with stiff-leaf capitals. All rather mechanical. – (Some good FURNISHINGS by *C. E. Deacon*, including e.g. the REREDOS, 1909, and NE chapel REREDOS, 1913. EH) – STAINED GLASS. The W window by *Kempe*, 1885. – PLATE. Set of 1725.

The VICARAGE is of 1880 by *Douglas*.

HOLY TRINITY, Norris Road, Blacon. Not of architectural interest, but in it is the C16 SWORD CASE from Holy Trinity, Watergate Street, and the PLATE from the same church: Cup and Cover by *William Mutton*, c.1570; Paten, 1694; two Flagons, 1727; Chalice by *R. Richardson* of Chester, 1752.

CHESTER COLLEGE, Parkgate Road. 1841–2 by *J. C. & G. Buckler*. By them the front to the street (i.e. E front), E-shaped with mullioned and transomed windows, though like the S front it has suffered alteration in recent years. A new building by the *Design Group Partnership* is awkwardly placed and defeats the scale of the college. – The CHAPEL is by *J. E. Gregan* of Manchester, 1844–7. (Dec. Rock-faced, with a spired turret. Ashlar interior. Steep hammerbeam roof and rows of STALLS facing each other. The chapel was partly built, and the FITTINGS almost entirely made, by students of the college, who were, in Ruskinian manner, instructed in manual labour and crafts, a forge being provided on the premises. – STAINED GLASS. E window also made by students and staff. – ORGAN CASE. 1856. Designed by the Rev. *T. N. Hutchinson*, vice-principal of the college and the son of Rickman's partner. – MONUMENT. Arthur Rigg, 1883 by *J. S. Westmacott*. EH)

MERSEYSIDE AND NORTH WALES ELECTRICITY BOARD, Sealand Road. 1968–70 by *Stroud, Nullis & Partners*. A large group, the main building Y-shaped and seven storeys high. The concrete frame allows a 53 ft clear span for the offices. The canteen building is 150 ft long and has an 80 ft clear span. Not complete at the time of writing.

NORTH EAST

ALL SAINTS, Hoole Road, Hoole. 1867 by *Dawkes*. Large, rock-faced, with a SW steeple and plate tracery. Dull interior. S aisle 1912.

ST COLUMBA (R.C.), Plas Newton Lane, Newton. By *L. A. G. Prichard, Son & Partners*. Five sides of an octagon; only the back flat with a steep pyramid steeple, and the jabbing roofs church architects at present like so much. – STAINED GLASS. Good abstract glass by *Hans Unger & E. Schulze*.

CONGREGATIONAL CHURCH, Hoole Road, Hoole. By *Paterson & Macaulay*, 1957–8. With an excessively steep roof starting very low.

By the roundabout at the end of HOOLE ROAD is the entrance to HOOLE HALL. Georgian at first sight, but probably Early Victorian.* Brick, five bays, two storeys, quoins, pedimental gable. Round the corner an elevation with two symmetrical bow windows, articulated by tiers of columns. Large conservatory.

EAST

ST PAUL, Boughton. By *Douglas*, 1876; the S aisle added by him in 1902 and the spiralet in 1905. The church is built on steeply falling ground, and hence the three-sided apse looks very impressive seen from below. The fenestration is mostly lancet. But the strength of this church is the internal timber-work, heralded by the brick-nogged exterior of the S aisle. The nave and original aisles, included under the main roof span and extending the full width of the broad apse, have a

* Though Twycross refers to a house having been built following the purchase of the property in 1757.

lofty wooden arcade, and there are big roof timbers including transverse braces. A brick and stone arcade separates the later S aisle. – Wrought-iron SCREEN. – Charming Arts and Crafts WALL DECORATION in paint, no doubt c.1902. – STAINED GLASS. In the N aisle *Kempe*, 1887. – In the baptistery by *Frampton*.* – All the rest by *Morris & Co.*, i.e. *Burne-Jones*. The E windows are of 1881, the SE window is 1887, the S aisle E window 1899, the rest are of the decline after the deaths of the two great men. The apse E window in particular is gorgeous. – PLATE. Chalice, 1804; Chalice, 1830.

CAMPBELL MEMORIAL HALL. 1894–7 by *Lockwood*. Brick, with shaped gables, and with half-timbered gables to the front and on the side elevation facing The Mount.

WORKHOUSE (former), Heath Lane, Great Boughton. 1857–8, yet still classical, though after e.g. Scott & Moffatt's workhouses. Long and low, with a three-bay centre.‡

PERAMBULATION. Beginning at The Bars, i.e. at the E end of Foregate Street, is the street called BOUGHTON. Almost immediately, on the S side, is the entrance to DEE HILLS PARK, where there are two notable houses. One is DEE HILLS (now government offices) by *Thomas Harrison*, 1814. Two storeys, stuccoed. To the river a segmental projection with Ionic columns. The other house, UFFINGTON HOUSE, 1885, was built for Thomas Hughes of the *Schooldays*. Brick, with a turret. By *Ould*, and obviously influenced by Douglas, whose pupil he was. To the N of Boughton is the SHOT TOWER, quite a big specimen. It was built in 1799. Then off Boughton, lying back on the S, SANDOWN TERRACE, with a frontage to the river. Italianate. A symmetrical terrace of three substantial houses, with a tower at either end. Probably early 1850s. In Boughton, near St Paul's, is a group of Late Georgian houses. The best are Nos. 125–127, with unfluted Ionic columns carrying a balcony, and Nos. 129–131, stuccoed, with giant pilasters with freely detailed capitals. (At THE MOUNT is an open space, marking the site of the burial ground of the medieval Hospital of St Giles. A half-timbered building at the fork in the street at the end of Boughton is by *Douglas & Minshull*, 1900, and groups well with St Paul's and the adjoining buildings. EH) About ⅜ m. SE in DEE BANKS is WALMOOR HILL (now the County Fire Brigade Head-

* According to Dean Addleshaw.
‡ Now demolished.

quarters), the house *John Douglas* built for himself in 1896. It
is a stone house of considerable panache, proof of the wealth
a successful provincial architect could assemble. Above the
portal is a private chapel, and next to them a turret. To the
river, owing to the steep fall of the ground, the house appears
of four storeys. Mullioned and transomed windows. Roofs
recessed behind parapets. In the same road Nos. 31–33 is,
according to Mr Howell's convincing suggestion, by *Douglas*
earlier on – 1869 – with one of the two houses for himself. A
pair, Gothic like North Oxford, and of brick with diapers.

SOUTH AND SOUTH WEST

St Mark, High Street, Saltney. 1892–3 by *Lockwood*. Brick,
with a bell-turret and lancets. Architecturally indifferent. –
Some post-Kempe STAINED GLASS by *Tower*.

St Mary-without-the-Walls, Overleigh Road, Handbridge. 1885–7 by *F. B. Wade* for the Duke of Westminster.
Large, with a w steeple, and mostly lancet windows. A high
interior, ashlar, with a high chancel arch. The piers are octagonal, but with concave diagonal faces – a sign that Wade
intended to be original. Another such feature is the two parallel
transverse wooden tunnel-vaults of the SE chapel, a third the
open triforium of the organ chamber. – The REREDOS is the
95   most interesting piece in the church. It was designed by
Frederic Shields in 1888 and made in cloisonné by *Clement
Heaton*. The reredos itself is a kind of North Italian Quattrocento handled extremely well and unsentimentally. The side
pieces are later – 1896 – and somewhat different in style –
more Burne-Jonesish. – (STAINED GLASS. Several windows
by *Edward Frampton*, 1887 and 1896. EH) – PLATE (from St
Mary-on-the-Hill). Elizabethan Cup and Cover; Credence
Paten, 1638; large Paten by *Nathaniel Bullen* of Chester,
1683; Flagon, London, 1712–13; Flagon by *Thomas Robinson*
of Chester, 1711–12; Flagon by *Thomas Robinson* of Chester,
1734; Spoon, 1750; Almsdish, 1822.
    The RECTORY is by *Grayson & Ould*.

Old Cemetery, Grosvenor Road. 1848–50. An eminently
picturesque layout by *T. M. Penson*,* originally with a lake. A
Norman CHAPEL by Penson remains. (N of the chapel a
MONUMENT to Chancellor Raikes † 1854, with sculpture by
Thomas Earp. EH)

City High School, Queen's Park Road. 1909–12 by *W. T.*
    * According to Mr Howell.

Lockwood. Symmetrical. Brick and much stone. Big shaped gables, but the centre pedimented, with a cupola, rather William and Mary.

CITY GRAMMAR SCHOOL, Queen's Park Road. 1939–41 by *Charles Greenwood.* Much chaster, squared-up Neo-Georgian.

WESTERN COMMAND HEADQUARTERS, Queen's Park Road. 1937 by the *War Office Directorate of Fortifications and Works.* A nonentity.

PERAMBULATION. In MILL STREET, at the S end of the Dee Bridge, are new flats, close to the river. They are by *Gilling, Dod & Partners.* At the E end of Queen's Park Road is QUEEN'S PARK, a residential estate laid out by *James Harrison c.*1851. Winding roads returning on themselves. Two or three Italianate villas remain, beside the river in LOWER PARK ROAD. (VICTORIA PATHWAY is a leafy, straight pedestrian walk, with small gabled houses of brick. EH) Next, return W to HANDBRIDGE. (Some buildings of recognizable Grosvenor estate character. Particularly, in OVERLEIGH ROAD, near the church, the HANDBRIDGE MEN'S INSTITUTE, 1895, which must presumably be *Lockwood,* and a COTTAGE at the SE corner of the churchyard, 1887 by *Douglas & Fordham.* EH) EATON ROAD (*see* below) leads off from here. Further W again to the roundabout at the end of Grosvenor Road. Here is the OVERLEIGH LODGE of Eaton Hall (*see* p. 212) and an entrance, past an Italianate lodge, to CURZON PARK, another villa estate. It must be of about the same time as Queen's Park, and has some original Italianate houses. Later houses include No. 11 CURZON PARK NORTH, 1967–8 by *T. O. Pottinger & Partners,* and in the same road No. 30, early C20 by *P. H. Lockwood.*

Finally an outlying item, GREENBANK, c. ½ m. S of Handbridge in EATON ROAD, of *c.*1812–25, and one of the best Georgian houses of Chester. Stuccoed. Two storeys. Seven-bay front. The centre three bays rise higher than the rest and have giant pilasters and also garlanded panels above the main windows. The doorway is of 1923 by Professor *Reilly* of Liverpool. Separate GATEHOUSE with pediment and running dog frieze also probably by *Reilly.**

* For many years the house belonged to Peter Jones, the Ellesmere Port industrialist for whom, as Mr Alan Crawford has discovered, cottages were designed by *C. R. Ashbee* (*see* p. 217) as part of an attempt to make of Ellesmere Port 'something better than the ordinary'. Mr Crawford refers to furniture and jewellery designed for Jones by Ashbee, and Reilly wrote enthusiastically of his enlightenment as a connoisseur and as a man of

At Heronbridge, s of Greenbank, between Watling Street and the river Dee, evidence of an extensive ROMAN SETTLEMENT has come to light. Several buildings and a dock have been located, associated with traces of industrial activity.

At Saltney also traces of ROMAN occupation were found, suggesting a small settlement site.

CHILDER THORNTON see HOOTON

5050
CHOLMONDELEY CASTLE

Cholmondeley Castle was built in 1801–c.30. The Old Hall was E of it. It was a building of 1571, of brick and half-timbering, and c.1713–15 *Sir John Vanbrugh* remodelled it. It was demolished when the new house was begun. Only one fragment of three bays with angle pilasters survives, and in addition the chapel.

The CHAPEL consists of a C14 to C15 chancel, timber-framed and encased in 1716, but with the original elaborate hammerbeam roof with blank as well as openwork tracery. The chapel itself was rebuilt and enlarged in 1652–5 and received transepts in 1829. The mid C17 FURNISHINGS are the most complete of their date in Cheshire. SCREEN. Dated
51 1655. High, with strapwork just turning gristly. – PULPIT r. of the screen and LECTERN l. of the screen. – COMMUNION RAIL. With the horizontal openwork ovals typical of the mid C17. – BOX PEWS. – FAMILY PEW. Raised, at the w end. With strapwork on a coat of arms against the w wall. The staircase is early C18. – STAINED GLASS. The familiar small Netherlandish roundels. – PLATE. German Chalice, German Paten, and German Almsdish. The Chalice is apparently Cologne-made and has Prussian coats of arms. The Paten is from Nuremberg and has Jacob and the peeled rods. The Almsdish has Prussian arms again and the date 1711.

Outside, two wrought-iron GATES and the W stair RAILING. They come from the Old Hall, and are in all probability by the *Davies Brothers*, a foretaste of things to come.
74 The castle was built in a better position, raised, with a view over fine landscaping with a lake. The house is large and all castellated. The earliest part dates from 1801–4 and was designed by the *Marquess of Cholmondeley* himself. To the

---

business. At the same time that Reilly was working at Greenbank, gates and railings, now destroyed, were supplied by the *Birmingham Guild* (EH).

entrance are two three-bay wings a little projecting, and between them a one-storeyed loggia. The E side corresponding to this part is contemporary. So is the Entrance Hall, a square room with Gothic wooden vertical and horizontal divisions. In one of the three E rooms in the part of 1801–4 is a chimneypiece of various dark marbles. Spacious staircase made splendid by the use of the *Davies* railing from the Old Hall.

In 1817 *Robert Smirke* was called in, no doubt on the strength of his medievalizing work at Lowther and Eastnor Castles. He added on the E front the r. end with the turret, and he added the l. turret. The extension of the low rectangular tower in the centre, however, by the addition of a large canted bay window dates only from after 1828 (cf. Neale's *Seats*). On the s side Smirke did the big round tower (1819) and the l. corner tower (1817) and thereby nearly but not quite hid the building of 1801–4.* The l. corner tower is of course the r. corner tower of the w front. On the N side also an extra tower was built. The effect was not only enlargement but also the introduction of romantic drama into the staid, conventional Gothic of 1801–4.

WHITE GATES, W of the castle. A capital work of the *Davies* 61 *Brothers*. The openwork turrets are characteristic (cf. Chirk). Also some wrought-iron stair-railings on the s side.

STABLES. Victorian; not ornate. Large, of brick, with a courtyard. Good gatehouse.

INNER GATEHOUSE. Plain. No doubt designed by the *Marquess of Cholmondeley*.

OUTER GATEHOUSE, to the E. 1854. With stepped gables and a turret.

CHORLEY HALL *see* ALDERLEY EDGE

CHORLTON *see* BACKFORD *and* MALPAS

CHRISTLETON   4060

ST JAMES. The tower is late C15, but not its top, with the higher stair-turret and the short set-back pyramid roof. That is *Butterfield*, and Christleton is Butterfield's only church in Cheshire. It was built in 1875–7. The interior spells his name clearly, though it has nothing of his aggressiveness. But the

* The dates of the Smirke additions were discovered by Dr Alistair Rowan.

stonework is red and white alternating and the proportions of nave and aisles are powerful. Goodhart-Rendel's notes say more; they could not be bettered, and so they are reprinted here: 'This is Butterfield with "Perpendicular" detail, and very characteristic none the less. Nave and chancel with aisles to nave. Continuous roof and a low tower, with solid tympanum masking the division between nave and chancel – no other distinction. Sanctuary roof richly ceiled but of same polygonal section as trussed rafter roof over remainder of chancel and nave. Two-light clerestory windows *over piers*. Three-light E window is very high over typical alabaster and mosaic reredos. Material red sandstone with a good deal of chessboard work in white sandstone informally. All windows under eaves have beams (wood) instead of rere-arches – and amusing corbels. Top stage of old tower most quaint and original – almost suggesting Douglas – a sort of square slated pigeonhouse with a spire roof set inside the battlements. Nice parapet stepped up very oddly and boldly. I think this an exceptionally interesting church.' – SCREEN. Of wrought iron. – Big REREDOS. *See above.* – STAINED GLASS. W window by *Gibbs*, 1877; disappointing. – Most of the other glass *Kempe*: 1884–1904. – PLATE. Almsbasin, 1595; Flagon, 1719–20, London; Flagon, 1722, London; Cup and Paten by *Richard Richardson* of Chester, 1723.

ALMSHOUSES. By the pond. By *J. O. Scott*. Black and white.

8050

CHURCH LAWTON

ALL SAINTS. The S doorway is Norman, with decorated multi-scalloped capitals and zigzag in the arch. Perp W tower, apparently of two campaigns. The large J. B. with a chalice refers to John Byber, rector. The nave is of 1803, brick, with along the sides a lunette, two round-arched windows and another lunette. – WEST GALLERY. – MONUMENT. John Byber † 1555. Plain tomb-chest under a plain four-centred arch. Byber's initials in the same kind of letters as on the tower.

LAWTON HALL. A C17 house, though that is not recognizable externally. But inside are two Jacobean fireplaces and a C17 staircase with vertically symmetrical balusters. The exterior is mid C18. Nine-bay front of two high storeys in the centre, but two and a half in the side parts. In addition lower wings, the r. one ending in a pavilion with a Venetian window and a tripartite lunette window over. The centre has a doorway with segmental pediment on Tuscan columns and a slightly enriched arched window over which cuts into the three-bay pediment. On the lake side the centre is a large canted bay, and this again has two storeys, whereas the side parts have two and a half. The end pavilion is treated as on the other side. The interior has two very fine rooms, the Entrance Hall and the Saloon which is in the canted bay. Both (and another room) have Rococo plaster ceilings and chimneypieces, that in the Saloon very high and ending in an open scrolly pediment.

BARLEYBAT HALL, Liverpool Road West. The façade has two segmental bows of two storeys with columns. The date is probably Regency. Fine tripartite doorway with a broken pediment, looking earlier.

CHURCH MINSHULL   *6060*

ST BARTHOLOMEW. The W tower is of 1702, the rest of 1704. Brick with stone dressings. Arched windows, their Venetian tracery probably of the restoration of 1861. The bell-openings have Y-tracery. Can that be 1702? The s porch looks 1861, the N doorway and round N window over have bolection mouldings and clearly represent 1704. The interior is also in the state of 1704 – rustic and engaging. Nave and aisles separated by round piers without entasis and with round minimum capitals. Shallow apse. The C18 church replaces a timber-framed one. – FONT. By *John Morfitt*, 1717. Ample baluster and gadrooned bowl. – BOX PEWS. – PLATE. Cup by *J. Bingley* of Chester, 1704. – (MONUMENT. One painted heraldic tablet, probably later C17.)

CHURCH FARMHOUSE, opposite. Timber-framed with a far-projecting square middle projection, now on columns. They don't look genuine, but something similar must have preceded them. Nice black and white group a little SE.

SCHOOL. 1858. Brick with diapers and a turret. Gothic.

WADE'S GREEN HALL, 1 m. SW. Probably early C17. Three very pretty dormers with timber criss-cross in the gables.

CHURTON   *4050*

CHURTON HALL. Timber-framed, with two gabled somewhat projecting end parts and a porch not yet set in the middle. It carries a date 1569 on a loose small board which may or may not date the house. It has herringbone bracing and also concave-sided lozenges. The sides of the porch are open and have flat balusters.

CLAUGHTON *see* BIRKENHEAD, p. 97

CLEULOW CROSS *see* WINCLE

5080
CLIFTON

(ROCK SAVAGE. Ruins of Sir John Savage's house of 1565, illustrated in Ormerod. Near the new Weaver Viaduct of the M56.)

CLONTERBROOK HALL *see* SWETTENHAM

4050
CLUTTON

CHARITY FARMHOUSE. Timber-framed. Dated early C17 by the MHLG. No ornamental motifs and no strict composition.

CARDEN HALL, a timber-framed C16 house, was burnt in 1912, but two lodges survive (and also an ICE-HOUSE, of red brick, round, with a saucer dome. MHLG) CLUTTON LODGE is very odd. Two square lodges, concave-sided and with canted corners holding niches. Domes with a terracotta urn on top. It is a Baroque conception, but the front windows are typical of say 1835–45. For such a date the rest is a puzzle. CARDEN LODGE is a grander affair, classical, tripartite, with giant columns flanking the outer bays. Only the middle bay is open. Attic on top. This also would be surprising for 1835–45. It looks rather like late C18 or early C19.

(LOWER CARDEN HALL. Half-timber. Dated early C17 by the MHLG. Much restored, though the s end looks authentic with, in its w gable, coves above the ground- and first-floor windows and much diagonal bracing. Interesting brick chimneystacks, with bricks in zigzag patterns and sets of crow-steps in the form of gablets – cf. Hill Farmhouse, Guilden Sutton. EH)

4050
CODDINGTON

ST MARY. 1833 by *J. Atkinson* (GR). The type of the Commissioners' churches, but handled oddly heavily. The buttresses for instance between the two-light windows with their four-centred arches are uncommonly deep. Also there is a square bell-turret of stone. The w porch is later.

COLLEYMILL BRIDGE *see* BOSLEY

6070
COMBERBACH

COGSHALL HALL, Senna Lane. The house is of brick, c.1830.

Seven by five bays with Ionic porches, one of four, the other of two columns. Ambitious LODGE with Tuscan columns *in antis*.

COMBERMERE ABBEY   5040

Combermere Abbey was a Cistercian house founded *c.*1130. Little of it remains, and what does, though always called part of the refectory, is not convincing as such. Whalley in Lancashire was colonized by Combermere. At the Dissolution the buildings went to the Cottons. An inscription refers to their building and gives the date 1563. What we see now is the Cottons' house, though much altered later. It is in a superb position overlooking a mere. From there an E-plan appears, though with the two recessed parts not having the same number of windows. The house is rendered and of two to three storeys. The windows are pointed and set in giant arches. This and the loggia are obviously of the early C19. Cooke in 1830 writes of recent Gothic additions, and designs by the Irish *Morrisons* are referred to by Neale in 1828. The r. wing is an addition of the 1870s. The entrance side is more confusing. The porch is recent and not in line with the front entrance. The wings are not regular either. Where the porch now is was a wing with the armoury. This dated from 1854, but the Gothic ground-floor decoration including the charming entrance hall with two screens of compound shafts is rather early than mid C19.

The principal room of the house is on the first floor. It is now the library, but it is this room that is supposed to be part of the monastic refectory. But the refectory surely was on the ground floor, and there three Gothic arches have recently been found. The library has an original Elizabethan screen of the Cotton period with pilasters and a chimneypiece with much mixed-up C16 to C17 woodwork. The coved ceiling looks early C19. Above it is a hammerbeam roof, presumably the roof of the hall of the Cottons' mansion. It is likely that the hall originally went through the two storeys and that the screen was moved when the dividing floor was put in.

STABLES. Large, of brick, with two gables and neo-Elizabethan turrets. First half of the C19 probably.

BRANKELOW FOLLY. A charming eyecatcher across the lake. Brick with battlements and pinnacles. Three bays. One oval room. Originally this was a keeper's cottage, and the end pavilions were kennels.

OBELISK. Behind the folly. It commemorates Field-Marshal Viscount Combermere † 1865.

ICE HOUSE. By the walled garden.

LODGES. One set stone, rendered, with gates. Tudor style; probably the *Morrison* lodge referred to by Neale. The other set half-timbered with two gables and a loggia between. Nice bits of decoration; probably second half of the C19.

COMPSTALL
9090

In a dip in the hills towards Derbyshire, though to the W close to suburbia.

ST PAUL. 1839–40, the chancel of 1866 by *James Hunt*. The usual lancets with thin buttresses between and the usual thin W tower with big pinnacles.

CONGLETON
8060

ST PETER. In a quiet place a little away and a little above the High Street. The church was built – rebuilt rather – in 1740–2, and the tower completed in 1786. The church is of brick, the tower of stone. The church is sizeable, seven bays long, with two tiers of windows – round-headed above, segment-headed below. The E window is Venetian. The porch is set oddly at an angle. It has two pairs of Roman Doric columns. The tower on the other hand is Gothick. The interior has preserved its three galleries carrying Tuscan columns. The ceiling is coved. – FONT. A marble baluster, better than many. – REREDOS. A fine piece of 1743 with a bold open pediment on pairs of Corinthian columns and a little Gibbonsish carving. – PAINTING. L. and r. of the E window in 1748 *Edward Penny* of Knutsford painted St Peter and St Paul. They are signed. Penny is the painter who painted the death of General Wolfe in 1764, i.e. before Benjamin West. – PULPIT. Still placed in the nave W of the communion rail in the middle. It comes from Astbury and is Jacobean. Detached colonnettes at the angles. – COMMUNION RAIL. C18; three-sided. – BOX PEWS. – CHANDELIER of brass. Dated 1748. – PLATE. Chalice, 1696; Paten, 1699; Chalice and Paten, 1706; two Chalices, three Patens, 1706, one pair made in London; Flagon, 1718; large Paten, 1721. – MONUMENT. Col. Sir Thomas Reade † 1849. By *Thomas & Edward Gaffin*. Kneeling Negro by a palm tree.

ST JAMES, West Street. 1847–8 by *J. Trubshaw*. A Commissioners' church, already with the developed chancel which the

Ecclesiologists demanded. Also already Second Pointed, i.e. with more than just lancets. The stepped triplet of lancets at the E end, however, is typical of Trubshaw. – PULPIT. Flemish, mid C17, ornately decorated.

ST MARY (R.C.), West Road, at the roundabout. 1826. By *Dr Hall*, a priest. A pretty brick façade with arched doorway, two large arched windows, and a pediment with an arched niche. The E end is shallowly polygonal and has a tripartite screen of columns with the wide middle arch segmental.

The PRESBYTERY is next door and looks contemporary, and opposite is a five-bay house called WOODLANDS which also looks 1820s.

ST STEPHEN, Brook Street. 1858–60 by *Joseph Clarke* of London. It cost about £3,000.* Nave and aisles, chancel with polygonal apse, bellcote on the E gable of the nave. The windows are of no interest. Inside five-bay arcades, the arches of alternating red and white stone. It was an odd idea to put small heads at the apexes of the arches. The chancel chapels are of one wide bay. The capitals Clarke designed are not in imitation of any Gothic ones.

The VICARAGE is by *Clarke* too, 1863, and decidedly successful. Note the huge pointed relieving arch over one window – banded white and red.

HOLY TRINITY, Mossley. By *C. & J. Trubshaw*, 1844–5. Rock-faced, nave and chancel; bellcote. Shafted lancets and some minor geometrical tracery. – STAINED GLASS. The E window has excellent *Morris* glass, dated 1889. Three lights, the Crucifixion above, three saints below. Morris's own floral quarries are a delight, as always.

CONGREGATIONAL CHURCH, Antrobus Street. 1876–7 by *Sugden* of Leek. Astonishingly carefree handling of the Gothic precedents, especially in the SW turret. One would guess 1900. Large W window with rich geometrical tracery.

TOWN HALL, High Street. *E. W. Godwin* is famous for spindly art furniture, for sympathy with *japonisme*, for building Whistler's house in Chelsea, and for theatrical initiative. But when he was young, he built Gothic, and he could handle the style on a substantial scale. He won the competition for the Northampton Town Hall in 1861, and on the strength of that building he was asked to design the Congleton Town Hall. Construction lasted from 1864 to 1866. Unfortunately the building is not detached. The tower in the middle of the front

* So Mr Spain tells me.

demands more space l. and r. Also five bays is not enough for
so ambitious a design. The five bays mean ground-floor arches,
originally open. On the first floor it is eight bays with stress on
the centre, in the tower by three niches, l., r., and above the
mid-window. Inside, the stone is left exposed, which creates
an awesome monumentality. The staircase runs up between
solid stone walls. Over each of the half-landings is a beehive
dome. The principal rooms have been regrettably altered. The
upper front rooms have beams on stone corbels. – PAINTINGS.
Three by *James Northcote*: Daniel in the lions' den, 1805;
Joseph betrayed by his Brethren, exhibited in 1813; Judgement
of Solomon, exhibited in 1814. – INSIGNIA. Silver-gilt Great
Mace, 1651; small Mace a little earlier. For Congleton is not
a C19 town. It received its first charter in 1272.

What the C18 and C19 contributed was industry. Congleton
started silk-weaving at the same time as Macclesfield. The
initiative was taken by John Clayton of Stockport and Nathaniel Pattison of London, and of Clayton's MILL in MILL
GREEN started c.1752 at least the two lowest floors survive,
with a new building behind them. In 1817 Congleton had
seventeen silk mills and five cotton mills. Cotton had come in
in 1785.

Of C17 black and white only two houses deserve a mention. Both
are pubs. The WHITE LION in High Street is small, with an
irregular front and herringbone bracing. It has on one of the
overhangs some carving, and in addition fleurons on the posts
and some plaster faces in the top overhang. The LION AND
SWAN at the E end of West Street is much larger but only
partly C17. It has a porch of Tuscan columns carrying a square
bay.

Of Georgian domestic architecture little needs pointing out. The
two best houses are in WEST STREET. The first, only a little
w of the Lion and Swan but on the other side, is of three bays
and has a Gibbs surround to its doorway and also to the window over, though the window is really too low for this treatment. The second is further out – OVERTON HOUSE – with
front garden and fine gatepiers. Five bays, two and a half
storeys, one-bay pediment, quoins of even length at the angles
and the angles of the middle bay. Doorway with triangular,
mid-window with segmental pediment. Is the date c.1730?
Other streets have minor Georgian houses, the nicest group
in MOODY STREET.

WATER TOWERS. The old one is 1881, by *William Blackshaw*,

circular, of red and yellow brick, with round arches where appropriate, the new one next to the old is utilitarian with tank and supports exposed.

CONGLETON VIADUCT. *See* North Rode, p. 294.

THE BRIDESTONES CHAMBERED TOMB. The surviving and visible portion of this monument consists of a stone-built chamber 18 ft 6 in. long and orientated E–W, divided into two compartments by a broken port-hole stone. Two further chambers, 6 ft 6 in. long, were originally incorporated in a long mound with the principal gallery, which was approached from a semicircular forecourt. Little of this covering mound (said to be over 300 ft long) now survives.

COPPENHALL *see* CREWE

COTEBROOK

5060

ST JOHN. 1874–5 by *Street*. Aisleless, with a thin NE turret. The turret has a blunt pyramid roof, as Street liked them, and the boiler chimney is typical Street as well. Lancet windows, a group of three at the E end and a much more original group of four at the W end. To its N the doorway facing W – an odd arrangement, and internally very unsatisfactory. The side windows very small. Surprisingly short chancel. Rather a tricky nave roof. – STAINED GLASS. The E window by *Kempe*, 1885. – PLATE. Elizabethan Cup.

In OULTON MILL LANE a new house by *B. Taylor & Partners* is of some interest. It is a substantial addition to an old cottage. The junction between old and the long new wing at the rear deserves to be looked at.

SANDY BROW, 1¼ m. NNE. Good iron gates.

COTTON HALL *see* HOLMES CHAPEL

CRABWALL HALL *see* MOLLINGTON

CRANAGE

7060

CRANAGE HALL, now part of a hospital. The original building is of 1829 by *Lewis Wyatt* (Ormerod), Tudor, brick, with dark diapers. To this was added a parallel later wing with a four-column porch projection (1932). Some recent buildings for the hospital by *Cruickshank & Seward*.

ALMSHOUSES. 1913. Brick, symmetrical, Tudor.

VILLAGE CLUB, close to the hospital entrance. 1907. A very
enterprising little job, basically à la Voysey, but more deliberately (picturesquely) irregular.

CREWE

INTRODUCTION

Crewe is the railway town *par excellence*. Swindon, the only
serious competitor, seems more something of its own as well,
and now of course has nearly twice as many inhabitants. There
was nothing on the site of Crewe but some farms when the railway arrived in 1837. By 1842 the station had become the focus of
four lines: from Birmingham, from Liverpool, from Chester, and
from Manchester. It is impressive on the map to see the lines
emerge from Crewe station fanning out absolutely straight. By
1842 also the locomotive works were getting ready to go into
production. So the stage was set for the development of a town.
The population was 5,000 in 1851, 43,000 in 1901. It is now
*c.*55,000. As at Wolverton (London & Birmingham Railway) and
at Swindon (GWR) the Grand Junction (which in 1846 became
a partner in the London & North Western) decided to build a
model town, and as at Wolverton and Swindon it amounted
architecturally speaking to pitiably little. Again as at Swindon
the one monumental building was the church. Housing layout
was planned, but little else was done, and what was done is now
mostly obliterated. A plan was drawn up in 1840 by *Joseph Locke*,
the railway engineer, and in 1842 *John Cunningham* of Liverpool
was appointed architect. The first 32 cottages were occupied by
the end of 1842, in 1848 there were 520, in 1858 well over 700.
Of the housing at Crewe *Chambers' Edinburgh Journal* wrote in
1846: 'The dwelling houses arrange themselves in four classes:
first, the villa-style lodges of the superior officers; next a kind of
ornamental Gothic constitutes the houses of the next in authority;
the engineers domiciled in detached mansions, which accom-
modate four families, with gardens and separate entrances; and
last the labourer delights in neat cottages of four apartments, the
entrances within ancient porches. . .'

If one tries to explore what is left of all this, the result will be
meagre – a building on the w side of Market Street, just one of
the four-family type, known as block houses, sw of Christ Church
at the s end of PRINCE ALBERT STREET, and the cottages in
DORFOLD STREET and the streets to its w, and also a terrace in
LYON STREET overlooking the railway. The block houses as well

as the early cottages were given some architectural treatment by individual bargeboarded gables. Later planned development N of VICTORIA STREET is just rows of brick cottages without any dignity.

CHURCHES

CHRIST CHURCH, Prince Albert Street. The parish church of Crewe in the main square of the new town, but not the original parish church, which was St Michael, Coppenhall (*see* below). Christ Church was built by the Grand Junction Railway in 1843 and was almost certainly designed by *Cunningham*. The *Railway Gazette* in 1845 went to the length of writing thus: 'This liberal art [of endowing churches] is one among many signs – the testimonials to Stephenson, Hudson, Saunders, and others – which seem to foretell that great, noble and national deeds and works, incidental only to railways, will come out of railways; such works as may chance to compete with our ancient cathedrals. Railways are the corporations of our time, which have the most real life and energy in them, and, like the corporations of olden time, will do noble deeds.' One had better not read this before looking at Christ Church especially if one considers in addition that the aisles came only in 1864, the tower in 1877, the present chancel in 1898–1901, and the NE chapel in 1906. The tower is by *J. W. Stansby*, engineer on the company staff. It is high and competent with geometrical tracery and was until recently finished by an iron crown made in the railway workshops. The interior has awkward octagonal iron piers, with something like intermediate capitals halfway up. They were for the galleries, which were removed only in 1901. At that time also the aisle windows received their free and simplified flowing tracery – an Arts and Crafts feature easily recognized.

(ALL SAINTS, Stewart Street. By *Robert Maguire* and *Keith Murray*. An exceptionally interesting church, every bit as good as those at Bow Common (London) and Perry Beeches (Birmingham) by the same architects. They were commissioned in 1961 and the church was built in 1964–5. Square plan with rounded corners, and with seating arranged round three sides of the altar. Font NE of the altar, with a segmental projection in the wall behind it. Pyramid roof punctuated by a vertical clerestory. The walls are of brick and the roofs of asbestos slate. Boarded ceilings inside. Tubular steel columns below the clerestory. At the NE corner the lower part of the roof continues over a hall (which itself has a good interior) and parsonage. The entrance is between church and hall. EH)

ST BARNABAS, West Street. 1885 by *Paley & Austin* at the expense of the London & North Western Railway. Common brick and red terracotta. No tower, but a shingled flèche close to the W end. Perp style with a seven-light E window. The dominant feature is the very big cross gables for the aisle windows, their tips timber-framed. The interior deserves a full description.* It is noble – clear, spacious, and open without being in the least bleak. Three-bay aisled nave with aisleless chancel. The piers are of pink stone, of Greek cross shape, chamfered, and they merge without capitals into terracotta arches. Everything else is of the same bare brick as the exterior. There is no clerestory and the aisles have transverse vaults, so that something of the effect of a hall-church is created. The choir is made by extending the chancel walls into the nave in an openwork screen which is then returned across the nave well in front of where the chancel arch would be. The choir is thus partly contained by the E end of the nave, rather like an apron stage. So there is a real spatial coherence about the whole building. The screen has three longitudinal sections and then seven across the width of the nave. The uprights are like turned table legs, but the spandrels are full of sinuous tracery with a distinctly Art Nouveau feel to it. The same is true of the altar screen and the panelling of the E wall. – Wooden SEDILIA with a big overhanging hood. – STAINED GLASS. The E window is of 1901, very full but fairly subdued. Whom can it be by?

The SCHOOL W of the church, 1887, gabled, low, and spreading, and the VICARAGE E of the church, in rather a Norman Shaw style, may well be by *Paley & Austin* too.

ST JOHN BAPTIST, Stalbridge Road. 1894–1901 by *Hicks & Charlewood* of Newcastle, and also at the expense of the railway company. Red brick, no tower. Windows of lancet type, but round-headed. Nave and aisle, transepts which do not project, chancel and chapels. The interior is brick-faced and has square piers and round arches. – STAINED GLASS. In the W rose window impressive Christ with Angels, by the *Bromsgrove Guild*. – (In the N chapel a window by *A. J. Davies* of the *Bromsgrove Guild*, 1929. EH)

ST MARY (R.C.), St Mary's Street. 1890–1 by *Pugin & Pugin*. Red brick, Dec details. High SW tower with a pyramid roof. Polygonal apse.

* Kindly provided by Dr Gomme.

ST MICHAEL, Ford Lane, Coppenhall. 1883–6 the chancel by *James Brooks*, 1907–10 the nave by *J. Brooks, Son & Adkins*. Red brick, with aisles and transepts and a flèche. High clerestory lancets. Lancets also otherwise. The interior is brick-faced and has high crossing arches. The chancel has aisles too, and they communicate with the transepts by twin openings with plate tracery. The w end is the baptistery, separated from the nave by a stepped triplet of arches. The ensemble is severe without any show of inventiveness except the capitals, which are not at all imitation Gothic, though they may be based on the waterleaf motif. They are Arts and Crafts at a remarkably early date. In the nave they are replaced by something simpler. The aisles open into the transepts by bold half-arches.

ST PAUL, Hightown. 1868–9 at the expense of the railway and by *Stansby*, the company engineer. Wide nave without aisles, covered by a hammerbeam roof. NE tower with a spire rising out of a saddleback roof. This is an addition of 1888 (GR). Windows with geometrical tracery and broad ornamental terracotta surrounds. The w baptistery and the CHURCH HALL, connected with the church by a cloister walk, are of 1893.

ST PETER, Earle Street. 1914–23 by *J. Brooke & C. E. Elcock*. Ashlar, Perp, with only a bellcote. Very high cross-gables. It was an odd idea to place single lancets between the wide Perp windows under the cross-gables. It makes a jumpy rhythm inside. The arcades are of three wide bays; the arches die into the piers. It is a conservative, dignified job of work.

PUBLIC AND PRIVATE BUILDINGS

MUNICIPAL BUILDINGS. By *H. T. Hare*, 1902–5. Disappointing, partly because placed in a terrace without space l. and r., and partly because the size of the motifs is too big for the scale of the building. Ashlar, of five bays only, three of them slightly recessed and with giant unfluted Ionic columns. Above the three main ground-floor windows pairs of large reclining figures in relief (by *F. E. E. Schenck*). Top cupola with a locomotive vane. The style is a kind of English Baroque.*

MARKET HALL, Earle Street. 1854 by *Charles Meason*. Immediately next to the town hall and its rawness doing damage to its neighbour. Yellow and red brick, vaguely Italianate. Tower added in 1871.

---

* INSIGNIA of 1877 by *T. & J. Bragg* included a badge of office with a shield illustrating the progress of transport from the packhorse to the latest L. & N. W. locomotive. (EH).

CIVIC CENTRE, E of Christ Church. By *W. S. Hattrell & Partners*. So far the POLICE STATION and the LIBRARY have been built, and they are the best recent buildings in a town which has built much recently and little of architectural interest. That applies for instance to the SHOPPING AREA of Tower Way and Queens Way. The police and the library are both of hard red brick, the library stressing the vertical, the police the horizontal in its fenestration. A high block is projected behind the library. So far the only high building at Crewe is the thirteen-storey RAIL HOUSE, by the station (1967–8 by *F. S. Curtis, R. C. Moorcroft*, and the architect team of British Railways).

COUNTY GRAMMAR SCHOOL, Ruskin Road. 1909 by *H. Beswick*, the then county architect. Free Neo-Georgian, with a cupola in the middle of its twenty-three-bay façade of red brick and red terracotta.

(SOUTH CHESHIRE COLLEGE OF FURTHER EDUCATION, Danebank Avenue. By the *Biggins Sargent Partnership* and *Edgar Taberner*, the County Architect, completed in 1966.)

(CREWE THEATRE, Heath Street. Built as the Lyceum Theatre in 1887. The interior in illustrations seems to be attractive.)

(Between Mill Street, Forge Street, and the railway are the original LOCOMOTIVE WORKS of 1840–3.)

(QUEEN'S PARK, Victoria Avenue. 1887–8. Given to the town by the London & North Western Railway to celebrate Queen Victoria's Jubilee and the fiftieth anniversary of the opening of the Grand Junction Railway. A notable example of Victorian public park design. Oval plan, with a principal central axis, a subsidiary cross axis, and an informal area with a lake. At the main entrance two stone and half-timber LODGES, by *John Brooke*, not quite a pair. CLOCK TOWER given by railway employees. SOUTH AFRICAN WAR MEMORIAL, 1904, with a model of a locomotive at its base. EH)

7050   CREWE GREEN

ST MICHAEL. 1857–8 by *Sir G. G. Scott*. Red brick and black brick. N turret, round apse. The style is the Second Pointed, i.e. late C13, with much outer shafting and much inner shafting. The shafts carry naturalistic foliage capitals such as Scott believed in. It is a surprise that so *comme il faut* an architect should have yellow brick with red brick bands as the inner facing material.

CREWE HALL ESTATE HOUSING. Close to the church the

VICARAGE, a largish Norman-Shawish house of 1889, red brick and half-timbering. By *Thomas Bower* of *Bower & Edleston*. The SCHOOL is dated 1882 and is bad Elizabethan. It carries a copy of the relief of Time rewarding Industry and punishing Sloth whose original is in Crewe Hall (*see* p. 193). Much prettier is the pair of cottages dated 1877, also brick and half-timbering. Along the road to Stoke is a cottage of red brick with diaper pattern and a bargeboarded gable. The style is Elizabethan. It is dated 1865, i.e. belongs to the years when *Nesfield* worked for the estate (cf. p. 194). Can he have designed this? Only the hipped gables are a motif known to be his.

CREWE HALL* *7050*

Crewe Hall is two buildings in one. Some people think of it as a [45] Jacobean house, others as *E. M. Barry*'s most ambitious mansion, but most people don't know it at all. In fact even those who have studied what there is of literature remain in the dark as to how much or how little Barry did to the Jacobean house. The dates are easily presented. Sir Randolph Crewe built the house in 1615–36. In the late C18 or early C19 the first Baron Crewe added a w service wing and made some alterations to the principal interiors. We know from Neale's *Seats* what the house looked like in the 1820s. Then in the late 1830s and 1840s the third Baron employed *Blore* to restore it. According to *The Gentleman's Magazine*, 1866, this cost £30,000 – an enormous sum. Then, in 1866, a fire almost entirely gutted the building, and in the same year Lord Crewe commissioned E. M. Barry to reinstate it. That job was done by 1870. Some alterations were made in 1896 by *Thomas Bower*.

As one approaches the building one division appears at once, that between the E and the w half. The w half is the Georgian service wing – an early instance of Jacobean revivalism, though later alterations, particularly the addition of a central gable, have made it look more authentic. *Bower* extended it further w and converted the kitchen in its SE corner into a billiard room. This has been dismantled, but the w end of the wing is his. The E half is Jacobean or looks it. The brickwork with the dark diapers is indeed largely original and some of the features also are, and though much was doubtless renewed by Barry, all was in accordance with the original design.

---

* This description and appreciation is the joint work of Edward Hubbard and myself.

This main block of the house thus essentially presents its
c17 appearance. The s front is of seven main bays and two
high storeys. The centre is a frontispiece, intact or facsimile,
with paired fluted Ionic columns, tapering pilasters, and a big
strap cartouche over. Top balustrade and achievement. The
end bays have canted bay windows and shaped gables, the
bays in between two-light windows. All windows have two
transoms.

The e side has four bays, two shaped gables, and a middle
cartouche. On the n side there is a big bow in the middle
behind which is the chapel. This is a Jacobean feature too,
though possibly coarsened by Barry. It ought to be noted that
here mezzanine windows appear between ground and first floor.
The w side is not wholly visible because of the w building
which on the n side is dominated – indeed at a distance the
whole mansion is dominated – by Barry's tower with its High
Victorian top. It is a cap of ogee outline with a break – neither
English nor French, just Victorian – and round it are four
chimneys acting as pinnacles.

Inside the house the question what is what is much more
intractable. The ENTRANCE HALL receives one at once as
pure Barry. To the e was the Jacobean great hall. Blore inserted an arcade between the screens passage and the room to
its w, and Barry made them both into one. The end wall is
opened in a screen of low columns with a wooden gallery over,
and through this screen one proceeds into the CENTRAL HALL,
a type of room which Jacobean houses of course did not
possess. It replaces an inner courtyard, and in its present form
is *Barry*'s, though a less ambitious, single-storey hall had been
introduced by *Blore*. There is a kind of cloister on all four
sides, and a gallery over. This, however, it will be noticed, is
not at the level of the upper floor but at an intermediate level.
It represents the mezzanine whose windows we have seen on
the n side, and whose sw room has a window hidden in the
upper part of the great transomed Jacobean window. The real
upper floor has a gallery round the central hall as well, but
that is walled off on the long sides and is incidentally tunnel-
vaulted. On the short sides, however, one can look into the
Victorian roof arrangement of timbers with a skylight over.

The DINING ROOM was the Jacobean great hall which, as
has been said, was e of the entrance. It retains its c17 form,
running as far as the e front with, strangely enough, no upper
end room divided off. It has also, to a large extent, been re-

stored to its C17 appearance, the ceiling and the traditional wooden screen apparently being correct facsimiles. The screen may also incorporate original woodwork, for the room partly escaped the fire, and the relief of Plenty in the overmantel must be original. It is known not to be *ex situ*, and no Victorian carver would carve so naïvely. The stone chimneypiece is huge, as are many of Barry's in the house, though this one seems to be by *Blore*, probably the only survival of his extensive enriching of the interior. The STAIRCASE is next to the 46 dining room on the E front. Exuberantly carved and on a fantastic plan starting with short flights from both E and W and continuing across the space at more than one level, it is another rebuilding job by Barry to the original design. It is an amazing piece; there is no other Jacobean staircase in existence running so complicatedly. The approach flight from the W is, however, a feature first introduced by *Blore*, in connexion with his central hall, and its present axial position is due to *Barry*. The ceiling and clerestory, surrounded by short columns, is Barry's. Beyond, the CARVED PARLOUR is again a facsimile of the original. Its chimneypiece is alabaster below (the original was of stone) and has a relief of Father Time with Industry and Idleness symbolized by two boys.*

N of the hall is the CHAPEL, small, but with an apse, and most lavishly decorated. Wooden screen with family pew in the form of a gallery above. Figural wall decoration by *Clayton & Bell*. Small medallions of the heads of biblical personages (by *J. Birnie Philip*), bronze in the side walls and alabaster in the arcading of the apse. The colouring of the ceiling etc. probably by *J. G. Crace*. The STAINED GLASS is by *Clayton & Bell*. Finally, W of the entrance hall is yet another major room, the OAK PARLOUR, with a great Jacobean wooden overmantel. This seems to be *in situ*, i.e. it survived the fire.

But that is not all. The Jacobean house had, as usual, a LONG GALLERY on the upper floor, and above the great hall

* Referring to Crewe in his *Lectures on Architecture*, published in 1881, Barry stated that 'the greatest care has been taken to recover the design of Sir Randolph [Crewe] for such of the work as it has been possible to restore . . . although with less roughness of execution and uncouthness of detail, particularly in respect of the human figure'. A comparison between the dining room overmantel and the figures of the Carved Parlour frieze and overmantel is instructive, particularly in the light of this interesting reflection of Victorian attitudes to restoration. Dr Mark Girouard drew attention to the passage.

7—C.

was the great chamber or DRAWING ROOM. With the LIBRARY and SMALL DRAWING ROOM they form a suite of state rooms, and were much embellished by Blore. All this *Barry* recreated, though the interiors with their exuberant plasterwork and stone chimneypieces etc. are largely or entirely of his own designing.* In the long gallery are busts of Sir Randolph Crewe and Bishop Crewe of Durham by *Henry Weekes*. The library has a frieze of scenes from Chaucer, Spenser, Shakespeare, Milton, Wordsworth, Homer, Virgil, Horace, Dante, Ariosto, and Tasso, by *J. Mabey*. Also statuettes by *Philip*. The other state rooms are two BEDROOMS, one with another large stone chimney piece, the other with a relief of Cain and Abel in the overmantel, which again is genuine, and escaped the fire.

The STABLES are largely genuine too. The centrepiece with the turret is *Blore*'s, but the brickwork of the shaped gables is evidently C17.

In the PARK much was done by *Repton*, though his lake immediately N of the house has vanished. GARDENS were laid out by *W. A. Nesfield*, but have doubtless been much simplified.

The ESTATE HOUSING is also of interest, and principally that built by *Eden Nesfield* between 1860 and 1866.‡ STOWFORD COTTAGES, 1864–5, a little E of the Weston Lodge directly S of the house, are a fair example, with their brick, tilehanging, and incised pargetting, their half-hipped gables on an overhang, and their high chimneys – Home Counties in derivation, but already at this early date without Gothic or Tudor motifs, intimate and informal. Nesfield at the time was in partnership with Norman Shaw, and the two of them created and propagated this style, Nesfield, it seems, a little before Shaw. In the SE corner of the park, N of Stowford Cottages, is SMITHY COTTAGE, of similar style, but now altered. The brick and stone Elizabethan WESTON LODGE is said also to be by *Nesfield*, but further W, on the S side of the road, are two more buildings definitely by him, in the more distinctive style: first FIR TREE, 1865, with a remarkably complicated roof,

* It is probable that these rooms had been much altered by the first Lord Crewe, and that Blore effected a complete neo-Jacobean transformation. Barry here seems not to have attempted any reproduction of C17 work, presumably because no record of the original treatment existed. *Crace* was responsible for decorating the principal rooms of the house, and Mrs Elfrida Mostyn suggests that much plasterwork may be his rather than Barry's.

‡ The dates are from Eastlake, but those of the drawings which are at the RIBA and which are dated are of 1864–5.

then a FARMHOUSE which has half-timbering as well as tile-hanging. On the N side of the park a LODGE by *Blore*, 1847. (CREWE HALL FARMHOUSE, ¼ m. SE of Crewe Hall, on the edge of the grounds. Brick; late C17. MHLG)

CROOK HALL *see* GOOSTREY

CROWLEY LODGE *see* ARLEY HALL

CROWTON

5070

CHRIST CHURCH. 1871 by *Pearson*, but nothing special, though of course well detailed. The only noteworthy feature is the two-tier bellcote. No aisles, but a N transept. The style is late C13. The former VICARAGE, according to Mr A. Quiney, is by *Pearson* too. It is partly brick, partly tile-hung, and partly half-timbered.

STONEHOUSES. 1685. With two symmetrical gables and still the mullioned windows of fifty years before.

DARESBURY

5080

ALL SAINTS. Perp W tower; the rest by *Paley & Austin*, 1870–2, Perp, like the tower. Nave and aisles; two-bay S chapel, one-bay N chapel and vestry. Bold roof with solid braces. – SCREEN. Square panels with very flamboyant design in the dado and on the chancel E wall. – PULPIT. Probably Jacobean. A very unusual design with angle figure-brackets. – PLATE. C17 Paten; Flagon inscribed 1738; Paten inscribed 1746; undated Chalice. – MONUMENT. Sarah Byrom † 1833. Large tablet, signed *Gibson*, Roma. She lies on a couch, her husband bends over her, an angel hovering on the r.

SESSIONS HOUSE, W of the church, next to the pub. 1841. Brick; only three bays and one storey.

DARESBURY HALL, ¼ m. E. Dated 1759. Brick, seven bays and three storeys; the three middle bays project and have a pediment. The doorway has a pediment on corbels, the windows have raised frames.

OAKLANDS, ¾ m. S, built in 1866, and now demolished, was Scottish Baronial, with a round turret with spire and stepped gables. Totally asymmetrical.

(THE COTTAGE. Cruck construction. MHLG)

DAVENHAM

6070

ST WILFRED. A large Victorian church, the result of a gradual rebuilding between 1844 and 1870, the latter date referring to chancel and transepts. The w tower with its very successful recessed spire is of 1850 and may be by *Sharpe* (GR). But who did the rest? Paley, Sharpe's partner and successor? The style is geometrical late C13 in the w, flowing early C14 in the E part. – STAINED GLASS. The aisle w windows are by *David Evans* of Shrewsbury in his typical style: large single figures in strident colours. – PLATE. Cup, London, 1570; Stand Paten, London, 1707. – WAR MEMORIAL. By *Sir Robert Lorimer*, with two screens across the s aisle. – MONUMENTS. Mrs France † 1814 by *S. & F. Franceys* of Liverpool, with a small free-standing figure of Faith on top. – Mrs Harper, 1833 by *Francesco Pozzi* of Florence, with a relief of mother and child.

RECTORY. Five-bay brick house with a one-bay pediment and a Tuscan porch. Late Gerogian.

DAVENHAM HALL, ½ m. s. Late Georgian, of six bays with a two-bay pediment and a porch of four freely detailed Tuscan columns.

WHATCROFT HALL, 1½ m. SE. Seven-bay s front with a fine doorway perhaps not *in situ*. Angle pilaster strips. The *clou* of the house is the spiral staircase in the middle, expressed outside by a bulbous dome. It is a flying staircase with an excellent trellis railing and a skylight on fan-like spandrels à la Wyatt. It must be *c*.1800.

DAWPOOL *see* THURSTASTON

7050

DEAN HILL

2 m. SE of Sandbach

Two dated houses stand side by side on the main road. One (SOUTH FARM) has a date 1621, probably *ex situ*; the brick front of the house must be a good deal later. WEST FARM says Randle Rode 1684, but must be earlier, for the Rode family moved to Dean Hill in 1668. Now plastered and rough-cast, but doubtless with close vertical studding underneath. At one end some exposed but mainly Victorian half-timbering. The inside, with a rather crude staircase and moulded doors, looks Early Jacobean.

¼ m. SE of these two is BROOK FARM, mid C17, with close vertical studs on the upper floor.

BETCHTON HALL, 1 m. ESE of Dean Hill. Mid C18, incorporating earlier fragments, all done up *c*.1800. Two storeys, of brick, with quoins. Seven-bay SE front with round-headed entrance doorway. Three-bay SW front, the centre pedimented and deeply recessed, with, on both floors, Venetian windows. Their centrepieces are semi-elliptical rather than semi-circular. Circular entrance hall of c.1800 and top-lit staircase hall. Adamish fireplace of c.1770 from a house in Oxfordshire.*

DEAN ROW see WILMSLOW

DELAMERE   5060

Delamere Forest was one of the three great medieval forests of Cheshire. It belonged to the Earls of Chester from the C11 and was enclosed only after 1812.

ST PETER. 1816–17 by *J. Gunnery*, but much altered in 1878. The tooling of much of the masonry is typical early C19. So are the one N window with its Y-tracery and probably also the W tower and the transepts. The more correct Gothic tracery is of course Victorian. – STAINED GLASS. The E window by *Kempe & Tower*, 1906.

SCHOOL, ⅜ m. W. 1846. Large for its date, and lavishly done. Gothic. A symmetrical front with two canted bay windows. Entrance is from the back.

ABBEY ARMS. At the A-road and B-road crossing. Late Georgian, a three-bay centre and one-bay lower wings.

PROMONTORY FORT (Kelsborrow Castle). The defences consist of a single bank and ditch, semicircular in plan, cutting off an area of 7¼ acres at the end of the spur. The rampart still rises some 6 ft above the floor of the ditch in places. No obvious entrance is now visible in the fortifications.

HILL FORT, at Eddisbury, ¾ m. NW of Delamere church. This is a univallate earthwork enclosing an area of 7 acres. In its first phase only the E part of the hill was defended by a single bank and ditch, forming an enclosure of 5½ acres. Later a second bank and ditch was added and the defended area increased by enclosing a further 1½ acres to the W. Little of the phase I fort is now visible, the rampart having been almost completely levelled, but the area of the site corresponds approximately with that of the large field in which it stands. Access to this first fort was by way of an entrance on the E. In phase II an elaborate inturned entrance was constructed on the W. The ramparts were slighted by the Romans, and on the N the site was refortified in the C10.

* The entry for Dean Hill is by Dr Gomme.

9080

DISLEY

Disley has a handsome little-town centre with a classical FOUNTAIN of 1823, the SCHOOL of the same year, with two-light windows on two floors and battlements, and the RAM'S HEAD, an Early Victorian Tudor inn with gables. The church lies up a steep bank behind the school and inn.

ST MARY. Perp w tower, built with the church by Sir Piers Legh who died in 1527. The church was then not yet completed. It was consecrated only in 1558. The church itself is now a re-building of 1824-35. Windows of three lights with intersecting tracery, low chancel, tall octagonal piers and four-centred arches. Three galleries. When the church was rebuilt, the excellent early C16 timber roof with its many bosses was preserved. – ORGAN CASE. By *Samuel Renn*, 1836. – STAINED GLASS. The E window is Netherlandish (or Swiss?) Early Renaissance. It represents scenes of the Passion, and under one scene one reads *Steynfrit* 1535. – Medieval fragments in other windows. – PLATE. Silver-gilt Set of 1769. – MONU-MENTS. George Barbor † 1779. Kneeling female figure by an altar. – Richard Orford † 1791 and others. By *Knowles* of Manchester. Mourning female figure by a sarcophagus. – Thomas Legh † 1857. By *A. Gatley*, 'Rome 1858'. An angel with a trumpet on a sarcophagus. Profile portrait head in the 'predella'. A work of considerable verve, though not large.

(WOODBANK. In the garden a four-storeyed TOWER, probably a belvedere. MHLG)

WYBERSLEY HALL, I m. NW. A farmhouse apparently converted in the early C19 into an eyecatcher. Centre and two projecting wings. The centre is castellated, the wings have stepped gables and giant arches for the front windows.

(Two houses by *John Brooke* are at Disley: WOODEND, Homestead Road, illustrated in 1894, and RED LODGE, ½ m. out on the road to Stockport, illustrated in 1893.)

7040

DODDINGTON HALL

The Doddington estate in the Middle Ages belonged to the Delves family, in 1727 through marriage and inheritance it came to the Broughtons. Doddington Hall was built for the Rev. Sir Thomas Broughton, but for the CASTLE which now stands like a great big eyecatcher in a field below and to the N of the Hall licence to crenellate was obtained by Sir John Delves in 1365 or by John Delves in 1403. It is not a castle strictly speaking, rather a North Country tower house like, say, Belsay. It has the typical embattled corner turrets and the typical tunnel-vaulted ground floor, below the stage of the doorway. But that doorway is now reached by an outer staircase with a wildly Jacobean balustrade of enriched quatrefoils, and at the foot of it, supporting the two top landings, are pilasters with a blob in relief on each stone, and between these stand rustically carved figures of the Black Prince, Audley, and his four squires. The balustrading and the statues come from the porch of the Doddington Hall which preceded the present one and which, according to old illustrations, must have been a C17 building.

The new building was erected on a new, higher site in 1777–98 to the design of *Samuel Wyatt*. It is Wyatt at his best in the sparing use of motifs and their delicacy, and also in the easy planning. The motifs themselves are typically Wyatt too. The house consists of basement and one and a half storeys, the basement being of smooth rustication, the rest totally smooth. The entrance is on the N side. That side has nine bays. The centre has a three-bay pediment. The doorway is reached by an outer staircase. Two columns set back support a blank round arch with a medallion. In the end bays the basement has a tripartite lunette window (rather an upsetting position for lunettes) and the *piano nobile* has one tripartite window again with a blank round arch and a medallion. The other windows are just cut in, without framing or moulding, but above those of the *piano nobile* are panels with garlands.

The S side is the same, except that the centre is a big three-window bow with the shallowest dome. The E side is fine too – only three bays, but the middle one treated like the end bays of the N and S sides. On the W side runs a low curved service wing which in its middle contained the kitchen.

As for the interior, only two rooms are treated lavishly, the entrance hall and the saloon, i.e. the middle rooms of the N and S sides. The ENTRANCE HALL has columns and pilasters of dark grey scagliola and the metopes repeat the pelican, the Delves crest. Painted panels with putti in imitation of stone. A fine cast-iron stove should also be noted. The SALOON is of course the climax of the house. It is circular and has dainty decoration on the pilaster-like vertical panels and on the ceiling. In the panels are painted plaques in imitation of Wedgwood, and in the frieze are painted panels of classical scenes in the style of *Biagio Rebecca*. The marble chimneypiece is outstanding too, with two elegant maidens and a Cupid in relief in the lintel. There is no reason to ascribe it to Italians.

The two STAIRCASES are of equal size and importance. They have simple iron and lead handrails and an oval skylight. Of the other rooms the most interesting are the DINING ROOM with two shallow apses – the tripartite windows behind them are blind – and decoration of vertical strips with vine-leaves and grapes, the room between it and the saloon with a coving and leaf decoration up its angles, the octagonal NE corner room, and three rooms on the bedroom floor, one because it has an apse towards the window, the other two because they are above the saloon and ingeniously together repeat its shape by being elongated hexagons with recesses in the long sides and groin-vaults over the centres – a complex composition easily over-looked, but relished by the connoisseur of spatial effects.

The STABLES are of brick, with a tripartite front, a centre pediment, and giant blank arches in the centre and the end bays.

Capability Brown landscaped the GARDENS. It is not easy to say what of his work remains, but it is known that he en-larged the LAKE. In the middle of this, until the early C19, stood a ROTUNDA, a domed summerhouse.

The NORTH LODGES are no doubt by *Wyatt*, two plain, square buildings with pyramid roofs. The church, ST JOHN, stands in the grounds. It was built in 1837 at the expense of the then Delves Broughton. It is of ashlar, with the familiar lancets and buttresses, and has a gauche front with bellcote and pinnacles. There is no separate chancel. Mr Howell re-ports that the design is of 1836 by *E. Lapidge*.

DODLESTON

ST MARY. 1870 by *Douglas*, except the lower part of the tower. The tower carries a short spire. Nave, chancel, and N aisle. Low, straight-headed windows with cusped lights. Five-light E window with panel tracery. Neo-Perp was exceptional in 1870. But the church had a medieval predecessor, probably Perp. Timber-framed N porch. Big nave roof. – FONT. Octa-gonal, presumably C17. – PLATE. Chalice inscribed 1732. – MONUMENTS. Several tablets.

(Dodleston is an Eaton estate village. There are many COTTAGES typical of those dating from the time of the first Duke of West-minster, and ½ m. SE is DODLESTON LANE FARM, a typical model farm. EH)

6050

DORFOLD HALL

Dorfold Hall has an ideal approach. It was made in 1862, when the lodge also was built. Past the lodge one is in a straight avenue of lime trees. The avenue is the work of *William Nesfield*, who landscaped the grounds. At the end of the avenue one passes ornamental iron gates bought at the Paris Exhibition of 1855 and faces the house.

The house was built in 1616 for Ralph Wilbraham. It is of brick, two-storeyed, and has a N façade of the type with recessed centre and projecting wings and with two insertions in the re-entrant angles, one for the porch, the other for the hall bay window, exactly as e.g. at Chastleton in Oxfordshire or Ludstone in Shropshire. These two insertions have top balustrades, the other parts straight gables. The windows are all mullioned and transomed except those in the gables, which are of three lights stepped. In front of the façade is a forecourt formed by the two L-shaped angle pavilions with curious shaped (ogee) gables and two Victorian screen-walls and end pavilions of the same pattern – a very happy idea. The s, i.e. garden, side of the house is flat and irregular, with two gables and a balustrade between.

The plan is odd, a double-pile plan, i.e. with subsidiary rooms behind the hall and behind the Great Chamber which lies above the hall. This latter, with the hall, is the grandest room of the house, and the other finest rooms are on the upper floor too. On the ground floor much was altered in the c18. A passage replaces the Jacobean screens passage, the hall has a panelled ceiling of *c.*1740, the room in the sw corner a richer ceiling of early Adam style. In its centre is a pair of cooing doves, referring probably to a wedding.

With the staircase one is back in the Jacobean work. The balusters are flat. Now for the Great Chamber. It has a tunnel-48 vaulted plaster ceiling with broad, moulded and studded bands in complicated interlocked geometrical patterns and with incongruous pendants. The tympana of the end walls are stuccoed too. Big chimneypiece with Roman Doric columns; panelling with tapering pilasters. The room has a large square bay window to the garden. This does not project externally because of the subsidiary rooms already mentioned. To the N the Great Chamber of course repeats the hall bay window. In another first-floor room is a chimneypiece with the arms of James I and the date 1621, and in yet another a wooden chimneypiece with coupled columns.

Re-erected GATEWAY from Roger Wilbraham's Alms-houses, Nantwich, mid C17, with two big niches and a raised pedimented centre.

ICEHOUSE, *c.* 200 yds SE.

DUDDON

5060

ST PETER. 1835 by *William Railton*. 'Of all the mean box-like Chapels,' wrote Goodhart-Rendel, 'this is nearly the meanest.' It is a box indeed, of brick, with a gawky bellcote, lancet windows, and no chapel.

DUDDON OLD HALL. The gabled projection has very rich black and white decoration – how far restored? Concave-sided lozenges, and also the baluster motif.

DUKINFIELD

9090

The only separation of Dukinfield from Ashton-under-Lyne, i.e. from Lancashire, is the river Tame, and that one hardly notices. Indeed the traditional industry of Dukinfield used to be cotton. One big typical mill rises prominently in FOUNDRY STREET: QUEEN MILL of 1901. The centre of the town is the TOWN HALL, 1899 by *John Eaton, Sons & Cantrell* of Ashton. It is of red brick, symmetrical, Gothic, and with a mid-tower. Opposite it is some new development of flats.

ST MARK, Church Street, is the parish church. It is a Commis-sioners' church, of 1848–9, by *Joseph Clarke*, with a new spire by *J. Eaton & Sons*, 1880–1. Nave and aisles, clerestory with round windows, the aisle windows coupled lancets. The tower is on the NW.

The VICARAGE is in the Late Georgian tradition, though probably later. Three bays, red brick, with a nice doorway.

ST JOHN, Oxford Road. 1838–40 by *E. Sharpe*. A Commissioners' church. Nave and aisles, paired lancet windows, W tower with lancets, short chancel. The aisles are separated from the nave by tall octagonal piers, but there are also galleries.

ST LUKE, King Street. 1889 by *Eaton & Sons*. Red brick, lan-cets, W lobby, no tower.

ST MARY (R.C.), Felland Street. 1854–6 by *Weightman, Had-field & Goldie*. Brick, pairs of lancets, no tower but a poly-gonal apse.

CONGREGATIONAL CHAPEL (OLD HALL CHAPEL), Old Hall Street, Globe Lane. Derelict at the time of writing. The chapel is of 1872, but its transept is the former domestic chapel of Dukinfield Hall, a house no longer extant. The chapel consists

of nave and chancel. Licence for a private oratory was granted
in 1398, but the building, according to the MHLG, is late C16
or early C17. (Hammerbeam roof inside. NMR)

METHODIST CHAPEL (former), Wellington Street. 1841. Large
and grim, with long lancets.

UNITARIAN CHURCH, facing the E end of Chapel Street. The
best building in Dukinfield. 1840–1 by *R. Tattersall*, but completed only in 1845. Stone, in the style of 1300, a very early
case of the use of the so-called Second Pointed. No tower.
Aisles and transepts. The lofty interior has thin quatrefoil
piers with cast-iron cores and galleries. Fine view from the E
into the Peak.

LAKES ROAD GIRLS' SCHOOL. Neo-Georgian, with a handsome arched cloister. Brick.

DUNHAM MASSEY   7080

ST MARGARET. *See* Altrincham.

ST MARK, Dunham Town. 1864 by *George & John Shaw* of
Saddleworth.

DUNHAM MASSEY HALL. There was a Norman castle on the
site, but of that only the motte tells us. It lies NW of the service
court of the present house The existence of a chapel is recorded for 1307. Sir George Booth, who lived from 1566 to
1652, built a house round a courtyard. It had a number of
gables, and walling of it may well survive. The S side, we are
told, came later. It was the work of the first Lord Delamer and
is assigned to 1655. Again we have nothing of this. From the
time of Sir George the MILL is preserved, a small gabled brick
building, with mullioned windows, quite picturesque on its
site. As to the present house, its story begins *c.*1720. To that
time belong the STABLES, two separate ranges, very handsome,
one S of the other. They have cross windows below and segment-headed windows above (the building further S has circular windows instead). The cross windows below are typical
later C17, the segment-headed windows above typical Early
Georgian. The centres of both ranges are a bay with Doric
pilasters carrying a pediment. The building further S has two
projecting wings and a wooden cupola with the date 1721.
Minor accents have one-bay brick pediments. The SERVICE
COURT of the house, N of the building further N, has the same
motifs and must be of the same date.

The HOUSE itself was rebuilt in 1732–40 by one *Norris*,

probably Richard,* for George Booth, Second Earl of Warrington and third Lord Delamer. This, with some alterations,
is the house we now see. *The Beauties of England and Wales* in
1801 call it 'one of the most beautiful residences in Cheshire',
the jaundiced Lord Torrington in 1790 'tasteless'. It is a brick
house with certain stone accents repeating the quadrangular
plan. The SOUTH FRONT stands at the far end of a front lawn
marked to the S by two high piers with lions and two lower
piers for the front drive which originally carried obelisks. The
S front is of eleven bays and two and a half storeys. The main
windows originally still had cross windows, a very conservative
motif. *J. Compton Hall* in 1905–7 replaced them in bays 3, 4,
8, and 9 by dormers, and gave the house the sumptuous,
chronologically incorrect frontispiece with columns in three
tiers and an open segmental pediment inside a normal pediment – a mid C17 motif. The whole frontispiece is of stone and
was of stone originally.‡

The WEST SIDE overlooks the service court and has on the
ground floor tall two-light windows with two transoms, this
also a conservative motif. Turning to the NORTH SIDE, there
are eleven bays with short projecting two-bay wings not quite
identical in width. Nor are they identical in design. The r.
pavilion continued the two-transom windows but now has the
ornate stone facing of *J. C. Hall*'s dining-room bay. By him
also are the stone centrepiece and outer two-arm staircase.
The EAST SIDE was altered by *John Shaw* in 1822. He gave it
the one-storeyed, wide segmental bow.

In the COURTYARD the principal feature is the great hall on
the S side of the N range, with its very tall three-transom windows. The stone frontispiece and that of the N side of the S
range are by *Hall*.

Hall also made alterations to some of the principal IN-
TERIORS. By him the entrance hall and the dining room in the
N range. The main staircase E of the hall may be 1822. Original,
i.e. of *c.*1740, is the GREAT HALL with its panelling, its doorcase, and its noble stone chimneypiece, totally undecorated
below, but with a richly carved coat of arms and supporters
above. The upper parts of the walls and the ceiling were decorated by *Percy Macquoid*. There are three minor original
staircases, and original also is the CHAPEL, which lies behind

* Though Lysons' *Magna Britannia* says John.
‡ Cf. one of the four paintings of *c.*1750 in the house which show all four
sides in their original state.

the great hall facing the N side and occupying three windows
E of the middle entrance. Curiously the altar is at the W end.
The chapel is said to have been made in 1655, but the fitments
do not go with so early a date. The panelling is clearly Early
Georgian, and the REREDOS looks 1675 and neither 1655 nor
1725. It has fluted pilasters, and in the middle a precious C17
SILK PANEL.* In the E range is the SALOON. It is the room
with the shallow bow. The bow is separated from the room by
dark green scagliola columns.

ORANGERY, NW of the house. Brick, of five bays, with tall
arched windows.

WELL HOUSE, N of the orangery. With a tree-trunk veranda
and bark decoration. The little house would be worth re-
storing.

DEER HOUSE, near the lodge. Brick, with lower lean-to extension on three sides. A beam carries the date 1740.

LODGE. By J. C. Hall, Tudor rather than Georgian.

OBELISKS. One SW of the house, dated 1714. A second N,
further away and in a wood.

TOMBS OF THE DOGS. N of the house in a row. The dates of
death stretch from 1702 to 1836.

WATER MILL. See above.

BOLLINGTON MILL, W of the estate. For this building,
see p. 108.

At DUNHAM WOODHOUSES two C18 farmhouses, both of three
bays. One has two rusticated corner piers to the front garden
and a good wrought-iron fence, the other two excellent gatepiers with urns and a date-plaque 1752.

DUNHAM-ON-THE-HILL ₄₀₇₀

ST LUKE. 1860–1 by *James Harrison*. Nave and chancel, rock-
faced, and a bellcote. The cost was estimated at £800. The
style is early C14. – CROSS. The church possesses a treasure, the 87
cross from over the choir screen of Chester Cathedral – typical
Skidmore of Coventry, who made it, typical *Scott*, who designed it, and typical High Victorian style in its elaboration
and its thick relief. It would be an ornament to any exhibition
of Victorian art. It was transferred from Chester in 1921.

* The famous *Grinling Gibbons* relief of Tintoretto's Crucifixion is on loan
at the Victoria and Albert Museum. – PLATE. Gorgeous Almsdish of 1706,
engraved by *Simon Gribelin* with a Deposition in the style of Annibale Car-
racci. – Chalice, Paten, and Flagon, also 1706. – Pair of Candlesticks, 1716. –
Paten or Almsdish, 1717. All these pieces by *Isaac Liger*.

DUNHAM WOODHOUSES see DUNHAM MASSEY

DUNSDALE see FRODSHAM

5070
DUTTON

DUTTON HALL. Timber-framed. When the house was demolished, fragments were removed to Sussex (on Dutton Homestall, *see The Buildings of England: Sussex*, p. 505).

(DUTTON VIADUCT. By *George Stephenson*, supervised by *Joseph Locke*. For the Grand Junction Railway, opened in 1837. Stone. Twenty arches.)

3080
EASTHAM

ST MARY. Ponderous W steeple, unhappily detailed. It must be late C13 to early C14 and has heavy diagonal buttresses with an oddly stepped-back top. The spire has broaches, and on them what can only be described as the most generalized pinnacles attaching themselves to the spire. It is very odd. There is a record of its having been rebuilt in 1751,* and the *Gentleman's Magazine* for 1762 reports that the spire was rebuilt 'about ten years since'. The rest of the church is largely Victorian outside, of the 1870s, when a drastic restoration by *David Walker* was done, but the four-bay arcades inside are Dec. The N chapel is Perp (but the arches to the chancel belong to the restoration). – FONT. Round and moulded instead of any decoration; C13 no doubt. – STAINED GLASS. Mostly by *Kempe*, 1889–1903. – MONUMENTS. Sir William Stanley † 1612. Tomb-chest with tapering pilasters and elementary geometrical ornament. – Sir Rowland Stanley † 1613. Table type, with crude columns. – Lady Haggerston † 1836. By *Bedford*. Kneeling female figure by an urn. – Sir Thomas Stanley Massey Stanley † 1841. Also by *Bedford*. The same ingredients plus a weeping willow.

S of the church is an ashlar-faced house, looking like a large lodge and being really three cottages. It has a wide canted porch with two Tuscan columns and a pediment.

The Eastham FERRY was a favourite ferry for travellers between Liverpool and Chester. Its usefulness declined with the opening of the railway from Chester to Birkenhead, but it enjoyed a period of prosperity with Eastham becoming a popular day resort. About 1845 Sir William Massey Stanley built the HOTEL by the ferry, five bays with some Early Victorian

* So the Rev. R. J. Pope tells me.

details round the windows and a jolly (later) wooden veranda and balcony.

At Eastham ends the Manchester Ship Canal, having run parallel with, and close to, the Mersey all the way from Runcorn. At Eastham also is the OIL DOCK, where tankers discharge the oil which is then conducted by pipes to the Stanlow Refinery. The POWER STATION was begun in 1947.

CARLETT PARK (West Cheshire Central College of Further Education). 1859–60 by *T. H. Wyatt*, brick and thoroughly bad. The CHAPEL is by *John Douglas*, c.1887, simple outside with plain lancets. NW turret. Ashlar interior, nicely done. Some STAINED GLASS by *Kempe*.* New good high block by the County Architect, *E. Taberner*, 1961–4.

EATON   8060
Near Congleton

CHRIST CHURCH. 1856–8 by *Raffles Brown*. W tower, nave and chancel. Ignorant Dec tracery.

(QUAKER BURIAL GROUND, but no meeting house left.)

EATON HALL. 1829 by *Lewis Wyatt*. Very large, of brick, in the Jacobean style with shaped gables; varied outline, no symmetry. The STABLES are dated 1831.

EATON   5060
Near Tarporley

A village with uncommonly many timber-framed houses.

ST THOMAS. 1896. Brick. Small.

EATON HALL   [EH]4060

Although Eaton Hall, as remodelled by *Alfred Waterhouse*, is no more (the demolition began in 1961), the remains of Waterhouse's work, together with numerous buildings in the park and surrounding villages, provide a record of an exceptionally interesting and important instance of Victorian aristocratic patronage. The first Duke of Westminster employed many architects in addition to Waterhouse. Those called in for individual jobs included e.g. *Bodley* for Eccleston church (*see* p. 213) and *Robson* for a school in Chester (*see* p. 159). Work given to the local architect *Thomas M. Lockwood* included some in Chester itself, but the majority of the Duke's estate projects were entrusted to *John Douglas*. The reputation of this Chester architect, whose buildings were illustrated with remarkable

* The house has been demolished. Happily, the chapel remains.

frequency in contemporary architectural journals, was not confined to this country alone, and Sédille and Muthesius in
praising him both singled out for special mention his work on
the Eaton estate.

Eaton came into the possession of the Grosvenors in the C15.
The first house on the present site, parts of which must have
survived until 1961, was built in 1675–83 and was designed by
William Samwell for Sir Thomas Grosvenor, third baronet. It
was as a result of Sir Thomas's marriage to the heiress of the
manor of Ebury that the family acquired its London property
which, with the developing of Mayfair and Belgravia, was to
bring fabulous wealth to subsequent generations. The seventh
baronet was created Baron Grosvenor in 1761, and Viscount
Belgrave and Earl Grosvenor in 1784. He was in 1802 succeeded by his son, who in 1831 became the first Marquess of
Westminster and who employed *William Porden* to rebuild the
house, c.1803–12. Porden was assisted by *Benjamin Gummow*,
and in 1823–5 wings were added by Gummow. The result was
the spectacular Gothic mansion which, with its delicate battlements, pinnacles, iron tracery, and plaster fan-vaults, remains
recorded in Buckler's illustrations. A heavy-handed attempt to
convert this into something more acceptable to the next generation was made in 1845–54 by *William Burn* for the second
Marquess (succeeded 1845), and the house in this state of compromise has sometimes been misleadingly illustrated (e.g. by
Eastlake) as being by Porden. There was no suggestion of
compromise in the transformation effected by *Alfred Waterhouse* in 1870–83 at a cost of £600,000. This was for the first
Duke of Westminster, who succeeded as third Marquess in
1869, and was created Duke in 1874. The work of encasing,
rebuilding, and extending was carried out in a style which,
though owing something to the C13 and something to France,
was an outstanding expression of High Victorian originality.
This Wagnerian palace was the most ambitious instance of
Gothic Revival domestic architecture anywhere in the country,
and to approach the w (i.e. entrance) front – scenically more
effective than the frequently illustrated E front – up the 1¾ m.
length of the Belgrave Avenue was an unforgettably dramatic
experience. The interior perhaps never possessed quite the
same degree of consistency and intensity as the exterior, and
many of its splendours, including decorative work by e.g.
Stacey Marks, had vanished long before 1961. NE of the main
block, and overlooking the terraces on the E (i.e. garden) side,

was the private wing, virtually a separate house. With a top-lit galleried hall and freely composed elevations, it was in itself something of a masterpiece. Would that it had been spared from the demolition, as were the chapel and clock tower and the stables.

CHAPEL, NW of the site of the main block, N of what was the forecourt. The altar is at the W end. Three-sided apse. Steep roof behind corbelled parapet. Geometrical bar tracery. Except for the upper stages of the clock tower and the spired termination of a staircase turret at the SE corner, the exterior is fairly plain compared with the exuberance that characterized the main block. Tower on the S, free-standing, though connected by a two-storey link and, at a higher level, by a bridge. Tall and slender coupled bell-openings. Clock stage corbelled out from the shaft and with corner pinnacles. Above it is a short but very eventful spire, commencing with an octagon with gables on four of its sides. The chapel interior, ashlar, and rib-vaulted throughout its length, is of narrow and lofty proportions. Five-bay nave, the end bay containing a low timber-vaulted narthex with gallery above. Three-bay chancel with low blank arcading. Heavily moulded chancel arch on clustered shafts. Four-light window behind the gallery. Two-light windows on one side of the nave and in the apse and adjoining bay. Two bays corresponding to the tower are occupied by the organ. The remaining bays have blank arches, the detailing of their tracery etc. and the arrangement of flanking shafts different from that of the windows. These blank arches are filled with MOSAICS designed by *Frederic Shields*, 1884. – STAINED GLASS. Also designed by *Shields* (commissioned 1876) and made by *Heaton, Butler & Bayne*. – MONUMENT. Duchess of Westminster † 1880. Recumbent effigy by *Sir J. E. Boehm*. – FURNISHINGS. Many items designed by *Waterhouse*.

The rebuilding of the STABLES was begun at the same time as the remodelling of the house. Although they formed a N continuation of the house, a different style was adopted, with a change of materials from light stone with slate roofing to brick, red stone, and half-timber with red tile roofing. Stone chimneys. Recognizable *Waterhouse* detailing. The stable court is immediately N of the chapel. The W range has a half-timbered upper storey and a gatehouse feature with two gables on both outer and inner sides. Flèches on this and on the lower E range. In the SE corner a fragment of the house, where the corridor from the main block met that linking the chapel and

the private wing. The N side of the court has a central gatehouse flanked by turrets (not quite symmetrical) which begin
polygonally, become circular, and end in conical roofs. On
either side are three gables above three bays of two-storey
arcades. Covered courtyard further N. Asymmetrical N end
elevation, with half-timbering, and rising to a considerable
height above the gateway. In the stable court, STATUE of a
rearing horse by *Boehm*.

GOLDEN GATES. Once the principal entrance to the forecourt, aligned on the axis of the house and the Belgrave Avenue.
The broad central pair of arched gates with overthrow and the
narrower screens on either side are early C18 by the *Davies
Brothers*. Open ironwork piers typical of them. Scroll and
foliated ornament. The remainder of the gates were designed
by *Waterhouse* and made by *Skidmore*, c.1871. Single-room
LODGES on either side by *Waterhouse*. In what was the forecourt is an equestrian STATUE of Hugh Lupus, Norman Earl
of Chester, by *G. F. Watts*.

The WALL between the park and the gardens etc. is by
Waterhouse, as are the following, N of the Golden Gates. First,
a set of GATES with a single-room LODGE, c.1871. Then
NORTH LODGE, 1881. A three-storey circular tower, French-
looking, with dormer and conical roof. Attached is a circular
stair-turret, also with conical roof. E of this is GARDEN LODGE,
1881–3. Picturesque and irregular, with a little half-timber
and pargetting. Near by a DRINKING FOUNTAIN, 1881, also
by *Waterhouse*. COACHMERE LODGE, s of the Golden Gates, is
probably of different authorship.

GARDENS. Landscaping is said to have been carried out in
the park by *Capability Brown*, though considerable remains
of axial layouts seem to have survived at the end of the
C18. Formal gardens were probably reintroduced by *W. A.
Nesfield* at the time of Burn's alterations to the house, but
the details of the C19 and C20 evolution of the gardens are
far from clear, and the story has been further complicated by
alterations made following 1961, which included the simplification of much of the planting and the removal of a number of
ornaments.

About the years 1897–8 designs for the ITALIAN GARDEN,
s of the house, were made by *Sir Edwin Lutyens*, and the present
layout probably reflects his work, though simplified.* The

* Mr Nicholas Taylor states that Lutyens was given the commission for
work at Eaton in 1896.

rusticated gatepiers at the s end are his too. Some way to the
e is a small LAKE, down to which extend FORMAL GARDENS
on the former axis of the house. The westernmost part of these
(between the site of the house and the cross axis known as the
Broad Walk) is of 1911, by *Detmar Blow*, and was made for the
second Duke (succeeded 1899) replacing Victorian terraces and
parterres with something on a grander scale. It incorporated a
canal on the axis. This part of the gardens has been altered
since 1961, however, and the topmost set of steps was destroyed with the house. Balustrading, terraces, curving steps,
etc., with gentle classical detail, and the pool at the centre of
the Broad Walk by *Blow*. On either side of the garden, cast-iron
Gothic balustrading, dating from the *Porden* and *Gummow*
period, but not in its original position. Two large groups of
STATUARY, 1852, by *Raymond Smith*. At the s end of the
Broad Walk was a Gothic TEMPLE by *William Cole*, built in
1822 to house a Roman altar discovered the previous year. The
altar and two fragments of Roman columns remain (*see* Chester,
p. 135), but the temple has been rebuilt, as a loggia with three
arches between Ionic columns. A Gothic structure by *Gummow*
at the opposite end of the Broad Walk was replaced by the
PARROT HOUSE, 1881–3 by *Waterhouse*. Rather surprisingly
it is classical and built of ochre-coloured terracotta. Circular
core, clerestoried and enclosed by a fluted Ionic colonnade.
Balustrades. Beyond the s end of the Broad Walk is the DUTCH
TEA GARDEN. The TEA HOUSE, 1872 by *John Douglas*, is of
cruciform plan with chamfered corners. Half-timber, with
small-scale enrichment, and a red-tiled roof which at the front
rises to a point in a broad concave sweep. Decorative work by
Stacey Marks does not survive. The present layout of the
Dutch Tea Garden is by *C. E. Mallows*, probably c.1905, but
no longer complete. Further e, a set of GATES communicating
with the Aldford Drive. Possibly by *Lutyens*.

NE of the stables are the KITCHEN GARDENS, where at least
some of the iron gates in the vast brick walls are probably by
Lutyens. Beyond is the former GARDENERS' HOUSE, by
Douglas & Minshull. Richly detailed brick chimneys, half-
timbering and brick and stone panelling etc. EATON COT-
TAGES, immediately N of the stables, are possibly by *Waterhouse*.*

Outlying lodges and buildings elsewhere in the park are

* Near them the former generator house, and to the e, beside the river,
former gas and water works.

most conveniently described in connexion with the several drives.

ALDFORD APPROACH. The ALDFORD LODGE, 1877 by *Douglas*, consists of two cottages. IRON BRIDGE. 1824 by *John Hazledine*, spanning the river Dee. A graceful cast-iron structure, over which the driveway gently rises. Segmental arch with Gothic ornament in the spandrels. A riverside LODGE of 1894 groups pleasantly with the bridge.

BELGRAVE AVENUE. An avenue existed here as part of a formal layout at any rate in the C18, and it may date from the time of the building of the C17 house. It was more than trebled in length early in the C19. BELGRAVE LODGE is of 1899. The OBELISK is by *Douglas & Fordham*, 1890.

BUERTON APPROACH. There are two LODGES, that near Bruera dated 1890. Near the junction of the drive with that from Aldford are two BRIDGES, one across a public road and the other, of three arches, across a tributary of the Dee. Both have iron Gothic balustrading like that which still survives in the gardens.

CHESTER APPROACH. OVERLEIGH LODGE and GATES, *c*.1893. One of the jobs for which the first Duke employed a London architect, in this case *R. W. Edis*. Neo-Jacobean lodge. Stone and brick with blue brick diapering. Conical-roofed turret. Elaborate brick chimneys. The first section of the drive is now disused. Beyond the junction of a branch from Eccleston is the marvellous ECCLESTON HILL LODGE, 1881–2 by *Douglas*, a three-storeyed gatehouse tower, with tourelles and, between them, a hipped roof so high and so steep as to be virtually a spire. The centre feature on the outer side consists of an armorial panel at first-floor level, a window above, and, as a termination, its own spirelet. Wings l. and r., that on the r. with conical-roofed staircase turret and half-timbered upper storey. Otherwise the materials are brick (with blue diapering) and stone, with red tile for the roofs. The gateway has two bays of rib-vaulting. EATON LODGE, *c*.$\frac{1}{2}$ m. beyond, E of the drive, was built as a gamekeeper's cottage and kennels, *c*.1873 by *Douglas*. Stone and some half-timber. The picturesque grouping includes a semicircular-ended wing, hipped gables, and a conical-roofed staircase turret. In the garden a SUNDIAL by *Lutyens*, originally in the Dutch Tea Garden.

ECCLESTON APPROACH. ECCLESTON LODGE and GATES. 1894 by *Douglas & Fordham*. Lodge of stone, half-timber, and diapered brick. Neat and smooth. Entrance recessed below a

gable. PARK KEEPER'S COTTAGE, a short way behind the
lodge. 1873 by *Douglas*. Largely half-timber, with some tile-
hanging and pargetting. Abreast of progressive taste at a time
when what Waterhouse was doing at the house itself was already becoming reactionary. ¼ m. inside the park, E of the drive,
is STUD LODGE, 1883 by *Douglas*, and the present ESTATE
OFFICE. The latter was built as the laundry, 1880, and is by
Waterhouse, but unremarkable. Behind the estate office is the
EATON STUD, for the rebuilding of which *Douglas* made in-
credibly ambitious designs in 1870. They remained unexecuted.

PULFORD APPROACH. Jacobethan PULFORD LODGES,
doubtless dating from the time of the second Marquess. They
are the only ones at Eaton not either built or rebuilt by the first
Duke. BLACK AND WHITE COTTAGES, ¾ m. beyond the hamlet of Poulton, s of the drive. Half-timber, with twisted brick
chimneys. By *Douglas & Fordham*.

VILLAGES. The villages round Eaton, with estate farms and
cottages, etc., and churches, schools, etc., built at Grosvenor
expense, are listed separately. (*See* particularly Aldford,
Eccleston, Pulford. Also Bruera, Dodleston, Lower Kinnerton,
Saighton, Waverton.)*

ECCLESTON   [EH] *4060*

The most notable and the most attractive of the Eaton estate
villages. Many cottages and other estate buildings.

ST MARY. Rebuilt in 1899 at the expense of the first Duke of 96
Westminster, who on this occasion employed *G. F. Bodley*. It
is one of Bodley's finest churches, and it formed the last of the
Duke's acts of patronage, for he died in the year in which it
was built. Red sandstone, ashlar. Nominally C14 with Dec
tracery. The exterior is characterized by an almost stark rectangularity. The W tower, with two long twins as bell-openings
on each side, battlements, and a curiously irregular disposition
of buttresses, is less uncompromising in outline than the rest,
though with its N and S walls flush with those of the high
clerestory, it forms a sort of vertical continuation of the nave.
It has lost the miniature spire which rose from the centre of its
roof. SW porch two-storeyed but windowless. External enrichment is almost entirely confined to statues in canopied niches

* Special thanks are due to Mr Peter Howell for many helpful comments
and for providing information which enabled many buildings by Douglas on
the Eaton estate to be identified.

in the upper part of the porch, the porch parapet, a frieze below the tower parapet, and quatrefoil patterns in the bell-openings. A long vestry block projects northwards. Flying buttresses to alternate bays. A greater sense of harmony pervades the interior, where the architect's refined and sensitive Gothic, redolent of scholarly and patrician Anglicanism, is seen at its best. Ashlar, and rib-vaulting throughout. Diagonal and ridge ribs. The N and S aisle windows differ in size and internal treatment. High arcades, but not excessively so. Unusual grouping of shafts and mouldings on the arcade piers neither strictly Dec nor strictly Perp. The arcade walls are pulled into unity by the rectangular crossing of the vaulting shafts with a string course which rests on the apexes of the arches but also touches the bottom of – not the clerestory windows – but recesses for them which in their lower part are blank. Black and white marble paving. Six bays, with no structural demarcation between nave and chancel. Carved enrichment of the simple and noble structure is virtually confined to the roof bosses, but *Bodley*'s genius for refined and inventive ornament, of C14 and C15 derivation, is lavishly expended on the FURNISHINGS. Particularly notable are the REREDOSES (executed by *Farmer & Brindley*) and the SCREENS which define the chancel. Above the tower arch the ORGAN CASE. All BENCH ENDS are carved. – STAINED GLASS. A complete set by *Burlison & Grylls*. – MONUMENT. First Duke of Westminster. 1901. Tomb-chest and canopy designed by *Bodley*. Effigy by *Farmer & Brindley*, the sculptor* being *Leon Joseph Chavalliaud*.

Trim and spacious CHURCHYARD with a broad avenue of trained limes aligned on the porch. GATES. A fine early C18 set, with overthrow, by the *Davies Bros*. The gates and the rusticated piers surmounted by urns were originally at Emral Hall, Flintshire. In the furthest, NE, part of the churchyard, adjoining what is now the Grosvenor burial place, is a fragment of the FORMER CHURCH of 1809–13 by *Porden*, including part of a window. Retained as a picturesque feature when the rest was demolished in 1900, but now much overgrown.‡

Former RECTORY, N of the church. Of *c*.1896 by *Thomas M. Lockwood & Sons*. Large. Elizabethan. Brick, blue brick

* This information kindly communicated by Miss Mary Bennett.

‡ TOMB of Earl Grosvenor †1909 aged four. Mr Nicholas Taylor, who kindly tells me that it was designed by *Detmar Blow* and *Fernand Billerey* and that the sculptor was *E. Madeline*, describes it as an enclosure with ornate openwork surround, all of bronze, in the Alfred Gilbert tradition, with statues of Edward I, St George, and St Hugh.

diapering, and stone bands and dressings, i.e. similar in style to Aldford Rectory.

The delightful toy-like SCHOOL is of 1878, by *John Douglas*. Built at the expense of the Duke. Stone, with varyingly traceried windows. Octagonal turret and spire. Projecting wing with unconventional things happening in the gable-end and culminating in a canopied niche under a pinnacle. In the niche a statue. A short link connects the school itself with the school house, which has a deeply projecting half-timbered gable. Douglas designed schools for other of the estate villages, but this, which must always have been the best, is the only one not spoilt by later alterations.*

PUMPHOUSE. 1874 by *Douglas*.

At the SW corner of the churchyard is a small brick and stone COTTAGE, 1870, with half-timber and tile-hanging in the end gables, by *Douglas*, and N of this a former CARRIAGE HOUSE AND STABLE, also 1870 by *Douglas*. Now converted into a residence, with the wide doors walled up. At the foot of the village, RIVERSIDE, early C18, rendered, has a timber doorcase with brackets and enriched frieze, pedimented. N of this is the MANOR HOUSE, now divided into cottages. Dated 1632. Mullioned and mullioned and transomed windows, originally five-light on the N side. Gabled projection flanked by chimneys. Finials. The oriel at the W end is apparently an addition. W of the church THE COTTAGE, a symmetrical early C19 Gothic house. On the W corner of the road leading to Chester, a group of COTTAGES, *c.*1889 by *Douglas & Fordham*, enclosing three sides of a little quadrangle. The central block has dormers with miniature Dutch gables. Twisted chimneys. The asymmetrical block of two COTTAGES, further W, with heavily pargetted gables, is by *Douglas*, dated 1882, though it could easily have been twenty years later.

THE PADDOCKS, immediately S of the village. Built for the Duke 92 of Westminster's agent *c.*1883. By *Douglas*. 'C'est un petit château!', exclaimed Sédille. Brick, with stone bands, dressings, etc. Blue brick diapering and carved stone enrichment. Some quite heavy gables and dormers set against the enormously high red-tiled roofs. At the E end a hipped-roofed block with conical-roofed circular turrets at the two corners. W of this runs a slightly narrower and lower range, the W end of which has, alas, been demolished. Entrance on the N side and, beyond it, the former ESTATE OFFICE, with pyramid roof over a gateway and

* But *see* Waverton, p. 377.

conical-roofed turret.* Further w is ECCLESTON HILL, built
for the Duke's secretary and also by *Douglas*. Less spectacular
than the agent's house, and more freely grouped in a friendly,
informal way, but built of similar materials, and also of considerable size. ¼ m. s of the village, beyond The Paddocks and
on the E of the road leading to Eaton Hall itself, is MORRIS
OAK, *c.*1875 by *Douglas*. Built as upper servants' houses, for
e.g. the Duke's chef. Two gables and, between them, two
dormers, all with pinnacles and brick Gothic panelling. E of
this ECCLESTON FERRY, with a prettily-sited ferry cottage,
1887, on the opposite side of the river.

WREXHAM ROAD FARM. Set back ¼ m. E of the main road from
Chester to Wrexham, 1 m. NNE of where it is joined by the
road from Eccleston. One of the most agreeable of all *Douglas*'s
model farms. About 1875–80. Farm buildings on three sides
of a quadrangle. Brick, with simple half-timbered gables. A
dovecote turret in one corner. The farmhouse, dated 1880, has
shaped gables and unmoulded stone mullions.

EDDISBURY *see* DELAMERE

EDGE HALL *see* TILSTON

5050
EGERTON

EGERTON HALL. In a field near by the ruins of a domestic chapel,
just two walls and hardly anything of detail. Ormerod guessed
C14; the MHLG says 'medieval'.

EGREMONT *see* WALLASEY, pp. 370, 371, 372

4070
ELLESMERE PORT

In the late C18 an attempt was made to start a watering place
where there is now Ellesmere Port. Then the Ellesmere Canal
from Chester, opened in 1795, changed the potentialities of the
site. *Telford* was in charge, and he created a tidal basin at the
Mersey end. This was completed in 1801. But activities gathered
strength only from 1825 onwards. Telford now, in 1830, laid
out an estate and began to build warehouses. A great increase
in the trade of Ellesmere Port came with the Birmingham &
Liverpool Junction Canal in 1835. *William Cubitt*, in charge after
Telford's death, built the sea lock in 1839–40 and a new dock.
Fifty years later it was the turn of the Manchester Ship Canal

* In paddocks to the E, stone and half-timber LOOSE BOXES by *Douglas*,
1871.

(1891),* and just over another fifty years later big industry began to settle down at and around Ellesmere Port. Shell, it is true, began refining oil at Stanlow as early as 1924, but the big expansion started only in 1949, and Vauxhall's came in 1958. Now Ellesmere Port is a boom town. Population was c.45,000 in 1961, and it is intended to allow an increase up to about 90,000. One-eleventh of the total county rates of Cheshire comes out of Ellesmere Port. The civic buildings show the wealth and pride of the town, even if no more.

CHRIST CHURCH. 1869–71 by *Penson & Ritchie*. Nave and chancel. Notable arrangement of the s tower with a gabled transept and gabled vestry. Nave later extended w.

The CIVIC HALL, 1954 by *Richard H. Kelly* (of *Gornall, Kelly & Partners*), and CENTRAL LIBRARY, 1962 by the same, are architecturally poor. The adjoining SHOPPING PRECINCT by *C. E. Wilford & Son*, 1958 etc., is no more distinguished. The new MUNICIPAL OFFICES, also adjoining, by the Borough Architect, *Norman Roberts*, in course of erection in 1968–9, are more promising, and there are banks of which Williams Deacons and Martins are pleasant. But it does not add up to a Civic Centre as it ought to. Ellesmere Port owed itself more than this.

Of the original Ellesmere Port there are still *Telford*'s CANAL WAREHOUSES, E-plan with three parallel wings, standing with rusticated segmental arches astride the canal. There is also a little of the earliest housing: Nos. 1–7 LOWER MERSEY STREET and 9–10 PORTERS ROW (N of Dock Street). *See* p. 441

(In and around BEECHFIELD ROAD, ¼ m. SW of the railway station, is an estate of cottages, designed for the Wolverhampton Corrugated Iron Company by *C. R. Ashbee c.*1906–9.‡)

Of new industrial and commercial buildings two deserve notice: the BOWATER PAPER CORPORATION, by *Farmer & Dark*, a number of large, well designed buildings, and in ROSSFIELD ROAD the BEMROSE PRESS, brick and shallow concrete arches, by *J. Roy Parker*.

ELWORTH 7060

ST PETER. By *John Matthews*, 1845–6. A Commissioners' church. Rock-faced. Nave and chancel and a bellcote. Lancet windows.

* Cf. Eastham, p. 207.
‡ Mr Alan Crawford told me about this estate, and Mr E. I. Johnson located it for me. Ashbee's client was Peter Jones of Greenbank, Chester (*see* p. 175).

ERINDALE *see* FRODSHAM

EVERSLEY *see* FRODSHAM

4050   ## FARNDON

ST CHAD. This sizeable church was so badly damaged in the
Civil War that it had to be all but rebuilt. Of 1658 are the
round piers with their elementary capitals, the single-chamfered arches, the mullioned windows of the clerestory, and also
the rere-arches of the chancel side windows. The aisle windows
are probably Victorian,* and only the lower parts of the tower
are medieval. The rusticated N porch must be Georgian. –
STAINED GLASS. One small window has panels of glass depicting some Cheshire Royalists of the time of the Civil War.
In the middle weapons and trophies, around attendant gentry
and pikemen, musketeers, etc. The technique is decidedly
Dutch. – PLATE. Paten Cover, 1688; Flagon given in 1781;
Chalice, 1791. – MONUMENT. Defaced effigy of a Knight,
c.1340–50, yet already no longer cross-legged.
BRIDGE. Between Cheshire and Wales. Built c.1345. Nine arches,
five of them over the water. The arches are segmental. Tri-
angular projections both sides.
The VILLAGE has a number of good houses, the best TOP
FARM, with an elaborate shaped gable, front and back.
On the road to Chester is the OBELISK to Major Barnston, by
E. A. Heffer, erected in 1858. It is peculiarly slim and starts from
a concave curve. The base has a similar curve, and as the monu-
ment stands on four lions, the whole makes a curious outline.

FLOWERY FIELD *see* HYDE

FOXHILL *see* FRODSHAM

2080   ## FRANKBY   [EH]

ST JOHN DIVINE. 1861–2 by *W. & J. Hay*. Red ashlar. E.E.
Bellcote over the junction of nave and chancel. N aisle. Chancel
ceiling decorated. – STAINED GLASS. Three excellent N aisle
windows 1873‡ by *Morris*, i.e. *Burne-Jones* designs. – The
easternmost window on the S of the chancel is of 1871 by
Kempe. – The remaining windows are by *Clayton & Bell*, and
the vestry S window is another early work by *Kempe*, 1870.

* There was a restoration by *Kelly & Edwards* (but with the SE chapel done
by *Douglas*), 1869.
‡ Date kindly supplied by Mr A. C. Sewter.

FRANKBY HALL. The grounds are now a CEMETERY for Wallasey. 1846–7. Red ashlar. Castellated and turreted. Converted to cemetery chapels and tall Gothic windows inserted in 1938–9 by *L. St G. Wilkinson*, Wallasey Borough Engineer and Surveyor.

On the N of the triangular village green is YEW TREE FARMHOUSE. Dated 1710. Brick, with stone quoins and dressings. Gable-ended. Two storeys and brick and stone dormers.

HILL BARK, ½ m. S. A house of 1891 by *Grayson & Ould, Edward Ould* presumably being responsible. Built originally for the soap manufacturer Robert Hudson, it began its life several miles away as Bidston Court, but was dismantled and re-erected here in 1929–31. The architects for this remarkable undertaking were *Rees & Holt*. For the original lodge, etc., *see* p. 97. The previous house at the Hill Bark site was, strangely enough, by *G. E. Grayson*, before Ould was taken into partnership. The present building was not only the largest and finest of the houses of outer Birkenhead, but is one of the most notable Victorian essays in half-timbered design anywhere in the country.* Brick and stone chimneybreasts and beautiful brick chimneystacks of differing design and great elaboration. Stone-flagged roof. U-plan enclosing an entrance court on the E. The S wing projects at an angle, and the irregular grouping of bay windows (based on those of Little Moreton Hall), porch, etc., is well contrived. Verses and mottoes and carved enrichment. The other elevations were treated more simply and were better suited to the restricted Bidston site for which the house was designed. The plan is arranged with ingenuity, and the great hall, running transversely through the centre of the W range, has an organ gallery, and open timber roof. Also a massive C17 chimneypiece and some screenwork apparently of the C15. A number of rooms were subdivided in connexion with the building's use as an old people's home, and its character has been seriously affected by the removal of the heavily-patterned leadwork from the windows. – STAINED GLASS. The W window in the great hall is almost certainly by *Morris*.

Hudson must have been one of those who, in Ould's own words, was 'a suitable client, one who is worthy of the privilege of living in a timber house', and the building, with its sense of craftsmanship, reflects Ould's enthusiasm for half-timber.

---

* The story that a replica was built at Potsdam for the Crown Prince Wilhelm is untrue, the Potsdam house being only vaguely inspired by Bidston Court.

'No style of building,' he wrote, 'will harmonize so quickly and so completely with its surroundings . . . and none continue to live on such terms of good fellowship with other materials, whether rosy brickwork, grey lichen-covered masonry, or pearly flag-slates, which last it loves the most of all. And then it is hard to say which season of the year most becomes it. In its cap of virgin snow, in its gorgeous garb of Virginia creeper or in its purple veil of wistaria it is equally bewitching. At noonday it throws the broadest shadows, and at eve (as no other building can) it gathers on its snowy breast the rose of sunset, and responds to the silver magic of the moon.'

HILL BARK FARM, ¼ m. E of Hill Bark itself. A model farm of 1875 by *John Douglas*. A stone and half-timbered group of house and farm buildings, with gables and steep hipped roofs.

FREEGREEN FARMHOUSE *see* LOWER PEOVER

5070
FRODSHAM

The MAIN STREET runs N of the railway and parallel with it. It is still the old-fashioned High Street, wide, with trees on both sides. The only building at once notable is the BEAR'S PAW, 1632, but much restored by *Douglas & Minshull*, 1903–4. Mullioned and transomed windows. E-plan front with five gables. Opposite a three-bay Georgian brick house with a hood over the door. The church lies ½ m. to the S, much higher up, and with a good view to the steep hill on which stands the War Memorial OBELISK.

ST LAURENCE. The church existed already in the late C11. As it is today it has conspicuous Late Norman remains, but looks externally almost entirely Dec and Perp, and even that largely under a Victorian overlay; for *Bodley & Garner* restored and partly rebuilt much in 1880–3. Late Norman are the W parts of the N arcade inside, and Bodley & Garner continued it. The piers are round with shallow leaf and crocket capitals and square abaci, and the arches are round and single-stepped. One pier is octagonal instead, and the W responds are rectangular. The clerestory also is (or was) Norman. The date is more likely to be *c.*1185 than *c.*1170. Bodley & Garner continued the arcade by a narrow arch S and N to link up with the chancel. They also rebuilt the S aisle. The N aisle, with its not over-elaborate flowing tracery, is original. The chancel is C14 too, cf. the arcades, but was extended in the C15, and the E and side windows are C15, the E window of seven lights. The N chancel chapel must be Late Perp. The difference is easy to see. The w tower must originally have been open to N and S, cf. internally the high blocked arches. Finally the porches. Bodley & Garner left them alone. So one is of 1715 (with pilasters), the other of 1724. – REREDOS. In the NE chapel, c.1700. Good, with two columns and two pilasters. – COMMUNION RAIL. Also c.1700, with twisted balusters. – ORGAN CASE. By *John Oldrid Scott*. – SCULPTURE. In the tower s wall, inside, one fragment of Norman zigzag and two interesting pieces of sculpture, more probably Saxon than Norman. One is of small, lively figures, the other of two larger figures, only their upper halves preserved, and even they totally defaced. – CHANDELIER. 1805. Brass, of Baroque shape. – PLATE. Mostly given c.1760. – MONUMENT. Tablet to William Allen and his wife who died in 1825. Profile heads, hers behind his. *See p. 441*

(OLD VICARAGE, E of the church at the corner of the B road. Good. The style suggests *Douglas*, and the little SCHOOL, ¼ m. SE, is his. EH)

TRINITY METHODIST CHURCH, Main Street. 1873 by *C. O. Ellison*. Late C13 style with SW steeple and cross-gables.

RAILWAY VIADUCT, to the NE. 1850. Of stone.

(Behind Rock House in the MAIN STREET opposite St Luke's R.C. church is a good recent house by *Robin Clayton*.)

EVERSLEY, 1 m. SE, near Newton Hall. By *William Owen*, c.1892. NEWTON HALL itself is Italianate.

(MICKLEDALE, 1 m. SSW. C17, with some minor medieval carving. MHLG)

(ERINDALE, ¾ m. SW of the church. By *R. T. Beckett*, 1910–11.)

(DUNSDALE, ¾ m. SW, is of 1876 by *Douglas*, and 1 m. SSE from it is FOXHILL, the DIOCESAN CONFERENCE CENTRE, with an extension by the *Design Group Partnership*. EH)

MESOLITHIC SITE. In the field E of Shepherd's House have been found a series of Mesolithic flint cores, flakes, and microliths.

IRON AGE HILLFORT, 1½ m. SE. This is a small univallate hillfort with external ditch enclosing an area of 1¼ acres. The defences are best preserved on the s and E. On the N the principal defence appears to have been the steeply sloping bank of a stream.

IRON AGE HILLFORT, 1½ m. SSW. This is a roughly rectangular fort whose defences enclose approximately 3¾ acres. The single bank is best preserved on the E side, where it still stands to a height of 5 ft and is 35 ft wide. On the w the line of defences is marked simply by a series of disjointed lengths of low bank, and it is possible that the site was never completed. There are no surface indications of a ditch, nor can the site of the original entrance be located.

GATLEY *see* CHEADLE

GAWSWORTH

There is nothing in Cheshire to compare with the loveliness of the church above the pool and the three great houses and one small house grouped round two further pools.

ST JAMES. A very strange church, in that it has no aisles, but a very wide nave and no structural separation of the chancel from that nave. It is all C15 to C16, the nave earlier than the chancel and w tower, which dates from the time of the rector Randle Fitton, i.e. from between 1497 and 1536.* The w tower has decorative friezes above the w doorway and beneath the battlements, and also three niches and eight pinnacles. The nave has battlements and pinnacles too. The s fenestration indicates that the E part, as if it were a chancel chapel, came later than the parts further w. The diagonally set buttress indicates that, and inside the reveal of an E window. Does that mean that there was a s aisle before the tower was built and the nave widened and the part E of the aisle added? It seems likely. Very decorated s porch, and large, splendidly character-ized hoodmould stops. – FONT. Big octagonal bowl; Perp. Two shields in panels on each side. – SCREEN. By *J. Oldrid Scott*, 1894, a copy of that of Elvaston in Derbyshire.‡ – MANORIAL PEW. The top part comes from *Pugin*'s Scarisbrick Hall in Lancashire. – STAINED GLASS. Many C15 fragments, also of figures. – The E window is by *Wailes*. – PLATE. Cup and Paten, unmarked, Edward VI or Elizabeth; Chalice, 1762–3. – MON-UMENTS. Four in the chancel, as if they were in chancel chapels. Francis Fitton, 1608. Table tomb, the effigy above, a skeleton below. Six short columns, the spandrels decorated with naïve branches. – Sir Edward Fitton † 1619 and wife. Two recumbent effigies, the children kneeling along the tomb-chest.

* Mr Raymond Richards pointed out to me that the whole nave is of yellow sandstone, but in the chancel only the lower courses. This indicates that when the tower arch was made for the new tower so much of the yellow stone of the w wall became available for the new chancel. It was used and, when exhausted, red sandstone took over.
‡ So Mr Richards told me.

Big wall-plate behind on the E wall. – Dame Alice Fitton
† 1627. Seated figure in widow's garb. Children kneeling in 52
front of and behind her. The monument is not in its original
shape. – Sir Edward Fitton † 1643 and wife. Big tomb-chest,
recumbent effigies, one little girl, big wall-plate on the E wall,
also a trophy on the S wall. There was originally a canopy over
this tomb.

RECTORY, the former school, by the churchyard. 1707, remodelled in 1949. The Late Georgian door surround comes from
Brook House, Knutsford.* (Inside, a Jacobean chimneypiece
from Pershore Hall, Worcestershire.)

OLD RECTORY. A large and impressive timber-framed house of
the late C15. It still retains its hall open to the roof. One truss
with queen-posts. The entrance to the porch is a reconstruction,
but the door is original. So are the three service doorways from
the former screens passage. The canted bay window is a C19
addition. The back wall of the hall was the former outer wall,
and here is a C15 window with ogee-headed, cusped lights,
exactly as at Bramall Hall. On the N a wing of 1872. To the l.
the LITTLE MANOR with a recent façade, but in its barn cruck
trusses.

OLD HALL. Another large timber-framed house, also with pre-
Reformation roof trusses, but in the original planning and the
function of the rooms still mysterious. It is of two and a half
ranges now, but was of three or four. Facing the former quadrangle, the E range has diagonal bracing and quatrefoil decorations. What remains of the S range, higher than the rest of the
house, has a frieze of patterned timberwork and a three-storey
canted bay window. About 1700 much was faced with brick,
and it is extremely interesting to hear that already then the
black and white pattern was painted on.‡ On the N front is the
Fitton coat of arms, carved in 1570 and including in the inscription the name of the carver, *Richard Rany* – an extremely
rare instance. Good woodwork inside, e.g. a chimneypiece with
inlay. In the library bookcases from *Pugin*'s Scarisbrick Hall.
In the Elizabethan GATEHOUSE a pedimented four-light
window.

NEW HALL. A surprisingly institutional large range of fifteen
by seven bays. It was begun in 1707 and left incomplete in
1712. Hipped roof and no external decoration, except the
recent doorway by *Sir Hubert Worthington*.

* Pulled down in 1949.
‡ I owe this piece of information to Mr Richards.

WHITE HOUSE, Warren, the former SCHOOL (1832). In it panelling and superbly carved late C17 doorcases from Wolseley Hall in Staffordshire. The carving is by *Edward Pearce*.

SE of the former in a spinney the TOMB of 'Lord Flame' or Maggoty Johnson, † 1773, one of the last paid English jesters. An entertaining rhymed inscription. Next to his tomb a Victorian slab of the same size with a further inscription in the Georgian tradition.

POST OFFICE TOWER, on the hills to the E. *See* Wincle, p. 387.

2080   GAYTON   [EH]

GAYTON HALL. The handsome SW front is early or mid C18 Two and a half storeys. Nine bays, the three central bays projecting slightly. Brick, with stone bands, quoins, parapet, and keystones. Doorcase with engaged fluted Ionic columns and curved open pediment. The glazing bars of the top storey are more closely spaced than those below, i.e. the panes are small, and this must be the original arrangement. Four-bay NW elevation. All this, as the other elevations show, is a refacing of an older house. The two-gabled SE end, where there is a bricked-up cross window with timber mullion and transom, must be largely C17, and work which is older still may be incorporated in the NE side. This is basically symmetrical in plan, though irregular in detail, with two gables, not identical, recessed in the centre. (Jacobean main and secondary staircases with turned balusters and square newels with ball-finials. MHLG) N of the house is a brick octagonal DOVECOTE. (Dated 1663.)

Gayton now forms a S continuation of Heswall. Some late C19 houses; but most are C20. In GAYTON LANE is GARTHLANDS, *c.*1930, Neo-Georgian, by *H. J. Rowse*. The chi-chi Italianate HESWALL GOLF CLUB HOUSE in COTTAGE LANE is also by *Rowse*, who seems to have been at his best only when handling jobs of greater size and complexity. Towards the NW end of LILLEYFIELD is a good modern house of 1965 by *Robin Clayton*. Vertical boarding above a ground storey of purple brick, with much glazing.

WINDMILL, immediately NE of Gayton, on the NE side of Telegraph Road. Two-storey battered stone-built tower, now much decayed.

GEE CROSS *see* HYDE

GODLEY *see* HYDE

1. *Landscape:* Peckforton Castle, by Anthony Salvin, *c.* 1844-50 (*foreground*), and Beeston Castle, *c.* 1220

2. (above) *Townscape:* Chester Walls, with the Water Tower,
1322–*c.* 1326
3. (above right) Chester Cathedral, font, possibly Early Christian
4. (below right) Sandbach, Crosses, ninth century

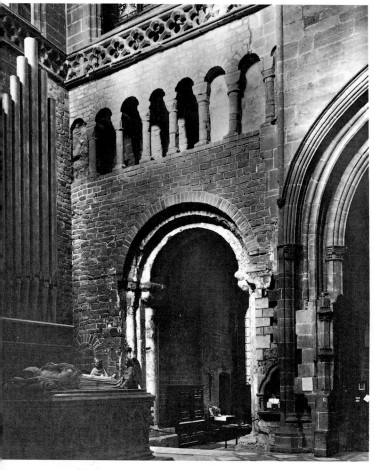

5. (above) Chester Cathedral, north transept, twelfth century
6. (right) Chester, St John, nave, twelfth and thirteenth centuries

7. (above left) Acton (near Nantwich) church, Norman stones
8. (below left) Norton Priory, doorway, late twelfth century
9. (above) Birkenhead Priory, former chapter house, twelfth century

10. (above) Chester Cathedral, thirteenth century and later

11. (left) Chester Cathedral, chapter house vestibule, early thirteenth century

12. (right) Chester Cathedral, chapter house, south wall, early thirteenth century

13. (below) Chester Castle, St Mary de Castro, late twelfth or early thirteenth century

14. (above left) Chester Cathedral, refectory, staircase to pulpit, late thirteenth century

15. (below left) Malpas church, iron-bound chest

16. (above) Chester, Browns Crypt Buildings, Eastgate Street, vaulted basement, probably after 1300

17. (right) Chester Cathedral, corbel in the choir, c. 1300

18. (above) Nantwich church, fourteenth century and later (*Copyright Country Life*)

19. (left) Nantwich church, chancel roof, fourteenth century

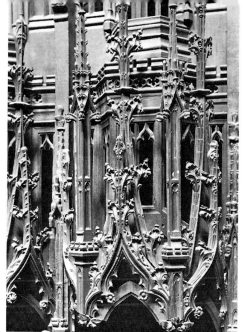

20. (right) Chester
Cathedral, choir
stalls, late fourteenth
century

21. (below) Great
Budworth church,
north arcade,
fourteenth century

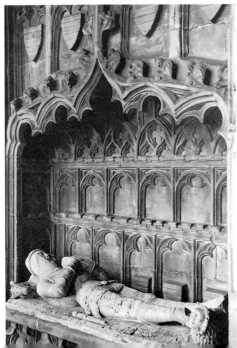

22. (above) Brimstage Hall, chapel, after 1398

23. (left) Acton (near Nantwich) church, monument to Sir William Mainwaring †1399

24. (above right) Astbury church, south aisle roof, late fifteenth century

25. (below right) Northwich, St Helen, Witton, c. 1500

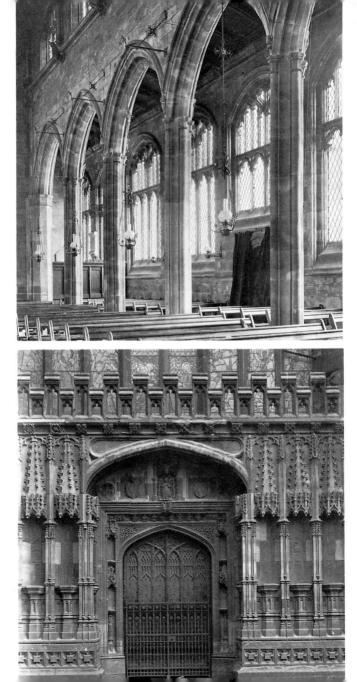

26. (above left) Bunbury church, north arcade, Perpendicular

27. (below left) Chester Cathedral, west doorway, early sixteenth century

28. (above right) Barthomley church, pier, Late Perpendicular

29. (below right) Nantwich church, pulpit, Perpendicular (*Copyright Country Life*)

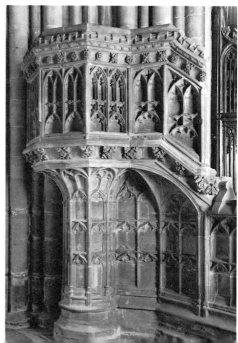

30. (above left) Daresbury church, screen, Perpendicular
31. (below left) Mobberley church, screen, 1500
32. (above) Saighton Grange, gatehouse, c. 1490

33. (below) Lower Peover church, fourteenth century, tower probably 1582
34. (above right) Marton church, fourteenth century
35. (below right) Holmes Chapel church, nave roof, Perpendicular

36. (top) Malpas church, monument to Randle Brereton †1522
37. (bottom) Macclesfield, St Michael, monument to Sir John Savage †1528
38. (right) Little Moreton Hall, mid or late sixteenth century

39. (above) Little Moreton Hall, courtyard, bay windows, 1559
40. (above right) Nantwich, Churche's Mansion, 1577 (*Copyright Country Life*)
41. (below right) Alderley Edge, Chorley Hall, sixteenth or seventeenth century

42. (above) Lyme Park, north front, frontispiece, *c.* 1570 (*Copyright Country Life*)
43. (above right) Brereton Hall, 1586 (*Copyright Country Life*)
44. (below right) Lyme Park, Long Gallery, chimneypiece, Late Elizabethan (*Copyright Country Life*)

45. (below) Crewe Hall, 1615–36, rebuilt by E. M. Barry, 1866–70
46. (above right) Crewe Hall, 1615–36, rebuilt by E. M. Barry
1866–70, staircase
47. (below right) Handforth Hall, staircase, 1562 or probably later

48. (above) Dorfold Hall, Great Chamber *c.* 1616 (*Copyright Country Life*)

49. (left) Astbury church, font cover, Jacobean

50. Over Peover, Peover Hall, stables, 1654

51. (left)
Cholmondeley Castle,
chapel, screen, 1655

52. (below)
Gawsworth church,
monument to Dame
Alice Fitton †1627

53. (above) Acton
(near Nantwich)
church, monument to
Sir Richard
Wilbraham †1643
and wife †1660

54. (right) Chester
Cathedral, monument
to John Leche †1639,
by Randle Holme

55. (right) Stoak church, monument to Henry Bunbury, 1668

56. (below) Wilmslow, Dean Row Unitarian Chapel, 1693

57. (left) Lyme Park, panelling in the Saloon, perhaps by Grinling Gibbons, 1680s

58. (below) Mottram-in-Longdendale church, monument to Reginald Bretland †1703

H. S. E.
Quicquid mortale fuit
REGINALDI BRETLAND A. L. S.
Familia non-ignobili orti.
Virtute, Doctrina, Ingenio Præclari

59. (above) Lyme Park, south front, late seventeenth century and 1720, the latter by Giacomo Leoni
60. (right) Chester, St John, monument to Diana Warburton †1693, by Edward Pearce

61. (above left) Cholmondeley Castle, White Gates, by the Davies Brothers, early eighteenth century
62. (below left) Adlington Hall, south front, probably by Charles Legh, 1757 (*Copyright Country Life*)
63. (above) Tabley House, by John Carr, 1761–7 (*Copyright Country Life*)

64. (above left) Mow Cop, Castle, 1754
65. (below left) Bruera church, monument to Sir Robert Cunliffe
†1778, by Joseph Nollekens
66. (below) Styal, Quarry Bank Mill, 1784

67. (above) Chester Castle, Propylaea, by Thomas Harrison, 1810–22 (*Copyright Country Life*)
68. (above right) Chester Castle, Shire Hall, by Thomas Harrison, 1791–1801 (*Copyright Country Life*)
69. (below right) Macclesfield, Roe Street Sunday School, 1813–14

70. Tatton Park, Entrance Hall, by Lewis Wyatt, 1807 etc. (*Copyright Country Life*)

71. (above) Lyme Park, Dining Room, by Lewis Wyatt, 1816–22
72. (below) Stockport, St Thomas, by George Basevi, 1822–5

73. (above) Birkenhead, Hamilton Square, by James Gillespie
Graham, 1825 etc.
74. (above right) Cholmondeley Castle, by the Marquess of
Cholmondeley and Sir Robert Smirke, 1801–*c.* 30 (*Copyright Country
Life*)
75. (below right) Bolesworth Castle, by William Cole, *c.* 1830

76. Macclesfield, St Alban, by A. W. N. Pugin, 1839–41

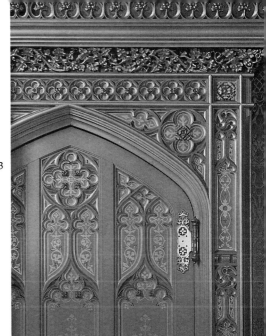

77. (right) Cheadle, Abney Hall (now Town Hall), door in the former Drawing Room, designed by A. W. N. Pugin, executed by J. G. Crace, 1852 etc.

78. (below) Great Moreton Hall, by Edward Blore, 1841–3

79. (above left) Peckforton Castle, by Anthony Salvin, *c.* 1844–50,
Great Hall (*Copyright Country Life*)
80. (below left) Chester General Station, by Francis Thompson,
1847–8
81. (below) Birkenhead Park, by Sir Joseph Paxton, 1843–7, Lower
Lake and Swiss Bridge
82. (bottom) Hyde, St Mary, monument to James Ashton †1841 and
John Ashton †1844, by Knowles of Manchester

AS A SACRED MEMORIAL
OF THE LATE JAMES ASHTON ESQ᷄ NEWTON LODGE,
WHO DIED JANUARY 23ᴿᴰ 1841, AGED 65 YEARS,
AND OF HIS SON, THE LATE JOHN ASHTON ESQ᷄ NEWTON HOUSE,
WHO DIED JULY 26ᵀᴴ 1844, AGED 44 YEARS,
THIS MONUMENT
WAS ERECTED BY THE OPERATIVES WHOM THEY EMPLOYED,
IN GRATEFUL REMEMBRANCE
OF THEIR KINDNESS AND BENEVOLENCE.

THE LAND ON WHICH THIS CHURCH
AND THE NATIONAL SCHOOL ARE BUILT,
WAS PRESENTED BY
THE SAID JOHN ASHTON ESQUIRE.

SACRED TO THE MEMORY OF
CHARLOTTE LUCY BEATRIX EGERTON.

83. (above) Rostherne
church, monument to
Lady Charlotte
Egerton †1845, by
Richard Westmacott
Jun.

84. (left) Sandbach
church, monument to
John Armitstead, by
G. F. Watts and
George Nelson, 1876

85. (above right)
Hooton church,
by J. K. Colling,
1858–62, dome over
the crossing

86. (below right)
Bromborough church,
by Sir George Gilbert
Scott, 1862–4

87. (left) Dunham-on-the-Hill church, cross from Chester Cathedral, by Skidmore of Coventry, designed by Sir George Gilbert Scott

88. (below) Crewe Hall, Stowford Cottages, by W. Eden Nesfield, 1864–5

89. Macclesfield, premises of Arighi, Bianchi, façade of cast iron and glass, 1882–3

90. (above left) Chester, corner of Bridge Street and Eastgate Street, by T. M. Lockwood, 1888
91. (below left) Chester, St Werburgh Street, by John Douglas, 1895–9
92. (above top) Eccleston, The Paddocks, by John Douglas, *c.* 1883
93. (bottom) Port Sunlight, The Dell and Park Road Cottages, by William & Segar Owen and Douglas & Fordham, 1892

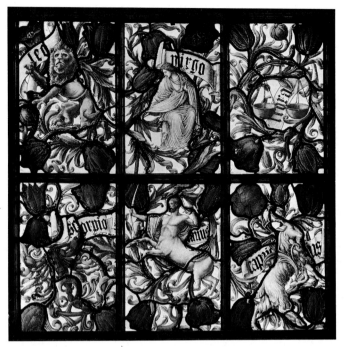

94. (above) Wilmslow, Pownall Hall, stained glass, by Shrigley &
Hunt, *c.* 1890
95. (right) Chester (Handbridge), St Mary-without-the-Walls, reredos,
by Frederic Shields, 1888

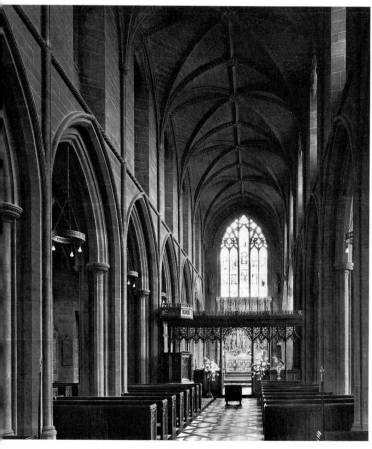

96. (above) Eccleston church, by G. F. Bodley, 1899
97. (above right) Stockport, St George, by Austin & Paley, 1896–7
98. (below right) Willington, Tirley Garth, by C. E. Mallows, begun
c. 1906–7

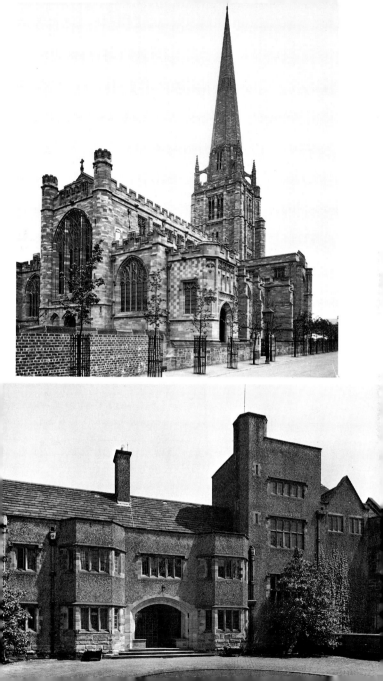

99. (above left) Marple, St Martin, font cover, by Henry Wilson, c.1900
100. (below left) Stockport Town Hall, by Sir Alfred Brumwell
Thomas, 1904–8
101. (above) Knutsford, The King's Coffee House, by Richard
Harding Watt, 1907–8

102. Stanlow, Shell Research Centre, by Sir Frederick Gibberd, 1956 etc.

GOLBORNE OLD HALL *see* HANDLEY

GOOSTREY 7070

ST LUKE. 1792–6. Brick, with W tower and arched windows. The nave side has a rusticated doorway and three windows. At the E end is a shallow polygonal apse. Lowish interior. – FONT. Perp, octagonal, with leaf quatrefoils and a panelled stem. – STAINED GLASS. The S windows are Victorian but not English. The probability is France or Belgium. – PLATE. Paten inscribed 1719; Flagon inscribed 1759; also an C18 Chalice. – MONUMENT. Tablet to W. Booth † 1810, by *Crake* of London. Naval still-life at the top.

BLACKDEN HALL, ¾ m. NE. Charming timber-framed house with two gables on the entrance side and various decorative motifs.

(TOAD HALL, N of Blackden Hall. A C16 cruck cottage. MHLG)

CROOK HALL, 1½ m. NE. Late C16, red brick, with three gables. The fenestration is altered. (Unusual staircase with twisted balusters. MHLG)

GOYT HALL *see* BREDBURY

GRAPPENHALL 6080

ST WILFRED. An interesting church. The earliest part is the Norman corbel-table preserved in parts in the nave S wall and visible from the aisle. Then follows the S chapel. It has square-headed Dec windows, and a chantry was indeed founded *c.*1334 by a Boydell. His MONUMENT is in the chancel, an excellent effigy of a Knight, cross-legged. Also preserved, though in bits and pieces, is the STAINED GLASS of the chapel, plenty of parts of figures, and plenty of the characteristic C14 green and yellow. The church was rebuilt about 1525–39: a date 1539 is on one arcade pier. Of this period are the W tower and the nave with the aisles. Seven bays; no chancel arch. Octagonal piers, clumsy capitals, double-chamfered arches. The clerestory was added in 1833, but in its present form must be of 1874 (restoration by *Paley & Austin*). Also Victorian and very successful is the long N transept. Here and in the chancel E window Perp is treated less elementarily, i.e. with proper panel tracery. The original chancel E window is now the N aisle E window. – FONT. Norman, big, oblong, with blank arcading. – STAINED GLASS. Three S aisle windows by *Mayer* of Munich. – PLATE. Flagon inscribed 1765; Chalice and two Patens inscribed 1797. –

8—C.

SUNDIAL, in the churchyard. A column, dated 1714. – STOCKS by the SW corner of the churchyard.

Grappenhall is still a village, in spite of the proximity to Warrington. It is a particularly attractive one, and retains cobbled paving. S of the church the RECTORY, early C19 Gothic, with two canted bay windows and Gothic treatment of the doorway too.

CAIRN, which covered several cremations in Food Vessels and urns.

₂₀₈₀   GREASBY   [EH]

OUR LADY OF PITY (R.C.). 1952 by *F. X. Velarde*. Tower at the SW corner. Brick interior with low transverse arches.

The DISTRICT BANK is a house dated 1680, altered. NW of it is a house with mullioned window and arched entrance. More notable is NEW HOUSE (or OLDFIELD MANOR FARM), 1 m. NW. Early or mid C17. Red sandstone with lighter dressings. Symmetrical. First floor with mullioned and transomed windows of five, four, two, four, and five lights. Ground floor with mullioned windows of five, four, four, and five lights, with arched doorway under an armorial panel in the centre. The house is said formerly to have had two gables, and the present hipped roof is obviously not original.

GREAT BARROW
₄₀₆₀

ST BARTHOLOMEW. W tower of 1744, well designed. The nave by *Douglas*, 1883, also carefully done. He only restored, however, and the N arcade with its depressed arches is probably trustworthy. Chancel of 1671 with mullioned windows with arched lights and inside one hammerbeam truss, quite grandly decorated, including shields. The chancel was built at the expense of a Dean of Chester Cathedral. – FONT. Octagonal, plain, dated 1713 – yet not a classical touch. – STAINED GLASS. By *Kempe* E 1884, N 1894. – MONUMENT. Mrs Wallis † 1848. By *Gaffin*. An angel kneels by an urn.

BARROWMORE HALL, by *Douglas* and admired by Muthesius, was destroyed in the Second World War.

GREYSFIELD. A large half-timbered house, with a brick and stone ground storey. First built in 1878, but shortly after much enlarged for Edward Paul, a Liverpool grain merchant and partner of H. Lyle Smyth, for whom Douglas designed Barrowmore Hall. W wing added in 1910.

GREAT BOUGHTON *see* CHESTER, p. 173

GREAT BUDWORTH

6070

ST MARY. This is one of the most satisfactory Perp churches of
Cheshire and its setting – *see* below – brings its qualities out to
perfection. The long N transept is Dec, as the E window with
reticulated tracery and the arch inside show, but the rest is all
Perp. Money was left to the building in 1498 and 1527, at the
latter date by Richard Starkey (cf. Over) for the rood-loft, i.e.
the church must have been complete then. Nearly the whole
church, tower, nave and aisles, S porch, N and S transepts, and
chancel and chancel chapels, is embattled. Nothing is ornate,
but all is substantial. W tower with a decorated doorway, an
inscription over, and a pair of twin bell-openings. It is so
similar to the tower at Northwich that the same mason, *Thomas
Hunter*, may be assumed. The arches inside are of six bays to
the chancel arch. The N arcade came first and was built from 21
E to W. The pier form changes from a square with four semicircular shafts to the standard Perp four shafts and four hollows.
The capitals have rounded forms. The arches are moulded in
quite big mouldings. On the S side the piers have four thin
triple shafts each side and four diagonal hollows, and the arches
have four mouldings. The chancel chapels are yet later – cf.
the polygonal parts of the capitals–and last came the clerestory.
The roof-line of the previous roof is visible above the arch.
When the clerestory was finally built, it was given E windows
too, as usual in the Cotswolds. Good nave roof of very low
pitch. – FONT. Perp, large, octagonal, with quatrefoils on the
bowl, heads against the underside, and a panelled stem. –
STALLS (S transept). Plain, and ascribed by Crossley to the
C13. – BENCH ENDS (S transept). Are they Elizabethan? The
ends still have close Gothic panelling, the fleur-de-lys poppyheads look Jacobean. – SCREEN, to the N transept. Stone, by
Salvin. – COMMUNION RAIL. Parts, with slim turned balusters; early C18. – STAINED GLASS. By *Kempe* the E window
(1883), the S aisle E window (1888), and the N aisle E window
(1901). – In the N transept Expressionist glass by *Fourmaintreaux*, 1965. – PLATE. Chalice and Paten, *c.*1571, by *William
Mutton* of Chester; Paten, London, 1685; two Flagons, 1719;
Chalice by *Richard Richardson* of Chester, 1763; two Chalices
by *Chawner* and *Emes* of London, 1796; Beadle's Staves, *temp.*
George III. – MONUMENTS. Sir John Warburton † 1575,
truncated alabaster effigy. Also inscription with good strap-

work surround. – Sir Peter Warburton † 1813. Large tablet
with a kneeling female figure with an urn above. – (On the
floor of the nave an unusually good Victorian brass to Joseph
Leigh † 1840, though its date must be later than this. EH) – In
the churchyard a SUNDIAL. Baluster-type; C18.

The immediate surroundings of the church make one of the best
pieces of villagescape in the county. Yet there is hardly a house
that would need a close look. The most interesting individually
is the former SCHOOL in the churchyard, low, of brick, with
mullioned windows. It is in SCHOOL LANE, and facing it is a
terrace of timber-framed cottages. Towards the church from
the N runs CHURCH STREET, quite narrow and all brick l.
and r. The HIGH STREET starts from the church and runs W.
Against the churchyard wall the STOCKS. The street is wider.
At the beginning the GEORGE AND DRAGON, 1875 by *Douglas*. (Also by him Nos. 54–57, brick. All the C19 building and
restoration in the village was under Warburton patronage,
i.e. for the Arley estate. There is a particularly attractive
COTTAGE by *Douglas* at the foot of the hill W of the village,
and N of this is THE DENE HOUSE, built as the Arley dower
house and by *Kirby*. EH)

*See
p.
441*

BELMONT HALL, I m. NW. 1755. A seven-bay brick S façade of
two and a half storeys with a decorated three-bay pediment and
two two-storeyed bow windows. The doorway with a wide
rusticated surround carries a pediment. Five-bay links with
pedimented archways in the centre connect the house with
three-bay wings set at r. angles. The garden side of the house
is absolutely plain, except for a smallish doorway with Gibbs
surround. The interior has quite sumptuous decoration in the
Rococo mode. The finest room is the so-called Adam Room
in the SW corner, with lush stucco wall panels and more delicate
ceiling decoration. Equally excellent the staircase hall. More
subdued the entrance hall and some other rooms.

8050

GREAT MORETON HALL

78 Built in 1841–3 for George Holland Ackers, a Manchester cotton
manufacturer. The architect was *Blore*, and it is one of his
largest and may well be his most successful mansion. It is all
castellated and Gothic – from Dec to Tudor – and consists of
a centre of two high storeys, ashlar-faced, with a deep vaulted
Gothic porte-cochère and angle turrets, the r. one polygonal,
the l. one square with a higher stair-turret, a long, much lower
one, and a half-storey wing and the extensive rock-faced

STABLES, more castle-like than the house. To the s the façade of the house is totally asymmetrical, with long two-light Dec windows, and a narrow polygonal and wide rectangular bay to mark the great hall and the staircase tower with higher thin turret rising behind and not axially. The interior is very completely preserved, with panelled ceilings, a hammerbeam roof in the hall, and a lierne-vault over the staircase. The accommodation is lavish and largely for display, the porte-cochère being followed by a large lobby and then a central hall with skylight. From here the screens passage continues the axis and ends in the narrow polygonal bay already referred to which is really a garden exit. From the central hall l. is the staircase, from the screens passage l. the great hall.

Castellated SUMMERHOUSE, SW of the house.

BOATHOUSE, on the lake, ¼ m. NW. A square C17 brick outbuilding of the Hall preceding Blore's, built before there was the lake. It has been, probably in the later C19, dressed up with Jacobean stonework, perhaps from the old hall.

EAST LODGE. 1858, with steep gables.

GREAT SAUGHALL   3070

The village is now mostly suburban Chester.

ALL SAINTS. 1895–1901 by *Medland Taylor* (GR), i.e. probably *Medland & Henry Taylor*. It is of fiery red Ruabon brick and has a number of Medland Taylor crotchets such as the placing of the E window in the polygonal apse just a little higher than the other windows, the rectangular shape of the central tower, the contrast between the height and depth of the s transept and the N attachment, and the prolongation of the nave roof by the s porch roof. The tower carries a low broach-spire. The N arcade has piers whose capitals are just blocks of stone flush with the piers.

The former SWINGING GATE pub, now a private house, opposite the Greyhound, is said by the MHLG to be of *c.*1490. It is of brick (but has a stone spiral staircase).

WINDMILL, I m. N. Just the tower of a tower-mill.

SHOTWICK PARK. By *Douglas*, 1872. A fine, large brick house with big tiled roof. Neo-Elizabethan, handled quietly. The façade is symmetrical except that to the big polygonal bay at the r. end and going round the corner corresponds at the l. end a tower forming a group of varied outline. Good STABLES too.*

* Mr Howell reports that the house was altered and partly rebuilt in 1907 after a fire.

3070
GREAT SUTTON

St John Evangelist. By *David Walker*, 1879–80, with a
perky sw turret with conical spire.

0070
GREAT WARFORD

The Mary Dendy Hospital is a large group of many scat-
tered buildings, some existing on the site when the hospital
(which is for the mentally sub-normal) was created by Mary
Dendy in 1902, but more built since. Close by are also the
David Lewis Hospital for epileptics and the Margaret
Barclay Home for spastics.

Baptist Chapel, close to the Mary Dendy Hospital. A barn
and cottage converted in 1712. Humble original interior. box
pews and pulpit. The windows have triangular heads. Is
that original?

GREENBANK *see* CHESTER, p. 175

4060
GUILDEN SUTTON

St John Baptist. 1815. Brick, small. Four bays, the round-
arched windows short and high up. The e window is pointed,
just with two mullions. Victorian bell-turret. – font. 1635.
Round, with the date and just one flower.

Hill Farmhouse. It has a chimneystack of a type the Victorian architects of estate housing were to like. Recessed vertical
panel up the whole height with a zigzag of tiles set in.*

HADLOW WOOD *see* WILLASTON

7080
HALE

Hale, Altrincham, Timperley, Sale, Bowdon are one and all Outer
Manchester. But Hale is distinguished from the others by one
group of memorable houses.

St Peter, Ashley Road. 1890–2 by *Tate & Popplewell*. Brick
and red terracotta. Nave and aisles. Geometrical tracery, sw
steeple with an octagonal upper part. The interesting feature
of the church is the very large clerestory of *c.*1910. – (stained
glass. By *Heaton, Butler & Bayne*.)

All Saints, Hale Road, Halebarns. 1966–7 by *Brian E. Bon-
skill*.

* Another such chimney is on the Cock Inn at Barton near Stretton
and on Lower Carden Hall, Clutton.

CONGREGATIONAL CHURCH, Ashley Road. 1911–13. Large.
Brick with arched windows. The front has a three-bay loggia
of stone with a raw granite vault inside, and the front tower is
square and high. The architects were *France & Laycock* of
Manchester.

UNITARIAN CHAPEL, Chapel Lane, Halebarns. 1723. Four
bays and two former doorways in the first and last bays. Brick,
with segment-headed windows. The PULPIT is in the middle
of the long side facing the two entrances. – BOX PEWS. –
STAINED GLASS. Caritas by *Morris & Co.*, i.e. designed by
Burne-Jones, but the lovely flower and leaf quarries designed
by *Morris*. The date is as late as 1906.

At the SW end of ASHLEY MILL LANE two very good recent
one-storeyed white brick houses by *Tom Mellor & Partners*.
Very well set in the landscape, too.

HALECROFT, Hale Road. 1891. Large and ambitious, brick,
stone, and half-timber. Mullioned and transomed windows.
Flower patterns in black on the white gables. Free Jacobean
staircase. This is by *Edgar Wood*, but he was very young when
he did it.

But further NW is a whole group of *Edgar Wood* houses, and they
are mature, of 1901–7. They are No. 226 HALE ROAD and
in PARK ROAD Nos. 116, 117, 119, and 121, and in PLANE-
TREE ROAD Nos. 20 and 27. They are one family, but ROYD
HOUSE, No. 224 Hale Road, which Edgar Wood built for
himself, 1914–16, is quite different. With its symmetrical
concave façade, its flat roof, and its jazzy mosaic in the middle
it points forward into the Modern Movement. The other
houses, less aggressive and hence more attractive, are typical
early C20, gabled, with Tudor connotations but, being
by Wood, at the same time never flagging in resourcefulness and full of delightful touches of façade and also of
planning (e.g. No. 121 Park Road). Wood uses indifferent
bricks, but they give him variations in colour and texture. He
even varies his doorways; he likes gables canted in plan and
segmental projections, and he knows where to introduce
weatherboarding. Nos. 223–233 are not by Wood but by *John
Cocker* of Altrincham, 1907–8.*

In BARROW LANE, Halebarns, in a district of curving, tree-
lined roads, is GRAYTHWAITE, c.1910 by *Frank B. Dunkerley*

* Information on all these houses was kindly supplied by Mr J. H. G.
Archer.

for himself. A large house, with much half-timbering and many gables.

HALEBARNS *see* HALE

HALTON

At the time of writing Halton village on its rock in the plain is still a village. Soon it will be New Runcorn (*see* p. 327) and may the planners fully realize what a visual treasure they have in this rock.

HALTON CASTLE. First built by Nigel Baron of Halton, to whom Halton had been granted by Hugh Lupus. The ruins tell little, and no intensive research has been done. Along the NW side some medieval masonry survives, including two crags at the N tip, a two-light window a little SW of it, a projecting late medieval tower with a three-light window, and a piece of wall with internal blank arches and cross loops at the W tip. The walls to the l. and r. of the back of the Castle Hotel are of *c*.1800, though built of medieval stone. They belong to a remodelling undertaken to make the castle an eyecatcher from Norton Priory.

ST MARY. By *Sir G. G. Scott*, 1851–2. On the brow. No tower, but a polygonal bell-turret on the nave E gable. The details in the style of 1300. Good, serious interior. – (STAINED GLASS. Christ and the Children window (N aisle) by *Holiday*.) – MONUMENT. Sir Richard Brooke, by *Douglas & Fordham*, 1889. Tablet with a stylized cross in a foliage frame.

At the entry to the churchyard the PARISH LIBRARY, built in 1733 by Sir John Chesshyre. Two bays only, with arched windows. Not classical yet, cf. the pedimental gable and the odd pediment over the doorway. The VICARAGE is opposite. It is dated 1739. Five bays, two storeys, a parapet, and a pedimental gable – still not a real pediment. Broad Tuscan porch. Windows with frames of small raised blocks.

CASTLE HOTEL, originally the Duchy of Lancaster Court House, and hence decidedly monumental. Seven bays with a recessed centre and a hipped roof. Open (asymmetrical) staircase to the entrance. Above this a coat of arms and another pedimental gable. The date is 1737–8.

In the MAIN STREET a number of good houses, best the SENESCHAL'S HOUSE, 1598, with three square projections, but not quite symmetrical. The side projections are bay windows and the fenestration continues round the corners. Then HALTON

HOUSE of 1779 and HOLLY BANK HOUSE of five bays with a splendid doorway with open curly pediment.

Behind the church to the E in THE COMMON is the OLD HALL, dated 1693 and yet still entirely Jacobean.

HALLWOOD was the house of Sir John Chesshyre. It must be of c.1710, and the stone-faced STABLES are grander than the house. They have a fine façade with giant pilasters, two pedimented doorways, and round windows above the normal ones. The house is of stone but has a brick front of five bays with a heavy pediment over the whole façade. Quoins of even length. Good, if small, interiors. The staircase has twisted balusters.

On Halton Brow, overlooking the Mersey above Runcorn, evidence suggesting Roman civil occupation has been found in an area of roughly pentagonal shape (c.350 by 240 ft) surrounded by a ditch.

HAMPTON OLD HALL *see* MALPAS

HANDBRIDGE *see* CHESTER, pp. 174, 175

HANDFORTH   8080

ST CHAD. 1897–8 by *John Brooke*. Red brick and stone dressings. The low façade with a small bell-gable and the twin-gabled S vestry are attractive features.

ST COLUMBA PRESBYTERIAN CHURCH. *See* Cheadle.

HANDFORTH HALL. Dated 1562 over the doorway. Timber-framed house, once much larger, though not necessarily quadrangular. What remains has a porch, and in the expected relation to it a square bay window, no doubt of the former hall. The posts of the porch are heavily carved. Staircase with 47 elaborate and unusual flat balusters.

HANDLEY   4050

ALL SAINTS. The W tower has an inscription and the date 1512 on its W face. The S doorway is Dec with continuous mouldings. Hammerbeam roof in the nave, dated 1662, with excellent corbels. The rest is by *James Harrison*, 1853–5. – STAINED GLASS. On the N side a window by *Wailes*, 1855 (TK). – PLATE. Elizabethan Cup; Flagon, inscribed 1747.

CALVELEY HALL, 1 m. NW. Seven bays, late C17, rendered and absolutely plain. (Staircase with double spiral newels and balusters. MHLG)

GOLBORNE OLD HALL, 1¼ m. NNW. 1682. Much altered, but provided with a doorway almost too grand for this size of a house. Pilasters and pediment – progressive for 1682 in Cheshire.

MANOR FARMHOUSE, Aldersey Green, 1¼ m. SW. Black and white, 1630, with lattice and herringbone decoration.

6040   HANKELOW

HANKELOW HALL. An Early Georgian brick house of ten bays and three storeys, with a startlingly high parapet. Two-bay centre culminating in a blank arch on pilasters raised yet higher than the parapet. Angle quoins, but pilaster strips at the angles of the centre. Porch of four unfluted Ionic columns. As it is known that the ground floor was remodelled by *William Baker* c.1755, that will be the date of the porch and the change in fenestration.

HANKELOW COURT. Big brick and black and white house of the 1870s, enlarged in 1901 and altered c.1958.

4060   HARGRAVE

ST PETER. A C17 church with a Victorian bell-turret. The C17 work, dated 1627, is simple and satisfying, and the inscription refers to the founder Sir Thomas Moulson, later to be Lord Mayor of London. Mullioned windows with arched lights, the E window also with a transom. Hammerbeam roof with pendants. No chancel arch. – PLATE. Beaker Cup, inscribed 1700.

6070   HARTFORD

ST JOHN BAPTIST. By *John Douglas*, 1874–5, the W tower with higher stair-turret of 1887–9. Sizeable, mostly with lancets. The aisles are of five bays and have very low windows, set in twins and two twins as a pair. Inside the pairs are separated by short detached shafts (cf. Sandiway). Low lancets in the clerestory too. Rough finish to the internal masonry. The interior is altogether interesting, especially the chancel, whose two sides are totally different, a Paley & Austin motif. Douglas was Paley's pupil.

WHITEHALL, ½ m. SE, in SCHOOL LANE. 1835 by *John Douglas Sen.*, a local builder, and father of the Chester architect. Stuccoed, of seven bays with a one-bay pediment and a porch with Ionic columns *in antis*. Side elevation with canted bay.

(HARTFORD MANOR, at the end of GREENBANK LANE. Two-storeyed five-bay ashlar front. Central segmental projection, with brackets, entablature, etc., to the first-floor window. Unfluted Roman Doric porch. Said to have been refronted for

John Marshall, a Northwich salt manufacturer, *c.*1820, though it looks later. EH)

HARTFORD BEACH, No. 228 CHESTER ROAD. The house belonged to Thomas Marshall, a salt manufacturer and brother of John (*see* above). 1802, but remodelled in 1814–24. Stuccoed. To the garden a delightful Gothick front with two canted bay windows and a balcony on Gothick shafts in the middle.

GRANGE SCHOOL, Kindergarten, NE of the church. 1938 by *Sir Leslie Martin*, an 'early Martin'. One storey, lightly built, with a veranda.

(In the grounds of FOREST HILL HOUSE, 1¼ m. WSW, at the junction of the A556 with the road to Hartford, is a good recent house by *R. Clayton*.)

HARTHILL   *5050*

ALL SAINTS. Probably 1609. Nave and chancel in one, and a thoroughly debased clock turret of 1862–3. The C17 work has mullioned windows with arched lights. Very wide nave; hammerbeam roof on brackets. – SCREEN. Only the rough framework is preserved. An inscription refers to 1609. – COMMUNION RAIL. C18. – PLATE. Set of 1773. – In the churchyard a columnar SUNDIAL; C18.

ESTATE HOUSES, opposite the church. 1844. A bit out of scale, but substantial and nicely different in design. ⅞ m. N, on the road to Tattenhall, a brick and stone Elizabethan-style FARMHOUSE, presumably one of the model farms which *James Harrison* deigned for the Bolesworth estate.

HASLINGTON   *7050*

ST MATTHEW. Two builds, handsome the one, handsome the other. The W part is of 1810, brick with arched windows and a narrower pedimented W or entrance bay. It has an arched doorway and a lunette window over. A cupola stands a little behind, on the nave W gable. The E end is of 1909, by the unknown *Reginald T. Longden*. The style is Dec, with a seven-light E window. The intention evidently was to rebuild the whole church.

HASLINGTON HALL. A large, timber-framed house, very attractive to look at. Several gables and, apart from herringbone bracing, quatrefoils and cusped concave-sided lozenges. (Inside, so the MHLG reports, are the roof timbers of a late medieval hall and a staircase with four main posts.)

HATHERLOW see BREDBURY

HATTERSLEY see HYDE

HAWK GREEN see MARPLE

9080
HAZEL GROVE

ST THOMAS, Norbury, but at the main centre of the A roads of
Hazel Grove. 1833–4 by *Hayley & Brown*, a typical Commissioners' church. Long lancets, thin buttresses, thin w tower,
prominent pinnacles, short chancel. Three galleries. – MONU-
MENT. Elizabeth Clayton, 1851 by *A. Gatley*. She is carried
heavenward by an angel.

COUNCIL HOUSE. A private early C19 house of brick, five
widely spaced bays and two pediments. Porch of two pairs of
unfluted Ionic columns.

HEALD GREEN see CHEADLE

HEFFERSTON GRANGE see WEAVERHAM

4070
HELSBY

ST PAUL. 1868–70 by *Douglas*, the s aisle and chapel 1909 by
Douglas & Minshull. On the mid-buttress of the w front sits
a stunted, slated bell-turret with slated spire. The church is
small and rock-faced, E.E. in style, with a polygonal apse.

PROMONTORY FORT. Only the s and E of this site are provided
with artificial defences. They enclose an area of $3\frac{1}{2}$ acres. These
defences consist of a bank 65 ft wide and 4 ft high; there is no
trace of an outer ditch. Outside the principal rampart are the
ploughed-out remains of a second bank about 3 ft high. The
original entrance is at the s w corner, where the line of the main
rampart is inturned. A second gap occurs on the s, but this
appears to be a comparatively modern trackway.

8070
HENBURY

ST THOMAS. 1844–5 by *Richard Lane*. Stone, lancets and a thin
w tower with broach-spire. Obviously later vestry with a high
chimney. The chancel must be altered too.

PARSONAGE. This could also be about 1845. With two symmetrical steep gables and a middle porch gable, all three gables
Gothically bargeboarded.

(HENBURY HALL. The house has been demolished, but the
former STABLES, C18 with cupola, remain.)

WHIRLEY HALL. Late C17 front of five bays, brick, with two
large shaped gables. In them horizontally placed ovals.

HERONBRIDGE *see* CHESTER p. 176

HESWALL   [EH] *2080*

ST PETER, Lower Village. Red sandstone. The lower stage of
the tower is C14. Bell-openings stage Late Perp, with three-
light openings and panelled battlements. Staircase projection
at the E end of the S face. The remainder of the church was
rebuilt in 1879 by *J. Francis Doyle*. Late C13 style with geometrical tracery in the E and W windows. Clerestory. The S
aisle, abutting against the tower, has a gable roof. Chancel interior of ashlar. In 1893 *Doyle* extended the chancel and added
the SE Brocklebank Memorial Chapel, the latter in somewhat
richer Perp. – REREDOS. 1890 by *C. E. Kempe*. – FONT. C18
baluster font at the W end of the nave. – STAINED GLASS.
Much by *Kempe*, e.g. E window 1881, SE window 1881, tower
window 1882, SW window 1907. – CHANDELIER, under the
tower. Late C17. – PLATE. Chalice, altered 1739; Flagon,
dated 1736; Paten, dated 1740. – MONUMENTS, under the
tower. John Glegg † 1619. Arms, acrostic inscription; figure
kneeling at a desk, incised on dark stone. – Katherine Glegg
† 1666. Armorial panel with scrollwork etc. under an open
pediment. – In the churchyard an C18 SUNDIAL of baluster
shape.

FRIENDS' MEETING HOUSE, Telegraph Road. 1961–2 by
Dewi Prys Thomas and *Gerald R. Beech*. Grey brick, with some
vertical boarding. Set diagonally to the road. Two blocks, with
a narrow passage between them, are connected by a first-floor
bridge. Both have low-pitched quarter-pyramid roofs. The
smaller block is the warden's house. The larger contains a
ground-floor foyer, glazed on three sides, above which is the
meeting room, with closely-spaced vertical slit windows on
two sides. An ingenious and highly sophisticated form of approach, with many changes of direction, leads under the
bridge, into the foyer, and to the upper room by way of a projecting oriel and a gently rising staircase between solid walls.
Immaculate detailing.

Writing in 1877 for the second edition of Ormerod, Thomas
Helsby referred to Heswall as 'having become a favourite place
of resort in the summer by the residents of Liverpool and
Birkenhead'. Today there is to be seen some residential

development of the C19 and much of the C20. THE ROSCOTE
in WALL RAKE was altered and enlarged c.1893 by *Doyle* for
Thomas Brocklebank, banker, and member of the Liverpool
shipping family. There are many C20 houses in this region
and further S, and in more heathery settings along the ridge,
but nothing which demands special mention. With the further
spread of commuter housing and with the growth of industry
on the oppposite side of Wirral, the destruction of the rural
character of the peninsula continues. Doubtless this is inevit-
able, but it is grievous that most of the recent housing, of
which much in and around Heswall is typical, should be of
such poor quality. Moreover, splendid opportunities are being
lost with fine sites overlooking the Dee estuary also being built
up with abysmal speculative development.

GOLF CLUB. *See* Gayton, p. 224.

5080
HIGHER WALTON

ST JOHN EVANGELIST. 1885 by *Paley & Austin* at the expense
of Sir Gilbert Greenall, the Warrington brewer. Not large, but
with an imposing crossing tower crowned by a recessed spire.
The decoration of the tower by chequer work was liked by
Paley & Austin. The windows of the church are free Dec,
some of them squarely framed. Fine S side with porch, transept, and vestry. Inside there is less to note, though the tower
has a stone rib-vault on shafts starting from leaf corbels, and
the PISCINA, SEDILIA, and vestry door in the chancel, all
square-headed, make a beautiful group.

WALTON HALL. Sir Gilbert's house, Early Elizabethan in style
and very large. Brick with red stone dressings. Of 1836–8.
Entirely asymmetrical. Later alterations and enlargement included the addition of a billiard room, 1870, forming the end
of a wing projecting on the E. (It contains a sculptural panel by
Warrington Wood.)★

The ESTATE HOUSING, both C19 and early C20, deserves a look.
½ m. N, at Wilderspool, is an extensive ROMAN SITE, now largely
between the Mersey and the Ship Canal, but extending to the
s. Occupation begins with a fort, probably of Agricolan date.
This is followed (c.85–90) by buildings associated with extensive industrial activities, including the working of iron, bronze,
and lead, the production of pottery and glass, and enamelling.

HIGHFIELDS *see* AUDLEM

★ This information kindly communicated by the Rev. V. G. Davies.

HIGH LANE

St Thomas. 1852, enlarged by *Medland Taylor* in 1866. The
original building is poor Norman, nave, chancel, and apse and
a thin s tower with a pyramid roof. Medland Taylor added the
equally poor N aisle and N arcade. – The PAINTED DECORA-
TION in the apse looks *c.*1866, not *c.*1852.

WYBERSLEY HALL. *See* Disley, p. 198.

HIGH LEGH

The recent past is sad. High Legh Hall (or East Hall) of 1782 has
been pulled down, and the chapel stands in a new villagescape of
prim detached houses. At the time of writing it must be called
derelict. West Hall has also been demolished. Its chapel is the
parish church. The grounds of both halls were laid out by *Repton,*
including a re-alignment of the Warrington–Knutsford road,
which was further altered in the mid C19. Repton's landscape
cannot now be recognized.

St MARY, the chapel of High Legh Hall, is low, of brick, and a
separate building. It was built *c.*1581 and had the s aisle added
in 1836. But the cross-gabled appearance of this looks more
like the restoration of 1858 by *Butterfield.* The chancel is by
J. Oldrid Scott, 1884. Inside the original timber piers.

An entrance to the new estate is by the LODGE of High Legh
Hall, 1833–4 by *James Hakewill,* and in the Italianate typical
of Loudon's *Encyclopaedia* of just those years. Of the subsidiary buildings of the Hall also the STABLES are still in existence.
Four brick ranges round an oblong court, the front range lower
than the back range. The latter carries the cupola.

St JOHN. The parish church. 1893 by *Kirby.* Timber-framed
with tile roofs. The details self-consciously picturesque, e.g.
the tower with its mullioned and transomed W window like a
domestic bay window. Below it an extra gable. This whole W
bay forms a lobby inside, and one can look up into the tower.
The interior of the church is brick-faced. So the half-timbering
outside is a sham. The stepped sills of the windows inside are
another deliberately unusual motif. Walls of the previous chapel,
which was by *Thomas Harrison,* and burnt in 1891, are incorporated.

(SWYNEYARD HALL, $1\frac{1}{2}$ m. W. Partly moated. The portion
which retains exposed half-timbering has a gable end with
ogee lozenges etc. at first-floor level and a heavy diagonal pattern in the gable itself. EH)

HILBRE ISLAND *see* WEST KIRBY

3070   HINDERTON   [EH]

HINDERTON HALL. An exceptionally early work by *Alfred Waterhouse*, dating from before his success in the Manchester Assize Courts competition. It was built in 1856 for Christopher Bushell, a Liverpool wine merchant and worthy. Rock-faced sandstone. Patterned slate roof. Of High rather than Early Victorian Gothic character, it is an early example of a familiar enough type, with its grouping of high main block and subsidiary service range and its tower and tall staircase window on the entrance front. Despite its historical significance it is immature, with the elevations not consistently resolved, and with the thin tower appearing to lack confidence and to have something of an Italianate villa feel about it. Hints of the architect's characteristic later style in the gables of the entrance front, the timber canopy above the doorway, and the terrace and area balustrading. An oriel rises out of a buttress on the end elevation. ENTRANCE LODGE. Single-storey, with triangular bay window and trefoil-headed entrance. STABLES, NE of the house, and beyond them a COTTAGE. Another similar COTTAGE ¼ m. SE, on the road to Willaston.

HINDERTON HALL FARM, S of Hinderton Hall and immediately W of Hinderton crossroads on the road to Neston. Possibly also by *Waterhouse*. Houses in this road include HINDERTON HEY, ½ m. SW, 1911 by *R. T. Beckett*.

HOCKENHULL HALL *see* TARVIN

HOLFORD HALL *see* PLUMLEY

9090   HOLLINGWORTH

On the way into the Peak District.

ST MARY. 1863–4 by *Clegg & Knowles*. Thin NW turret.
ARROWSCROFT MILL is two dignified stone mills with towers.
THORNCLIFF HALL, up Spring Lane. Neo-Jacobean, with shaped gables.
The house at the E end, MILLBROOK HOUSE, with shaped gables and a tower, is initially of before 1805, and belonged to the Sidebottom family of local millowners. Originally a cotton mill adjoined the house, but this was demolished and the house enlarged in 1882.
WATER FILTRATION PLANT, connected with the Manchester

Reservoirs higher up. A small but impressive building, reminiscent of Frank Lloyd Wright. By *S. G. Besant Roberts*, the
Manchester City Architect, 1963.

HOLLYHEDGE FARM *see* WESTON

HOLME STREET HALL *see* TARVIN

HOLMES CHAPEL   7060

St Luke. Perp w tower, but the body of the church seemingly
early c18. This is deceptive, however, as the brickwork is only
a new casing for an exceptionally large Perp timber church.
Arcades of four bays, with octagonal piers with eight thin rolls.
They continue above the capitals with posts of the same moulding to support the tie-beams and their arched braces. There are
also longitudinal tie-beams. The aisle roofs are lean-tos. It is a
very interesting arrangement, and one wonders only if the
heightening of the nave posts is not later. The brick casing has
two tiers of windows, round-arched and segment-arched. There
are entrances in the second and sixth bay, and they still have
the steep pediments of the late c17. The two entry bays are
singled out by giant pilasters. The chancel is lower than the
nave. – SCREEN. A top frieze with the date 1623 now over the
w door. – SOUTH and WEST GALLERY dated 1705. – CHAN-
DELIER of brass. 1708. – PLATE. Stand Paten, London, 1698;
Paten, inscribed 1700; Flagon, London, 1719; Stand Paten,
London, 1722; Cup, London, 1723; also an inscribed set without date. – MONUMENT. Tablet to Harriet Vyse † 1836. By
William Spence. Inscription on drapery.
RAILWAY VIADUCT. 1840–1 by *G. W. Buck*. Of twenty-three
brick arches each of 63 ft.
COTTON HALL, 1 m. W. One timber-framed gable with angle
brackets and several decorative motifs, including balusters.

HOOLE *see* CHESTER, p. 172

HOOLGROVE MANOR *see* MINSHULL VERNON

HOOTON   3070

St Paul, at Childer Thornton. 1858–62 by *James K. Colling*,
author of *Gothic Ornaments* (1850) and *Details of Gothic Architecture* (1856). The church was built by R. C. Naylor, the
Liverpool banker, and his second wife. It cost £5,000. Colling

just before (in 1856–8) had built the Albany in Liverpool for
Naylor, a spectacular eleven-bay palace of commerce in a very
mixed Italianate style. St Paul also is, whatever one may think
of it, a spectacular building – unquestionably one of the most
spectacular churches of Cheshire. It is also under the aspect of
Victorian historicism one of the most interesting. The 1840s
had seen a great vogue in the *Rundbogenstil*, the style of the
round arch, whether Norman or Italian Early Christian to
Romanesque. The vogue was over by 1850; so Colling was
doing something the Scotts, the Butterfields, the Streets, and
of course the Ecclesiologists would all have disapproved of.
But though round-arched, the church is not Norman, nor
purely Italian Romanesque, even if the w porch and the Lombard friezes are. The church is of stone, red ashlar, white ashlar, and – a complete surprise – red rock-faced stone. The
three materials are not separated; they interact. The windows
are not all Romanesque either. Colling uses with them pointed
windows with plate tracery. The nave and aisles are three bays
long. Then follow transepts and an octagonal crossing tower
or lantern, not as one would assume rising over the square of
nave, transepts, and chancel, but somehow smaller in diameter.
The interior explains this, as we shall see. The total height is
95 ft. The choir has aisles too, and they continue as an ambulatory, a French, not an Italian motif. Finally, there is a private
entrance for the family, connected with the church by a short,
formerly open cloister walk. The entrance porch itself was open
too, and it has a truncated pyramid roof, an open upper stage
with columns, and a pyramid top.

Inside, the arcades have Petershead granite columns and
carry capitals which are not Romanesque at all, but free French
Early Gothic. In the chancel there are instead much slimmer
coupled shafts set in depth. Where did Colling get that idea
from ? From Sens, or rather from Italian cloisters ? For the one
his shafts are too thin, for the other too thick. But the climax
is the crossing, and here Colling is entirely original. The crossing
piers are Romanesque, but on them, and on pendentives, an
ashlar dome rises, and that dome stops half-way up and carries
the crossing tower or lantern. The feeling is Byzantine, but
neither the motif nor the form is. – FONT. Square, of dark
green serpentine, 1851. It received a medal at the Great Exhibition. – BUST of Caroline Naylor, unsigned.

ST MARY OF THE ANGELS (R.C.), ½ m. NW. 1879 by *E. J.
Tarver*. Aisleless and towerless, but with a polygonal apse, and

a w porch with lean-to roof up to a rose window. Ashlar facing inside, and good carving of corbels. The style is late C13.

HOOTON HALL has been demolished. It was by *Samuel Wyatt* – an early work, of 1778, and Victorianized for R. C. Naylor by *Colling*. Only the LODGES, by *Wyatt*, near St Paul, remain, a very fine pair connected by a semicircle of unfluted Ionic columns, and the gatepiers. The lodges are square, with few openings and wreath and garland panels. Pediments turned towards the way in.

HOUGH 7050

WESLEYAN CHAPEL. 1901. In a field. Red brick and stone, with lancets and big pinnacles. Small and naïve.

HOUGH HOUSE. Early Georgian. Five bays, two storeys, segment-headed windows, pilaster strips at the angles and those of the centre bay. Doorway with apsidal hood. (In one room panelling with pilasters. MHLG)

HOYLAKE [EH]2080

HOLY TRINITY, Trinity Road. 1833 by *Sir James Picton* of Liverpool. An early work of his which later he may well have regretted. Red sandstone. Aisleless nave of Norman style, its detailing over-scaled, most noticably on the w front. Chancel E.E. Chancel arch Norman. The nave interior has large head corbels. s porch and w gallery added 1856.

ST CATHERINE AND ST MARTINA (R.C.), Birkenhead Road. 1926–8 by the firm of *Edmund Kirby & Son*. Unexciting exterior. Rustic brick, dormer windows. The interior comes as a surprise. Narrow passage aisles included under the roof span. The nave bays below the dormers are carried up to a triforium (having cubist-like enrichment built up in brick) with the dormers forming a clerestory above. The intermediate bays are spanned by a barrel roof. An intended chancel was not built.

ST HILDEBURGH, Stanley Road. 1897–9 by *Edmund Kirby*. Exterior of pressed brick and terracotta. An unusually good brick interior, warm and mellow. Five-bay nave, including a narrow w bay, with arcade columns of polished granite. The E window tracery includes quatrefoils up the sides and a cross in the centre, the clerestory windows are multi-foils, and the windows of the projecting w baptistery are square with tracery. Lancets elsewhere. Virtuoso brickwork, particularly in the interior of the chancel, with two heavily moulded transverse arches defining the choir, three small arches giving into the SE

chapel with arcading above them, etc. – Woodcarving of
REREDOS and PULPIT, very sumptuous. – STAINED GLASS.
In the SE chapel some by *J. Wilson Forster*, 1921–3. An amus-
ing period piece.

ST JOHN BAPTIST, Birkenhead Road, Meols. 1911–13 by
Edmund Kirby. Chancel incomplete. Lofty, with a high clerestory. Lancets. Ambitious W front with two turrets. Rather an
unhappy mixture of materials externally. The brick interior,
with stone columns and dressings, and the unusual arcading
which frames the aisle windows, is far more successful. –
STAINED GLASS. Baptistery windows and two lancets E of
them in the N aisle by *H. Gustave Hiller*.

CONGREGATIONAL CHURCH, Station Road. 1906 by *Douglas
& Minshull*. Brick and stone. Perp with Douglassy details.
Transepts, polygonal apse. The spire, which rose from the roof,
was not replaced after bomb damage.

RAILWAY STATION. *See* below.

LIGHTHOUSE, Valentia Road. Disused, and forms part of a
private house. The remaining one of a pair rebuilt in 1865.
Tapering octagonal brick tower, surmounted by a recessed
lantern stage.

The existence of Hoylake as a bathing resort dates from 1792,
when Sir John Stanley built a hotel, though little residential
development work took place prior to the later C19 and the
coming of the railway. A railway first appeared in 1866, but in
1888 a link was made with the Mersey Railway and thus with
Liverpool. Electrification, begun in 1903, was extended to this
line in 1938, when the RAILWAY STATION in STATION
ROAD was rebuilt, in a modern idiom, and presumably influenced by Charles Holden's London Transport stations. It was
designed in the Architects' Section of the office of *W. K. Wal-
lace*, Chief Civil Engineer to the L.M.S. Railway Co.

Stanley's ROYAL HOTEL of 1792 survived until recently in
STANLEY ROAD. Houses here date from 1835, though most
are early C20. Larger houses in MEOLS DRIVE, e.g. ETHAN-
DUNE, 1904 by *Woolfall & Eccles*. Asymmetrical E-plan frontage. Brick and half-timber and some stonework.

MESOLITHIC SITE at Meols, 1 m. E. From the shore have come
a series of flint tools suggesting coastal settlement by Mesolithic hunters and fishers.

HULME HALL

see ALLOSTOCK *and* CHEADLE HULME

HULME WALFIELD   *8060*

St Michael. 1855–6 by *Sir George Gilbert Scott*, an attractive
building, and one for which money must have been spent generously. Rock-faced, of nave, N aisle, and chancel. Bellcote on
the E gable of the nave. The N side has cross-gables besides the
porch. Geometrical tracery and naturalistic capitals and hoodmould stops for the aisle arcade.

HURDSFIELD   *9070*

Hurdsfield is no more than an outer district of Macclesfield. It is
largely industrial, with a recent industrial estate among whose
buildings those for Geigy, the Swiss pharmaceutical firm,
excel. Two two-storeyed blocks connected by a covered way
with the entrance. Both blocks have heavy bands of concrete.
The architect is *Martin H. Burckhardt* of Basel. Near by also,
in Carisbrook Avenue, are the only two high blocks of
flats of Macclesfield.

Holy Trinity, also typical Outer Macclesfield. 1837–9 by
William Hayley, and entirely like a Commissioners' church.
W tower with clumsy pinnacles, lancets in stepped groups of
three, no structural chancel. The E window is obviously later
Victorian.

HUXLEY   *5060*

Lower Huxley Hall, NW of the village. The centre part of
a once larger brick house. It lies in a moat which is crossed by
a bridge which ends in an archway with a curly top, typically
Jacobean. The house as it is at present has a recessed centre
with two three-light mullioned and transomed windows behind
which is the hall. At the back of the house shows the big chimneybreast of the hall chimney. On the front, a square projection
on the l. of the hall originally had the entrance, a square projection on the r. has the hall-bay. Both projections have a five-light
front window. On the r. there is then a lower projecting wing
in which one room has a simple stucco ceiling, also Jacobean.
The corresponding l. wing is missing.

HYDE   *9090*

One of the Cheshire cotton towns close to the Lancashire border.
St George, Church Street. 1831–2 by *T. & C. Atkinson*. A
Commissioners' church. W tower, lancets, the usual clumsy

pinnacles. The interior with tall round piers with octagonal
capitals and four-centred arches – a curious combination. Galleries halfway up the piers. The chancel is of 1882–3. – ORGAN
CASE. Gothic, by *Samuel Renn*, 1838.

The same lancets and the same pinnacles as in the church
also in the SCHOOL, which dates from 1835–6. Also a HEARSE
house, dated 1841.

ST JOHN BAPTIST, High Street, Godley. Also built with aid
from the Commissioners. 1849–50 by *E. H. Shellard*, the
steeple of 1878. It has a higher stair turret. The style of the
details of the church is *c.*1300. Aisles and short chancel. Quite
a large building.

ST MARY, Bowers Street, off Talbot Street, Newton. A Commissioners' church too, and the most memorable building of
Hyde, though architecturally a bad building. 1838–9 by *Hayley
& Brown* of Manchester. Big and Norman, with a high façade
with two stunted turrets. Lancet-like round-arched windows.
Three galleries inside. Long chancel added by *M. & H. Taylor*,
1876–7, in the same Norman, a little richer inside, but with
none of the jokes of Holy Trinity (*see* below). – MONUMENT.
82   James Ashton † 1841 and John Ashton † 1844, by *Knowles* of
Manchester. A very odd, almost sinister tablet, the ornament
being of a fleshy kind difficult to place. The inscription is un-
rolled from a scroll held at the bottom by marble nails, most
improbably.

ST PAUL (R.C.), St Paul's Street, Newton. 1853–4 by *Weightman, Hadfield & Goldie*. The chancel of 1899.

ST STEPHEN, Bennet Street, Flowery Field. 1889–91 by *J. Eaton*
of Ashton-under-Lyne. Sizeable, with NW steeple and polygonal apse.

ST THOMAS, Lumm Street. 1867–8 by *Medland & Henry Taylor*. Medland Taylor was a joker – and a rogue as well, in
Goodhart-Rendel's sense. There is this façade: crazy-paving
and red brick dressings with the roof pitch changing its degree
to distinguish between nave and aisles. But there are no aisles,
as one realizes at once on entering. Timber roof on big moulded
corbels. Short chancel. – FONT. C18, of baluster type. –
STAINED GLASS. Several late *Morris* windows.

HOLY TRINITY, Higham Lane, Gee Cross. 1873–4 by *Medland
& Henry Taylor*. The tower was added in 1903 and is incred-
ibly retrograde for that date. Medland Taylor's joke this
time is to give bargeboards to all his roofs. Inside he has another roguery: the chancel arch is tripartite, i.e. short, fat

columns divide off narrow passages. Through the l. one of them the parson reaches the pulpit. Tricky timber roof, as Medland Taylor liked them.

CONGREGATIONAL CHURCH, Union Street. 1843. A good, severe façade of brick with pediment and an entrance with two high unfluted Ionic columns *in antis*.

UNITARIAN CHURCH (HYDE CHAPEL), Stockport Road, Gee Cross. The appearance is of a parish church in its urban church-yard. – w tower with broach-spire, nave and aisles and chancel of the length normal in churches whose tracery is geometrical. The date is indeed 1846–8, when progressive church architects had adopted the so-called Second Pointed, and *Bowman & Crowther* were progressive architects. Only this is a Unitarian chapel, and in this lies the historical importance of Hyde Chapel. It is the first Nonconformist church to be so entirely – seating and the placing of the altar as well – a copy of a building for the Established Church.

UNITARIAN CHURCH, Newton Street, Flowery Field. 1878 by *Thomas Worthington*. Perp, but with some liberties. NW tower with higher stair-turret.

TOWN HALL, Market Place. 1883–5 by *J. W. Beaumont* of Manchester. Uninteresting. Red brick, two-storeyed, with a mid-tower with a domed cap. Nearly but not quite symmetrical. The style is imprecise. A Neo-Georgian extension with a stately portico is in Greenfield Street. It dates from 1937 and is by *J. H. Ward*.

Opposite the Town Hall is a new SHOPPING PRECINCT by *Leach, Rhodes & Walker*.

POST OFFICE, Corporation Street. 1899–1900 by *W. T. Old-rieve*. Two-storeyed, asymmetrical, red brick and much yellow terracotta.

THEATRE ROYAL, Corporation Street. By *Campbell & Horsley*, 1901–2. Red brick, high, nothing special.

(HALLBOTTOM SUNDAY SCHOOL, Garden Street. Built *c.*1820 by the millowner James Ashton.)

GREENFIELD COUNTY PRIMARY SCHOOL, Greenfield Street. 1928–9 by *Farmer*. Neo-Georgian block, with a mid-cupola and two projecting wings.

ASHTON BROTHERS, Newton Street, Flowery Field. A big brick mill, built *c.*1810.

HATTERSLEY. A number of high blocks among the recent housing.

(APETHORN FARM, Apethorn Lane. A four-bay cruck frame,

probably c15. One end-cruck has vanished. The central one
has carved capitals.)

(NEWTON HALL, Dukinfield Road. Also cruck-framed, the span
being 22½ ft. Three bays. The house is assigned to the late c14,
and is being restored at the time of writing.)

IDDINSHALL HALL *see* TARPORLEY

4070   INCE

ST JAMES. The chancel is Dec, the tower Perp, the rest, including
the tower top, by *Hodkinson*, 1854. But the chancel roof is dated
1671 and has moulded corbels. – COMMUNION RAIL. Late
c17; with twisted balusters. – CHANDELIER of brass; 1724. –
STAINED GLASS. In the chancel two *Kempe* windows; 1897. –
PLATE. Flagon and Paten, inscribed 1710; Chalice, 1788–9.

In the village, the Square is marked by a surprisingly formal, low
five-bay house with a three-bay pediment. Turn l. to the
mysterious remains of a Late Perp manor house.

MANOR HOUSE. It belonged to the Abbots of Chester,* and
what remains is part of a fine hall, later no doubt by at least a
century than the licence to crenellate, which dates from 1399.
The hall has four windows to the road, of two lights, straight-
headed and transomed, set under segmental arches. On the
opposite side and one short side the windows repeat. The fourth
side is broken. At r. angles is a second building, longer and
buttressed on both sides. Several simple doorways and one
simple window. Also heavy roof timbers.

INGERSLEY HALL *see* BOLLINGTON

2080   IRBY   [EH]

IRBY HALL. On the site of a manor house of Chester Abbey.
Early c17. Basically an H-plan. The E (entrance) front has a
red sandstone ground floor with half-timbering above, though
it was all half-timber prior to a reconstruction in 1888. Two
large gables project at either end, and a smaller gable, over the
porch, adjoins one of them. First-floor windows transomed,
of six lights in the end projections. Diagonal timberwork. The
remaining three sides all stone, with mullioned windows. Massive chimneystack on the N.

* Their other country houses were Saighton Grange and Little Sutton. Of
the latter nothing survives.

JODRELL BANK   *7070*

A telescope by means of a lens receives light-waves; Jodrell Bank receives radio-waves. The bowls or dishes replace lenses. Jodrell Bank is the radio astronomy laboratory of the University of Manchester. It has five of the receiving bowls, and with their supporting framework on their astounding scale they look like a huge piece of science fiction. But then what they perform is more than any science fiction twenty years ago could have dreamt up. They also look like today's abstract sculpture. They must be the envy of certain young English sculptors. Of the five instruments the largest, Mark I, is also the oldest. The design was initiated in 1949–51 and the telescope was built in 1952–7. It was able, just before completion, to track the first sputnik. The engineers for all five were *Husband & Co.*, the director is, as everyone knows, *Sir Bernard Lovell*. Mark I has a circular bowl 250 ft in diameter. The supporting lattice triangles l. and r. are 180 ft high. The great lattice semicircle behind is for stabilizing. Mark I is still the largest fully steerable radio telescope in the world. Mark II dates from 1960–4. Its bowl is an elliptic paraboloid 125 ft along its longer axis. The 8 ft cube attached by four struts to the rim of the bowl is a laboratory. The frame of the bowl is of prestressed concrete. Mark III (1963–6) has a bowl of open one-inch mesh. The smaller telescope adjacent to the Control Building was completed in 1963 and serves almost wholly the tracking of space probes. The bowl is 50 ft in diameter; the frame is concrete. So is the fifth bowl, the one in the NE corner of the area. This was also completed in 1963 and is also 50 ft in diameter. It has the most massive concrete pillar. There are also two 25 ft bowls and other aerials.

JODRELL HALL (Terra Nova School). Georgian, brick, of five bays and three storeys, with a three-bay pediment. The lower l. wing is C18 too; the r. wing is by *Douglas*. By him must also be the porch, dated 1885. (The main block, which is of 1779, has a stone staircase and a stone Doric screen at the first-floor landing. MHLG)

KELSALL   *5060*

St Philip. 1860 by *T. Bower*. Rock-faced, nave and chancel late C13 Gothic, with the bellcote awkwardly on the nave E gable. Ashlar interior.

Lockup, opposite the Royal Oak, a pub of 1900. The lockup is of big stone blocks and windowless.

CELTIC FIELDS, just w of Longley Farm. The most noticeable features are the lynchet banks running E–W across the ridge, but less well defined banks, much reduced by ploughing, also run N–S, forming a group of small rectangular fields. The field system is undated and may be either Iron Age or Romano-British.

KELSBORROW CASTLE see DELAMERE

9070

KETTLESHULME

GLEBE HOUSE. By *Ernest Newton*, 1911–12. Built as the vicarage for a church never provided. A three-bay house of two storeys with a typical Newton hood over the doorway.

KINDERTON HALL see MIDDLEWICH

1070

KINGSLEY

ST JOHN EVANGELIST. 1849–50 by *Sir George Gilbert Scott*. Built for the Commissioners. Small, with a w tower embraced by two side chambers, not part of aisles. There is in fact a short N aisle, but that has a timber arcade. Inside the w end is a composition of three arches, the middle one, i.e. the tower arch, much higher. The church is in Scott's favourite Second Pointed, i.e. the style of the late C13. – SCREEN. Of wrought iron, as Scott liked it.

KINNERTON see LOWER KINNERTON

7070

KNUTSFORD

Knutsford, with about 10,000 inhabitants, is the most attractive town of its size in Cheshire. It has a nicely winding main street, King Street, and to the w of that rises a hill on which stands the church and beyond it the Sessions House. Newer development of wealthy villas extended s along Toft Road and Legh Road, and minor developments of this century followed on the hill to the E of these streets. Moreover, immediately N of the N end of King Street the park of Tatton Hall starts. One sequence of the villas s of the centre marks the beginning of the architectural activities of the incredible Mr *Watt*.

ST JOHN BAPTIST, Church Hill. 1741–4 by *J. Garlive*. It cost £4,000. Brick with stone dressings. w tower, nave and aisles of five bays with arched windows in two tiers. The apsidal chancel was replaced in 1879 by a flat one (*Alfred Darbyshire*). s doorway with pilasters and pediment. Interior with Tuscan giant columns and two galleries. Lord Torrington called it 'in the Venetian ballroom stile'. – FONTS. One of 1741 (by the lectern). This has a baluster stem and a fluted bowl. – The other is of 1865 and is ornately High Victorian Gothic and utterly out of place. Not for the High Victorians the *genius loci*. – CHANDELIER of brass; 1763. – PLATE. Chalice and Paten, mid C17; Flagon, given in 1768. – MONUMENT. Elizabeth Leigh † 1823. Below the inscription is an urn in a wreath. Signed by *R. Westmacott* with his address. – In the churchyard a baluster SUNDIAL; Georgian.

ST CROSS, Mobberley Road, in a fine position E of the old town. By *Paley & Austin*, 1880–1. Brick and red terracotta, with a strong crossing tower. Perp in style. The nave arcades differ in a way typical of Paley & Austin, two bays S, three bays N. The justification is the vestry placed surprisingly into the SW angle. As the vestry is two-storeyed and the main entrance is from the W into the N aisle, the result is a W front again asymmetrical. The chancel chapels on the other hand are identical l. and r. The finest effect of the church is the light which streams into the crossing from windows N and S above the (non-projecting) transepts. – SCULPTURE. Small bronze relief of the Deposition of Christ, curiously composed and Mannerist in the figures. It is signed HK, 1607. – STAINED GLASS. By *Morris & Co.*, incorporating *Burne-Jones* designs, are the W window, c.1894, and the S aisle easternmost window, 1899.*

UNITARIAN CHAPEL, Adam's Hill, at the S end of King Street. 1689. Of brick, with two-light windows. The front has the entrances in the first and last bays and staircases running parallel with the front from the centre outward to upper entrances above the lower. They lead to upper galleries, their parapets being of flat shaped balusters. The type of building is exactly the same as in the Unitarian chapels of Macclesfield (1689) and Wilmslow (1693). – PLATE. A Cup of 1694–5.

METHODIST CHURCH, Princess Street. *See* Perambulation.

CEMETERY, 1¼ m. NW. The chapel by *Robert J. McBeath*, 1901,‡ is freakish in design, an octagonal centre and a loosely attached tower also in its upper parts octagonal.

TOWN HALL (former), Toft Road, at its N end. By *Waterhouse*, 1870–2, and typical of him in its matter-of-fact fulfilment of function. Red and dark brick, Gothic. Gabled entrance in the first bay, then five pointed arches originally open. Above them

* Information from Mr Sewter.
‡ Information given me by David McLaughlin.

just the five pointed windows of the Council Room. In the roof three dormers with round windows. The side elevation equally straightforward, and at the back just segment-headed windows as if the Gothic had been forgotten.

SESSIONS HOUSE, Toft Road. 1815–18 by *Thomas Harrison*. A duly grave building of ashlar stone, in a very free Grecian. Projecting centre with a portico of unfluted attached Ionic columns with a niche l. and r. In the recessed parts l. and r. of these just one very large, heavily rusticated arched doorway. Yet further recessed plain, mostly windowless wall. Good Sessions Hall with polygonal end. Behind the building was originally the gaol.

CARNEGIE LIBRARY, Brook Street. 1903–4 by *Alfred Darbyshire*. Elizabethan, asymmetrical, with gables and mullioned and transomed windows.

HOSPITAL, Stanley Road, the former WORKHOUSE. The front of 1897, but the large utilitarian brick range of the workhouse behind.

PERAMBULATION. We start from the church. CHURCH HILL leads down to KING STREET, the main shopping street. It is an attractive street, though without highlights, unless one is ready to call the GASKELL MEMORIAL TOWER and THE
101 KING'S COFFEE HOUSE of 1907–8 a highlight. It brings us up for a first time to *Richard Harding Watt* (1842–1913) and his remorseless imposing of crazy grandeur on poor Knutsford.[*] His style, wherever it appears, is hard to define. It is at its best a parallel to Barcelona at the same time. Stonework is heavy, fenestration random, and motifs may be Italian or Byzantine or just Watt. The Georgian of King Street has no chance against this barrage, especially the pretty, two-storeyed brick cottages at the s end. Further N the ROYAL GEORGE HOTEL, brick, with quoins and an archway. The assembly room at the rear is a later C18 addition. (Good staircase, and also good decoration in the assembly room and the circular card room. MHLG) Another house worth noting is No. 98. Opposite is BARCLAYS BANK (former Union Bank), 1856, round-arched Gothic with Venetian tracery. No. 131 must be late C17, with pilasters in two orders. This is at the corner of

[*] It should be added that his role was that of patron and client, and that he employed professional architects (*W. Longworth* in the case of this building) to execute his ideas, though obviously they were little more than draughtsmen carrying out his orders. Much information on Watt has been supplied by Mr McLaughlin, and further details of the story are to be found in a thesis by Miss Julia Beck at the Manchester College of Art and Design.

DRURY LANE, where *Watt* perpetrated the RUSKIN ROOMS, with a row of COTTAGES beyond. They are of 1899–1902. The composition is again totally irregular. There is a domed turret and a minaret at the lower end of the row of cottages, though the group has lost some original features. The roof has pantiles. Pair of COTTAGES behind, 1904.

The N end of Knutsford is the KNUTSFORD LODGE of Tatton Park (*see* p. 354). Large pedimented arch and two lower arches l. and r. Roman Doric columns – a dignified, noble introduction to the property. 1810 by *Lewis Wyatt*.

(W of King Street near the S end of Moorside Road is SWINTON SQUARE, 1902, another *Watt* job.)

By the side of the churchyard CHURCH HILL rises. In it a lively three-bay early C18 house, the doorway with a Gibbs surround, the windows with rusticated lintels. At the top turn r. into PRINCESS STREET, where on the E side the SAVINGS BANK, a small Grecian ashlar façade of 1840–1, by *Robert Gregson*,★ and adjoining it the incongruous METHODIST CHURCH of 1864–5 by *T. R. Clements*, Gothic, with a wild SW tower which has lost its spire. On the W side No. 12, a handsome Georgian three-bay brick house. E of the N end of Princess Street is the HEATH, and on its S side (GASKELL AVENUE) two Georgian houses, Nos. 17 and 19.

Interest in the newer parts of Knutsford is concentrated in the S of the centre.

LEGH ROAD can boast the maddest sequence of villas in all England, all needless to say by *Watt* and his architects, all four of whom (*Walter Aston, John Brooke, Harry S. Fairhurst,* and *W. Longworth*) were employed here. The beginning, as one comes from the N, is harmless enough, just Italianate, reminiscent of 1840 rather than 1900. But then the Witches' Sabbath starts, incredible top crestings where the chimneys are, and stone-domed turrets and Italian villa towers and harmless Ionic porches. THE OLD CROFT, Watt's own house, has a tower of 1907 (*Longworth*) added to a more conventional structure of 1895 by *Brooke*. Brooke, it seems, was unwilling to be subject to Watt's orders, and for MOORGARTH, 1898, he was replaced by *Fairhurst*. BRAE COTTAGE is of 1898 by *Paul Ogden* (later extended) and unconnected with Watt.

At the S end of Legh Road in LEYCESTER ROAD is WOOD-GARTH, a good, large, rendered L-shaped house by *Sir Percy Worthington*, 1903. In CHELFORD ROAD in its own grounds is

★ Again information from Mr McLaughlin.

BOOTHS HALL, built in 1745 but totally remodelled c.1850 by *Edward Habershon*. It is now red and Italianate with an over-columned porte-cochère and a very odd dome at the back.

Finally in TOFT ROAD one of *Baillie Scott*'s best early houses, BEXTON CROFT, 1895–6. It is quite small, or at least appears so on the entrance side. This, with its half-timbering, is more conventional than the garden side. Here the Voyseyish rendering dominates, and there are four bay or oriel windows, nearly but not quite symmetrically arranged. The ground-floor windows are still mullioned and transomed in the tradition of historicism. On the other hand there is, e.g., the entirely original little motif of the carved cat-stone to the r. of the entrance. Inside Baillie Scott already has his favourite motif of a two-storeyed hall, even if it is no bigger than a moderate-sized drawing room. There is instead of an upper gallery a tiny balcony with one of the oriel windows behind it, and on the opposite side opening shutters communicate with the landing. There is a recessed fireplace once with a big copper hood, as one still survives in the dining room. This and the drawing room are connected with the hall by sliding doors. The hall walls are covered not by tapestry but by Irish damask linen bedsheets painted gold.

LANDICAN *see* WOODCHURCH, BIRKENHEAD,
pp. 106, 107

LANGLEY

9070

LANGLEY HALL. 1696. Seven bays, two storeys, hipped roof. The windows have flat raised surrounds, the doorway a remarkable shell hood of two concentric semicircles of shell pattern. The hood stands on carved brackets.

LAWTON *see* CHURCH LAWTON

LEA HALL *see* WIMBOLDSLEY

LEA HALL FARM *see* ALDFORD

LEASOWE *see* WALLASEY, pp. 372, 373

LINDOW *see* WILMSLOW

LISCARD *see* WALLASEY, pp. 370, 371, 372

LITTLE BUDWORTH

5060

ST PETER. Square Perp w tower of c.1526 with three-light bell-openings. The church itself is of 1798–1800. The money was given by a Manchester merchant. Arched windows, thin incorrect minimum tracery probably of the restoration of 1870 (by *Douglas*). Shallow plaster vault inside. – FONT. C18; a gadrooned bowl. – PULPIT. Pretty; probably of *c.* 1800. – FAMILYPEW. – PAINTING. 'Entombment'; Italian C17; good (but not at all Caravaggio). Presented by an Egerton. – PLATE. Silver-gilt Flagon by *F. Garthorne*, 1697(?); silver-gilt Chalice and Paten by *J. Ward*, 1711.

ALMSHOUSES, 200 yards w of the church. Probably of *c.*1700. Five bays, two storeys, brick. Three-bay projection. Big rusticated arched entrance. Two-light mullioned windows.

OULTON PARK. The house was burnt in 1926. The large ARCHWAY remains, with low pedimented side-pieces. Above the arch an odd fluted short bit of attic. Several garlands. Inside, in the former grounds, the MONUMENT to John Francis Egerton. By *Scott & Moffatt*, 1846 or 1847. Gothic with a polygonal upper part, decorated with statues. Pinnacles and a spire.

LITTLE LEIGH   6070

ST MICHAEL. 1878–9 by *Kirby*. Hot orange in colour. Lancets, and a spire over the central space. This space is inside emphasized very successfully by two arches, as if a real tower had been projected. The interior also has the bricks exposed. Over-large E rose-window, also, as it turns out, very successful. – REREDOS. Last Supper in terracotta, so that the brick colour dominates even here.

LITTLE MORETON HALL   8050

Little Moreton Hall is the most popular of all English black and 38 white houses, yet as it comes into sight – happily reeling, disorderly, but no offence meant – it seems at first unbelievable, and then a huge joke. This is due to the s range, the gatehouse range, leaning forward in overhangs in all three outer directions. Outer; for Little Moreton Hall is a courtyard house like Bramall, like Speke, like probably Ordsall, though on the w side the courtyard was never closed and a gap remained.

The house was built essentially for three members of the Moreton family, William who lived *temp.* Henry VII, his son William who was busy on alterations and additions in 1559, and the second William's son John, who was still alive in 1580. So there is pre-Reformation and post-Reformation work here, Henry VII and Elizabeth, pre-Renaissance and

Renaissance. But in spite of some Renaissance decoration and some Elizabethan fireplaces, it is ridiculous to speak of Renaissance in a house which structurally and in the visual consequences of its structure is so entirely in the medieval tradition. It is timber-framed throughout except for the mighty brick chimneybreasts of all three ranges and some later buttressing by brick walls.

The oldest part, late C15, is the N range with the GREAT HALL and its porch towards the courtyard. The hall has one truss with elegant arched braces and, in the place where the original screen stood, the two speres, partly now hidden. Spere trusses in this position are again as at Ordsall and also as at the more famous Rufford Old Hall, a number of other Lancashire halls, and Adlington Hall in Cheshire. At Moreton they are roughly moulded. Some time in the C16, probably c.1559, an intermediate floor was put in, and the band of upper window to the N made. The chimneypiece is yet later, say c.1600. The HALL PORCH is elaborate late C15, its spiral-moulded colonnettes still Gothic and not Renaissance. So are the odd little colonnette brackets in two tiers above the entrance. This motif incidentally repeats in the W wing, next to the porch, and this seems also to belong to the late C15. (Inside it on the upper floor is the castellated brick chimneypiece.) The framing of hall and W wing is simple. In the W wing it is a little heavier, and there are here spiral octagonal corner shafts as in the hall porch. It should be noted that the coving has quatrefoil decoration – an early case. The house at that time was in all probability roughly H-shaped, with the service rooms W of the hall and the living rooms E. In 1559 – so an inscription tells very explicitly, mentioning William Moreton and also *Richard Dale*, the carpenter – the living quarters were remodelled, and in the course of this work the two big polygonal bay windows were made towards the courtyard. One is accessible from the hall and is no doubt the replacement of a former hall bay window, the other belongs to the Withdrawing Room in the E range. The house, in 1559 – that has recently been proved – ended with the S wall of the Withdrawing Room (see e.g. the herringbone bracing in that wall, but also the roof construction). The two big bays have their own overhangs and, as they nearly touch, are connected by a kind of bridge on horizontal struts. The quatrefoils of the overhangs are here only painted on plaster, whereas the coving of the earlier work is framed in timber.

At the time when this work went ahead, the s range was probably being built too. This is the range which one approaches across the moat – a well preserved moat. Here the doorway is surrounded by friezes with typical Henry VIII–Renaissance motifs, not yet the strapwork motifs of Elizabeth's reign. The variety of black and white decorative motifs on the other hand – cusped concave-sided lozenges especially – is Elizabethan. To the r. of the portal is one of the brick chimneys, to the l. a garderobe projection discharging into the moat. What contributes to make this range look so uniquely crazy is the decision to put on its top a LONG GALLERY all along its length. It has almost continuous window bands to N and S and a window to the w (and originally to the E as well). The roof has two tiers of cusped, concave wind-braces and in the end tympana poor plaster decoration illustrating the Spear of Destiny whose rule is Knowledge and the Wheel of Fortune whose rule is Ignorance. There are leaf scrolls l. and r. of them. The devices are taken from *The Castle of Knowledge* published in 1556, i.e. brand-new if the long gallery is of *c.*1559 and not an afterthought of *c.*1575, as the late H. Avray Tipping thought.

In the room off the long gallery above the porch is an Elizabethan plaster chimneypiece with the figures of Justice and Learning, and that indeed must be later than 1559. But dating is difficult all round. Much is evidently conservatism of timber construction. For instance the moulded beams of the big room on the first floor of this range, i.e. below the E half of the long gallery,* are much the same as those of the Withdrawing Room at the N end of the E range, and could be 1500 as well as their real date. The latter is in fact dated *c.*1500 by Mr Lees-Milne.

The most confusing example of this conservatism is in the part of the E range s of the Withdrawing Room. It is the slightly projecting upper window with the purely Gothic frieze. Yet this part is later, even if only a little later, than 1559. It connects with the CHAPEL, whose chancel projects E of the E range. It still has its screen *in situ*, though repaired. Finally the WITHDRAWING ROOM. Here is another plaster overmantel of the time of Queen Elizabeth (cf. her coat of arms).

THE MOUNDS. There are two, one inside (NW), the other outside the moat (SW). Their purpose is not known. Maybe they were simply gardening features of the C16.

---

* The big corbels must be a C17 addition.

6070
LOSTOCK GRALAM

ST JOHN EVANGELIST. The church was built in 1844–5, but must have been victorianized; it looks 1870s. The first work can be easily distinguished from the second on the N side. The nice spire is of course part of the Victorian work, and the one actually enjoyable feature.

3060
LOWER KINNERTON

BRIDGE FARMHOUSE. 1685. E-shaped front with Dutch gables. Quite an impressive house.
Also EATON ESTATE HOUSING.

7070
LOWER PEOVER

33 ST OSWALD. The W tower is said to be of 1582, though this may refer only to a repair. The rest is of the C14 and timber-framed. As a timber-framed church Lower Peover is very important. Professor Horn regards it as quite possible that the arcades with their octagonal piers, although apparently C14, may be as ancient as the C13 – a chapel is known to have existed here in 1269. The church originally had aisles under the same roof as that of the nave, though *Salvin* in 1852 gave the three vessels three separate roofs. They are all three now mostly by Salvin, but the nave roof has original timbers of mighty scantling. Cambered tie-beams on big braces. The original aisles were lower and narrower than they are now. The S chancel chapel is of c.1610, the N chancel chapel of 1624. The exterior is much restored all round. It has plenty of diagonal bracing. – FONT. A large round piece with mouldings at top and bottom and a simple band as its only decoration, and a Jacobean FONT COVER. – SCREEN. Jacobean, of flat balusters. – PARCLOSE SCREENS. Jacobean; the N chapel one dated 1624. – Specially handsome the S chapel one, with closely set balusters. – PULPIT. With two tiers of the usual blank arches and fine inlay in the panels (cf. Over Peover). – LECTERN. Jacobean. – BOX PEWS. Very simple. – CHEST. A mighty dugout of the C13. – PLATE. Flagon, London, 1687; Cup, 1715 by *Richard Richardson* of Chester; two Stand Patens, 1715 by *Richard Richardson* of Chester. – MONUMENTS. In the S chapel Godfrey Shakerley † 1696. Standing monument, not large. Two columns and an open scrolly pediment. – Katherine Shakerley, 1725. Still (very late) with twisted columns and an open scrolly pediment.

COMBERBACH SCHOOL, SW of the church. Founded 1710.
Brick and very small.

FREEGREEN FARMHOUSE, ½ m. E. Brick. Is this a C17 house?
The windows (five bays, two storeys) are later, but how should
one date the angle turrets with their pyramid roofs?

LOWER WHITLEY   6070

CHURCH. An unpromising exterior, with the funny NW turret.
But the small, low church is interesting enough. It was built
at some time early in the C17, has mullioned windows with
arched lights, and inside a glorious Jacobean hammerbeam
roof with big scrolly brackets easy to study in so low a room.
The roof covers the nave and a central space W of the sanctuary.
The sanctuary is a polygonal apse. The church is of brick and
was over-restored in 1864 and at other times in the C19.

LYME PARK   9080

The mansion lies in a marvellous park, large and taking advantage of the rising and sinking landscape of the Peak. The size
of the quadrangular block – the largest house in Cheshire, with
its 190 by 130 feet* – stands up to the scale of the surroundings.

EXTERIOR. The house receives you with gatepiers, gates, and
railings of the 1720s in the grand French manner and with the
craziest Elizabethan FRONTISPIECE, set in the middle of the 42
N side of the N range. How can any mason of about 1570 have
composed like this, and how can a client have approved? The
archway has two perfectly harmless Roman Doric colums and
niches l. and r., but then, on the first floor, are three Doric
columns carrying a pediment – a duality started c.1550 at the
end pavilions of Somerset House and taken over e.g. by the
projecting bays of Longleat – and as the second floor has three
columns again, one of them stands on the tip of the pediment.
Moreover, the third tier changes from three to the more normal four columns and crowns it all with a shell pediment of
Venetian derivation. Above that incidentally is an open scrolly
pediment with an agitated Minerva – late C17 evidently, and a
foretaste of things to come. The whole N range is in fact Elizabethan, although only two windows with ogee-keeled mullion
and transom crosses and two small doorways on the S side of
the range prove it. There are other Elizabethan features to
which we shall return, in one room of the S range and two of

* Always excepting of course the late Eaton Hall.

the E range, and even if they are all not necessarily *in situ*, in all probability all the ranges are Elizabethan.

That house was built by Sir Piers Legh, not the first Piers or Peter in the family at Lyme. The first died in 1399, and his monument is in Macclesfield parish church. Lyme had been in his family from 1346. A house is recorded in 1466. Our Sir Piers is number seven and died in 1590. What his house may have looked like appears in a stucco relief in a room. The façade seems E-shaped and behind it was a tower. This was only taken down in 1810. That its top was re-erected will be told later.

The windows of the NORTH FRONT are no longer Elizabethan; they are sashed. So they belong, like the top pediment of the frontispiece, to the late C17. There is a reference in a letter of 1676 to windows, and there are rainwater heads with the same date. Yet for sashing 1676 is about ten years too early; so maybe altering went on. The sash windows are in four bays l. and four bays r. of the frontispiece. But the ends of the range are very different. Their classicity is C18, and we must revert to them in another context. Meanwhile turn the r. corner to the WEST FRONT, and you will find a front of the late C17 – three-storeyed, of nine bays with two wings projecting by one bay. The ground floor is rusticated, the upper floors are smooth.

59　　　　This motif was taken over on the SOUTH FRONT by *Giacomo Leoni* (to whom the W front also owes a little – particularly the doorway). He was called in by yet another Sir Peter – Peter X – in 1720. Leoni was Venetian and had worked for the Elector Palatine before coming to England, where he did Lathom and Bold Hall in Lancashire at about the same time as he worked at Lyme. Already in 1715–16 he had edited Palladio in English. But his great S front is not a Palladian front. It has a rusticated ground floor with arched windows and above that two storeys culminating in a four-column portico of detached fluted Ionic giant columns carrying a pediment. The whole front is of fifteen bays and all of them have giant pilasters. That is not a Palladio motif, even if the upper portico is. Such porticoes had been done in England slightly before Lyme especially at Wanstead (by Campbell), and Lord Burlington and other Palladians believed in them. But giant pilasters all along a façade belongs rather than to Palladio to the Baroque, even if not the extreme, but it does not on the other hand belong to Italy. The nearest parallels are in France, e.g. Boffrand's unexecuted design for the Ducal Palace at Nancy which dates from 1717. In England the nearest parallel would be the W side of Chatsworth of 1700–3. But Chatsworth has much more decoration, and the porticoes at Chatsworth and Nancy are of course not detached. So Leoni was more original at Lyme Park than one might at first sight have realized. It is interesting by the way that Lord Torrington in 1790 pronounced himself reminded of Chatsworth. The odd top hamper on the S front incidentally is not by Leoni; it was added by *Lewis Wyatt*, who worked at Lyme for Thomas Legh in 1816–22. It was to provide servants' bedrooms. The EAST FRONT of the house was also altered by *Wyatt*. He set, projecting in its middle, a one-storeyed block containing a dining room. The two canted end bays of this side may well be Elizabethan in structure. Such bays after all are quite a current Elizabethan motif.

Finally, to return to the start of this survey of the façades, the three-bay end pavilions of the N front must be an attempt by Leoni to modernize that front, which was for him sadly compromised by the Elizabethan frontispiece. There are in these pavilions the same rusticated ground floor and the same upper giant pilasters as on the S façade.

One more contribution of Leoni is now left. He altered the COURTYARD by giving it a rusticated cloister all around, and above that varying architecture on the different sides: on the W a one-bay centre with a pedimented window between two Doric pilasters, on the S and N three such windows and four such pilasters, and on the E his grand entrance, a portal in a Tuscan aedicule and an open staircase with iron rails leading up to it. The *piano nobile* windows here all have pediments.

INTERIOR. The interior is confusing, partly owing to a change of levels which Leoni made because he had to work in an existing shell, partly for other reasons. The notes on rooms are therefore not made in the order in which the public sees them. Leoni's change of level is that he dropped the floor of his ENTRANCE HALL by twelve feet, thereby keeping it at a lower level than the first-floor state rooms but at a higher level than the old ground floor. The hall has been interfered with early this century, and the grand chimneypiece e.g. is Edwardian. What else here – and in other rooms – is a C19 or early C20 remodelling has never yet been sufficiently investigated. The hall has giant pilasters, a screen of three fluted Ionic columns – three is an odd number – and the doorway to the courtyard with an open scrolly pediment.* S of the entrance hall is the

* Mr Buttress suggests that the columns mark the position of the Elizabethan W wall. He also advances the theory that the Elizabethan house was of

LIBRARY, victorianized without glamour, E Wyatt's DINING
71 ROOM, interesting as a rare example of so early a use of the
Wrenaissance. The stucco ceiling and the carved overmantel
are evidently meant to look late C17. The frieze is less deceiving.
White marble chimneypiece. N of the entrance hall (and on the
upper floor) are the two principal Elizabethan rooms. The
DRAWING ROOM is gorgeously panelled, with intersecting
arches – an exceptional motif – and a delicate frieze of mar-
quetry above. L. and r. of the doorway are tapering pilasters.
The ceiling has intricately conducted broad studded bands,
the broad frieze below strapwork cartouches. But the climax is
the huge stone overmantel with pairs of atlantes and caryatids
framing the arms of Queen Elizabeth. The decoration round
the figures is wild, at the top much more classical. The bay
window is obviously altered, and the present arrangement of
the room may well owe something to *Wyatt*. The STAINED
GLASS from Disley church is Elizabethan and later. Next door
is the small STAG PARLOUR with its fabulous though amazingly
inept chimneypiece. On it is a hunting scene with the Elizabethan house in the middle, and hunting scenes go on on the
stucco frieze. The chimneypiece incidentally has the arms of
James I, and so must be a little later than that of the drawing
room. The room forms part of *Wyatt*'s dining room wing, so
its features must be viewed with caution. The frieze at any rate
must be C19.

Other Elizabethan rooms are the STONE PARLOUR, in the s
range on the ground floor, again with a mighty stone chimneypiece (probably *ex situ*), and the LONG GALLERY on the top
floor of the E range. The bay windows off the two ends of the
gallery especially are Elizabethan usage, and the gorgeous
44 chimneypiece, the most elaborate of all, has the arms of the
Queen. Again it may not necessarily be in its original position,
and of the rest much, including the ceiling, is copy or imitation.
Next to the gallery, also on the top level, is the GHOST ROOM
with yet one more Elizabethan stone chimneypiece. Is the
ceiling of this room original?

The Leoni period has less to show of such a spectacular
nature. The grand STAIRCASE is spacious and has a juicily
Baroque plaster ceiling, but leads to no grand rooms, as it

E-plan, rather than quadrangular, based on the present E range, and that, as
suggested by Dr R. B. Wood-Jones, the frontispiece of the N front is *ex situ*,
and originally formed the centre of the w side of the E range.

starts only at state-room level. At the top landing are square, fluted Corinthian pillars. The balusters with their goblet-like lower part are entirely c17 in character, and the SALOON so much so that it has been doubted whether its wooden decoration can be of the 1720s. References to *Grinling Gibbons* in 1684 and to the new parlour in 1687 have been adduced for an earlier date. The panelling is articulated by coupled Corinthian pil-57 asters, and cascades of limewood carving entirely in the Gibbons style hang down in panels, representing the fine arts, music, and the four seasons. Equally luscious is the overmantel. Grand doorway from the staircase. The ceiling of the room on the other hand is evidently of the 1720s.

This leaves only the CHAPEL unmentioned. It is on the ground floor in the NE corner, has windows perhaps gothicized in this moderate way by Wyatt, but inside again sumptuous carving in the late c17 style, especially the openwork foliage parapet of the family PEW and the openwork foliage of the COMMUNION RAIL. The screen of square fluted Corinthian pillars on the other hand is like that of the staircase.

ORANGERY. 1862 by *Alfred Darbyshire*, a mixture of classical pilasters with mullioned and transomed windows. The centre is a canted projection.

STABLES. Nine bays, with weakly segment-headed windows. Even the archway, though with pilasters (they are blocked in two places) and a pediment, is segment-headed. This is *Darbyshire* again, 1862–4 apparently.

(TOWER in Lantern Wood, ¼ m. away. This is the re-erected top of the tower of the house, as it appears in the relief in the Stag Parlour. *Wyatt* took it down and used its top thus.)

LYME CAGE, on the bare hill, l. of the approach road. A square 'standing' with corner turrets with caps, built for watching hunts. What is its date? Elizabethan seems most likely – cf. e.g. Chatsworth.

(THE BOWSTONES, c.1500 yds SE. Standing stones.)

LYMM

6080

Lymm is a surprising place so near Warrington. It is a real little town, the streets run most intricately, and there is a rocky ravine right in the town and a lake right below the church.

ST MARY. 1850–2 by *Dobson* of Newcastle, the high W tower 1888–90 by *Crowther* of Manchester. The church is long and rather dull, the motifs are 1300 to early c14. Transepts (with galleries) are still used in the pre-Pugin, pre-Scott way. – FONT. Octagonal, with one repeating geometrical motif, probably 1660s. – PULPIT. Plain, very satisfying C17 work, dated 1623. – In an ogee-headed TOMB RECESS from the old church of c.1322 an object supposed to be a Roman ALTAR. – WALL PAINTING in the S aisle; 1883. – STAINED GLASS. In the S aisle three windows by *Wailes*. – Good E window with large figures of Christ, Angels, and Saints as one composition. It is of 1865. – In the N aisle one *Kempe* window of 1897. – PLATE. Cup and Paten Cover, London, 1691; Stand Paten, London, 1691. – MONUMENTS. John Leigh † 1806. Sarcophagus with drapery. – Mrs Leigh † 1819. She kneels by an urn. – Two plain, but excellent tablets to members of the Fox family, †1830 and 1833 and † 1835 and 1845 (S transept).

CONGREGATIONAL CHURCH, Brookfield Road. 1862–3 by *Edward Walters* of Manchester. E.E.

LYMM HALL, Rectory Lane. E-shaped Elizabethan house with a porch carrying a balustrade. Much restored. The house is reached by a BRIDGE with a lively balustraded parapet. Fine landscaped grounds, which must owe something to a layout by *Edward Kemp*, 1849. By the approach a mysterious building, probably C17, with a roof of pointed barrel shape and also such gables. Along the long side a balustraded parapet. Style, preservation, and history are all obscure.

The centre of the town is the CROSS. For this also dates are missing, but it must be early or mid C17. Steps in the live rock, and then an obelisk reaching up and through a canopy with gables and ball finials. By the cross a replica of the STOCKS.

DANE BANK (Hotel), N of the Cross. Georgian, of five bays and two storeys. Three-bay pediment. Round both corners canted bay windows.

(THE LIMES, at the corner of Brookfield Road, and Eagle Brow. Is this the house built to the designs of *Waterhouse*, 1859 ? EH)

W of Lymm the long THELWALL VIADUCT of the M6 Motorway, not at all as good as the recent bridges of motorways.

MACCLESFIELD

INTRODUCTION

Macclesfield is a medieval town, as the parish church testifies. It received its first charter in 1261. Nothing however tells otherwise of a medieval past, except street patterns and street names.

The fame of Macclesfield is silk, and the first silk mill was built by Charles Roe in 1743. He was a Derbyshire man, and at Derby John Lombe had established his silk mill already in 1717. Great wealth ensued. Torrington in 1792 writes: 'They seem in prosperity . . . and are building away. . . . The silk and copper trades are in a most flourishing state'; for Mr Roe in 1758 also started copper works. *The Beauties of England and Wales* only nine years later than Torrington tells of many cotton factories and thirty silk mills. A number of the early mill buildings indeed survive. They are architecturally the most interesting feature of Macclesfield. Major Georgian houses also are more frequent than in other Cheshire towns. From the townscape point of view there is only one aspect which ought to be sought out – the view from the railway station. From here the parish church looks spectacular; for it is built on top of a steep escarpment. Once one has managed the 108 steps to it, one is on top, and there are no further contrasts of level.

CHURCHES

St Michael (formerly All Hallows). It was consecrated in 1278, and of that date there are just two mementos: the w responds of the former nave with round deeply moulded capitals. They will be found w of the tower. So the c13 nave was no wider than is the s aisle now, for the tower is now a sw, not a w tower. That it is medieval the masonry shows, that it is Perp the tower arch and the tierceron-vault with large bell-hole inside, but the generous decoration is by *Sir Arthur Blomfield*, who also rebuilt nearly the whole rest of the church in 1898–1901, not pulling down the medieval church, but its successor of 1739–40. What remains of the pre-Blomfield time must be looked for on the s side. The Savage Chapel was built by Thomas Savage, Archbishop of York, between 1501 and 1507. It is only two bays long, but has to the w a sumptuous three-storeyed porch. It has decoration over the doorway, two canopied niches l. and r., an oriel on a carved underside above, and another niche above that. The chapel is open to the s aisle of the church by means of a small doorway and two arches, serving, as we shall see, for monuments. The s and E windows have simple Late Perp details. The blocked w window was the original E window of the Legh Chapel, which was founded c.1422. In 1620 it was rebuilt. The s window of the rebuilt chapel is canted, of 2, 5, 2 lights with arched tops to the lights.

FURNISHINGS. FONT (nave E), a robust baluster and a
fluted bowl; 1744. – REREDOS, ALTAR TABLE, and COMMUN-
ION RAIL were designed by *Sir Charles Nicholson*. – WARDENS'
PEW. Jacobean, with tapering pilasters. – CHANDELIERS of
brass, one given 1744 remodelled 1822, the other 1822. –
STAINED GLASS. One *Kempe* window of 1901 (N aisle), with his
mark, the wheatsheaf. – The choir E window is by *Powell*, 1901,
the nave W window and N aisle W window by the same, 1902

Macclesfield church, Pardon Brass of Roger Legh † 1506

and 1904 .– By *Shrigley & Hunt* Legh Chapel *c.*1900–5. –
Many late *Morris & Co.* windows. – PLATE. Two Chalices
and Patens of 1624; two Flagons of 1724 and 1731; two Dishes
of 1757; Tray given in 1812. – (CURIOSA. Bellringers' Jugs.)
MONUMENTS. Macclesfield has more large monuments than
any other Cheshire church. They are therefore mentioned here

by position. In the chancel N wall an alabaster Knight of c.1475. – In the S wall Sir John Savage † 1495 and wife. Alabaster effigies, holding hands. Kneeling figures against the tomb-chest l. and r. of shields. They are the children of the couple, including the future Archbishop (W side). – In the Savage Chapel in the N arches to the chancel Sir John Savage † 1492, also alabaster, and John Savage † 1527, alabaster again. The change in the fashion of shoes from pointed to broad may be noted. – Against the W wall the famous Pardon Brass, Roger Legh † 1506. Only he, kneeling, and sons behind him remain, and the inscriptions. The upper one tells us that the pardon for five Paternosters, five Aves, and one Creed is 26,000 years and 26 days. – Next to this Sir John Savage † 1597 and wife, erected three or four decades later. Recumbent effigies, she above and behind him. Columns carrying obelisks, a shallow coffered arch, and two figures reclining on it. – On the S wall from W to E. Effigy of a civilian, c.1500, the whole middle part of the effigy left in the block, i.e. not carved at all. Tomb-chest with angels in panels. – Sir John Savage † 1528 and wife. Two alabaster effigies. Tomb-chest with mourners and angels. – S aisle E. Earl Rivers, 1696 by *William Stanton*. Black and white marble, semi-reclining effigy with demonstrating hand. Animated drapery and accomplished treatment of the wig. He still lies on the half-rolled-up straw mat which the Dutch had introduced in the 1530s and which was popular in Elizabethan and Jacobean English monuments.

ST ALBAN (R.C.), Chester Road. Rightly appearing here immediately after the parish church; for this is a *Pugin* church of considerable size and unstinted design. The building cost c.£8,000, and some of it was given by the Earl of Shrewsbury. It was designed in 1838, begun in 1839, and opened in 1841, and it is still not E.E. but Perp, and none the worse for it. In 1840 or 1841 Pugin turned to the Second Pointed, i.e. the style from Westminster Abbey to the early C14, as the one and only style. St Alban has a big W tower unfortunately never finished, aisles with five-light windows, a clerestory of ten closely set windows, and a seven-light E window. There is a straight-ended S chapel as well, but no N chapel. The piers are extremely slender, of the standard four-shafts-and-four-hollows section, and carry moulded four-centred arches. The roof is steep. – The church has its SCREEN, as according to Pugin every Catholic church ought to have. – The PULPIT, the stencilled WALL DECORATION of the chancel, and the chapel ALTAR could also be to his design. – STAINED GLASS. The E window by *Warrington.**

CHRIST CHURCH, Catherine Street. A large brick church with a very high tower, built in 1775–6 at the expense of Charles Roe. The tower was heightened a little later to satisfy Roe's former demand that it should appear as high on the skyline as the tower of St Michael, which was built on higher ground. Seven-bay nave with a monumental stone portal in the middle of the N side. The middle bay has a pediment, and the doorway itself has a pediment on columns. Arched windows, a Venetian window on the E side between four subsidiary doorways; parapet. Three galleries inside, not at all lavishly treated. – COMMUNION RAIL with turned balusters. – STAINED GLASS. The E window by *Wailes*, treated pictorially. – MONUMENT. Charles Roe, founder of the Macclesfield silk industry. Large tablet by *Bacon*, 1784. Seated woman holding the portrait medallion. On the seat reliefs of the church, the old Park Green Mill with its water-wheel, and Roe's copper works with smoking chimneys.

ST GEORGE, High Street. Built as a Congregational church in 1822–3, but on speculation, and the speculation failed. Brick, three by seven bays, the long side with giant pilasters. Two tiers of windows all comprised under giant arches. The façade has a porch of four Tuscan columns with a Venetian window again comprised under one giant arch. Broken pediment. The chancel is later. (Inside, three galleries. NMR)

The SCHOOL to the SW was built in 1835 by *William Grellier*. It is a handsome design. Brick, of five bays and two storeys, with pediments over bays one and five. They rest on very elongated coupled pilasters. Arched entrance.

ST PAUL, Brook Street. 1843–4 by *W. Hayley*, a Commissioners' church, and quite large, as Macclesfield needed it. The steeple dominates, thanks to size and even more to the elevated site of the church. The church is long, with aisles and a many-windowed clerestory. The aisles have the typical Commissioners' lancets, here with Y-tracery and four-centred arches, and thin buttresses. The coarse pinnacles are equally typical. Octagonal piers and four-centred arches inside, and a thin hammerbeam roof.

ST PETER, Windmill Street. 1849 by *C. & J. Trubshaw*. Also a Commissioners' church. Lancets and plate tracery, a SW tower (intended to carry a spire), and a long chancel, i.e. according

* Information given by Mrs Stanton.

to the new Cambridge Camden precept – a decisive step away from St Paul, which is, however, the better design.

CEMETERY. Opened in 1866. The chapels are by *J. Stevens.*

CONGREGATIONAL CHURCH, Park Green. 1877 by *C. O. Ellison.* Gothic, with a SW tower, i.e. like a church with too little ground to stand on. Its neighbour forces this lesson home.

METHODIST CHURCH, Sunderland Street. 1779; enlarged or rebuilt in 1799. Further enlarged or beautified at the expense of John Ryle († 1808). Four bays along the street; windows in two tiers. Brick.

BRUNSWICK METHODIST CHURCH, Chapel Street. 1823. Five bays, brick, with two tiers of arched windows. Segmental porch of Tuscan columns. Thin three-bay pediment.

METHODIST CHURCH, Park Street. 1836. Brick, five bays plus two entrance bays with demi-columns. The front has no pediment.

UNITARIAN CHAPEL, King Edward Street. 1689. The same design as at Knutsford and Wilmslow, i.e. a long side with mullioned windows in two tiers, entrances in the end bays, and upper entrances above them, reached by staircases which run up outwards along part of the side.

PUBLIC BUILDINGS

TOWN HALL. 1823–4 by *Francis Goodwin.* A fine ashlar front of nine bays with a tetrastyle portico of unfluted Ionic columns and a pediment closing the vista from Chestergate. The side windows are tripartite. The portico repeats to the S towards the churchyard. In fact this was Goodwin's original building. The wider front to the market place is an addition of 1869–71 by the local architect *James Stevens.* – INSIGNIA. Great Mace, silver-gilt, 1693; Lesser Mace, Jacobean.

CHADWICK LIBRARY, Park Green. By *James Stevens,* 1874–6. Small and very Gothic.

KING'S SCHOOL, Cumberland Street. 1911, Neo-Georgian, with cupola. L. of it the earlier building of 1854–6 (by *F. Bellhouse*), r. of it another Neo-Georgian building with cupola, this of 1938. More recent buildings at the back.

COUNTY HIGH SCHOOL FOR GIRLS, Fence Avenue. Three storeys; fourteen bays. Brick, with stone ground floor and frontispieces. Freely Neo-Georgian with cupola. 1908–9 by *H. Beswick,* the County Architect.

SUNDAY SCHOOL, Roe Street. 1813–14. Remarkably large, as 69 is the Sunday School at Stockport. It cost £5,639 13s. 1d.

Brick, of ten bays and four storeys. Four-bay attic, and on the ground floor four corresponding arched windows. Two doorways with Tuscan columns. – The MONUMENT in front is of 1846 and commemorates John Whitaker, who founded the school in 1796.

INFIRMARY, Cumberland Street. 1867–72 by *J. Stevens*. The original buildings symmetrical, with a centre with columns in two tiers and a French pavilion roof – to a certain extent probably French C17 in inspiration. The NURSES' HOME is very much a period piece now. It looks to us like nothing in particular, but it is by *Sir Frederick Gibberd*, was won in competition in 1937 and illustrated in *The Architectural Review* in 1939. The building is not large. It is of brick, with horizontal windows, and two large staircase windows up the whole height. We forget how the pioneer style of the 1930s has become run-of-the-mill today.

WEST PARK HOSPITAL, Prestbury Road. The former WORK-HOUSE. By *Scott & Moffatt*, 1843–5. It is with workhouses that Scott started, and they are Tudor and no longer classical. Two middle gables and a cupola. Several more gables, well articulated chimneybreasts and chimneystacks. Lower wings to front and back. Several later additions.

PARKSIDE HOSPITAL, Victoria Road. By *Griffiths* of Stafford, 1868–71. Red brick, yellow brick, and stone. A large composition with two symmetrical towers with ogee caps and a higher clock tower behind. All in the *Rundbogenstil*. An old guidebook called the style Italian.

DRILL HALL, Bridge Road. 1871. Brick, Gothic, with a machicolated tower.

WEST PARK. In the park near the NW end are three Anglo-Danish CROSS SHAFTS. They represent a type also occurring in North Staffordshire and Cumberland (Gosforth, Penrith) which is characterized by being square above but circular below, the transition being made by pendant lunettes or lobes, one to each side. It is likely that Macclesfield was the centre of this type. One of the crosses has an interlace pattern, the others panels.

PERAMBULATION

This is in search of Georgian houses – there are of an earlier date no more than a few cottages – and of early mills.

Starting by church and Town Hall No. 8 MARKET PLACE was once a handsome house, with a little decoration of the middle windows and a doorway with columns. Five bays. N in JOR-

DANGATE is first the MACCLESFIELD ARMS HOTEL of 1811: five bays, three and a half storeys plus one-bay lower attachments with a Venetian window. Then an irregular house with a Venetian window on the ground floor, and opposite JORDAN-GATE HOUSE, an excellent Early Georgian specimen, dated 1728, of five bays and three storeys, with quoins, moulded window surrounds, and a doorway with fluted pilasters and a pediment. Front area with piers and iron railing.

w from the s end of Jordangate is KING EDWARD STREET with the former COUNTY POLICE OFFICE. This is of 1845–50, Tudor, two-storeyed, of stone, with three gables. Opposite the RURAL DISTRICT COUNCIL, a fine house of 1758 with an addition of 1927. The original house is of seven bays and three storeys with pediments over bays one, four, and seven. Doorways with Tuscan columns and pediment. On the ground floor Venetian windows l. and r. of the centre. Opposite a former MILL, six by six bays, three storeys, all arched windows. At the end of King Edward Street are STANLEY'S ALMSHOUSES, 1871, Gothic.

w from the Market Place is CHESTERGATE. Nos. 60–62 is a five-bay house of c.1700. Three storeys, windows with moulded surrounds, doorway with open scrolly pediment. In CATH-ERINE STREET to the s is a FOUNDRY, not large, but with a show window to display goods. The details are the same as at St George's church of 1822.* CHESTER ROAD is the continuation of Chestergate. At the corner of Oxford Road is a monumental mill known as THE CARD FACTORY, four-storeyed, of seventeen bays, with a five-bay pediment and a cupola.

s from the Market Place Mill Street descends to PARK GREEN, a fine centre of Macclesfieldiana.‡ There is the MILL of W. Frost & Sons at the e end, of thirteen bays and four storeys with a pedimented three-bay projection with a cupola. The building is dated 1785. To its l. is a Victorian addition of six bays. Then, at the corner of Sunderland Street is a late c18 house of five bays with a big curving-up attic storey with a tri-partite lunette window, a Venetian window under, and a door-way with columns in antis, all this enclosed in a giant blank arch. On the n side is MARTINS BANK, originally built in 1841–2 as the Savings Bank, and as such highly ambitious, Peri-clean, with a Greek Doric tetrastyle portico, a triglyph frieze, and a pediment. Next door preposterously the Congregational

* Mr Buttress told me of this factory.
‡ (The WAR MEMORIAL is of 1921 by J. Millard. D. Buttress)

Church, and next door to that, equally preposterous, the bijou DISTRICT BANK, brick, with much stone, one-storeyed with Baroque, Jacobean, and Arts and Crafts elements insouciantly *See* mixed. In PARK LANE a MILL of four storeys and twenty-two p. bays with a four-bay pediment, dating from *c.*1810–20, and in 441 PARSONAGE STREET a terrace of workers' cottages. There are more such terraces than can be recorded, as there are plenty more Georgian cottages with nice doorways.* In WARDLE STREET off Park Lane yet another early MILL. Eleven bays, four storeys, five-bay pediment, very coarse Ionic doorcase with pediment.

Finally, to the E, across the railway, in COMMERCIAL ROAD 89 Messrs ARIGHI, BIANCHI, with a front mostly of arched cast iron and glass. The building is late for its style – of 1882–3 – but one of the most perfect specimens of that style in the North of England.

E of the railway also new blocks of flats. The estate is called after VICTORIA PARK.

BRONZE AGE BURIAL, Beech Hall School. When the new swimming pool was being constructed in 1960 a collared urn containing the cremation of an adult female was discovered.

9070 ## MACCLESFIELD FOREST

Macclesfield Forest was created by the Norman Earls of Chester and became royal in 1237. The Kings to the C14 hunted here. Very little now remains, and E of this, about 1200 ft up, is the Forest Chapel.

FOREST CHAPEL. Rebuilt in 1834. Small, of coursed stones. Short W tower with saddleback roof. The windows are with a transom at the springing of the arch and a mullion only up to the transom. No structural chancel.

MAIDEN CASTLE *see* BROXTON

4040 ## MALPAS

Malpas is a tiny town, not a village. It has a CROSS (of 1877) at the crossing of the main streets – paved already in Leyland's time – and in the streets a few old houses of interest. The church dominates from the distance, but is invisible from the cross.

* Mr Buttress cites the following streets as having further examples of industrial housing: Paradise Street, Hope Street West, Pitt Street, Lord Street, Park Lane (Nos. 82–94, part of an intended larger development), and higher-class housing in Prestbury Road (Nos. 34–46).

ST OSWALD. A Perp church, one would say, with its battlements and pinnacles, but in fact to quite a considerable extent pre-Perp C14. These parts are as follows: the chancel in its lower masonry with the SEDILIA and PISCINA and the N vestry door, the chancel arch, which dies into the walls, the tower arch, and the lower parts of the tower – cf. the W doorway. The W window appears Dec but is of 1864 by *Clutton*. The most characteristic Dec motif is the sunk quadrant moulding. This also appears in the arches of the Perp arcade, and the NE respond indeed still has the springer of the much lower Dec arcade. So the arch voussoirs of the present arcades are redone. Even the outer walls are pre-Perp. The four large cusped recesses in the N aisle look no later than 1300, and so do the SEDILIA and PISCINA in the S aisle, though the additional PISCINA in the SE corner seems fully Dec.

Now the Perp church as a whole can be taken in. There are dates of donations 1488 and 1508. The chancel was given large windows with panel tracery and decorated buttresses. The aisle buttresses are decorated too. The aisle windows are of four lights and also have panel tracery. Two-storeyed S porch. The only post-Reformation element is the handsome vestry of 1717, brick, with two windows E, one and a doorway N, and prominent quoins. Inside, the arcade is of six bays. The piers have four shafts and four subsidiary diagonal shafts. Only the E responds are simply large faces. The capitals differ considerably. In order of time NE must come first, then the rest on the N side and one on the S, and last the other S ones. The Perp arcades carry a Perp clerestory of four-light windows. The tower has a vault inside with ribs leading starwise to a large bell-rope hole. This is presumably Perp too. On the top of the tower the start for a spire has been identified. It was probably never built. The Perp nave roof is glorious, of very low pitch, with many bosses and many angels with spread wings – not all original. The aisle roofs have quatrefoil panels. (Below the E end is a vault with single-chamfered ribs.)

FURNISHINGS. FONT. Octagonal; Perp. Quatrefoils on the bowl, fleurons on the base, panelling on the stem. – STALLS. In the chancel and the S chapel. Simple, with small faces on the arm rests. Three MISERICORDS: two Knights in combat, a Mermaid, a monster. – SCREENS. To the S and N chapels, the Brereton and Cholmondeley Chapels, high and structurally identical, but of different tracery. That on the N side has the small forms set in the usual circles, that on the S has very busy

small-scale Flamboyant forms. Both carry Orate inscriptions
('Pray, good people . . .'). – BOX PEWS with nice brass fittings
(s aisle w).–(One pew top is a BEAM with the date 1680). –
15   CHEST. A gorgeous piece, thanks to the intricate iron scrolls. –
PAINTING. 'St Peter's Denial of Christ', by *Hayman*, given in
1778. A large piece, now above the chancel arch. – STAINED
GLASS. In the N chapel a good panel of *c.*1500 (Presentation in
the Temple) and several C16 panels – all probably Flemish. –
Many Netherlandish C16–17 medallions. – In the s aisle one
Kempe window; 1902. – PLATE. Cup by *Thomas Mangy*, made
in York, 1673; Chalice, inscribed 1674; Cup, by *Richard
Richardson* of Chester, 1717; two Patens, 1742; three 'early
Chalices' (Richards); two Flagons, 1795.

MONUMENTS. Arranged topographically. In the chancel
tablet to Charles Wolley Dod † 1904, by *Edward Hilton*. Bronze
Art Nouveau trees round the inscription. – In the nave incised
slab to Urian Davenport † 1495, rector of Malpas. – In the s
36   chapel Randle Brereton and wife, 1522. Superb alabaster
piece with the excellently portrayed two recumbent effigies on
a tomb-chest with three by seven little recesses with statuettes.
– In the s aisle: tablet to John Stockton † 1700, a scrolly cartouche. – Mrs Bridget Kynaston † 1644. Tablet with two ugly
standing angels. The ornament is just turning gristly. – In the
N chapel: Sir Hugh Cholmondeley and wife; 1605. Alabaster.
Tomb-chest with strapwork pilasters and the kneeling children.
Also one baby in swaddling clothes. Good recumbent effigies. –
Lady Cholmondeley † 1815. By *Westmacott*. Two draped
floating angels joining from l. and r. to embrace. – In the N
aisle Lt. Col. Henry Tarleton † 1820. By *Edwards & Co*. of
Wrexham. Urn and trophy.*

GATEPIERS and iron GATES, two sets and minor gates. The
piers are dated 1725 (E approach) and 1764–5 (main gates).
See p. The s porch gates are of 1767 by *Thomas Tomlinson*.
442 Of the houses in the town little need be said. At the main crossing
is the MARKET HOUSE with open ground floor and eight
Tuscan columns; early C18. In CHURCH STREET is a wide-
bayed, three-bay brick house, with a pedimental middle gable.
The middle bay is flanked by two tiers of pilasters, and the
doorway has a steep pediment. The house is dated 1733 but
is in the style of the late C17. Then the CHOLMONDELEY

* In the Cholmondeley Vault – so Mr Richards told me – a lead effigy was
found with the body of a woman inside. A photograph is with the Council for
the Care of Churches.

ALMSHOUSES of 1721, one-storeyed, with a big steep pedimental gable. At the far end of the HIGH STREET the OLD
SCHOOL HOUSE, a curious composition, curious for its date
1745. Two storeys, three bays with two giant pilasters flanking
the middle bay, parapet with closely set pilaster strips. One-
storeyed wings imitating this reactionary style were added in
1833 and 1845.

HAMPTON OLD HALL, 1¾ m. NE. Dated 1591. The front is
timber-framed and has three gables. Recessed on the l. a fourth
bay with gable. This bay has a doorway with pediment, a
carved angle-bracket, decorated bressumers, and the familiar
baluster motif. But round the corner the house continues in
brick and stone with mullioned windows and yet further in
ashlar. There must be quite an interesting story behind all this.

(CHORLTON HALL, 1½ m. NW. Quite a large gabled house,
dated 1666, with C19 alterations. Staircase with shaped and
pierced flat balusters.)

(OVERTON HALL, 1¼ m. NNW. Partly half-timbered, of the
early C17.)

MARBURY
Near Comberbach
6070

MARBURY HALL. The house has recently been demolished. It
is a great pity. It was originally by *Gibbs* and totally remodelled
by *Salvin* c.1850. The style had Louis XIII pavilion roofs with
French dormers as well as Queen Anne elements, the mixture
something like Wellington College of 1856–9. So it was quite
a document of architectural history. (There remains a pair of
massive gatepiers, rusticated, and with urns. Are they by
Gibbs? EH)

MARBURY
Near Wrenbury
5040

ST MICHAEL. Beautifully set above a mere. Not a large church.
Perp, with battlements and pinnacles. Three-bay nave only,
but with clerestory. Perp W tower with two bands of fleurons,
some in the form of grotesques. The chancel was rebuilt
c.1822, but re-gothicized by *Douglas & Fordham* c.1891–2. –
PULPIT. Perp, with crocketed ogee panels. – MONUMENT.
William H. Poole † 1855. Gothic canopy.

At the approach to the church on the l. a timber-framed C17
house with its gable on a coving.

(MARBURY HALL, ⅜ m. S of the church, and also well sited overlooking the mere. 1810 according to Ormerod. EH)

MARPLE

Marple is splendidly placed close to a valley with steep banks, and it also has the Peak Forest Canal at its junction with the Macclesfield Canal. That gives ideal canalscape, especially along LOCK-SIDE, with narrow lock after lock – sixteen in all – and humpbridges. It also has to the NW close to the railway the AQUE-DUCT, where the canal is conducted above the River Goyt. This dates from 1801–8, and is by *Benjamin Outram*.

The chief promoter of the Peak Forest Canal was Samuel Oldknow, who started his muslin factory at Stockport in 1785 and his cotton mill at Marple in 1790, working with apprentice children on a large scale. He got his supply from poorhouses and the foundling hospital. His mill was E of the river, at the NW end of Old Hall Lane. It was five storeys high and twenty-five bays long and had two-storeyed, nine-bay wings. Little else survives of his activities, though his CANAL WAREHOUSE remains in St Martin's Road, and near the junction of Strines Road and Arkwright Road are the partly ruinous LIME KILN FARM and LIME KILN COTTAGES. Oldknow went in for lime-burning as well, and the two ranges with arched ground floors as well as the larger arches built into the bank behind are connected with that. They date from 1797. Oldknow also built the first church at Marple.

ALL SAINTS, Church Lane. Oldknow built this church in 1808–12. It does not stand any longer. We have only its tower and the new church next door. In the tower are kept some of the MONUMENTS. The best is *Flaxman*'s Rev. Kelsall Prescott † 1823, a tablet showing him – he died young – standing and gently instructing boys. – Samuel Oldknow's own monument is disappointing, though it is by *Chantrey*. He died in 1828. Draped altar with a profile head. – Nathaniel Wright † 1818. A cherub with an extinguished torch. – Elizabeth Isherwood † 1835. By *Manning*. A woman kneeling by an urn on a base. – John Clayton † 1848. A standing woman with a lamp and a torch.

NEW ALL SAINTS, Church Lane. By *Medland & Henry Taylor*, 1878–80. It never received its NW tower. Interior of no special interest. – FONT. A Georgian baluster. – PLATE. Chalice of 1762. – Next to the church and the old tower is the HEARSE HOUSE, with three pointed-arched openings.

ST MARTIN, Brabyns Brow. The church was built at the expense of Miss Maria Anne Hudson. *Edmund Sedding* was to design it, but he died, and so his far more talented brother *J. D. Sedding* was commissioned. The church was built in 1869–70. It is a quiet design of nave and chancel and bellcote and a half-timbered s porch. Yet in the rhythm of the s fenestration one can sense a designer of uncommon sensitivity. But at St Martin it is Sedding's pupil *Henry Wilson* who made the church into something of more than county interest. Wilson in 1895-6 added the N chapel, and *c.*1909 the N aisle, with arches dying into the square piers. The lovely N apse has a vault with a row of trees and a flight of birds. He gave the apse also an ALTAR TABLE and a COMMUNION RAIL of charming inlay,* and he was responsible for the large STATUE of St Christopher in a niche in his aisle which causes a projection in the outer wall. Finally also by him is the bronze War Memorial RELIEF of 1924. And that says nothing of the Art Nouveau FONT COVER and the 99 DOOR FURNITURE of the aisle w door. – STAINED GLASS. The E window is by *Morris*, 1869–70. Many individual figures; the pale patterns on the background quarries have disappeared. – By *Morris* also two chancel s windows, 1873. – The w and sw windows by *Christopher Whall*. – Two N windows are by *Herbert Bryams*, obviously a pupil of Kempe. – The plaster relief of angels on the chancel s wall is by *Sedding*.‡

By *Sedding* also the SCHOOL and COTTAGE behind, of 1869 and 1871, and the remarkably progressive VICARAGE in St Martin's Road. This was built in 1873, and has on the ground floor mullioned and transomed windows of original design, wooden casement windows in a different rhythm over, and a hipped roof – i.e. no gothicizing any longer but progress towards the free neo-William and Mary comparable to some of Webb's designs.

METHODIST CHURCH, Church Lane. A recent addition along the street is by *Heywood, Ashworth & Partner*.

CONGREGATIONAL CHURCH, Hollins Lane, Marple Bridge. 1885 by *Barker & Ellis* of Manchester. A lively group on a steep site. Perp, with straight-headed windows.

COUNTY GRAMMAR SCHOOL FOR GIRLS, Hilltop Drive. 1965 by *W. S. Hattrell & Partners*. Very good, both in grouping and detailing.

The C17 Marple Hall has been demolished, and of other things little need be appended. (At the s end of OLD HALL LANE, s of the site of Oldknow's mill, is BOTTOMS HALL, whose

* The REREDOS is by *Christopher Whall*.

‡ So are PULPIT and ROOD SCREEN (information from the Rev. H. H. Thomas).

outbuildings were used by him for the housing of his pauper children. It is a house of three bays and three storeys, c.1792. At the N end of BRABYNS PARK, by a lodge to the former mid C18 Brabyns Hall, is a cast-iron BRIDGE, 1813. THE SHANTY, No. 135 CHURCH LANE, is by *Barry Parker*, c.1895.) Off STRINES ROAD in Barlow Wood is a PACKHORSE BRIDGE of one long segmental arch. At HAWK GREEN, ⅜ m. S of the parish church, is a COTTAGE dated 1686. It has mullioned windows, of three lights l., but four lights r. of the doorway. ⅞ m. S of the church, at the end of RIDGE ROAD, is RIDGE END FARM, a C17 farmhouse, with mullioned windows and two symmetrical gables.

(OLD MANOR FARM, 1 m. W, in STOCKPORT ROAD. Small medieval manor house. The central part timber-framed, probably C15, with two-bay hall of cruck construction. Later wings, the service wing of stone, the other half-timber.)

MARTHALL

7070

ALL SAINTS. 1839, enlarged in 1887. Brick, with round-arched windows and an apse.

(COLHURST MILL, Sandlebridge. A three-storeyed brick watermill, still working. MHLG)

MARTON

8060

ST JAMES AND ST PAUL. One of the timber-framed churches of Cheshire – all except the E end. The church was founded in 1343, according to Randle Holme, or perhaps in 1370. The tower is specially interesting. It has an aisle with lean-to roofs to the W, N, and S, like the Essex towers. The sturdy posts survive carrying the shingled turret, and scissor-bracing to the W. The nave arches are of three bays with octagonal piers and arched braces longitudinally as well as transversely. Certain later alterations should be noted, e.g. that the original windows were of two, not three lights, and that the aisle roofs were different. The windows date from a restoration by *Derrick*, 1850, and some alteration was made to the tower timbers by *Butterfield* in his restoration of 1871. Professor Horn has stated, on the strength of his experience of Continental timber building, that Marton and Lower Peover are the earliest longitudinal timber churches of Europe. – FONT. Square, of timber, High Victorian. It may date from the time of Butterfield's restoration. – LADDER. In the tower. It looks original. – PULPIT. 1620. – WALL PAINTINGS. On the W wall, only outlines

34

preserved. – PAINTING. Moses and Aaron holding the tables of the Commandments. From the former reredos. C18. – STAINED GLASS. Two figures and fragments in the W window. – PLATE. Chalice, London, 1597. – MONUMENTS. Two defaced effigies of Knights, probably mid or later C14.

MELLOR

ST THOMAS. The church lies exposed on the hill, with marvellous far views into the Peak. Short Perp W tower, but the church early C19, the nave with round-headed windows, the chancel with pointed windows. – FONT. Early Norman, drum-shaped, with large, utterly barbaric carvings of a man on horseback, two other quadrupeds, and a seated child (?). – PULPIT. Carved out of one block of wood. Perp, with simply traceried panels; also leaf motifs in small panels below. – PLATE. C18 pieces.

MELLOR HALL, NE of the church. A fine seven-bay late C17 house. Can a date 1688 on an outbuilding apply? Two storeys, hipped roof, cross windows, and a doorway with a bolection-moulded surround and an absurdly steep open scrolly pediment.

(PEAR TREE FARM, Mill Brow, has a BARN with crucks. MHLG)

MEOLS see HOYLAKE

MERE

(MERE OLD HALL is essentially a Regency house and has some good Regency decoration. MHLG)

MERE NEW HALL was built in 1834 and is neo-Elizabethan of brick, with brick diapers. It is a mansion indeed, for though the centre is only of medium size, there is a long L-shaped wing attached to one side. The centre has a porte-cochère on the entrance side and is symmetrical towards the garden. Interiors in the Elizabethan style too.

MICKLEDALE see FRODSHAM

MIDDLEWICH

Middlewich is not an attractive town, and one is not tempted to walk. The MHLG in fact found very little to list.

ST MICHAEL. St Michael on the other hand is an impressive church, almost entirely Perp. Inside, however, the curiously narrow E arches of the arcades with one round pier each side

and the responds are Late Norman. They have typical leaf
capitals, and the piers also decorated bases. The narrow arches
are single-stepped. The rest of the arcades is Perp, with octagonal piers, fleurons on the capitals, and double-chamfered
arches. The ceiled roof of the nave has a date 1621.* Now the
Perp exterior. Big NW tower, projecting beyond the N front.
It is of *c*.1500 and has two pairs of bell-openings under one
ogee arch (cf. Sandbach). The aisles are embattled and have
pinnacles. The nave has three-light clerestory windows. The
one distinguishing feature of the church is the S aisle W and E
ends, both canted. It is said that on the W side the road made
this device necessary, and that on the E side it was repeated for
symmetry's sake. The whole exterior was over-restored by
Joseph Clarke in 1857–60. – SCREEN and STALLS. With many
Flemish panels, including C16 parchemin panels and C17
scenes of small figures. – SCREEN formerly of the Kinderton
(NE) Chapel. Dated 1632. The very large and bold top parts
remain, with strapwork and a coat of arms. – STAINED GLASS.
The E window of *c*.1860 must be Continental, probably French
or Belgian. – PLATE. Chalice and Paten, dated 1666; some C18
pieces. – MONUMENTS. Totally defaced stone effigy in the S
chapel. – In the N chapel two C17 tablets, typical of first versus
second half.

METHODIST CHURCH, Lewin Street. *See* below.

CEMETERY. The twin chapel is by *Bellamy & Hardy*, 1859. The
two parts are separated by an archway crowned by a rather
wildly detailed spire.

TOWN HALL, W of the church. 1844. Brick, Gothic, with mullioned and transomed windows and open arches below. The
side to the churchyard is plain but embattled.

In LEWIN STREET first a Gothic brick SCHOOL of 1854, then
the METHODIST CHURCH, red brick and stone dressings and
characteristic of *c*.1900, and then the VICTORIA TECHNICAL
SCHOOL and LIBRARY, dated 1897 and just as typical. Red
brick and red terracotta, with a cupola but otherwise vaguely
in the Loire style.

MIDDLEWICH MANOR, ¾ m. SW. Probably of *c*.1830 or 1840.
Ashlar, the front with two canted bay windows and a very
handsome segmental porch of fluted Ionic columns. Here and
there lengths of oversized Greek key.

KINDERTON HALL, ½ m. NE. Early C18. Five bays, two storeys,
wooden cross windows and a moulded door surround.

* It was heavily restored in 1858.

RAVENSCROFT HALL, 1 m. N. 1837 and 1877. The front is of
1837. Five bays with an Ionic porch. A pediment on the side
round the corner. On the other side extensions with a moderate
tower which look 1850s rather than 1870s.

STANTHORNE HALL, 1¾ m. W. Built in 1804–7. Three bays,
two and a half storeys. Dark brick. Doorway with broken
pediment on attached Tuscan columns.

The Roman site of SALINAE straggles for about ½ m. along King
Street. Fragmentary evidence suggests the existence of mainly
timber buildings of C2 and C3 date. As the name implies, salt
production was an important industry.

MILLBROOK

9090

ST JAMES. 1861–3 by G. & J. Shaw of Saddleworth. N tower
with prominent spire, geometrical tracery, a number of enterprising minor features. The PARSONAGE with its steep gables
might well belong.

ST RAPHAEL (R.C.), N of St James. 1963 by Massey & Massey,
with low concrete dome on a low drum and a long entrance
colonnade with segmental concrete arches. – Good STAINED
GLASS by Fourmaintreaux, made by Powell's, 1963.

MINSHULL VERNON

6060

ST PETER. By John Matthews, c.1847–9. Nave and chancel, bellcote, lancets. Rock-faced. The church was built for the Commissioners.

CONGREGATIONAL CHURCH, Cross Lanes, ¾ m. NW. 1809.
The façade is victorianized, but one original arched window
remains.

(HOOLGROVE MANOR, ¾ m. SW. C17, brick, gabled. Pilasters
at the angles. Pediment on a slight central projection. MHLG)

MOBBERLEY

7070

For twenty or thirty years in the first half of the C13 Mobberley
had an Augustinian priory, but no trace seems to remain.

ST WILFRID. Broad w tower of c.1533 (mason: Richard Platt),
yet the bell-openings with Y-tracery. The rest C14–15, except
for the E end, which is by J. S. Crowther, of 1889. What made
him choose intersecting tracery for his E window? The PIS-
CINA, which is genuine work of c.1300? The arcades are of four
bays with Dec arch mouldings; only the w bay differs (capitals
with fleurons), as it was built to link up with the new tower.

The chancel arch is of 1889. The nave roof is of low pitch with big cambered tie-beams and panelling. Fine openwork tracery above the tie-beams. Over the rood screen a ceilure. – FONT. Minute, gadrooned Georgian bowl. – SCREEN. The best in the county, with richly traceried dado, trails of foliage up the reveals of the arcade, ribbed coving with bosses to the w and E, and brackets for the former loft parapet. The screen is inscribed and dated 1500. – TOWER GALLERY. 1683, but looks mid C17. Openwork, with two big ovals. – WALL PAINTINGS. In the nave a St Christopher and some unrecognizable further representations. – STAINED GLASS. In the s aisle windows many fragments. – (Leigh-Mallory memorial window † 1924 by *A. K. Nicholson*. EH) – PLATE. Cup, London, 1571. – MONUMENT. Painted board of odd shape, with the effigy in a shroud. (Mr Buttress reports that it mentions Elizabeth and Nathaniel Robinson and has a date 1665, though the style looks a little later.)

BOYS' SCHOOL, Warford House. By *S. G. Besant Roberts*, the Manchester City Architect; recent.

MARGARET BARCLAY SCHOOL. Part of it is NEW HALL, a neo-Elizabethan house of 1848. Also buildings by *Leonard C. Howitt*, former Manchester City Architect.

OLD HALL. Jacobean, with some late C17 alterations.* Irregular, of brick with stone dressings, two storeys high. Mullioned and transomed windows. Evidently only a fragment.

ANTROBUS HALL, Knolls Green. A fine front dated 1709. Five bays on the ground floor, four on the upper floor. Cross windows of wood. Rusticated gatepiers.

DUKENFIELD HALL, at the Knutsford end. Brick, early C17, with a symmetrical front of E-type. The short projections and the middle porch are all gabled. (Inside, a stucco ceiling. MHLG) Good gatepiers.

(Mr McLaughlin adds to this the following houses by *Sir Percy Worthington*: BAGUELEY GREEN FARM, THE BEECHES, GORSEY BROW.)

MOLLINGTON

CRABWALL HALL. The façade with porch projection and polygonal angle turrets must be early C19. Brick; Flemish bond. Doorway with heavy Gothic shafting. The windows are renewed. At the back older brickwork.

---

* A date 1686 is on an outbuilding.

MOORE

MOORE HALL. Early C18, brick, roughcast. Five bays, rusticated angle pilasters. The porch looks mid C19 Palladian. (Fine staircase. MHLG)

VILLAGE FARMHOUSE. Mid C17. Stone. Three bays, symmetrical, with a string course running all along and round the doorway.

MORETON see GREAT MORETON HALL and LITTLE MORETON HALL and WALLASEY, pp. 369, 371, 373

MOSS HALL see AUDLEM

MOSSLEY see CONGLETON

MOTTRAM-IN-LONGDENDALE   9090

ST MICHAEL, Church Brow. The usual dedication for churches on hills. St Michael indeed lies right on the brow, outlined against the sky as seen from the village, and it has wonderful views into the hills. The church is Perp but much renewed. It is a large building with a W tower, aisles, and chapels. The tower is of c.1486. Three-light windows with cusped heads, stepped, and no tracery. Transomed five-light E window. The interior is almost entirely of 1854 (*Shellard*). – PULPIT. High Victorian, alabaster, with much elaborate figurework. – PAINTINGS. Now over the chancel arch the former reredos, with Moses and Aaron and the usual texts. – Big brass CHANDELIER, 1755. – MONUMENTS. Two early C15 stone effigies, defaced (s chapel). – Incised slab to John Pycton, rector, † 1517, almost totally defaced (chancel). – Reginald Bretland † 1703. Stanton style. Semi-reclining, and wearing a wig. (N chapel; badly placed.)

Close to the church the CROSS. Basically medieval, but restored in 1760 and in 1897.

(CONGREGATIONAL CHURCH. 1791. It was originally Methodist.)

SCHOOL, Church Brow. 1832. Six bays, two tiers, entrance in castellated attachments l. and r.

MOTTRAM OLD HALL. A five-bay early C19 stone house of two storeys with a three-bay pediment. Porch with thin Tuscan columns. Good LODGE of six Greek Doric columns with a pediment, the middle intercolumniation being wider than the others.

MOTTRAM ST ANDREW

MOTTRAM HALL. Built *c.*1753 and much too little known. A brick mansion, its centre of five bays with slim giant Doric pilasters and pediment with a Rococo cartouche right across. Triglyph frieze. Delicate doorway with a broken pediment and flower decoration. Wings of three bays, then turning forward to add another five by three. The wings have in the centres of the parts parallel with the house and at r. angles to the house rusticated doorways, four in all. What were they needed for? The one to the r. of the centre gave access to the CHAPEL whose panelling and w pew seem original. The altar space must be a Victorian alteration and change of direction. Along the centre of the house runs a corridor with fine stucco vaulting of the late C18 including fan lunettes. The staircase and one room also have restrained late C18 stucco ceilings. The other ceilings and the doorcase seem to be interfered with. The façade of the centre towards the garden is plain, with just some decoration of the middle windows.

MOTTRAM OLD HALL. C17, timber-framed and sizeable.

MOTTRAM CROSS. Medieval the steps and part of the shaft. Above that 1832.

MOULDSWORTH

ST CUTHBERT (R.C.), by the station. Brick, with a detached campanile with recessed spire. The mullions of the side windows are stylized figures. The church was designed by *F. X. Velarde* and completed in 1955.

MOULTON

ST STEPHEN. 1876–7 by *Douglas*. Nave and chancel under one unbroken roof. The chancel with geometrical, the nave with freely Perp tracery. Characteristic w spirelet. The two sides have different fenestration. The N vestry has a boldly outlined chimney. Interior of exposed yellow and red brick, whereas the exterior is faced with small stones. Big timber roof.

BOSTOCK HALL, 1¾ m. SE. An interesting mansion, not sufficiently investigated. Built in 1775, and that represents the essential brickwork and the two segmental bows of the façade. Is the Venetian window also original? Then, about 1850, this quiet house was forcefully italianized. The motifs are evident in many places, especially the porch. Yet later, say in the seventies, more was done, and probably all the spires and spirelets. Even the good late C18 STABLES received a spire. There is also a prominent water tower with spire. Inside, one fine late C18 chimneypiece of white marble with two maidens l. and r., and in the same room a gorgeously painted ceiling with flowers and peacocks, and in another room a painted frieze of big leaves – excellent work no doubt of the time of the later C19 work, i.e. the seventies.

MOW COP   8050

Mow Cop is over 1000 ft high. It belongs to the Cheshire outliers of the Peak. The rock (Yoredale Rocks) is the oldest in the county, a little older than the Millstone Grit to its N and the Coal Measures further NE along the Lancashire border where industry settled.

(ST LUKE. 1875. The architect seems unrecorded. Dr Gomme reports a chancel with polygonal apse, an aisleless nave, lancets, and at the W end of the S side a cruciform window with a STAINED GLASS representation of the Holy Spirit.)

ST THOMAS is in Staffordshire.

WESLEYAN CHAPEL. 1862, yet still with an ashlar façade in the Georgian tradition. Three bays, arched windows, and a low hipped roof.

CASTLE. This very considerable folly was built in 1754 (MHLG) 64 by Randle Wilbraham as an eyecatcher from Rode Hall. It is a very early sham ruin, only a little later than Sanderson Miller's. It consists of a large ruinous round tower, a high and wide arch, and some walling, and lies right on the outcrops of jagged rock. If only the bungalows were not so near.

RAMSDELL HALL. *See* Rode, p. 323.

NANTWICH   6050

Nantwich, now a friendly country town of about 10,000 inhabitants, was from Roman times to the C19 the centre of the English salt industry. The other 'wiches', i.e. salt towns, were Middlewich and Northwich, and they carried on when the Nantwich industry declined. In Domesday Book Nantwich had eight salt houses; Leland speaks of three hundred. By 1624 there were still about a hundred, but the industry declined from the C17 and had ceased by the mid C19.

ST MARY. Until the C17 a chapel of ease, yet a large, impressive 18 church and rather earlier than most of the other major Cheshire parish churches. It is essentially of the C14, but taking in the change from Dec to Perp in a particularly abrupt manner. If one starts looking at the exterior from the square, i.e. the w, one must first of all discount *Sir George Gilbert Scott*'s inexcusable replacement of a Dec doorway and a Perp window by two pieces in his beloved Second Pointed, i.e. late C13 style. He restored the church in 1854–61. Then, as one looks up, one sees at once the crowning motif of the church, the octagonal crossing tower, and the bell-openings are Dec. So along the s side with an added Perp porch of two storeys – lierne-vaulted inside – and then the aisle windows, the same as on the N side. They have cusped intersecting tracery with ogee-headed lights. In the s transept one window is like that; the rest are Perp. On the N side the N transept has a three-light Dec E window and a Dec N vestry. Now to the chancel. Here the side windows are all very rich Dec, with crocketed gables and also much decoration on the buttresses and pinnacles. But the E window of seven lights is pure Perp, though also under a crocketed ogee gable. Openwork parapet.

The chancel interior reinforces the problem. SEDILIA and PISCINA are Dec (ogee arches), and the pretty AUMBRY and the three doorways are all Dec in their mouldings. The vaulting-shafts have a Dec section, and they carry a gorgeous lierne-vault, which of course could as well be Dec as Perp. Are we to assume then, as Crossley did, that all this is one building operation, perhaps interrupted by the Black Death? Or is the E window a substitution?

Anyway, the rest of the interior must be taken into consideration, the many-shafted crossing arches, the springers for a crossing vault, the springers for a vault in the outer bay of the N transept separated from the rest of the transept by a strong arch, and the nave arcades. They are of four bays, the piers with four shafts and four small flat diagonal projections, the arches with Dec mouldings. The clerestory of eight windows is later. The aisles have flying buttresses across, each with an additional shank to make them into pointed arches. Now what will be the actual dates? We have none. Was the beginning *c.*1340, was the end *c.* 1400? A chantry was endowed in 1405, and that creation has been attributed to the s transept.

FURNISHINGS. STALLS. Late C14, with gorgeous canopies. Twenty seats have MISERICORDS. Among them are a Woman beating her husband with a ladle, the Devil pulling a nun's mouth open, Samson and the Lion, Virgin and Unicorn, Skinning a stag, a Pelican, the Fox pretending to be dead, a Nun reading, St George and the Dragon, a Mermaid, Wrestlers,

several Dragons. – PULPITS. An excellent stone pulpit is in 29
the crossing with pillar and body and back wall all panelled. –
The other pulpit is in the nave. It is dated 1601 and has the
usual two tiers of blank arches. The maker was one *Thomas
Finche*. – PAINTING. The Widow's Mite, by *Jules Bouvier
Sen.*, Nazarene in style. It is a small piece and hangs in the s
aisle. – STAINED GLASS. Original fragment in the tracery of
one chancel window. Little that is complete, but the superb
colours typical of the early C14 keep their full effect. – s transept s by *Wailes*, 1858. – N transept E by *Hardman*, 1862 and
1864. – N transept w by *Kempe*, 1876, and one of his best. – s
aisle by *Harry Clarke*, 1919; remarkably Expressionist. – w by
Clayton & Bell. – PLATE. Chalice, 1604; Cup and Paten, 1618;
Chalice, 1623, Cup, 1633, two Flagons, 1659, two Almsdishes,
1732–3, all London–made; also a C17 Paten. – MONUMENT.
In the s transept an alabaster effigy of the late C14; damaged.

The church is the centre of the town. Along the N side of the
churchyard is the DISTRICT BANK by *Waterhouse*, Gothic,
of 1864–6, and the later, smoother, equally Gothic BAR-
CLAYS BANK of 1876 by *Thomas Bower*, subsequently enlarged
and altered. The MARKET HALL of 1868 (by *George Latham*)
has iron columns inside but is no great shakes. Then NE of the
church in MONKS LANE the surprisingly metropolitan DY-
SART BUILDINGS, a perfectly even brick terrace of nine
houses, two and a half storeys high. Opposite are the CON-
GREGATIONAL CHURCH of 1842, three bays, brick, with a
pediment across, and the CONGREGATIONAL SCHOOLS of
1903, typical of the date and denomination. Fiery brick.

On the w side of the churchyard runs the HIGH STREET. It
starts from the bridge (*see* below) and runs up in a curve. Its
line has been spoiled by a recent opening up just in the bend.
(Nothing is earlier than 1583, in which year much of the town
was destroyed by fire. No. 12 is half-timber and may well date
from immediately after the fire. No. 20, late C18, has a Venetian
window with slender detached columns and a lunette window
in a pediment. No. 20 is half-timber with a gable. EH) Then
the CROWN HOTEL, known to have been rebuilt soon after
the fire, with an impressive flat front of timber-framing with
close studding. Three storeys with continuous second-floor
windows. At the back is an C18 assembly room. The WEST-
MINSTER BANK is typical Baroque of *c*.1900, three bays, three
storeys. No. 42 and Nos. 44–46 are two timber-framed houses,
both with two gables. Carved brackets. There is a three-gable

frontage to Castle Street. Turn into MILL STREET, where the
LIBERAL CLUB occupies a fine, spacious five-bay house of
1736 with segment-headed windows and a one-bay pediment.
At the end of Mill Street is the COTTON MILL of John Bott,
late C18, large, of four storeys, brick, with an undersized cupola. Off Mill Street in BARKER STREET is a nice group of
Georgian brick houses.

(Returning to the HIGH STREET, on the E side, No. 45 has a
small single-gable half-timbered frontage. No. 41 is a much
larger timber structure, of three storeys below a gable. Overhangs on carved brackets. Ogee lozenges in the first-floor panels
and two kinds of patterns in those of the second floor. An inscription, *ex situ*, records the date 1584, the name of *Thomas
Cleese*, carpenter, and the aid given by the Queen in the rebuilding of the town after the fire. N of the churchyard the
three-gabled building which includes MARTINS BANK is also
timber-framed, with patterning and carved brackets. Blocked
remains of a former continuous run of window lights, a feature
also to be seen on No. 42, above. EH)

From the recent opening in the bend in the High Street BEAM
STREET runs E. No. 20 is a timber-framed cottage with a
Georgian doorway. At the far end the CREWE ALMSHOUSES
of 1767, a sad sight at the time of writing. They are of thirteen
bays, brick, one and a half storeys high, with a three-bay pediment and a stone doorway with Tuscan columns.*

The continuation of High Street is PILLORY STREET, and Nos.
1–5, the building on the curved corner, are of 1911 by *E. H.
Edleston* of *Bower & Edleston* (MHLG). From here HOSPITAL
STREET runs E. On the l. is the LAMB HOTEL, 1861 by
Bower, decent, staid, mid C19 with a Tuscan porch. Then Nos.
55–57, SWEETBRIAR HALL, timber-framed with a big poly-
gonal bay window. On the other side further out the UNI-
TARIAN CHAPEL of 1726, small, with a big shaped gable. Then
No. 148 with a pretty Gothick doorway and No. 154, COMBER-
MERE HOUSE, with an equally pretty classical doorway. At the
end on the l. the side of THE ROOKERY, a square and stately
C18 brick house with two projecting wings and a mid-doorway
with Roman Doric columns and a pediment, and on the r.
CHURCHE'S MANSION, an outstanding piece of decorated
half-timber architecture. It has a date 1577, i.e. is of before the
fire. It has a plan like Dorfold Hall near Nantwich, i.e. two big

40

---

* From here by turning r. Churche's Mansion in Hospital Street can be
reached.

gabled endpieces and a centre of hall with porch and corresponding bay window. Three- to five-light mullioned and
transomed windows. Several of the usual ornamental motifs,
including diagonal ogee braces. The builder was *Thomas Cleese.*

The continuation of Hospital Street is LONDON ROAD. At its
start WRIGHT'S ALMSHOUSES. 1638. Built by a Lord Mayor
of London. Six brick cottages of two low storeys. Mullioned
windows. The best thing is the archway into the front garden,
with two big volutes and Tuscan columns.

But the best street of Nantwich is WELSH ROW, the continu-
ation of the bottom end of the High Street beyond the bridge.
The BRIDGE is of 1803. In Welsh Row little at the beginning.
The first noteworthy building is Victorian, the PEARL ASS-
URANCE, formerly Savings Bank, of 1846 with a big shaped
gable. Then No. 48, timber-framed with overhangs, No. 50
Georgian, of four bays, and No. 52, TOWNWELL HOUSE,
Early Georgian, of five bays and two and a half storeys with a
big pedimented stone doorway. THE GATEWAY is the handsome Late Georgian stable entrance of No. 64. The windows
are in giant arches, and so is the centre with the archway. One-
bay pediment. No. 64 lies back. On the other side No. 83 is a
plain five-bay house. The METHODIST CHAPEL is dated 1840
and has its pediment across the façade. At the end WILBRA-
HAM'S ALMSHOUSES, C16, timber-framed and at the time of
writing derelict. Two low storeys. The façade seems to heave
visibly.

BARONY HOSPITAL, Middlewich Road. The oldest part was
the WORKHOUSE. It dates from 1780 and has a long front with
two long wings receding. One-bay pediment with two tiers of
Venetian windows under.

ALVASTON HALL, 1½ m. NE. By *E. Salamons & A. Steinthal,*
1896–7. Brick and half-timber, with gable and dormers.

COLLEGE OF AGRICULTURE (REASEHEATH HALL), 1½ m.
NNW. Brick, many-gabled, Tudor and Stuart in style and of
good quality. 1878; enlarged 1892.

POOLE HALL, ½ m. N of the former. A house of 1817, six by
three bays, with a semicircular porch of unfluted Ionic columns
and an exceptionally fine interior. Generous staircase with cast-
iron balustrade and skylight, drawing room with an elegant
segmental tunnel-vault, a screen of two columns, and a Grecian
chimneypiece with two detached maidens, and dining room
with a shallow lower segmental recess. By the approach to Poole
Hall is REASEHEATH OLD HALL, another Georgian house,

plain, five bays, chequer brick, with a one-bay pediment and a tripartite lunette window under.

AUSTERSON OLD HALL, 1½ m. s. Half-timbered. The N part has closer studding than the the s wing.)

2070   NESTON   [EH]

At the commencement of the C19, Neston, with 1,486 inhabitants, was the most thriving and populous place in Wirral, and the population was not exceeded by that of Birkenhead until 1831. Prosperity had resulted from the decline of the port of Chester, which, with the silting up of the river Dee, Neston superseded in importance. In 1557 and 1560 collections were made in churches throughout the land for the completion of the New Quay, construction of which extended over a long period, but which in due course was abandoned in favour of the quay at Parkgate (*see* p. 299). Remains of the New Quay, sw of the town, still exist, now confusingly known as the OLD QUAY. Until the early C19 decline of Parkgate's Irish traffic, Neston flourished as a market town and coaching station.

ST MARY AND ST HELEN. The tower is C14, but with Norman masonry re-used in the lower two storeys. Bell-openings of two cusped lights under a trefoil. (Squinches indicate that a spire existed or was intended.) A plaque dated 1697 must refer to a restoration, not necessarily of the tower. The top storey of the tower is C19, presumably added when *J. Francis Doyle* rebuilt the remainder of the church in 1874–5. Clerestory and gabled aisles. E.E. turning Norman at the w end, commemorating the C12 work which survived prior to 1874. – FONT. Perp. Octagonal with roll-mouldings. Quatrefoils on the bowl and cusped panels on the stem. – STAINED GLASS. By *Morris*, i.e. *Burne-Jones*, are the s aisle second window from the E, 1888, and the N aisle easternmost window, 1894. – Later work by the *Morris* firm in the N aisle: third window from the E, 1901, second from the E, 1906, and E window, *c.* 1927.* – Two windows by *Kempe* in the s aisle: second from the w, 1900, and westernmost, 1905. – PLATE. Large Paten, London, 1683; Cup, London, 1717. – MONUMENT. C14 priest. A slab with cross fleury. – CROSSES. Fragments of pre-Conquest crosses. Part of a circular head with cable-moulding and knotwork, and the top of what seems to be the shaft belonging to it, with cable-moulding and interlaced bands. Also two fragments of the shaft of another cross,

---

* Dates supplied by Mr A. C. Sewter.

cable-moulded. The upper part has two fighting figures on one side and a winged figure on the other. Lower part with interlacing on one side and the figure of an ecclesiastic on the other. (Built into the wall of the tower at bell-openings level is a stone depicting two fighting equestrian warriors.) – In the churchyard a Georgian SUNDIAL of baluster type.

St WINIFREDE (R.C.), Burton Road. By *A. W. N. Pugin*. Very humble. With Pugin's mind overflowing with religious ardour and rich Gothic splendour, the financial restrictions which all too frequently hampered his creative genius may be seen as one of the saddest aspects of his tragic life. Built as a school in 1840, and adapted as a chapel in 1843, when the present presbytery, adjoining, was enlarged. Later alterations include an extension, presumably at the altar end, in 1852, almost certainly not by Pugin. The s porch has a doorway at the side and the front wall carried up as a diminishing bellcote above a moulding which indicates the roof pitch behind.

TOWN HALL, High Street. 1887–8 by *David Walker*.

In PARKGATE ROAD some early C18 brick houses. On the N side VINE HOUSE, two storeys of four bays with pilaster strips at the corners. Above the cornice a storey with two windows and a sundial between. Doorcase with bracketed canopy. ELMHURST is two-storeyed with at either end a projecting wing with partly-segmental front.* Adjoining, ELM GROVE HOUSE, three-storey, four-bay, with pilaster strips, but rendered. On the s side MOORSIDE HOUSE is of three storeys with four irregular bays. Doorcase with shell canopy. Further w, on the N side the VICARAGE, *c*.1906, and in the cul-de-sac beyond it COLONUS, 1967 by *J. Roy Parker*. In LEIGHTON ROAD the four-storey tapering brick tower of a WINDMILL. (C17. MHLG)

NETHER ALDERLEY

St MARY. A sizeable Perp church, in spite of two Dec doorways with continuous mouldings – w and s. Stately w tower very similar to that of Mobberley. The N and s sides of the church are unexpectedly and picturesquely irregular. On the s side there is the two-storeyed addition of the Jacobean Stanley family pew, on the N side is a Jacobean dormer window. The chancel is of 1856 by *Cuffley & Starkey*, and much restoration

---

* Built in 1717 with alterations including work by *W. Aubrey Thomas* (MHLG).

was done by *Paley & Austin* in 1877–8. The interior has three-bay Perp arcades of standard elements. Good canted nave roof, and good aisle roofs. – FONT. Circular, with large heads projecting, only two of four preserved. They point to the C14. – FAMILY PEW. Elevated like an opera box. The parapet is Jacobean, but the surround is Gothick, presumably late C18. – STAINED GLASS. The E window is by *Wailes*, 1856. – In a s window late *Morris* glass. – PLATE. Paten given in 1714; Flagon given in 1753. – MONUMENTS. The Rev. Edward Shipton † 1630. The inscription reads

'Here lies below an aged sheepheard, clad in heavy clay,
Those stubborne weeds which come not off unto the judgment
day,
Whilom he led and fed with welcome paine his careful sheepe,
He did not feare the mountaines highest top, nor vallies deepe,
That he might save from hurte his faithful flock which was his
care,
To make them strong he lost his strength and fasted for their
fare:
How they might feed, and grow, and prosper, he did daily tel,
Then having shewe'd them how to feede, hee bade them all
farewell.'

– First Lord Stanley of Alderley. 1856 by the younger *R. Westmacott*. Recumbent effigy in a Gothic recess noticeable from outside by an arcaded slight projection. Stiff-leaf capitals. – Second Lord Stanley of Alderley † 1869. Tomb-chest with Cosmati mosaic decoration, i.e. an Italian C12–13 type. Against it a bronze plaque with the mourning family – the *pleureurs* of medieval tomb-chests brought up to date. Recumbent alabaster effigy. The artist is not recorded. – John Constantine Stanley † 1878. Tablet with portrait medallion by *Boehm*. – Stanley Mausoleum, in the churchyard. 1909. A rectangular block in a restrained neo-Jacobean.

OLD SCHOOL, at the entrance to the churchyard. It was built in 1693 and has small mullioned windows. An extension at the back of 1817 has mullioned windows too, and the two with the mausoleum form a pretty group.

OLD MILL, E of the church, on the main road. A C16 water-mill with its machinery recently restored (National Trust). Big expanse of stone-flagged roof with small dormers.

OLD HALL, close to the mill, E of the church. The house looks late C16. It is partly brick with mullioned windows, partly timber-framed with elementary geometrical motifs. Square SUMMERHOUSE of brick. Across the lake in a field an OBELISK crowned by the Stanley eagle. It dates from 1750.

ALDERLEY PARK. The house of the Stanleys of Alderley does not exist any longer, but the STABLES, the DOVECOTE, and a SUMMERHOUSE are there, all of brick. CHURCH LODGE, irregular, with an Italianate-looking tower but Elizabethan features, is dated 1817. The site has in the meantime attracted ICI, and they have their Pharmaceutical Research Division here. The buildings are by *Harry S. Fairhurst & Sons* and were started c.1956. They include a restaurant by a pool. This was built in 1967.

The C17 half-timbered EAGLE AND CHILD COTTAGE, at the corner of the lane leading to the church from the main road, has quatrefoils on the cove of a small gable, and a similar feature appears at NUT TREE, ½ m. N.

SOSS MOSS HALL, 1 m. W. Timber-framed; dated 1583 on a chimneystack. Three-gable front with herringbone bracing and some busier decoration. Colossal chimneybreast round the l. corner.

THE MOSS, 1 m. N of Soss Moss Hall. 1900. With a semicircular porch.

NETHER TABLEY *see* TABLEY

NEWBOLD FARM *see* BRUERA

NEW BRIGHTON *see* WALLASEY, p. 373

NEW FERRY   [EH] *3080*

ST MARK, New Chester Road. Rock-faced sandstone. 1865–6 by the younger *Edward Haycock*. Five-bay nave, clerestory, W bellcote. Chancel (ashlar-lined) 1910 by *Deacon & Horsburgh* as part of an intended complete rebuilding, the abandonment of which is to be regretted. – STAINED GLASS. Series of aisle windows. English Saints etc. Six windows 1880 by *Holiday*, alternating with Apostles etc. Three windows 1876–7 by *Morris*, i.e. *Burne-Jones*.

NEWTON *see* CHESTER, p. 172, *and* HYDE

NEWTON HALL *see* FRODSHAM

NOCTORUM *see* BIDSTON, BIRKENHEAD, p. 96

NORBURY *see* HAZEL GROVE

NORLEY

ST JOHN EVANGELIST. By *Pearson*, 1878–9.* Not large, and not alas vaulted, but masterly without a doubt. The church is in the later C13 style and has a central tower, broad and sturdy, and a N transept. The tower has two pairs of bell-openings to each side, and its large S window is deliberately contrasted against the more ornate N transept N window. The chancel has a square end with three long windows with Y-tracery, shafted inside. The shafting however is subdued compared with the shafts of the tower arches. N aisle of four bays.

NORLEY HALL, ¼ m. NE. Largish and rendered. Rebuilt 1782 in, it is said, Gothic style. However, Twycross in 1850 referred to it as having been recently enlarged and improved, and indeed with its Tudor motifs and gables it looks *c.*1830–40. Stable court with gatehouse.

At RULOE, 1¾ m. E, is a house by *Douglas*,‡ of brick, and with some of his typical motifs. It is of *c.*1873.

ROUND BARROW, at the W end of Gallowsclough Hill, 1 m. S. The barrow is 50 ft in diameter and 5 ft high and has been considerably reduced by ploughing. Beneath the mound was found an eccentrically placed pit containing the cremated remains of an adult male.

PROMONTORY FORT. Only the N and E sides of this fort are protected by artificial defences. They consist of a single bank and ditch. On the W and S natural defence is provided by the river. The bank still stands to a height of 6 ft in places, and the irregular nature of the ditch suggests that the site may be unfinished. Excavation has shown the ditch to be 50 ft wide and 10 ft deep. The defences are broken by four gaps, that on the S having the appearance of an original entrance.

NORTH RODE

ST MICHAEL. 1845 by *C. & J. Trubshaw*. Rock-faced, with a W tower with a higher stair-turret. Bad late C13 detail.

Wider views include the POST OFFICE TOWER (cf. Wincle, p. 387) and the CONGLETON VIADUCT of many arches, built in 1849, engineer *J. C. Forsyth*, for the North Staffordshire Railway.

---

* Mr Quiney suggests *c.*1875 for the design.
‡ Information from Mr Howell.

NORTHWICH

Northwich is one of the three wiches, i.e. salt towns, and contrary to Nantwich it kept its industrial prosperity until it could switch over to chemicals. The town has little to attract – hardly anything except the parish church on its hill. Look around from the hill and you see the ICI Winnington works in the distance, and the new shopping centre, Memorial Hall, etc., by WATLING STREET nearer by, not at all architecturally valuable. The high gasholder in the very centre does not help matters of course.

ST HELEN, Witton. The first impression is Victorian in its 25 smoothness and evenness. In fact it is Perp outside and partly Dec inside. But the restorations of 1842, 1861, and 1884 have done a lot. The C14 is represented by the arcade piers, with a section of four semicircular attachments and small hollows in the diagonals. The capitals are very raw, the moulded arches are contemporary. The Perp work has recorded dates of 1498 and 1525. The N arcade was then rebuilt further N to create a wider nave, the chancel arch, whose S respond survives, was taken down, and the stones were re-used in the E arch of the N arcade. Chapel arches were opened in the former chancel walls (cf. the finer arch mouldings than those in the nave), and a new E end was built. This is a bold, well-lit polygonal apse – à la Lichfield. It was rebuilt in 1861, and it is said that the tracery was altered. Of c.1525 is the gorgeous nave and chancel roof, panelled with big and small bosses – good enough for Somerset. Several initials of William Venables, lord of the manor at the time. The W tower (by *Thomas Hunter*) is Late Perp.* Wills of 1498 and 1525 refer to it, but the tower arch towards the nave goes with the arcades. The tower has two decorative bands. It is, like the whole church, of four and five lights, and in the clerestory in one place even six. The apse has decorated buttresses and transomed windows. – SCREEN. In the vestry, top beam with inscription, dated 1641. – REREDOS in the S chapel, of stone, Dec. A row of ogee-headed niches with brackets for statuettes, and a frieze above. – STAINED GLASS. In the S aisle *Kempe* glass: 1895, 1906, 1907.

HOLY TRINITY, Castle Street. 1842. Built by the Weaver Navigation Trustees for the use of the watermen. The architect is not recorded. Ashlar, geometrical tracery, tower with a thin, prominent broach-spire, very short and narrow chancel. Open

* The Rev. G. L. Davies queries the attribution to Hunter, pointing out that parts of the inscription are in other places, e.g. the inside of the porch, though Hunter's name is indeed on the tower.

timber roof – i.e. all pre-archaeological. – The PULPIT is no doubt also of the time of the church.

ST WILFRID (R.C.), Witton Street. 1864–6 by *E. Kirby*, enlarged in 1901–2. Brick with diapers and a flèche. Lancet windows. Wooden piers and open timber roof. The detailing is of the 'rogue' type, as Goodhart-Rendel calls this kind of wilfulness.

CONGREGATIONAL CHURCH, Castle Street. 1882 by *Maxwell & Tuke*. Large, brick, with mostly lancets. Not at all churchy.

LONDON ROAD METHODIST CHURCH. 1888–9. Italianate, with pilasters and attached columns. Two short towers with pyramid roofs. Brick and terracotta decoration.

POLICE HEADQUARTERS, Watling Street. 1966–8 by the County Architect and the *Biggins Sargent Partnership*. The best modern building in Northwich.

POST OFFICE, Witton Street. Super black-and-white.

BRUNNER LIBRARY, Witton Street. 1909. Timber-framed and symmetrical.

TECHNICAL SCHOOL (former), London Road. By *Joseph Cawley*, 1897. Brick and red terracotta with nice figures in relief and a scene of small figures representing science and the arts. Angle cupola.

SIR JOHN DEANE'S GRAMMAR SCHOOL, The Crescent, London Road. Rebuilt in 1908, a gift of Sir John Brunner (*see* Winnington). Brick and stone dressings. Symmetrical front with large mullioned and transomed windows and a cupola.

WEAVER HALL, the former WORKHOUSE, now a hospital, London Road. 1837. Brick. A friendly nine-bay front, only of two storeys. Centre with three-bay pediment and turret. Close glazing of the windows. A wing runs back from the centre.

VIADUCT. The railway viaduct of 1869 runs right through Northwich. It is of stone, not of brick.

Northwich is the site of Roman CONDATE. A dense scatter of Roman material from ¼ m. S of Castle Hill is from a settlement which may possibly have originated as a military site close to Watling Street.

NORTON

NORTON PRIORY was founded for Augustinian canons *c.*1133 at Runcorn and moved to Norton in 1134. It was quite a large house, still with fifteen canons in 1381. In the C15 it became an abbey. After the Reformation the buildings were replaced by a house for Sir Richard Brooke, and this was remodelled by

Wyatt for another Sir Richard Brooke about 1775, after having been rebuilt earlier in the C18. Very little remains of any of the buildings. The only visible fragment is an arched loggia which was the porch to the house. Inside the loggia is a Late Norman doorway from the priory, duplicated for symmetry's sake probably in the late C18. (Of the monastic buildings all that survives is a Norman undercroft of seven and a half bays with round piers carrying round multi-scalloped capitals. The vaults have plain ribs.)*

WATER TOWER, on a hill S of Norton village. Built for the Liverpool Corporation by the municipal water engineer, *G. F. Deacon*, c.1890–2.

OAKLANDS *see* DARESBURY

OAKMERE HALL *see* SANDIWAY

OAKWOOD HALL *see* ROMILEY

ODD RODE *see* RODE

OLLERTON   7070

KERFIELD HOUSE. A Neo-Georgian remodelling by *Sir Percy Worthington*, 1912.

OLLERTON GRANGE. 1901 by *J. Brooke*.‡

OUGHTRINGTON   6080

ST PETER. By *Slater & Carpenter*, 1871–2. An ambitious, but externally not a satisfactory church. The fault lies in the NE steeple. The pinnacles against the high octagonal bell-stage are unjustifiable, and the spire is too thin for so substantial a church. The chimney on the S vestry also is lacking in propriety. The large polygonal apse is the best external feature. The interior is serious, the W group of four long lancets and a rose comes off well, and the ensemble culminates in the stone rib-vaulting of chancel and apse. – STAINED GLASS. The apse windows by *Kempe*, 1894. – Also by him S aisle W.

OUGHTRINGTON HALL (now part of a school). Early C19. It has been rendered, which is always a pity. The ground floor has a

* Recent excavations undertaken by Mr F. H. Thompson on behalf of the Runcorn Development Corporation have produced the ground plan of the church: long nave and N aisle, transepts, and straight-ended chancel. One chancel chapel N and one S of the chancel, both later. The cloister lay S of the church. The surviving undercroft was the W range.

‡ Information kindly conveyed by Mr McLaughlin.

porch of pairs of Tuscan columns in a not quite standard arrangement, and l. and r. are tripartite windows with a blank
segmental arch over.*

BURFORD LANE FARM, ¾ m. ESE. By *Douglas*, *c.*1869.‡

OULTON PARK *see* LITTLE BUDWORTH

OVER *see* WINSFORD

OVER PEOVER

ST LAURENCE. A W tower of 1739, much like that of Knutsford,
a miserable brick church of 1811 by *William Turner*, and attached to it on the S side a coarsely done Perp chapel and on
the N side a chapel of *c.*1648–50, amazingly pure in its classicity. The tower has round windows and arched bell-openings
with pilasters, the S chapel rather ugly window tracery and an
octagonal pier with canted projections, the N chapel ashlar
masonry, an E pediment, lunette windows high up, and three
round entrance arches on piers. The exterior looks 1720
rather than 1650. The chapel ceiling has a boldly carved coat of
arms in the middle (cf. the N chapel of Sandbach church, dated
1661). The furnishings are exceptionally rich. – FONT. Perp,
with a quatrefoil frieze and a panelled stem. – PULPIT. Two
tiers of blank arches. In them inlay panels (cf. Lower Peover).
– N chapel SCREEN. – by *F. H. Crossley*. STAINED GLASS.
C15 fragments in the S chapel; also figured ones. – PLATE.
Set inscribed 1772. – MONUMENTS. Probably John
Mainwaring † 1410 and wife. Alabaster effigies, uncommonly good. In the chancel. – Randle Mainwaring † 1456 and
wife. Alabaster effigies in a recess. The recess has an ogee arch.
In the S chapel. – Incised alabaster slabs to Philip Mainwaring
†1573 and wife, and to Sir John and wife, 1586, both also very
good. – William Littleboys † 1624. Small painted panel with
skeleton and the tools of death. Long inscription. – Philip
Mainwaring † 1647, in whose memory the N chapel was built.
Sarcophagus with garlands and shields and on it two white
marble effigies. – Also in the N chapel a suit of ARMOUR.

PEOVER HALL. The house was built by Sir Ralph Mainwaring
and is dated 1585. It is part of a larger house, the remainder of
which either was never built or has been demolished. Brick,
with mullioned and transomed windows. The parts of that date

* Mr Howell suggests that *Harrison*, who is known to have designed gates
and a lodge here, may have had something to do with it.
‡ Information from Mr Howell.

are partly two-storeyed with gables, partly three-storeyed with flat tops. A later C18 range has recently been demolished and the new frontage tudorized. The drive is by gatepiers with splendid Rococo iron GATES from Alderley Park. Then on the l. STABLES of 1654, an important building. Long low brick front with middle entrance and three mullioned five-light windows l., three r. The upper storey with just three rounded windows altogether is later. Interior with Tuscan columns and arches, a strapwork frieze, and a sparse plaster ceiling, all original. The adjoining COACH HOUSE has a date 1764. It is a very handsome building, long, of lighter brick, and also with middle entrances. They are three arches, and on top is a three-bay pediment and a cupola.

FREEGREEN FARMHOUSE. *See* Lower Peover.

OVER TABLEY   7080

ST PAUL. 1855–6 by *Salvin*. Of little merit; small and rock-faced. The bell-turret must be later. (TOMBSTONE to H. L. B. Langford-Brooke by *Eric Gill*, 1909. The carving above the inscription by *Macdonald Gill*.)

OVER TABLEY HALL, just N of the motorway interchange. Part of a larger Gothick house of before 1780 (Ormerod). Brick, with pointed windows, and centre with angle pilasters and doorway decorated by large fat fleurons and a gable top with pinnacles. The side parts, now only two bays long, have a top frieze also with pinnacles. It is all handled a bit clumsily, but all the more engaging for that. Older outbuildings with mullioned windows.

OVERTON *see* MALPAS

OXTON *see* BIRKENHEAD, p. 99

PARKGATE   [EH] 2070

The rise of Neston (*see* p. 290) and Parkgate resulted from the decline of the port of Chester. In the C18 Parkgate had become a principal port for traffic to and from Ireland. Mrs Delaney, sailing from here in 1754, wrote: 'Had we not come to Parkgate as we did, we should not have found room. People come every day and the place is crowded.' *The Beauties of England and Wales*, 1801, recorded that it 'has become a convenient and fashionable bathing place. It is also celebrated as the station for some of the packets for Ireland'. By *c.*1820–30, however, it had, like Chester before it, fallen victim to the silting of the river Dee, though it survived as a resort for some time after the passenger traffic had moved to Liverpool and Holyhead, and only since the 1930s has marshland replaced the tidal waters of the Dee.

ST THOMAS. Apparently built in 1843 as a Congregational chapel. A small sandstone box. Lancet windows with iron glazing bars in petaloid patterns.

MOSTYN HOUSE SCHOOL. The range facing The Parade is a recasting of a former inn. Behind this the CHAPEL, begun in 1895 by the then headmaster, *A. G. Grenfell*. – FURNISHINGS by *Frederick Fraser*. – STAINED GLASS. Apse and w windows by *Morton & Co*. Several of the N and s windows form a notable series, from 1905 onwards, by *R. Anning Bell*. – The central, half-timbered, part of the range N of the chapel is also 1890s by *Grenfell*.*

THE PARADE. Largely composed of C17 to early C19 houses and cottages. Much of the rendering is doubtless later. The small block of shops by *J. S. Allen* containing the POST OFFICE now looks a mild and unremarkable manifestation of the Modern Movement, though it was considered important enough for illustration in *The Architectural Review* in 1935. The group N of it includes an iron balcony on lofty and delicate columns. In BOATHOUSE LANE, HAMILTON CLOSE is a layout of houses by *J. Roy Parker*, 1965.

7090   PARTINGTON

ST MARY. 1884 by *G. Truefitt*. Rock-faced, with a SE tower with short spire.

OUR LADY OF LOURDES (R.C.), Chapel Lane. 1964 by *Reynolds & Scott*.‡

TOWER HOUSE, Chapel Lane, has alas disappeared. According to the MHLG it was in the spirit of the Watt buildings at Knutsford.

5050   PECKFORTON CASTLE

Peckforton Castle was built about 1844–50 by *Salvin* for the first Lord Tollemache. His riches were his estates. The family (in 1883) owned 35,726 acres producing £43,345 annually. Peckforton Castle cost £60,000; Lord Tollemache, however, built

* According to the present headmaster, Mr Julian Grenfell. *Frederick Fraser & Warburton* may also have been involved.
‡ Information from Mr D. Evinson.

not only for himself but also for his tenants. He put up fifty-five
farmhouses at a cost of £148,000 and as much again for cottages.
Though a Tory, he was praised as a model landlord by Gladstone and Joseph Chamberlain.* Of Peckforton Castle *The
Illustrated London News* in 1851 said that it 'seems to exhibit
the peculiar beauties of Carnarvon Castle without its inconven-
iences', but Sir George Gilbert Scott, younger than Salvin by
a crucial twelve years, obviously referred to Peckforton when
in 1858 he called 'the largest and most carefully and learnedly
executed Gothic mansion of the present' 'the very height of
masquerading'.

So we must see for ourselves. Peckforton is indeed the only
fully deceptive of all the English C19 castles, not just generally
medieval and with windows clearly of the C19 as at Smirke's
Lowther and Eastnor and Hopper's Penrhyn, but a real castle
in a position which might have been chosen by any medieval ˌ
ingenerius. It also faces Beeston in the most challenging way.
The approach is romantic, by an asymmetrically composed
outer gatehouse with a round turret, and through the wood
whose trees are of course now higher than they were meant to
be in proportion to the castle. The moat, it is true, never carried water, but once one approaches the inner ward the illusion would be complete if it were not for the picturesque tree in
the ward.

The inner gatehouse looks forbidding with its triple-cham-
fered giant arch above the gateway arch and its broad battlements. On the r. is the small chapel. A hexagonal bell-turret is
on the E gable of the nave. The vestry has a dramatic pointed
tunnel-vault with transverse arches. Facing the gatehouse is
the hall range. The great hall is entered by a porch which leads
into a screens passage. The screen is of wood. The hall has the
correct two-light transomed windows of the late C13 castles 79
and mansions, a polygonal bay window, and a pointed tunnel-
vault with arches and ribs forming four large areas each crossed
diagonally by a pair of ribs. At the high-table end starts a long
gallery – not a C13 or C14 feature this – and behind this is the
drawing room with large two-light windows to the outside and
two deep, diagonally set canted bay windows. The gallery has
a large, irregularly shaped recess for a billiard table. At the far
end of the gallery is the octagonal library and a subsidiary
staircase in a higher square turret. Behind the hall is the main
staircase. It has an open well visible as one ascends through

* I owe all this information to Mrs N. Franklin.

openings in solid walls. The massive stonework is exposed here and everywhere. Behind the staircase rises the highest stair-tower of the castle, circular, with a higher stair-turret. In this is the dining room, an octagonal room with a vault of eight radial ribs. Below is the wine cellar, circular, with a ring-shaped tunnel-vault on a short round pier. Far away on the w side of the ward are the kitchen and service rooms. They are on a lower level, and the kitchen has a huge fireplace.

But all these descriptive details cannot convey any idea of the overwhelming solidity and the marvellous workmanship. There are plenty of stone fireplaces. Some of the principal interiors are plastered, with stone dressings, but others are ashlar throughout, as are even some of the minor passages, if anything at Peckforton can be called minor. Every doorway is detailed precisely, in full earnest.

Lord Tollemache evidently wanted the size and scale, but Salvin had to cope with the problem of how to make a genuine castle habitable. And it is habitable, or would be, if such a scale were still in demand. As it is, the house is empty. What can its future be? Who could take it over? Some enlightened American university? Some luxury hotel?

PEEL HALL *see* ASHTON

PEOVER HALL *see* OVER PEOVER

4070   ### PICTON

MANOR FARMHOUSE. A pity the house has been dolled up by painting coarse half-timber decoration. It must have been a dignified place with its brick exposed. Two slightly projecting two-bay end pavilions with big Dutch gables. One would date it 1660–70.

In the village below a square house with straight-headed Tudor windows with hoodmoulds, probably of *c.*1840.

4070   ### PLEMSTALL

ST PETER. The tower is of 1826, entirely Georgian in style. The church is Perp – cf. the side window with panel tracery and the six-bay N arcade and the hammerbeam roof. There is no chancel arch. – The Rev. *J. H. Toogood*, incumbent from 1907 to 1946, carved the extremely copious WOODWORK, except for a few pieces which are old. By him most of the rood screen, the top of the PARCLOSE SCREEN, which is early C16 (linenfold dado), the reredos and its surround, the choir stalls, the lectern,

the baptistery screen, and more. – Three-decker PULPIT dated
1722. – FONT. Octagonal, only two sides carved. Probably of
the 1660s, or perhaps Laudian. – DOOR. Simple, but good;
C15. Studded. – PEW, dated 1697, with a canopy on twisted
columns. – STAINED GLASS. Old fragments in a s window. –
PAINTED INSCRIPTION referring to benefactions from 1660
onwards (to 1684?). More refined lettering in an added inscription of 1718. – MONUMENTS. Painted heraldic tablet; C17,
undated. – Elizabeth Hurleston † 1727. Large tomb-chest outside the church, with a skeleton carved on. Also an elaborate
tablet. – In the churchyard a baluster SUNDIAL; C18.

PLUMLEY   7070

HOLFORD HALL. Part of a timber-framed mansion approached
by a stone bridge across the moat with two semicircular,
heavily detailed projections. The gabled front is gaily decorated
by concave-sided lozenges, double-curved diagonal braces,
and angle pilasters in two orders.

POOLE HALL see NANTWICH

PORTAL see TARPORLEY

PORT SUNLIGHT   [EH] 3080

INTRODUCTION

William Hesketh Lever, born in 1851, was the son of a Bolton
wholesale grocer. Taken into partnership by his father, he expanded the already prosperous family business before beginning,
in 1884, to specialize in the marketing of soap. Sold under the
registered name 'Sunlight', it was made to his own formula by
various manufacturers until, in 1886, in partnership with his
brother, he began production on his own account in a small
factory at Warrington. Sunlight Soap differed from most types
then available in being made largely of vegetable oils instead of
tallow and – a notable innovation – it was sold neatly packaged
and stamped with its name. Business was boosted by efficient
salesmanship and advertising, the scale of which was to expand
over the years and reveal Lever's seldom-erring flair for astute
publicity. With production having risen, in a short space of time,
from 20 to 450 tons a week, new premises became necessary, and
Lever conceived the idea of building a factory with a model village adjoining. In consultation with the Warrington architect

William Owen the present site was chosen, and construction of the Port Sunlight factory began in 1888. In the same year Lever took up residence at Thornton Hough (*see* p. 357). From an early date the firm pursued policies of international expansion, of amalgamation with, and taking over of, other concerns, and of gaining control of the supply of raw materials. After the First World War multiplicity of business, including the development of margarine manufacture, led to the moving of headquarters from Port Sunlight to London, and in 1929 Lever Brothers and a group of Dutch-founded margarine companies amalgamated to form the Unilever organization.

Lever became a baronet in 1911 and a baron in 1917 (when he used the maiden name of his wife, Elizabeth Hulme, † 1913, to form the title Leverhulme) and was created Viscount Leverhulme in 1922. One of the most celebrated of enlightened employers (albeit a paternalistic one), he introduced shorter working hours and benefit and welfare schemes, though the creation of Port Sunlight remained his chief exercise in 'prosperity sharing', and his record as a benefactor is closely allied with his interest in architecture and town planning. For work executed under his patronage in, e.g., his native Bolton and at Rivington, *see* the *Lancashire* volumes of *The Buildings of England*. He presented Stafford (i.e. Lancaster) House to the nation, and the £91,000 damages for libel, received from *The Daily Mail* and other newspapers following 1906, was partly devoted to saving the Liverpool Blue Coat Hospital from demolition and endowing the Chair of Civic Design at Liverpool University. He was a Congregationalist and a Liberal, and was M.P. for Wirral from 1906 to 1909. He died in 1925.

At Port Sunlight, two separate traditions in the history of English town planning met for the first time. On the one hand there was a social tradition, in the form of the C19 movement for improved working-class dwellings. Previous examples of housing and amenities provided by employers in connexion with their factories such as New Lanark, Copley, Akroyden, Saltaire, and, ¾ m. from Port Sunlight, the little-known Bromborough Pool Village (*see* p. 116) contained conventional terraces, with open spaces as mere adjuncts. Hence the significance of Port Sunlight in incorporating the visual tradition of the sylvan suburb. Derived from C18 romantic landscaping via Nash, with greenery forming an integral element of a spacious plan, it had previously been applied to the planning of resorts and middle-class suburbs. Bournville (which was to have a more direct influence on the

garden suburb and garden city movement and which differs from
Port Sunlight in that its tenancy is not restricted to company employees) dates from 1879, but its large-scale planned development
began only in 1893.

Adjoining Bromborough Pool (which provided dock facilities
for the factory), the land purchased in 1888 consisted of about
56 acres, of which 24 were allocated to the factory and 32 to the
village, and a group of 28 houses by *William Owen* was built
*c.*1889–90. With the acquisition of more land, the site of the village reached its present area of about 130–40 acres, and a layout
plan was drawn up by *Lord Leverhulme*. A series of channels –
formerly tidal inlets from Bromborough Pool – traversed the site,
and the village was planned round them, with curving roads,
skirting their edges. One became a sunken garden (The Dell),
and a bridge carried the principal cross axis (Bolton Road, aligned
on the spire of Bebington church) across the widest. For the most
part a 'superblock' plan was adopted, with land behind the cottages laid out as allotment gardens (an idea later developed by
Unwin), and at the perimeter of the site the village is outward-
looking, with cottages facing the boundary roads, the factory,
and, on the E, a railway. By the turn of the century over four
hundred of the present total of more than a thousand houses had
been erected, with the perimeter almost entirely built up and with
a little building also having taken place in the centre of the site.
In 1910 (when it had become practicable for the channels to be
filled in) a competition to revise the plan and to provide a village
centre was held, open to students of the Liverpool School of
Architecture and Department of Civic Design, and was won by
Ernest Prestwich, a third-year student at the School of Architecture. His scheme involved the filling in of all the channels except
The Dell, the enlargement of the central open area (The Diamond)
into a major formal element, the making of a second broad vista
at r. angles to it aligned on the church (The Causeway), and the
formation of roads radiating from the opposite side of the church.
A formal square of public buildings, including an art gallery, was
planned s of The Causeway linking the church with already-
existing public buildings (Hulme Hall and the Bridge Inn) in
Bolton Road. An Edwardian *Beaux Arts* plan (cf. Hampstead
Garden Suburb) was thus imposed on the partly-completed village, but although the broad outlines were carried out, the radiating roads were never built up, and the project was revised in
execution by *Lord Leverhulme* and *J. Lomax-Simpson*, with the art
gallery being re-sited and the other public buildings not mater-

ializing. Bolton Road remains unsatisfactorily related to the formal layout.*

Besides *William Owen*, who was joined in partnership by his son *Segar Owen*, the architects most extensively employed were *Douglas & Fordham* (and later *Douglas & Minshull*), *Grayson & Ould*, and *J. J. Talbot* of *Wilson & Talbot*. There is little by *Jonathan Simpson*, Leverhulme's life-long friend, but much by his son *J. Lomax-Simpson*, who in 1910 joined the company, and almost everything built after that date is by him.‡ London architects represented include *Maurice B. Adams*, *Ernest George & Yeates*, *Sir Edwin Lutyens*, and *Ernest Newton*, but their buildings do not stand out as being superior to those by local men. There is said to be a block of cottages by *W. Curtis Green*, and *Edmund Kirby* and *Sir Charles Reilly* were also employed.§

The cottages are mostly in groups of between two and ten, though some of the blocks, no two of which are identical, are larger. The earliest houses are quite simple, but by the time Park Road was being built (1892 etc.) the more ambitious variations of external design and the costly elaboration which were to be features of the village were already apparent. Materials and textures are generally hard and crisp, with red pressed Ruabon brick much in evidence, though with the work of *Lomax-Simpson* a greater sensitivity, characteristic of the early C20, is introduced. Accommodation of two standard types was provided – the 'kitchen cottage' with kitchen, scullery, and three bedrooms, and the 'parlour cottage' with, in addition, a parlour and a fourth bedroom. W.C.s were in outbuildings and bathrooms were mostly on the ground floors. An admirable modernization scheme, by the *Estates Department of UML Limited* (i.e. Unilever Merseyside Ltd), was commenced in 1963. Garages and individual gardens are being provided in the former allotment areas, and the cottages are being modernized, sometimes with considerable replanning being involved, without alteration to the frontages. A ragged effect is resulting from the removal of the chimneypots,

* The widest of the channels was bordered by Corniche Road and Church Drive. Branches occurred at Lodge Lane, between Lower Road and Windy Bank, at The Causeway, and at Park Road. The latter became The Dell, and the curves of the other branches, except for that at The Causeway, can still be traced in the lines of pre-1910 cottages.

‡ His work as company architect included factories in many parts of the world, and Unilever House in London.

§ As were *W. Naseby Adams*, *H. Beswick*, *Bradshaw & Gass*, *Cleland & Hayward*, *C. E. Deacon & Horsburgh*, *Garnett, Wright & Barnish*, *Thomas M. Lockwood & Sons*, *Huon A. Matear*, *Ormrod & Pomeroy*, *Pain & Blease*, *T. Taliesin Rees*.

with just one for each cottage remaining, but otherwise the treatment of the buildings is exemplary.*

CHURCH

CHRIST CHURCH, Church Drive. 1902–4 by *William & Segar
Owen*. Built at the expense, not of the company, but of Lord
Leverhulme himself. Undenominational, but in the trustee-
ship of the Congregational Union of England and Wales and
served by a Congregational minister. Red sandstone. Ashlar
outside and in. Stone-flagged roof. Neo-Perp of an Austin &
Paley type, with predominantly horizontal emphasis and Arts
and Crafts touches in e.g. the conventionalized tracery. Cruciform, with double N transepts and a tower in the angle between
chancel and s transept. The exterior is fresh and lively, but in
comparison the interior seems mechanical and uninspired.
Indiscriminately rich FURNISHINGS made by *Hatch & Sons*.
– STAINED GLASS. W window 1914 by *Heaton, Butler &
Bayne*. – Two aisle windows *c*.1950 by *Ervin Bossanyi*. –
Adjoining the w end is the LADY LEVER MEMORIAL, 1914
by *William & Segar Owen*, a rib-vaulted loggia, richly treated
with pinnacles, canopied niches, heavy bosses, etc. It contains
MONUMENTS to Lady Lever † 1913, and Lord Leverhulme
† 1925. Bronze effigies by *Sir W. Goscombe John*.

PUBLIC BUILDINGS ETC.

BRIDGE INN, Bolton Road. 1900 by *Grayson & Ould*. Opened
originally as a 'temperance hotel'. Roughcast rendering. Timber bargeboards, balustrades, etc. Two projecting wings enclose a small forecourt. Side elevation with big chimneystack
and half-timbered gable. The building has been enlarged, and
the entrance front and interior altered.

DELL BRIDGE, Bridge Street. A pedestrian bridge of 1894 by
Douglas & Fordham.

FIRE STATION, or, as it more correctly proclaims, Fire Engine

* It should be added that some demolition took place in the inter-war period,
including that of a reproduction of Shakespeare's Birthplace by *Edmund
Kirby*, of a bandstand in The Diamond by *Lomax-Simpson*, and of an open-air
theatre in The Dell by *Grayson & Ould*. The Victoria Bridge, 1897 by *William & Segar Owen*, vanished when the channel over which it carried Bolton
Road was filled in. Its former existence explains the name of the near-by
Bridge Inn. With the present Post Office soon becoming inadequate for its
original function as a village shop, a new and larger shop by *Douglas & Fordham* was built at the corner of Bolton Road and Bridge Street, but was destroyed by bombing and not rebuilt. Cottages which suffered war damage
were, however, almost without exception, faithfully restored or rebuilt.

Station. Behind Greendale Road, between Park Road and
Wood Street. 1902.

FOUNTAINS, The Diamond. 1949 by *Sir Charles Wheeler*.

GLADSTONE HALL, Greendale Road. 1891 by *William & Segar
Owen*. The first of the village institutions, built as a recreation
hall and men's dining room. Much tile-hanging and some half-
timber.

HESKETH HALL, Boundary Road. 1903 by *J. J. Talbot*. Originally Technical Institute.

HULME HALL, Bolton Road. 1901 by *William & Segar Owen*.
Originally a women's dining hall. Single-storey, of brick and
stone, with mullioned and transomed windows and big half-
timbered gables. Signboard with timber post.

LADY LEVER ART GALLERY, The Diamond. 1914–22 by
William & Segar Owen, with *Segar Owen* apparently being responsible. Provided by Lord Leverhulme (the contents being
part of his own huge collection) as a monument to his wife.
Of reinforced concrete clad in Portland stone, it is 364 ft long.
Restrained and accomplished *Beaux Arts* classical. On each
of the four fronts is a projecting entrance feature, those at the
N and S ends with concave re-entrants. All have recessed porticoes of fluted Ionic columns, except for that on the W, where
the columns are engaged. The N and S entrances are identical,
but the others differ in the disposition of their columns and in
the treatment of flanking windows. Except for these windows,
the elevations are without fenestration. Towards either end is
a shallow dome, each set above a rotunda with colonnades of
coupled Ionic columns. Main hall of elongated H-plan. With
its contents reflecting the taste of its founder, the building was
until recently itself an unaltered period-piece reflecting the
taste of its day. Alterations have, however, now been made by
J. Quentin Hughes, and have included the recasting of a number
of rooms and the changing of the original black and white
colour scheme of the main hall.

LEVER CLUB, Greendale Road. Originally Men's Social Club.
1896 by *Grayson & Ould*. Extended in 1968 by the *Civil Engineers' Department of UML Limited*.

LEVER LIBRARY and DISTRICT BANK, Greendale Road. 1896
by *Maxwell & Tuke*. Built as a girls' hostel. Upper part half-
timbered, with four gables. Pargetted frieze below the first-
floor windows.

LEVERHULME MEMORIAL, Queen Mary's Drive. In front
of the W entrance of the Lady Lever Art Gallery. 1930 by

J. Lomax-Simpson, who re-designed the w end of Windy Bank
to provide an axial setting. Sculpture by *Sir William Reid Dick*.
A polished granite column rises from a fluted base. One allegorical figure on top and three in front. An interesting design,
but surely superfluous. *Si monumentum requiris, circumspice.*

LYCEUM, Bridge Street. 1894–6 by *Douglas & Fordham*. Originally the school, and until the church was built services were
held here. Brick, with stone bands and dressings. Blue brick
diapering. Shaped gables. Mullioned and transomed windows,
some with tracery, under shallow-curved hoodmoulds. Quite
loosely grouped, with low, cross-gabled parts on either side of
the main block. Broad octagonal clock tower with short recessed spire.

POST OFFICE, Greendale Road. 1891 by *Grayson & Ould*, together with the adjoining cottages. Built as the village shop.
Half-timber, with a large gable to Greendale Road.

ROSE GARDEN, Jubilee Crescent. A terrace and monumental
arch of *c.*1937 by *Lomax-Simpson*, terminating the vista at the
s end of The Diamond.

SCHOOL, Church Drive. 1902–3 by *Grayson & Ould*. Built at
the edge of one of the channels: hence the sharp change in
levels at the rear.

SOCIAL CENTRE, King George's Drive. 1913 by *Lomax-Simpson*, together with the adjoining cottages. Originally the Girls'
Club. Pebble-dashed, with stone dressings and a little half-
timber. Symmetrical centre with two tall mullioned and transomed canted bays.

WAR MEMORIAL. At the intersection of the axes of The Causeway and The Diamond. 1919–21. The designer and sculptor
was *Sir W. Goscombe John*. The theme is 'defence of the home'
and it provides a rare example of a war memorial which is
genuinely moving and which avoids sentimentality. The stonework is granite and the sculpture bronze. In the centre rises a
runic cross, at the base of which are two soldiers defending a
wounded comrade and groups of women and children. Around
the surrounding parapet are relief panels of more children, and
groups representing the armed and medical services.

FACTORY

The FACTORY has a frontage to Wood Street. Though much enlarged, the original building of 1888–9 by *William Owen*, with
a tower at its SE corner, remains. Facing the end of Greendale
Road is the OFFICE BUILDING. Ornamented stone frontage

and office areas on either side of the entrance hall by *William & Segar Owen*, 1895. Behind is a higher block by *J. Lomax-Simpson*, 1913–14, containing another enormous office, with galleries, built on the axis of the entrance and above one of the soaperies. COMPOUND MILL, at the E end of the factory group and visible from New Chester Road. Shell concrete roof structures. It is of 1962 by *Sir Frederick Snow & Partners*.

HOUSING

The streets, with selected examples of housing, are here listed alphabetically, but the following is a suggested route for a perambulation which would also include the public buildings etc. Begin with the earliest houses around the junction of Bolton Road and Greendale Road. Then the part of Greendale Road S of them. Park Road, Poet's Corner, Wood Street, Bridge Street, Cross Street, Bath Street, Riverside, The Ginnel, Water Street, and the remaining (i.e. E) part of Bolton Road. Jubilee Crescent, The Causeway, Church Drive, Windy Bank, The Diamond (i.e. King George's Drive and Queen Mary's Drive), Lower Road, Central Road, Primrose Hill, Circular Drive, Boundary Road, New Chester Road, Corniche Road, Lodge Lane, Pool Bank, Bebington Road, Brook Street, and the remaining (i.e. N) part of Greendale Road.

BATH STREET. Nos. 3–33, with Nos. 9–10 RIVERSIDE, are of 1896 by *J. J. Talbot*. The longest ranges of the group enclose two sides of a lawn. Free Elizabethan with C17 touches. Brick with stone dressings. Dormers and many gables, some of them shaped. *See also* Cross Street.

BEBINGTON ROAD. Nos. 57–65, c.1899 by *William & Segar Owen*, have steep-roofed end pavilions and pedimented dormers. Nos. 67–79 are of 1897 by *Ernest Newton*. Asymmetrical, but incorporating overlapping symmetry. Nos. 89–97 are of c.1899 by *Talbot*.

BOLTON ROAD. The blocks which comprise Nos. 1–13 and Nos 2–12, and also a further block which was destroyed by bombing, were the first houses to be built at Port Sunlight. They all are by *William Owen*, c.1889. (For the S continuation of this group *see* Greendale Road.) The few larger houses built in the village for professional men and heads of factory departments etc. include Nos. 17–21, c.1890 by *William & Segar Owen*. At the turn of the century the minister, doctor, and schoolmaster were living here. Nos. 64–78, c.1912 by *William & Segar Owen*, are symmetrical, though freely grouped, with end blocks projecting at an angle. Pebbledash, with brick mullions, massive chimneystacks, etc. *See also* Cross Street, The Ginnel.

BOUNDARY ROAD. The blocks which comprise Nos. 1–43 and include two shops are by *Grayson & Ould, c.*1905.

BRIDGE STREET. By *William & Segar Owen,* 1894, are Nos. 1–9, with No. 26 PARK ROAD, and also Nos. 16–22, with No. 24 PARK ROAD and No. 25 WOOD STREET.

BROOK STREET. *See* Greendale Road.

THE CAUSEWAY. *See* Church Drive, The Diamond, Greendale Road.

CENTRAL ROAD. Nos. 66–72, with Nos. 51–59 LOWER ROAD, are of *c.*1906 by *J. Lomax-Simpson.*

CHURCH DRIVE. Nos. 1–5, with Nos. 5–7 THE CAUSEWAY, *c.*1901 by *William & Segar Owen.* The frontage to The Causeway is set at an angle, indicating the originally intended line of the road, skirting one of the channels.

CIRCULAR DRIVE. Nos. 28–38, with Nos. 1–7 POOL BANK, are of *c.*1899 by *William & Segar Owen.*

CORNICHE ROAD. Nos. 17–23, 1897 by *Lutyens,* have two rendered gables in the centre with first-floor Venetian windows. On either side the main roofs descend and widen out as porch roofs. Tile-hung end blocks, different from each other. Doors placed diagonally at the corners of the porches. Nos. 31–35 are of 1897 by *Jonathan Simpson.*

CROSS STREET. Nos. 1–9, with No. 1 BATH STREET and No. 20 BOLTON ROAD, *c.*1896 by *Grayson & Ould,* have Gothic ornament in the gables and large French C15 dormers of terracotta.

THE DIAMOND. On the E are the blocks comprising Nos. 1–22 KING GEORGE'S DRIVE with Nos. 8–12 THE CAUSEWAY and with the SOCIAL CENTRE. On the W are the blocks comprising Nos. 23–50 QUEEN MARY'S DRIVE with Nos. 13–17 THE CAUSEWAY. All are by *J. Lomax-Simpson,* 1913. The centres of the E and W sides are recessed, opposite each other, and both have three gables, but although similar in massing, the two sides differ. Resourceful but unobtrusive variations of grouping, detailing, and materials (rustic brick, roughcast rendering, stone, half-timber, weatherboarding etc.). At the N end of QUEEN MARY'S DRIVE, Nos. 10–14, *c.*1925, and Nos. 15–22, with No. 5 WINDY BANK, *c.*1926, are also by *Lomax-Simpson.* The latter, part of a scheme for providing a setting for the Leverhulme Memorial, is irregular, with the centre symmetrical in massing but not in detail.

THE GINNEL. All by *Lomax-Simpson*, c.1914, together with Nos. 60–62 BOLTON ROAD and Nos. 2–4 WATER STREET.

GREENDALE ROAD. DUKE OF YORK'S COTTAGES, with frontages also to BROOK STREET and PRIMROSE HILL, are pensioners' cottages of 1933 by *Lomax-Simpson*. Nos. 11–17, c.1902 by *Talbot*, half-timbered on an E-plan, are a scaled-down version of the now demolished Kenyon Peel Hall in Lancashire. Nos. 25–29 are of c.1901 by *Ernest George & Yeates*, Nos. 30–32 c.1901 by *Grayson & Ould*. Nos. 33–39 are of c.1901 by *Ernest George & Yeates*. Roughcast rendered. Large block with a hipped roof. Differing gabled blocks project at either end. Nos. 40–43 are of c.1902 by *Grayson & Ould*, Nos. 44–48 with Nos. 18–24 THE CAUSEWAY c.1902 by *Talbot*. Nos. 49–53, with Nos. 1–4 THE CAUSEWAY, c.1901 by *Grayson & Ould*, have a corner pavilion with the roof developing into an octagonal spire. Nos. 59–63 are of c.1899 by *Maurice B. Adams*. The blocks comprising Nos. 71–82 are by *William Owen*, c.1890, and form a continuation of the earliest group of houses (*see* Bolton Road) and are of similar simple design. Red pressed brick, with tile-hung gables and white-painted oriels and glazing bars. Nos. 83–87, together with the POST OFFICE, are of 1891 by *Grayson & Ould*.

JUBILEE CRESCENT. All c.1938 by *Lomax-Simpson*.

KING GEORGE'S DRIVE. *See* The Diamond.

LODGE LANE. Nos. 12–20, with Nos. 69–75 POOL BANK, 1898 by *Grayson & Ould*.

LOWER ROAD. Nos. 15–27, c.1906 by *Sir Charles Reilly*, form a shallow crescent. Veranda with Reillyish ironwork. Large sweep of roof punctuated by round-headed dormers. Nos. 29–33 and Nos. 35–49, c.1906–7 by *Lomax-Simpson*, are at r. angles to each other, facing a fine beech tree. *See* also Central Road.

NEW CHESTER ROAD. Nos. 178–190, 1897 by *Ernest George & Yeates*, are roughcast-rendered, on an E-plan, with the side wings long enough to form a courtyard. The cottages in this road extend for more than ½ m., and include many by the several architects most active at Port Sunlight in the 1890s, particularly *Grayson & Ould*.

93 PARK ROAD. The N side is all of 1892. Nos. 1–7 and Nos. 9–17 are by *William & Segar Owen*. The former, with half-timbering, has elaborate pargetting in the gables and in panels below. The latter has half-timbering and a row of five gables. Nos. 19–23 are by *Douglas & Fordham*. No. 23, BRIDGE COTTAGE, is of flint with stone dressings and has a fanciful end elevation

with projecting chimney and corner bay window. Lord Lever-hulme lived here in 1896–7 while Thornton Manor underwent alteration. The remainder of the block has a half-timbered upper storey. Cusped windows. Twisted chimneys. On the S side (i.e. on the opposite side of The Dell), the following are all by *William & Segar Owen*: Nos. 2–4, 1892; Nos. 6–12, 1894; Nos. 14–22, 1893; and Nos. 28–36, with Dutch gables, 1893. *See* also Bridge Street, Poet's Corner.

POET'S CORNER. The reproduction of Shakespeare's Birth-place, by *Edmund Kirby*, which stood here, has been demol-ished. Nos. 2–8, with Nos. 50–52 PARK ROAD, c.1895, are probably by *Kirby*.

POOL BANK. Nos. 9–17, c.1902 by *Talbot*, are near-symmetrical, freely using some C17 elements. Nos. 27–39 are of c.1899–1901 by *Talbot*. Stone and pebbledash. Segmental bow windows with unmoulded mullions. Nos. 55–67 are of c.1899 by *Douglas & Minshull*. *See* also Circular Drive, Lodge Lane.

PRIMROSE HILL. Nos. 30–38 are of c. 1899 by *Jonathan Simpson*, Nos. 52–56 also c.1899, by *Maurice B. Adams*. *See* also Greendale Road.

QUEEN MARY'S DRIVE. *See* The Diamond.

RIVERSIDE. Nos. 1–8 are of c.1895 by *Grayson & Ould*. *See* also Bath Street.

WATER STREET. Nos. 1–7 and Nos. 9–21 are of c.1912 by *William & Segar Owen*. *See* also The Ginnel.

WINDY BANK. Nos. 6–11 and Nos. 12–18, c.1902 by *Grayson & Ould*, were built following the line of one of the channels. A continuation of this group, and some cottages in Greendale Road, were demolished in connexion with the providing of a setting for the Leverhulme Memorial. The present axial vista was formed, and Nos. 1–3 and 2–4 built, c.1926 by *Lomax-Simpson*. Nos. 19–22 are of 1913 by *Lomax-Simpson*, together with the SOCIAL CENTRE. *See* also The Diamond.

WOOD STREET. Nos. 17–23 are of 1892 by *Douglas & Fordham*. Nos. 27–35 and Nos. 37–47, c.1895 by *Grayson & Ould*, are of brown brick with stone dressings. Heavy stepped gables and some odd detailing. *See* also Bridge Street.

POTT SHRIGLEY

ST CHRISTOPHER. The medieval church of a small village up in the hills. Perp throughout, except perhaps the very odd tre-foil, not quatrefoil, pier of the two-bay N arcade. The S arcade is clearly Late Perp. Perp also the W tower and the chancel. The

Perp work on s aisle and tower may be connected with the foundation of a chantry in 1491. Original chancel and nave roofs. The diagonal buttresses at the w end of the nave prove that this originally did not presuppose a tower. – FONT. An C18 baluster font. – BOX PEWS. – STAINED GLASS. The E window has much of its original glass, even if with considerable restoration in 1872. – PLATE. Paten of 1576; Chalice of 1622; Set of 1711, London made. – MONUMENTS. Two with only inscriptions in architectural surrounds, one by *Bacon* † 1798, remarkably elegant, the other by *Gatley* † 1840.

SHRIGLEY HALL, now a school of the Order of the Salesians of St John Bosco. A very fine Regency house of eleven bays and two storeys.* Ashlar, with a porch of four unfluted Ionic columns. The windows of the end bays are tripartite under a blank segmental arch. The centre of the house has a three-bay pediment. Good interiors. The staircase has unfortunately been taken out, and only the luxuriantly decorated coving to the glass skylight and the columns of the upper landing remain. As at Tatton Park, an adjoining room is open through both floors to a skylight too, and also has upper columns. It must have been a very fine composition. Plaster ceilings in two big ground-floor roooms too.

CHAPEL. This large building was added in 1936–8 to the designs of *Philip Tilden*. Externally it is conventional in its motifs – portal of three round-headed arches, groups of three stepped lancet windows – but once inside one realizes that this is a piece of imaginative and resourceful spatial planning. It is a Greek cross with a slightly elongated nave arm. The arches are round, the upper windows groups of lancets. The centre has an octagonal domical vault and is indeed octagonal outside. The arms of the cross are lower, and in the diagonals are yet lower chapels set diagonally.

POULTON *see* PULFORD *and* WALLASEY, p. 370

3080   POULTON LANCELYN   [EH]

POULTON HALL. Scirard de Lancelyn is known to have held the manor in 1093. In the C16 the estate passed to Randle Greene on his marriage to Elizabeth Lancelyn, and has remained in the possession of the Greene family ever since. The present L-shaped house, dating from 1653,‡ has been much

* 1825 by *Emmett*, according to Twycross.
‡ According to Mr Roger Lancelyn Green.

altered and enlarged. It is now roughcast rendered. A C17
staircase, rising through two upper storeys, has twisted balusters and flat-topped newels to which Gothic embellishments
have been added. To the E is an early C18 addition containing,
on the first floor, an interesting and unusual library. This is
quite small, and planned with three recesses on either side.
There is a window in both the end bays on the N side, and the
openings to these two recesses are straight-headed. The remainder have shallow arches. Pilasters between the openings
and a heavy cornice above. Woodwork detailing simple and
unlettered. Subsequent additions included the building, in the
1840s, of a dining room in the internal angle of the C17 block.
N of the house, the former BREWHOUSE, C17, of brick with
stone quoins, is doubtless indicative of the original style of the
house.

SPITAL, 1 m. N of Poulton Hall. On the corner of POULTON
ROAD and SPITAL ROAD is LANCELYN COURT, flats, forming part of a recent development scheme by *James & Bywaters*.
W of this, on the N side of BRIMSTAGE ROAD, a PINFOLD,
i.e. cattle pound. Like Bromborough, which it adjoins, Spital
developed as a district of large Victorian villas, of which hardly
a trace now remains, though a few entrance lodges survive as
hints of its former character.

POWNALL HALL *see* WILMSLOW

POYNTON   *9080*

ST GEORGE. 1858–9 by *Crowther*, the S steeple 1884–5 by *Medland & Henry Taylor*. Late C13 style. Fine W front with two
very slim lancets and a small rose window over. Dull interior.
– STAINED GLASS, N aisle E, 1885. A remarkably crisp piece
derived from the Pre-Raphaelites. By *J. Aldam Heaton*. – According to Mr Sewter the chancel E and S windows are most
probably by *O'Connor*.

PRENTON *see* BIRKENHEAD, p. 100

PRESTBURY   *9070*

Prestbury is or was a specially handsome village, its main street
passing the churchyard with no buildings that would hurt, though
unfortunately with plenty of shops trying to posh up the ground
floors of the houses. It has spoiled the reality of the street distress-
ingly. The best individual house is the DISTRICT BANK, timber-

framed, small, with two projecting square bays.* Close gables face all three sides. At the S end of the main street across the vista is a larger, white Early Victorian house, three storeys with two pedimental gables and a fan-motif above the upper windows below the gables. Good recent housing tucked away behind, w of the street. Two ranges of three storeys, with slightly stepped façades. By *Leach, Rhodes & Walker*, 1965. The scale of the ranges may be rather urban, but one does not see them in conjunction with the village. Facing Prestbury Green is some more housing, also right in scale but architecturally deplorably indifferent.

CHAPEL. In the churchyard is the Norman predecessor of the church, largely rebuilt in 1747. Nave and chancel only. The W portal alone is intact, but alas in a state which makes the appreciation of the sculpture difficult. Two orders of columns, the arch with one order of heads, one of zigzag, one of pellets. In the tympanum Christ in a halo held by angels. No details recognizable. Above a row of seven figures whose identity is not clear.

ST PETER. The interior is earlier than the exterior. It shows a late C13 church of the same size more or less as the present one. Both arcades are C13, S with quatrefoil piers with fillets, N with alternating round and octagonal piers. The E and W responds are the same on both sides. One S capital has stiff-leaf decoration. In the chancel one charming window remains of that time. It is now internal. Three lights divided by triple shafts. The five-light E window dates from the restoration of 1879–85 by *Sir G. G. Scott* and *J. O. Scott*. Earlier than all the rest is the tympanum of the chancel doorway: it has a trellis pattern and is not *in situ*. The C17 altered the S aisle windows into the plain mullioned type. But the S doorway with continuous mouldings is Dec. The N aisle was rebuilt in the C18 and is now of the time of the restoration. Good W tower of *c*.1480. Built with help from Reginald Legh, who died in 1482. – PULPIT. 1607. With one tier of the usual blank arches. – TOWER SCREEN. Jacobean with strapwork. The balcony over is of 1637. – CHAPEL SCREEN. Classical, dated 1739. – CHANCEL SCREEN. Later C18. A fine classical piece of 1739 with fluted pillars and a pediment.‡ – COMMUNION RAIL (Leigh Chapel). C17. – PEWS, at the W end; Jacobean. – CHANDELIERS of brass. In the chancel 1712, in

See p. 442

* Recently restored.
‡ Excellently restored in 1969.

the nave – much grander – 1814. – PAINTINGS. In the spandrels of the arcades are demi-figures of the Apostles; 1719 – gay and reminiscent of Continental rather than English churches. – PLATE. Chalice of 1646; two Cups, London, c.1665; Flagon of 1668; two Chalices 1670; two Patens 1770. – MONUMENTS. Incised slabs of 1482 (Reginald Legh, *see* above), of 1495 (partly re-cut), of 1558, and of 1592. – Charles Legh, 1785. By *Joseph Turner* of Chester. Urn before obelisk, elegantly done. – In the churchyard is part of an Anglo-Danish cross found in 1841. Coarse fat interlace; also an elephant-like quadruped.

VICARAGE, off the main street, to the W, at the end of a passage and lane. By *Ernest Newton*, 1893. In the Home Counties style, including tile-hanging.

PUDDINGTON

3070

PUDDINGTON OLD HALL. Roughcast. To the outside the house does not betray that inside a delightful little turfed courtyard timber-framing of before the Reformation is displayed, including a doorway and traces of an open gallery. (C18 DOVE-COTE. EH)

PUDDINGTON HALL. Of the house of c.1760 only two eight-bay wings with hipped roofs are preserved.

PULFORD   [EH] 3050

ST MARY. Rebuilt in 1881–4 at the partial expense of the first Duke of Westminster. Red sandstone with bands of lighter stone. NW tower and spire. With the arcaded panelling below the bell-openings, the distinctive outline of the shingled spire and pinnacles, and the tiny dormers in the spire it is unmistakable *Douglas*. Porch below the tower. Aisleless nave. Transepts opening off the choir, that on the S forming an organ chamber and vestry. Dec windows. Plate tracery (N transept window) and bar tracery (E and W windows). The nave windows rectangular but heavily traceried. Ashlar interior with some unusual detailing, e.g. the corbelling of the transept arches. A passage connects nave and N transept. Nothing very remarkable, but there is a freshness and a sureness of touch which raises the church well above the level of mere competence.

GROSVENOR ARMS. For the Duke of Westminster. Said to be by *Beswick*, but it is not clear if this means *H. Beswick*, the then County Architect.

To the N some characteristic EATON ESTATE BUILDING, and

$\frac{5}{8}$ m. N, set back W of the road, a particularly good farmhouse now known as GREEN PADDOCKS. This is of 1872, by *Douglas*. Brick, employed with inventiveness and virtuosity. Three bays, steep hipped roof, two storeys, and heavy dormers with shaped gables. Central projection containing the entrance and a pargetted gable. Brick is resourcefully used, e.g. for the mullions and curved heads of the window lights, but more particularly for panelling in the gables and in a frieze which runs between the ground- and first-floor windows. All meticulously detailed. 1 m. further N is BELGRAVE, not even a hamlet, but notable for having given its name to the square and to a whole district of the London Grosvenor estate where, incidentally, several other local place names are to be found. Some *Douglas* COTTAGES.

The hamlet of POULTON, $1\frac{1}{4}$ m. E, has more ESTATE HOUSING, including some dating from the 1850s and 60s, i.e. from the time of the second Marquess. Also a SCHOOL, 1866. Immediately S of the drive to Eaton Hall is a FARMHOUSE, presumably C17, restored, and $\frac{3}{8}$ m. further S is CHAPEL HOUSE FARM, late C17, two gables front and back. (Rectangular well staircase to the second floor with twisted balusters. MHLG)

QUEEN'S PARK *see* CHESTER, p. 175

3070   RABY   [EH]

SCHOOL. Gothic, built at the expense of Joseph Hirst of Wilshaw (*see* Thornton Hough, p. 357) and thus doubtless by *Kirk & Sons*.

WHEATSHEAF INN. Dated 1611. Thatched, with some half-timbering.

THORNTON FARM (formerly STANACRES), $\frac{1}{4}$ m. N, with lodge gate on the main road to Bebington. 1851 by *Charles Verelst* (i.e. *Charles Reed*). Gothic. Octagonal summerhouse. Garden layout by *Edward Kemp*.

9070   RAINOW

HOLY TRINITY. 1845–6 by *Samuel Howard*. A cheap Commissioners' church built of small coursed stones. Two-light lancets with four-centred arches and Y-tracery. The E window is of three lights and has intersecting tracery. – WEST GALLERY; BOX PEWS.

JENKIN CHAPEL, Saltersford, $2\frac{1}{4}$ m. ENE. All alone in the Peak, and reached only by steep minor roads. Built in 1733, the tower

added in 1754–5. A trim little building, of small coursed stones.
The short w tower has a saddleback roof. The side windows
are square, with small glass panes in Georgian glazing bars. –
WEST GALLERY; BOX PEWS; two-decker PULPIT.

RAMSDELL HALL see RODE

RAVENSCROFT HALL see MIDDLEWICH

REASEHEATH HALL see NANTWICH

RIDLEY   5050

RIDLEY HALL. This includes a gateway of stone with on both
  sides a segmental arch on responds. Is it Elizabethan? The
  mouldings look yet earlier.
SCHOOL. 1876. Wildly irregular Gothic; worth seeing.
WOODHEY, 2 m. SE. Of Woodhey Hall nothing survives, except
  two outbuildings of brick, one with five regularly spaced four-
  light windows in two storeys, and the gatepiers. What does
  survive is an Elizabethan loggia at the end of a terrace, and,
  later attached to it, a chapel of c.1700. The chapel is quite plain
  with on each long side an entrance with a round window over
  and three arched windows. At the E end just two such windows.
  The loggia has Roman Doric columns, a scrolly frieze, and
  two-light side windows. The sides are brick in English bond;
  the chapel has Flemish bond. (The chapel has the PULPIT in
  the middle of the E wall, STALLS N and S, and the FAMILY
  PEW on a w gallery.)

RINGWAY   8080

ST MARY. By *Preston & Vaughan*, 1894–5 (GR). Brick and red
  terracotta. Quite a roguish w front with a NW tower of open
  timberwork on a brick base and a little spire and the façade of
  the church proper provided with a w porch set asymmetrically.
  Half-timbered gable. N arcade of wooden piers. – PLATE. Cup
  and Stand Paten, London, 1726.
MANCHESTER AIRPORT. The earliest buildings are of 1937–8,
  by *Noel Hill* (consultant *Norman & Dawbarn*). In 1962–3 the
  Manchester City Architect *Leonard C. Howitt* built a new
  terminal building. The more important interiors are by *James
  Cubitt & Partners*.

ROAD STREET HOUSE see TARPORLEY

ROCK FERRY and ROCK PARK see BIRKENHEAD, p. 102

ROCK SAVAGE *see* CLIFTON

RODE

ALL SAINTS, Odd Rode. 1864 by *Sir George Gilbert Scott*. Nave with bellcote and a rather restless front. s aisle under its own roof, s chapel also under a separate roof, and chancel. Late C13 style. Small brown stone and tiled roofs. Arcade of quatrefoil piers. The chancel arch and the twin marble columns to the s chapel have capitals of naturalistic foliage. Goodhart-Rendel noted: 'Taking things all round, I like this best of any Scott church I have seen.... Everything seems to me a triumph of the academic type of good Gothic design.... Here is nothing but safety first – but it *is* safety.' – Ornate stone PULPIT and alabaster FONT. – STAINED GLASS. The w window by *Kempe & Tower*, 1907, but who did the excellently coloured E window in 1864?

RODE HALL.* A quite big, somewhat eccentric house with a complex building history. As one approaches, one sees first the tall early C19 front of the main house, and then to one side a much humbler range obviously of about 1700. This latter was in fact the entire house built soon after the estate had come into the possession of the Wilbraham family, and described by Randle Wilbraham (the first) as newly completed in 1708. Though the inside has been much pulled about, the exterior survives largely untouched. It is long and low, and looks lower by the side of its tall neighbour: two storeys with hipped roof. The middle five bays are slightly recessed and still have cross windows; the wings have Venetian windows under *œils de bœuf*, which must be a mid C18 insertion, like the door with its semicircular head with Gibbs surround. The pretty octagonal oniondomed cupola (which is repeated on the stable block) must also be later than the original house. The external angles oddly have quoins on the ground floor only.

In 1752 Randle Wilbraham (the second) built a completely new house NW of the old one, which was turned into the servants' wing and joined to the new by an arcaded courtyard (filled in in the early C19). The second house also survives, though greatly altered about sixty years later. It was very plain, two and a half storeys high, five bays by four, the entrance front now facing NW so that the house turned its back on the old one. A picture of Randle Wilbraham holding an elevation indicates that the main façade originally had architrave sur-

* Contributed by Dr Andor Gomme.

rounds to the windows: this is confirmed by the upper string course stopping a few inches short of the sides of each first-floor window. It seems also to have had a big Venetian doorway, but this may never have been built. There is however still a Venetian window on the first floor at the back lighting the staircase. Today, without the architraves, the NW front of the house looks very calm and spacious, with its windows unusually widely spaced. Its length was extended into two-storey polygonal bays (cf. those at Barlaston Hall, Staffordshire, and – differently placed – at Ramsdell Hall). Again quoins on the ground floor only. Some indirect evidence on a surviving plan of 1752 suggests that the architect may have been one of the *Hiorne* brothers: David Hiorne's fondness for Venetian windows lends some support. The big Doric order of the portico must be later than the main block and perhaps dates from *See* p. 442 c.1790, when Richard Wilbraham Bootle, son of Randle Wilbraham (the second), was planning alterations to the grounds. *Repton* supplied a Red Book, though apparently his client had declared that it 'would not be requisite'; it is hard to tell now how far his proposals were carried out. The portico could perhaps be as late as the big early C19 alterations, but why should the old main entrance have been made so grand just when a new one had been devised?

By 1818 the house could again be described as 'recently enlarged'. Randle Wilbraham (the third) not only covered the whole house in stucco, but entirely reorganized and reorientated it, bringing the main entrance back to the SW. The polygonal bays were made nearly semicircular and continued to the full height of the house, and the new entrance front made approximately symmetrical by the addition of another bow, leaving two flat bays rather awkwardly in the centre. In 1927, when the stucco was removed, *Darcy Braddell* ingeniously pulled the design together with the big tetrastyle Ionic portico which fills the gap between the bows. The back of the house was also extended but left with a single bow. The doorway on this side was given a strange and massive stone aedicule with colossal square half-columns but no entablature to join them over the door.

Of the interiors only the staircase hall survives from the mid C18 house. Stair with two columns per tread and exceptionally richly carved tread-ends; the columns are fluted and have elaborate scrolly cups near the bottom. A good deal of Rococo plasterwork, including a fine eagle under the landing. The

II—C.

staircase is immediately behind the original entrance hall, which was turned into an anteroom and made octagonal with niches in alternate sides; it has severe Soanish doorcases with rosettes in the corners and an equally Soanish white marble fireplace. The new entrance hall, much bigger than the old, has a screen of wooden Tuscan columns immediately inside the door and another three-quarters of the way along. Of other decoration there is almost none either here or in the main rooms on the NW front. The most interesting of the new rooms is the dining room on the NE side of the house, made by extending the former library. It has a shallow segmental vault, with a shallow apse at one end decorated with rays of stiff plaster foliage. On each long wall are two dark green scagliola columns with chunky Ionic capitals carrying a small piece of entablature and then a wide arch across the vault. Otherwise again almost no decoration except for strawberry-mace carving on the big black marble fireplace.

Who can have designed these ambitious early C19 additions and reconstructions? They are ingeniously contrived even if the architectural result is not entirely happy. It is unlikely to be purely local work, though within the capacities of a good provincial mason who kept himself informed about new developments. If a London name is wanted, and if 'recently enlarged' can be interpreted generously, *Henry Holland*'s might be as good as any. But Holland died in 1806. Some things look Soanish, but there is no evidence to suggest that Soane had any connexion with the house. The primitivist stone doorcase on the NE front might suggest *C. H. Tatham*, who worked at Trentham across the Staffordshire border in 1808. All three architects were closely connected; and perhaps the most one can say is that stylistically the work is somewhere in the triangle of which they are the apices.

The STABLES, standing SW of the first house and at r. angles to it, must be part of the rebuilding of the 1750s. They are on higher ground and tend somewhat to overshadow the little old house; yet they seem to have been consciously built in keeping with it. Six bays wide, the middle two projecting under a pediment with twin segmental archways meeting very oddly on a central column. All the ground-floor windows are round-headed and the upstairs ones circular. Hipped roof and a cupola like that on the old house.

ESTATE COTTAGES by *William White*, c.1854, brick, with pointed windows, but nothing more that would be strictly

Gothic. Examples are BROOK COTTAGE, N of Rode Hall, the schoolmaster's house s of the church, a little off the road to the w, and Nos. 182–184 CONGLETON ROAD NORTH.*

RAMSDELL HALL, 1¼ m. ENE of the church. A curious house. It has two fronts, of *c.*1720 and of *c.*1760, the former L-shaped with the entrance diagonally across the angle, the latter straight, so that the entrance hall which serves both sides assumes an irregular shape. The older front has a tripartite doorway with Gothick touches, nicely framed windows over, and a segmental gable on corbels, not higher than the parapet; the other side has two canted bay windows and a Venetian doorway. There are on this side also low links to pavilions with a cupola, a Venetian window, and a tripartite lunette window over. Pediment again lower than the parapet.

OLD PARSONAGE, N of Ramsdell Hall. Three bays plus a fourth on the l. Two later canted bays and a porch with stately Corinthian columns.

RODE HEATH see RODE

ROMILEY   9090

ST CHAD. 1864–6 by *J. Medland Taylor*. With a NW steeple, transepts, and a polygonal apse. The aisle arcades have very unorthodoxly treated Early French Gothic capitals. Note the buttress of the tower growing out of the staircase projection and the gable over where the clock-face was intended; also the s transept doorway with its one short column. – Altar PANELLING. Partly Jacobean; from a church at Chester.

CHADKIRK CHAPEL, Lower Chadkirk Lane, under the canal. A humble church. The s side is of 1747, but the timber-framed chancel is medieval. Much rebuilding in the 1860s. – FONT. Probably C18, perhaps 1747.

The adjoining house is of 1748 and has a rusticated doorway.

OAKWOOD HALL, down Oakwood Road and along a long drive to the house, which lies steeply above the river Goyt. Stone Tudor-Gothic. Slender octagonal tower. By *Edward Walters* of Manchester, 1844–5, for Ormerod Heyworth. His MILL was built in 1833–7. It was a cotton gassing mill.

ROOKERY HALL see WORLESTON

* I owe the reference to White to Dr Muthesius, who also told me of shops by White at Audley in Staffordshire, only 4 m. away.

ROSTHERNE

ST MARY. Beautifully placed above the Mere – entirely rural, only two miles from Bowdon. w tower of 1742–4 by *John Rowson*, replacing one of 1533. The bell-openings are of the Venetian type, the parapet curves up at the corners. The rest is Perp externally, save for the chancel and vestry, which were built by *Sir A. W. Blomfield* in 1888. The side windows are typically Late Perp, i.e. mullioned with uncusped arched lights. However, the N doorway has Dec mouldings and the vestry a Dec w window; so the church is older. It is indeed; for the N arcade has unmistakably E.E. round piers. The octagonal piers of the s arcade may be early C14. Perp tower arch (tower of 1533), two-bay chancel aisles. The Blomfield entrance to the vestry has a big traceried opening, as the Victorians liked it. – REREDOS and two figures above l. and r. of it. Mosaic of 1910. – PLATE. Two sets of 1771. – MONUMENTS. Recumbent effigy of a Knight; C13, badly preserved. – John Egerton † 1738. Tablet with a free-standing putto holding a portrait medallion. – Jonas Langford Brooke † 1784. By *Bacon*. Urn before an obelisk. – Samuel Egerton, 1792, also by *Bacon*, one of his most ambitious monuments, but sadly disjointed. A centre obelisk with an urn, two smaller side obelisks with urns, and in front of them the figures of Patience and Hope, excellent, as so many of Bacon's allegorical figures are. – Thomas Langford Brooke † 1815, by *Bacon Jun*. Urn before obelisk. – Elizabeth Leigh † 1807 by *Westmacott*. Tablet on which she is rising to heaven. – Lady Charlotte Lucy Beatrix Egerton † 1845, by *Westmacott Jun*. White marble. She is seen asleep and an angel kneels by her, a free-standing figure, all the more impressive as the monument does not stand against a wall.

(At the s end of the village is ST MARY'S SQUARE, Tatton estate housing of *c.*1909–10.)

ROWTON

METHODIST CHAPEL. With its shaped gable, the shaped gable of the porch, and the hoodmoulds to the windows it looks early C19, or 1840 at the latest, and only the materials used may make one doubt. The date inscribed is in fact 1865.

RULOE *see* NORLEY

RUNCORN

Runcorn is miserable to look at; so the best of luck to the New

Runcorn at the time of writing just beginning to emerge. The old town with its population of 26,000 (1961) has of course the two bridges, and at least the newer of them delights the eye, but otherwise there is near to nothing. Leland in the C16 called it 'a poor townlet by a salt creke'. It began to grow when in 1773 the Bridgewater Canal had been extended to end at Runcorn.

ALL SAINTS, Church Street. Well placed by the river and in a street with, opposite the church, one very minor Late Georgian brick terrace. The church is by *Salvin* and was built in 1847–9. It has a high S W steeple, E.E. details, a clerestory with round windows, and inside five bays of arcades with stiff-leaf capitals. – PLATE. C16 Cup made by *William Mutton* of Chester; Cup and Paten inscribed 1670; Flagon dated 1704. – There are quite a number of MONUMENTS to the Brooke family of Norton Priory. Thomas † 1737, a large tablet, mostly architectural. – Sir Richard, 1792 by *Bacon*, with a large putto unveiling an urn. – Sir Richard, 1796, also by *Bacon*. With a typically Bacon female figure by an urn with profile medallion. – Thomas † 1820. By *B. F. Hardenberg* of London. A plain demi-column and a plain elongated demi-urn on it. – Also John Barclay † 1866. By *Williams & Clay* of Warrington. Ornately Gothic.

ST EDMUND (R.C.), Ivy Street. 1956 by the firm of *E. Kirby & Sons*.

ST MICHAEL, Greenway Road. 1884–92 by *T. D. Barry* of Liverpool. Quite a good design, apparently meant to have a S tower. Dec in style, with a large polygonal apse. Indifferent interior.

HOLY TRINITY. 1838 by *Joseph Hartley* of Runcorn; the short chancel of 1857. Of the Commissioners' type, i.e. with a thin W tower with clumsy pinnacles and pairs of lancets along the sides.

CONGREGATIONAL CHURCH, High Street. 1835, and reminiscent of Commissioners' churches. Ashlar, embattled, without a tower. Two tiers of windows; short chancel.

METHODIST CHURCH, High Street. 1865–6. Built at the expense of Thomas Hazlehurst, a soap manufacturer (£8,000). Grand, in a free Renaissance. Broad front with two short towers.*

METHODIST CHURCH, Halton Road. 1871. Also built at the expense of Thomas Hazlehurst (another £8,000). Five-bay, Italianate stone front, the windows with Venetian tracery.

* (It has now been demolished. The town centre has thus lost its one distinctive building. E H)

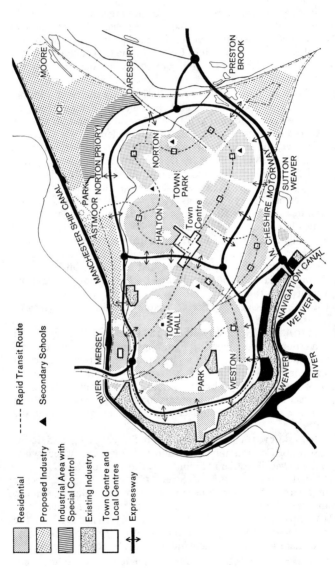

Runcorn New Town, diagram of master plan

Residential

Proposed Industry

Industrial Area with Special Control

Existing Industry

Town Centre and Local Centres

Expressway

----- Rapid Transit Route

▲ Secondary Schools

MOORE

ICI

DARESBURY

PRESTON BROOK

MANCHESTER SHIP CANAL

ASTMOOR NORTON PRIORY PARK

NORTON

TOWN PARK

N. CHESHIRE MOTORWAY

SUTTON WEAVER

HALTON

Town Centre

RIVER MERSEY

TOWN HALL

PARK

WESTON

NAVIGATION CANAL

WEAVER

RIVER WEAVER

CEMETERY, Greenway Road. 1859–60. Two chapels, one with a little steeple on one side.

TOWN HALL. If this is not as cramped as the other public buildings of Runcorn, this is due to the fact that the town took over a mansion, Halton Grange, built in 1853–6 to the design of *Charles Verelst*, formerly *Charles Reed*. Italianate villa, rendered, two-storey, with the typical angle tower à la Osborne. Next to it a big curtain-walled addition of 1965.

THE BRIDGES. The RAILWAY BRIDGE is of 1864–8, of iron, with fortress-like stone pylons. The TRANSPORTER BRIDGE (really *transbordeur*) of 1901–5 has been replaced by a new road bridge. The ROAD BRIDGE of 1956–61 is by *Mott, Hay & Anderson*. It is a single steel arch rising elegantly into the air and carrying hanging from it the roadway. The span is 1,082 ft, the total length 1,628 ft. It was the largest steel arch in Europe when it was built, and the third largest in the world. The structure consists of two arches connected by zigzag lattice work. The outer arch starts in a double curve, slightly concave before it becomes convex.

None of the other public buildings deserves more than a few words. The POST OFFICE, High Street, stone, symmetrical, is of an unusual design, and the BATHS in Bridge Street were built as the Market Hall in 1856, by *Michael Barker*. The POLICE STATION in the same street is of 1831 and later.

And private houses? No. 53 HIGH STREET is good Georgian, brick, of three bays with a lower two-bay wing. Doorway with pediment on Tuscan columns.

BRIDGEWATER HOUSE, off the E end of Algernon Street, is an imposing six-by-five-bay block of two and a half storeys, standing all alone by the former end of the canal. Doorway with broken pediment. The house was put up as an occasional residence for the Duke while the canal was building.

THE ELMS, Highlands Road, Beaconhill, is of five bays with lower wings and has a fine doorway with segmental pediment.

In HALTON ROAD by the Methodist church are two pairs of Early Victorian houses each with one quite monumental stone window.

So to the NEW TOWN. At the time of writing what has already been built does not join up to form a coherent picture. This being so, an account of what the New Runcorn is going to be like follows here. It was kindly written for me by Mr R. W. Cresswell of *Arthur Ling & Associates*, the appointed planners.

In 1964 the Runcorn Development Corporation was established in order to provide additional employment and housing
for people from the North Merseyside Area. The population
figure for the whole of Runcorn was set at *c*.90,000, as against
the present *c*.30,000. The master plan was published early in
1967. The designated area measures 4½ by 3 m. The undulating site with fine landscape is E of the old town, dominated
by Halton Castle rock and by the road and rail bridges across
the River Mersey and the Manchester Ship Canal.

The new town centre is S of Halton. It will have open and
covered pedestrian shopping areas and a full range of commercial, cultural, and entertainment facilities. The centre will
be linked to Halton Village and the castle rock. The existing
town centre becomes a district centre serving the N W area of
the town.

The main new residential areas form a series of communities
of 8,000 population, surrounding a park and linked by a rapid
transit system of buses on a reserved track. The residential
communities are planned so that everyone is within five min-
utes' walking distance of the local social and shopping centres
where rapid transit stops are located. Each community com-
prises four neighbourhoods of 2,000 people housed in a variety
of residential groups of thirty to sixty families. The secondary
schools are grouped in campuses and linked to the residential
communities by the rapid transit system. The primary schools
are associated with the local centres. The buses will pass through
the local centres of the communities and their route forms the
spine of a figure of eight system with the new town centre at its
intersection. Supplementary loops will serve the industrial
areas on the flatter land on the edge of the town. An expressway system encircles the residential areas and connects with
the town centre, the industrial areas, and the regional roads.

The plan provides for an increase of 19,000 jobs in manu-
facturing industry, mainly in three large industrial estates.

A large new park is located to the E of the town centre. This
encompasses the best existing landscape features of the site.
Greenways will link the surrounding communities to the park
and provide a continuity of open space from the private garden
to the public park.

Visible evidence of the industrial phase of building were at
the time of writing the ASTMOOR INDUSTRIAL ESTATE,
housing of the CASTLEFIELDS COMMUNITY with in the end
1,379 deck-access flats, 510 terrace houses, and 333 patio

houses, i.e. a population of 7,500, and beginnings of the TOWN
CENTRE. The chief architect is *F. Lloyd Roche.*

SAIGHTON

4060

SAIGHTON GRANGE. This was the principal country house of
the Abbots of Chester.* Of that time is the gatehouse, which 32
was rebuilt by Abbot Ripley *c.*1490. The large house now attached to it is by *E. Hodkinson* and was built in 1861 for the
second Marquess of Westminster and enlarged in 1874. The
gatehouse has – not to the front but to one side – an oriel, with
a figure in the merlon above and a higher staircase tower next
to it. The front of the gatehouse has two big buttresses l. and r.,
but the upper part of the building, by means of angle corbels,
manages to have its wall flush with the face of the buttress.

On top of the hill is a castellated C19 WATER TOWER.

(In the village Eaton estate buildings, dating from the time of
both the second Marquess and the first Duke. COTTAGES by
John Douglas include, e.g., the group with tile-hanging, towards
the s end of the village street on the E side. SAIGHTON LANE
FARM, ½ m. NNE, is a model farm by *Douglas & Fordham* and
a particularly nice one. Half-timber and diapered brick. The
farmhouse has twisted chimneys and a big half-timbered gable.
EH)

SALE

7090

Sale, Altrincham, Hale, Timperley, and Bowdon are one and all
Outer Manchester. Sale has a bit of a centre by the town hall and
little else.

ST ANNE. 1854, with enlargements of 1860, 1864, and 1887. But
who did what ? The original architect was *William Hayley,* and
due to him must be the thin iron piers, set as twins in depth and
endowed with ignorant E.E. details. Most of the rest looks
later. Dec tracery. NW steeple, nave and aisles, transepts and
short chancel. *John Lowe* was the architect for the 1864 and
1887 work.

ST JOSEPH (R.C.), Hope Road. 1884–5 by *W. H. Raule.* E extension 1929. Fiery red brick, lancets, no tower.

ST PAUL, Springfield Road. 1883–4 by *H. R. Price,* the NW
tower by *Bird & Oldham,* 1911. Geometrical tracery, piers of
polished granite, polygonal apse.

TRINITY METHODIST CHURCH, Trinity Road. Grand, ashlar-
faced façade with two giant columns *in antis.*

* The others were Sutton and Ince.

UNITARIAN CHAPEL, Chapel Road. 1739. Small; of only two bays. Brick.

TOWN HALL. 1914–15 by *C. T. Adshead*. Free neo-William-and-Mary. Brick and stone dressings. Seven bays. A cupola over the centre.

(MONUMENT to Dr Joule, Worthington Park. By *John Cassidy* of Manchester.)

ODEON CINEMA, at the N end of Washway Road. By *Drury & Gomersall*, 1933. With Egyptian motifs outside (and inside). It was originally called The Pyramid.

The houses Nos. 263 etc. WASHWAY ROAD are an ancient monument. They are now over thirty years old and exhibit the International Modern of the thirties, a style at that time still rare in England. The architects were *R. A. Cordingley* and *D. McIntyre*. The houses were illustrated in 1936.

SALTERSFORD see RAINOW

SALTNEY see CHESTER, pp. 174, 176

7060   SANDBACH

Sandbach is quite a good little town to walk through. As one walks from the bridge at the E end past the church and up the hill there is a nice sequence of street and open spaces.

ST MARY. Largely by *George Gilbert Scott*, 1847–9, and original in masonry only part of the s side. But the prominent w tower for instance is said to be an exact reproduction of the original Perp one. Note the pairs of two-light bell-openings under one ogee gable (cf. Middlewich), and note also what can't be overlooked – the high open porch in the tower, open to w, N, and s. Embattled clerestory of seven closely set bays. All details Perp. Inside, the arcades are largely old, with thin octagonal piers and double-chamfered arches, but Scott made the chancel and chapels part of his nave and added a new chancel. Some of the roof corbels are original. The roofs are dated 1661, and that of the N aisle – former N chancel chapel – has a big coat of arms in a wreath (cf. the Mainwaring Chapel at Over Peover of *c*.1650). – FONT. Dated 1667, a very unusual design. Stone, octagonal, with big juicy leaves. – SCULPTURE. Outside the church defaced fragments of two Saxon crosses (cf. Market Place), two broken coffin lids, and one headstone, among them one with a standing figure. – STAINED GLASS. By *Wailes* N chapel E (signed), s chapel E, and chancel N and s. – By *Kempe*

N aisle NW, of 1887. – PLATE. Chalice and Paten given 1656, London made; Almsdish, 1709, London; two Chalices, inscribed 1734; Almsdish, inscribed 1737. – MONUMENTS. John Ford † 1839. With a life-size female allegorical figure by an altar. – Rev. John Armitstead, 1876 by *G. F. Watts*, executed 84 by *George Nelson*. White marble, three-quarter figure in relief, very carefully carved folds of the alb.

ST JOHN, Sandbach Heath. By *Scott*, 1861. A successful ensemble, with its crossing tower. The style is Scott's favoured Second Pointed, i.e. mid to late C13, characterized by geometrical plate tracery. There are many seriously considered details: the shafted arcading of the chancel, the contrast of the groups of W and E windows, the proportions of the spire. The materials are more or less brick-size yellow stone and red sandstone dressings. Ashlar-faced interior. Rich foliation of the capitals around the crossing. The former organ chamber opens in a large windowlike treatment to the chancel. Several dates with inscriptions are carved in black letter in the stone. – The woodwork in the chancel was carved by *Jessie B. Kennedy*; note especially the big flowers l. and r. of the altar. – The SCREENS etc. are typical *Scott*.

TOWN HALL. 1889 by *Thomas Bower* of Nantwich. Brick, Gothic, angle tower with a resourceful roof. Four open arches below, windows with plate tracery above.

LITERARY INSTITUTE. 1857 by *Scott*. Gothic, of brick, a well balanced, even façade of three three-light windows on the first floor, three tall two-light windows on the second developed into dormers. To the l. the polygonal entrance and staircase bay, treated frankly as an attachment. Ornate doorcase into the upper rooms.

SAVINGS BANK, to the r. of the above. Gothic, brick with diapers, picturesquely composed. It is dated 1854 and could be by *Scott*.

FOUNTAIN, in the High Town Square, facing the Literary Institute. By *Thomas Bower*, 1897. With Tuscan columns and top motifs of the earlier C17. The style is reminiscent of Jackson.

SANDBACH SCHOOL, Crewe Road. A grammar school of C17 foundation. The original buildings on the present site by *Scott*, 1849–50, i.e. the Gothic gatehouse and the main parts along the front (except the l. wing, which is of 1911). Several later buildings, especially Gym and Pool (1969 by *Leslie Nunn & Partners*).

Opposite the church is the OLD HALL HOTEL, timber-framed
and dated 1656. Of that date the r. half. Decorative motifs are
balusters and barbed lozenges.

The MARKET PLACE, r. of the High Street, is unusually attractive in that it retains its cobbles. It is entered between two
timber-framed houses, WILLIAMS DEACONS BANK and the
BLACK BEAR, dated 1634. In the Market Place stand the famous
4 SANDBACH CROSSES. They had stood there already in the
mid C16, but were broken up in the C17 and finally reinstated
on a 3 ft high base in 1816. What we see now is parts of two
high crosses. The N one has its whole shaft and the base of the
head, the S one only its shaft. The head belongs to another,
smaller cross. The N shaft is nearly 16 ft high, the S shaft now
10 ft 9 in. As for the date of the crosses, Sir Thomas Kendrick
suggests c.850, Mr Ralegh Radford c.800. In detail the NORTH
CROSS has all four faces decorated. The decoration ends at the
bottom in triangles clasping the angles of the shaft. On the E
face are angels in the triangles, then a circle with three figures,
one being Christ. Above this are another three figures, one
being once more Christ (here with a staff). The scene is the
Transfiguration. Then follows the Nativity, and above it the
Crucifixion with the Signs of the Evangelists. Above the
Crucifixion small panels with one or two figures. On the W
face are many small panels with single figures. At the bottom
are two interlaced animals, and about the middle scenes from
the Passion of Christ, e.g. Christ before Pilate and Christ
taken away to be crucified. On the N face are again many small
panels with single figures. At the top is a big dragon. The S face
has vine scrolls, and at the top interlace.

The SOUTH CROSS has the same triangles near the bottom
as the other. The W and E faces have a plaited border with
human masks. On the W side at the base are very small panels
with single figures, above three larger figures, the middle one
probably Christ (Resurrection ?). On the E side are again small
panels with single figures. The S and N sides have more panels
with single figures.

The two crosses evidently are of the same time and from the
same workshop. They have always been a pair, as are those of
Gosforth, Penrith, and Beckermet St Bridget in Cumberland.
No others have so many single figures. In stylistic elements
they resemble such crosses as those of Wolverhampton in
Staffordshire, and also for the single figures and single heads
under arches those of Melsonby in Yorkshire and Heysham in

Lancashire, but the vine-scroll is a Northumbrian motif though it is at Sandbach, as Sir Thomas Kendrick wrote, 'ragged . . . late and derived'.

ALMSHOUSES, The Hill. 1865–7. Brick, gabled. Four groups, each with three gables and three dwellings; vaguely Gothic.

(ABBEYFIELDS. Of *c*.1800, with a good iron trellis veranda on the S porch. MHLG)

(Three old mills survive: CHIMNEY ROW MILL, Newcastle Road, of 1830 – no longer a mill – BROOK MILL of *c*.1810, also Newcastle Road, and NEWFIELD MILL, Congleton Road, dated 1844.)

SANDIWAY   6070

ST JOHN EVANGELIST. 1902–3 by *John Douglas*, who was born at Sandiway, and became lord of the manor. He donated the site of the church and contributed towards the cost of the building. Aisleless, with a small W tower. Ashlar interior. Competent Perp, except for the E window, which is a free Dec with rather bald flowing tracery. The chancel is higher than the nave. The low windows are in pairs of two lights, of different rhythm N and S. Small piers detached to the inside separate the twins of each pair (cf. near-by Hartford). At the W end some rather quirky fenestration.

Also by *Douglas* cottages by the church and SANDIWAY MANOR, ¼ m. ESE. Near the junction of two A roads, 1¼ m. SW of the church, is OAKMERE HALL, built for John Higson, a Liverpool merchant, again by *Douglas* but much earlier. The date 1867 is inscribed in the tower. This tower, with a bold pavilion roof, is on the E side of the house and is its dominant motif. But there are several others, equally bold, e.g. on the W side the porte-cochère, and on the narrow S side two round angle turrets and the fenestration between as random as if the date were 1967, not 1867. Inside, now subdivided, is a great hall reaching up to the pitched roof, and with a gallery with dainty balusters at first-floor level. It forms a bridge where the staircase rises, not otherwise separated from the hall. Hall and staircase are S of the porte-cochère.

SANDLEBRIDGE see MARTHALL

SANDY BROW see COTEBROOK

SAUGHALL see GREAT SAUGHALL

SEACOMBE *see* WALLASEY, pp. 370, 372

SHAW HEATH *see* STOCKPORT, pp. 340, 342

4040
SHOCKLACH

ST EDITH. A small Norman building – cf. the very crudely decorated s doorway with zigzag, rope, and lozenges broken by ninety degrees. Nave and chancel, and double bellcote. C14 chancel arch and E window. Also C14 the N doorway. The odd w baptistery squeezed between the two buttresses looks a rustic C17 job. Nice C18 nave ceiling with rosettes. – FONT. Was it re-cut in the later C17? See the stylized flower motifs in the panels. – PULPIT. 1687; plain. – COMMUNION RAIL. C18.

3070
SHOTWICK

ST MICHAEL. The church has a Norman s doorway, poorly preserved. Scalloped capitals; the arch stones decorated with a kind of random chequer pattern. The chancel doorway is probably Transitional, though the chancel E window and the N chapel E window are Dec (reticulation units). The N aisle windows have cusped lights and a straight head – C15 probably. Perp w tower of *c.*1500 with a sparsely decorated frieze at the level of the springing of the w window arch. The s windows are plainly mullioned, a post-Reformation alteration. – Much woodwork is preserved, notably the Georgian three-decker PULPIT, the CHURCHWARDENS' PEW, dated 1709 on the canopy which is carried by two balusters, the C17 COMMUNION RAIL with turned balusters, the BOX PEWS, and also the C15 DOOR, studded with nails.* – CHANDELIER of brass; late C18. – STAINED GLASS. In the tracery of the N aisle E window a C14 Annunciation, contemporary with the window. – PLATE. Chalice inscribed 1685, by *Peter Pemberton* of Chester.

Shotwick in the Middle Ages was a port. Henry II left for Ireland from Shotwick, and Edward I in 1278 for Wales. Of the CASTLE adjoining the quay nothing remains. Shotwick's chance was the silting-up of the Dee, depriving Chester of its sea traffic. However, now the land of the estuary is all reclaimed.

SHOTWICK HALL. Brick. Dated 1662 inside. The façade lies at the end of a front garden with gatepiers. It is of E-shape, the wings plainly gabled, the porch with a smaller and lower stepped

---

* It is said that most of the woodwork came in 1812 from a church at Chester.

gable. The window frames are of wood, mullioned and transomed and under relieving arches. (Inside, some plasterwork
and other original features.)

SHOTWICK PARK. *See* Great Saughall, p. 229.

SIDDINGTON

ALL SAINTS. Charmingly placed above a rill. The church presents itself nearly all black and white. It was in fact a timber-
framed building. Money was left to it in 1474, and it is said
that glass in the E window had a date 1513. But as it is now,
the front is all black painted on whitened brick, and this is true
of much of the interior too. The nave in fact has its brickwork
exposed. The tracery of the windows is probably of *c.*1820.
Genuine is the chancel. It is of two narrow bays with timber
wall-shafts and timber arched braces. Herringbone bracing in
the walls. Original S porch too. – PULPIT. 1633. Plain panelling. – SCREEN. Single-light divisions with ogee heads and
foiled circles in the spandrels. The tracery panels in the chancel
E wall may come from the rood-loft parapet.

CAPESTHORNE. *See* p. 125.

SMALLWOOD

ST JOHN BAPTIST. 1845 by *C. & J. Trubshaw.* Nave and lower
chancel; bellcote. Lancets and Y-tracery, the E end with three
stepped lancets, a Trubshaw predilection. Hammerbeam roof.

SMALLWOOD HOUSE, probably also *c.*1845. Brick and diapers.
Steep-gabled.

SOMERFORD
Near Congleton

CHAPEL, belonging to Somerford Hall. The chapel was built in
1725. It is of chequer brick, four bays long, with arched windows. The E window is unfortunately altered. It was probably
Venetian. Quoins, cupola, W doorway with moulded surround.

(SOMERFORD HALL was built *c.*1720, wings were added *c.*1820,
and the house was altered and enlarged by *Salvin* in 1859. It
has largely been demolished, though Dr Gomme reports that
remains include one wing, the end of which is castellated, and
the STABLES, thirteen bays, with pediment and lunette
windows. Also, ⅓ m. W, an C18 ICEHOUSE.)

SOMERFORD BOOTHS HALL, 1 m. NE. Dated 1612, but altered
by *Webb* of Stafford before 1824. The façade is alas rendered.
Three gables and three lower gables in front of them for two
bay windows and the porch.

(GROVEHOUSE FARMHOUSE, Mill Lane, Somerford Booth, has a pair of crucks. MHLG)

SOSS MOSS HALL *see* NETHER ALDERLEY

SPITAL *see* POULTON LANCELYN

5050
SPURSTOW

SCHOOL. 1872, built for Lord Crewe. Very much what Good-hart-Rendel called 'rogue architecture'.

OAKLANDS. Brick with much stone, *c.* 1850, Italianate.

(HAUGHTON HALL. Rebuilt in 1891–2 by *J. Francis Doyle* for Ralph Brocklebank of the Liverpool shipping family, but subsequently much altered. Doyle also worked for Brocklebank's brother at Heswall, *see* pp. 237, 238.)

9090
STALYBRIDGE

There is no break between Stalybridge and Dukinfield, nor is there much of a break between Stalybridge and Ashton-under-Lyne in Lancashire. In fact Stalybridge used to be a cotton town. The earliest cotton mill was established in 1776.

ST GEORGE, Church Walk. 1838–40 by *Sharpe*. A Commissioners' church, i.e. the usual W tower, the usual long windows along the sides separated by thin buttresses. What is however very remarkable is that these long windows have geometrical tracery – two lights and an uncusped circle – which before 1840 is entirely unexpected. The galleries inside have been removed.

ST PAUL, Huddersfield Road. 1839, according to Mr Colvin by *Tattersall*. Open to the hills on the S. Lancets in pairs, thin buttresses and a W tower. The clerestory and the S transept by *Brakspear*, 1872. – STAINED GLASS. The E window by *Wailes* (White).

The VICARAGE and the SCHOOL appear to belong to the same build. Kelly gives 1841 as the date of the school. The date of the vicarage is however 1851 (addition 1881).

ST PETER (R.C.), Spring Bank Road. 1838–9 by *Weightman & Hadfield*. Lancets; no tower; a wide undivided nave.

HOLY TRINITY, Trinity Street. 1851–2 by *E. H. Shellard* of Manchester. Nave and aisles, W tower; Perp.

CONGREGATIONAL CHURCH, Trinity Street. By *Poulton & Woodman*, 1861. No tower, but otherwise churchy.

METHODIST CHAPEL (former), Caroline Street. 1872–3 by

Gregory Gill; enlarged in 1895. Big, of brick, with giant columns in the front.

TOWN HALL. 1831–2. A three-storeyed block with a pediment over front and back, and a one-storeyed portico of Tuscan columns with pediment also front and back. The ground floor was originally the market hall. Addition of 1882.

VICTORIA MARKET. 1866 by *Amos Lee*, Borough Surveyor. Brick and much stone. Mid-tower with steep hipped roof. The style may be called a mixed Renaissance. Iron structure inside.

LIBRARY and POST OFFICE, 1901 by *J. Medland Taylor*, form an acceptable group in Trinity Street.

Another group, in Stamford Street, is the COUNTY SECONDARY SCHOOL FOR GIRLS, brick and yellow terracotta, 1909–10 by *George Rowbottom*, symmetrical, and the NORWEB offices, 1904 by *W. H. George & Sons*, in a successful Baroque.

But the best school building was formerly a private house, the WEST HILL CENTRAL SCHOOL in Stamford Street. The house was built in 1822 for William Harrison, a cotton manufacturer. Five bays and two storeys; ashlar. Enclosed porch with four columns. Round the corner, further back, one bay with giant pilasters and a pediment. Why this emphasis?

In the HUDDERSFIELD ROAD, E of St Paul, is COPLEY MILL, a big stone building of quite some dignity. Rows of workers' cottages opposite. The very high polygonal chimney of another mill is W of St Paul. At the E end of Huddersfield Road PARK-HILL, an Early Victorian three-bay house, with an exceptionally elaborate iron porch.

(STALY OLD HALL, N of Stalybridge, off Huddersfield Road, at the end of Howard Street. C16, two-storeyed, with wings and a two-storeyed porch and mullioned windows.)

STANLOW 4070

STANLOW ABBEY was founded in 1172 and transferred from the waterlogged site to Whalley in Lancashire in 1294. Sully in 1889 writes that one doorway, part of a wall, and four columns remained then, built into farm buildings.*

The first oil dock was built at Stanlow in 1916–22. Shell-Mex began refining in 1924. A second oil dock followed in 1933, but the big expansion started only in 1949.

SHELL REFINERY. The vast area mostly of oil tanks, mysterious pieces looking much like sculpture of 1960, and cooling towers also contains the RESEARCH CENTRE, a group of low, well 102

* The site is now inaccessible.

designed buildings by *Sir Frederick Gibberd*, 1956 etc., and the
ADMINISTRATION BUILDING, an eight-storey slab by the
Building Design Partnership (then *Grenfell Baines & Har-
greaves*), also 1956 etc., but a little more restless.

STANTHORNE HALL *see* MIDDLEWICH

6040   ## STAPELEY

STAPELEY OLD HALL. Late Georgian. Seven bays, rendered,
with the doorway in an uncommonly big bow.
STAPELEY HOUSE (Rural District Offices). This is a five-bay
brick house of 1778. Two and a half storeys; quoins. But *Salvin*
about 1845–50 remodelled it, i.e. gave it the stone frontispiece,
very restrained classical, and the two bleakly undetailed canted
bay windows. He also put a 'campanile' (Burke's term) in the
centre which is no longer there and may just have been an
Italianate belvedere.

4070   ## STOAK

ST LAWRENCE. 1827 by *George Edgecumbe* (GR), but of the preceding church the small chancel (Perp) and the nave roof (with
convex angle bracing) remain. – PULPIT. Late C17. – WEST
GALLERY. With panels of the rood screen dado. They have at
the top two tiers of tiny openwork cusped arches, a Welsh type.
Early C16. – COMMUNION RAIL. With twisted balusters. Late
C17. – PLATE. Cup and remade Paten Cover, C16 by *William
Mutton* of Chester. – MONUMENTS. Large and spectacular
55   marble cartouche tablet for Henry Bunbury; 1668. – Many of
the painted heraldic tablets by one of the *Randle Holmes*. The
dates lie between 1627 and 1702.

8090   ## STOCKPORT

INTRODUCTION

Stockport is a medieval town, though, apart from the chancel of
the parish church, nothing tells of that. It received a first charter
about 1220. Of its castle we know that it existed in the later C12,
that it stood NW of the church, and that its ruins were finally demolished about 1775. On the site Sir George Warren built a
circular building with battlements, and this was a cotton mill – so
The Beauties of England and Wales reports. Lord Torrington
refers to it in 1790 and says that it looked 'like one of the grandest
prisons in the world'. So, although the silk industry came first,
by then Stockport was launched on her career as a cotton town.

The border to Lancashire runs in fact almost immediately N of what survives of the old town. This old town lies in the valley of the Mersey and rose steeply to the market place and the parish church. But when the town began to spread, it spread on the higher ground. Here St Peter's church was built in 1768, and a good deal further s St Thomas in 1822–5. Of other early C19 buildings the Sunday School dates from 1805–6 and 1835–6, the Infirmary from 1832. Names of streets such as Wellington Road* and Waterloo Road are telling too. The population was 22,000 in 1801, 53,000 in 1851, 93,000 in 1901, 142,500 in 1961. It is thus the largest town in Cheshire, with Birkenhead a close second (1961 141,700 inhabitants).

Architecturally Stockport is rarely praised, but it has one tremendous asset, the difference of level between the older and the newer town which allows the iron BRIDGE in St Peter's Gate (1868) to cross Little Underbank above the roof level of the shops below, and the railway to cross the valley by a VIADUCT of twenty-seven arches (1839–40, by *G. W. Buck*). Very recently architects in providing new and more metropolitan shopping have made full use of these possibilities.

INNER STOCKPORT

CHURCHES

ST MARY, Market Place and Churchgate. The chancel is Dec, though externally it is too restored for the unaware to recognize it. But inside the SEDILIA with crocketed gables and the (also over-restored) DOUBLE PISCINA remain, and opposite a recess with a three-centred arch, and in it the badly preserved MONUMENT to Richard de Vernon † 1334, rector of Stockport. The piscina has blank Kentish tracery and a thickly foliated gable. But most of the church was rebuilt to *Lewis Wyatt*'s design in 1813–17. It is Perp Gothic, with a w tower and two tiers of windows along the long sides to indicate the galleries inside. The walls are canted towards the tower, and here two porches are attached. The interior has high thin piers of Perp section and plaster tierceron-vaults. – PLATE. Cup with Cover Paten, London, 1580; Plate, London, 1674, by *G. G.*; Stand Paten, London, 1715; Ewer by *Josiah Daniel*, London, 1716; Flagon by *Thomas Mason*, London, 1719; Paten by *Thomas Wright*(?), London, 1760. – MONUMENTS. For Richard de

* Wellington Road was built as a by-pass turnpike road, avoiding the streets of the old town.

Vernon *see* above. – William Wright † 1753, by *Daniel Sephton* of Manchester, his *chef d'œuvre*. Huge tablet with volutes and garlands l. and r. of the inscription and a bust on top, palm branches r., oak (?) l. – Sir George Warren (*see* Introduction) † 1801. By *Sir Richard Westmacott*. Standing female figure by an urn on a pillar. – The Rev. Charles Prescott † 1820, also by *Westmacott*. Dignified seated effigy; Grecian character (s aisle). – James Antrobus Newton † 1823. By *Bacon Jun.* and *S. Manning*. Female figure kneeling by a broken column. – Mrs Hawall † 1852. By *Latham* of Manchester. Angels hovering over her body (s aisle).

St Joseph (R.C.), Tatton Street, St Peter's Gate. 1861–2 by *M. E. Hadfield*. Towerless. Dignified façade in the style of 1300. Polygonal apse. Nave and aisles; round piers.

Our Lady and the Apostles (R.C.), Shaw Heath. 1905 by *Edmund Kirby*. Very typical Kirby. Large, of fiery red brick, without a tower, but with a monumental front with two turrets and two portals and a large rose window set in a giant arch. The continuous brick mouldings are especially typical. Interior with granite columns. The area round the s transept and the narrow ambulatory is ill managed.

St Peter, St Peter's Gate. 1768. Built at the expense of William Wright (*see* below). A modest church, though not small. Brick, with arched windows and a w tower with an octagonal top stage and a cap. The chancel was added in 1888 – a tactful job. Inside only a w gallery. – PLATE. Chalice and Paten, 1768. – MONUMENT. William Wright † 1770. Against an obelisk an urn with a garland pegged on to it.

Next to St Peter's is St Peter's School. 1844. Brick, five bays, with arched windows.

Also by the church is the COBDEN MONUMENT, by *George G. Adams*, 1862.

St Thomas, St Thomas' Place, Wellington Road South. By *George Basevi*, 1822–5, the only Commissioners' church of the first grant in Cheshire and one of the most expensive. It cost over £15,000; ashlar of course. The high w tower stands at the end of a vista from Wellington Road. Its top is an open cupola. The sides have two tiers of windows – round-arched above, segmental below – and coupled angle pilasters. But the surprise is the E end; for it is here that the grand portico of six fluted Ionic columns is placed, as if it were the entrance side.* Inside

* I hear from Mr Skillern that originally it was the entrance side. Wellington Road was made after the church had been started. The portico thus originally faced the only available street.

the portico is a recess in which the staircase to the galleries rises – a fine touch to open up behind the portico. Inside on the galleries fluted Corinthian columns. The chancel was re- 72 modelled in 1890 – by *Medland Taylor*, but unobtrusively.

NONCONFORMIST CHAPELS. An early one is the former IN-DEPENDENT, i.e. CONGREGATIONAL CHAPEL in Waterloo Road, *c.*1788–90, brick, of three bays with a pediment, two doorways with pediments and Venetian windows between. There is also a remarkable number of really large chapels in the centre of Stockport. First the TIVIOT DALE CHAPEL (Methodist), Tiviot Dale (in Lancashire), 1825–6 by *Richard Lane*. Classical ashlar front of three bays, with one-bay porch attachments. No pediment, just a big parapet. The main porch is in the middle and has four unfluted Ionic columns. Then, totally different, the UNITARIAN CHAPEL in St Peter's Gate, 1841–2 by *Richard Tattersall*, stone, with lancet windows (à la Commissioners). Then three grand more or less vaguely Italianate ones, debased and showy. The earliest was the best (now demolished): MOUNT TABOR METHODIST, Wellington Road South, 1865–8 by *William Hill* of Leeds. Five-bay stone front with giant Corinthian portico; round-arched windows. Of 1880–2 the former EBENEZER METHODIST CHAPEL, also Wellington Road South, by *T. H. Allen* of Stockport He managed to mix Gothic bits into the Renaissance brew. Finally TRINITY METHODIST, again Wellington Road South but further S, 1884–6 by *William Waddington & Sons*. Italianate, with two short polygonal turrets. The centre is two windows flanked by pairs of giant columns.

PUBLIC BUILDINGS

TOWN HALL, Wellington Road South. 1904–8 by *Sir Alfred* 100 *Brumwell Thomas*. Of white stone, in a free William-and-Mary with a super-Wren middle tower a bit too high and too heavy for the body of the building. Below the tower two very Baroque pedimented projections with columns and a big porch between them. Marble-faced staircase hall and a lush foliage balustrade of iron. Square Council Chamber with a dome on segmental lunette arches.

MASONIC GUILDHALL, Wellington Road South. 1869 by *T. H. Allen*. Originally a Methodist Sunday School, Gothic to Jacobean, asymmetrical.

WAR MEMORIAL ART GALLERY, Wellington Road South.

Staid classical. 1925 by *J. T. Halliday* of *Halliday, Paterson & Agate* of Manchester.

CENTRAL LIBRARY, Wellington Road South. 1912–13 by *Bradshaw, Gass & Hope*. Very free William-and-Mary, with a corner dome. Brick with stone trim.

COLLEGE OF TECHNOLOGY, Wellington Road South. The old building was the technical school. It is of 1888–9 by *G. Sedger* of London. Mixed Tudor and Georgian with a cupola.

STOCKPORT SUNDAY SCHOOL, Duke Street. 1805–6, enlarged in 1835–6. A remarkably large building of brick: four-storeyed, of fourteen bays. The lowest and the two middle windows on the first and second floor in blank arches. Attached to it is the CENTENARY HALL, 1905–9 by *Potts, Son & Hennings*. Long, of red brick and yellow terracotta, asymmetrical and lively.

INFIRMARY, Wellington Road South. 1832 by *Richard Lane*, a long, stately ashlar front of two storeys with a central tetrastyle Greek Doric portico and pediment and the angle pavilions with pilasters and pediments. It makes the town hall opposite look very bumptious. The total length is twenty-one bays. Good, if small staircase with a Venetian window.

ST THOMAS' HOSPITAL, Shaw Heath. The oldest part was the WORKHOUSE, 1841 by *Bowman*, but not Gothic. Utilitarian, brick, a large range, three- and four-storeyed, altogether thirty-three bays. A cupola on the five-bay centre.

PENDLEBURY HALL, Old Road and Lancashire Hill (in Lancashire). Formerly Pendlebury Memorial Hall and Orphanage. Built in 1880–2 by *J. W. Beaumont*. Red brick; a high tower with a domed cap.

ARMOURY OF THE CHESHIRE REGIMENT, Greek Street. 1862 by *Bowman*. Gothic, with a polygonal tower with steep spire or roof and a main block to its r. with a big hipped roof. Upper windows of two lights; only slits below.

MARKET HALL, Market Place. 1861, iron and glass, nothing special.

PRODUCE MARKET, Market Place. 1852 by *J. Stevens* and *G. B. Park*. Originally one-storeyed. The upper storey with attached columns and a parapet was built in 1875 to house the library.

COBDEN MONUMENT. *See* p. 340.

PERAMBULATION

Little except the churches and public buildings.
Georgian houses are few and (really) far between. The best is the

OLD RECTORY in CHURCHGATE, of 1744, five bays, brick, of two and a half storeys, with a doorway with columns and pediment and an enriched window over. Other, very minor houses in Churchgate, e.g. No. 96. In NEW BRIDGE LANE another five-bay brick house with three-bay pediment and porch (derelict at the time of writing). More in GREEK STREET (one date 1838) and also in the old town: the MANSION HOUSE in HIGH STREET, again five bays (but added to and at the time of writing neglected).*

There is nothing else that would make the High Street a High Street. The best preserved pre-Georgian buildings are in GREAT UNDERBANK, and chiefly the former Underbank Hall of the Ardern family (*see* Bredbury, p. 113), now DISTRICT BANK, Elizabethan, timber-framed, of two storeys and gables, twice coved forward. Three gables, but the porch not symmetrically placed. Decoration with concave-sided lozenges and crosses set diagonally.‡ Nos. 30–32, a little further w, is a smaller house with the same motifs, but only two gables. Several bogus Elizabethan black and white buildings.

Immediately w the new SHOPPING CENTRE by *Bernard Engle & Partners*, including the big new COOPERATIVE STORE by the *Co-op Architects' Department*. The latter is rather wild, both the tower of various vertical brick slabs and the remorseless concrete pattern of the façades. But the scheme as a whole is very ingenious, with elevated walks, a shopping arcade, and all sorts of vistas.

MERSEYWAY was made in 1936–40 by covering up a stretch of the Mersey. It has been pedestrian since 1968, and is incorporated in the new shopping precinct.

Also recent and uncommonly good is the new HOUSING in LANCASHIRE HILL (in Lancashire), 1967–9 by *J. S. Rank*. Two splendidly slender, twenty-two-storey slabs and lower maisonettes well grouped. No one will extend this praise to the lumpy high blocks immediately SE of the town hall (1964–6 by *J. S. Rank*).

OUTER STOCKPORT

NORTH WEST AND NORTH

For HEATON CHAPEL, HEATON MERSEY, HEATON MOOR, HEATON NORRIS, and REDDISH, see *The Buildings of England: South Lancashire*.

---

* Mr Buttress mentions three Georgian houses in MIDDLE HILLGATE, particularly No. 18, with a rain-water head dated 1715.

‡ The structure of the house is assigned to *c.*1500.

NORTH EAST AND EAST

St Alban, Offerton Lane. 1899 by *Preston & Vaughan*. Brick and red terracotta. New galilee immediately to the w by *Cruikshank & Seward*, 1966.

St Paul, Carrington Road. 1849–51 by *Bowman & Crowther*. Perp, with a good high w tower which has alas lost its spire. Nave and aisles, octagonal piers, three-bay chancel – in short a Cheshire Perp church. – STAINED GLASS. Some very pretty domestic glass from Brinnington Manor House, no doubt by *Powell*. Flowers and birds.

VERNON PARK was laid out in 1858. In it a MUSEUM built in 1860 (enlarged in 1865–6).

In WOODBANK PARK is WOODBANK by *Thomas Harrison*, 1812, for Peter Marsland, a cotton manufacturer. (Ashlar, two storeys, three bays with tripartite ground-floor windows under segmental arches and a segmental four-column Ionic porch. Side and rear elevations with a ground-floor order of Ionic demi-columns. Entrance hall with coffered segmental ceiling and relief panels over the doors. Top-lit staircase hall with more relief panels. Good staircase. EH)

SOUTH EAST AND SOUTH

97 St George, Buxton Road. By *Austin & Paley*, 1896–7, at the expense of George Fearn, a brewer. This is by far the grandest church of Stockport and, even nationally speaking, a masterpiece of the latest historicism, designed just before the most original younger English architects began to turn away from the strict Gothic Revival. Not that Austin does not introduce original touches in many places – e.g. the panelling of externa wall surfaces – but they concern details rather than the general conception. St George is a church on a splendid scale. From the road it builds up from the seven-light E window between heavy buttresses to a high, powerful crossing tower with its spire between thin flying buttresses connecting it with four pinnacles (the Louth motif). The total height is 230 ft. The style of the church is of course Perp. The w window has seven lights too, the aisle windows have four. Inside there are six bays before the crossing and the transepts. One is allowed to look into the crossing tower, where squinches provide for the spire. Prettily decorated ceiling. In the chancel is a high entry arch into the N chapel, a low one into the S vestry. The ORGAN CASE is by *Austin* too.

George Fearn also gave the extensive SCHOOL on the s side

(1905) and the VICARAGE. In the CEMETERY opposite is his
MONUMENT – he died in 1911 – which is a reduced replica of
the church spire.* (The remaining cemetery CHAPEL is Gothic,
and is by *Bowman*, c.1857.)

ST SAVIOUR, Buxton Road. By *R. B. Preston*. Begun in 1915.
Neo-Romanesque, of brick. Passage aisles and segmental ar-
cade arches. High single-light clerestory. Much freer than
Preston mostly was.

CHURCH OF THE LATTER DAY SAINTS (Mormon), Bramhall
Lane. 1961–3 by *Ivan Johnston & Partners* of Liverpool. Very
steep, large roof and very steeply gabled dormers jabbing forward. Tower of two sheets of timber.

GRAMMAR SCHOOL, Buxton Road. 1914–16 by *Spalding &
Theakston*, a weak building of theirs, in a conventional wild
Jacobean. New addition by *Dex Harrison* with a zigzag roof.

GIRLS' HIGH SCHOOL, Beech Road. 1908–9 by *Spalding &
Spalding* and *E. G. Theakston*. Brick and stone dressings, neo-
Early-Georgian. The tower is surprising in position and detail.

WEST

ST AUGUSTINE, St Augustine's Road, Stockport Road. 1893 by
Preston & Vaughan. Conventional Perp, of brick with red
terracotta dressings. The interior is terracotta too, even the
octagonal piers. The only surprise is the very capricious timber-
framed upper part of the N tower.

ST MATTHEW, Grenville Street. 1855–8 by *J. S. Crowther*. High
W tower with a good broach-spire. Late C13 details. Along the
churchyard the SCHOOL, 1871.

(TRAVIS BROOK MILL, Heaton Lane. Actually in Lancashire.
1834–6 by *Sir William Fairbairn* for Ralph Orrell. Mr
Buttress reports that the building is still there, its columnar
chimney truncated, and that there is factory housing as well,
including a long terrace. The housing is in Brinksway Road.)

STOCKTON HEATH   *6080*

This is really outer Warrington.

ST THOMAS, by the border of Cheshire and Lancashire. 1868
by *E. G. Paley*. A large church with a big SE tower. The church
is faced with small stones, and the tracery is of c. 1300. S aisle
arcade with stiff-leaf capitals. N chapel of two bays with odd

* Mr Buttress kindly told me of this.

details of the arch springing. – The TILE DECORATION of the chancel is the one thing one will remember.

STOKE *see* STOAK

STORETON   [EH]

STORETON HALL. Storeton came into the possession of the Stanley family in the C13, and it is from the Stanleys of Storeton that the Earls of Derby are descended. Incorporated in the farm buildings of Storeton Hall Farm are extensive remains of the house built *c.*1360 by William Stanley. It was of H-plan, with the great hall running from N to S between a N wing containing upper end chambers and a S service wing. What survives is the two-storey N wing and the E wall of the hall, though farm buildings have been erected against the outer side of this wall, i.e. the inside face now forms an outside face. Buttresses occur at the W corners of the N wing, and in the gable-end (which does not quite rise to its original height) is a window which lit the solar, pointed, and with hoodmould, though now blocked. In the centre of the N wall, at first-floor level, are the remains of a fireplace. Adjoining the NE corner is a smaller block, again with buttresses, the ground floor of which was a chapel. On the S side of the N wing can be seen the point at which it was joined by the W wall of the hall. In the E wall of the hall there is, at the N end, a doorway which gave access to stairs in the angle between the hall and the N wing. Then follow traces of two blocked windows, and at the S end is the entrance doorway, which would have communicated with the screens passage, and which, though blocked, retains its pointed moulded arch. A jamb and arch springing is all that remains of the S wall of the hall.

Through the village runs part of the system of AVENUES, laid out in 1912–14 by *J. Lomax-Simpson* for the first Viscount Leverhulme (*see* Thornton Hough, p. 360). The former SCHOOL was built in 1865 at the expense of the shipowner Sir Thomas Brocklebank, the then landlord.

STRETTON
                      Near Appleton Thorn

ST MATTHEW. 1870 by *Scott*, replacing a Commissioners' church of 1826–7 by *Hardwick*. The ever observant Goodhart-Rendel noticed that the chancel (with its plate tracery) does not look like Scott, yet cannot be of 1826. Was there then someone

else involved, say about 1860? Scott's work is E.E. W tower,
nave and aisles. Scott can be depended on to do an earnest and
dignified job, provided the money available was adequate.
Goodhart-Rendel calls the church 'solid, decent, well designed
and unamusing'.

STRETTON HALL, ½ m. S. 1664, black and white, with three
gables of different sizes. Big square porch on later supports.
Few decorative motifs.

Two good Georgian three-bay houses W of the Hall, on the A
road. WALLSPIT is dated 1791 and has quoins and a rusticated
arched doorway.

STRETTON   4050
1¼ m. SW of Clutton

Three noteworthy brick houses – from N to S.

STRETTON LOWER HALL. 1660. A flat front with dentil bands
and two big shaped gables with big semicircular tops.

STRETTON OLD HALL. One big gable of a more complex
shape, and a single-storey porch with a simpler shaped gable.

STRETTON HALL. Two storeys. Stone dressings. Front with a
central canted bay holding the pedimented doorway. Five-bay
garden front. Single-storey wings with Venetian windows on
the garden side. (1765, altered and added to. Ionic screen in
the hall. MHLG)

STYAL   8080

QUARRY BANK MILL. Samuel Greg of Belfast in 1784 built a 66
silk mill in the wooded valley of the Bollin. It was enlarged later,
but the oldest part survives. It consists of the r. part of three
bays with the typical pediment, the typical cupola and a pedimented doorway, the detached chimney, and a l. part of eight
bays and four storeys, a little recessed. The five-bay continuation is later, and yet later the seven-bay, five-storey addition
with a gambrel roof. To the river is a low and unbecoming addition of 1810. (Although part of the buildings is of the fire-
proof filler-joist system, for the most part the floors are timber.)
   To the S of the mill buildings the river is dammed. The
Manager's House is to the S too; QUARRYBANK HOUSE, the
former owner's house, is to the N. The APPRENTICES'
HOUSE (shades of the Hammonds!) is up the hill, some distance
away. Housing on the hill was no doubt built for the employees.

NORCLIFFE HALL. Of c.1830–40, brick, Elizabethan. Built for
Samuel Greg's son.

H.M. PRISON. Built as COTTAGE HOMES for children by the Chorlton (i.e. Manchester) Board of Guardians in 1898. The architect was *Frederick H. Overmann*. It is interesting as an early case of the replacement of the workhouse type of architecture by something more human. 600 children lived in twenty-eight houses, informally arranged. The large CHAPEL is timber-framed and has a bell-turret and cross-gables.

SUTTON LANE ENDS
9070

ST JAMES. 1840 by *Hayley*, the lower chancel and apse of 1871 by *C. Hodgson Fowler* (GR). The debased tower with its four gables in front of the start of the spire is Hayley's, the chancel is no better. The church has lancet windows.

PARSONAGE. Of the 1840s, with steep, bargeboarded gables, totally asymmetrical As attractive as the church is unattractive.

SCHOOL. 1841. Small, symmetrical.

(SUTTON HALL. Now divided up. An irregular building with a complicated building history. Some C17 half-timber. Gable with brackets. Also quatrefoils and a zigzag frieze.)

SUTTON WEAVER
5070

(SUTTON HALL. Largely early C17. Inside, decorated beams and joists. The roof has 'very ornamental Perp style trusses'. Jacobean staircase. MHLG)

SWETTENHAM
8060

CHURCH. A funny church, with its imitation Norman arcade piers and square Early French Gothic capitals, its S aisle fenestration Victorian Gothic, its W tower brick of *c.*1717–22, its chancel chequer brick of about the same time, but the brick casing hiding a two-bay chancel of timber, with raw posts. Probably of *c.*1720 the segment-headed N window too. The Capesthorne Chapel with its odd oval windows is said to date from 1717. The normanizing is by *Derrick*, 1846, the gothicizing seems, according to the Tipping MONUMENTS in recesses of the S aisle, *c.*1865. The monuments are foliated cross slabs. – FONTS. One is Norman, no doubt of *c.*1846, the other an C18 baluster shaft. – COMMUNION RAIL. Three-sided; early C18. – PLATE. Chalice of 1705 by *Pemberton* of Chester; Paten, London, 1713.

SWETTENHAM HALL. A C17 house with Late Georgian remodelling in the Gothic direction. The entrance side is castellated, the garden side has two gables and between them a big canted bay window also castellated. Good C17 outbuildings, especially one symmetrical two-storeyed one.

CLONTERBROOK HALL, 1¼ m. E. Late C17, five bays, two storeys, with wooden cross windows.

SWYNEYARD HALL *see* HIGH LEGH

TABLEY

The Leicesters are the family for which both Tabley Old Hall and the present Tabley were built. TABLEY OLD HALL, together with a chapel, stood picturesquely on an island in a lake. Although it had been reduced in size, there remained the hall of a medieval timber-framed house to which alterations and additions had been made in the C17, particularly in 1670. In the 1920s it became unsafe, due to subsidence rather than old age, and it has since quietly collapsed. The ruin still stands as a brick shell, and can just be seen from the A556. The chapel, however, was rescued, and re-erected W of Tabley House.

CHAPEL OF ST PETER. Moved to its present site in 1927–9, but built originally in 1675–8, a late date considering the fact that the windows still have arched lights. They are transomed, and the arches repeat below the transoms. The E has two transoms and a shaped gable of convex curves only. At the W side is a thin tower. The building is of dark brick. The room inside has a segmental plaster vault and wooden panelling. The furnishings are reminiscent of those of Oxford colleges. – PULPIT. High up, with a sounding-board and an HOURGLASS. – WEST SCREEN. The doorway has an open pediment on columns. – COMMUNION RAIL. With twisted balusters. – PEWS. The ends have plain, largish balls. – STAINED GLASS. Small pieces of Netherlandish glass. – One window by *Morris & Co.*, i.e. designed by *Burne-Jones*; *c.* 1895 and good. – PLATE. Pieces of 1678, including a Collecting Box.

TABLEY HOUSE, the replacement of the Old Hall, was built in 1761–7 by *John Carr*. It is a mansion of red brick with stone dressings and has an exceptionally splendid ENTRANCE SIDE with wings and two later archways (by *Robert Curzon*, *c.*1830) creating an effective cross-axis. They have pediments, and there are also two pairs of gatepiers. The house is of seven bays and one and a half storeys above a basement. It has a three-bay pediment and porch added in 1914. The basement, really a low ground floor, is of stone, rusticated. The windows of the *piano nobile* have parapet balustrades. The mid-window is Venetian.

The framing of the top-floor windows is rather reactionary for its date. The wings are connected with the house by quadrant links, oddly enough convex, not concave. The wings themselves are of four bays with two-bay pediments and canted bay windows to the forecourt and the outside.

On the far side of the forecourt, facing the entrance, are the STABLES, long and simple.

63   The GARDEN SIDE was originally the entrance side. Two curved outer staircases sweep up to the former main doorway. This side has nine, not seven, bays and an upper portico of Tuscan columns carrying a pediment. The *piano nobile* windows here have pediments, triangular in the side parts, segmental behind the portico.

The side elevations differ, though both have a central canted bay window. On the E side the arrangement is Carr's, on the W side it is an adjustment of *c.*1825. The arched windows are a sign of the earlier and later dates.

The INTERIOR ought to be seen in the original way, entering by the outer stair flights. The original ENTRANCE HALL is a fine apartment with chaste white stucco decoration on blue and two statues in niches. Very spacious STAIRCASE, its balustrade with three slender turned balusters to each step and a screen of columns, twice two in depth, on the upper landing. Ceiling with lunette lighting. To the E of the entrance hall is the DRAWING ROOM with a fine fireplace and a panelled stucco ceiling with foliage frames. The smaller room N of this has its fireplace in the bay window. The W side is the former PICTURE GALLERY. (The first Lord de Tabley (the creation was of 1826) had a famous collection of paintings.) It is tripartite with segmental arches, of 1827 by *Thomas Harrison.* The present ENTRANCE HALL, on the ground floor N, was remodelled *c.* 1825.

In the link between the house and the chapel a chimneypiece from the Old Hall has been re-erected. It is a very barbaric piece with caryatids and Lucretia and Cleopatra in niches.

By the lake are the Gothic BOATHOUSE and a round TOWER. N of the house, on the Knutsford Road, is a pair of single-storey LODGES. Square, of brick and stone.

5060   TARPORLEY

ST HELEN. The exterior seems almost entirely Victorian, so over-restored is most of it. Only the Perp N and S chancel chapels still show some of the original handwriting. Yet it is basically a medieval church – only, according to Mr Richards: S chapel remodelled 1861, chancel remodelled 1865, tower remodelled 1878, nave remodelled 1879 (Ormerod: 1869). The remodelling was done by *J. Crowther* of Manchester. The tower stands on the s w end and now has a pyramid roof. To the w end a baptistery was added in 1931–2 by *Sir Percy Worthington*. The interior has nave arcades of four bays and chancel arcades of three, separated by a chancel arch. The piers are Perp, of octagonal shape. – SCREEN. Of iron, High Victorian, yet as late as 1890. But the gates are said to be from Siena and c16. – STAINED GLASS. The s aisle w window by *Kempe*, 1899. – PLATE. Inscribed 1711 a Chalice, a Paten, and a silver-gilt Flagon; another Chalice and Paten probably 1724 by *Richard Richardson* of Chester; two Almsdishes, early c18. – MONUMENTS. Sir John Done † 1629. Tablet of the later c17 with relief bust in oval. – Next to it tablet to John Crewe † 1670. The same composition but a little more advanced in style. Both, however, have hanging garlands. – Sir John Crewe † 1711. Semi-reclining white marble figure praying. Sorrowful little boys at head and feet. The architectural setting is missing. – Jane Done † 1622, her sister Mary Crewe † 1690, and the latter's little grand-daughter † 1674. White marble. The young woman recumbent, the old propped up on one elbow. The child stands by her feet and holds a bunch of flowers. The monument is of 1698.

In the churchyard the DONE RECREATION ROOM, built as a school in 1636. Brick with blue brick diapers, one-storeyed, with coat of arms in a strapwork setting.

The OLD RECTORY, NW of the church, has a good staircase from Utkinton Hall. This looks c.1700, with twisted balusters.

The church lies back from the HIGH STREET. At the s end of this, set across, is the MANOR HOUSE, with a date 1586. Rendered, with a symmetrical N front. Three gables. Then, walking N, on the E side GABLE HOUSE, brick, with the gable facing the street. In it a window with a lintel, as if it belonged to a Venetian window. Then a piece of a three-storeyed brick terrace of the late c18. Opposite the stately SWAN HOTEL, brick, of 1769. Three storeys, with two canted bay windows and windows like those of Gable House. Next to it the MARKET COURT, lower, also brick, of five bays with a recessed centre which on the ground floor was originally open. At the top in the middle a one-bay open pediment. On the other side more but minor Georgian brick houses, interrupted by the METHODIST CHAPEL of 1867. (Stone, style of 1300, no tower.)

At the N end of the High Street is a fork of A roads. To the NW is first SALTERSWELL HOUSE, brick, of *c.*1783 (MHLG). Three bays and three storeys, with rusticated window lintels and a broken pediment over the door. Fine iron garden railings. Then, ¾ m. further WSW, ROAD STREET HOUSE, early C18. Brick, two-storeyed. Four-bay front. The two-bay centre has giant angle pilasters and a pediment. Doorway with shell-hood. Yet ¾ m. further out is IDDINSHALL HALL, brick, of two and a half storeys, with quoins and stone cross windows, on the ground floor seven of them, above less. It looks late C17.

ARDERNE HALL, E of Tarporley, was demolished in 1958. It was then a house of the 1870s, but there had been a predecessor. There remains a curious, large hexagonal lodge with steep bargeboarded gables. It stands N of Portal.

PORTAL, ½ m. NE of Tarporley, was built *c.*1900–5 to designs of *W. E. Tower*, better known as Kempe's partner in the flourishing stained-glass business. It is a *tour de force* in accurate but scaled-up imitation of timber-framed mansions. The side to the garden is symmetrical and has three very large identical bay windows of five sides of an octagon. Round the corner is the entrance side, which in itself is again symmetrical. The entrance is in the middle, and leads to a screens passage and into the great hall, which rises to the roof and has a big stone Jacobean chimneypiece. Behind the hall is a courtyard. There is also plenty of re-used old timber, including boldly moulded C15 beams in one room, structural timbering also probably of the C15 by the staircase, and panelling in the hall and other places. Also Swiss C16 STAINED GLASS. (Similar in style to the house itself are the ENTRANCE LODGE and, on the E side of the grounds, a COTTAGE and a house known as OAKSTONE LODGE. EH)

4060

TARVIN

ST ANDREW. Approached from the street through C18 gate-piers with urns and a short avenue of lime trees. It leads to the doorway in the Perp W tower, a doorway flanked by niches and crowned by an ogee gable above which runs a quatrefoil frieze. The high arch to the nave however has C14 mouldings. The S aisle is largely a Victorian remodelling of an C18 job – cf. the one remaining Venetian window. The S chapel is Dec and has a good E window with reticulation units. The N aisle and N chapel are Perp and have enriched buttresses and battlements.

But the window tracery cannot be original.* The chancel was a C18 rebuilding – cf. one N window inside – but is now Victorian. The N arcade is Perp, five bays with short octagonal piers, the S arcade is the earlier, i.e. C14, and has four piers instead and then one to the S chapel plus a narrow panelled arch once used no doubt for a monument. The N capitals are moulded, the S capitals foliated but drastically re-cut or re-made. The nave roof is quite a sumptuous piece – dated 1650, but still in the Gothic tradition, e.g. with hammerbeams. It is only such details as the brackets that tell the real tale. The S aisle roof is C14. It is single-framed, and the braces give it a semi-circular section. – FONT. Perp, octagonal, with quatrefoil decoration and a panelled stem. – REREDOS. With reliefs, five saints and four scenes of small figures. They are of c.1500, and probably Flemish. – SCREEN. To the S chapel, a genuine Dec piece with six ogee-headed openings either side of the entrance and a pierced quatrefoil frieze at the top. – STAINED GLASS. By *Kempe* the E window (1892) and one chancel S window (1884). – CHANDELIER of brass; Late C18. – PLATE. Several pieces inscribed 1775 and 1777.

Along the churchyard W of the church a row of brick cottages, and as their continuation at the street corner one timber-framed one with diagonal bracing and some decoration. Next to this two modest timber cottages and then the two best houses of Tarvin, a pair dated 1756 – there had been a fire at Tarvin in 1752. They are of brick, two and a half storeys high and each of four bays. One has a triangular, the other a segmental pediment over the doorway. The windows have rusticated lintels. Looking down the HIGH STREET is TARVIN HALL, a simpler brick house, three bays, with the first-floor side windows minimum Venetian, but without the posts that would make them tripartite. Front garden with brick wall and gatepiers.

HOCKENHULL HALL, ¾ m. SW. The two main façades are of c.1720, brick, two-storeyed, with stone-framed windows and giant angle pilasters. There was originally a top parapet. The former entrance side, one of the two main façades, is of nine bays, with the end pairs of bays a little projecting. Doorway with open segmental pediment. Dr Gomme is inclined to attribute the work to *Francis Smith* of Warwick. The two ranges have between them, visible at the back, earlier work, probably of the late C17.

* Though the Rev. G. E. Rundell tells me that the N aisle E window is considered to be original as is the S aisle westernmost.

(PACKHORSE BRIDGES, ½ m. w of Hockenhull Hall. Three,
with the path passing all three. They are narrow, though two
have been widened, and they span each about 12 ft. MHLG)
(HOLME STREET HALL, N of Hockenhull Hall on the A road.
C17. Brick and stone with mullioned windows. Central projection, gabled. EH)
POOLBANK, ¼ m. NE of the village. Early C19. Doric porch and
two segmental bay windows.

TATTENHALL

4050

ST ALBAN. By *Douglas*, 1869–70, except for the Perp w tower.
But not apparently an original design of Douglas. – STAINED
GLASS. Two beautiful little early C14 figures of saints complete
with the characteristic canopies of C14 stained glass. Also
the characteristic yellow and green. Some red, but no
blue. – E window by *Hardman*, *c.*1870. – w window by *Lavers
& Westlake*, *c.*1870. – s aisle E by *Kempe*, 1897. – CHANDELIER
of brass, dated 1755. Specially sumptuous. – PLATE. Flagon
and Chalice, 1762; two Patens, 1767.
THE ROOKERY, N of the church. Late C19 or early C20 black
and white, and apparently the result of a partial rebuilding
*c.*1909.
TATTENHALL HALL. Jacobean, an irregular façade with mullioned and transomed windows. One part is recessed, and the
doorway is placed in the gabled part projecting from the recess
at r. angles to the front.
Unusually rewarding village with brick terraces, timber-framed
cottages, and imitation timber-framing.
ROSE CORNER. 1927 by *Clough Williams-Ellis* – almost a folly
for the Bolesworth Castle estate. A Palladian façade with a
tetrastyle portico and pediment, set in a prominent place in
the village scene, but containing just two cottages and leading
to a few not rebuilt ones.

TATTON PARK

7080

The estate went to the Egertons in 1598 and remained with them
until it came to the National Trust in 1958. After a long gest-
ation the new house was finally begun *c.*1788–91 for William
Egerton to designs by *Samuel Wyatt*, brother of the more
famous but no more talented James Wyatt, and completed for
Wilbraham Egerton from 1807 onwards by their nephew *Lewis
Wyatt*. Samuel intended a house of eleven bays, and began the
execution of his plan, Lewis reduced the size to the present

seven bays and had to come to terms with what Samuel had already built. This explains the awkward relation between entrance hall and staircase. Otherwise the plan is simple. Entrance hall, staircase hall, and library form the centre and are all three of the same width. Two rooms lie to their E, two and a passage to their W. From the passage access is to a subsidiary wing, originally one-storeyed. There is however one complication. The dining room W of the library has a Rococo interior clearly of *c.*1750. It is not likely that it should be *ex situ*. Is it then part of the preceding house?*

The house is ashlar-faced, of two storeys, with sparingly set and detailed windows, every inch a testimony to the Wyatt style. The S front is of seven bays, in a 1–5–1 rhythm. The centre has a giant Corinthian portico, the end bays a tripartite window with a blank segmental arch over. Paterae in the tympana; garland panels above the main windows behind the portico. The N front is simpler, and the two-column porch is not really enough to mark the centre. The capitals of the columns are of a free leaf shape. The five-bay E side has giant pilasters all along. On the W side is the wing already referred to. The seven-bay colonnade is now two-storeyed, but the upper storey was added in 1861–2 by *G. H. Stokes*, Paxton's son-in-law. W of this is a part with much yellow terracotta, and this is supposed to have been designed by *Lord Egerton* himself. Yellow terracotta also the forecourt of the N front with its two pedimented archways.

The ENTRANCE HALL (by *Lewis Wyatt*) is tripartite, with [70] screens of columns marking the middle bay, although it leads nowhere. Shallow coffered tunnel-vault in all three parts. This is no doubt the finest room of the house. The LIBRARY is the other main room. It has a plaster ceiling which, despite its Victorian appearance, is original, and bookcases with delightful grilles of intersecting segmental curves. The recess in the MUSIC ROOM was intended for an organ.

The STAIRCASE HALL is spacious. It is *Samuel Wyatt*'s, but the square room, which is the required total size and forms a spatial unity with it, was added by *Lewis Wyatt*. The staircase itself has a simple iron railing, and there is a balcony all round the room. Oval skylights on fan-shaped pendentives. The square addition is separated by a screen of columns. The ground

* There is indeed a cellar below the library, and in this is a date 1718. The dining room has recently been attributed by Mr John Harris to *T. F. Pritchard*. Its chimneypiece with a Bacchanalian relief is by *Westmacott*.

floor here communicates with the upper floor only by a circular opening. Again fan pendentives. The skylight is round. The subsidiary staircase in the w wing comes from Hough End Hall, Manchester. With its sturdy balusters and the big balls on the newel posts, it must be of the later C17.

The TERRACING s of the house is very probably by *Paxton*, 1859–60.

ORANGERY. By *Lewis Wyatt*, c.1818. Seven bays with canted ends and Doric pillars.

TOWER in the TOWER GARDEN. Two storeys, brick, negligible.

ROTUNDA, the so-called TEMPLE, at the end of the BROAD WALK. A variation on the theme of the Lysicrates Monument. By *William Cole*, c.1820. On a terrace platform with stairs up to it.

SHINTO TEMPLE and JAPANESE BRIDGE. The temple was actually imported from Japan c.1910.

STABLES. By *Samuel Wyatt*. Red brick, eleven widely spaced bays. A sober design, but with its two pedimented bays l. and r. of the gateway and in its square cupola quite individual.

TATTON MERE is a genuine mere, but a second lake is the result of subsidence in the 1920s. Some work seems to have been carried out in the PARK to designs by *Repton* following 1791.

(OLD HALL. The house incorporated a timber-framed building of before the Reformation. The hall has a splendid roof with carved wall-plate, carved beams, and three tiers of quatrefoil wind-braces. At r. angles to the hall range is a wing with part of another roof with quatrefoil wind-braces.)

KNUTSFORD LODGE. *See* Knutsford, p. 253.

MERE LODGE. Octagonal, with a Tuscan veranda.

ROSTHERNE LODGE. 1833 by *James Hakewill*. Hexastyle, with Greek Doric columns and a pediment, but the middle intercolumniation wider than the others.

TETTON *see* WARMINGHAM

6080

THELWALL

ALL SAINTS. 1843 by *J. Mountford Allen*. The nave is of that date, with a long side of single lancets à la Commissioners, and with a bellcote. The chancel is of 1857, the N aisle and no doubt the w porch by *W. Owen* of 1890. The nave was lengthened to the E in 1857, to the W probably in 1890. All is rock-faced. – MEMORIAL to Edward the Elder, who founded Thelwall in 923. By *Eric Gill*, 1907. A triptych, with its middle pediment like a small Venetian altarpiece. Gill's work is all _{See} painted inscriptions. Can Gill also have done the framework? ^{p.}₄₄₂

HOME FARMHOUSE, ½ m. E. Dated 1745, and yet still with mullioned windows, though all of two lights, all of upright form, and all with raised frames.

CHAIGELEY SCHOOL (Greenfield House) was once a fine Georgian house. The bay windows have spoiled the façade. Fine doorway and a somewhat enriched window over.

THELWALL VIADUCT (M6). *See* Lymm.

THORNTON HOUGH   [EH]³⁰⁸⁰

The transformation of Thornton Hough into a model estate village was the work of two landlords – Joseph Hirst († 1874), a textile manufacturer of Wilshaw, Yorkshire, and, more particularly, William Hesketh Lever, first Viscount Leverhulme. Lever bought Thornton Manor in 1891, having rented it since 1888, the year in which construction began at Port Sunlight (*see* p. 303). By him the village was, except for Hirst's contributions, almost entirely rebuilt, with a number of the architects who were active at Port Sunlight being employed.

The village groups around its two churches which, despite being near to each other, act as separate visual nuclei. The Congregational church forms a particularly effective focal point.

ALL SAINTS. Built in 1867 at the expense of Joseph Hirst. His architects were *Kirk & Sons* of Huddersfield. Rock-faced red sandstone with lighter dressings. Geometrical. Cruciform, with SW tower and spire.* Fairly rich-looking outside, but the interior is thin and starved. Aisleless nave. A N chancel aisle forms an organ chamber, and although the S chancel aisle is now a vestry, its partition screen is not original, and there is a fireplace. Could it, at this late date, have been a family pew? Substantial stone REREDOS. Originally the RAILS and the PULPIT were of similar character, and the church is not helped by the present feeble replacements.

Adjoining the churchyard are the VICARAGE and, to the N, the former SCHOOL. Both are of *c.*1866–8 at the expense of Hirst, so doubtless by *Kirk & Sons*.

---

* On the N side of the tower is a fifth clock face, added because Hirst was unable to see the lower face from his house.

ST GEORGE (Congregational). 1906–7. Designed for Lord Leverhulme by *J. Lomax-Simpson*. Norman in style, at Lever's suggestion. The building reflects his Nonconformity combined
with his love of richness in architecture and dignity in worship.
Sandstone, with stone-flagged roof. Ashlar interior. Cruciform.
Broad central tower with recessed pyramid roof. Rib-vaulted
apse. No aisles. Very thorough and costly, with strong concen-
tration of diverse ornament and detail, especially inside – cf.
e.g. the crossing arches and the treatment of the windows, all
different and all very elaborate. Norman is employed in quite
unprecedented ways, particularly in the FURNISHINGS. – At
the lowest point of the churchyard is a hexagonal COVERED
ENTRANCEWAY, also Norman. It is well placed to form a feature in the village.

COUNTY PRIMARY SCHOOL (formerly Lever School). 1904 by
Jonathan Simpson. Long and symmetrical. Pebbledash with
sandstone dressings. Unmoulded mullions and transoms.

VILLAGE CLUB (originally Liberal Club). By *Grayson & Ould*,
c.1904. A screen wall links two shops which have half-timbered
upper storeys.

SMITHY, at the foot of Neston Road. 1905 by *J. Lomax-Simpson*.
Half-timber. Recessed in the centre in the Wealden manner.
Very pretty, and there is even a spreading chestnut tree.

At the head of the village is WILSHAW TERRACE. Built for
Hirst, 1870, and presumably by *Kirk & Sons*. Gothic. A row
of cottages and a shop with conical-roofed tower, strategically
sited. All the following houses in the village belong to the Lever
period. Immediately N of the Congregational church a semi-
detached pair (one of them SUNNYSIDE) and also THICKET
FORD. Both are by *William & Segar Owen*, 1892, the latter for
Lord Leverhulme's sister. Then WEALD HOUSE (formerly
the Manse). 1904 by *Grayson & Ould*, and built for the Congregational minister. Below, Nos. 1–6 MANOR ROAD are by
William & Segar Owen. A varied group of cottages. Stone,
half-timber, etc. Brick chimneystacks. Crude Tuscan porches
provide a touch of deliberate rusticity. More varied still is the
group round the corner, Nos. 1–7 NESTON ROAD, 1893 by
Douglas & Fordham, which, with its mixing of styles and
materials, seems a self-conscious attempt to be frivolously
rural. It is, however, carefully detailed, and there is some quite
rich ornament on the half-timbered parts. Opposite is a recreation ground, forming an open space in front of the parish
church, and on the opposite side is THE FOLDS. Cottages here,

predominantly half-timber, include Nos. 7–11, 1892 by *William & Segar Owen*. Others are by *Grayson & Ould*. In RABY ROAD are single-storey half-timbered cottages by *Grayson & Ould*, and a terrace, stone with roughcast rendering, by *Lomax-Simpson*, 1906.

Immediately NE of the village is THORNTON HOUSE, Joseph Hirst's house, rebuilt in 1895 by *Grayson & Ould* for James Darcy Lever, Lord Leverhulme's brother. It must have been a fine house, even before additions by *J. Lomax-Simpson*, 1906, greatly improved the effectiveness of the composition. Stone and half-timber, picturesquely combined. L-shaped, with the main block and a service wing enclosing two sides of a forecourt. The principal feature of the entrance front is a large gable, inspired by the now-demolished Darcy Lever Hall in Lancashire, and forming a particularly happy instance of Ould's half-timber revivalism. To the S of this the frontage is all of stone, and, except for a short length adjoining the gable, of 1906. The upper storey of the garden front is all half-timber, with four gables, that on the r. belonging to the 1906 extension. Rectangular chimneys, some set diagonally. The richly fitted interior is now divided up. ENTRANCE LODGE by *Grayson & Ould*.

To the NW, on the W side of MANOR ROAD, are three more large houses. They are as follows.

HESKETH GRANGE. 1894 by *Grayson & Ould* for Lord Leverhulme's father. Of L-plan. The ground storey is stone and the upper storey heavily and elaborately pargetted. The principal features of the entrance front are a large gable, also pargetted, and a Norman-Shavian oriel.

COPLEY. Rock-faced stone. Gothic, with a high tower. The ENTRANCE LODGE, dated 1867, is a jolly High Victorian piece, though shorn of its bargeboards, etc.

Finally, THORNTON MANOR. As bought by W. H. Lever in 1891, it was a modest Early Victorian house, and a series of separate alterations and additions transformed it into the present Neo-Elizabethan mansion.* First, some minor alterations were made by *Jonathan Simpson*, followed by more substantial work, apparently c.1896, by *Douglas & Fordham*, of which two shaped gables and semicircular bay windows on the SE (i.e. entrance) front remain. Later work includes the music room

---

* Thanks are due to the present Viscount Leverhulme and to Mr J. Lomax-Simpson, who supplied almost all the facts contained in this account, and also much information relating to Thornton Hough village.

by *J. J. Talbot*, forming a large block NE of, and at an angle to, the main part of the house. It has a 'Wrenaissance' interior, though there is a two-storey feature, framing a fireplace recess below and forming an organ screen above, which is of earlier stylistic derivation. Tunnel-vaulted ceiling. Kitchen and service quarters are by *Grayson & Ould*. The long E-plan SW or garden front, by *J. Lomax-Simpson*, came in 1913, involving the demolition of Douglas & Fordham work. The ground-floor rooms in this range are all in different styles, and contain some earlier fittings, e.g. a marble chimneypiece in the hall said to be by *Canova*.

GATEHOUSE. 1910 by *Lomax-Simpson*. Stone below and half-timber above, with a deep cove.

The STABLES, dated 1899, adjoin the house on the NW. They have a loggia facing the garden and are by *Talbot*.*

The GARDENS were laid out from 1905 onwards by *Thomas H. Mawson* and *Lord Leverhulme* himself, but are less notable than the results produced by the same partnership at Rivington in Lancashire and at The Hill, Hampstead, London. Some formal layout, particularly NW of the house. The KITCHEN GARDEN lies behind a LOGGIA of 1912, which is arcaded, with a terrace walk above, and which was intended to extend further. It is (like the small LOGGIA SE of the house) by *Lomax-Simpson*. Further NW is a small structure known as THE LOOKOUT, 1896 by *Douglas & Fordham*, but not in its original position. The LAKE, $\frac{1}{4}$ m. W of the house, includes a length of formal canal, but lacks the buildings which were planned in connexion with it.

To the N and NE of the village is a system of AVENUES, laid out in 1912–14 by *Lomax-Simpson*, with a total length of about 5 m.

₄₀₇₀

THORNTON-LE-MOORS

Close to the vast oil refinery, with its oil tanks and weird machinery, ST MARY. Mainly Dec; cf. the SW tower, the S aisle doorway, surprisingly large and with continuous mouldings, and the S aisle windows, the priest's doorway in the chancel, and also the chancel E window with its very odd tracery. The chancel S windows are Perp, those on the N post-Reformation. The hammerbeam roof is Perp too. The S arcade continues

---

* The First World War prevented the execution of a scheme by *Lomax-Simpson* for further enlarging the house, involving the refacing of the entrance front and the formation of a quadrangle, with ranges linking up with the gatehouse.

along the s side of the tower. The s chapel is clearly Perp, and the capitals indicate a late date. The chapel arch is C19. – See p. 442 FONT. C17. A big cup, strongly fluted. – COMMUNION RAIL. With twisted balusters. Dated 1695. – DOOR. 1725, simple and fine. – PLATE. Cup and Paten Cover, c.1567, possibly by *William Mutton* of Chester; C18 Paten, possibly by *Richard Richardson* of Chester. – MONUMENTS. Several painted heraldic ones, probably by *Randle Holme*. Dates 1634 to 1687.

RECTORY. Late C17. Five bays, two storeys, wooden cross windows.

THREAPWOOD

4040

ST JOHN. 1815, and still entirely Georgian, i.e. of brick with a pediment along the front, a cupola over, and pedimented doorways in the front and the middle of the s side. Arched windows. No projecting chancel at all. – Three GALLERIES on iron columns and with iron parapet. The N and s galleries curve round to the w gallery. – Two CHANDELIERS of brass; 1817. – Churchyard GATES of wrought iron.

A derelict WINDMILL to the SE; it is a brick tower mill.

THURSTASTON

[EH] 2080

ST BARTHOLOMEW. Rebuilt in 1885 by *John Loughborough Pearson*.[*] Red sandstone, with ashlar interior. Late C13 style. No aisles. Over the choir is a not altogether gainly tower and spire. A vestry abuts on the s, like a shallow transept. The interior is superb. It is very small, and, in its contrast to the external height, the quite massive tower and spire, and the generous N porch, it comes as something of a surprise. Typically Pearsonic are the cool and careful regularity of plan and proportions, the use of quadripartite vaulting, and also the effects of spatial complexity, here achieved with economy of means within a very limited volume. Three-bay nave. The chancel is divided into choir and sanctuary, with two transverse arches defining the choir. The w choir arch is filled with a stone tripartite traceried screen; the sanctuary vaulting is at a slightly higher level than that in the nave and choir and is divided into two narrow bays; the sanctuary windows have single shafts and recessed soffits, and the large E window has bar tracery. The result is that changing spatial relationships and

---

[*] A scheme for rebuilding had been prepared in 1871 by *Philip Webb* – one of his rare ecclesiastical designs.

increasing richness are presented to the visitor – and the communicant – progressing eastwards. – The REREDOS accentuates the richness of the E end. It is characteristic of *Pearson* furnishings in its heavy rectangularity. – ORGAN CASE. 1905 by *R. Norman Shaw*. Side panels painted by *Robert Christie*. – STAINED GLASS. Some by *Clayton & Bell*. – PLATE. Chalice, 1706; Paten, 1707.

In the churchyard is a meagre battlemented TOWER, a survival of a rebuilding of the church in 1824.

THURSTASTON HALL. Immediately W of the church, with which it groups on the S of a tree-lined green. The house is approached axially between high gatepiers, and is of charming appearance, tranquil and mellow. The entrance (i.e. N) front is of U-plan, with wings projecting on either side of a symmetrical centre. The W wing, of stone, is medieval, and is said to be C15, though it seems earlier. On its E wall, adjoining the internal angle of the centre block, are two blocked pointed-arched doorways, one of them partly obscured. Inside, a third arch is visible. Might they have been the service doors of the screens passage? A further arched doorway occurs elsewhere in the wing. Pointed first-floor window in the gable-end, with hoodmould and head-stops. Two collar-braced roof trusses remain, and there are cusped wind-braces. On the W front is a chimney-breast and a W projection which was either rebuilt or remodelled in, according to a datestone, 1680. The principal staircase, in the W wing, with twisted balusters and flat-capped newels could be of this date. The central block of the house must also be 1680, or a little later. It has a three-bay brick front with stone dressings. Two storeys below a cornice. Cross windows with timber mullions and transoms, and with leaded quarries remaining on the first floor. Bolection-moulded doorcase, with oval window above, and surround of unfluted Corinthian demi-columns and broken pediment with armorial shield. Above the cornice is a third storey, or rather a screen wall masking the roof. It has finials and dummy oval windows. Hall with bolection-moulded chimneypiece, and overmantel of Jacobean work cut to fit its present position. A small room to the rear of the hall and a first-floor room have crude bolection-moulded panelling. The E wing is of 1836, in a simple Elizabethan style. Its principal room has a chimneypiece of Renaissance design with Gothick tendencies. Is this 1836? The stone GATEPIERS, dated 1733, are both of cruciform plan, fluted, with shallow niches on their inner faces.

Near by stood DAWPOOL. As rebuilt in 1882–4, for the ship-owner Thomas Henry Ismay, it was one of *Norman Shaw*'s major domestic works, and was one of the first to be destroyed. Fragments known to exist include the dining-room chimney-piece, now in Birkenhead (*see* p. 95), but what became e.g. of the stained glass representation of Shaw holding a roll of drawings and a model of the house? The group of buildings N of the church and Thurstaston Hall includes a SCHOOL of c.1858–9 and a LODGE, also of the pre-Ismay period, but the former STABLES (now called THE CLOCK TOWER) are un-doubtedly by *Shaw*, as is the LODGE at the corner of the main Chester road. The stables are rock-faced sandstone, with red-tiled roofs. There is a broad, low tower with a battlemented parapet and pyramid roof.

TILSTON

4050

ST MARY. Ormerod says: rebuilt in 1877–8 except for the tower and the N chapel. It is true that the tower is Perp and that the chapel in spite of its purely Perp windows is of 1659. But more of the old materials remains – the S and N doorways and also something of the deep concave surrounds of the wide, straight-headed windows. – PULPIT. Plain C18. – COMMUNION RAIL. Flat openwork balusters, entirely Jacobean, yet dated 1677. – PLATE. Chalice and Paten, early C18.

EDGE HALL, 1½ m. E. A Jacobean house with a curious insertion of c.1700. The Jacobean house has five gables, two l. and three r. of a recess whose façade is the contribution of c.1700. This short piece has quoins of even length, windows with raised moulded frames, a balustrade, and a cupola. Fine large door-way with Corinthian pilasters and an open segmental gable. Behind this part is an entrance hall with a screen of Ionic col-umns and a staircase with (renewed) twisted balusters. In the Jacobean part to the l. is a room with the original plaster ceiling and chimneypiece.

GRAFTON HALL, a large Jacobean house, has recently disap-peared. The STABLES remain. They are of c.1884 by *John Birch* (who restored the house at the same time) and are not re-markable. Birch earlier designed THE WETREINS, a model farm ¾ m. NW.

TILSTONE FEARNALL

5060

ST JUDE. Built c.1836 at the expense of Lord Tollemache. Of the Commissioners' type, but not connected with them. Lancet front with two big corner pinnacles and a bellcote. Pairs of lancets along the sides. No aisles, no chancel. – MONU-MENTS. Gothic tablet to Vice-Admiral J. R. Delap Tollemache † 1837 by *Bedford*. – Gothic tablet (but different) to his wife † 1846.

TILSTONE LODGE. Handsome, rendered, early C19 three-bay house with a porch of two pairs of Tuscan columns.

TILSTONE HALL FOLLY is the name in the MHLG lists of a structure just s of Tilstone Hall which looks much more like the ruin of a Jacobean gatehouse *in situ* and once of two storeys. It has an archway in the middle and mullioned windows with pediments, and in addition odd pediments on the string course between ground floor and first floor.

TIMPERLEY
7080

Timperley is indistinguishable from Altrincham and part of the Manchester spread.

CHRIST CHURCH, Thorley Lane. 1849, neo-Norman, by *J. Bayley*. The transepts, also Norman, 1864–5 by *John Lowe*. The chancel is of the same date by the same architect, but much busier and also later-looking. Inside, the windows have terracotta details, and the walls an all-over tile pattern. – REREDOS. Early C20; worth noticing. – BOX PEWS.

TINTWISTLE
0090

At the bottom of the long, gently curving Manchester reservoirs which fill the Etherow valley.

CHRIST CHURCH. 1837. Lancets with Y-tracery, thin buttresses; thin w tower. Short low chancel.

TIRLEY GARTH *see* WILLINGTON

TIVERTON
5060

At the entrance to the village a nice group of two pairs of brick ESTATE COTTAGES at r. angles and between them the METH-ODIST CHAPEL with a jolly front of 1864.

TOAD HALL *see* GOOSTREY

TOFT
7070

ST JOHN EVANGELIST. 1854–5 by *W. & G. Habershon*. In the late C13 style. Nave and chancel and N aisle under a nave roof

extended at a different pitch. Ignorant and busy s w steeple –
all quite small.

T O F T   H A L L. A strange house whose architectural history would
deserve to be elucidated. Thirteen-bay E-plan front, with the
porch projection carried up as a tower. There is a second tower
immediately behind it on the opposite side. Stuccoed early in
the C 19, prior to which the building was of brick with stone
quoins, having the appearance of a C 17 house in which sash
windows had later been inserted. Fine wide avenue to the N E.

TRANMERE see BIRKENHEAD, p. 104

TUSHINGHAM 5040

S T   C H A D. 1862–3. The architect is not recorded. Walls of crazy
paving. Nave and transepts; chancel. The w tower is of 1896.
– S T A I N E D   G L A S S. By *Kempe*, w 1897; N transept 1904.

O L D   S T   C H A D, in the fields, ⅔ m. E S E. Built in 1689–91 by
donations especially from John Dod, a London mercer. Brick,
nave and chancel in one. Narrow w tower with pyramid roof.
Straight-headed two-light windows, but round-headed in the
E window. Tie beams inside, and above them charming openwork panels of complex star shapes. – F O N T. Jacobean. A fat
baluster and a tiny bowl. Could this not be a bedpost later
adapted? – P U L P I T. A real three-decker. – S C R E E N. The dado
of flat balusters. – Two family P E W S. – Plain, honest-to-good-
ness B E N C H E S. – M O N U M E N T. Thomas Vernon † 1833. Big
Grecian tablet by *Spence*.

(T U S H I N G H A M   H A L L, 1 m. S E. Symmetrical stuccoed front
with Gothic porch, dating from a remodelling of *c.* 1815.
Late C 17 staircase, brought in. E H)

TWEMLOW 7060

(T W E M L O W   H A L L. C 17 and 1817. Brick, five bays. Late C 17
staircase with twisted balusters. M H L G)

UPTON (WIRRAL) see BIRKENHEAD, p. 104

UPTON 4060

Upton is suburban Chester, and an affluent suburb.

H O L Y   A S C E N S I O N. 1852–4 by *James Harrison*. w tower with
recessed spire, nave and chancel. The transepts are of 1958
and 1967 (by *A. C. Bennett* of the *Design Group Partnership*)

and help a great deal. The style is early C14. – STAINED
GLASS. By *Kempe* W 1883, E 1885.*

CHESTER ZOO. The house in the centre, called OAKFIELD, of
1892 is a rebuilding by *H. Beswick*. Earlier a ballroom had
been added by *Ould*, who did a near-by LODGE in 1884. The
house is brick, with dark diapering. Elizabethan, and nothing
special. The STABLES with their steep pavilion roof really have
more to offer.

DEVA HOSPITAL. The main block is of 1827–9 by *William Cole*
– seventeen bays long, of brick, a basement and two storeys.
Slightly projecting end pavilions, and equally projecting centre raised by half a storey. Pediment over the centre. Ionic
porch.

WINDMILL, Mill Lane, S of the church. The tower of a tower-
mill.

UTKINTON

5060

UTKINTON HALL. The home of the Done family. To the road
gatepiers and a front with details of *c.*1700, e.g. wooden cross
windows. Brick, with stone quoins, etc., but set on an earlier
stone basement which has mullioned windows. Further back
a room in whose middle stands an octagonal wooden pier which
goes up into the first floor. It looks Perp and must have belonged to something on a large scale. For the staircase *see* Tarporley, Old Rectory, p. 351.

VALE ROYAL

6060

Vale Royal was founded by Edward I for Cistercians. The building
of the ABBEY was begun in 1277. It is a late foundation as
Cistercian settlements go, and it was the largest in England.
Hardly anything, however, is visible above ground. The so-
called Nun's Grave has made use of a base which with its four
main attached shafts and four minor attached shafts‡ looks
convincingly late C13. Other fragments used in the Nun's
Grave are a C17 column and the head of a churchyard cross
with the Crucifixion. The Nun's Grave might well be where
the altar of the church was. From there one can take one's
bearings. The present house stands S of the site of the church.
The cloister roughly corresponded to the area enclosed by the
main block of the house and the SE wing. The W end of the
church was slightly W of the W end of the NW wing of the house.

* And three more of 1871–3.
‡ But at one corner it is triple instead.

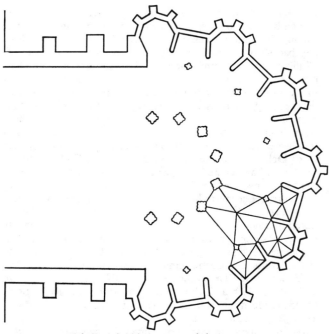

Vale Royal Abbey, east end, begun 1359.

The church was *c*.420 ft long. It had nave and aisles, transepts with the usual Cistercian straight-ended chapels attached to their E, three N and three S, and a unique E end, the contract for the building of which (by *William of Helpeston*) is dated 1359. It consisted of an apsidal choir with ambulatory and seven separate radiating chapels of six sides of a heptagon connected by smaller, nearly rectangular chapels with slightly tapering short sides. There is no really similar Cistercian E end anywhere, and it is a great shame that the result of the excavations is not indicated on the grass.

At the Dissolution the site went to Sir Thomas Holcroft. In 1616 it came to Lady Cholmondeley, and the Cholmondeleys Lords of Delamere held it into the C20. The HOUSE is large and has a façade of the E-type. I.e. there is a main block with a porch and SW and NW wings. There is also a long SE wing, so that the plan is really of H-shape with one arm missing. An illustration of 1616 shows the present plan form existing, but with longer front wings and completely irregular elevations, and with the main entrance, reached by a large outer staircase, leading right into the centre of the great hall. This is a mode of approach entirely un-Elizabethan and very rare still by 1630 (cf. Chillingham, Northumberland). All along the façade are giant pilasters, a motif used in the Elizabethan period at Kirby and in the mid C17 often, and they and the windows may be of this date, though there is reason to suppose that they are C18. Similar elevational treatment is applied to the wings, but these show different, smoother ashlaring than the recessed centre, and they were indeed remodelled by Thomas Cholmondeley, later Lord Delamere, in the late C18 or early C19.* The fronts of the wings have canted bay windows and mullions and transoms – a remarkably early instance of Elizabethan revivalism. The entrance seems to have been moved from first- to ground-floor level at the same time, and the present crude Gothic porch is almost certainly the C16 or early C17 one re-used. Its former position is occupied by a canted bay similar to those in the wings. The SE wing was half-timbered above a stone base said to contain monastic remains. It seems, however, to have been altered by *Blore* in the 1830s, and the present wing, large and gabled, with a clock turret, seems to be entirely of 1860. On the E side of the main block is a pretty porch and oriel dated 1877. By *John Douglas*.‡

As one enters the main door, one is in lowish rooms gothicized evidently in the late C18 or early C19. To the S is the main staircase, with heavy twisted balusters and heavy turned newel posts – say *c.*1670–80. This now forms the approach to the great hall, the decoration of which is partly C19 – the doorcases – and partly yet later. The big timber arches appear in Joseph Nash's picture and the whole roof is there much more richly decorated. In the SW wing is the dining room, with a coved ceiling and late C18 decoration. However, the splendid doorcase with columns and pediment looks 1750 and is hence probably *ex situ*. N of the great hall is a room with assorted C16–17 woodwork, brought in. The best piece is a smallish relief of the Annunciation, from the wing of an altar, Flemish, *c.*1500. In the Victorian SE wing one room has some poor Early Renaissance panels with heads and roundels.

The main DOOR is medieval.

* 1796 according to Lysons.

‡ The account of the house thus far owes much to Mr Hubbard, who also suggests that the 1860 wing may be a very early work of *Douglas*.

½ m. NE the VALE ROYAL VIADUCT of the Grand Junction Railway, opened in 1837. Of stone.

WADE'S GREEN HALL see CHURCH MINSHULL

WALLASEY

3090

INTRODUCTION

Wallasey has a little over 100,000 inhabitants, and it is a County Borough, but it is not a town. It is an appendix of Birkenhead which is an appendix of Liverpool. Or, to put it another way, it is a number of overgrown villages plus New Brighton. New Brighton has undeniable character; nothing else has. There is for instance no centre. The parish church lies about a mile and a half from the town hall, and in between it is nearly all dormitory. Development began with the steam ferry to Seacombe, and this started in 1823. For the DOCKS see Birkenhead. The following description therefore treats Wallasey all as one, except for New Brighton.

CHURCHES

ST HILARY, Claremount Road, Wallasey Village. The church was rebuilt in 1858–9 by *W. & J. Hay*. Of the old church the tower remains, C13 below, with blocked arches to W and N, and Henry VIII bell-openings, i.e. with arched uncusped lights. Money was given for the tower in 1527. The Victorian church is big and has a crossing tower (with stair-turret) and fussy tracery. Goodhart-Rendel noted: 'Extremely ill-detailed . . . typical Victorian bathos on a large scale.'

Wallasey Village lies below to the W, and in BRECK ROAD, a little to the S, No. 180 is the OLD GRAMMAR SCHOOL, dated 1799.

ST ALBAN (R.C.), Mill Lane, Wallasey, ¾ m. SE of the parish church. 1852–3 by *Stephen R. Eyre* and *J. A. Hansom*. With a NW steeple and an interior of no interest.

Close to the church is the WATER TOWER, a substantial piece with Norman detail. It dates from 1860.

ALL SAINTS. *See* New Brighton.

CHRIST CHURCH, Upton Road, Moreton, 2½ m. SW of the parish church. 1862–3 by *Cunningham & Audsley*. Ignorant details and a niggly SW steeple. Goodhart-Rendel found 'the detail spiky', and the proportions 'odiously bad'.

ST COLUMBA, at the s end of Seabank Road, Egremont, $1\frac{1}{4}$ m. E. 1902–23 by *C. E. Deacon*. Hard red brick, no tower. In the details some influence of the Arts and Crafts, especially in the interior, which is much more interesting than the exterior. Two bold arches run across separating the choir from the nave and the sanctuary. The piers are of odd shape. Their capitals were intended to be carved. Where the carving has been done it is decidedly Art Nouveau. Passage aisles; canted ceiling. – FONT. Latest Grecian with a spreading Doric shaft as its stem.

EMMANUEL. *See* New Brighton.

ENGLISH MARTYRS (R.C.), St George's Road, $\frac{1}{4}$ m. NW. By *F.X. Velarde*, 1952–3. Light brick, with a SE campanile. Much decoration with sculptured figures, even on window mullions. Round-arched windows, in the high clerestory arranged not in a row but four cruciformly disposed, then two single, then again four cruciform etc. – an odd idea. Low round piers inside, and jagged decoration in the 1925 style.

ST JOHN, Liscard Road, the parish church of Egremont, $1\frac{1}{8}$ m. ESE. 1832–3 by *H. Edwards*. Externally this is without question the finest church at Wallasey. It is ashlar-faced, with a five-bay front to which is attached a portico of Greek Doric columns with pediment. A heavy attic terminates the composition. The sides have six slender pedimented windows. The interior suffers from being deprived of its galleries and from the remodelling of 1892. The church is aligned on the wide CHURCH STREET, which in Mortimer's time, i.e. in 1845, had 'many excellent buildings'. It has not now.

OUR LADY STAR OF THE SEA (R.C.), Wheatland Lane, Seacombe, $1\frac{1}{2}$ m. SE. 1888–9 by *Edmund Kirby*. No tower; apse with geometrical tracery. The w front is the most successful element. Large rose set in a chamfered giant frame.

ST LUKE, Breck Road, Poulton, $\frac{3}{4}$ m. SSW. 1899–1900 by *Harry May*. – FONT from St Hilary. Norman, drum-shaped, with blank arcading.

ST MARY, Withens Lane, Liscard, $\frac{7}{8}$ m. E. 1876–7 by *E. W. Nobbs*, with *Grayson* as a consultant. A sensible, sound exterior. w tower; Perp tracery. Without aisles, but with transepts. Disappointing inside.

ST NICHOLAS, Groveland Road. 1910–11 by *J. Francis Doyle*. Big, rock-faced, with a central tower (with stair-turret) and Perp details. Routine interior.

ST PAUL, St Paul's Road, Seacombe, $1\frac{1}{2}$ m. SE. 1846–7 by the

Hay brothers, enlarged in 1859 and 1891. Nothing of note.
NW steeple; style of 1300.

(SACRED HEART (R.C.), Moreton. 1957 by *Reynolds & Scott*.
Gothic. EH)

EGREMONT BAPTIST CHURCH, Liscard Road, close to St John.
1924–6 by *J. E. Bladon*. Surprising for a Baptist church. Light
brick, Romanesque, with a campanile.

TRINITY METHODIST CHURCH, Manor Road, Egremont, E
of St John. Brick and red terracotta. Perp. Façade with a SW
turret.

PRESBYTERIAN CHURCH, Seabank Road, Egremont, 1 m. E.
1907–8 by *Briggs, Wolstenholme & Thornely*. Large. Arts and
Crafts Gothic with a big NW tower. Good inside as well as out,
and excellently composed with the hall at r. angles and in a
Tudor style with mullioned and transomed windows.

MEMORIAL UNITARIAN CHURCH, Manor Road, Liscard, ¾ m.
E. 1898–9 by *Waring & Rathbone*. A low, asymmetrical, secu-
lar-looking building with a large mullioned and transomed
window, a turret, and a porch or loggia set at an angle. (On the
wall behind the communion table are panels of *Harold Rathbone*'s so-called Della Robbia ware, manufactured at his Birkenhead Pottery Works. Some of the furnishings were decorated by *Bernard Sleigh* of the *Bromsgrove Guild*. Electric
light fittings by *Walter Gilbert*.)★

PUBLIC BUILDINGS

TOWN HALL, Brighton Road, Egremont. 1914–20 by *Briggs,
Wolstenholme & Thornely*. Spectacularly overlooking the Mersey, and a strikingly monumental building for so unmonu-
mental a town. Fifteen by nineteen bays, ashlar, with rusticated
ground floor, giant upper columns and pilasters in strategic
positions, and in the middle a high tower with, at the top, four
porticoes, and then stepped back a copper cap. (On the first
floor is a suite of rooms in *Beaux Arts* Classical with Neo-
Grec detailing. The Civic Hall, with tunnel-vaulted ceiling,
occupies the street frontage. It lacks something of its original
display, with the organ not having been reinstated after bomb
damage. Behind the hall is a circular reception room, the principal staircase, and, overlooking the river, the council chamber. EH)

Opposite is a jolly Gothic pub, THE BRIGHTON. Asymmetrical, with foliate details round the porch. Built in 1886.

★ Thanks are due to Mr Roger Billcliffe for providing this information.

POLICE STATION, Manor Road, Liscard, ¾ m. E. Built c.1890. Quite large and quite enterprising. Brick and stone trim with a domed angle turret, shaped gable, mullioned and transomed windows, and a big doorway with columns and segmental pediment – i.e. all in all a mixture of English C17 elements.

FERRY BUILDINGS, Seacombe. 1930–3 by *L. St G. Wilkinson*, the Borough Surveyor. In the uneventful simplified Classical of the twenties. Brick and stone dressings.

CENTRAL LIBRARY, Earlston Gardens, ¾ m. NE. 1910–11 by *R. B. MacColl & G. E. Tonge*. Behind is a house of c.1840 in the Tudor style.

COLLEGE OF FURTHER EDUCATION, Withens Lane. This is the old building of the Grammar School, 1907–10 by *Willink & Thicknesse*, symmetrical, Neo-Georgian, brick, with a cupola, and some good new extensions of 1959–61 and 1969–70 (by *W. P. Clayton*, the Borough Architect).

SCHOOL OF SCIENCE AND ART, Central Park, Egremont, 1 m. SW. Originally the house of Sir John Tobin. It is a serious classical design, probably of c.1830. Five by six bays. Porch of two pillars and two columns with pediment, middle window with pediment on pilasters. Round the corner a two-bay pediment, and below it a pair of windows with pilasters under one pediment.

WALLASEY GRAMMAR SCHOOL, Birket Avenue, Leasowe, 1½ m. WSW. By *Richard Sheppard, Robson & Partners*, 1966–8. A very simple plan, and consequently the main façade symmetrical. That on the entrance side the corners do not comply with that symmetry is a pity. The plan provides an entrance hall in the middle of that front with on the l. the assembly hall, on the r. an inner courtyard visible from the l. façade by way of a loggia. Most of the teaching rooms are upstairs. The gymnasium is connected with the main building by a covered way. The buildings are of load-bearing brick construction with brick and timber facing.

MANOR ROAD SCHOOL, Manor Road, Liscard, 1 m. E. By *Kirby*, 1905.

HOME FOR AGED MARINERS, Seabank Road, Egremont, ⅝ m. NW of the Town Hall. 1882–91 by *David Walker*. Not of architectural value. Brick and stone, symmetrical, with a mid-tower carrying tourelles and a spire.

RAILWAYMEN'S CONVALESCENT HOME. This is LEASOWE CASTLE, Leasowe, 2 m. W. The house looks confusing now. It started life as a 'standing', i.e. a stand for watching races, built by Ferdinando Earl of Derby in 1593. It was just an octagonal tower. Very soon after, however, in the four diagonals square gabled attachments were built. Two only remain. The house then was one of those with a decided pattern in plan. At some stage an extra storey was added to the tower, and in 1818 *Foster* of Liverpool enlarged the house. By him is the symmetrical castellated entrance front and the tower behind, higher than the original one.

LEASOWE LIGHTHOUSE. 1824. The datestone of 1763 belonged to its predecessor. A tall brick tower, looking sad now, out of operation.

(E. R. SQUIBB & SONS LTD, Reeds Lane, Moreton. A recent factory by *Gerald Beech & Partners*. Pre-cast concrete facing. Separate office block with green-tinted glass curtain walling. EH)

NEW BRIGHTON

3090

James Atherton of Liverpool in 1830 bought 127 acres to develop them as a resort, and a prospectus, issued probably in 1832, stated: 'As New Brighton is likely to become a favourite and fashionable Watering Place, several Gentlemen have proposed to erect there a handsome Hotel, and a convenient Dock or Ferry . . . and to establish a communication by Steam Packets between that place and Liverpool.' It went on to say that 'The proprietors intend to avail themselves of the natural advantages afforded by the undulations of the ground and to erect Villas on such sites that one shall not interrupt the view of another,' and in 1847 Mortimer reported that, 'nature, so far as regarded scenery and local attractions, had done wonders towards the adaption of the ground to the purposes of a marine residence. Rising out of the sea by a succession of lofty ridges it offered an inducement for the erection of villas, retreating one above another, without the view from the upper ranges being in the slightest degree intercepted, by the houses below them.' However, despite an ambitious street plan being laid out and many villas being built, the speculation never really got off the ground. No grand hotels were built, nor terraces, and the New Brighton of the last hundred, and especially seventy or eighty, years is a miniature Blackpool chiefly for Liverpool day trippers.

Some large villas in landscaped grounds have vanished, and there has also been demolition in the two chief early streets – MONTPELLIER CRESCENT and WELLINGTON ROAD. Some of the nicest houses are gabled and bargeboarded, stuccoed, but the two best remaining of the early villas are ashlar-faced. One is No. 33 Montpellier Crescent of *c.*1841, with a porch of four fluted Ionic columns and above it a recessed window below a small pediment. The sea frontage has a segmental centre projection with a segmental bay window on either side. The other is REDCLIFFE in Wellington Road, by *Elmes,** *c.*1845. Tudor, with a balcony on arcading to the sea. Recently mutilated. In ST GEORGE'S MOUNT on the topmost ridge is an Italianate house with a tower.

To-day's New Brighton appears at the end of Wellington Road, not in an architecturally satisfactory guise. PORTLAND COURT of 1938–9 by *H. Thearle* is bad 1930s, with long window bands. CLIFF ESTATE by *Stephenson, Young & Partners* of 1962 is two high blocks, bad too.

ALL SAINTS, Hose Side Road. By *Sir Giles Gilbert Scott,* 1927–39; incomplete. Light brick. Broad w tower with a very tall window with flowing tracery. High clerestory. Chancel 1963, a poor substitute. Broad nave with narrow passage aisles. Rendered walls, with some stone dressings, particularly the short circular piers of the arcades. The arches are slightly pointed, though they appear semicircular. Flat timber ceiling with decorated beams. Not a notable or an inspired work.

EMMANUEL, Seabank Road. 1899–1909 by *C. E. Deacon.* Very red brick; no tower. Recognizable Deacon characteristics, but also many oddities, e.g. the transeptal arrangement. The transepts are two bays deep from w to E, and the arcade acknowledges that by raising the apexes of the two arcade arches and introducing heavy piers. Capitals Art Nouveau.

ST JAMES, Victoria Road. By *Sir George Gilbert Scott,* 1854–6. NE steeple with thin broach-spire. Polygonal apse. Goodhart-Rendel writes very nicely: 'This is a perfectly decent church of which after a fortnight, I have forgotten all characteristics, except that it is large, "handsome", and typically Scott.' – PAINTINGS in the apse, and on the chancel walls and ceiling, on the walls apparently reduced in area. They look 1850s, but are of 1899 (by *A. D. Hemming*). – Of about the same time – 1897 – is the REREDOS (by the same).

   Opposite is the CHURCH HALL. This is of rustic brick, long and gabled. 1912–13 by *Sir E. Guy Dawber.*

ST NICHOLAS, Groveland Road. *See* above, p. 370.

ST PETER AND ST PAUL (R.C.), Atherton Street. 1932–5 by *E. Bower Norris.* Very large and ambitious, and a fine landmark,

---

* A discovery of Mr Hubbard.

but not really valuable as architecture. Light brick and much
stone, with a dome on a drum and two short w towers. Plan
and interior obviously derived from the Roman Gesù type,
but all internal mouldings, indeed all relief, is planed away –
modern by negative means.

Close to the church, a little to the w, is the much more 'real'
GORSEHILL WATER TOWER, round-arched, castellated, and
with a higher turret. 1902–5.

FORT PERCH ROCK. Sited off what is now Marine Promenade,
i.e. at the NE corner of the Wirral peninsula, guarding the
seaward approach to Liverpool. 1826–9 by Captain *John Sykes
Kitson*, R.E. A real fort, with four round angle towers and a
portal with columns. It looks C17 rather than C19. This and
the following are the beginning of architectural activity at New
Brighton – pre-Mr Atherton, it will be noted.

PERCH ROCK LIGHTHOUSE. 1827–30 by *John Foster Jun.* in
his capacity as Liverpool Corporation Surveyor.

TOWER. 1897–1900 by *Maxwell & Tuke*, who had built Blackpool tower in 1891–4. Both are (or were) lattice towers of steel.
But otherwise the New Brighton tower was a much more ambitious affair, 621 ft as against the 500 ft of Blackpool, and
rising from a very large, totally detached brick structure, a
square set diagonally and with chamfered corners to which
attachments were added with their own towers and turrets. It
was a thing thoroughly to amaze visitors from Liverpool.
Alas, the tower was taken down in 1919–21, and the rest has
been demolished after a fire in 1969.

FLORAL PAVILION, Marine Promenade. The iron porch, happily preserved, is of 1913.

WALTON SUPERIOR *see* HIGHER WALTON

WARBURTON   6080

Warburton is *Douglas* land. John Douglas built the church and
various other buildings for R. E. Egerton-Warburton. Douglas's
church outside the village was a replacement of the old church
in the village.

OLD ST WERBURGH. A lovable muddle, starting at once with
the confusing fact that the small tower is an E, not a W tower.
It is dated 1711, built of brick, and has a brick extension with
E archway. This was the hearse house. The N side of the church
is timber-framed, and the interior indeed has timber posts. But
the w and part of the s side are of stone and carry the proud
date 1645. What then is the date of the original building, as

preserved in the cosy interior ? Pre-Reformation or post-Reformation ? – FONT. Plain, octagonal, with an inscription and the small date 1603. – PULPIT. Jacobean, with the usual two tiers of blank arches. – COMMUNION RAIL. Round three sides of the altar space. C17, with balusters. But how can it have a bench all along the inner side ? The answer is – so the Rev. R. S. Moore tells me – that they are seats for the choir and were put there in 1857. – STAINED GLASS. E window by *Wailes*, 1857 (TK).

NEW ST WERBURGH. By *Douglas*, 1883–5. A broad, strong building – no gimmicks, no profusion. Solid N tower, wide nave, goodly roof, the window details a free Dec or a free Perp – it cannot be said with certainty.★

CHURCH HOUSE, next to the church. 1889 by *Douglas*. The Douglas motifs are easily seen, e.g. the stepped brick lozenges.

BENT FARM, opposite the church. A heavy restoration and re-modelling by *Douglas*, 1880.

Also by *Douglas* the SCHOOL, 1871–2, the POST OFFICE, 1893, and several village houses.

WARDLE

6050

Here is the junction of the former Chester and Nantwich Canal with the branch to Middlewich to join the Trent & Mersey Canal. Handsome bridge with sweeping parapets.

WARDLE OLD HALL. Early C18, brick. Five bays, two storeys, hipped roof. Giant pilasters each carrying a triglyph, at the angles and flanking the middle bay. Pedimented doorway.

WARMINGHAM

7060

ST LEONARD. The W tower is of 1715, of dark brick with stone dressings and alternately bulgy quoins. Still recognizably C18, despite a gothicizing of 1899. The church was timber-framed but rebuilt to designs of *Hussey* in 1870. He chose the Perp style, being very progressive or very old-fashioned. – (Dull interior, with narrow aisles erupting into would-be transepts. – No trace of the *Clayton & Bell* PAINTING on the W wall which is said to have existed. – STAINED GLASS. S transept and E by *Maréchal & Champigneule* of Metz, 1870. – N transept and S aisle by *Heaton, Butler & Bayne*, 1878E. (H) – PLATE. Cup and Paten, London, 1663. – Rococo MONUMENT to William Vernon † 1732.

★ The Rev. R. S. Moore informs me of a FONT COVER of 1595, brought from the old church.

CHURCH HOUSE. A delightful late C16 or early C17 façade with closely set uprights and closely set diagonal braces forming double lozenges or, if you like, arrows upward and arrows downward.

w of the church a group of two pairs of cottages, and between them the BEAR'S PAW. One house is dated 1870. All are of brick and half-timbering, and especially the pub is very cheerfully done. The three belong to the Crewe Estate enterprises (cf. Crewe Hall, p. 191).

YEW TREE FARMHOUSE, Tetton, 1¾ m. NE. Quite small, and now isolated. Dated 1658. Timber-framed, with big baluster motifs and also ship's wheel motifs.

WARREN see GAWSWORTH

WAVERTON 4060

ST PETER. Perp w tower with C19 recessed pyramid roof. Nice doorway with decorated spandrels, a figure and shields above, and a big w window. But that probably belongs to the restoration of 1888.* Much else was done then; yet the timber-framing of the chancel must be original, and the windows, also of the clerestory, and the s doorway look convincingly Latish Perp or even post-Reformation. The nave roof is in fact dated 1635.

(The SCHOOL, 1877, was built at the expense of the first Duke of Westminster, and it can unhesitatingly be ascribed to *John Douglas*. Stone, with three gables against a high roof. School house partly half-timbered. A pleasant group is formed by church, school, and a FARMHOUSE which lies between them and which, although owing much to the C19, is apparently a C16 or C17 house restored. s of the church some EATON ESTATE COTTAGES dating from the 1860s, i.e. built for the second Marquess of Westminster. Those built for the first Duke include two pairs to the N by *Douglas & Fordham*, one of them dated 1889. N of the village is COTTON ABBOTS FARM, by *Douglas*, with the farmhouse dated 1873. The RAILWAY STATION (now closed), ¾ m. w of the village, was built for the Duke, expensively, in 1897. EH)

WEAVER BANK FARM see WIMBOLDSLEY

WEAVERHAM 6070

ST MARY. A Late Perp church with a bold, robust w tower and aisles. The tower is said to have been begun before 1485;

* (Which must undoubtedly have been by *Douglas*. EH)

otherwise all is later. The interior is impressive by the absence
of a chancel arch. There are thus five bays of arcades without
any break. All piers are octagonal, all capitals coarse. The first
three on the N side are smaller than the others. The aisles are
both wide, but of different width. The aisle windows are of
four lights, and so barren in design that one can understand
their date having been suggested as post-Reformation. The N
aisle has a good panelled roof of very low pitch. The three
parallel E windows are of more normal Perp motifs. (Restorations by *Salvin*, 1855, and *Douglas*, 1877. PF) – PANELLING
round the altar. Linenfold, i.e. probably *temp.* Henry VIII. –
Parclose SCREENS. 1636, with sparse balusters. – COMMUNION
RAIL. 1709; with twisted balusters. – PEWS. Incorporated in a
pew in the children's corner is part of the C16 screen. This
must be of *c.*1530, cf. the heads of a man and a woman. – The
sidesmen's pew re-uses the woodwork of the former three-
decker PULPIT, which was erected in 1774. – FONT. The font
is a short C13 column, the base typical of the date. The bowl
is later, C14 or C15. – CHANDELIER of brass; C18. – PLATE.
Queen Anne Ewer; Paten inscribed 1716, made in London. –
MONUMENT. Pretty tablet to George Wilbraham † 1852.

GRAMMAR SCHOOL (former), 38 Forest Street. C17, two-
storeyed, with three-light mullioned windows. The doorway
is close to the l. end. The school was founded in 1638.

GRANGE HOSPITAL. Part of the hospital is HEFFERSTON
GRANGE, brick, dated 1741. It is still Early Georgian, of
seven bays, with quoins of stones of even length and a recessed
three-bay centre. The doorway has a segmental pediment.
Handsome staircase ceiling with Rococo stucco decoration. A
similar stucco ceiling in a first-floor room. The STABLES have
normal quoins and a cupola.

4070
WERVIN

CHAPEL. Behind a farmhouse. Nothing certain seems to be
known about it. What remains is the E wall, but nothing of the
E window – i.e. just two cliffs of red sandstone.

WEST END *see* WISTASTON

2080
WEST KIRBY   [EH]

ST BRIDGET. Church Road. Nave, aisles, chancel (inclining to
the N), and N chancel aisle, all with gable roofs. The church
was almost completely rebuilt, and the S aisle was added, in

1869–70 by *Kelly & Edwards* of Chester. Further restored and a N porch added in 1876. Some C14 masonry survives, particularly in the S and E walls of the chancel, though the windows, including the reticulated tracery of the E window, are renewed. SEDILIA and PISCINA also renewed. C14 masonry in the N chancel aisle and adjoining vestry, including a trefoil-headed doorway. Some old work also in the N aisle. Late C15 or early C16 tower with pairs of two-light bell-openings. Its upper stages are unbuttressed and, except for panelled battlements and a W doorway with label-mould and tablet flower enrichment, etc., it is quite plain. The S porch has head-stops representing Queen Victoria and William Jacobson, Bishop of Chester, and at the W end of the N aisle is a Gladstone and Beaconsfield gargoyle. – SCREENS. Iron chancel screens by *C. E. Kempe.* – STAINED GLASS. All windows, except the two easternmost on the S of the chancel, are by *Kempe.* Ranging over almost forty years, and including much early work, they illustrate the development of his style. They include, e.g., chancel SW 1870; S aisle 1882; N aisle 1890–3; dormers 1906–7. – PAINTING. Over the chancel arch. 1906.*

ST ANDREW, Meols Drive. Begun in 1889–91 by *Douglas & Fordham* and completed in 1907–9 by *Douglas & Minshull.* Sandstone. Ashlar interior. Neo-Perp. Cruciform, with clerestory. The S transept forms a chapel and the N transept an organ chamber. The choir occupies the crossing, from the roof of which rises a diagonally-placed slate-hung spire, with four pinnacles at its base. The chancel roof is higher than that of the nave, which is higher than those of the transepts. The E crossing arch is higher than the S and N arches, which are higher than that on the W, and the detailing of the arches varies. Nave arcade columns octagonal. 'Nothing except the belfry is unusual,' wrote Goodhart-Rendel, 'but everything is satisfactory.' Very satisfactory. – REREDOS. 1911 by *Geoffrey Webb.* – STAINED GLASS. S transept, N aisle, and E windows by *Bryams*, a pupil of Kempe, whose influence is apparent.

COUNTY SECONDARY SCHOOL FOR GIRLS, Frankby Road, Newton. 1964–6 by *Edgar Taberner*, County Architect. Steel frame with curtain walling. Two three-storey classroom blocks and separate assembly hall etc.

GRANGE BEACON, Column Road. Built in 1841 as a landmark

---

* Professor A. R. Myers states that it is by *Kempe*, with wooden figures from Oberammergau.

to aid navigation of the Dee and Mersey channels. Unfluted Doric column with ball-finial.

WAR MEMORIAL, Grange Hill. 1922. An obelisk flanked by two bronze figures by *C. S. Jagger*.

In VILLAGE ROAD, E of the church, are a few C17 and C18 cottages, particularly THE NOOK, thatched and whitewashed. Beyond this village nucleus the remainder of West Kirby dates almost without exception from after the coming of the railway in 1878, when the line was extended from Hoylake. A link was established with Liverpool in 1888. HILBRE HOUSE, near the shore, beyond the S end of SOUTH PARADE, does however pre-date the railway, and at the head of WARWICK DRIVE is KIRBY MOUNT, where the house now known as No. 1 Kirby Mount has a pedimented frontage of *c.*1810 (MHLG) with a block of 1709 at the rear. Adjoining is a good group of recent houses. The layout is by *Robert Gardner-Medwin* and all the houses are by him (including No. 6 for himself) except for No. 4, which is by *Carl Pinfold* for himself. No. 2 was converted from former outbuildings.

To the NW, in the mouth of the Dee estuary, is HILBRE ISLAND. Until the Dissolution, a cell of Chester Abbey was maintained here, and a fragment of a Saxon cross has been found.

WESTON
Near Crewe

7050

ALL SAINTS. 1838 (Kelly) or 1842 (White). With a terrible apsidal chancel of 1893. The church is of brick and the nave has lancet windows. No tower. – STAINED GLASS. In the apse late *Morris* glass.

VICARAGE. 1846. Elizabethan, and much more serious than the church.

WESTON HALL. Dated 1677 in brick numerals. Five bays, two storeys, hipped roof.

HOLLYHEDGE FARM, ½ m. N, i.e. ½ m. SSE of Crewe Hall. 1647. A good timber-framed house with only a little decoration of ogee-sided lozenges.

WESTON
S of Runcorn

5080

ST JOHN EVANGELIST. 1895–8 by *Douglas & Fordham* (GR). Blackened stone. Very short W tower with short broach-spire. One set of lucarnes. The chancel is higher than the nave. Lancet windows, also in groups. (Good interior. Ashlar, with

few mouldings. The embraced w tower has E, N, and S arches.
Also arches l. and r. of it forming a triple-arcaded end to the
nave. Narrow N passage aisle with timber posts and beams. –
STAINED GLASS. E window by *Kempe*, 1898. EH)

OLD HALL, S of the church. 1607; much restored. Two gables,
recessed centre with porch in the r. re-entrant angle. Mullioned and transomed windows. (E of this MANOR FARM-
HOUSE, C17, with mullioned windows. EH)

ICI OFFICES, Heath. 1957–68 by *Sir Frederick Gibberd &
Partners*. Very large, of three parallel three-storeyed ranges
connected by a three-storeyed cross wing. In the SE corner is
the square one-storeyed canteen. Grouping and details are both
sound and attractive. The structure is pre-cast concrete columns and beams. The facing is reconstructed Portland stone,
timber, and coloured glass.

CHRIST CHURCH, Weston Point. Right in the docks. Built in
1841 by the Trustees of the Weaver Navigation for the use of
the watermen. Thin w tower with broach-spire. Nave and
transepts. Geometrical tracery.

(The DOCKS at Weston Point adjoin the Manchester Ship Canal.
They originated, however, in connexion with the Weaver Navigation, which dates from 1721, but which was extended to
Weston from Frodsham by means of *Telford*'s Weaver Cut,
authorized in 1807. EH)

WETTENHALL   6060

ST DAVID. 1870 by *J. Redford* and *J. A. Davenport* (GR). Brick.

WHARTON   6060

CHRIST CHURCH. 1843 (Ormerod second ed.) or 1849 (Kelly).
Of small red stone, Perp, without aisles but with transepts
which, according to Kelly, are part of a former building. N
tower – the one unexpected motif. Altogether, the pre-archeo-
logical material is well handled.

WHATCROFT HALL *see* DAVENHAM

WHEELOCK   7050

CHRIST CHURCH. 1836–7. Brick, lancet windows, and a chancel
of 1903 by *Alfred Price*.

WHITEGATE   6060

ST MARY. By *Douglas*, 1874–5, at the expense of Lord Delamere,
replacing a church of 1728 whose S portal and gatepiers (dated

1736) remain. Inside, the octagonal timber piers go yet further back – to the original Perp church, which evidently was timber-framed. Douglas's church is placed so happily against trees on a hillside that it makes the perfect, comforting picture of the Victorian village church. Red brick and timber-framed E gables; heavily timbered lychgate exactly E of the E end. Timbered S porch too. Shingled spire of concave outline on the W tower. The nave roof sweeps down in one pitch over nave and aisles. Strong roof-timbers inside. – REREDOS and chancel arcading of c. 1876–7, much heavier, more High Victorian, clearly not by Douglas. – PLATE. Set given in 1832.

VICARAGE. 1878 by *Douglas*, and also paid for by Lord Delamere. It is ¼ m. NNW of the church, sited above a small lake.

WHITEHALL *see* HARTFORD

9060

WILDBOARCLOUGH

The most beautifully placed of all Cheshire villages. In a fold of the Peak, sheltered yet close to the wide spaces of the hills.

ST SAVIOUR. 1908–9. Low W tower. Nave with a dormer; chancel.

CRAG HALL. Early C19. Five-bay front continued l. and r. by big bows round the corners. Porch of four unfluted Ionic columns. The porch is reached up some steps. Handsome railings. The house was that of the manager of a cotton mill close to the church.

POST OFFICE. Originally part of Crag Mill, c.1770. Seven bays, three storeys, stone. In the middle bay an arched doorway, a window with triangular pediment over, a window with segmental pediment over that, and a broken pediment as the conclusion.

WILDERSPOOL *see* HIGHER WALTON

3070

WILLASTON
Wirral

CHRIST CHURCH. 1854 by *Fulljames & Walker* (GR). Nave and chancel; bellcote on the nave E gable. The nave roof is unusually steep and rests on very elaborate foliage corbels of stone. In 1926 *Bernard Miller* added a N aisle. The piers are no longer an imitation of the past. The roofs are somewhat mannered. – STAINED GLASS. The E window must be by *Wailes*. – S windows and a N window by *Kempe*.

WILLASTON HALL. A fine, compact Elizabethan front. Red

brick and red stone. Two square bay windows and a square porch in the middle. Three storeys and gables. Mullioned and transomed windows of three and four lights. The front is completely symmetrical, and the hall is indeed not only in the centre of the house but also approached centrally through the porch. Ormerod reports the date 1558 on a chimneypiece on the first floor. This is an extremely unlikely date for such an enlargement. One would not expect to find it before 1600, and even for 1610–20 it is still a rarity. (There is only one early chimneypiece on the first floor now, and it has no date. Maybe the date was painted on and misread for 1558. The date over the entrance was cut only in the C19. Staircase with crude newels and flat balusters and with strapwork on the string. E H).

WINDMILL, ½ m. NW. A high brick tower with cap. (1800. MHLG)

HADLOW WOOD, ¾ m. S. 1909–10 by *Woolfall & Eccles*.

WHITE GATES, Birkenhead Road. 1935 by *Hubert A. Thomas* – an early case of the C20 style in this part of England.

WILLASTON HALL *see* WILLASTON *and* WISTASTON

WILLINGTON

WILLINGTON HALL. A neo-Elizabethan square brick house of 1829. The brick has blue diapers. Straight gables on two sides, but on the principal side Dutch gables instead. The façades are symmetrical. The entrance front has a porch of four Tuscan columns, an entirely Georgian motif. Does it perhaps date from the time when a large extension of 1878 was removed?

TIRLEY GARTH, ¾ m. E. The *magnum opus* unquestionably of C. E. *Mallows*, an architect in the Voysey–Baillie-Scott succession and a brilliant draughtsman. Tirley Garth is a large house. It was begun *c.* 1906 – for one of the Monds of the firm which became ICI, and completed for R. A. Prestwich, a director of Burberry's. The 'garth' in Tirley Garth comes from the internal courtyard with cloister walks around, each side three depressed arches, nicely moulded. There are living ranges to S, W, and E, but on the N there is nothing behind the outer wall of the cloister. The centre is a sunk circular pond reached by curved steps. The main front, with a fine view to Beeston and Peckforton, is to the S, broad and high and symmetrical, with gables, the centre one of a steep personal shape. Beneath it is the big three-transomed bow window of the great hall. To the l. and r. a bay with a broad segment-arched window on the first floor, not a motif belonging to the Elizabethan or Jacobean style of most of the rest. The house is pebble-dashed with ample stone dressings. Mullioned and transomed windows. The entrance side is more informally composed and incorporates a big tower. The gardens, both formal and land-scaped (a delightful dell), are by *T. H. Mawson*. The great hall is in the s range and runs through two floors. It has an open timber roof and a gallery on three sides. There are plenty of charming details, e.g. the hidden staircase to the gallery. In the w range was the billiard room. This has a shallow plaster dome, and there are two smaller domes at the two ends of the corridor behind the hall serving as lobbies. The SOUTH LODGE, the NORTH LODGE, and a HOUSE near the North Lodge are all Mallows too, and more on the scale he had usu-ally to deal with.

8080

WILMSLOW

ST BARTHOLOMEW. Still with views into fields to the w. The impression, as usual in Cheshire, is of a Perp church, and one has to look carefully to notice the Dec N and s doorways with their typical mouldings. Dec is confirmed by the arcades (octagonal piers, double-chamfered arches), except for the chancel arches, which with their crude capitals must be Latest Perp. In fact the remodelling was began *c.* 1490, and the chan-cel was rebuilt by Henry Trafford, the then rector, in 1522. That must be about the date of the nave clerestory too (mull-ioned windows with uncusped arched lights). Low w tower of *c.* 1490 etc. with Victorian battlements and pinnacles. N organ chamber by *Brakspear*, who restored the church in 1862–3. By *Crowther*, 1878, are the NE vestry and the s porch (the latter said to be to the original design), and probably also the replacement of the parapet and pinnacles of the tower. Chancel clerestory by *Bodley & Garner*, 1898. On the s side is the family pew of 1700 of the Hawthorne family. Separate pews inside it. – SCREENS. The parclose screens are mostly original Perp work. Single-light divisions with tracery, an ornamental frieze, and a cresting. (The chancel screen, though incorpora-ting old work, is largely by *Bodley*, though now reduced.) – STAINED GLASS. The three *Morris & Co.* windows of 1920 by *Dearle** are a come-down after Morris himself and Burne-Jones. – Some fragments of original glass in the s pew and the

---

* Information from Mr Sewter.

tracery of two N aisle windows. – MONUMENTS. In the N aisle
defaced effigies of Humphrey Newton † 1536 and wife. In two
ogee-headed recesses. – Henry Trafford † 1537. Recumbent
effigy, also defaced. – (Brass to Robert Booth † 1460 and wife.
His figure is 3¾ in. long. At the time of writing, on the chancel
floor.)

(ST JOHN EVANGELIST, Lindow. 1873–4 by *J. W. Beaumont*.)

FRIENDS' MEETING HOUSE, Altrincham Road. 1830, when the
Quakers no longer built so humbly as at first. Five bays, brick,
with arched windows and the doorway in the middle.

UNITARIAN (originally Presbyterian) CHAPEL, Dean Row, 1½ 56
m. E. 1693, and very similar to those at Macclesfield and
Knutsford. Brick, oblong, with two tiers of two-light mullioned
windows set regularly. In the two end bays entrances on ground
and gallery level, the upper entrances reached by stairs rising
along the façade. – BOX PEWS. – The PULPIT was originally in
the middle of the long side facing the entrances.

Of the town as such, a village developed into a Manchester dormitory area, little need be said. The STATION has recently
been rebuilt, quite crisply and with a curtain-walled offices
attachment. BARCLAYS BANK have a new building too, at the
corner of Grove Street. It is by *Green, Lloyd & Son* of London,
1963–4, and is easily remembered. Two storeys all of pre-cast
concrete members, just posts and segmental arches all the way
through. New shopping terraces in Manchester Road (ST
ANNE'S HOUSE by *Neodix Construction*, 1963–6) are good too.

COUNTY GRAMMAR SCHOOL FOR GIRLS, Dean Row Road.
By *W. S. Hattrell & Partners*, 1965. Brick with white fascia-
boards. Well composed and detailed.

In addition three country houses now in the town.

HAWTHORN HALL, Hall Road, is dated 1698. It is of brick,
many-gabled, and has a pretty cupola and windows with very
close glazing. It is good to look at, though conservative for its
date. (The staircase has twisted balusters. MHLG)

FULSHAW HALL, Alderley Road, is of 1684. Brick and stone
dressings. Symmetrical, with two gables and stone cross windows. The door-hood is probably later.[*] Victorian wing.

POWNALL HALL, Carwood Road. The house was initially a
plain five-bayer, ashlar on the front with a one-bay pedimental gable and a porch. It was built *c.*1830–5. Then, in 1886,
Henry Boddington, the brewer, started on it with the help of
William Ball of *Ball & Elce* of Manchester. Whether they

---

[*] Earwaker refers to an enlargement and alterations *c.*1733.

13 + C.

or he chose the remarkably progressive team for the decorating and furnishing, we don't know. Foremost among them is the *Century Guild*, which had been founded four years before by Mackmurdo, Horne, and Selwyn Image. The Guild was responsible for furniture, metalwork (wild vegetable forms of typical *Mackmurdo* character), and general decorating such as plaster ceilings. The result is unique in its presentation of the most advanced the Arts and Crafts could do in 1886–90. By 1891, when the *Art Journal* published the house in great detail, all was essentially ready.* The façade received a lot of pretty, small-scale Gothic bits of decoration. *De Morgan* supplied tiles, *Shrigley & Hunt* stained glass, the most delightful of it that of the Signs of the Zodiac in foliage in the hall. This hall has massive roof timbers and some timbering in the walls as well. On the fireplace are inscribed the days of the week with their Anglo-Saxon names. Altogether Mr Boddington loved inscriptions, and they are found all over the house, from one recording the names of the designers and craftsmen to the names of the bedrooms. In the former library are plaster panels of the Seven Ages of Man by *J. D. Watson*, who also painted the scenes from 'As you like it' in the cove of the overmantel. The former dining room has a big Century Guild chimneypiece with atlantes by *Creswick* and a painted panel by *Image*. The staircase has unfortunately been changed. It had on the intermediate landing a big alcove with seating and a fireplace, and the glass by *Shrigley & Hunt* (the Four Winds) was visible immediately behind it. There was also stained skylight glazing. On the upper floor the finest piece is the former nursery hall with an open timber roof and two levels at one end: music room and school room. It has, however, been subdivided. Of the bedrooms the most attractive is Fytton, which is in two parts intricately subdivided, with a bed alcove and a fireplace alcove. The CHAPEL has been pulled down, and the PICTURE GALLERY altered and denuded, though some original woodwork remains. Mr Boddington had, among many others, thirty-three paintings by Ford Madox Brown.

6060

WIMBOLDSLEY

LEA HALL, 2 m. SW of Middlewich church. Early C18; the perfect brick box, delightful if just a little funny to look at.

* I am deeply grateful to Peter Howell, who discovered the article and the house, for allowing me the use of his unpublished discovery. There are further illustrations in the *British Architect*, vol. 36, 1891.

Brick, of five bays in a 2–1–2 rhythm, with a big hipped roof and a doorway with open scrolly pediment. Slightly Victorianized. Re-set gatepiers.

WEAVER BANK FARM, 1 m. SSW of Lea Hall. By *Douglas*,* *c*.1869. Brick with timber-framed gables. Mullioned windows with arched lights.

WIMBOLDS TRAFFORD

4070

WIMBOLDS TRAFFORD HALL. The date 1756 is on a rainwater head. It is a five-bay brick house of two and a half storeys, with quoins at the angles of the centre bay. Doorway with four columns. Round the corner the staircase window, Venetian, and above it a tripartite lunette. Fine staircase of three twisted and decorated balusters for each step and carved tread-ends.

WINCLE

9060

In the Peak; reached on steep roads.

ST MICHAEL. The tower is of *c*. 1820, the rest of 1882 by *Edward Witts*.

WINCLE GRANGE, ½ m. SW. An odd house. It has on three sides pre-Reformation windows, i.e. straight-headed windows with cusped lights, but no convincing plan can be made out.

CLEULOW CROSS, in a group of trees on a hill 1 m. NW. Of the round-shaft type.

POST OFFICE TOWER, 2 m. NW. Concrete with a round shaft. It is 225 ft high and belongs to the telephone and television microwave network.

WINNINGTON

6070

WINNINGTON HALL now belongs to ICI. Their Winnington works was the beginning of their empire. It was started in 1873 by John Brunner (born in 1842), son of a Swiss father, and the German Ludwig Mond (born in 1839), and their statues of bronze stand rightly in front of the Research Laboratory, Mond by *Lanteri*, 1912 in a greatcoat with a big floppy hat, Brunner by *Goscombe John*, 1922 in his morning coat, much more forthcoming. Winnington Hall belonged to Lord Stanley of Alderley and he sold it to the young firm. The LODGES of Winnington Hall indeed now lead right into the works. The house is at the back timber-framed of the C16 or C17 and much

* Information from Mr Howell.

restored (smooth front, five even gables), at the front a beautiful addition of the late c18 (the date is perhaps *c.* 1780) which
may possibly have been intended as the first part of a complete
rebuilding. Seven bays, one and a half storeys, ashlar, with
very sparing decoration – just panels with garlands above the
main windows. Round both corners a canted bay window. The
junction with the old work, which is shorter, is not so satisfactory, but there is a large Venetian window there. The room
behind was an Orangery – a strange thing to have as part of a
house. One of the *Wyatts* has been suggested as the architect
and seems more than likely. The work is probably too early
to be by *Lewis Wyatt*, but either *James* or *Samuel* could have
been responsible, and the latter would seem probable, if one
compares with Tatton Park and Doddington. Exquisite interiors, especially the Octagon Room, the anteroom to it with
an apse, the dining room with a larger apse, and especially the
hall or gallery along the middle of the house, with four groin-
vaults and lunette lights. Attached columns and niches along
the walls. *Darcy Braddell* restored the house *c.*1920 and did
some redecorating; it is not quite clear how much. The black
Wedgwood vases anyway are of his time. Above the Octagon
Room is another decorated room, and the anteroom of this has
an apse towards the window and a screen of two columns towards the Octagon. Is that original too ?*

Brunner and Mond were pioneers in manufacturers' responsi-
bility for the well-being of their employees. As early as 1889
Brunner addressed a mass-meeting of the workers urging them
to join a trade union. The firm became a limited company in
1881 and ICI in 1926.

St Luke. This must be one of the most disappointing churches
Pearson ever designed. It is true, it lacks its projected s tower,
but even so the brick is dull to look at, and little has been made
of the possibilities of the fall of the site. The interior is exposed brick too, and more satisfying. The nave has no aisles.
The style is of course c13, and the church was built in 1896–7.

6060   WINSFORD

Winsford and Over are one and the same. One can't separate
them. Over is the w fringe, with the church on its own at the s
end and Delamere Street at the NW end, Winsford is the rest,

---

* For an apse towards a window cf. Doddington. In the c19 Winnington
Hall was a girls' school, and it is the one where Ruskin spent holidays, happy
to be surrounded by adolescent girls.

with the new shopping and its own little church. It is a centre of the Cheshire salt industry.

ST CHAD, Church Hill, Over. A remodelling took place in 1543, and most of the church is Perp, but the E window with reticulated tracery is Dec. Is it original? The architectural history of the church is not quite clear. Perp W tower with three-light bell-openings, built as late as 1543. Two-storeyed Perp S porch with lavishly decorated STOUP, aisles with four-light and five-light windows and battlements. The two E bays are new; so is the whole N wall. The W parts are by *Douglas*, 1904, though incorporating two old windows, the E part of 1926. (*Christian* and *Teulon* restored the church in 1870. PF) The interior is impressive by its length – nine bays, though that is due to the C20 lengthening. Octagonal piers, double-chamfered arches. The two N bays with the continuous mouldings are of 1926. Genuine however is the N wall of the chancel with the robust, wholly unrefined MONUMENT to Hugh Starkey, who rebuilt the church c.1543. Decorated sarcophagus in a recess, brass effigy, 39 in. long, big lettering on the back wall, and H.S. on the wall above the recess. – SCULPTURE. Small piece of Anglo-Saxon interlace (chancel N). – STAINED GLASS. Fragments, medieval and C19, in a N window. – In the N aisle three *Kempe* windows. – PLATE. Chalice, inscribed 1663; Paten and two Flagons, inscribed 1747.

CHRIST CHURCH, High Street, Winsford. Close to the river. Built by the Trustees of the Weaver Navigation for the use of the watermen in 1882. The preceding church of 1844 by *Sharpe* was demolished owing to subsidence. The new, by *Richard Beckett*, is of timber-framing, and constructed so as to be raised up in the event of subsidence. Brick infilling, thin tower.

ST JOHN EVANGELIST, Delamere Street, Over. 1860–3 by *John Douglas* for Lord Delamere, his early patron.* Rock-faced and boldly modelled. Geometrical tracery. SW tower with a thin broach-spire. Prominent vestry with the chimney on the gable. Small aisle and clerestory windows. Indifferent interior.

CONGREGATIONAL CHURCH, Over. By *Douglas*, 1864–5. Very ugly and not, it seems, in a deliberately challenging way. Red and yellow brick. Façade of two-column loggia and Transitional windows above. Turrets l. and r. and quadrant pieces to connect with the sides.

* It is at present the earliest known Douglas building.

CROSS, Delamere Street, Over. This is a mystery. The stepped
base is huge (*c.* 9 ft) and contains the local lockup. The cross
itself is small and undecorated. Is it all C17?

The centre of Winsford is in the process of radical change, and
its final visual quality cannot yet be assessed. The N side of the
HIGH STREET has brick public buildings of the late C19, not
specially good but worth the use in connexion with the new.
But the new so far is too distant, and the two parts are separated
by a depressing no-man's land. Yet the SHOPPING PRE-
CINCT and the CIVIC HALL, 1963–9 by *Noel Tweddell*, are
fair examples of their kind.

BRUNNER GUILDHALL. 1899 by *A. E. Powles* of Northwich.
Presented by Sir John Brunner (*see* Winnington). Brick and
red terracotta. The style is free Tudor with French touches;
symmetrical.

VERDIN GRAMMAR SCHOOL. 1895 by *Woodhouse & Willoughby*
of Manchester. Brick and red terracotta. Less enterprising, but
in a more accurate Jacobean.

SECONDARY SCHOOL. 1906. Lower, and nothing special.

WIRSWALL

5040

WICKSTED HALL. Late C19. Brick and half-timbering with a
stone portal. Symmetrical towards the garden.

WISTASTON

6050

ST MARY. 1827–8 by *George Latham* of Nantwich. Still entirely
Georgian. Brick, four bays of arched windows. Narrow W
tower. The chancel was lengthened and the transept added in
1884 – in the original style, which is remarkable. – PLATE. Set,
'over 200 years old'.

WEST END, ¾ m. NNW. Timber-framed; C17. One gable-end has
carved brackets and an angle pendant.

WILLASTON HALL, ¾ m. SW. A house whose architectural history is not clear. It looks a uniform Early Georgian. Brick with
pronounced quoins, three bays of two and a half storeys and
one-bay wings of only two storeys. Parapet with urns. However,
the tripartite windows might be a later Georgian alteration.
Yet the dates suggested are *John Bailey*, 1713 (MHLG), and
1731 with the wings 1833 and 1838 (White). In addition there
are rainwater heads with the date 1737. The handsome staircase could as well be 1713 as 1737, though the latter is more
probable.

WITTON *see* NORTHWICH

WOODCHURCH *see* BIRKENHEAD, p. 105

WOODFORD   *8080*

CHRIST CHURCH. The impression is C17 – brick, four bays, no separate chancel, mullioned windows of three lights, the E window of four. Only the thin W tower has something of the early C19. Yet the whole church is of 1841 – a baffling case of conservatism. A good deal of victorianizing seems to have been done later, e.g. inner surrounds of the doorway and windows. – WEST GALLERY with amphitheatrically rising seats. – ALTAR PANELLING and PULPIT no doubt also later.

(WOODFORD OLD HALL, Old Hall Lane. Timber-framed. Nice gable with trellis and pointed-quatrefoil motifs. NMR)

WOODHEAD   *0090*

ST JAMES, the highest chapel in the Etherow valley, three-quarters of the way along the Manchester reservoir, and 4 m. from the pass, where the A road reaches over 1,000 ft before descending towards Sheffield. The chapel is minimum indeed, two arched windows and a doorway; small bell-turret. – C18 FONT, deeply fluted.

By Woodhead Station the TUNNEL begins. It is 3 m. long, and when it was opened in 1845 it was the longest in the world. Engineers: *Vignoles*, then *Joseph Locke*. By the side of the present tunnel entrance is the original one: two parabolic arches and one of formerly three turrets. These two early tunnels are of 1845 and 1852, the new one is of 1954.

WOODHEY *see* RIDLEY

WORLESTON   *6050*

ST OSWALD. By *C. Lynam* of Stoke-on-Trent, 1872. Remarkably good. Cruciform without aisles, with a flèche over the crossing carried by a rib-vault. The rest of the roofs canted and ceiled. The church is built of rough rubble blocks; the window tracery is of the plate variety. It is a low, but well proportioned building. – STAINED GLASS by *Kempe*, 1872 (E) and 1882. – Also a late *Morris & Co.* window.

PARSONAGE, to the E. Also good, in the Douglas style.

ROOKERY HALL, ¾ m. SE. Asymmetrical, neo-Elizabethan, rather classical ashlar exterior, the result of the alteration of a Georgian house about 1900 for Baron Schroeder.

WRENBURY

5040

ST MARGARET. A Perp church, but the chancel was rebuilt in
1806, a nave rainwater head says 1791, and the s porch is said
to have had a date 1795. The chancel was re-gothicized in 1865.
Short w tower. Five-bay nave with clerestory. The arcades
differ in details, and the N side seems earlier. Money was given
for the building by Richard Cholmondeley in 1488. – PULPIT.
A nice late C18 piece. – The Gothick WEST GALLERY looks
*c.*1800. – BOX PEWS. – CHANDELIER. Of Baroque shape; yet
given 1839. By *Cocks & Son* of Birmingham. – PLATE. Sweet-
meat Dish, *c.*1630; Cup, 1664–5, London; Paten, possibly
Dutch, C17; Flagons, 1707–8 and 1719–20, both made in
London; Cup, 1727–8 by *Richard Richardson* of Chester. –
MONUMENTS. Sir Lynch Salusbury Cotton, 1777. By *Turner*
of Chester. Urn before obelisk. – John Jennings. By *Bacon Jun.*,
1809. On an obelisk a pair of figures. – Thos. Starkey † 1802.
By the same. Faith stands by the dying man's couch. – Elinor
Starkey. By the same, 1815. Female figure against an obelisk
with an urn. All three good. – Viscount Combermere † 1865.
By *Theed.* Grecian still. Three figures and a segmental top
with portrait medallion.

SCHOOL. 1875. Brick, Gothic, and very idiosyncratic.

WRENBURY HALL. Parts seem to date from the C17, but the
present entrance front must be late C19 or early C20. Elizabethan style. Asymmetrical with stepped gables. (Open-well
staircase with twisted balusters. MHLG)

WREXHAM ROAD FARM *see* ECCLESTON

WYBERSLEY HALL *see* DISLEY

WYBUNBURY

6040

ST CHAD. By *James Brooks*, 1892–3,* except for the high Perp
w tower of five stages with an elaborate w side including five
original but partly recarved statues, two bishops, the Annunciation, and the Trinity. The two two-light bell-openings are
under one ogee moulding exactly as e.g. at Sandbach. Brooks's
chancel has been demolished. He gave the tower arch a
segmental form and used arches which die into the piers.
– FONT. Perp, octagonal, with simple motifs. – PLATE.
Cup, London, 1641; Tankard, London, 1677, by *T. K.*;
Tazza, London, 1702; Spoon, *c.*1720, by *R. W.* (possibly

* Estimated cost £7,000, as Mr Spain found in *The Builder.*

Ralph Whalley of Chester); Flagon, London, 1726, by *I. P.*; Chalice, 1728 by *Richard Richardson* of Chester; Chalice and Paten, London, 1790, by *Henry Chawner*. – MONUMENTS. Brass to Rafe Delves † 1513 and wife; 34 in. figures. – Sir Thomas Smith † 1614. Uncommonly fine. All parts closely decorated. Two recumbent effigies, he wearing a beard. Coffered arch on heavy corbels; also two pairs of columns. Much strapwork on the back wall and also in the top achievement.

DELVES CHARITY SCHOOL, ½ m. SSW. 1822. Five-bay front of one storey. Arched windows and doorway.

GLOSSARY

ABACUS: flat slab on the top of a capital (q.v.).

ABUTMENT: solid masonry placed to resist the lateral pressure of a vault.

ACANTHUS: plant with thick fleshy and scalloped leaves used as part of the decoration of a Corinthian capital (q.v.) and in some types of leaf carving.

ACHIEVEMENT OF ARMS: in heraldry, a complete display of armorial bearings.

ACROTERION: foliage-carved block on the end or top of a classical pediment (q.v.).

ADDORSED: two human figures, animals, or birds, etc., placed symmetrically so that they turn their backs to each other.

AEDICULE, AEDICULA: framing of a window or door by columns and a pediment (q.v.).

AFFRONTED: two human figures, animals, or birds, etc., placed symmetrically so that they face each other.

AGGER: Latin term for the built-up foundations of Roman roads; also sometimes applied to the banks of hill-forts or other earthworks.

AMBULATORY: semicircular or polygonal aisle enclosing an apse (q.v.).

ANNULET: see Shaft-ring.

ANSE DE PANIER: see Arch, Basket.

ANTEPENDIUM: covering of the front of an altar, usually by textiles or metalwork.

ANTIS, IN: see Portico.

APSE: vaulted semicircular or polygonal end of a chancel or a chapel.

ARABESQUE: light and fanciful surface decoration using combinations of flowing lines, tendrils, etc., interspersed with vases, animals, etc.

ARCADE: range of arches supported on piers or columns, free-standing: or, BLIND ARCADE, the same attached to a wall.

ARCH: round-headed, i.e. semicircular; pointed, i.e. consisting of two curves, each drawn from one centre, and meeting in a point at the top; segmental, i.e. in the form of a segment; pointed; four-centred (a late medieval form), see Fig. 1(a);

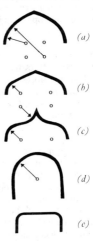

Fig. 1. Arches

Tudor (also a late medieval form), see Fig. 1(*b*); Ogee (introduced *c.* 1300 and specially popular in the C14), see Fig. 1(*c*); Stilted, see Fig. 1(*d*); Basket, with lintel connected to the jambs by concave quadrant curves, see Fig. 1(*e*) for one example; Diaphragm, a transverse arch with solid spandrels carrying not a vault but a principal beam of a timber roof. *See also* Strainer Arch.

ARCHITRAVE: lowest of the three main parts of the entablature (q.v.) of an order (q.v.) (*see* Fig. 12).

ARCHIVOLT: a continuous moulding on the face of an arch and following its contour.

ARRIS: sharp edge at the meeting of two surfaces.

ASHLAR: masonry of large blocks wrought to even faces and square edges.

ATLANTES: male counterparts of caryatids (q.v.).

ATRIUM: inner court of a Roman house, also open court in front of a church.

ATTACHED: *see* Engaged.

ATTIC: topmost storey of a house, if distance from floor to ceiling is less than in the others.

AUMBRY: recess or cupboard to hold sacred vessels for Mass and Communion.

BAILEY: open space or court of a stone-built castle; *see also* Motte-and-Bailey.

BALDACCHINO: canopy supported on columns.

BALLFLOWER: globular flower of three petals enclosing a small ball. A decoration used in the first quarter of the C14.

BALUSTER: small pillar or column of fanciful outline.

BALUSTRADE: series of balusters supporting a handrail or coping (q.v.).

BARBICAN: outwork defending the entrance to a castle.

BARGEBOARDS: projecting decorated boards placed against the incline of the gable of a building and hiding the horizontal roof timbers.

BARREL-VAULT: *see* Vault.

BARROW: *see* Bell, Bowl, Disc, Long, *and* Pond Barrow.

BASILICA: in medieval architecture an aisled church with a clerestory.

BASKET ARCH: *see* Arch (Fig. 1*e*).

BASTION: projection at the angle of a fortification.

BATTER: inclined face of a wall.

BATTLEMENT: parapet with a series of indentations or embrasures with raised portions or merlons between. Also called Crenellation.

BAYS: internal compartments of a building; each divided from the other not by solid walls but by divisions only marked in the side walls (columns, pilasters, etc.) or the ceiling (beams, etc.). Also external divisions of a building by fenestration.

BAY-WINDOW: angular or curved projection of a house front with ample fenestration. If curved, also called bow-window: if on an upper floor only, also called oriel or oriel window.

BEAKER FOLK: Late New Stone Age warrior invaders from the Continent who buried their dead in round barrows and introduced the first metal tools and weapons to Britain.

BEAKHEAD: Norman ornamental motif consisting of a row of bird or beast heads with beaks biting usually into a roll moulding (q.v.).

BELFRY: turret on a roof to hang bells in.

BELGAE: aristocratic warrior bands who settled in Britain in two main waves in the CI B.C. In Britain their culture is termed Iron Age C.

BELL BARROW: Early Bronze Age round barrow in which the mound is separated from its encircling ditch by a flat platform or berm (q.v.).

BELLCOTE: framework on a roof to hang bells from.

BERM: level area separating ditch from bank on a hill-fort or barrow.

BILLET FRIEZE: Norman ornamental motif made up of short raised rectangles placed at regular intervals.

BIVALLATE: of a hill-fort: defended by two concentric banks and ditches.

BLIND ARCADE: see Arcade.

BLOCK CAPITAL: Romanesque capital cut from a cube by having the lower angles rounded off to the circular shaft below. Also called Cushion Capital (Fig. 2).

Fig. 2. Block capital

BOND, ENGLISH or FLEMISH: see Brickwork.

BOSS: knob or projection usually placed to cover the intersection of ribs in a vault.

BOWL BARROW: round barrow surrounded by a quarry ditch. Introduced in Late Neolithic times, the form continued until the Saxon period.

BOW-WINDOW: see Bay-Window.

BOX: small country house, e.g. a shooting box. A convenient term to describe a compact minor dwelling, e.g. a rectory.

BOX PEW: pew with a high wooden enclosure.

BRACES: see Roof.

BRACKET: small supporting piece of stone, etc., to carry a projecting horizontal.

BRESSUMER: beam in a timber-framed building to support the, usually projecting, superstructure.

BRICKWORK: *Header:* brick laid so that the end only appears on the face of the wall. *Stretcher:* brick laid so that the side only appears on the face of the wall. *English Bond:* method of laying bricks so that alternate courses or layers on the face of the wall are composed of headers or stretchers only (Fig. 3a). *Flemish Bond:* method of laying bricks so that alternate headers and

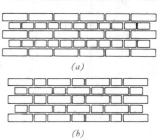

(a)

(b)

Fig. 3. Brickwork

stretchers appear in each course on the face of the wall (Fig. 3*b*). *See also* Herringbone Work, Oversailing Courses.

BROACH: *see* Spire.

BROKEN PEDIMENT: *see* Pediment.

BRONZE AGE: in Britain, the period from *c.* 1600 to 600 B.C.

BUCRANIUM: ox skull.

BUTTRESS: mass of brickwork or masonry projecting from or built against a wall to give additional strength. *Angle Buttresses:* two meeting at an angle of 90° at the angle of a building (Fig. 4*a*). *Clasping Buttress:* one which encases the angle (Fig. 4*d*). *Diagonal Buttress:* one placed against the right angle formed by two walls, and more or less equiangular with both (Fig. 4*b*). *Flying Buttress:* arch or half arch transmitting the thrust of a vault or roof from the upper part of a wall to an outer support or buttress. *Setback Buttress:* angle buttress set slightly back from the angle (Fig. 4*c*).

CABLE MOULDING: Norman moulding imitating a twisted cord.

CAIRN: a mound of stones usually covering a burial.

CAMBER: slight rise or upward curve of an otherwise horizontal structure.

CAMPANILE: isolated bell tower.

CANOPY: projection or hood over

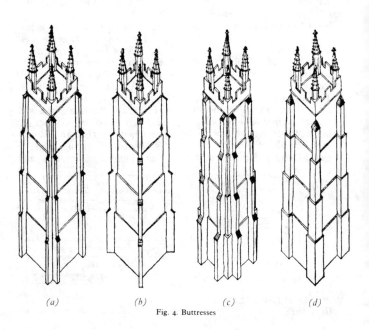

(a)   *(b)*   *(c)*   *(d)*

Fig. 4. Buttresses

an altar, pulpit, niche, statue, etc.

CAP: in a windmill the crowning feature.

CAPITAL: head or top part of a column. *See also* Block Capital, Crocket Capital, Order, Scalloped Capital, Stiff-leaf, *and* Waterleaf.

CARTOUCHE: tablet with an ornate frame, usually enclosing an inscription.

CARYATID: whole female figure supporting an entablature or other similar member. *Termini Caryatids:* female busts or demi-figures or three-quarter figures supporting an entablature or other similar member and placed at the top of termini pilasters (q.v.). Cf. Atlantes.

CASTELLATED: decorated with battlements (q.v.).

CELURE: panelled and adorned part of a wagon roof above the rood or the altar.

CENSER: vessel for the burning of incense.

CENTERING: wooden framework used in arch and vault construction and removed when the mortar has set.

CHALICE: cup used in the Communion service or at Mass. *See also* Recusant Chalice.

CHAMBERED TOMB: burial mound of the New Stone Age having a stone-built chamber and entrance passage covered by an earthen barrow or stone cairn. The form was introduced to Britain from the Mediterranean.

CHAMFER: surface made by cutting across the square angle of a stone block, piece of wood, etc., usually at an angle of 45 to the other two surfaces.

CHANCEL: that part of the E end

of a church in which the altar is placed, usually applied to the whole continuation of the nave E of the crossing.

CHANCEL ARCH: arch at the W end of the chancel.

CHANTRY CHAPEL: chapel attached to, or inside, a church, endowed for the saying of Masses for the soul of the founder or some other individual.

CHEVET: French term for the E end of a church (chancel, ambulatory, and radiating chapels).

CHEVRON: Norman moulding forming a zigzag.

CHOIR: that part of the church where divine service is sung.

CIBORIUM: a baldacchino (q.v.).

CINQUEFOIL: *see* Foil.

CIST: stone-lined or slab-built grave. First appears in Late Neolithic times. It continued to be used in the Early Christian period.

CLAPPER BRIDGE: bridge made of large slabs of stone, some built up to make rough piers and other longer ones laid on top to make the roadway.

CLASSIC: here used to mean the moment of highest achievement of a style.

CLASSICAL: here used as the term for Greek and Roman architecture and any subsequent styles inspired by it.

CLERESTORY: upper storey of the nave walls of a church, pierced by windows.

COADE STONE: artificial (cast) stone made in the late C18 and the early C19 by Coade and Sealy in London.

COB: walling material made of mixed clay and straw.

COFFERING: decorating a ceiling

with sunk square or polygonal ornamental panels.

COLLAR-BEAM: *see* Roof.

COLONNADE: range of columns.

COLONNETTE: small column.

COLUMNA ROSTRATA: column decorated with carved prows of ships to celebrate a naval victory.

COMPOSITE: *see* Order.

CONSOLE: bracket (q.v.) with a compound curved outline.

COPING: capping or covering to a wall.

CORBEL: block of stone projecting from a wall, supporting some feature on its horizontal top surface.

CORBEL TABLE: series of corbels, occurring just below the roof eaves externally or internally, often seen in Norman buildings.

CORINTHIAN: *see* Order.

CORNICE: in classical architecture the top section of the entablature (q.v.). Also the term for a projecting decorative feature along the top of a wall, arch, etc.

CORRIDOR VILLA: *see* Villa.

COUNTERSCARP BANK: small bank on the down-hill or outer side of a hill-fort ditch.

COURTYARD VILLA: *see* Villa.

COVE, COVING: concave undersurface in the nature of a hollow moulding but on a larger scale.

COVER PATEN: cover to a Communion cup, suitable for use as a paten or plate for the consecrated bread.

CRADLE ROOF: *see* Wagon Roof.

CRENELLATION: *see* Battlement.

CREST, CRESTING: ornamental finish along the top of a screen, etc.

CRINKLE-CRANKLE WALL: undulating wall.

CROCKET, CROCKETING: decorative features placed on the sloping sides of spires, pinnacles, gables, etc., in Gothic architecture, carved in various leaf shapes and placed at regular intervals.

CROCKET CAPITAL: *see* Fig. 5. An Early Gothic form.

Fig. 5. Crocket capital

CROMLECH: word of Celtic origin still occasionally used of single free-standing stones ascribed to the Neolithic or Bronze Age periods.

CROSSING: space at the intersection of nave, chancel, and transepts.

CROSS-VAULT: *see* Vault.

CROSS-WINDOWS: windows with one mullion and one transom.

CROWN-POST: *see* Roof (Fig. 15).

CRUCK: cruck construction is a method of timber framing by which the ridge beam is supported by pairs of curved timbers extending from floor to ridge.

CRYPT: underground room usually below the E end of a church.

CUPOLA: small polygonal or circular domed turret crowning a roof.

CURTAIN WALL: connecting wall between the towers of a castle. In C20 architecture, a non-load-bearing wall which can be applied in front of a framed structure to keep out the weather; sections may include windows and the spans between.

CUSHION CAPITAL: *see* Block Capital.

CUSP: projecting point between the foils (q.v.) in a foiled Gothic arch.

D ADO: decorative covering of the lower part of a wall.

DAGGER: tracery motif of the Dec style. It is a lancet shape rounded or pointed at the head, pointed at the foot, and cusped inside (Fig. 6).

Fig. 6. Dagger

DAIS: raised platform at one end of a room.

DEC ('DECORATED'): historical division of English Gothic architecture covering the period from c. 1290 to c. 1350.

DEMI-COLUMNS: columns half sunk into a wall.

DIAPER WORK: surface decoration composed of square or lozenge shapes.

DIAPHRAGM ARCH: *see* Arch.

DIOCLETIAN WINDOW: semi-circular, with two mullions.

DISC BARROW: Bronze Age round barrow with inconspicuous central mound surrounded by bank and ditch.

DOGTOOTH: typical E.E. ornament consisting of a series of four-cornered stars placed diagonally and raised pyramidally (Fig. 7).

DOMICAL VAULT: *see* Vault.

DONJON: *see* Keep.

Fig. 7. Dogtooth

DORIC: *see* Order.

DORMER (WINDOW): window placed vertically in the sloping plane of a roof.

DRIPSTONE: *see* Hoodmould.

DRUM: circular or polygonal vertical wall of a dome or cupola.

DUTCH GABLE: *see* Gable.

E .E. ('EARLY ENGLISH'): historical division of English Gothic architecture roughly covering the C13.

EASTER SEPULCHRE: recess with tomb-chest (q.v.), usually in the wall of a chancel, the tomb-chest to receive an effigy of Christ for Easter celebrations.

EAVES: overhanging edge of a roof.

EAVES CORNICE: cornice below the eaves of a roof.

ECHINUS: convex or projecting moulding supporting the abacus of a Greek Doric capital, sometimes bearing an egg and dart pattern.

EMBATTLED: *see* Battlement.

EMBRASURE: small opening in the wall or parapet of a fortified building, usually splayed on the inside.

ENCAUSTIC TILES: earthenware glazed and decorated tiles used for paving.

ENGAGED COLUMNS: columns attached to, or partly sunk into, a wall.

ENGLISH BOND: *see* Brickwork.

ENTABLATURE: in classical architecture the whole of the horizontal members above a column (that is architrave, frieze, and cornice) (*see* Fig. 12).

ENTASIS: very slight convex deviation from a straight line; used on Greek columns and sometimes on spires to prevent an optical illusion of concavity.

ENTRESOL: *see* Mezzanine.

ESCUTCHEON: shield for armorial bearings.

EXEDRA: the apsidal end of a room. *See* Apse.

F

FAN-VAULT: *see* Vault.

FERETORY: place behind the high altar where the chief shrine of a church is kept.

FESTOON: carved garland of flowers and fruit suspended at both ends. *See also* Swag.

FILLET: narrow flat band running down a shaft or along a roll moulding.

FINIAL: top of a canopy, gable, pinnacle.

FIRRED: *see* Roof.

FLAGON: vessel for the wine used in the Communion service.

FLAMBOYANT: properly the latest phase of French Gothic architecture where the window tracery takes on wavy undulating lines.

FLÈCHE: slender spire on the centre of a roof. Also called Spirelet.

FLEMISH BOND: *see* Brickwork.

FLEURON: decorative carved flower or leaf.

FLUSHWORK: decorative use of flint in conjunction with dressed stone so as to form patterns: tracery, initials, etc.

FLUTING: vertical channelling in the shaft of a column.

FLYING BUTTRESS: *see* Buttress.

FOIL: lobe formed by the cusping (q.v.) of a circle or an arch. Trefoil, quatrefoil, cinquefoil, multifoil, express the number of leaf shapes to be seen.

FOLIATED: carved with leaf shapes.

FOSSE: ditch.

FOUR-CENTRED ARCH: *see* Arch (Fig. 1*a*).

FRATER: refectory or dining hall of a monastery.

FRESCO: wall painting on wet plaster.

FRIEZE: middle division of a classical entablature (q.v.) (*see* Fig. 12).

FRONTAL: covering for the front of an altar.

G

GABLE: *Dutch gable:* a gable with curved sides crowned by a pediment, characteristic of *c.* 1630–50 (Fig. 8*a*). *Shaped gable:* a gable with multi-curved sides characteristic of *c.* 1600–50 (Fig. 8*b*).

GADROONED: enriched with a series of convex ridges, the opposite of fluting (q.v.).

GALILEE: chapel or vestibule usually at the W end of a church

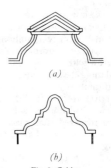

(a)

(b)

Fig. 8. Gables

enclosing the porch. Also called Narthex (q.v.).

GALLERY: in church architecture upper storey above an aisle, opened in arches to the nave. Also called Tribune and often erroneously Triforium (q.v.).

GALLERY GRAVE: chambered tomb (q.v.) in which there is little or no differentiation between the entrance passage and the actual burial chamber(s).

GARDEROBE: lavatory or privy in a medieval building.

GARGOYLE: water spout projecting from the parapet of a wall or tower; carved into a human or animal shape.

GAZEBO: lookout tower or raised summer house in a picturesque garden.

'GEOMETRICAL': see Tracery.

'GIBBS SURROUND': of a doorway or window. An C18 motif consisting of a surround with alternating larger and smaller blocks of stone, quoin-wise, or intermittent large blocks, sometimes with a narrow raised band connecting them up the verticals and along the face of the arch (Fig. 9).

GROIN: sharp edge at the meeting of two cells of a cross-vault.

GROIN-VAULT: see Vault.

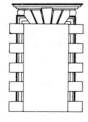

Fig. 9. 'Gibbs surround'

GROTESQUE: fanciful ornamental decoration: see also Arabesque.

HAGIOSCOPE: see Squint.

HALF-TIMBERING: see Timber-Framing.

HALL CHURCH: church in which nave and aisles are of equal height or approximately so.

HAMMERBEAM: see Roof (Fig. 18).

HANAP: large metal cup, generally made for domestic use, standing on an elaborate base and stem; with a very ornate cover frequently crowned with a little steeple.

HEADER: see Brickwork.

HERRINGBONE WORK: brick, stone, or tile construction where the component blocks are laid diagonally instead of flat. Alternate courses lie in opposing directions to make a zigzag pattern up the face of the wall.

HEXASTYLE: having six detached columns.

HILL-FORT: Iron Age earthwork enclosed by a ditch and bank system; in the later part of the period the defences multiplied in size and complexity. They vary from about an acre to over 30 acres in area, and are usually built with careful regard to natural elevations or promontories.

HIPPED ROOF: see Roof.

HOODMOULD: projecting moulding above an arch or a lintel to throw off water. Also called Dripstone or Label.

ICONOGRAPHY: the science of the subject matter of works of the visual arts.

IMPOST: bracket (q.v.) in a wall, usually formed of mouldings, on which the ends of an arch rest.

INDENT: shape chiselled out in a stone slab to receive a brass.

INGLENOOK: bench or seat built in beside a fireplace, sometimes covered by the chimneybreast, occasionally lit by small windows on each side of the fire.

INTERCOLUMNIATION: the space between columns.

IONIC: see Order (Fig. 12).

IRON AGE: in Britain the period from c. 600 B.C. to the coming of the Romans. The term is also used for those un-Romanized native communities which survived until the Saxon incursions.

JAMB: straight side of an archway, doorway, or window.

KEEL MOULDING: moulding whose outline is in section like that of the keel of a ship.

KEEP: massive tower of a Norman castle. Also called Donjon.

KEYSTONE: middle stone in an arch or a rib-vault.

KINGPOST: see Roof (Fig. 14).

KNEELER: horizontal decorative projection at the base of a gable.

KNOP: a knob-like thickening in the stem of a chalice.

LABEL: see Hoodmould.

LABEL STOP: ornamental boss at the end of a hoodmould (q.v.).

LACED WINDOWS: windows pulled visually together by strips, usually in brick of a different colour, which continue vertically the lines of the vertical parts of the window surrounds. The motif is typical of c. 1720.

LANCET WINDOW: slender pointed-arched window.

LANTERN: in architecture, a small circular or polygonal turret with windows all round crowning a roof (see Cupola) or a dome.

LANTERN CROSS: churchyard cross with lantern-shaped top usually with sculptured representations on the sides of the top.

LEAN-TO ROOF: roof with one slope only, built against a higher wall.

LESENE or PILASTER STRIP: pilaster (q.v.) without base or capital.

LIERNE: see Vault (Fig. 23).

LINENFOLD: Tudor panelling ornamented with a conventional representation of a piece of linen laid in vertical folds. The piece is repeated in each panel.

LINTEL: horizontal beam or stone bridging an opening.

LOGGIA: recessed colonnade (q.v.).

LONG AND SHORT WORK: Saxon quoins (q.v.) consisting of stones placed with the long sides alternately upright and horizontal.

LONG BARROW: unchambered Neolithic communal burial mound, wedge-shaped in plan, with the burial and occasional other structures massed at the broader end, from which the mound itself tapers in height; quarry ditches flank the mound.

LOUVRE: opening, often with lantern (q.v.) over, in the roof of a room to let the smoke from a central hearth escape.

LOWER PALAEOLITHIC: see Palaeolithic.

LOZENGE: diamond shape.

LUCARNE: small opening to let light in.

LUNETTE: tympanum (q.v.) or semicircular opening.

LYCH GATE: wooden gate structure with a roof and open sides placed at the entrance to a churchyard to provide space for the reception of a coffin. The word *lych* is Saxon and means a corpse.

LYNCHET: long terraced strip of soil accumulating on the downward side of prehistoric and medieval fields due to soil creep from continuous ploughing along the contours.

MACHICOLATION: projecting gallery on brackets (q.v.) constructed on the outside of castle towers or walls. The gallery has holes in the floor to drop missiles through.

MAJOLICA: ornamented glazed earthenware.

MANSARD: *see* Roof.

MATHEMATICAL TILES: small facing tiles the size of brick headers, most often applied to timber-framed walls to make them appear brick-built.

MEGALITHIC TOMB: stone-built burial chamber of the New Stone Age covered by an earth or stone mound. The form was introduced to Britain from the Mediterranean area.

MERLON: *see* Battlement.

MESOLITHIC: 'Middle Stone' Age; the post-glacial period of hunting and fishing communities dating in Britain from *c.* 8000 B.C. to the arrival of Neolithic communities, with which they must have considerably overlapped.

METOPE: in classical architecture of the Doric order (q.v.) the space in the frieze between the triglyphs (Fig. 12).

MEZZANINE: low storey placed between two higher ones. Also called Entresol.

MISERERE: *see* Misericord.

MISERICORD: bracket placed on the underside of a hinged choir stall seat which, when turned up, provided the occupant of the seat with a support during long periods of standing. Also called Miserere.

MODILLION: small bracket of which large numbers (modillion frieze) are often placed below a cornice (q.v.) in classical architecture.

MOTTE: steep mound forming the main feature of C11 and C12 castles.

MOTTE-AND-BAILEY: post-Roman and Norman defence system consisting of an earthen mound (the motte) topped with a wooden tower eccentrically placed within a bailey (q.v.), with enclosure ditch and palisade, and with the rare addition of an internal bank.

MOUCHETTE: tracery motif in curvilinear tracery, a curved dagger (q.v.), specially popular in the early C14 (Fig. 10).

Fig. 10. Mouchette

MOURNERS: *see* Weepers.

MULLIONS: vertical posts or uprights dividing a window into 'lights'.

MULTIVALLATE: of a hill-fort: defended by three or more concentric banks and ditches.

MUNTIN: post as a rule moulded and part of a screen.

NAIL-HEAD: E.E. ornamental motif, consisting of small pyramids regularly repeated (Fig. 11).

Fig. 11. Nail-head

NARTHEX: enclosed vestibule or covered porch at the main entrance to a church (*see* Galilee).

NEOLITHIC: 'New Stone' Age, dating in Britain from the appearance from the Continent of the first settled farming communities *c.* 3500 B.C. until the introduction of the Bronze Age.

NEWEL: central post in a circular or winding staircase; also the principal post when a flight of stairs meets a landing.

NOOK-SHAFT: shaft set in the angle of a pier or respond or wall, or the angle of the jamb of a window or doorway.

NUTMEG MOULDING: consisting of a chain of tiny triangles placed obliquely.

OBELISK: lofty pillar of square section tapering at the top and ending pyramidally.

OGEE: *see* Arch (Fig. 1c).

OPEN PEDIMENT: *see* Pediment.

ORATORY: small private chapel in a house.

ORDER: *see* Fig. 12. (1) *of a doorway or window:* series of concentric steps receding towards the opening; (2) *in classical architecture:* column with base, shaft, capital and entablature (q.v.) according to one of the following styles: Greek Doric, Roman Doric, Tuscan Doric, Ionic, Corinthian,

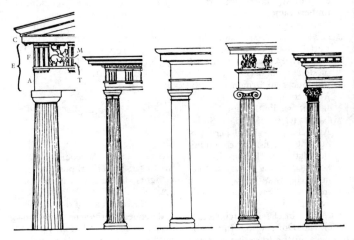

Fig. 12. Orders of columns (Greek Doric, Roman Doric, Tuscan Doric, Ionic, Corinthian)
E, Entablature; C, Cornice; F, Frieze; A, Architrave; M, Metope; T, Triglyph

Composite. The established details are very elaborate, and some specialist architectural work should be consulted for further guidance.

ORIEL: *see* Bay-Window.

OVERHANG: projection of the upper storey of a house.

OVERSAILING COURSES: series of stone or brick courses, each one projecting beyond the one below it.

OVOLO: convex moulding.

PALAEOLITHIC: 'Old Stone' Age; the first period of human culture, commencing in the Ice Age and immediately prior to the Mesolithic; the Lower Palaeolithic is the older phase, the Upper Palaeolithic the later.

PALIMPSEST: (1) *of a brass:* where a metal plate has been re-used by turning over and engraving on the back; (2) *of a wall painting:* where one overlaps and partly obscures an earlier one.

PALLADIAN: architecture following the ideas and principles of Andrea Palladio, 1508–80.

PANTILE: tile of curved S-shaped section.

PARAPET: low wall placed to protect any spot where there is a sudden drop, for example on a bridge, quay, hillside, housetop, etc.

PARCLOSE SCREEN: *see* Screen.

PARGETTING: plaster work with patterns and ornaments either in relief or engraved on it.

PARVIS: term wrongly applied to a room over a church porch. These rooms were often used as a schoolroom or as a store room.

PASSING-BRACE: *see* Roof (Fig. 16).

PATEN: plate to hold the bread at Communion or Mass.

PATERA: small flat circular or oval ornament in classical architecture.

PEDIMENT: low-pitched gable used in classical, Renaissance, and neo-classical architecture above a portico and above doors, windows, etc. It may be straight-sided or curved segmentally. *Broken Pediment:* one where the centre portion of the base is left open. *Open Pediment:* one where the centre portion of the sloping sides is left out.

PENDANT: boss (q.v.) elongated so that it seems to hang down.

PENDENTIVE: concave triangular spandrel used to lead from the angle of two walls to the base of a circular dome. It is constructed as part of the hemisphere over a diameter the size of the diagonal of the basic square (Fig. 13).

PERP (PERPENDICULAR): historical division of English Gothic architecture covering the period from *c.* 1335–50 to *c.* 1530.

PIANO NOBILE: principal storey of a house with the reception rooms; usually the first floor.

PIAZZA: open space surrounded by

Fig. 13. Pendentive

buildings; in C17 and C18 England sometimes used to mean a long colonnade or loggia.

PIER: strong, solid support, frequently square in section or of composite section (compound pier).

PIETRA DURA: ornamental or scenic inlay by means of thin slabs of stone.

PILASTER: shallow pier attached to a wall. *Pilaster Strip: see* Lesene. *Termini Pilasters:* pilasters with sides tapering downwards.

PILLAR PISCINA: free-standing piscina (q.v.) on a pillar.

PINNACLE: ornamental form crowning a spire, tower, buttress, etc., usually of steep pyramidal, conical, or some similar shape.

PISCINA: basin for washing the Communion or Mass vessels, provided with a drain. Generally set in or against the wall to the s of an altar.

PLAISANCE: summer house, pleasure house near a mansion.

PLATE TRACERY: *see* Tracery.

PLINTH: projecting base of a wall or column, generally chamfered (q.v.) or moulded at the top.

POND BARROW: rare type of Bronze Age barrow consisting of a circular depression, usually paved, and containing a number of cremation burials.

POPPYHEAD: ornament of leaf and flower type used to decorate the tops of bench- or stall-ends.

PORTCULLIS: gate constructed to rise and fall in vertical grooves; used in gateways of castles.

PORTE COCHÈRE: porch large enough to admit wheeled vehicles.

PORTICO: centrepiece of a house or of a church, with classical detached or attached columns and a pediment. A portico is called *prostyle* or *in antis* according to whether it projects from or recedes into a building. In a portico *in antis* the columns range with the side walls.

POSTERN: small gateway at the back of a building.

PREDELLA: in an altarpiece the horizontal strip below the main representation, often used for a number of subsidiary representations in a row.

PRESBYTERY: the part of the church lying E of the choir. It is the part where the altar is placed.

PRINCIPAL: *see* Roof (Figs. 14, 17).

PRIORY: monastic house whose head is a prior or prioress, not an abbot or abbess.

PROSTYLE: with free-standing columns in a row.

PULPITUM: stone screen in a major church provided to shut off the choir from the nave and also as a backing for the return choir stalls.

PULVINATED FRIEZE: frieze (q.v.) with a bold convex moulding.

PURLINS: *see* Roof (Figs. 14-17).

PUTHOLE or PUTLOCK HOLE: putlocks are the short horizontal timbers on which during construction the boards of scaffolding rest. Putholes or putlock holes are the holes in the wall for putlocks, which often are not filled in after construction is complete.

PUTTO: small naked boy.

QUADRANGLE: inner courtyard in a large building.

QUARRY: in stained-glass work, a small diamond- or square-shaped piece of glass set diagonally.

QUATREFOIL: *see* Foil.

QUEENPOSTS: *see* Roof (Fig. 16).

QUEEN-STRUTS: *see* Roof (Fig. 17).

QUOINS: dressed stones at the angles of a building. Sometimes all the stones are of the same size; more often they are alternately large and small.

RADIATING CHAPELS: chapels projecting radially from an ambulatory or an apse.

RAFTER: *see* Roof.

RAMPART: stone wall or wall of earth surrounding a castle, fortress, or fortified city.

RAMPART-WALK: path along the inner face of a rampart.

REBATE: continuous rectangular notch cut on an edge.

REBUS: pun, a play on words. The literal translation and illustration of a name for artistic and heraldic purposes (Belton = bell, tun).

RECUSANT CHALICE: chalice made after the Reformation and before Catholic Emancipation for Roman Catholic use.

REEDING: decoration with parallel convex mouldings touching one another.

REFECTORY: dining hall; *see also* Frater.

RENDERING: plastering of an outer wall.

REPOUSSÉ: decoration of metal work by relief designs, formed by beating the metal from the back.

REREDOS: structure behind and above an altar.

RESPOND: half-pier bonded into a wall and carrying one end of an arch.

RETABLE: altarpiece, a picture or piece of carving, standing behind and attached to an altar.

RETICULATION: *see* Tracery (Fig. 22*e*).

REVEAL: that part of a jamb (q.v.) which lies between the glass or door and the outer surface of the wall.

RIB-VAULT: *see* Vault.

ROCOCO: latest phase of the Baroque style, current in most Continental countries between *c.* 1720 and *c.* 1760.

ROLL MOULDING: moulding of semicircular or more than semicircular section.

ROMANESQUE: that style in architecture which was current in the C11 and C12 and preceded the Gothic style (in England often called Norman). (Some scholars extend the use of the term Romanesque back to the C10 or C9.)

ROMANO-BRITISH: a somewhat vague term applied to the period and cultural features of Britain affected by the Roman occupation of the C1–5 A.D.

ROOD: cross or crucifix.

ROOD LOFT: singing gallery on the top of the rood screen, often supported by a coving (q.v.).

ROOD SCREEN: *see* Screen.

ROOD STAIRS: stairs to give access to the rood loft.

ROOF: *see* Figs. 14–18. *Single-framed:* if consisting entirely of transverse members (such as rafters with or without braces, collars, tie-beams, etc.) not tied together longitudinally. *Double-framed:* if longitudinal members (such as a ridge beam and purlins) are employed. As a rule in such cases the rafters are divided into stronger principals and weaker subsidiary rafters. *Hipped:* roof with sloped instead of vertical ends *Mansard:* roof with a double slope, the lower slope being larger and steeper than the upper. *Saddleback:* tower roof shaped like an ordinary gabled timber roof. The following members have special names: *Rafter:* roof-timber sloping up from the wall-plate to the ridge. *Principal:* principal rafter, usually corresponding to the main bay divisions of the nave or chancel below. *Wall-plate:* timber laid longitudinally on the top of a wall. *Purlins:* longitudinal members laid parallel with wall-plate and apex some way up the slope of the roof. These are side purlins and may be *tenoned* into the principal rafter, or they may be *through purlins,* i.e. resting in slots cut into the back of the principals. *Clasped purlins:* purlins held between collar-beam and principal rafter. *Collar purlin:* a lengthwise beam supporting the collar-beams, found in the context of crown-post roofs, which do not have a ridge-piece. *Tie-beam:* beam connecting the two

slopes of a roof at the height of the wall-plate, to prevent the roof from spreading. *Cambered tie-beam roof:* one in which the ridge and purlins are laid directly on a cambered tie-beam; in a *firred tie-beam roof* a solid blocking piece (firring piece) is interposed between the cambered tie-beam and the purlins. *Collar-beam:* tie-beam applied higher up the slope of the roof. *Strut:* an upright or sloping timber supporting a transverse member, e.g. connecting tie-beam with rafter. *Post:* an upright timber supporting a lengthwise beam. *Kingpost:* an upright timber carried on a tie-beam and supporting the ridge-beam (*see* Fig. 14). *Crown-post:* an upright timber carried on a tie-beam and supporting a collar purlin, and usually braced to it and the collar-beam with four-way struts (*see* Fig. 15). *Queenposts:* two upright timbers placed symmetrically on a tie-beam and supporting purlins (*see* Fig. 16); if such timbers support a collar-beam or rafters they are *queen-struts* (*see* Fig. 17). *Braces:* inclined timbers inserted to strengthen others. Usually

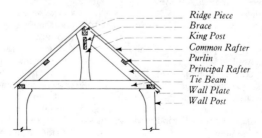

Ridge Piece
Brace
King Post
Common Rafter
Purlin
Principal Rafter
Tie Beam
Wall Plate
Wall Post

Fig. 14. Kingpost roof

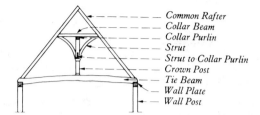

Common Rafter
Collar Beam
Collar Purlin
Strut
Strut to Collar Purlin
Crown Post
Tie Beam
Wall Plate
Wall Post

Fig. 15. Crown-post roof

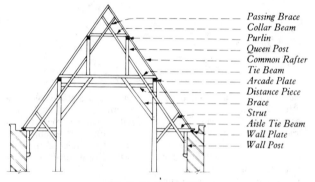

Passing Brace
Collar Beam
Purlin
Queen Post
Common Rafter
Tie Beam
Arcade Plate
Distance Piece
Brace
Strut
Aisle Tie Beam
Wall Plate
Wall Post

Fig. 16. Queen post roof

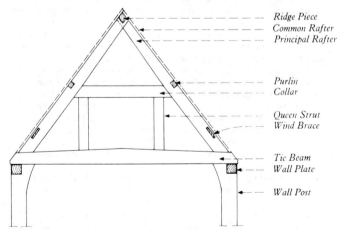

Ridge Piece
Common Rafter
Principal Rafter

Purlin
Collar

Queen Strut
Wind Brace

Tie Beam
Wall Plate

Wall Post

Fig. 17. Queen-strut roof

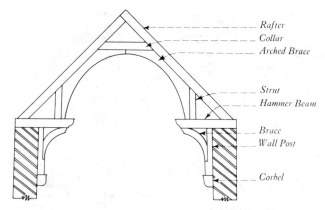

Fig. 18. Hammerbeam roof

braces connect a collar-beam with the rafters below or a tie-beam with the wall below. Braces can be straight or curved (also called arched). *Passing-brace:* a brace, usually of the same scantling as the common rafters and parallel to them, which stiffens a roof laterally by being halved across one or more intermediate timbers within its length (*see* Fig. 16). *Hammer-beam:* beam projecting at right angles, usually from the top of a wall, to carry arched braces or struts and arched braces (*see* Fig. 18). *See also* Wagon Roof.

ROSE WINDOW (or WHEEL WIN-DOW): circular window with patterned tracery arranged to radiate from the centre.

ROTUNDA: building circular in plan.

RUBBLE: building stones, not square or hewn, nor laid in regular courses.

RUSTICATION: *rock-faced* if the surfaces of large blocks of ashlar stone are left rough like rock;

smooth if the ashlar blocks are smooth and separated by V-joints; *banded* if the separation by V-joints applies only to the horizontals; *vermiculated,* with a texture like worm-holes.

SADDLEBACK: *see* Roof.

SALTIRE CROSS: equal-limbed cross placed diagonally.

SANCTUARY: (1) area around the main altar of a church (*see* Pres-bytery); (2) sacred site consist-ing of wood or stone uprights enclosed by a circular bank and ditch. Beginning in the Neo-lithic, they were elaborated in the succeeding Bronze Age. The best known examples are Stone-henge and Avebury.

SARCOPHAGUS: elaborately carved coffin.

SCAGLIOLA: material composed of cement and colouring matter to imitate marble.

SCALLOPED CAPITAL: develop-ment of the block capital (q.v.) in which the single semicircular

Fig. 19. Scalloped capital

surface is elaborated into a series
of truncated cones (Fig. 19).

SCARP: artificial cutting away of
the ground to form a steep slope.

SCREEN: *Parclose screen:* screen
separating a chapel from the rest
of a church. *Rood screen:* screen
below the rood (q.v.), usually at
the W end of a chancel.

SCREENS PASSAGE: passage
between the entrances to
kitchen, buttery, etc., and the
screen behind which lies the hall
of a medieval house.

SEDILIA: seats for the priests (usually three) on the S side of the
chancel of a church.

SEGMENTAL ARCH: see Arch.

SET-OFF: see Weathering.

SEXPARTITE: see Vault.

SGRAFFITO: pattern incised into
plaster so as to expose a dark surface underneath.

SHAFT-RING: motif of the C12
and C13 consisting of a ring
round a circular pier or a shaft
attached to a pier. Also called
Annulet.

SHAPED GABLE: see Gable.

SHEILA-NA-GIG: fertility figure,
usually with legs wide open.

SILL: lower horizontal part of the
frame of a window.

SLATEHANGING: the covering of
walls by overlapping rows of
slates, on a timber substructure.
Tilehanging is similar.

SOFFIT: underside of an arch,
lintel, etc. Also called Archivolt.

SOLAR: upper living-room of a
medieval house.

SOPRAPORTA: painting above the
door of a room, usual in the C17
and C18.

SOUNDING BOARD: horizontal
board or canopy over a pulpit.
Also called Tester.

SPANDREL: triangular surface
between one side of an arch, the
horizontal drawn from its apex,
and the vertical drawn from its
springer; also the surface between two arches.

SPERE-TRUSS: roof truss on two
free-standing posts to mask the
division between screens passage and hall. The screen itself,
where a spere-truss exists, was
originally movable.

SPIRE: tall pyramidal or conical
pointed erection often built on
top of a tower, turret, etc. *Broach
Spire:* a broach is a sloping half-
pyramid of masonry or wood introduced at the base of each of
the four oblique faces of a tapering octagonal spire with the
object of effecting the transition
from the square to the octagon.
The *splayed foot spire* is a variation of the broach form found
principally in the south-eastern
counties. In this form the four
cardinal faces are splayed out
near their base, to cover the
corners, while oblique (or intermediate) faces taper away to a
point. *Needle Spire:* thin spire
rising from the centre of a tower
roof, well inside the parapet.

SPIRELET: see Flèche.

SPLAY: chamfer, usually of the
jamb of a window.

SPRINGING: level at which an
arch rises from its supports.

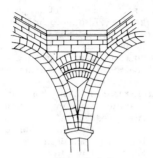

Fig. 20. Squinch

SQUINCH: arch or system of concentric arches thrown across the angle between two walls to support a superstructure, for example a dome (Fig. 20).

SQUINT: a hole cut in a wall or through a pier to allow a view of the main altar of a church from places whence it could not otherwise be seen. Also called Hagioscope.

STALL: carved seat, one of a row, made of wood or stone.

STAUNCHION: upright iron or steel member.

STEEPLE: the tower of a church together with a spire.

STIFF-LEAF: E.E. type of foliage of many-lobed shapes (Fig. 21).

Fig. 21. Stiff-leaf capital

STILTED: see Arch (Fig. 1d).

STOREY-POSTS: the principal posts of a timber-framed wall.

STOUP: vessel for the reception of holy water, usually placed near a door.

STRAINER ARCH: arch inserted across a room to prevent the walls from leaning.

STRAPWORK: C16 decoration consisting of interlaced bands, and forms similar to fretwork or cut and bent leather.

STRETCHER: see Brickwork.

STRING COURSE: projecting horizontal band or moulding set in the surface of a wall.

STRUT: see Roof.

STUCCO: plaster work.

STUDS: the subsidiary vertical timber members of a timber-framed wall.

SWAG: festoon (q.v.) formed by a carved piece of cloth suspended from both ends.

T ABERNACLE: richly ornamented niche or free-standing canopy. Usually contains the Holy Sacrament.

TARSIA: inlay in various woods.

TAZZA: shallow bowl on a foot.

TERMINAL FIGURES (TERMS, TERMINI): upper part of a human figure growing out of a pier, pilaster, etc., which tapers towards the base. *See also* Atlantes, Caryatid, Pilaster.

TERRACOTTA: burnt clay, unglazed.

TESSELLATED PAVEMENT: mosaic flooring, particularly Roman, consisting of small 'tesserae' or cubes of glass, stone, or brick.

TESSERAE: see Tessellated Pavement.

TESTER: see Sounding Board.

TETRASTYLE: having four detached columns.

THREE-DECKER PULPIT: pulpit with clerk's stall below and reading desk below the clerk's stall.

TIE-BEAM: *see* Roof (Figs. 14–17).

TIERCERON: *see* Vault (Fig. 23).

TILEHANGING: *see* Slatehanging.

TIMBER-FRAMING: method of construction where walls are built of timber framework with the spaces filled in by plaster or brickwork. Sometimes the timber is covered over with plaster or boarding laid horizontally.

TOMB-CHEST: a chest-shaped stone coffin, the most usual medieval form of funeral monument.

TOUCH: soft black marble quarried near Tournai.

TOURELLE: turret corbelled out from the wall.

TRACERY: intersecting ribwork in the upper part of a window, or used decoratively in blank arches, on vaults, etc. *Plate tracery: see* Fig. 22(*a*). Early form of tracery where decoratively shaped openings are cut through the solid stone infilling in a window head. *Bar tracery:* a form introduced into England *c.* 1250. Intersecting ribwork made up of slender shafts, continuing the lines of the mullions of windows up to a decorative mesh in the head of the window. *Geometrical tracery: see* Fig. 22(*b*). Tracery

characteristic of *c.* 1250–1310 consisting chiefly of circles or foiled circles. *Y-tracery: see* Fig. 22(*c*). Tracery consisting of a mullion which branches into two forming a Y shape; typical of *c.* 1300. *Intersecting tracery: see* Fig. 22(*d*). Tracery in which each mullion of a window branches out into two curved bars in such a way that every one of them is drawn with the same radius from a different centre. The result is that every light of the window is a lancet and every two, three, four, etc., lights together form a pointed arch. This treatment also is typical of *c.* 1300. *Reticulated tracery: see* Fig. 22(*e*). Tracery typical of the early C14 consisting entirely of circles drawn at top and bottom into ogee shapes so that a net-like appearance results. *Panel tracery: see* Fig. 22(*f*) and (*g*). Perp tracery, which is formed of upright straight-sided panels above lights of a window.

TRANSEPT: transverse portion of a cross-shaped church.

TRANSOM: horizontal bar across the openings of a window.

TRANSVERSE ARCH: *see* Vault.

TREFOIL: *see* Foil.

TRIBUNE: *see* Gallery.

TRICIPUT, SIGNUM TRICIPUT: sign of the Trinity expressed by

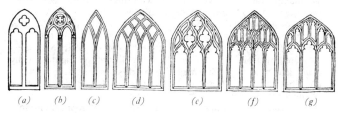

(*a*)   (*b*)   (*c*)   (*d*)   (*e*)   (*f*)   (*g*)

Fig. 22. Tracery

three faces belonging to one head.

TRIFORIUM: arcaded wall passage or blank arcading facing the nave at the height of the aisle roof and below the clerestory (q.v.) windows. (*See also* Gallery.)

TRIGLYPHS: blocks with vertical grooves separating the metopes (q.v.) in the Doric frieze (Fig. 12).

TROPHY: sculptured group of arms or armour, used as a memorial of victory.

TRUMEAU: stone mullion (q.v.) supporting the tympanum (q.v.) of a wide doorway.

TUMULUS: see Barrow.

TURRET: very small tower, round or polygonal in plan.

TUSCAN: see Order.

TYMPANUM: space between the lintel of a doorway and the arch above it.

UNDERCROFT: vaulted room, sometimes underground, below a church or chapel.

UNIVALLATE: of a hill-fort: defended by a single bank and ditch.

UPPER PALAEOLITHIC: see Palaeolithic.

VAULT: *see* Fig. 23. *Barrel-vault: see* Tunnel-vault. *Cross-vault: see* Groin-vault. *Domical vault:* square or polygonal dome rising direct on a square or polygonal bay, the curved surfaces separated by groins (q.v.). *Fan-vault:* late medieval vault where all ribs springing from one springer are of the same length, the same distance from the next, and the same curvature. *Groin-*vault or *Cross-vault:* vault of two tunnel-vaults of identical shape intersecting each other at r. angles. Chiefly Norman and Renaissance. *Lierne:* tertiary rib, that is, rib which does not spring either from one of the main springers or from the central boss. Introduced in the C14, continues to the C16. *Quadripartite vault:* one wherein one bay of vaulting is divided into four parts. *Rib-vault:* vault with diagonal ribs projecting along the groins. *Ridge-rib:* rib along the longitudinal or transverse ridge of a vault. Introduced in the early C13. *Sexpartite vault:* one wherein one bay of quadripartite vaulting is divided into two parts transversely so that each bay of vaulting has six parts. *Tierceron:* secondary rib, that is, rib which issues from one of the main springers or the central boss and leads to a place on a ridge-rib. Introduced in the early C13. *Transverse arch:* arch separating one bay of a vault from the next. *Tunnel-vault* or *Barrel-vault:* vault of semicircular or pointed section. Chiefly Norman and Renaissance.

VAULTING SHAFT: vertical member leading to the springer of a vault.

VENETIAN WINDOW: window with three openings, the central one arched and wider than the outside ones. Current in England chiefly in the C17–18.

VERANDA: open gallery or balcony with a roof on light, usually metal, supports.

VESICA: oval with pointed head and foot.

VESTIBULE: anteroom or entrance hall.

VILLA: (1) according to Gwilt (1842) 'a country house for the residence of opulent persons'; (2) Romano-British country houses cum farms, to which the description given in (1) more or less applies. They developed with the growth of urbanization. The basic type is the simple corridor pattern with rooms opening off a single passage; the next stage is the addition of wings. The courtyard villa fills a square plan with subsidiary buildings and an enclosure wall with a gate facing the main corridor block.

VITRIFIED: made similar to glass.

VITRUVIAN OPENING: a door or window which diminishes towards the top, as advocated by Vitruvius, bk. IV, chapter VI.

VOLUTE: spiral scroll, one of the component parts of an Ionic column (see Order).

VOUSSOIR: wedge-shaped stone used in arch construction.

WAGON ROOF: roof in which by closely set rafters with arched braces the appearance of the inside of a canvas tilt over a wagon is achieved. Wagon roofs can be panelled or plastered (ceiled) or left uncovered. Also called Cradle Roof.

WAINSCOT: timber lining to walls.

WALL-PLATE: see Roof.

WATERLEAF: leaf shape used in later C12 capitals. The waterleaf is a broad, unribbed, tapering leaf curving up towards the angle of the abacus and turned in at the top (Fig. 24).

WEALDEN HOUSE: timber-framed house with the hall in the centre and wings projecting only slightly and only on the jutting upper floor. The roof, however, runs through without a break between wings and hall, and the eaves of the hall part are therefore exceptionally deep. They are supported by diagonal, usu-

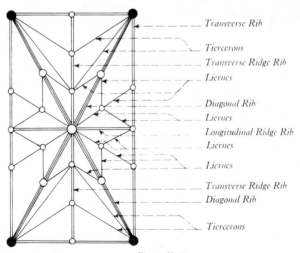

Transverse Rib
Tiercerons
Transverse Ridge Rib
Liernes

Diagonal Rib
Liernes
Longitudinal Ridge Rib
Liernes

Liernes

Transverse Ridge Rib
Diagonal Rib

Tiercerons

Fig. 23. Vault

ally curved, braces starting from the short inner sides of the overhanging wings and rising parallel with the front wall of the

Fig. 24. Waterleaf capital

hall towards the centre of the eaves.

WEATHERBOARDING: overlapping horizontal boards, covering a timber-framed wall.

WEATHERING: sloped horizontal surface on sills, buttresses, etc., to throw off water. Also called Set-off.

WEEPERS: small figures placed in niches along the sides of some medieval tombs. Also called Mourners.

WHEEL WINDOW: *see* Rose Window.

INDEX OF PLATES

INDEX OF ARTISTS

INDEX OF PLACES

Edge Hall, *see* Tilston, 363
Egerton, 216
Egremont, *see* Wallasey, 31, 370, 371, 372
Ellesmere Port, 12, 43, 216, 441
Elworth, 217
Erindale, *see* Frodsham, 221
Eversley, *see* Frodsham, 221
Farndon, 23n, 24, 27n, 218
Flowery Field, *see* Hyde, 246, 247
Foxhill, *see* Frodsham, 221
Frankby, 36, 39, 218
Freegreen Farmhouse, *see* Lower Peover, 259
Frodsham, 11, 13, 14, 18, 43, 48, 220, 441
Gatley, *see* Cheadle, 127
Gawsworth, 15, 16, 17, 20, 21n, 22, 25, 46, 222
Gayton, 224
Gee Cross, *see* Hyde, 246, 247
Godley, *see* Hyde, 246
Golborne Old Hall, *see* Handley, 25, 233
Goostrey, 225
Goyt Hall, *see* Bredbury, 113
Grappenhall, 16, 27n, 225
Greasby, 226
Great Barrow, 23, 27n, 226
Great Boughton, *see* Chester, 30, 173
Great Budworth, 15, 16, 17, 20, 27n, 28, 227, 441
Great Moreton Hall, 29, 32, 228
Great Saughall, 35, 229
Great Sutton, 230
Great Warford, 230
Greenbank, *see* Chester, 175
Guilden Sutton, 230
Hadlow Wood, *see* Willaston, 383
Hale, 23, 42, 43, 230
Halebarns, *see* Hale, 230, 231
Halton, 18, 22, 33, 38, 232
Hampton Old Hall, *see* Malpas, 21, 275
Handbridge, *see* Chester, 134, 174, 175

Handforth, 21, 233
Handley, 16, 23, 25, 26n, 233
Hankelow, 234
Hargrave, 23, 234
Hartford, 234
Harthill, 23, 27n, 235
Haslington, 21, 235
Hatherlow, *see* Bredbury, 31, 113
Hattersley, *see* Hyde, 247
Hawk Green, *see* Marple, 278
Hazel Grove, 236
Heald Green, *see* Cheadle, 129
Hefferston Grange, *see* Weaverham, 378
Helsby, 11, 35, 50, 236
Henbury, 236
Heronbridge, *see* Chester, 51, 176
Heswall, 27n, 237
Higher Walton, 32, 51, 238
Highfields, *see* Audlem, 26, 69, 441
High Lane, 32, 239
High Legh, 23, 36n, 239
Hilbre Island, *see* West Kirby, 380
Hinderton, 240
Hockenhull Hall, *see* Tarvin, 353
Holford Hall, *see* Plumley, 303
Hollingworth, 240
Hollyhedge Farm, *see* Weston, 380
Holme Street Hall, *see* Tarvin, 354
Holmes Chapel, 17, 27, 241
Hoole, *see* Chester, 172
Hoolgrove Manor, *see* Minshull Vernon, 281
Hooton, 12n, 33, 241
Hough, 243
Hoylake, 32, 36n, 48, 49, 243
Hulme Hall, *see* Allostock, 58, *and* Cheadle Hulme, 129
Hulme Walfield, 33, 245
Hurdsfield, 31, 43, 245
Huxley, 245
Hyde, 27n, 32, 34, 35, 245

ADDENDA

(NOVEMBER 1970)

p. 69 [Audlem, Highfields.] The house was the home of the architect *William Baker* (1705–71), and was altered and enlarged by him. He seems to have used half-timbering – an exceptionally early instance of black-and-white revivalism.

p. 101 [Birkenhead, St Stephen, Prenton.] The SE chapel is being decorated and re-furnished by *S. E. Dykes-Bower*.

p. 110 [Bowdon, St Mary.] The C14 knight was a Baguley. Canon Ridgway refers to another knight, early C14, with his r. hand on his sword hilt and uncrossed legs. Above the head a small crocketed gablet, formerly cinquefoil.

p. 164 [Chester.] N of the District Bank, in FRODSHAM STREET, work is now well advanced on MERCIA SQUARE, a development scheme by *Michael Lyell Associates*.

p. 217 [Ellesmere Port, Canal Warehouses.] These have, alas, been gutted by fire and almost entirely demolished. There remain the rusticated arches of the lowest stage of two of the wings.

p. 221 [Frodsham, St Laurence.] The chandelier, Mr Sherlock tells me, was supplied by William & Homer Silvester of Birmingham and cost £50 18s. 0d.

p. 228 [Great Budworth.] The cottage by *Douglas* w of the village is of 1868, but with its incised pargetting etc. is entirely Late Victorian in character. Yet more remarkable is a small cottage on the s side of the HIGH STREET on the corner of MOUNT PLEASANT. Brick, half-timber, and apparently originally with pargetting. It was described by Raffles Davison in *The British Architect*, vol. 22, 1884, as being by *Nesfield* and built 'twenty-two years ago', i.e. in 1862. It is thus an exceptionally early and interesting example of the style invented and popularized, with such influential effect, by Nesfield and Shaw. Cf. Crewe Hall, p. 194. (EH)

p. 272 [Macclesfield.] The mill in Park Lane has been demolished.

p. 274 [Malpas, St Oswald.] The main gates and those of the E
        approach are apparently from Oulton Park, and they
        are attributable to the *Davies Brothers*.

p. 316 [Prestbury, St Peter.] The chandelier of 1712 is, according
        to Mr Sherlock, by *William Davenport*, the one of 1814
        by *John Cocks* of Birmingham. The latter was origi-
        nally in the Macclesfield Sunday School.

p. 321 [Rode, Rode Hall.] In a recent letter Sir Randle Wil-
        braham states that the Doric portico is not a later
        addition, and that it is shown on the original plans of
        the main block.

p. 357 [Thelwall, All Saints.] The Rev. Derek A. Smith adds
        that, according to an inscription, the memorial was
        designed by *F. C. Eden* and made by *Helfer Brothers*.

p. 361 [Thornton-le-Moors, St Mary.] The Rev. E. Williams
        adds that there is a second FONT, dated 1673.

THE BUILDINGS OF ENGLAND

COMPLETE LIST OF TITLES

Bedfordshire and the County of Huntingdon and Peterborough *1st ed. 1968 Nikolaus Pevsner*

Berkshire *1st ed. 1966 Nikolaus Pevsner*

Buckinghamshire *1st ed. 1960 Nikolaus Pevsner, revision in progress*

Cambridgeshire *1st ed. 1954, 2nd ed. 1970, Nikolaus Pevsner*

Cheshire *1st ed. 1971 Nikolaus Pevsner and Edward Hubbard*

Cornwall *1st ed. 1951 Nikolaus Pevsner, 2nd ed. 1970 revised Enid Radcliffe*

Cumberland and Westmorland *1st ed. 1967 Nikolaus Pevsner*

Derbyshire *1st ed. 1953 Nikolaus Pevsner, 2nd ed. 1978 revised Elizabeth Williamson*

Devon *1st ed. in 2 vols. 1952 Nikolaus Pevsner, 2nd ed. 1989 Bridget Cherry and Nikolaus Pevsner*

Dorset *1st ed. 1972 John Newman and Nikolaus Pevsner*

Durham, County *1st ed. 1953 Nikolaus Pevsner, 2nd ed. 1983 revised Elizabeth Williamson*

Essex *1st ed. 1954 Nikolaus Pevsner, 2nd ed. 1965 revised Enid Radcliffe*

Gloucestershire: The Cotswolds *1st ed. 1970, 2nd ed. 1979, David Verey*

Gloucestershire: The Vale and the Forest of Dean *1st ed. 1970, 2nd ed. 1976 reprinted with corrections 1980, David Verey*

Hampshire and the Isle of Wight *1st ed. 1967 Nikolaus Pevsner and David Lloyd*

Herefordshire *1st ed. 1963 Nikolaus Pevsner*

Hertfordshire *1st ed. 1953 Nikolaus Pevsner, 2nd ed. 1977 revised Bridget Cherry*

Kent, North East and East *1st ed. 1969, 3rd ed. 1983, John Newman*

Kent, West, and the Weald *1st ed. 1969, 2nd ed. 1976 reprinted with corrections 1980, John Newman*

Lancashire, North *1st ed. 1969 Nikolaus Pevsner*

Lancashire, South *1st ed. 1969 Nikolaus Pevsner*

Leicestershire and Rutland *1st ed. 1960 Nikolaus Pevsner, 2nd ed. 1984 revised Elizabeth Williamson*

Lincolnshire *1st ed. 1964 Nikolaus Pevsner and John Harris, 2nd ed. 1989 revised Nicholas Antram*

London 1: The Cities of London and Westminster *1st ed. 1957 Nikolaus Pevsner, 3rd ed. 1973 revised Bridget Cherry*

London 2: Except the Cities of London and Westminster *1st ed. 1952 Nikolaus Pevsner, being revised, expanded, and reissued under the following three titles*

London 2: South *1st ed. 1983 Bridget Cherry and Nikolaus Pevsner*

London 3: North West *1st ed. in progress, Bridget Cherry and Nikolaus Pevsner*

London 4: North and North East *1st ed. in progress, Bridget Cherry and Nikolaus Pevsner*

NOTES